THE FOXFIRE 40TH ANNIVERSARY BOOK

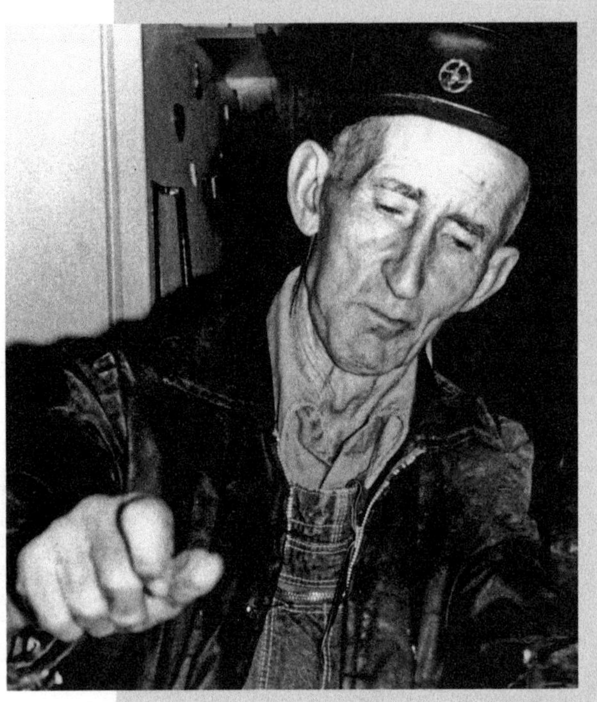

THE FOXFIRE
40TH ANNIVERSARY BOOK

FAITH, FAMILY, AND THE LAND

Edited by ANGIE CHEEK, LACY HUNTER NIX,

and FOXFIRE STUDENTS

ANCHOR BOOKS

A Division of Random House, Inc.

New York

AN ANCHOR BOOKS ORIGINAL, SEPTEMBER 2006

The Foxfire Fund, Inc.
P.O. Box 541
Mountain City, GA 30562-0541
706-746-5828
www.foxfire.org

Most material in this book originally appeared in *The Foxfire Magazine.*

Library of Congress Cataloging-in-Publication Data
Foxfire 40th anniversary edition ; faith, family, and the land / edited by Angie Cheek,
Lacy Hunter Nix, and Foxfire students.
p. cm.
Includes index.
1. Rabun County (Ga.)—Social life and customs. 2. Appalachian Region, Southern—Social life and customs. 3. Country life—Georgia—Rabun County. 4. Country life—Appalachian Region, Southern. 5. Folklore—Georgia—Rabun County. 6. Folklore—Appalachian Region, Southern. 7. Handicraft—Georgia—Rabun County. 8. Handicraft—Appalachian Region, Southern. 9. Rabun County (Ga.)—Biography. I. Cheek, Angie. II. Nix, Lacy Hunter, 1979– III. Foxfire Fund. IV. Title: Foxfire fortieth anniversary edition.
F292.R3F713 2006
975.8'123—dc22 2006045311

Anchor ISBN-10: 0-307-27551-6
Anchor ISBN-13: 978-0-307-27551-5

www.anchorbooks.com

Printed in the United States of America
20 19 18 17 16 15 14 13

We are honored to dedicate The Foxfire 40th Anniversary Book: Faith, Family, and the Land, *to Ann Moore, president of The Foxfire Fund, Inc.; to Robert Murray, curator of the Foxfire Center; and to Kaye Carver Collins, former student and staff member. Their determined efforts, belief in Foxfire's mission, espousal of an innovative approach to teaching and learning, and undying support have kept Foxfire growing and glowing.*

Unparalleled is Ann's commitment to Foxfire and its many facets. As president, Ann Moore is the pilot who keeps us all on course. Having been with Foxfire for thirty years, Ann understands who we are and what we do. She gives advice to the book editors and counsels The Foxfire Magazine *senior editors and staff. With her loving but firm hand, she has steered us through sunny skies and rough storms.*

Having been with Foxfire for twenty years, Robert, who jokes about being the ditchdigger, maintains the upkeep of the center, conducts tours of the land and cabins, and is a veritable cornucopia of old-timey lore. Robert's discussions of "dead as a doornail" and "sleep tight," his "cracking" a bullwhip for onlookers (and letting them try it, too), and his making a toothbrush for them from a sweet birch twig mesmerize those who visit our museum of artifacts. His wit and knowledge have made him a popular favorite with us and with our visitors.

Kaye Carver Collins was one of the early students in The Foxfire Magazine class at Rabun Gap-Nacoochee School. She served on the Foxfire staff for thirteen years, was a member of the Community Board, was coeditor of Memories of a Mountain Shortline *and* Foxfire 11 *and* 12, *oversaw the scholarship program, and facilitated the summer work/leadership program. Also, before she became an elementary educator, Kaye was ex officio adviser to* The Foxfire Magazine *for several years. Obviously, we owe her much.*

Realizing the vital part each of you has played in our continuing work, we truly thank the three of you. Your dedicated commitment to this work and to an ideal has had a positive impact on our success.

Furthermore, without the willingness of our many contacts who, over the years, opened their hearths and hearts to us and the other dedicated students who participated in our work, Foxfire could not have carried out its mission: to chronicle and preserve the language, culture, and heritage of the people of Appalachia. Therefore, we also dedicate this, our 40th Anniversary Book, *to you, our contacts and students.*

CONTENTS

ACKNOWLEDGMENTS

We are so proud to share with you forty years of Foxfire in this volume. Over those years those involved with Foxfire have grown to know and love the elders in our area and beyond, and we have sought to share their poignant stories with you, our readers. To preserve this history is our honor and privilege. Compiling this publication, a sentimental endeavor, was a quiet stroll under the canopy of memories. We would like to thank some folks who aided us in our efforts to complete this volume, a labor of love.

As always, we want to thank our contacts who have graciously taken the time to share their remembrances with us. Over the years, they have remained our friends. We certainly want to thank the many students who, since 1966, have spent hours interviewing, photographing, transcribing, and archiving in order to preserve a legacy we will leave to future generations.

As usual the Foxfire staff was there when we needed them. We would like to thank Ann Moore, Foxfire's president, for encouraging us, for helping to proof every page of this publication, and for troubleshooting. Also, we bombarded Robert Murray with questions such as "What does 'to scotch something' mean?"; "What's the difference between sorghum and molasses?" (I told you he was a cornucopia of information!) Thank you, Robert, for your patience and for checking on lightbulbs that went defunct and air conditioners that didn't "condition."

Help also always comes from our friend Lee Carpenter, computer and camera whiz extraordinaire. Thank you, Lee, for being our resident photographer and for rescuing us from the mire of computer glitches. (Lee took the picture you see of us in the back of this publication.)

Jimmy Hunter, Lacy's dad, also needs a special pat on the back. He received so many phone calls from our workroom: "Where's Bald Mountain?" "What's a 'grab'?" "Who, what, where, when, why?" Thanks for being patient!

Our Foxfire board of directors provides leadership to help steer us into the future, and our community board members help keep us afloat with their active involvement in our everyday workings and special events. Thank all of you for your past and continuing interest in our mission.

We would also like to acknowledge teachers everywhere who are using the Foxfire Approach to Teaching and Learning and allowing their students to have a voice in that learning. Permitting young people to take responsibility for their own learning enables these students not only to become intrinsically motivated but also to develop self-esteem, to learn to work as part of a team, and to gain an understanding and appreciation for what they learn and how they learn—important life skills.

Finally, we give a heartfelt thanks to you, our readers, supporters, and friends. We here at Foxfire are grateful for your continued patronage and encouragement and hope you will be part of the Foxfire readership family in years to come.

INTRODUCTION

As God, the Creator, walked upon the earth millions of years ago, His feet formed the deep valleys and pushed the earth up to form the beautiful, green Appalachian Mountain Range. (As my husband and I travel, I always marvel at the different ways folks pronounce "Appalachia." I have noticed that many call this range "Appa-lay-chuh." Around here, it's "Appa-laa-chuh.") This range extends approximately 1,600 miles from southern Quebec, Canada to central Alabama. Did you know that millions of years ago, the Appalachians were taller than the Rockies? I didn't know that fact until Foxfire student Sherie Dixon interviewed a geologist about a Rabun County wonder, the Tallulah Gorge, a two-mile-long chasm 900 feet in depth located right here in Rabun and Habersham Counties in Northeast Georgia.

Besides the gorge, Rabun County has another claim to fame: In our northeast corner of the state, the famous Appalachian Trail begins and stretches approximately 2,050 miles to Mount Katahdin in Maine. I know several adventurous souls who have hiked part or all of the trail, and they do have some stories to tell! Our area also has hundreds of hiking and biking trails, and many of us have our own tales.

Several years ago, my best friend, Cathy, who also grew up in Rabun County and has been my best friend for fifty years now, got a wild hair to do something challenging. (Because she's always planning adventures for the two of us and our husbands, the three of us call her the camp director.) Anyway, on an early spring morning, my husband, Bobby, with our friends Cathy and Mike Corrigan, who now live in Macon, Georgia, drove toward Mount Le Conte, the highest peak in the Great Smoky Mountains, a beautiful part of the Appalachian Mountain chain. Cathy had decided that we should hike to the top of this peak—I'm certain the hike was easier for God!

With equipment packed, we drove north. In the space of an hour or so, we who live here in the corner of Georgia can pass Clingmans Dome—unless the road's closed in the winter because of ice and snow—and be enveloped in the mists (hence its name) of the Great Smoky Mountains. Driving the Blue Ridge Parkway through the Smokies will take your breath away, not only because of the majestic beauty but also because of the precipices right at the road's edge—not to mention the signs that warn motorists to "Watch for falling rock"! This area is truly one of our nation's scenic wonders.

When the four of us arrived at the parking area below Mount Le Conte, we donned our backpacks, took a deep breath, and headed up Boulevard Trail. A hiker has a choice of several trails up the mountain. Boulevard Trail, because it was not as steep and rocky, seemed the least physically damaging even though it was seven miles long, longer than the other trails. After what seemed a lifetime, we arrived at the top and spent the night in one of the few rustic cabins (and "pottied" in the central outhouse). We ate dinner and breakfast in the dining hall (llamas bring up the food; we joked about avoiding llama scat on the trail); then, the next morning, we came down Alum Cave Trail, a much more arduous hike. I still can't believe I hiked to the top of Mount Le Conte. I can't believe I was *able* to! Every time I go to get-togethers and play that silly game of "Guess Who Did That," on my "secret" card I always write: "I climbed the highest peak in the Smokies." Others are supposed to "guess who did that"—no one ever guesses correctly.

Though the going was sometimes difficult, as I look back on that adventure, one of my cherished memories, I revel in those two days. We persevered toward our goal, we gloried in our mountaintop experience, and after we faced and survived the challenge, we headed toward home. Along the way we saw beautiful sights, met some nice folks, and accomplished our purpose. What did we accomplish? What did we get? Sometimes the greatest reward is not what we get but what we become by persevering and meeting the challenge, by accomplishing a purpose.

The stalwart trekkers who have hiked the Appalachian Trail that wends its way along the East Coast of the United States never remain unchanged. Like our hike to the top of Mount Le Conte, in many aspects hiking the Appalachian Trail, with its hills and valleys, its smooth flats and treacherous terrain, its expected sights and sudden surprises, is like traveling the trail of life. Traversing this trail brings forth moments of exhilaration and periods of pain. The experience makes hikers stronger, builds their endurance, and gives them a sense of accomplishment. In facing the challenges of hiking the trail, the trekkers learn not only about the trail itself and others on the trail with them but also about themselves.

When Cathy, Mike, Bobby, and I headed home down the more difficult Alum Cave Trail, we were tired from hiking up the day before, we found the trail steeper and rockier, and we were on unfamiliar territory; however, we kept walking because we were headed home. There we would find rest. Isn't this trek like our walk through life? As we go through life, we will have sun, we will see beauty, and we will enjoy our relationships with others; however, we will also face rain and endure the cold, and we will face adversity, obstacles that we must overcome. The challenge is having the fortitude to persevere; the good news is that we will find rest when we get home. Meeting and overcoming challenges and hardships is the story of the people of Appalachia. We who worked on this edition want our readers to know the hearts, the spirits of these people.

When Ann Moore, president of The Foxfire Fund, Inc., mentioned the possibility of publishing a Foxfire 40th anniversary edition and asked me if I'd be interested in editing it, I had to think—for about a second! Kaye Carver Collins and I had edited *Foxfire 12* two years ago, and though we felt the pressure of meeting a deadline, the work was most rewarding, for I felt I had a hand in preserving the language and culture of the people of Appalachia, my people. Fortune smiled, and I was able to choose the folks with whom I would work on this new volume. All are former or current exemplary magazine students of the Rabun County High School Foxfire Magazine class, a class which I facilitated from 1992 until I retired in May 2005.

My coeditor, Lacy Hunter Nix, graduated from high school in 1997 and then attended Brenau University, where she received a degree in Music. Lacy married Chris Nix, also a former magazine student, and they now live in North Carolina with their daughter, Libby. Amanda and Diana Carpenter, twins, graduated in May 2005, and are majoring in education at Piedmont College. April Argoe, currently a senior editor in the Foxfire Magazine class at Rabun County High School in Tiger, Georgia, plans to further her education to become an early childhood teacher.

When Lacy and I met in May 2005 to discuss our vision for this 40th anniversary Foxfire book, we batted some ideas back and forth across the table. At one point, I mentioned a couple of lines I had written in the dedication and "Personality Portraits" introduction for *Foxfire 12* concerning our people's reverence for God, their love for their families, and their regard for the land. Lacy said, "That'd make a great format for the new book." So there you have it—the heart of *The Foxfire 40th Anniversary Book*. As you can see, this anniversary book is divided into three parts: "Faith," "Family," and "The Land." This volume is truly a "Foxfire's Greatest Hits," for Lacy, Amanda, April, and I carefully perused forty years of *Foxfire Magazines*, and even a few books, and searched for anecdotes to give you a glimpse into the hearts of these stalwart people. (Note: In reading this edition, you will many times see a season and a year after a contact's name. That season and year indicate the particular *Foxfire Magazine* from which the interview came. Many of you are familiar with the *Foxfire* books but do not know that students at Rabun County High School publish a journal twice a year—we would love to have you as a subscriber! Those magazines provide the backbone for our books.) Also, Diana, who works in our archives in the summer, spent some time with us as a researcher, looking through our archive files for contact photographs and information.

One of the most important of Foxfire endeavors is to fulfill the mission of recording and preserving the language, culture, and heritage of the people of Appalachia. We are recording a history. A native of Young Harris, Georgia, Zell Miller, a former governor of Georgia and a member of the United States Senate, said, "History is how people lived, and that's what Foxfire tells us about. It is how people really lived" (Fall/Winter 1996, 160).

Faith, family, and the land is a triad that reveals the soul, heart, and mind of a proud people, courageous men and women of Southern Appalachia who have walked in sunshine and rain and have faced happiness and hardship with equanimity and unwavering hope and faith. They have descended into the valleys, and their indomitable spirits have enabled them to face change and overcome adversity in order to reach the peaks. Their lives are testaments of strength and courage and integrity.

Overcoming adversity builds character, and character determines our destiny. We know that no matter the twists and turns on the trail of life, the path is the way home. Oh, the legacy of wisdom our elders could leave us—if we would but follow in their footsteps.

—*Angie Cheek*

To every thing there is a season and a time to every purpose under the heaven:
A time to be born, and a time to die; a time to plant, and a time to pluck up that which is planted;
A time to kill, and a time to heal; a time to break down, and a time to build up;
A time to weep, and a time to laugh; a time to mourn, and a time to dance . . .
A time to get, and a time to lose; a time to keep, and a time to cast away . . .
A time to love, and a time to hate; a time of war, and a time of peace. (Ecclesiastes 3:1–8)

The preceding oft-quoted passage of Ecclesiastes (Is anyone else humming the song now?) is a familiar reminder to us all about the nature of life: Everything changes; nothing stays the same. All our lives have seasons, and we each experience the same cycle of life. This year marks a unique season in Foxfire's life, one we hope to share with you through this 40th anniversary edition.

When Angie Cheek and I sat down to discuss the focus of the book, we knew that we had an opportunity to reflect on not only the success of Foxfire but also the great changes that have come to the mountains over the last forty years. Most of Foxfire's original contacts have passed away. The old way of life that Foxfire originally sought to document is almost nonexistent these days. Even the language has changed. When Foxfire students first went into the community to talk to local folks, their interviews were about a way of life that was disappearing with the advent of modern conveniences. Now, when Foxfire students venture out to interview folks who are practicing a way of life without modern conveniences, they are often interviewing people who've chosen that life. In fact, as a student I interviewed a man who'd learned about his craft in one of the original Foxfire books. Later, when I was an adult teaching school in Florida, one of my fellow teachers and dear friends told me that her parents-in-law had used the original Foxfire book as a back-to-simplicity manual when they had moved to the Canadian countryside years ago.

As a product of the Foxfire educational process, I believe in Foxfire. I believe that young people can benefit from having a voice in their own learning. I believe that education is often more effective when young people produce a real, tangible product. I believe that the education of the young should invariably involve people from the communities in which they live, people who know the history of the community, people who are willing to share their roots with the young.

I was fortunate enough to have had excellent instruction from caring teachers. All that I learned served me well as I made my way through college into adulthood. However, I have now spent as much time married as I spent in college, and an idea expressed in passing by Olene Garland—a woman I met during a Foxfire interview—regarding how to make a marriage successful has remained with me to this day. I am sure that my own marriage has been better because I remembered what she said and have tried to put it into practice. After all, who better to tell me than a woman who'd had years of experience making her own marriage work? I feel strongly that little, if anything, I learned in a textbook can compare in importance to that one piece of advice Mrs. Garland gave me years ago. In case you are wondering what that advice was, I will share it with you. Mrs. Garland told me that she thought many young couples burdened themselves with debt by trying to acquire early in their marriage all the things that their parents, who'd been married for years, had. She felt that a large amount of debt was too much stress on a young marriage. I agree wholeheartedly. That connection to the community and to the wisdom of our elders is what is so often missing in our current system of education, and that is why Foxfire is so very important still today.

Coming back to Foxfire, no longer as a student but as a woman with a family of her own, has been more meaningful than I expected. While I had always found the stories of yesteryear fascinating, I had never become emotionally involved in them. An event in my own life during this past year, however, has forever changed the way I view the world around me. I've entered a new season in my own life: I'm now a mother. The responsibility I bear for my daughter's life is a filter through which I view all other events. Now, as a mother, my heart breaks for Harriet Echols—a woman you'll meet later in this book who spoke of losing two babies during the Depression—in ways that I could not have imagined before. Only a few nights ago, my baby girl was having trouble sleeping. Just as I was beginning to bemoan my lack of sleep, I thought about Mrs. Echols, and I held my own baby closer and thanked the Heavens above that she is healthy enough to fuss while teething. And, yes, in case you're wondering, I gladly rocked her until she was content once more.

Finally, I cannot end a volume about family without telling you the significant place Foxfire occupies in the life of my own family. Ten years ago, during my first summer working for Foxfire, I met Chris Nix (you can see his work in *Foxfire 10*), the man who would later become my husband. Then he was a cute college student who was home on summer break to help a new crop of magazine students as part of his scholarship requirement, and I was a sixteen-year-old girl with an impossible crush. As with most other journeys in life, our path was filled with plenty of twists and turns, but six years later, I married that boy (who was by then a grown man—and did I mention that he's still handsome?). This past year, as I gave birth to a brown-haired baby girl, a new family was born. Right now we're young; our days are filled with diapers and toys and little baby giggles, but I know that life is all too short. My grandmother, Juanita Kilby, remarked recently, "You'll just be goin' along and livin' your life, and then one day you'll wake up and discover that you're now seventy! You won't believe it, but then you'll look at your baby and realize that she's now a grandmother and your grandbaby has a baby, and you'll know it's true—somehow you're seventy years old. And you'll wonder, Where has the time gone?"

Fortunately, one of the great lessons I've learned from my Appalachian heritage is how to make the most of our short time in this world: Love my Creator first and most and center my life around my family and cherish them. With those values in place, for all of its suffering, life can be sweet.

Though many of the men and women Foxfire has documented over the years may have gone—their seasons here on Earth have ended—their essence still touches us today, coloring our world and helping us learn about who we are. To them, we are grateful. This book is a tribute to them and to those still with us. Their lives and examples teach us how to approach the new seasons in our own lives with confidence and joy.

—Lacy Hunter Nix

WHAT IS FOXFIRE?

Mark Twain and Sterling North both use "foxfire" in their respective books *Huckleberry Finn* and *Rascal*. In *Rascal*, author Sterling North describes foxfire as "a real curiosity—a phosphorescent stump which gleamed at night, as luminescent as all the lightning bugs in the world—ghostly and terrifying to boys who saw it for the first time." A more practical Twain describes a scene with Tom Sawyer and Huck as they make plans to dig a tunnel under the cabin where the slave Jim is being held. They discuss the fact that a lantern will make too much light and may call attention to their activities. Tom tells Huck: "What we must have is a lot of them rotten chunks that's called foxfire, and just makes a soft kind of glow when you lay them in a dark place."

A dictionary would describe foxfire as "an eerie phosphorescent light; the luminescence of decaying wood; any of various luminous fungi as *Armillaria mellea* that cause decaying wood to glow; the phosphorescent light emitted by certain fungi in rotted wood." Other common fungi responsible for the glow are *Clitocybe illuden* and *Panus stypticus*, members of the Basidiomycete class.

How can decomposing wood and the fungi associated with it actually glow? Foxfire is the result of a complicated chemical reaction within the fungi pigment molecules. According to studies done by plant physiologists, phosphorescence is a product of photosynthesis. Photosynthesis, as most of us know from junior high science, is the process by which a plant manufactures its own food. Photosynthesis requires light; therefore, phosphorescence requires light, too.

The process starts when the luminous fungi absorb light energy either directly from sunlight or through ultraviolet rays, which can penetrate wood, stumps, or soil to reach them. Another possible scenario exists: From a lifetime of absorbing light energy, the excess energy left in a stump or piece of wood could be released in the form of phosphorescence as the stump decomposes if the correct fungi are present. When the proper fungi are present and conditions are right, decomposing wood, through the process of oxidation, glows. Marie Mellinger, a local plant guru, says, "Foxfire is not a plant but a process. Foxfire will happen anywhere there is fungus. You can't say it is a fungus or a plant: You have to call it a process. When the fungus starts to decay, to decompose, it gives off light . . . After the fungus is all decomposed, the foxfire is just not there anymore."

When you dig around a stump in the dark, Clyde Hollifield told us, "It will look like a castle, like deep openings and a light coming from deep down in the ground. All around the stump will look like a castle with a party going on inside. Once, we pulled up an old stump; where the tree came out of the ground, it left a cavity, and that cavity was just a city down there all lined with lights. At night, foxfire looks like a jewel, but the next day it's just rotten wood."

Clyde continued, "On moonlit nights you can hardly see foxfire—there's too much light. If it's lying on the ground, it looks like moonlight on dry leaves. Foxfire could be everywhere, and you'd think it was moonlight scattered about. It takes a real pitch-black night to see it." Apparently, foxfire is everywhere in the mountains. On a summer night, walk along any stream or creek where it's damp and where roots are hanging over the creek. If you look under the overhang of roots, you have a good chance of seeing foxfire. "Practically every old rotten poplar log lying on the ground or just the stump has foxfire in it," Clyde averred.

Glowing objects are the stuff of the fantastical: witches' brews, sorcerers, elfin people, magic. Foxfire is truly a conundrum, a mystery of the magical mountains. Perhaps foxfire's mystical qualities are characteristics that appealed to the students at Rabun Gap-Nacoochee School in 1966, when they were choosing a name for their proposed publication. Instead of *Parchment and Pine, Rabun Gap Literary Magazine, Red Hills Reader, Soul Plus,* and others, they chose *Foxfire*—how apt.

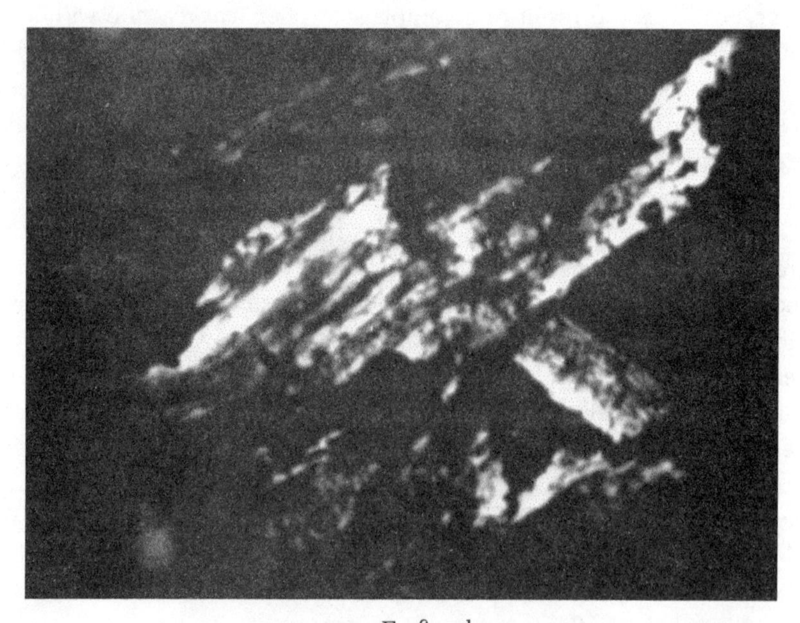

PLATE 1 Foxfire glows.

Like foxfire, in the shadowy valleys, the dark woods, and the damp coves and on the sunlit mountains, are the determined people whom we love and respect. Forty years ago, we began our efforts to record and preserve a dying language, culture, and heritage. Foxfire still glows in these hills and mountains, and the spirit of our stalwart elders still lights our paths today.

—*Angie Cheek*

[Adapted from Chet Welch and Al Edwards, "Why Does Foxfire Glow?"; research by Curt Haban. *The Foxfire Magazine*, Spring/Summer 1985. 26–34, and Spring/Summer 1996. 8–17.]

FOXFIRE: A HISTORY

Forty years, four decades, twoscore years, almost half a century—whichever way you choose to say it, Foxfire has been around for quite a while. So much about the world has changed in these years that it's almost impossible to imagine that any small grassroots movement begun and grown in a high school class could still be alive today, yet Foxfire is still here.

The magazine program, founded in 1966, helped a perplexed, overwhelmed teacher reach students who until that point could not envision a need for English class. Written for a "real" audience, the original magazines were a combination of interviews with local old-timers as well as student work. Students then went into the community to collect donations for the cost of the first printing, and the magazine was launched. The benefits from the production of the magazine were twofold. First, with a product that would reach real readers, intrinsically motivated students began to take pride in their work and feel a sense of accomplishment from their learning. Furthermore, at a time when rural mountain communities were being mocked about their "hillbilly" roots, students listened to local elders discuss a way of life that required strength and determination, a way of life that was dying; these young people began to feel a sense of pride in their own roots.

Two years after the creation of the magazine, Foxfire's founder established The Southern Highlands Literary Fund, which would later become The Foxfire Fund, Inc. Establishing a nonprofit organization for educational purposes, specifically the preservation of Appalachian folklore and the promotion of the Foxfire philosophy of education, allowed the fledgling organization to accept the donations and grants crucial to the continued survival of the magazine.

As the magazine's popularity increased, requests for subscriptions poured in, and people began to ask for back issues, many of which were no longer available. An idea for publishing interesting past articles and photos metamorphosed into *The Foxfire Book.* Thus began the best-selling *Foxfire Book* series, twelve of them thus far, prior to this edition, and various other publications.

In 1973, after several months of discussion concerning the need for a place to store the artifacts the organization had been collecting over the years, the board voted to allow the purchase of property located on Black Rock Mountain in Mountain City, Georgia. Shortly thereafter, Foxfire students moved a gristmill to "the mountain," the first of many such relocations of historic log buildings.

Then, in 1977, needing a place more readily accessible to tourists, community residents, and commercial deliveries, Foxfire purchased another tract of land in Mountain City, on Highway 441, on which to house the Foxfire Press. Most of Foxfire's daily operations, as well as a bookstore, moved to this property in 1986, along with the addition of a one-room museum. The organization completed a gift shop in 1991.

Also in 1977, upon the consolidation of the local high schools into one large county high school, Foxfire moved from Rabun Gap-Nacoochee School to Rabun County High School. Until the completion of the new high school building, the community students from the northern end of Rabun County had attended Rabun Gap-Nacoochee School because the then current high school building had been too small for all of the local students. However, in 1976, when the construction of a new building to house all local students grades seven through twelve neared conclusion, Foxfire's staff and founder made a decision—albeit a difficult one—that the program belonged with local students rather than dormitory students. Rabun Gap-Nacoochee School became a private preparatory school where most of the students were boarding students not native to the area. The decision to move the program was based on the realization that the local students were the ones with ties to the area and a belief that these students' education should include a connection to their own community.

Foxfire shifted its focus in 1986 with the acceptance of the Bingham and Dewitt-Wallace grants. Though the Foxfire Magazine class continued at Rabun County High School, Foxfire's attention largely turned away from local and heritage programs to focus outward on national programs. For much of the next two decades, Foxfire focused its efforts on the dissemination of the Foxfire educational philosophy and teacher-training programs.

In 2000, Foxfire again refocused its efforts, this time on Georgia and the Southeast Region. Though the teacher-training program continues in conjunction with Piedmont College, Foxfire has focused once again on local and heritage programs. Over the last four decades, through an endowment, the nonprofit has awarded local Foxfire students almost three-quarters of a million dollars in scholarships. Furthermore, the organization continues to advise and support the local Foxfire Magazine program, and thousands continue to visit the museum, which houses hundreds of old-timey artifacts. Then, in an effort to streamline the organization and reduce the cost of operations while still maintaining the flexibility required for growth, Foxfire sold the property on the highway in Mountain City and relocated once more to the mountain, one hundred and ten acres now known as The Foxfire Museum and Heritage Center.

Currently, Ann Moore, who has been with Foxfire for thirty years, is the president of The Foxfire Fund, Inc. Under her direction, Foxfire is celebrating forty years of promoting its hands-on philosophy of teaching and learning, providing a way for students to connect with their community, and preserving the mountain culture of Appalachia, a culture that is rapidly disappearing. Though the last forty years have seen enormous changes in both our beloved mountains and in the organization itself, Foxfire not only survives but continues to glow.

FORTY YEARS OF FOXFIRE:
A Partial Timeline of Events and Accomplishments of The Foxfire Fund, Inc.

1966 Eliot Wigginton and students create *The Foxfire Magazine.*

1967 Students publish the first issue of *The Foxfire Magazine.*

1968 Foxfire incorporates and establishes "The Southern Highlands Literary Fund," a nonprofit 501(c)3 organization.

1972 Students publish *The Foxfire Book.*

1973 Students publish *Foxfire 2.* Foxfire establishes the Foxfire Community Board, and the organization's name is changed from The Southern Highlands Literary Fund to The Foxfire Fund, Inc. Foxfire purchases 110 acres of property, now known as The Foxfire Museum and Heritage Center, and moves and reconstructs the first historic log building at the center.

1974 Foxfire publishes *Moments* and *You and Aunt Arie.* The Foxfire Fund, Inc., establishes the national advisory board, and the board holds its first meeting in Rabun County.

1975 Students publish *Foxfire 3.* Foxfire holds the first Annual Celebration of Community and honors its "contacts" and creates the Foxfire Student Summer Jobs Program. *The Foxfire Book* passes 1,000,000 in sales.

1976 Foxfire establishes the Foxfire Scholarship Program, as well as the Video and Music programs at Rabun Gap-Nacoochee School. Foxfire publishes *Memories of a Mountain Shortline,* and students publish the tenth birthday issue of *The Foxfire Magazine.* Ann Moore joins the Foxfire staff.

1977 Students publish *Foxfire 4.* Beginning with the 1977/78 school year, Foxfire moves its programs from Rabun Gap-Nacoochee School to Rabun County High School and starts environmental courses there. Foxfire music students record their first album, *North Georgia*

Mountains, with Joyce Brookshire of Cabbagetown. Foxfire purchases the Highway 441 property in Mountain City and receives the NHPRL grant to organize its archives.

1978 The organization signs a contract with Hume Cronyn and Susan Cooper for dramatic rights to book series material for the play *Foxfire.* Foxfire music students create the Foxfire String Band, now known as "The Foxfire Boys."

1979 Students publish *Foxfire 5,* and the organization holds the first Foxfire National Conference in St. Louis, Missouri.

1980 Students publish *Foxfire 6. Foxfire,* the play, opens in Stratford, Ontario. Music students release the album *It Still Lives.*

1981 *Foxfire,* the play, opens at the Guthrie Theatre in Minneapolis, Minnesota.

1982 On the tenth birthday of *The Foxfire Book,* students publish *Foxfire 7,* and the organization builds the passive solar house on the Mountain City property. The play *Foxfire* opens in Baltimore, in Boston, and on Broadway, and Jessica Tandy wins a Tony Award for her performance. The Foxfire String Band releases its first cassette tape and performs at the World's Fair in Knoxville, Tennessee.

1983 The Foxfire Press publishes *Aunt Arie: A Foxfire Portrait.* The organization moves the Rothell House from Toccoa, Georgia, to the Mountain City property. The Foxfire String Band performs on *The Grand Ole Opry* and changes its name to "The Foxfire Boys."

1984 The organization publishes *Foxfire 8* and *The Foxfire Book of Appalachian Cookery.*

1985 Foxfire publishes *The Foxfire Book of Toys and Games* and *Sometimes a Shining Moment.*

1986 The organization receives the Bingham Grant and begins networks and national teacher-training programs. Foxfire celebrates its twentieth birthday, and Robert Murray joins the staff.

1987 Foxfire publishes *The Foxfire Book of Winemaking.*

1989 Students publish *Foxfire 9.*

1990 Foxfire publishes *A Foxfire Christmas.* The Hallmark Hall of Fame movie, *Foxfire,* based on the play, airs on national television.

1991 Foxfire's founder takes a sabbatical from the organization to teach at the University of Georgia. The organization creates the Foxfire Museum and publishes *Foxfire: 25 Years.*

1992 Students publish *Foxfire 10* and the hundredth issue of *The Foxfire Magazine.* Angie Cheek, a Rabun County High School teacher, becomes the Foxfire Magazine class facilitator. Foxfire's founder resigns.

1993 Due to limited staffing, Foxfire closes the museum gift shop.

1994 Foxfire hires Bobby Ann Starnes as the new Foxfire president. Joyce Green, a Rabun County High School teacher, joins Angie Cheek as a Foxfire Magazine class facilitator.

1995 Foxfire reopens the museum gift shop and holds the first annual Foxfire Fall Heritage Festival in Rabun County.

1996 The organization starts *Active Learner: A Foxfire Journal for Teachers,* and students publish a special thirtieth anniversary issue of *The Foxfire Magazine.*

1998 Foxfire publishes *Considering Assessment and Evaluation: A Foxfire Teacher Reader.* The Foxfire Museum and Heritage Center becomes a Community-Based Vocational Instructional worksite for local area schools. Foxfire begins a strategic-planning process.

1999 Foxfire publishes *Foxfire 11, From Thinking to Doing, Considering Creativity and Imagination: A Foxfire Teacher Reader,* and *Considering Reflection.* President Starnes resigns.

2000 Foxfire completes its strategic plan and refocuses its efforts on Georgia and the Southeast. Ann Moore becomes Foxfire's acting president and executive director.

2001 Foxfire celebrates its thirty-fifth birthday and holds a special Annual Community Celebration event. State Senator Carol Jackson recognizes Foxfire's thirty-five years of achievements by awarding the organization with a commemorative resolution that she drafted and introduced in the Georgia General Assembly. *The Foxfire Magazine,* published continually since 1967, releases issues number 135/136 and 137/138.

2002 Foxfire's Board of Directors appoints Ann Moore president and executive director. Establishing the Artist-in-Residence program, Foxfire invites Sharon Grist/The Village Weaver to join The Foxfire Museum and Heritage Center.

2003 Foxfire partners with Piedmont College in Demorest, Georgia, to provide teacher-training courses in the Foxfire Approach to Teaching and Learning.

2004 Foxfire relocates off of the Highway 441 property back to The Foxfire Museum and Heritage Center on the mountain. The organization publishes *Foxfire 12* and *Teaching by Heart: The Foxfire Interviews.*

2005 Angie Cheek retires from teaching; Holly Billingsley Cabe, a former Foxfire student, becomes the new facilitator in the Foxfire Magazine class at Rabun County High School.

2006 Foxfire celebrates its fortieth birthday with the release of *The Foxfire 40th Anniversary Book: Faith, Family, and the Land,* and a special fortieth anniversary issue of *The Foxfire Magazine.* To date, the Julia Fleet Scholarship Program has awarded over $710,000 to 310 Rabun County High School students.

A FOXFIRE PORTRAIT: AUNT ARIE CARPENTER

Foxfire could not publish a 40th anniversary book without remembering our beloved Aunt Arie. Though we knew her only a few short years before she passed away, Arie Carpenter became a part of our lives, and we remember her and honor her.

Aunt Arie was born to Christine Tilithia Henson and Davie Leander Cabe on December 29, 1885, in Macon County, North Carolina, and was raised there. She had four brothers. In all of her ninety-two years, she never left Macon County except on short visits, and these visits apparently never took her more than thirty-five miles from home.

When she was thirty-eight, she married in Dillard, Georgia, for the first time. Her husband, Ulysses, was also from Macon County. Their one baby was premature and stillborn, probably when Aunt Arie was around forty. Ulysses died November 19, 1966, and left his wife to live alone on their eighty-acre farm in the log house they had built together. They'd been married forty-three years.

Foxfire, only four years old, first met the now-famous Aunt Arie Carpenter in her dark, smoke-stained kitchen in the fall of 1970. The kitchen may have been dark, but light emanated from the white-haired woman in the shapeless dress. Her bright eyes, beautiful smile, and lilting laugh mesmerized those who visited her. Aunt Arie loved to laugh: "I don't reckon th' Devil'll get me fer laughin', but if he does, he'll shore get me, 'cause I've always done more 'n my share o' th' laughin' in the world." Her warmth and humor made folks love her instantly.

That visit was the first of many. She showed us her handmade quilts and baskets. She fed us Sunday dinner—souse (meat soaked in liquid or pickling) meat, chicken and dumplings, leather breeches (dried green beans), hominy, egg custards, peach cobbler, and bread—which she prepared on her woodstove and in her Dutch oven in the fireplace; and she shared with us many tales and words of wisdom. We took food to her, carried firewood and put it next to the front door, and restocked her kitchen supply of kindlin'. We wound her clock for her (after she told us "I can't wind that clock t' save my life"), worked most Saturdays in her garden, and took her to church and to lunch. We also brought her to school where, dressed in her Sunday best, she entranced high school students with the stories of her life.

Her life was difficult: "Yeah, we worked hard. Made a good life. Why, you just had t' work 'r starve, one. [Laughs] . . . Pays a body t' work more'n it does starve." She confided that she almost starved one cold winter when her food cellar door froze shut.

On one of our visits, Aunt Arie also confided, "Y' know what I miss? Me and Ulyss' would sit right here at this table for hours at a time and talk. . . . I love t' set and talk. . . . We talked till midnight many a night. Yes, sir. That was silly, but that's what we done." We can believe it—we loved to talk with her, too. Another time she told us, "Well, it's might lonesome—'specially days like when it comes storms and things like that. That's not s' good." But she went on to say, "And still I don't mind it a bit in th' world. I never have been afraid o' nothin' in my life." She continued, "Livin' by yourself ain't all roses—and it ain't all thorns." Aunt Arie did, however, tell us that a big snake came out of her kindlin' and that she never got over it. Of course, her husband, Ulysses, had been bitten by a copperhead on a Fourth of July, and she told us she'd been afraid to put her feet down on a snake ever since. Conspiratorially, she admitted, "I've got a good number twelve shotgun in there if I need it. I've shot it many a time. I used t' shoot with th' boys, and I was pretty good with a gun."

Once Arie Carpenter's story appeared in *Foxfire* books, she would never be totally alone again. Although her good neighbors brought her what she called "m' rations": coffee (which she drank hot out of a saucer—never in a coffee cup) and medicine, people who read about her in *Foxfire* books and magazines drove hundreds of miles to see her and take photographs. A continuous stream of tourists would find their way to her mountain cabin, and she loved to chat.

In the mid-seventies, Aunt Arie developed a suspicious lump on her chest that seemed to be growing, but before she could have surgery to remove the tumor, she developed pneumonia. She went into Angel Memorial Hospital in Franklin, North Carolina, on February 9, 1974, for treatment, and while she was there, doctors removed the tumor, which was benign. However, her time of living alone in her isolated mountain cabin had come to an end. She had always wanted to outlive her brothers so she could see them buried properly—she outlived her last brother by three months. Aunt Arie died of a stroke on September 10, 1978, at the age of ninety-two.

Aunt Arie Carpenter was a courageous woman who faced life head-on. In the winter of her life, she did think about the end: "I don't know what I'll have t' do before I die. May have t' lay out in th' rain somewhere. I hope I don't. I think God will take care o' me." God did take care of her. Aunt Arie did not have children of her own, but she had dozens and dozens of children who adopted her. She would not be alone when the end came. She loved us, and we loved her in return. She was always glad to visit: "I hope ever' one of you a safe journey through life. And if y' ever have th' opportunity t' come back in here, remember the door's open; come pull th' latch string anytime you'uns want to." Those who pulled her latch string found their journey through life better for having entered into the home and heart of this independent woman with a zest for living. Through the many reminiscences which she shared with us, we learned lessons we'll never forget. Thank you, Aunt Arie, for the legacy you left us. We at Foxfire have written your name on our leaves for others to know you, too. Your memory lives.

—*Angie Cheek*

[Adapted from Linda Garland Page and Eliot Wigginton, eds. *A Foxfire Portrait: Aunt Arie.* University of North Carolina Press, 1992.]

PLATE 2 Aunt Arie Carpenter

WORDS FROM THE WISE: OUR BELOVED CONTACTS

Forty years ago, Foxfire began recording the culture and heritage of the folks of Appalachia. In fulfilling our mission, preserving the past by chronicling the poignant stories of those older and wiser, we have formed a connection with stalwart folks who had true strength of character.

Beginning in 1966, we have known and loved so many contacts, folks who have impacted not only our lives but the lives of our readers. These elders have left all of us an inheritance of down-to-earth wisdom that reverberates today. Though they have passed from this temporal world, we remember them and feel honored that they allowed us to be part of their lives, and we feel grateful for their having left us a legacy: their secrets of living with hope and their words of wisdom. Can you hear their voices whispering through the verdant valleys and echoing from the misty mountains?

—Angie Cheek

"I have done some hard work and made it honest, and what I've got, I worked for. Nobody gave it to me. By gosh, I believe them old days were good 'cause I don't believe hard work would hurt anybody."

—Lawton Brooks

"People used to go see one another, and they didn't have no way to go but walk or ride a horse. Now they're livin' a lot faster than we did back then. Nowadays, they ain't got no time to go see anybody. They're goin' all the time, and they don't go nowhere either." **—Claude Darnell**

"Love is the thing that's missing today. That's the main thing. If people loved one another, they wouldn't want to harm each other but would want to help each other like they did back in my childhood days." **—Lillie Nix**

"I see older people who seem kind of soured on life, and they feel they haven't had a chance in life. I feel we make a lot of our chances."

—Lola Cannon

"We made a mistake sellin' our land. Once the money's gone, it's all gone, and what is there left? Money ain't worth nothin'." **—Furman Arvey**

"I'll tell y', be a neighbor, and you'll have neighbors. Now I've tried that by experience. I do try t' be good t' everybody, and I try t' treat everybody just as I'd have them treat me. I don't care th' goodness you do, you'll always get repaid for it—double, fourfold. You children remember that. Th' more you do for people, th' more they'll do for you. Always remember, t' have a friend, be one." **—Aunt Arie Carpenter**

"If I was boss of the mountains, I would put it back there like it was when it was a wild country." **—Richard Norton**

"Set a goal for yourself and try not to follow everybody else. There's a tendency to be just like the others, but don't do wrong things because you see others doing them. Set a goal and try to keep your life clean and pure. You'll never be sorry." **—Ada Kelly**

"There's never been a time as hard to live the Christian life as there is now. There's so many things to get the attention of people and draw them away." **—Preacher Ben Cook**

"They ain't anybody up and down this country here that will tell you that they ever met me but what I'd speak to 'em and treat 'em nice. And if they wadn't so good, well, that 'as all right. Go right ahead anyway—speak to 'em. Treat 'em nice and go on." **—Thad "Happy" Dowdle**

"I don't think it makes much difference what y' wear—it's how yer heart is." **—Kenny Runion**

"Back when I came up, people didn't sell things—they gave to each other. . . . Seems like our country now is more for money, regardless of how it comes or how it goes or who suffers, who lives or who dies. . . . Me and money, we're so far apart. I like to make it and I like to have it. But just following after money like I see some people do, that's the least thing I think about." **—Beulah Perry**

"I like t' be close t' people, but I don't like them t' live in my door! I like t' be where, if I take a notion to fuss, I can fuss. Oh, I'd be like a bird in a cage. Catch a bird and put it in a cage. Livin' in town—that'd be like a bird in a cage." **—Annie Perry**

"As you grow older, you've got to have hope and trust in somethin'. We need somethin' to cling to, and our hope and trust in a higher power is it. We know that we're here, and we just didn't grow up out of the ground. And we look all around us, and we see how everything goes on and the beauty of everything. You learn to love people. You learn to love everything."
—Harriet Echols

"Sometimes I think if these people had to go back and live about fifty, sixty years ago, just turn back time from 1910 up to 1920 and let 'em share just what people had at that time, I wonder what this world would be."
—Aunt Addie Norton

"When you've got old, you're not a-goin' t' lay down and die just because you're old. Feller's got t' have somethin' t' do." **—Hillard Green**

"Some people say the only way out now is for people to go back to th' way they's livin' fifty years ago. Wonder how th' young people'd feel about that? It'd be hard, I'll tell you." **—Margaret Norton**

"It'd just be terrible to think about some of these old people comin' back here today and see how it was then and how it is now." **—Clarence Lusk**

"Generally, I don't think people live as close as they did back then. But people are still neighborly up here on Betty's Creek [in Dillard, Georgia]. They go and help each other if they need it. They always come to the rescue if you need help." **—Billy Long**

"I believe that children were a little more afraid of their parents, or the rules were more strict for us then. Children were more obedient. You give a child a nickel now, and he doesn't want it. He wants *money,* he says, and holds out for a quarter." **—Anna Tutt**

"Pay your debts, if you die hard. If somebody's good enough to let you have somethin' on credit and you promise to pay them, you pay them! And tell the truth." **—Lelia Gibson**

FAITH

Why, you know that there's

a higher power if y' just look out . . .

They's somebody, somethin', behind it.

—*Kenny Runion*

I advise you not to be carried away with the ways of the world. The Bible says, "Love God, and love your neighbor." That's the commandment that Jesus gave: Love God and love your neighbor. In order to do that, you've got to study the Bible a whole lot, and you've got to go to church and hear the Gospel preached. You've got to mix and mingle with Christian people, and you've got to worship your Maker. We were put here for a purpose. This world was made for man's enjoyment—for man's use. Man was put in charge of the world and everything that's in it. We don't realize it, but the Spirit of the Lord is present at any time. You can call on It any time. If you call on It in faith, you'll get an answer.

—Esco Pitts

So-called modern folks have faith. We have faith in the sun: When we awaken in the morning, the sun's rays will be warming the earth. We have faith in gravity: We can step with assurance, for we do not believe we will float away into space. We even have faith that the chair over which we are hovering will hold us if we sit in it. Some have faith in the almighty dollar, in other people, in science. Others even have faith in faith. This faith, however, is not the "faith of our fathers, living still."

Why do so many people in our crowded, modern, technologically advanced world today feel isolated and alienated, depressed, empty, and afraid? Our world seems full of danger: The "nice" man next door is a child molester, robbers and rapists break into our homes, terrorists attack our homeland. The news media reports random acts of violence; the film industry depicts catastrophic forces threatening the very existence of Earth and its inhabitants: *Independence Day, The Day After Tomorrow, War of the Worlds,* and so many others. Nuclear weapons, toxic waste, and global warming threaten our habitat. The future looks bleak. Robert Burns wrote about man's perspective in his poem "To a Mouse": "And forward though I cannot see, I guess and fear." Many are indeed fearful of what tomorrow holds for mankind.

In the midst of such seeming chaos, many in society today search for some meaning and purpose for their lives. They wonder if the quest for meaning and purpose is realizable. Viktor Frankl, in his work *Man's Search for Meaning*, purported a truism applicable to society today: "[P]eople have enough to live by but nothing to live for; they have the means but no meaning" (142). For some, God is a myth. Atheists, for example, do not believe in what they see as an unprovable deity; therefore, Epicurus reigns: "Eat, drink, and be merry, for tomorrow you may die." Some ascribe to Nietzsche's philosophy: God is dead. Perhaps God did exist, but He died. Others espouse existentialism or nihilism: Life is a meaningless accident. Still others believe in the concept of naturalism: Cosmic forces conspire against humanity; environmental and biological determinism ensure our failure, no matter how mightily we struggle. To others God is a laissez-faire deity, some nebulous being somewhere who set the earth spinning and now watches to see how the creatures formed from dust fare. Furthermore, an afterlife is also "unprovable": Heaven is a fantasy; hell hath no fury. Dust to dust, and it's over.

In contrast, folks whom we interviewed did not seem to harbor any such philosophies and fears. They are people whose sustaining faith enables them to live with calm assurance, for they believe in the reality of the resurrection. These elders talked to us about being raised in the church, about being saved, about some specific practices of their religion, about spiritual gifts, and even about heaven, hell, and the last days. They are people of faith—the assurance of things hoped for, the certainty of things unseen (Hebrews 11:1)—a deep, abiding faith in a Maker Who is actively involved in their lives, a triune God Who cares for them. Because of Him, they can face tomorrow. They have a purpose: to glorify God. They believe Jeremiah 29:11: " 'For I know the plans I have for you,' declares the Lord, 'plans to prosper you and not to harm you, plans to give you a hope and a future.' " The belief that God has a plan for them gives their lives meaning and hope. Their hope, however, is not in the things of this world but in the reality of the next: the unseen, eternal world of the spirit.

—*Angie Cheek*

GOD

I think how thankful people ought to be that they're living in this beautiful world, and I wonder how they can ever think that there is not a higher power.

—Aunt Addie Norton

When I was in college at Georgia Southern University, a Christian college professor (I am aware that, to many, "Christian" and "college professor" seem oxymoronic) talked to us about his beliefs. He began by telling a story: Out in space aimlessly floated steel, Plexiglas, aluminum, vinyl, copper . . . you get the picture. Anyway, all these materials were minding their own business when, for some unknown reason or provocation, they came together—*hard!* Out of the aftershock of that huge wham of a consummation flew a 747! The professor used that analogy to explain to us that such an event made as much sense to him as the Big Bang theory. Even after all this time—years!—that analogy has stuck with me, and I have used it myself.

In his book *Grendel* (*Beowulf* told from the monster's point of view), author John Gardner depicts a wounded Grendel's speaking his final words as he sits on the edge of the bottomless chasm and prepares to hurl himself into the abyss: "Poor Grendel's had an accident . . . so may you all" (174). Grendel's search for meaning led this human-like monster to aver that life's events are mere accidents, that the only meaning for our lives is the meaning we ourselves ascribe to our existence. Is our existence accidental? The answer to that question is one each of us must discover for himself/herself.

We all desperately desire to discover the whys of life's triumphs and tragedies. Where is God when we need Him? Why do bad things happen to good people? Why do the wicked seem to prosper? Why, why, why? Our whys lead us to question God. We realize we know *about* Him, but we don't *know* Him. We are "Oh, Best Beloved," like Rudyard Kipling's "Elephant's Child," "full of 'satiable curiosity' ":

I know a person small—
She keeps ten million serving-men,

Who get no rest at all:
She sends 'em abroad on her own affairs,
From the second she opens her eyes—
One million Hows, two million Wheres
And seven million Whys.

We search for meaning. Viktor Frankl, a Holocaust survivor, author, and psychoanalyst, in his work *Man's Search for Meaning,* among the most influential works of psychiatric literature, maintains that we choose our own way; that even though everything we have can disappear, we can choose our own attitude in any given set of circumstances. After being imprisoned in Auschwitz—"the very name stood for all that was horrible" (Frankl, 22)—and then in other concentration camps for a period of over five years during World War II, Frankl wrote the following: "What was really needed was a fundamental change in our attitude toward life . . . *it did not really matter what we expected from life, but rather what life expected from us*" (85).

Many in today's world, those who do believe in a supernatural creator, have a "vending machine" mentality concerning God. We say, "I've put in my quarter. I've prayed. Now give me what I want. Bless *my* will." We're concerned with only that perpendicular pronoun I. We fail to ask God what He expects of us.

As you meet our Foxfire contacts, you will become aware of their deep desire to discover what God expects from them. They pray fervently. You will hear their deep convictions about their God, a God Who is alive and well, and about His mighty power, a saving power not only for tomorrow but for today. He, to them, is Savior, Sustainer, Comforter, Counselor, Friend. They seem not to question His will or His way. They trust and obey and thus live with the joy and peace of the Spirit.

—*Angie Cheek*

"I sit here and study by myself when I have a lot of time, and I think about things. I've got so I can't read my Bible much because I can't see to read for long at a time. I think how thankful people ought to be that they're living in this beautiful world, and I wonder how they can ever think that there is not a higher power. Who makes all these pretty flowers? We can make artificial flowers, but they don't smell and are not as pretty as the flowers that we pick out there. We can't make flowers like the Almighty.

"You've got to have faith to believe in God. You've got to have faith to know that He'll do what you've asked Him to do if it's in His will. When we pray, we've got to say, 'If it's Your will, God, do so and so.' If you don't have faith enough in God, you can't live a very good Christian life.

"I think that asking God for things is healthy. I think that God will grant what I ask for if it is His will. Sometimes we ask for things that's not God's will. And we sometimes don't have any faith in our prayers. You know, we forget the faith; and we think, I don't know if God will do that for me or not."

—Aunt Addie Norton, Summer 1979

"Well, it's right here b'fore your eyes. You can see things a-happenin' ever' day. Different things. I was sittin' here th' other day, and a ol' hen was comin' through here that had chicks. She'd go a little piece. Then she'd cluck. Now what caused her t' do that? I studied about that—just sat here

PLATE 3 "I wonder how they can ever think that there is not a higher power." —Aunt Addie Norton

and watched. She'd go a little piece; then she'd cluck again. Now what makes her do that? 'At's Mother Nature. . . .

"Why, you know that there's a higher power if y' just look out. Now they talk about goin' t' th' moon, and they may've went. I don't know. But that moon . . . is it standin' still or movin', or what about it? Rises here [points], and th' mornin' it's here—plumb across th' world. What d' y' think about that, now? And when it goes, it's dark nights. And when it starts up, it's a bright light thing. It's little and gets bigger and bigger. What changes that? They's somebody, somethin', behind it." **—Kenny Runion, Fall 1971**

PLATE 4 "It's right here b'fore your eyes. You can see things a-happenin' ever' day." —Kenny Runion

"There's just a few times in my life that I've ever been afraid. My dad taught me not to be afraid. Now, he was quite religious. He grew up in the Methodist church. He was superintendent of the Sunday school, and he had this incredible faith.

"He always told me that there's nothin' in one place that's not goin' to be in another. He told me not to be afraid at night out at a camp because I would be in just as much danger there as I'd be sittin' on my porch at home. He built up this immunity to fear in me at an early age, when I was four or five years old. Now, we lived about a fourth of a mile from the main store. All the men went there at night and gathered at the store. He'd let me go with them down there, and then, when I got tired, he let me walk home by myself. He always told me to just go on, that nothin' was goin' to bother me, and nothin' ever has.

"Have faith in the universal life that you are connected to. Now they think of God as a man sittin' up in a high throne with a long beard and white hair, but God is everywhere. It doesn't make any difference what you call Him. You can call Him 'Universal Mind,' 'Allah,' 'Jehovah,' or anything you want to call Him, but He is still everywhere. I always think of it as electricity. You can't see it, but you know it's there. And you can always plug into this Uni-

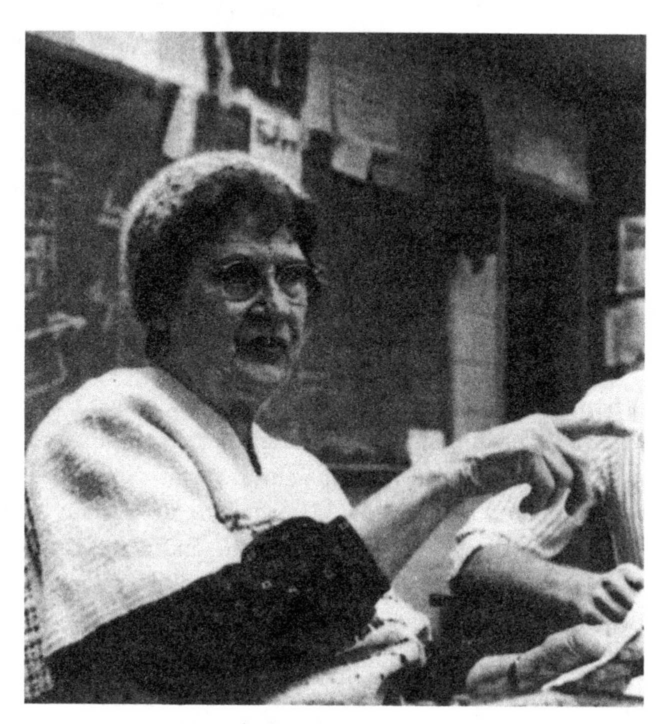

PLATE 5 "Have faith in the universal life that you are connected to." —Lyndall "Granny" Toothman

versal Mind and have faith, and that will take care of you. It's just like electricity. You can take an iron, and you can't heat it unless you plug it in. You've got to be in connection, and if you're in connection, there's nothing in the world that you can't do that your mind can conceive and dream."

—Lyndall "Granny" Toothman, Fall/Winter 1991

"I've lived up here in the mountains, and I don't see nobody or talk to nobody much, but I think the bigger majority of people this day and time put all their values on money and things money can buy. They put all their values on the world and the things of the world, and they're leavin' God out of it. . . .

"You know, I think the Almighty made the world, made the moon and stars and everything in the world. He made the sun, and all of it is His. He put it where He wanted it. Do we have any authority to go up there and bother with it?" **—Aunt Addie Norton, Fall 1976**

"I don't believe they went to the moon. I don't know. But I just don't believe they did. Why, the moon is a . . . I never studied science in my life. I never did go t' school farther than th' seventh grade, and I'm glad I got that much. Children, I'm eighty-three years old. And that's the reason I never did care for science. And I read the Good Book, and the Good Book said that the moon was made to rule the earth and all the heavens therein, fishes of the sea an' the fowls of th' air and even man's body. And the moon rules the vegetation. I don't think they landed up there. You just know what they said. And how do y' know but what they carried them rocks with 'em? Possibility's that they did. And if it was made t' fool with, it'd a-been put down in th' reach of man. I believe that, too, 'cause we know that God created ever'thing.

"I think that the world has made great progress, but they's a few things that I think is money spent foolish, and that is tryin' to go t' th' moon! I don't think that's fair at all. God made everything. He made man t' rule th' earth and all the inhabitants therein. And He didn't make th' moon for man t' play with. If He did, He'd put it down for man to reach. He'd put it, anyhow, where man could get on a stepladder and go up! I don't think that it's . . . well, it's just no means! Th' moon is th' moon. Leave it alone! There's not a thing in the world up there but just th' moon. And if they read th' first chapter of Genesis, they'll find out what th' moon is—first and second chapters, I believe it is—they'll find out how God created the earth. And He made everything. Man was created. The earth was made. I'm not educated, of course, but it's true. We had it in Sunday school yesterday about th' Creation." **—Annie Perry, Summer/Fall 1975**

PLATE 6 "I think that the world has made great progress, but they's a few things that I think is money spent foolish, and that is tryin' to go t' th' moon!" —Annie Perry

"It's through God we have all of our enjoyments, all of our good things. It's through Him that we get it. We know that for sure. We see some of His handiwork every time we look out and see somethin' because He made everything on the earth, and He is the Creator of all the beauties everywhere.

"The first thing when I get up of a mornin' that I want to do is get to a door or window and look out, and I stand there and look and thank the Lord for bein' able to see that beauty one more time. It's a wonderful thing to try to live a Christian life and to love the Lord. We have so much to be thankful for." **—Beulah Perry, Summer 1974**

"Who is it that can make that little bush now right there? Can man? Who is it that can make the fountain of water eternally flow down out there and never stop—flow day and night and never quit? You can go to bed and go to sleep and never wake up 'til in the mornin'. When you get up, the creek is still a-flowin'—a beautiful sight! Who makes the sun shine every day that we live? Who makes the beautiful flowers bloom you look upon? Can man do it? That's why I know there's a God . . . If you just look out there, you know that mankind never done that. Mankind can't have a thing to do in that."

—Garland Willis, Spring 1973

"God has richly blessed me, and I praise Him. God just helps me enjoy every day, and with Him I find something to laugh about every day."

—Clara Mae Ramey, Fall/Winter 1996

"Heartfelt religion will make ye shed a few tears, become humble. We've got people that is full of pride today that they don't want t' shed a tear. It might mess up their makeup—ruins their looks. But our Lord cried; He shed tears. I can't preach much 'til I get t' cryin'; then I enjoy hit a sight in the world. You don't see many tears shed in the pulpit today—honorin' Him with their lips, but their hearts are far from Him. There ain't no way to be a Christian without some emotion. If they ain't no emotion, they ain't no love of God there.

"God is a-gonna have some praise. These people who are too stubborn and are too full of sin to praise Him here, they'll praise Him in hell, but hit'll be too late.

"My method of preachin' is this: I don't write out any sermons, don't prepare any. I read that Book, and then I get on m' knees. If God says, 'Preach hell hot and heaven sweet,' hit'll just come." **—Garland Willis, Spring 1973**

"People don't pay enough attention to the Lord this day and time. You've heard people say, 'I've got so-and-so. I've got so many acres of land. I've got this; I've got that.' Honey, let me tell you somethin': We've not got a foot of land to our name. It all belongs to the Almighty God, and He just gives it to us, just to live on what time that we live here in this world, to do what we please with it. But it does not belong to us. We've not got anything, honey. What could we do? Can you tell me anything in the world that we can do if it wasn't for the power of the Almighty God? We wouldn't have ever breathed. We couldn't have done anything."

—Aunt Addie Norton, Fall 1976

"I'm not a monkey, and I'm not akin to a monkey. The Bible says man was created in the image of the Lord, so He wasn't a monkey either."

—Randy Grigsby, Fall 1988

"I've lost a husband and two children, and that's the worst thing I've ever done in my life is givin' up my children. Now my husband, that hurt—it hurt; I lost two of my children. That was about the hardest thing I've ever done. I've went through some mighty tough times, but God's been good to me. He sure has been good to me. He took me through all of this. . . .

"Now, I've been through it, and I've had a lot of hardships and sufferin', but I'm still hangin' in there. I'm ready to see what's gonna happen next!" **—Fannie Ruth Martin, Fall/Winter 2002**

"Faith in God—the most important thing. I've always believed that we'd know one another in heaven. My boy, y' know, he got killed when he was seventeen years old. After Mommy died, I'd come home. I was up there, an' I'd been plowin' that day. They was plenty o' beds, but I had a urge t' sleep where Mommy had slept. That was in the front room where the couch was a-settin'. An' I slept there. I jest laid down, an' I wasn't asleep. I was awake. An' I'd studied a lot over that, an' I'd prayed over hit. An' that night I'd laid down, an' Mommy and Kenneth, my son, they appeared on the side o' that couch, and they 'as the brightest, shiniest people. An' they had their arms around one another a-talkin'. Now I couldn't hear a thing they said. An' I just lay there and watched, an' they jest passed. An' I know God sent them to show me that Mommy and Kenneth knowed one another in heaven th' same as they had on Earth. An' I have never worried another minute. An' I live with that hope of all these loved ones and friends, ye know—when I'm out of this world, I'll be with 'em, and I'll know 'em. So I guess faith in God is the one thing I couldn't live without.

"But it's easy to backslide. I have done it in my life. I have backslid. But God'll whup ye out when you do, an' when God whups ye, that's the worst whuppin' you'll ever get. Several years back when my younguns was awful small was the worst experience—I'll never forget. I had backslid, an' God brought me down sick on the bed. An' He spoke t' me and told me I'd either come back to Him or He'd take me away from my little younguns.

"Now I prayed all night long 'til early the next mornin'—that's been several year ago—and God accepted me back in, an' I said I'd have to be plumb crazy to ever turn my back on God again." **—Ethel Corn, Fall 1973**

"Religion is everything to me." —*Eunice Hunter*

"Religion is everything to me. That's just life. If you don't know the Lord, then you don't know anything. To me, you just don't have a life, because without Jesus Christ, I couldn't do anything. I grew up in church. My grandmother used to take me to church when I was little, and she'd have handkerchiefs. She ironed every one of 'em, and they were real pretty handkerchiefs. She would tie my pennies up in a corner of a handkerchief to take to church with me. I was tiny, and I still remember that. I've just always gone to church. I was saved when I was twelve, and over the years I think I have grown more and more to realizing exactly what that means to me because when something comes up or anything, you know, we just can't do anything on our own. Without Christ there's no way. There's just absolutely no way. So Philippians 4:13, that's my favorite verse to go by because I can do all things through Christ. I may not do it like anybody else. I may not be perfect doin' it. But I can do it . . . Acceptin' the Lord and having Him as my Savior is the happiest and most important time of my life."

—Eunice Hunter, Spring/Summer 2004

"While at Sister H.'s this afternoon, she told me of how a poor widow, a Mrs. N., made a coat for an idiotic brother of a rich man, a member of the church. He asked his wife what *she* thought it was worth; she replied, 'Forty cents.' He then sent the poor woman a bushel of corn, which was worth very little in payment for the coat. Not long afterwards, this man's chimney, though seemingly secure, without any apparent cause, came crashing to the ground. This same woman sent to another man, a member of the church, too, her last dime to get some [corn] meal. He sent her word he could not sell her so small a quantity. In a short while afterwards, his mill was blown all to pieces. These casualties seem to have been the visitations of Divine Justice on these two men for their oppression of the poor."

—Reverend R.O. Smith, Winter 1972

"We can't see God. We can't see th' Holy Ghost. We can't see Jesus. They're all up yonder. But the Holy Ghost is here, but He's somethin' that you can't see here on the earth . . . God is a person, but you can't see Him. I believe that's the reason so many people don't believe in Him."

—Reverend Browning, Spring 1973

"God didn't put us here to stay. He didn't give us children to keep either. It was hard to give up my youngest son, but I don't question God why 'cause he would really have suffered if he had lived on . . . he had cancer. He told me one day, he said, 'Mom, you're not supposed to bury children. Children are supposed to bury their parents.' I said, 'No, God needs younguns the same as He needs olduns.' It was hard, though. God knows best."

—Frances Harbin, Fall/Winter 2004

"God answers your prayers. He showed Himself to me whenever I would pray and ask Him to do something like to help Doc, my husband, when he was sick. He always did help y'all because y'all are still livin' today. I guess

PLATE 7 "I guess the most valuable thing I have ever had is God changin' my life from a sinner to a Christian." —Estelle Chastain

the most valuable thing I have ever had is God changin' my life from a sinner to a Christian." —**Estelle Chastain, Fall/Winter 2003**

"Now you take old people. Why, don't th' Bible tell you 'honor your father and mother'? Don't make no difference when they get old. Why, don't do anything agin' [against] 'em. Young folks think they're far ahead of their own parents because they've got a little education from man's work—not from th' work of God but from the work of mankind." **—Hillard Green, Fall 1970**

"My mother died on Sunday, she was buried on Tuesday, and the following weekend my father was remarried. He chose to live in the Atlanta area with his new wife. He left my brother and me in our little house in Youngcane [Georgia] to look after ourselves.

"The winters get sort of severe over there. I can remember waking up sometimes, and I'd have ice frozen across my face from the condensation of my breath. I think being cold was one of the things I remember most. It would be dark by the time the school bus got me home. Some mornings I didn't properly cover the coals in the fireplace before I left for school. I would come in by myself in the evening; the fire would be completely out, and I'd not have kerosene to start a new fire.

"There were times I could almost literally leave my body, and it was like the cold, the hunger, the troubles were happening to someone else. I could just step aside, and I wasn't cold anymore. I wasn't hungry. The Japanese have this theory that one can drink tea from an empty cup. That's the way I think I got. . . .

"I think that if it had not been for my faith in Jesus Christ as being my friend, I probably would have died. I felt like He was the only friend I had, and He would be there when no one else was. When Mother was living, we didn't go to church that much. It was just something that I have felt strongly about all my life. Christ was the one friend that would never let me down. Even now, I don't go to church regularly. I don't belong to a particular church or anything, but I feel very close to my Creator. As a child, I think that I had more openness, and I had not learned to hate. So that's the reason I felt so much closer."

—Carolyn Stradley, Fall 1984 and *Foxfire: 25 Years*

"Our pastor had preached about Jesus's love to us, and it was on a Sunday before Easter. In my child's mind I could see the three crosses and Jesus dying for me. The invitation hymn was 'I Gave my Life for Thee, What Wilt Thou Give to Me?' I responded to the invitation that morning, accepting Christ and becoming a Christian [and] the call to become a missionary." **—Dr. Edith Burney, Spring/Summer 2001**

PLATE 8 As missionaries, Dr. Burney and her husband, Bob, pose with fellow Nigerian teachers.

"My parents gave me advice. They teached us how to live right and treat everybody alike, and that way we would have no enemies at all. They told us to just live for the Lord and all will go right."

—Icie Lou Ester Carpenter Dills, Fall/Winter 2003

"So God does all things well. Just look how He's blessed us. Boys, you need t' never fear t' trust in th' Lord 'cause I don't care what you do: If you do it in th' right way and in th' right spirit and do it for th' glory o' God, He'll return it to you fullfold. He'll sure do that. Now, I've tried that. Me and Ulyss' [her husband] both tried that. Yes, sir."

—Aunt Arie Carpenter, *Foxfire: 25 Years*

"I have some advice for younguns—I sure do—if they'll do it. If all you young people would get y'self in a good church somewhere and turn y'self over to the Lord—I'm talkin' about get saved, start servin' God—we'd have a good country to live in everywhere. That's the advice I'd give them today, and that's the only hope we have. If they don't turn to God, it's gonna get worser, and time is gonna get worser than what we see right now if people don't come back to God and do their first work. You just can't get that across to people today. God will always be with you through good and rough times." **—Lois Martin, Spring/Summer 2002**

THE BIBLE

The Bible will give you prayers for a lifetime.
—Naomi Welborn McClain, Spring/Summer 2004

In church, little children sing about the Bible, God's Holy Word: "God's Word is a lamp unto my feet and a light unto my path." Believers see the Bible as the inspired, God-breathed Word of God, a book of prophecy and promise, the prophecy of the coming Messiah, the promise of life eternal with Him in heaven. It is a history of God's chosen people; it is the story of the birth, life, death, and resurrection of the Savior, a beacon to light "the narrow way" to life everlasting. It " 'as made fer us t' go by."

Those with whom we shared discussions on religion told us about growing up in homes where their mothers or fathers read the Scripture regularly. These folks see the Bible as a guide that reveals God's plan for their lives.

They understand Jesus to be the preincarnate Word—the Way, the Truth, and the Life. The Bible is a revelation of the truth.

—*Angie Cheek*

"My people went more on the Bible times, you know. We'd go to church and hear the preacher and read our Bibles. Now, we don't keep up with it like they did: They read it and went by that Bible . . . Parents took up a lot of time with their children. It wasn't just once in a while. My parents, on rainy days or at nighttime or in the mornin', would read a little Bible Scripture, or they'd tell us about somethin' that was said in Sunday school . . . Most of these people now just say, 'Well, go ahead. I don't want to be bothered.' They didn't say that when I came along. They had time.

"My religion's the only part of my life that stays with me today. My Bible teachin' and trainin' from back as far as I can remember, that's the sweetest part of my life. The Bible is our guide. We wouldn't know how to serve the Lord if we didn't know a little about the Bible."

—Beulah Perry, Summer 1974

PLATE 9 "My Bible teachin' and trainin' from back as far as I can remember, that's the sweetest part of my life." —Beulah Perry

MRS. DOWDLE: My mother taught me about th' Bible and that they was a hell and a heaven. Lots o' people argue with y' that they ain't no hell. Today, they say th' hell is here on earth.

MR. DOWDLE: That's what a lot of 'em's tryin' t' claim. Now what about people like that? Boys, it won't do! Accordin' t' my a-lookin' at it, it just won't do.

People believed on th' Bible more then. They appreciated th' Bible more'n they do now. Yes sir, they's lots o' folks come in here, and I'd ask 'em t' have prayer 'r somethin' or t' read some Bible t' me. They'd glance up, and mebbe they didn't want t' do it. See, now that's th' way it is.

We had some neighbors—they're not Christian—and I asked 'em if either of 'em prayed. They said no.

I said, "Well, we have prayer. If you want t' stay fer prayer, it's about bed-time. I'm gonna pray. I'm gonna read some Scriptures here, and we're gonna have a prayer." And they didn't come back fer th' longest time. They never come back now. Well, that's all right. If that's all they know now and all they can learn, why, I ain't responsible. I tried t' show 'em what 'as right there, and I tried t' tell 'em.

Never go t' disputin' that Bible, folks. You're doin' th' wrong thing. That 'as made fer us t' go by.

—Mr. and Mrs. Thad "Happy" Dowdle, Spring/Summer 1971

"It'll make you wise, that Bible will—ain't a thing wrong with it. It's the truth. It has helped to keep me outta jail. By just knowin' what it said, it's kept me outta jail and not to do things that I know is wrong."

—Harold Houck, Spring/Summer 2001

"I never started the day without reading the Bible. I had a book called *Herbert's Story of the Bible.* I've used three editions of that book up. I still have it for my grandchildren. But the children would often ask during the day, if we had any spare time, 'Read us a story from the Bible.' We always had the Bible reading and a pledge to the flag. I still feel like sometimes when I go back to substitute teach that it just doesn't feel right without starting the day with a prayer and a reading of a Bible story."

—Mildred Story, Summer 1986

"I'll tell you somethin'—you all may not know this—the book of the Psalms will help you live a sure enough life. Read that Book of Psalms! Every time I would just about get ready to quit, I'd read my night lesson in Psalms, and I'd find somethin' to bring me up. That's the truth. But, boys, I just wouldn't take nothin' for the Book of Psalms. I love it."

—Viola Lenoir, Fall 1981

"I just knew we was all gonna be washed away." *—Flora Youngblood*

"When I was real little, we lived down in a low place, kinda in a valley like. Well, it came a lot of rain that time—just rainin', rainin', rainin', rainin'—and I'd heard the grown-ups talk about the floods, you know. My daddy had been reading to me about Noah's Ark in the Bible, back when the Flood came. Well, I was too small to understand what it was all about, but I knowed just a flood came and washed everybody away. That's all I had in my mind. Well, it rained and rained, and we couldn't go to school because it was so rainy. I got out in the yard one day and came runnin' back in the house: 'Mama, Mama, it's comin' a flood!'

"Mama said, 'How do you know it's comin' a flood?'

"I said, 'There's just water everywhere.' I was scared, just as scared as I could be.

"Then my daddy called to me. He said, 'Come here. Let's get this straight now. Back in them olden days, back when people was wicked, God seen people destroyin' the first world. A flood came and washed everybody away, but the ones that was ready to go, Noah had built an ark for them. The ones that wasn't ready to go in the ark . . . well, they was washed away.'

"So that kinda satisfied me a little, and I calmed down. [Laughs.] I just knew we was all gonna be washed away, you know, 'cause there was water everywhere! My daddy told me the big Flood's already been, and it took away all the mean people. Well, that satisfied my mind right there."

—Flora Youngblood, Spring 1985

"When Sunday mornin' come, everybody recognized the house of the Lord. They didn't work on Sunday like they do now. You never found anybody who worked on Sunday.

"I just don't give a tull about long hair 'cause the Bible says it's a shame for a man to have long hair. Hit's the right thang fer a woman t' do [1 Corinthians 11]. Does that mean that a person with long hair can't be a Christian? No, sir, if that Bible tells ye somethin' to do and ye don't do hit, ye lack that much bein' a Christian. Hit says a drunkard shall not inherit the kingdom of God . . . [The drunkard says,] 'I can't get this 'cause I'm a drunkard.' See what I mean? We're gonna live or die. Choice—where we're gonna live eternally or die eternally. 'Now choose this day whom you will serve.' "

—Garland Willis, Spring 1973

"I advise you not to be carried away with the ways of the world. The Bible says, 'Love God and love your neighbor.' That's the commandment that Jesus gave: 'Love God and love your neighbor.' In order to do that, you've got to study the Bible a whole lot, and you've got to go to church and hear the Gospel preached. You've got to mix and mingle with Christian people, and you've got to worship your Maker. We were put here for a purpose. This world was made for man's enjoyment, for man's use. Man was put in charge of the world and everything that's in it. We don't realize it, but the Spirit of the Lord is present at any time. If you call on It in faith, you'll get an answer." **—Esco Pitts, Summer 1979**

"We were raised in a good, old-time Christian home. What our parents said was right—there wasn't anything else said about it.

"Now, my parents would sit and spend the evenin', the night, their whole daytime and read the Bible to us. And my father would have a prayer every night and most of the time in the mornin's—'round the table. Sometimes my father would have to get up early and leave before we were up, and my mother taught me and my older sister t' pray. She would say, 'Now you all got to pray this mornin'. Your papa had to leave early.' And we didn't know anything about prayin', and Mama said, 'Well, you'll have to learn. Don't you know how it's done? You know how to ask me and your father for things, and you know how to thank us for things.'

"We said, 'Yes, ma'am.'

"And she said, 'Well, that's just the way you talk to the Lord.'

"You know a lot of people are blamin' the young folks for a lot of things, like losin' interest in the Bible and church life. Well, I don't. I'll be different. I believe we older people, people who have children, are responsible for part of it. They just haven't taken the time, and, you know, it takes time. People have got to have a lot of patience with children. We didn't go to bed without havin' that prayer. We'd go to the table in the mornin'—we had a great big country dinin' room with a big bench; it would seat about six of us on one bench—and we would have the mornin' prayer. Then we would eat. Rainy days, maybe, we'd have a little leisure, and Mother would get it down and read the Bible to us. Nowadays, people don't have time, or they don't make time. Back when I was a girl, people's mothers and fathers worked at home—they didn't go out and work. It was on the farm, around the house. . . .

"My people went more on the Bible times, you know. We'd go to church and hear the preacher and read our Bibles. Now we don't keep up with it like they did. They read it and went by that Bible."

—Beulah Perry, Summer 1974

"Religion has played a part in all I have ever had. It wasn't much of a life until I found the Lord. I don't read the Bible as much as I did, but I still read it. I love to read the Bible. Everybody ought to read the Bible. There's many a thing in there that you can learn about. If you don't read the Bible and study it, then you wouldn't learn nothin' about it."

—Estelle Chastain, Fall/Winter 2003

CHURCH

I think the church is the greatest institution on earth. To be a true Christian, we have to put Christ first in our life. If it wasn't for the church today, this world wouldn't last an hour.

—Preacher Ben Cook

Church was important to the life of the community as well as to the spiritual life of the individual believer. Many horseback- or buggy-riding circuit preachers have a place in the history and folklore of mountain churches. These dedicated men whom God had called to preach had to traverse ten, fifteen, or more miles over treacherous trails and winter's icy streams to conduct both morning and evening Sunday services, Wednesday-night services, and revivals. Revivals, special times in the life of the church, were "extra" worship services meant to "revive" or renew people's faith and zeal for the Lord or to bring individuals to salvation. Revival meetings could last as long as one month or as short as a few days. Preachers, usually invited to come speak to the congregation and visitors, often conducted one service a day, but two or more services a day were not uncommon.

Ministers of the Gospel feel they received a divine call to preach, and though some initially tried to ignore or deny God's call, His knocking on the doors of their hearts became a summons they could not resist. Ben Cook, a Southern Baptist preacher from whom we learned much about mountain religion, once told us, "You've got to turn yourself loose to the Lord." Preacher Cook and others like him have a deep and abiding faith that God is alive and well and working His plan in the lives of His children, that "in all things God works for the good of those who love him, who have been called according to his purpose" (Romans 8:28).

To hear these circuit preachers, many churchgoers walked several miles, or they rode in horse-, mule-, or ox-drawn wagons. To see "five or six old steer wagons" tied up in the churchyard was not unusual. Church was not only a place to commune with God but also the social gathering place for the community. Several told us about dinners on the grounds, "sock suppers," or square dances about which their parents and other adults knew nothing. Many a young man dated by attending church services and activities and then walking his "date" home. Daisy Justice,

"Mama Daisy" to most of the folks around here, told us, "Usually when you 'as a-datin', somebody'd ask at church to go home with you, and they'd just walk y' home."

We had heard about some churches still practicing the phenomena written in Mark 16:16–18. After Jesus's resurrection, He appeared to many. One of those appearances was to the eleven apostles as they were eating:

> He said to them, "Whoever believes and is baptized will be saved, but whoever does not believe will be condemned. And these signs will accompany those who believe: In my name they will drive out demons; they will speak in new tongues; they will pick up snakes with their hands; and when they drink deadly poison, it will not hurt them at all; they will place their hands on sick people, and they will get well." (NIV)

I feel obligated to tell you that a footnote in my *NIV Study Bible* notes that "serious doubt exists as to whether these verses belong to the Gospel of Mark. They are absent from important early manuscripts and display certain peculiarities of vocabulary, style, and theological content that are unlike the rest of Mark. His Gospel probably ended at 16:8, or its original ending has been lost" (1530).

Nevertheless, over a nine-month period, Foxfire students visited a mountain church to witness firsthand some of the practices we had heard or read about: snake handling, handling fire, speaking in tongues, and the laying on of hands. I wish we could give you the true feel of these five-hour services—the songs, the noise, the preaching by several ministers and laymen, the drama. Hopefully, the photographs and anecdotes we've included will give you some idea. We also visited with other contacts who told us about these "gifts" and other practices such as footwashings.

We did not attempt to judge what was happening, for all of us are struggling to discover our own truths. But no matter what you think about the above practices, you will find the churches to be alive and the churchgoers whom we interviewed to be strong believers with total commitment to God and to each other.

—*Angie Cheek*

BEING RAISED IN THE CHURCH

"Raise up a child in the way that it should go, and when it is old, it will not depart from it." You raise your child up. We have to start when that youngun is little. —Aunt Addie Norton

You don't have to talk with very many of our elders to discover what an important part the church has played in their lives. In fact many told us they were in church whenever the doors opened. Though they informed us that they truly wanted to go, they also admitted that going to prayer meeting was not a choice: Their parents made sure they went.

A basic doctrine they hold is that the foundation of the church, the cornerstone, is Jesus Christ; the church is the body of Christ. Christ is the head; believers are the body, the bricks, the church. Everyone has a special task to perform as part of the body. (See 1 Corinthians 7:7 and 1 Corinthians 12.)

Because of "being raised in the way they should go," the Appalachian folks we interviewed, though they might have "backslid" for a time, have, like the prodigal son, come back to the Father. They attend church and worship the Lord, and they are quick to tell you that going to church and being part of the body of Christ has impacted and changed their lives.

—Angie Cheek

" 'Raise up a child in the way that it should go, and when it is old, it will not depart from it.' You raise your child up. We have to start when that youngun is little. Just as soon as it gets old enough to talk and things like that, we've got to begin to train that child.

"It may go wild for a while—'sow wild oats,' a lot of folks call it. And after a while it's gonna come back if you raise it in church and raise it like it ought to be.

"I've made an awful boo-boo a lot of times with mine. My husband wasn't a Christian. He didn't belong to the church, and we didn't have prayer in the home and things like that like people ought to. And I regret a lot of things I didn't do. I prayed *for* them, but I didn't pray *with* them. That's what helps is to pray *with* them. Take them to church. Don't *send* them to church; *take* them to church.

"I always have loved to go to church all my life. That's somethin' I've always loved to do. And I feel like it's my duty when Sunday comes to go to church. . . .

"I don't think it's right to have so many denominations. I think that we all belong. Now, let me ask you, what's the use of all these different denominations? We all have the same Bible. Now, baptism is a little different in some of them. I can't see why we can't all be together. I think Christ's church is one. It's not a dozen. His church is just one church. I don't know if it's a Baptist or a Methodist. I don't guess He has any denominations. I love the Methodists and the Presbyterians, and I'm a Baptist."

—Aunt Addie Norton, Fall 1976

"Well, as far as religion in my life, I joined the Methodist church when I was nine years old. Jack Waldroop was our preacher. He took up a lot of time with me. I guess he realized that I needed help. I believe just like the Bible verse says: 'Raise up a child in the way that he should go, and he won't depart from it.' I think that's very true. You can kinda lose your way every once in a while, but then you find your way back and realize your mistakes because your conscience is always there. You know when you're wrong.

"My parents always taught me to go to church, listen to your preacher's counsel, and obey your parents. The main thing that impressed me was the way my parents lived their life—not full of greed but willing to help people—and the way they overcame hardships."

—Malcolm Dillard, Spring/Summer 2003

"The person who inspired me the most in my life, I guess, was my father. Ever'body says that I sing just like him. I don't think I can sing as good as he did. I always wanted to be just like my daddy. Another thing that inspired my life was my Christian home. It made me want to always live right. I had a good Christian daddy and mother, and they always taught us right. They always taught me to do right and be good to ever'body and love 'em."

—Senia Southards, Spring/Summer 2003

"My daddy used to take me to church when I was a little girl, and he used to knock the dew off the corn and weeds so I could get through without gettin' my shoes and my dress dirty. I remember it so well because I was really happy goin' with him. Getting up early Sunday mornin' to get to go with Daddy were some of my happiest days. After church we went to our grandpa's to eat dinner, and we played with all the rest of the children that came to my grandpa's.

"Religion has played a big part in my life because my parents were both Christians. They taught us to be better Christians. We never wanted to do anything but go to church. When I got married, my husband and I both got saved. All my children got saved and are leading a Christian life today. My grandchildren are, too."

—Naomi Welborn McClain, Spring /Summer 2004

"My parents taught me the values of going to church early because that is something good to do. I do not remember not going to church. The only difference is we were out in the country. We did not have a full-time preacher. It was once a month the preacher would come up. He lived in Atlanter, and he would come and preach on a Saturday afternoon and again on Sunday. I would remember on a Saturday that they would have a conference, so they would take up tithes and whatever was necessary. Then after the business was taken care of, the preacher would preach. One hour was the length of the service for preaching. After you had your business and your hour of preaching, you were ready to go home. . . .

"My grandfather gave the land for the Baptist church where my wife and I were both baptized. Religion has been a big part of my life. I do not remember what year it was that I joined the church. I was a deacon pretty early in my life. I taught Sunday school classes."

—Thomas Coy Cheek, Fall/Winter 2003

"People don't make the children go to church or school like they used to. Now sometimes when we're goin' to church, the road is full of little children playin' ball. If you don't train them when they're little, which way are they goin' when they grow up? I blame the parents for that. They could send the children to church now, and when they get grown and want to change, that would be their business . . . On Sundays, we automatically got up goin' to Sunday school and church. My grandmother didn't have to ask us, 'Are you all goin' to Sunday school?' We just got up and got ready. We didn't stay out like the children do now either. We went back home after church. Sometimes we'd go to the B.Y.P.U. [Baptist Young People's Union], and if we went to church at night, our neighbors chaperoned us.

"Our grandmother gave us all a nickel apiece, and we didn't spend it on candy or anything else. We didn't dare do anything like that. We put that nickel in the Sunday school plate like we thought maybe she could see through us and know what we did." **—Anna Tutt, Spring 1978**

"You could take a crowd of children to the church if you wanted to, but you didn't hear no 'hoopin' an' hollerin'. Uh-uh."

—Carrie Stewart

PLATE 10 "If you don't train them when they're little, which way are they going when they grow up?" —Anna Tutt

"People taught the children so different then. You could take a crowd of children to the church if you wanted to, but you didn't hear no 'hoopin' an' hollerin'. Uh-uh. They'd go in there and would sit quiet. But now people leave their children at home and go to church and leave them there to cut up. I don't know, it's so different to what it once was. There's so many things that children don't know anything about now. Well, I guess everything is changed.

"I was just thinkin' that in the church on one side the women would sit, and on the other side the men would sit. The women and men didn't all sit on the same side. I wondered why that was.

"I bet a million times I sat on a church bench with my little ones strowed 'long there, you know, my children sittin' up on the bench. I would always take a little half-gallon bucket of water and a little tin cup. We had pint cups and half-pint cups back then. I'd take that little bucket of water and a little half-pint cup, and I'd set all my little ones on the bench. My oldest daughter, Ella, would slide off the bench and give the little children a drink of water if they wanted one. I never allowed my children to run in and out of the church.

"I had one son; he was very comical. There was a preacher that, I don't know, he just liked this boy because he was kind of comical—like, you know, loved to do things. So one Sunday he wanted to know—asked the preacher—could he sit up there in the pulpit with him. The preacher said, 'Yes! You can sit up there.'

"My boy said, 'Well, can I sing?'

"The preacher said, 'Yeah, you can sing if you want to.' And, you know, I had to keep punchin' him to keep him from singin' too loud!

" 'Way back then, they had outside door toilets, you know, and these children would go there to this toilet and spread paper over the holes, and they'd have prayer meetings there. I was just thinkin' about how funny it was.

"They'd have prayer meetin's, you know. And they'd pray, and they'd shout. Well, they wasn't makin' like children—they was makin' it real. And they'd have what they call 'the mourner's bench.' They'd say, 'Well, he wants to be converted, wants to turn to Christian.' And he'd go to the mourner's bench. Well, some of the older ones'd go to talk to him, you know, and tell him how to pray and all like that. And after a while, one would jump up, you know, and just shout and holler. But they don't have times like that now. Children don't play like that." **—Carrie Stewart, Fall 1981**

"Walkin' to church—we used to walk to church. It was on Warwoman [Road], and it would take us about an hour and a half to get to Pleasant Hill. We'd go to prayer meeting. We would mostly just go to church once a week, but when they'd have revival, we'd go every night. We had a church bell. They'd rang that bell. When anybody died in our community, somebody went and rung the church bell however old they was—we would guess. We knew everybody, about who it was that was that age. We had dinners at the church out on the ground. Then, finally, we built us a homemade table outside. I guess that was the greatest thing of growin' up."

—Effie Mae Speed Bleckley, Spring/Summer 2004

"The church service, they had every Sunday, of course. Then they had revival meetings which would last a week long. All the men would sit on one side, and the women, on the other. They had a lot of shoutin'. They would sing without music 'cause they didn't have any kind of instrument to play. 'Course, everybody always went to the revivals 'cause that was entertain-

PLATE 11 "When anybody died in our community, somebody went and rung the church bell however old they was—we would guess."
—Effie Mae Speed Bleckley

ment back then, and that was the only place to go. That's one reason a lot of people went to church back then.

"The church service was in the schoolhouse. 'Course, they didn't have a church. Preacher preached a lot about hell. He didn't have an education. He may have finished the seventh grade, but he knew a lot about the Bible 'cause that's the only book he read.

"We had a 'mourner's bench.' If you were sittin' in the back and you felt convicted, you would go up to the front; then you would kneel down, and the other Christians would come up and pray with you. Sometimes if you were sittin' in the back (and they knew who was Christian and who wadn't), some of the good sisters would come back and grab you by the arm: 'Now come on!' That's true. You hadn't heard of that, had you? Oh, yeah, they'd go back and embarrass y', y' know. Most people'd go up just to get rid of 'em.

"They always went to see the neighbors after church, which may be two or three miles apart. At church everybody would invite you home with 'em: 'Go home with me.' Sometimes y' did, y' know. You were welcome everywhere you went. They were glad to see somebody 'cause they were lonely livin' way out by themselves.

"When anybody died, the neighbors would go in, an' they would wash the body. My mother, back then, made most of the burial clothes. The men would make the casket. They would make caskets out of wood, and they would line it with some kind of cloth or somethin'. The service was usually held at the cemetery. Back then, they didn't take 'em to church. They took 'em to the cemetery. People would mourn and carry on. Anyway, they would let 'em down with ropes down into the grave. They didn't have any vaults. To me, that was sad that you had to watch them go down in there. Then they'd throw the dirt on 'em.

"Sometimes they would bury 'em near their home. It depends what the family wanted to do. There was lots of graves out near homes. Most of my folks were buried in a regular cemetery because my grandfather had given the plot for it. I can go back there now, and there's all my ancestors.

"Most times, the way you'd meet some boy was he might come home with your brother, or you would meet him at a church and revival meetings. It's real funny—the young boys would never go inside the church, but they'd be there. They'd be out in the yard lookin' in the windas, winkin' at the girls. We'd wink back at 'em. Then when you came out the church, if a boy wanted to take you home, he'd come up and take you by the arm, and if you didn't like him, you'd just push his arm off or, most times, kick him. He realized you didn't want him. If you went home with him, he had that arm 'til you got home.

"You walked home. Everywhere, we walked. An' many times we'd hear of a revival meeting maybe five miles away, an' we would get up a crowd, y' know, an' walk over there—laugh and talk on the way—go to revival and come back. Right neat." —**Lois Duncan, Spring /Summer 2000**

PLATE 12 "Preacher preached a lot about hell. He didn't have an education. He may have finished the seventh grade, but he knew a lot about the Bible 'cause that's the only book he read." —Lois Duncan

"We had a preacher come once a month, but we had superintendents to run the church when the preacher wasn't there. We had a lot of singin's . . . One of the neighbors would let the young people come to their house and sing for a while. Then they'd fiddle with the banjos and 'juice' harps [jew's-harps]. The singin's usually turned into a big square dancin'. A lot of them never did know we were square dancin'. They might have surmised it, but they never said anything about it."

—Martha Roane, Winter 1983

"We had church services every Sunday. We had Bible school and the little catechism. We had church on Sunday night and church on Wednesday night. We attended them, too. We knew to. We didn't say no. The preacher went home with us on Sunday for dinner. We didn't give him a weekly pay. He would always go home with someone and eat dinner. Seems like he always went home with our family. My mama and daddy had to feed the preacher on Sunday. I'm sure he was just like we were. He lived on a farm. He had a horse and one wagon with two benches behind the wagon seat that he used for everything. We always had to get out on Saturday and clean the chickens for his dinner on Sunday. The preacher's wife came to dinner with him. She'd always be right there."

—Rose Ester Shirley Barnes, Fall/Winter 1997

PLATE 13 "We had church on Sunday night and church on Wednesday night. We attended them, too. We knew to." —Rose Ester Shirley Barnes

PLATE 14 Claude "Buck" Gragg, a member of Flat Creek Baptist Church in Rabun County, Georgia

"I remember goin' to church when I was little. There would be hogs under the floors, and when the preacher was a-preachin', you could hear them under there. They only had one kind of heat—I call 'em pot stoves. Most of the time there wasn't that many people goin' back then, and we would all gather up and get warm around that thang. There were only a few people goin', but it was a great place. Today we have a beautiful church, and it is really growin'!" —**Claude "Buck" Gragg, Spring/Summer 2004**

"The church that we were goin' to, Mount Pleasant Baptist Church in Westminster, South Carolina, was a small country church. It was just a buildin'. A sanctuary was all there was to it. There was no classrooms for Sunday school or nothin'. First, let me tell you when the church was organized. It was organized in 1905. I don't know when that buildin' was built after the church was organized, but they didn't even have a buildin' when the church was first organized. I think there was about nineteen charter members that built the buildin'. It was just one long buildin' with a side door, a front door, and two rows of pews. There was no rooms for classrooms, but the few members would gather by age groups in corners here and yonder all over the buildin'. They'd teach the Bible to the children, young people, and adults.

"In the latter part of the 1920s and the earlier part of the thirties, the women began to talk about needin' classrooms built onto the church. We started a plan about makin' a quilt and sellin' it to the highest bidder and chargin' a dime for everybody that wanted their name on the quilt, and this is the quilt that was made. This quilt that I helped make is famous. It's a Waterlily quilt, and that quilt has made history . . . those names on it . . . everybody's name who's on it paid a dime. We embroidered their names in the corner of a square. Then the quilt was finished an' quilted and sold to the highest bidder.

"Have y'all ever heard of a box supper? When I was growin', they used to have 'em when they raised money for anything. The young girls would get a candy box or somethin'. They'd decorate it up, wrap it in crepe paper, and fix it to look pretty. They'd fix a meal—sandwiches and cake or cookies or somethin'—and put it in that box. The boxes were sold, and the men did the biddin' on the box—he didn't know whose box he was buyin'. The highest bidder got the box, and he had to eat supper with the girl that fixed it.

"We had a sock supper when we was goin' to sell the quilt. Everybody, women and girls, brought a pair of men's socks, and we would put fruit in the toes of the socks. We'd put crackers, nuts, or wrapped candy and fill that sock full of somethin' like that. The socks were sold. The men bid on the socks, and he had to find the girl that made his sock and eat supper with her. Then we had cakewalks. The women baked cakes, and they'd play music. The couples would walk around; when the music stopped, they would get a cake. The main thing was the auctionin' of that quilt. My boyfriend's brother-in-law bought it for him, and he gave it to me for a weddin' present. It brought seven dollars and a half, but this quilt was sold, I think, in 1933, or somewhere along about then, in the early thirties anyway. That was just durin' the Depression. Nobody had much money, but the Lord always blesses what you try to do." [**Editor's Note:** This Waterlily quilt *is* famous: It was on the cover of the Blue Ridge Electric Corporation's *Memorial Calendar of Quilts,* it was in the McKissick Museum in Columbia, South Carolina, in *Early American Quilts,* and it was in the book *Quilt Making in America.*] **—Frances Harbin, Fall/Winter 2004**

"I didn't really go to church when I was young, but I was supposed to. What I did was go downtown and hang out with the boys durin' church hours, but when I met my wife, she turned me around one hundred and

PLATE 15 Waterlily fund-raising quilt of pieced solid-color cottons, 75 inches × 65½ inches, made by women of Mount Pleasant Baptist Church near Westminster, South Carolina. Back-to-front edge treatment machine and blue quilting thread, seven stitches per inch, as well as colored threads in French knot, outline, and buttonhole stitches. Collection of Frances Harbin. Photo by Terry Wild Studio (courtesy of Frances Harbin)

eighty degrees. She had been a Baptist since she was a baby. Every time the church was in, we were there. I'd go with her. So people thought I was a member there, but I wasn't even baptized until 1947. My oldest boy was getting baptized, so I thought it was time for me to get baptized."

—Paul Power, Spring /Summer 2003

"June 18: We had a temperance meeting at the church today for the purpose of praying for the barkeepers in this place and for the removal of the whiskey hells. The meeting was very impressive. Brother Hodges gave us an interesting account of his experience in selling spirituous liquors. He stated that he began with sixty dollars, made fourteen thousand dollars, and finally wound up with a quantity of Confederate money with an old plug of a mule—less than he started with."

—From the journals of Reverend R.O. Smith, Winter 1972

"Go to a meetin' an' see five or six ol' steer wagons tied around up in th' woods, y' know. They's more people then, seems like, that went to church than they do now'days.

"Now'days, you can go to church, an' if you ain't got no money t' pitch in, you may just as well stay home. They don't care whether you die or not if you ain't got somethin' t' throw in th' dadblamed pot. Back in them days, they wasn't no pot t' pass around nor nothin'. If a man had anything t' give the preacher, they'd give him somethin' t' eat." **—Lawton Brooks, Fall 1973**

"We walked to church and everywhere most of the time, unless we went in the wagon. The churchyard was filled up with wagons, buggies, horses, and vehicles, except for them who walked. Some that was fortunate enough, now very few were, but if they were, they had a car. They would not let you ride. They felt better than you. I'd be a-walkin' home from church; they would go by me, and I'd say, 'That's all right. One day I'll have a car!' We walked to school, and we walked to church. There was a bunch of us teenagers, and we would all walk to church. It looked like a big crowd on the road just a-walkin' to church. Once in a while, Daddy would take us in the wagon at night." **—Fannie Ruth Martin, Fall/Winter 2002**

"I was raised up with th' local folks, and I love 'em. We all went to church and Sunday school. I love t' go t' church. I certainly do appreciate workin' for the Lord. I want to feel like I'm at home when I go t' church. It ain't helped Betty's Creek [a community, Dillard, Georgia] one bit for all these outsiders to come in. It sure ain't. I believe the older generation is the strongest and the best in their religion." **—Pearl Martin, Spring 1975**

"This Mr. Moore—he's one of the funniest men we have down at our congregation—he told me, says, 'You know,' says, 'I believe you'd be a pretty good woman if you didn't talk so much. What makes you talk so much?'

"I says, 'Because I got a tongue.' His wife, it just tickled her to death. But they are the sweetest couple.

"Oh, I had a good time, though, workin' in the church, and I'm still stickin' with it." **—Viola Lenoir, Fall 1981**

PLATE 16 "I want to feel like I'm at home when I go t' church." —Pearl Martin

"The church over in the old orchard . . . was more interdenominational even though it must have become a Baptist church for a while because the Methodists, back in 1920 or '21, along in there, begun to build a church where the present church is located. Then the Baptists, they begun to build in the very close proximity to the Methodist church. I think both churches were built in their present location because of the school [Tallulah Falls School, a private boarding school in Tallulah Falls, Georgia] so that the school students could come down to the church."

—Reverend James Turpen, Sr., Fall/Winter 2002

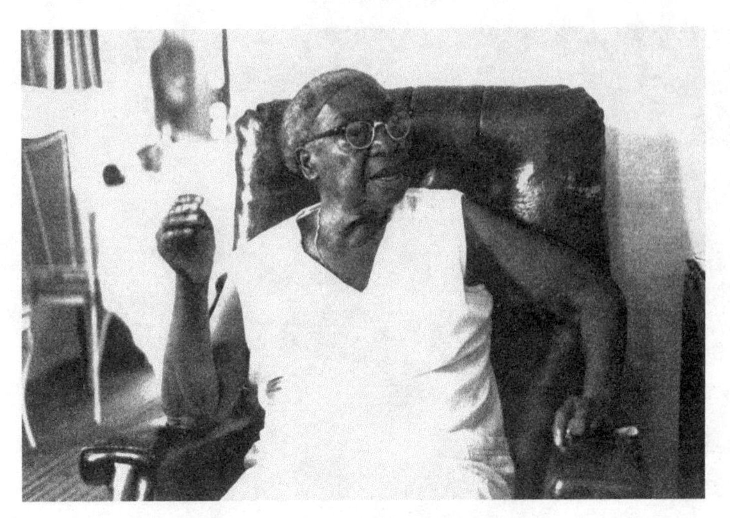

PLATE 17 "You know, I'm still stickin' with it [church]." —Viola Lenoir

"A lot of people don't like to hear you talk about things like that [Christianity] in schools. In a lot of places, it's forbidden, but that's what's wrong with our country this day and time." ***—Frances Harbin***

"We were brought up in a Christian home. We wadn't sent to church: We were carried to church, and we worshiped together. It was a big part of our life. It's a good start when you get out and start a home of your own, too, 'cause a home is not complete 'til a man and a woman takes Christ into it. A lot of people don't like to hear you talk about things like that in schools. In a lot of places, it's forbidden, but that's what's wrong with our country this day and time. It's gettin' worse. I'm sorry for the children comin' up now 'cause parents don't carry children to church like we were carried. They may send the little ones, but their parents don't go. They don't set the example for 'em that should be. I think that's the biggest thing that's wrong with our generation comin' on." —**Frances Harbin, Fall/Winter 2004**

"When I 'as thirteen years old, I joined th' Baptist church. I've been a Baptist ever since. I don't fall out with th' other denominations because hit's not th' church that saves y'. Don't do you any good t' join th' church if you ain't saved.

"I'm a-lookin' forward to a better time than I've got. I've enjoyed life. I've had a lot o' sorrow. I'd a-never went through it all if it hadn't a-been for th' Lord.

"My parents treated us strict. There were parties. We never went to 'em. My daddy said dances would lead you wrong. They trained me that they was a Lord over us all. And they'd read th' Bible to us every night. Had a big fireplace. I can see m' old daddy. After supper he'd throw in a piece o' pine wood, lean his chair back, and read th' Bible to us. I wuz th' oldest. Then he'd get his songbook, and he'd set there and sing. We enjoyed it. We knowed t' behave. I think that has a lot t' do with our young people. Young people get into mischief, but you'll think about what Daddy and Mommy said." **—Aunt Celia Wood, Winter 1972**

"The road from my dad's place to Murphy was eight miles, and it went up the river nearly to town. I'll never forget that day I walked to school—Mother told my brother to put me on the side of the road away from the river so I wouldn't fall in. I've always been afraid of water. I've said I'd never be a Baptist because I wouldn't get under the water!"

—Harriet Echols, Fall 1976

"A lot of church today is form. Back in the days of Jesus, those Pharisees had control of the temple, and Jesus didn't have anything to do with the

PLATE 18 "I've said I'd never be a Baptist because I wouldn't get under the water!" —Harriet Echols

temple. He couldn't: He was born in the manger and wrapped in swaddling cloth. That showed that pride could never enter into the Kingdom of God. Now you've got to get down to the manger if you're ever born into the Kingdom of God. That's how Jesus came into the world. He said, 'Pride is an abomination in the sight of God.' I think that's what's wrong with the churches today. They're not reachin' the lost world. It's been several years since I've seen an old man saved. Today, you've also got to get young people to join the church.

"I think, however, that the church is the greatest institution on earth. To be a true Christian, we have to put Christ first in our life. If it wasn't for the church today, this world wouldn't last an hour."

—Preacher Ben Cook, Fall 1979

"To my parents thirteen children were born . . . My parents were staunch Presbyterians. Since there were so many of us, usually two trips were made to take us to Sunday school and church. We were given a penny to put in the collection plate. Later, my sister Sue taught me that the tenth for a tithe belongs to God to carry His teaching. Sue was then a teacher in Toccoa School [Toccoa, Georgia]. She came home on the weekends. She would make out a check to our church: Hopewell Presbyterian Church. It was the most money I had ever seen. Knowing we did not have that much, I could not understand, and she read to me in our Bible that a tenth of our income belongs to the Lord and should be brought into the storehouse. This impressed me, and my husband and I have continued this in our married life."

—Ruby Mae Miller Cheek, Spring/Summer 2005

"Our grandparents lived on the top of the hill. We would visit with them, and very frequently we went up and took our Sunday school material to be studied with Grandmother. We would have little cards instead of Sunday school books. They were little individual cards, and I can see 'til this day those little cards. They were as big as a postcard with colored pictures. One would be Moses and the basket in the river with his sister, Miriam. I can remember them, and we saved those cards. On a Sunday afternoon, we'd just play with them all afternoon. We would lay them out and read them to our dolls. We were very quiet on Sunday afternoons. We did not get to play noisy games. The boys couldn't play games. We could not even cut with scissors. We could color with crayons if we wanted, but we just could not make doll clothes. There were some rules about Sunday." **—Iris Daniel Engel Barnes, Fall/Winter 2003**

"When we 'as growin' up, we went to church all the time, an' we sang a lot in church. An' after I got right with the Lord, we went to church more than I did before. I played my guitar, an' we sang a lot. They ran a revival up in North Carolina for nine weeks; we didn't miss a night, an' I worked ever'day. Boy, I enjoyed it! There is one thing about it: Salvation ain't got old yet. No, I really enjoy it. There's nothin' like it. An' there is one thing about it: We can live it if we want to."

—Ervin Chastain, Spring /Summer 2005

"I will never forget, one time it was rainin', and along after dinner it went to thunderin' and lightnin' and everything got so dark. And it went to hailin'. You never heard the like! It was a tin roof, you know, and it was just a-hailin' like everything—big ol' hail! Everybody in the church was cryin'. They was scared to death. Mr. Kirk, the mail carrier, was in his buggy, and the kids went up there to the mailbox to talk to him. He said, 'Boys, that was rough! I was comin' up the road, and that hail was just a-beatin' her like everything.'

"We had church meeting every fourth Saturday and every fourth Sunday. That was all the meetings we had unless it was revival. Then we had Sunday school every Sunday. We'd go over there, and they'd sing and have Sunday school and then sing some more. We'd leave here about a quarter 'til ten or twenty minutes 'til, and we wouldn't get back home 'til one o'clock. They'd have to cook dinner for forty. They didn't hurry up. They just took their time and sung several songs before and after Sunday school. They'd come here and eat dinner, especially on preachin' day. Mama has cooked dinner for a house full many a time.

"There was houses all the way around the church then. We had a church full every Sunday school. . . . We always had a big crowd. Back when you had revivals, all the churches watched out and didn't have their revivals when the other churches were havin' it. Everybody would come to Wolf Creek [Lakemont, Georgia]; then they had revival the next week somewhere else, and everybody went there. We've walked many a time from here to Lakemont Church and here to Camp Creek [Lakemont, Georgia]. Sometimes we didn't get home 'til twelve at night. Kids would come home with us, and we'd go to the field and get tomatoes and apples and sit out there in the yard and eat apples. We didn't get in the bed 'til one or two o'clock. Then we got up about five o'clock. We had to get our farmin' done and get ready to go to church at eleven when a revival was goin' on." **—Bernice Taylor, Summer 1990**

PLATE 19 A visiting preacher conducts a revival service.

BEING SAVED

I was down under a bench when I was saved. I had to give up everything; I had to forget everything; I had to die to everything. . . . That's my beginning. —Preacher Ben Cook

In a person's life, "being saved" usually follows the period of conviction. Being "under conviction" is a time in a person's life when he or she realizes that life is incomplete without accepting Christ and the teachings of Christianity. For some, it represents a time of worry and concern, as they are not one of the "saved." The Holy Spirit convicts. God has already chosen each of us; each of us must "choose Him back." "Being saved" means claiming the promises of God's Word. It means that one accepts Jesus as his/her personal Lord and Savior and believes the truth of His teachings. In a Southern Baptist church, baptism by immersion follows. The time between being saved and baptism varies from church to church and person to person. Some believers experience baptism in the church's baptismal font; others, in a creek, river, or lake. Claudine Palmer Cantrell and her husband, Fred, on their memorable trip to the Holy Land, were rebaptized in the Jordan River. Baptism does not save. Being saved is the act of choosing to follow Christ and making Him Lord of your life, the act of the submission of one's will to the will of the Lord. One must subjugate self:

> [Y]ou will never make a good impression on other people until you stop thinking about what sort of impression you are making. Even in literature and art, no man who bothers about originality will ever be original. . . . Give up yourself, and you will find your real self. Lose your life and you will save it. Submit to death, death of our ambitions and favourite wishes every day and death of your whole body in the end; submit with every fibre of your being, and you will find eternal life. Keep back nothing. Nothing that you have not given away will be really yours. Nothing in you that has not died will ever be raised from the dead. (Lewis 226–227)

Dying to self is difficult, but obsessively trying to maintain an illusion is debilitating. If you put yourself on a pedestal, you worry constantly about falling off. The submission of your own will in obedience to God means living by faith. It means having a place prepared for you after this life is over; it means living for eternity in heaven with the Lord, and that truth is no illusion.

The folks we interviewed related many poignant stories of their being saved and the impact that that moment has had on them. Many consider that moment as the most important in their lives. As Eunice Hunter put it, "If you don't know the Lord, then you don't know anything"; Claudine Palmer Cantrell wrote in her journal, "Without faith in our Risen Lord, life for me would have no meaning"; and Mama Daisy confided to us, "I don't think I'd ever made it without God." Because they are saved, our contacts live their lives courageously, for they believe what the Lord told Joshua:

> Be strong and courageous. Do not be terrified; do not be discouraged, for the Lord your God will be with you wherever you go. (Joshua 1:9)

They also profess that "with God all things are possible" (Matthew 19:26 and Mark 10:27); "Everything is possible for him who believes" (Mark 9:23). Their joy sometimes overflows, and many saved believers in the South will shout, for shouting is a vocal, outward display of spiritual joy, and, as Preacher Ben Cook put it, "To be delivered from the power of sin and death is somethin' to shout over."

—*Angie Cheek*

"I was about, I guess, sixteen years old. You know, back then they believed in waiting 'til they got up in age. My father was a minister, and he and old Frank Arrington was in a revival meeting at John's Creek [Jackson County, North Carolina]. It was a school building back then, and I went there—me and my brother and Ham Mash—we were all converted at the same time. I was about sixteen years old, and I got under conviction. I wanted to be saved, but I wanted it to be done in secret, to see if I could live right. Then I'd tell it. (I found out you can't do it that way.) I prayed all week and was under conviction. I got to feelin' good, but I wasn't satisfied. I went there to the altar at John's Creek, an old school building, and down under a seat—they had those old-time seats there in the school building. I don't know what happened, but there was a light that shone brighter than the sun. It shone from the top of my head all over me, and everything was just as white as snow. The congregation looked like angels, and the people that I hated, why, they were the first ones that I put my arm around. The people that I'd called hypocrites back when I was a sinner were the first that I got ahold to, and I loved them. I shouted all over the church. I don't know what happened. Before I got home, the devil tried to make me doubt it, and he tried to make me believe that it was just excitement. But I prayed, and the Lord gave me a sign that I was saved. My brother was saved, too, in the same meeting, and we joined the Balsam Grove Baptist Church and were both baptized together. Ham Mash professed religion that night, and Lem Parker, an old man, was saved the same night. We were all baptized out there in the creek.

"I never did doubt my salvation. I was down under a bench when I was saved. I had to give up everything. I had to forget everything. I had to die to

PLATE 20 I baptize you, my brother, in the Name of the Father and of the Son and of the Holy Spirit.

PLATE 21 Buried with Him in the likeness of His death; raised in newness of life.

everything. When I was born of the Holy Spirit of God, it shone all over me and through me; it made me love everyone. That's my beginning."

—Preacher Ben Cook, Fall 1979

"Seek Christ in your life 'cause life's nothin' without Him. I don't mean that everybody has to be a Baptist. I'm a Baptist. I fully believe in Baptist beliefs, but there's good and there's bad in every denomination. I think that God places in all of us a conviction to know when we need the Lord. I'll never forget the time that I first felt God's call to repent and accept Christ. I was about thirteen when I first felt the need for repentance, but I was about fifteen before I ever really accepted the Lord, joined the church, and was baptized. It was the best decision I ever made. He'll never leave me. I think it's His Holy Spirit that convicts every individual when they need a savior, and it's up to that individual what they do about it."

—Frances Harbin, Fall/Winter 2004

> **"They's some people that join the church, and it don't make no difference in their lives. You've got to live right every day—can't live it just on Sundays." —*Coleman Lyday***

"I wouldn't say I've led a good life. I done what I wanted to do. I didn't live like I should, you know. I was mean as a rattlesnake for years. I didn't go to church. I was tough. I used to drink whiskey and cuss real bad and all that kinda stuff. But the Lord changed me.

"The way it started out was I went to a revival meeting in Asheville, North Carolina. I was about thirty or forty years old when I went to that revival. B. F. Jones was a big healing preacher there, and I went up there with some people who was goin' to get healed—hear the man preach and get healed. They had a big tent meeting, and Jones said for all of 'em to stand up that wanted the congregation to pray for 'em. I couldn't help it. I stood up. He said to come to the front of the tent. Well, I said I wasn't goin' anywhere, but I went to walkin'. I couldn't help from walkin' to save my life. It was like I was walkin' downhill. When I got up there, I felt different all the way around, lightened up. I thought about all the things I'd done, and it changed my life. . . . I hear some people call the Lord's Name in vain, and that just ruins me. It don't come to my mind to say no bad words no more. Why, if somebody offered me a thousand dollars to sell a gallon of liquor or drink a gallon, I'd refuse it. I wouldn't do it.

"After I became saved, money wouldn't have enticed me to backslide. . . . In the revival, I was struck heavy. I couldn't do a thing but just walk. I didn't mean to go either. . . . They's some people that join the church, and it don't make no difference in their lives. You've got to live right every day—can't live it just on Sundays." —**Coleman Lyday, Winter 1979**

"Prayer meetings were held in different homes in the mill village. At the time, my uncle Cliff Palmer, Dad's brother, was preaching. That night I

PLATE 22 "I didn't go to church. I was tough. I used to drink whiskey and cuss real bad and all that kinda stuff. But the Lord changed me." —Coleman Lyday

decided to go, and on January 6, 1938, I was saved. When Uncle Cliff finished his sermon, I went to the bench in the center of the room and knelt by a chair. Everyone in the room gathered around me and began to pray for me. I had never gone to church much, but I knew I was lost. I stayed on my knees until my legs went to sleep. I was determined to wait until I was sure I was saved. Different people were singing, but I just didn't feel satisfied. Finally, near midnight, I prayed, 'I'm willing to give up everything if You will save me.' I was numb from my toes to my waist when I came up. I cannot describe the joy I felt. All the women were hugging me, and the men were shaking my hand. It was as if my singing was going straight into heaven. I will always remember the song. It was 'There's nothing between my soul and the Savior. Jesus is mine; there's nothing between.' Uncle Cliff Palmer baptized me. . . .

"Without faith in our Risen Lord, life for me would have no meaning. My faith has sustained me through most of my life. Many times I have been discouraged. I remember at one time in my life when I felt so helpless and alone, all I knew to do was pray, for I knew that my God could do all things. There is nothing too big for God, and I knew when we come to Him in faith, believing, that He can move in on the scene. God has been a present help in times of trouble all my life . . . I have seen Him work miracles in my life and in the lives around me. I know I don't deserve this wonderful love, but I'm so glad He loves me in spite of my faults and failures. God said in His Word, 'If thou can believe, all things are possible to him that believeth.' "

—From the journals of Claudine Palmer Cantrell, Spring /Summer 2005

> **"When I got up, I don't know what happened, but I know that somethin' came outta me. I jumped up off the floor and shouted all over her house." —*R. A. Miller***

"I got right with the Lord one night when I went to a meeting at the little Methodist church down there. There was a little preacher runnin' a revival. Me and my old lady went there. One night, that little preacher came to me while I was sittin' on a bench in the church. He got on his knees, and I never heard a man pray a prayer like that one in my life. If you've ever been saved, you know how it is. I was hard-hearted before I got saved at a revival.

"Later at home, me and my wife went to bed. Just me and her lived in the house, and somethin' spoke to me. I got to shakin', and the Lord spoke to me: 'I tell you, you better get right, son.' I stood there on the floor, and I believe I shook the bed where she was layin'. 'Lord, if you'll let me live 'til I get back here to Mother's house, I'll make it right.' I put it off. So one night, I came in there, and God said, 'You better get right.' I came in the house, and my mother was sitting in an old chair. I'll never forget. She said, 'Get down, son. Let's go to prayin'.' She was a good woman. We got down there, and I prayed, I don't know how long, but there was a special time I can't tell you about. When I got up, I don't know what happened, but I know that somethin' came outta me. I jumped up off the floor and shouted all over her house . . . We used to have good revivals. You don't hear of any revivals now that are like we used to have." —**R. A. Miller, Fall 1989**

"I remember one time when we were havin' a revival at our church in Waco [Georgia]. Dr. Parish was the preacher. He was a fine evangelistic preacher. The week he was there, he lived in our home. Preachers that came in like that always stayed at our home. It was usually my daddy who brought them in. Anyway, that preacher was preachin' about this train that was goin' down this hill so fast with brakes that wouldn't hold. The train wrecked. He said some of the people on the train were saved, and some of the people were not. Those that were saved didn't have anything to worry about. However, those that were not saved were goin' to the devil. I thought to myself, if anything was to happen to me, I'd like to be saved—I believe tomorrow I'll join the church.

"The next day, he preached about how it was easier for a camel to go through an eye of a needle than it was for a rich man to enter into the kingdom of heaven. That worried me. Of course I was young then. I didn't understand the true message the preacher was talkin' about. Anyway, I consulted my uncle Grady on the matter. I didn't ask my daddy because he would only tell me to take the Bible and study it. I said, 'Uncle Grady, I was goin' to join the church today, but the preacher talked about how it was easier for a camel to pass through the eye of a needle than it was for a rich man to enter into the kingdom of heaven.'

"Uncle Grady, bein' the great trader he was, said, 'Walker, wait until tomorrow. Maybe he'll make you a better proposition.' "

—Walker Word, Summer 1991

"I believe in shouting. I think pride has just almost killed the Spirit of God. My mother shouted as long as she lived. When Jesus Christ comes back to earth again, He's coming with a great shout, isn't He? David said, 'Let them shout from the tops of the mountains.' I think we've got somethin' to shout about if we're born of the Holy Spirit of God. To be delivered from the power of sin and death is somethin' to shout over.

"These old pioneer mothers, back forty or fifty years ago, were always shouting in church. In the revival meetings, there were some of the old mothers that could do things the preacher couldn't do. When some of those old Christian mothers began to shout, it convicted sinners. I think that shouting is just a gift of God, and I think it's a part of the service of God. I love to see the day when they glorify God." —**Preacher Ben Cook, Fall 1979**

"Shoutin' is not appreciated in our churches today. Makes me think of a feller I know. He said, 'Boys, I don't know . . . I've seen peoples happy an' shout, and I can't shout.'

"I said t' him, 'No, no doubt ye can't. An' as long as ye stay a-deer-huntin' on Sunday, you'll never shout. You gotta do somethin' for the Lord.' Some people shout; some cry—different emotion. He'll show up somewhere. Th' preachers now say, 'Anyone here want prayer, ever' head bowed, ever' eye closed.' Why do they want ever' head bowed, ever' eye closed? God is a-lookin' on the sin, an' if a sinner is ashamed before man to confess to the Lord, then He said, 'I'll be ashamed to confess you before My Father and before the angels.' Instead of bein' ashamed of the Lord, we should be proud of Him." —**Garland Willis, Spring 1973**

PLATE 23 "I love to see the day when they glorify God." —Preacher Ben Cook

"I'll tell you another thing that was th' happiest time in my life was when we used t' have a revival meetin' in Coweeta [Otto, North Carolina], and ever'body in the church would get t' shoutin'. That's th' happiest time I ever see'd in my life. Ever'body was as happy as they could be. You don't see many o' them days now, though. Scare a body t' death if they 'as t' see anybody shout nowadays, wouldn't it? [Laughter.] Sure 'nough, I ain't seen nobody shout lately. That was th' happiest time in my life, when I got back t' that church. Now that's th' truth. Words can't express th' feelin' you had. No, sir. I was just th' happiest that I could be."

—Aunt Arie Carpenter, *Foxfire: 25 Years*

"I have missed one year out of thirty-eight years preachin'. January 1, 2002, praise the Lord, we just come out of two weeks of revival that 'as as good a one that I have been in, in I don't know how long. A preacher from Westminster, South Carolina, preached for us for two weeks. People got healed and saved and set free, praise the Lord, but I just thank God. I pray.

PLATE 24 "Scare a body t' death if they 'as t' see anybody shout nowadays, wouldn't it?"
—Aunt Arie Carpenter

I said, 'God, just let me have one more soul before you take me out of the world.' Praise the Lord, I am lookin' for that soul all the time, wantin' God to save that soul that is lost and undone without Him because I done went to hell. I done know what that is. God let me go to hell, praise the Lord, to show me how hell was, and I don't wanna go to hell. I don't wanna see no one else go to hell. It's up to us to live the Word of God, to make heaven our home. Don't perish and die and go to hell."

—Clarence Martin, Spring/Summer 2002

"Daddy [Charlie Bry Phillips] was a Baptist, but he did not knock other denominations. He got up and preached the Bible, and he just did not believe in compromising with the devil. If you're goin' to stand for God, you've got to stand for God all the way. If you don't, then He don't do nothin' for you. It can't be half and half. My dad's life was lived for God—every day, every hour, every minute. The way he said it, 'Put everything you've got on the altar and crawl on with it. Go whole totally out for the Lord. You've got to live it, you've got to dress it, you've got to preach it, and you've got to act it day by day because,' he said, 'somewhere there's somebody a-watchin' you. And if they're lookin' for mistakes in me, they're gonna find some, of course. You've got to do your best for the Lord. You cannot get up and use your mouth to preach the Word of God and then turn around and curse somebody. You cannot do it. It's not right.' "

—Catherine Weaver, Spring 1984

SNAKE HANDLING

Last Sunday, I believe if there'd been a den o' lions 'ere, if it had been God's will, I believe I coulda opened the door an' walked right in there because they's no fear in my heart. —Spring 1973

In 1909, the Gospel of Mark, Chapter 16, so struck George Went Hensley that, the story goes, he chased down a rattler, held a meeting of his neighbors, handled the serpent, and passed it among them. The snake bit no one, and Hensley launched a movement.

Hensley himself, after supposedly being bitten 446 times, finally died of the 447th during a meeting in an abandoned blacksmith shop outside of Altha, Florida. He was seventy-five years old. Refusing to allow anyone to call a doctor, he died "belching blood and writhing on the floor" according to the 1973 eyewitness report of Don Kimsey, an *Atlanta Journal* correspondent.

Since that time, numerous others have died either of the same cause or of drinking poison. Despite these deaths and despite the fact that most states outlaw the practice, the movement that Hensley founded, though largely underground, is still active.

Foxfire students visited a church that practices Hensley's doctrines. At the request of the preacher, we cannot reveal the location or the name of the church, which was founded in 1931. Two years after its founding, the members began to handle serpents.

The preacher, Reverend Browning, tells us about the beginning:

"I was thirty-four years old. Th' Lord called me t' preach this. He began t' reveal th' faith t' me. It was through the revelation of Him.

"It was revealed t' me in this Bible when it said t' take 'em up; and I was preachin' one day, and I didn't know that verse was to us. I thought it was to th' apostles. And th' Lord revealed it t' me, and then I got t' preachin' it. And they brought one [snake] one time and said, 'Can we bring it in?'

"And somebody said, 'Yeah, bring it in.'

"And they said, 'Th' preacher'll have t' tell us.' And I went out to 'em and hollered to 'em t' bring it in.

"They've been bringin' it ever since."

Of the guidelines laid down in Matthew, Mark, Luke, John, and Acts, books they consider the most important, the belief that sets this sect apart from other Church of God churches is the rigid adherence to the idea of the spiritual gift. From baptism and anointing, the faithful must prove their faith by having "victory" over snakes, fire, poison, or all of these.

Sunday, nine-thirty in the morning, people begin arriving early for an annual homecoming service that promises to be a big one, with family members coming in from as far away as Ohio and Indiana and Florida. In no time at all, the church is packed.

The real center of interest before the service is Dexter Callahan, who arrives bearing two sinister-looking flat boxes. On the end of one, in white paint, are the words "In Jesus's Name." Inside the box are live rattlesnakes and copperheads. As Mr. Callahan reaches the building, people crowd around, and the rattlers inside buzz furiously. Then he pushes through the crowd, carries the boxes up to the front of the church, and slides them under a low bench behind the pulpit.

The service begins with hymns—the congregation knows them by heart; there are no hymnbooks—but after that, the service happens as the spirit leads. A series of different preachers stand and talk, and people in the congregation do, too. They testify or ask for prayer. Music starts—guitars, some

PLATE 25 Proving his faith by having "victory" over snakes

of them electric, and children with tambourines—and serpents are brought out in periods of intense activity. The long, complicated service goes on for hours. —**Spring 1973**

A preacher fires up the congregation:

"I love t' be with God's people that love Jesus. Praise th' Lord. Hallelujah to God! I want more of God! I want more of His Spirit!

"I believe in God's signs! I believe in th' Word of God. I believe in God. I believe in takin' up serpents with all my heart. I believe in drinkin' strychnine 'n' deadly poison. I believe in whatever God puts on me t' do; that's what I want t' do! I believe in God. If we're led by th' Spirit of God, hallelujah to God, and feel with th' Spirit o' God, that it won't be no harm come t' us.

"Praise God! His great big eye's watchin' ever' one of us. Hallelujah to God! I'm glad tonight that I'm sheltered in the arms of th' Lord. [Softer and almost tearfully] I'm glad th' Lord's savin' souls tonight. Hallelujah to God! . . . Perfect love casteth out fear. Hallelujah t' God! If a man's got perfect love, he's got no fear in his heart. Hallelujah t' God. [Shouting] I've got perfect love in m' heart! Glory t' God in th' name o' Jesus. I believe with all my heart. Last Sunday, I believe if there'd been a den o' lions 'ere, if it had been God's will, I believe I coulda opened the door an' walked right in there because they's no fear in my heart." —**Spring 1973**

"Once there was this preacher on Cullowhee Mountain [North Carolina] who had a rattlesnake on the pulpit in a box. Some preachers in these mountains, you know, hold snakes and things to prove their faith. Well, he had this snake on his pulpit—said if the Lord ever told him that it was all right to hold it, he'd have it handy. Well, one day he was preachin' away and got to feelin' good; he reached right in that box in front of the crowd and grabbed that snake and pulled it out, and it didn't make a sound—tame as it could be. He held it for a while and then put it back and didn't get bit at all.

"Later, all the people wanted him to do it again. He didn't much want to, but they kept at it; finally, he reached in to get it again, and it bit him. He lived . . . but just. When he was well, he said that the first time he had done what the Lord wanted him to do, and the next time he had done what the people wanted him to do; that was what made the difference."

—Daniel Manous, March 1967

"Everybody's got a certain amount of faith. If your intentions are goin' back home, you've got faith that you're goin' t' make it.

"Take my little boy. When he was about three years old, he didn't really understand what he was doin'. He said, 'Daddy, I want t' handle a big one [serpent].' I gave him a big one. I just give him a big one. And he held his hand out and took it, and I started tellin' him, I said, 'Son, if you do this, you gotta live with it.' " —**Brother Huff, Spring 1973**

"I've seen people put snakes around their necks—in their bosoms. There was a woman once that had pretty, long hair, and a copperhead crawled right up in her hair. Th' copperheads ain't as dangerous as th' rattlers. Copperheads will bite you quicker, but th' rattlesnakes'll kill you. They bust a man's heart. I heard a man say th' doctor said one man's heart was busted. He was killed.

"I've been bit one time. It just stung for a few minutes, and I never felt it n' more—just a little sting. I might not a been anointed. I just went t' stick m' hand out t' take it, and it bit me right in th' palm of my hand. It never did bite me before, and it never did bite me since. [His wife believes that the

PLATE 26 "Hallelujah to God . . . they's no fear in my heart." —Reverend Browning

bite might have been designed to be a sign to the congregation that even though he was bitten, he didn't get sick because he had the proper faith in God. As she said, "Believin' gives you th' power."]"

—Reverend Browning, Spring 1973

"I was pastor of a church up there at Yellow Mountain [North Carolina] when there was a preacher up there that believed in the handling of snakes. I knew about that. He tried to make a big show of it, you know, but I don't believe in tempting God. I think that those things are dangerous. I don't think Paul knew that that serpent was in there when he picked up to build that fire, but when it got warm, it [the snake] thawed up and bit him. They thought he'd die, but he didn't. He shook it off. Now this preacher up here on the Cullowhee Mountain—I was pastor up there and Yellow Mountain not too far from where he was—told them to bring a snake on Sunday night, and he would handle it. There were two guys there, and I don't think that they had the right kind of spirit. They caught a rattlesnake and deviled it all week just to make it ill. It would strike at everything, you know. They took it in. He took it out, and it bit him. He threw it down on the floor. They told him to pick it up, and it bit him again. I do know that they used all the medicine that they could find on that fellow, and it liked to have killed him."

—Preacher Ben Cook, Fall 1979

"Well, I'll tell you, that's [snake handling] more of a show than anything else. I'm afraid of snakes and always have been. If a man gets wrought up to where he thinks a snake won't bite him, he's just badly mistaken. Some of those [who practice snake handling] have been bitten and died holding those snakes. Jesus told the devil to not tempt the Lord. The Bible says not to tempt the Lord thy God. There's not many people that have faith enough [to handle snakes or drink poison]. The snake doesn't know you've got faith! . . . It didn't say anything about takin' him up and playin' with him and messin' with him, tryin' to prove a point. There's other ways to worship Christ without that. Plenty." **—Esco Pitts, Spring 1978**

HANDLING FIRE

Faith will kill the power of fire. —Brother Huff

The practice of handling fire is almost impossible to believe—unless you see it with your own eyes. The faith to handle fire and not be burned is based on Daniel 3:26–27, the story of Shadrach, Meshach, and Abednego and their refusal to denounce their one true God by obeying King Nebuchadnezzar's order to bow to the ninety-foot-high and nine-foot-wide golden statue. Their refusal caused the angry king to bind them with a rope and throw them into the fiery furnace. When the viewers peered in, the three men were walking around unharmed in the flames:

> Nebuchadnezzar then approached the opening of the blazing furnace and shouted, "Shadrach, Meshach, and Abednego, servants of the Most High God, come out! Come here!"

> So Shadrach, Meshach, and Abednego came out of the fire, and the satraps, prefects, governors, and royal advisers crowded around them. They saw that the fire had not harmed their bodies, nor was a hair of their heads singed; their robes were not scorched, and there was no smell of fire on them. (NIV)

Because the three young men remained faithful and true to God, He rewarded them by protecting them from harm. They remained untouched by the fire and heat; the fire burned only the rope that bound them. Believers confidently contend that no fetters can bind us if God desires us to be free. Born-again Christians believe that God's protection transcends earthly understanding; thus, the power that delivered Shadrach, Meshach, and Abednego is available to believers today, even the power to hold flames and remain unscorched.

—*Angie Cheek*

PLATE 27 "When I hold fire, it feels cool, just like there's no fire there." —Brother Huff

"Several containers rested on the pulpit. Two of them were filled with kerosene and had large wicks in their necks. One was a Pepsi bottle; the other, a metal canister. Despite the activity swirling all around, it was hard not to notice when one of these was lit, for the flames rose a foot or more into the air.

"Men at a pitch of intensity stripped off their shoes and socks and held the flames for minutes at a time under their bare feet. A woman thrust the fire right into her hair and held it up, and not a hair was singed.

"Faith will kill the power of fire. Fire's got power, you know. It will burn you. It will burn up a whole woods. It will burn up a house or whatever it gets to.

"Now I've seen this little bottle of propane gas bein' handled, and that's hot. And there was another man one time that said he could handle that fire, and he got his hands burnt to two big crispers."

—Brother Huff, Spring 1973

"[H]e come up a-jumpin', and he took one of them carbide lights right by th' face. And th' blaze should have burnt his hands off, but one of them fellows checked his hands for burns—no burns there."

—Brother Huff

PLATE 28 "I . . . stuck the flame to my sock and left it there plenty long enough t' cut my sock apart." —Brother Huff

"My father one time was layin' on th' floor sick, and they come in and prayed for him. They had carbide lights back then. Money was hard t' get ahold of. And so when they prayed for him, they said he come up a-jumpin', and he took one of them carbide lights right by th' face. And th' blaze should have burnt his hands off, but one of them fellows checked his hands for burns—no burns there.

"When I hold fire, it feels cool, just like there's no fire there. One time I thought in myself I had a little faith, and I wanted to handle it in such a way that people couldn't doubt that fire. You know, y' see people that kindly waver. I wanted them t' know there was no doubt about it. Well, I had a little faith, and I pulled my shoe off and stuck the flame to my sock and left it there plenty long enough t' cut my sock apart. And about that time it come apart. It had been there long enough t' catch it on fire."

—Brother Huff, Spring 1973

SPEAKING IN TONGUES

And then th' Holy Ghost came in, and I was speakin' I didn't know what. I knowed my tongue was movin', but I didn't know what I was sayin'. —Spring 1973

Handling serpents, drinking poison, and handling fire and remaining unharmed are proof to some believers of the anointing of the Holy Spirit. Believers receive this initial anointing; then, in a moment of supreme ecstasy, they receive a blessing from the Holy Ghost Himself and subsequent gifts, proof that they have been rewarded for their unquestioning faith and devotion. These gifts are spiritual knowledge, prophecy, discernment, and speaking in tongues. The preacher, Reverend Browning, of the church we visited, contends that until the member of the congregation has reached this plateau, he or she is still damned.

Many often challenge Reverend Browning on this point, but his defense is that though the Bible does not specifically say that one must speak in tongues, it does say that when the apostles received the Holy Ghost, they did speak in tongues; and when the Gentiles received the Holy Ghost, they did also, and on and on through example after example. And that's good enough for him.

Some of our readers might not be familiar with the idea of speaking in tongues. This practice is based on Acts 2:1–6:

> When the day of Pentecost came, they were all together in one place. Suddenly a sound like the blowing of a violent wind came from heaven and filled the whole house where they were sitting. They saw what seemed to be tongues of fire that separated and came to rest on each of them. All of them were filled with the Holy Spirit and began to speak in other tongues as the Spirit enabled them.
>
> Now there were staying in Jerusalem God-fearing Jews from every nation under heaven. When they heard this sound, a crowd came together in bewilderment, because each one heard them speaking in his own language.

Important to note is the fact that the gift of speaking in tongues is not necessarily connected to snake handling or fire handling. Several passages of Scripture in 1 Corinthians 14 discuss speaking in tongues, and Paul gives some admonitions concerning this spiritual gift. With this gift, the Holy Spirit empowers an individual with the ability to speak in unknown languages (it can be an earthly language but is usually an unknown, angelic language). Some believe the Holy Spirit gives that individual not only the ability to speak in unknown tongues but also the ability to translate; however, others believe one believer speaks the unknown language and another receives the power to translate for other believers. Another belief is that a person receives the ability to speak in tongues in order to speak directly to God without the devil's interference, for the devil would be unable to understand the unknown tongue.

Although this spiritual gift has become controversial over the last two decades, many believers in churches in Appalachia do still speak in tongues.

—*Angie Cheek*

"The pinnacle of an intense service is the receiving of the Holy Ghost, just as it came upon the apostles at Pentecost. Acts 2:17–18 reads, 'And it shall come to pass in the last days, saith God, I will pour out my Spirit upon all flesh: And your sons and your daughters shall prophesy, and your young men shall see visions, and your old men shall dream dreams: And on my servants and on my handmaidens I will pour out in those days of my Spirit; and they shall prophesy.

"We sit here and you see th' wind blow and we hear th' sound and we hear th' roar of the wind but we can't tell when it's coming and we can't tell where it's going. It goes on. 'So is everyone born of th' Spirit,' said th' Spirit. Say you get th' Holy Ghost and you speak in tongues . . . I can hear th' sound, but I can't tell what you're sayin'. Well, your tongue is gonna speak when He comes—the Holy Ghost. 'When He comes, He shall testify of Me.' We read that here in John 15:26.

"First time I got th' Holy Ghost, I spoke in tongues, and then I didn't speak in it no more for a long time . . . I was gonna pray ten hours before I went to church. I was gonna pray 'til time t' go to church. And my wife went off and let me. And I got on th' altar and got down to pray. I was just layin' there and prayed. I prayed from six o'clock to nine o'clock, and I know what I was sayin'. I was sayin', 'Lord, take my life and give me the Holy Ghost.'

"And then th' Holy Ghost came in, and I was speakin' I didn't know what. I knowed my tongue was movin', but I didn't know what I was sayin' 'til that moved on.

"I guess it lasted fifteen minutes—or maybe not that long. Then I came to myself, and I could talk back. That's a mystery, ain't it? That's a mystery."

—Spring 1973

"If you're speakin' in tongues and interpretin', we're gettin' what you're sayin'. See, you'll stop speakin' to God, and you'll go to speakin' to us, tellin' what the Holy Ghost is sayin' through you. Then it edifies us. But if you can't interpret it, you're still speakin' to God. . . .

"If they speak in tongues, nobody understands 'em but God. But God can anoint you t' interpret, and then you can tell what I'm a-sayin' if I'm speakin' in tongues . . . It's got to come from th' same Spirit.

"My wife'll go t' speakin' in tongues, and we'll not nary a one know what she's sayin'. She'll speak in tongues maybe for an hour and then interpret it herself—tell us what she's sayin'." **—Reverend Browning, Spring 1973**

FOOTWASHING

If you're humble enough to get down and wash your brother's feet, that's all right. —Esco Pitts

Footwashing is a practice patterned after New Testament Scripture. John 13:1–17 depicts Jesus as the model servant. Washing guests' feet was a task for a lowly household servant, but Jesus, wrapping a towel around his waist, washed and dried His disciples' feet. He, God in the flesh, was willing to serve others: Those who would be great leaders must be willing servants.

Other accounts of footwashing occur in the Bible. Luke 7:36–50 recounts Jesus's having dinner at the house of a Pharisee when a woman comes in, wets His feet with her tears, wipes them with her hair, and pours perfume on them. John 12:3 is a like account.

Although very few churches today include footwashing as part of the service, some churches do continue the practice as an expression of humility, love, and a servant heart. The Bible depicts Christ again and again as servant, and many believe that a maturing Christian strives to be more and more like Christ; thus a biblical basis for footwashing does exist.

—*Angie Cheek*

"I've seen footwashin's in our church—not too many times. But there was a pastor there that believed in it, and some of the deacons believed in it. I haven't seen it lately. This day 'n' time, people take baths and have shoes to keep their feet off the ground. Back in those days when Jesus washed the disciples' feet, they wore sandals, and they were full of mud and dust. But He did that as an example of humility. If you're humble enough to get down and wash your brother's feet, that's all right. That humble spirit is the thing—not what you do but how humble your heart is. It's not necessary to wash feet, but it is necessary to be humble enough to do it if it's necessary."

—Esco Pitts, Spring 1978

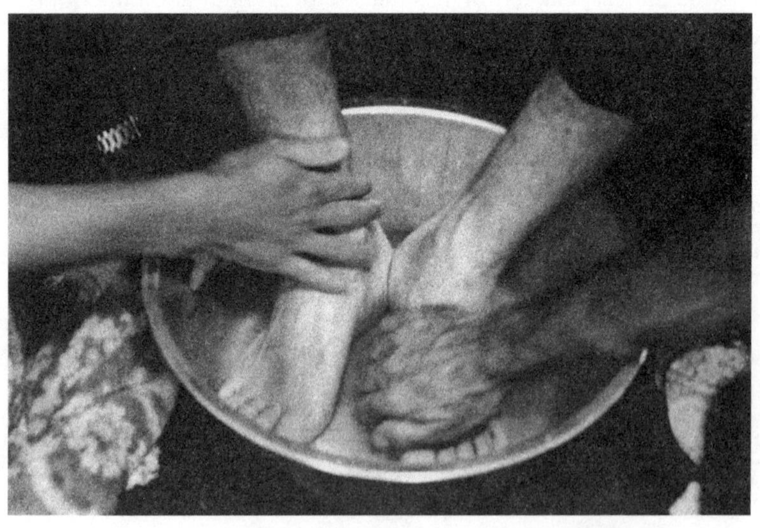

PLATE 29 "That humble spirit is the thing—not what you do but how humble your heart is." —Esco Pitts

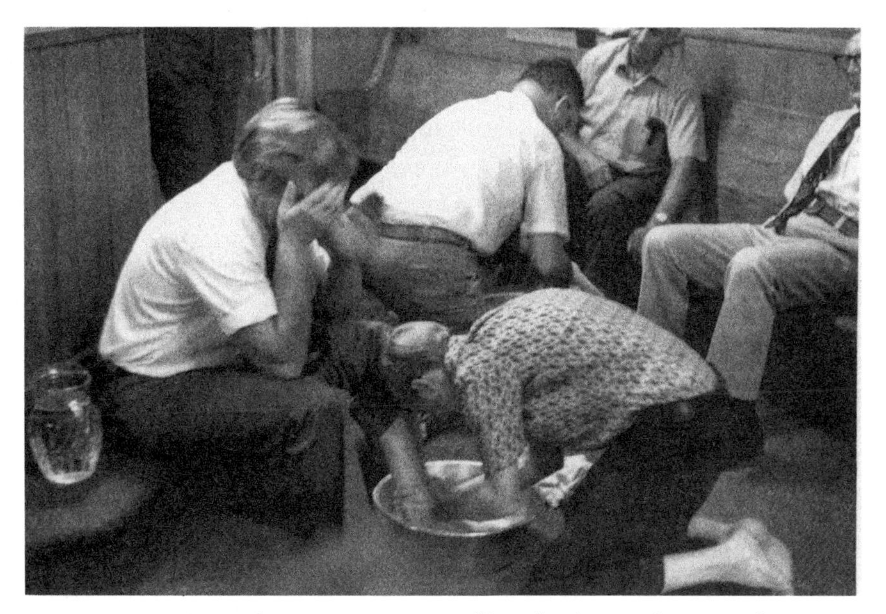

PLATE 30 Footwashing is an expression of humility, love, and a servant heart.

"We'll go out before the whole Association and I'll read the thirteenth chapter of John; if they're not goin' to observe that and not goin' to let that be Bible, let's just tear it out." ***—Preacher Ben Cook***

"We still have them [footwashings] over here at New Hope [Otto, North Carolina] yet. When this church was established twenty-one years ago, it went to get in the Association. We had some modern preachers that objected to a footwashin' church bein' taken into the Association. We had a council, and I went back in there with all the preachers of this county that was in the Tuckaseegee Association. I said, 'These old pioneer preachers practiced footwashin', and Jesus Christ practiced it. If you're tellin' me that I can't be a Baptist and can't follow the teachings of the Lord Jesus Christ and do the things He did, I don't want to be in the Association. We'll go out before the whole Association and I'll read the thirteenth chapter of John; if they're not goin' to observe that and not goin' to let that be Bible, let's just tear it out. We'll put it before the whole Association and see what they think about it.' They agreed to let us have footwashin's and be in the Association.

"We put the ladies on one side of the church and the men on the other side. The men wash the men's feet, and the women wash the women's feet. That's about the best service you've ever been in! We have communion at the same time." **—Preacher Ben Cook, Fall 1979**

FAITH HEALING

I think Jesus Christ has just as much power today as He had when He was here on earth. . . . I believe that people are being healed today.

—Preacher Ben Cook

Divine healing is healing aided by God. This healing can be gradual or, in some cases, instantaneous. Most Baptists, along with other denominations, also believe in medical professionals and procedures as an extension of God's work.

In the Southern Appalachians today, some folks still claim to be able to heal by faith. Now, before you become a naysayer, many people around these parts swear they've experienced a healing personally or know someone who has. When I was in high school, I remember hearing about a young mother whose child pulled a pot of boiling water off the stovetop onto its head. Instead of taking the child to a doctor, the mother took it to her neighbor who "talked out" the fire. The child had no blisters or scars. I personally know people who can "talk off" or "conjure" warts. "How can this be?" you ask. I don't know.

The Bible clearly speaks of this power. In John 14 is an account of Jesus's attempting to answer Thomas and Philip's questions about ascertaining where He was going and discovering the nature of God. Jesus assuages the disciples' doubts in verses 12–14:

> I tell you the truth, anyone who has faith in me will do what I have been doing. He will do even greater things than these, because I am going to the Father. And I will do whatever you ask in my name, so that the Son may bring glory to the Father. You may ask me for anything in my name, and I will do it. (NIV)

The elderly healers we interviewed were quiet, simple, strong, and sure. They were people of faith. They have faith in themselves, and they have faith in their God because they believe that it is through Him that their words have power. They do not heal in the tent before throngs. They do not accept money for their work. They speak words from the Bible quietly or silently, and many who seek them out find healing.

Folks seek out these healers primarily for their skills in four areas: stopping blood, drawing fire, curing "thrash" [thrush], and conjuring warts. Each healer with whom we spoke claimed he or she could cure at least one of the above ills. Some said they could cure them all. Each of the healers had some personal variation in the actual method of treatment, but all maintained that an essential part of the treatment was a certain verse from the Old Testament.

As for your being a skeptic, do you not admit that the world is full of mysteries? Haven't you heard that God works in mysterious ways? Can you set aside your skepticism for a moment and ponder the possibility of God's hand's working through healers? After all, Jesus said, "Anyone who has faith in me will do what I have been doing" (John 14:12). Hear what these healers say and judge for yourselves.

—*Angie Cheek*

"I don't think anybody doesn't believe in divine healing. I think Jesus Christ has just as much power today as He had when He was here on Earth. I don't think that that's ever been done away with. I believe that people are being healed today.

"I'll tell you one experience I had and the reason why I believe in divine healing. I was up at Cathan's Chapel [North Carolina], the church where I first started preachin'. I was at a revival meeting. We were havin' a good meeting there, and I was the only preacher. In the evenin' I took sick; my bowels were runnin' off, and I was vomiting—just as sick as a man could be. Time began to run out before the service, and there wasn't anybody to preach. I went across the little creek there—I can go yet today to the very place I went to—and I said, 'Lord, I believe you're in this revival meeting. People's being saved. I don't have any medicine, and if you want me to preach, heal me now.' The Lord healed me that minute. That's been fifty-three years ago, and that's just as right to me today as it was then. I could go to that place today and show you the spot of earth where that happened. Now that happened to me, and that's been a great grace for me. Lots of times when doubts and things come, I could go back to that spot of earth where that took place. I believe in divine healing." —**Preacher Ben Cook, Fall 1979**

"I believe in divine healing. I'll tell you, it's just sort of like believing that God will answer your prayer. If you pray sincerely, He'll answer you. I've had prayers answered many a many times. Two years ago, I couldn't walk, but now I can get up and go to the mailbox and go to church. My family had to carry me to Atlanta in the ambulance. I went to a bone specialist. He took a long needle and ran it through my knees. It'd nearly take your breath, but it eased you. I asked the Lord to ease the pain if it was His will, and He did."

—Esco Pitts, Spring 1978

"I can't tell y' how healin' is done because it's handed down from th' beginnin'. It's in th' Bible. If y' tell somebody, y' lose yer . . . in other words, like a man doin' somethin' t' destroy his rights, y' know.

"In that now, I could learn two women, or three, I think it is, and then one of 'em that I'd learnt could learn a man-person. So about th' biggest point I get in that is t' add a little mystery t' th' party that don't believe, maybe we'll say, in fire drawin'." **—Harley Carpenter, March 1968**

"I can blow fire out. I can stop blood. I can cure th' thrash [thrush]. I do all that by th' help of th' Lord. I don't do that by myself. If I ain't got th' Lord wi' me . . . All I've got's been a gift from God, and it's perfect. But

PLATE 31 "I can't tell y' how healin' is done because it's handed down from th' beginnin'." —Harley Carpenter

PLATE 32 "When people gets old, younger people don't pay much attention to 'em."
—Mrs. Andy (Bashie) Webb

when people gets old like me an' him [my husband], younger people don't pay much attention to 'em. They don't come to 'em for advice like they should." —**Mrs. Andy (Bashie) Webb, Summer 1979**

"There's some of these churches that think they can heal y'. They make y' believe they can heal y', but I don't know if it's true or not. I never have had enough faith in it t' try it myself. There's folks around that make y' believe that they can. There's a neighbor that lives over in th' next holler, and his wife was down on her knees until she just couldn't hardly walk at all. She was just in th' bed. They went t' this church on a lark and had th' members of th' church t' pray fer her, and she come back home walkin'. They must've had th' faith. I don't know whether I'd have that much faith 'r not. I'd be too doubtful, I guess." —**Mrs. Don Burnette, Fall 1971**

"I'll tell you one on my brother. There was a fellow who had a big knot come on his head, and my brother told him, 'I know a person over in Floyd County who is a faith doctor. I'll take you to him. He'll do somethin', and the knot will disappear.' The fellow declared he didn't believe in such stuff, but he'd try it. So he did. The faith doctor done somethin' to the knot and said, 'Now your troubles are over. Within a day or two, it will come off.' Well, what happened was another knot come on his head; he had two knots instead of one." —**Clay Collins, Fall 1988**

LAYING ON OF HANDS

Then if th' anointin' gets in my hands, then I know it. You can feel it—like electricity. —Spring 1973

The laying on of hands in the Old Testament period was used to confer blessing, to transfer guilt from sinner to sacrifice, and to commission a person for a new responsibility. In the New Testament period, the laying on of hands also ordained people for service, as illustrated in Acts 6:6, when the Twelve ordained the seven newly elected deacons. The laying on of hands further signified the Holy Spirit's imparting of the power of healing to an individual or individuals. Empowered by the Spirit, these healers could lay hands on the afflicted who would be healed. Acts 5:12 records that "the apostles performed many miraculous signs and wonders among the people." Those powers, Christians believe, are Christ's legacy to those of faith. One or two can lay hands on the sick, or clusters of people can encircle a person who is ill and has asked for prayer. Believers' hands reach out to touch the afflicted, and those outside the inner circle touch those who are touching the afflicted.

Believers trust what the Bible says: "they will place their hands on sick people, and they will get well" (Mark 16:18). I know individuals who practice this spiritual gift; I and some of my friends have witnessed supernatural healings. The grace of God through the power of the Holy Spirit, flowing through a believer's hands, can transform lives spiritually and physically. Christ, before He ascended into heaven to sit at the right hand of the Father, comforted the disciples and told them they would "do even greater things than these (John 14:12). People of faith take Jesus at His Word and consider His Words a promise.

—Angie Cheek

"Maybe Mrs. Browning will be anointed, and the rest of them will be prayin'. The anointing is what it takes to do it. But you don't know some-

PLATE 33 "They will place their hands on sick people, and they will get well."
—Mark 16:18 (NIV)

times. Say you're sick. I don't know whether I'll be anointed 'til I come to you and pray. And then if th' anointin' gets in my hands, then I know it. You can feel it—like electricity.

"They brought a child to one of these here all-day meetin's—and she was three or four year old—that couldn't walk. They'd set her down, and her feet'd just go all around. She couldn't stand on her feet. They brought her up there and prayed for her. And then they brought her back, and she'd walk—about four year old. It was old man Couch's granddaughter. And it was just like th' man at th' beautiful gate that hadn't never walked."

—Spring 1973

"This boy of mine had a cancer on his chin. And we took him out t' th' doctor, and he said, 'I don't know what it is, but I'll cut this off and see what it is.' And when he come back with it—got the report on it—it was cancer. And before I got t' th' doctor with him, It [the Spirit] showed my wife at home that it was a cancer. And she laid hands on him and healed him.

"My wife can get in th' Spirit and pick out a man that's sick and know he's sick, and she don't know his name ner never seen him before. She can find he's sick. That Spirit in her will let her know. Don't have t' nobody tell her."

—Reverend Browning, Spring 1973

"They'd tell them if they laid their hands on them, they'd be healed, and they *was* healed. If you tell me that you've got the gift of healing, and she's sick, then I'd say, 'If *she* believes it, you can heal her.' Cindy Causey got

PLATE 34 "My wife can get in th' Spirit and pick out a man that's sick and know he's sick, and she don't know his name ner never seen him before." —Reverend Browning

healed of a cancer that was big around as a half-dollar. It just healed over. She's th' singin'est woman I ever did know!" —**Spring 1973**

"My mother suffered terrible from a pain in her cheek, a pain so strong it would nearly take her life. Pills wouldn't knock it, and the doctors couldn't cure it. We'd heard of a healer, so we took her to him—a two-day trip, goin' and comin'. That was back in the twenties. We hitched up a pair of mules to a wagon and put in food and quilts and fodder and rode to Letcher County [Kentucky] and on across Pine Mountain and on past Bad Branch, nearly to the Virginia line where the healer lived. His woman didn't want him to do it, but he done it anyway. He come out to the wagon and said somethin' to my mother and touched her cheek or somethin'. He done somethin' to my mother—I don't know what. We headed back home, and my mother never had another attack as long as she lived. She lived to be way up there."

—**Sam Stamper, Fall 1988**

STOPPING BLOOD

You don't have t' be religious. You don't have t' be a preacher. An' you don't have to be a big church member, just as long as you got that faith. —Charley Tyler

Those who claim to be able to stop blood purport they can do so not only in humans but also in animals. Those who are healers of this ailment all admit that an essential part of the treatment is a certain verse from the Old Testament. Like other cures, this ailment has its own appropriate verse as well. One healer told us, "You don't have t' turn over very far in Ezekiel to find that about bleedin'." I looked. What the secret words are eludes me. No healer was willing to tell us the entire secret for fear of losing the power. Each healer can teach others, but only a certain number of people and only those of a certain gender. Though doctors and others scoff at the idea of stopping blood, scientifically explaining why profuse bleeding stops within minutes after the incantation of a healer is impossible.

—Angie Cheek

"Old Aunt Caroline Korn could certainly take fire out of you if you got burnt, and old Uncle Joe Teague could certainly stop bleedin'. Once they 'as a logger cuttin' timber and cut his foot. He went to see Uncle Joe that evenin'. His shoe 'as just about full o' blood, and he wanted him to stop it. And Uncle Joe said, 'How long'll it take y' t' go home?' The logger said, 'About twenty minutes'; and Uncle Joe said, 'All right.' Well, when he got t' th' house in about twenty minutes, that blood stopped and never did bleed n' more.

"And he 'as over at Sapphire at that little hotel there, and they said t' him, they said, 'They say you can stop blood.'

"He said, 'Yeah.'

" 'All right,' said, 'We'll just let y' try your luck on this beef.'

"He said, 'All right, but it'll ruin your beef, man.'

" 'Aw, shucks.'

"They killed it 'n' stuck it. It never bled a drop. Blood stayed right in th' flesh an' ruined it—couldn't eat it. He shore could stop the blood. It's in the Bible. You can get that stoppin' blood out o' th' Bible. It's in the Old Testament somewhereabouts. I've read it, but it's been s' long."

—Lester Norton, March 1968 and Spring /Summer 1996

"It's just a gift from God. I just commenced at it."

—Mrs. Andy (Bashie) Webb

"My son Jim, his child's nose commenced bleedin' one night at th' supper table, and they live away down yonder in Georgia. An' he said t' his brother, 'I'm a-gonna take him t' Mama.'

"Well, when they come, they had him rolled up in a sheet, and that blood—hit was just about as bloody as it could be. Y' couldn't tell whether it 'as a sheet or what. And he just come in th' door and said, 'Here, Mama, I want y' t' stop Lewis's nose from bleedin'.'

"I said, 'All right.' And he laid him down in m' lap, and it'd just squirt. Ever' time his pulse 'd beat, y' know, it'd squirt. And it wasn't long, though, 'til it stopped bleedin', and it's never bled another drop.

"To do it, you don't have t' touch the person. I can just talk t' th' Lord, and it's all right. And when y' blow fire, you blow on th' burned place an' say somethin'—it's out o' the Bible, but I can't read a word of th' Bible, not a

PLATE 35 "You can get that stoppin' blood out o' th' Bible. It's in the Old Testament somewhereabouts."
—Lester Norton

PLATE 36 "To do it, you don't have t' touch the person. I can just talk t' th' Lord, and it's all right."
—Mrs. Andy (Bashie) Webb

word. I can't read, and I can't write. It's just a gift from God. I just commenced at it."

—Mrs. Andy (Bashie) Webb, March 1968 and Spring/Summer 1996

"I tell y' what I see'd her [my wife] do one time. We lived on Mud Creek up yonder. One of our neighbors' boys here had a big black horse. He 'as back over at a little place at work and throwed his mowin' blade down. Th' horse 'as a-pickin' around there, and he happened t' run against it and cut his front leg plumb in t' th' bone. And that horse had bled 'til he 'as s' weak he couldn't hardly walk. They 'as goin' t' try t' get a doctor up there t' see about him, and [someone] told 'em wan' no use, just t' stand still a few minutes. And they said in less 'n five minutes, that horse's leg was quit bleedin'."

—Andy Webb, March 1968 and Spring/Summer 1996

"You don't have t' turn over very far in Ezekiel to find that about bleedin'." —*Aunt Nora Garland*

PLATE 37 Andy Webb tells us about seeing his wife stop blood.

"My mother told me where t' find it at in the Bible, so I found it. And it's somethin' every doctor ought t' know. It's simple, and you don't have t' turn over very far in Ezekiel to find that about bleedin'. You don't have t' read any farther than th' sixteenth chapter. You memorize it by heart, but don't leave one little error out. If you do, it won't stop. . . . My mother . . . could stop blood. She's th' first 'un I knew could.

"There 'as a lady—she 'as expectin' t' go t' th' hospital at any time. All th' time durin' that time, her nose had almost bled her t' death. So this man rid [rode] up inta th' yard one night, and that's been twenty year ago, I guess. And he said, 'I want y' t' go t' my house.' It 'as way down on Church Road. He said, 'My wife's nose is a-bleedin' her t' death.' Said, 'I don't believe she'd be alive 'til I get back.'

" 'Oh, yes, she will.'

"He said, 'Would y' go?'

"I said no. It 'as after dark. I said, 'No use in me a-goin' down there. It'll be okay as soon as you get back.'

"So th' next day I see'd him in town an' asked him about her. Said, 'It 'as stopped when I got back.'

"I don't have t' know their name . . . don't have t' know a thing about them.

You just think about 'em and say it three times. I've been sent for from Lakemont [Georgia] and different places t' come and stop th' blood; and I say, 'There's no use in me a-comin'. I could do it in New York if they 'as t' call me.

"I'll tell y', we 'as a-milkin' one Sunday night, and you can see th' scar there [points to her forehead]. There 'as twenty-six stitches took up an' down there, and a blood vessel bursted over here. A cow kicked me in th' head. And Dr. Dover, he just didn't know a thing in th' world t' do. And that blood 'as a-comin' up and spillin' back down in my face after he got th' other places fixed up and m' head sewed up, and he says, 'I just can't get that stopped t' save my life.' And I never thought t' do it. I never thought th' first time . . . it hurt s' bad.

"He said, 'Try your luck on it.'

"We tried, and it stopped right quick. I believe I can stop it.

"I don't believe I could do it if I started chargin' money for it. It's from th' heart. Dr. Neville wanted to know how t' stop blood. He offered me twenty-five dollars in money to tell how t' stop it, but I wouldn't."

—Aunt Nora Garland, March 1968 and Spring/Summer 1996

"Stoppin' blood's just like drawin' out fire. It's th' same identical thing. You do it with th' same verse and th' same words and ever'thin' except where

PLATE 38 "I don't have t' know their name . . . don't have t' know a thing about them. You just think about 'em and say it three times." —Aunt Nora Garland

y' ask for th' fire to be taken out, you ask for th' blood t' be stopped. That's th' only difference is th' blood an' the fire you ask for. Rest of it's all th' same thing.

"Doctors don't like it. They just plain don't like it. They just plain tell you it's not so; you can't do it. But they're wrong. It can be done. An' y' can show a doctor that y' can do it, and still he'll argue with y' that it's just not right. I'd tell one doctor, I'd say, 'Well, Doc, you like I am. I just don't believe you got sense enough t' know right from wrong.' Doc'd say, 'Aw, you go on; shet your mouth.' [Laughs.]

"I'd stop blood on a mule—doctorin' an old mule, y' know. Cut his foot on a slop pan. Two handles on it, y' know. Hold it in th' dirt, an' th' mule'll pull it 'til it loaded. You've see'd 'em, I guess. Well, that sort o' thing'll get more wi' it than a wheelbarrer will, y' know.

"An' that slip pan hit a root, an' somehow 'r 'nother hit turned over—jerked it loose from th' man an' caught th' mule right just between that holler place back of his leg an' like t' cut that foot off. An', Lord, did it bleed!

"An' Doc Dover's down thar, an' they had th' mule's foot tied up, pulled up, tied, 'cause Doc 'as afraid it'd kick him—might would, I guess. And he's a-workin' with it, and look like th' more he worked, the worse it 'as a-bleedin'. But it wudn't. It 'as just pourin' th' blood, 'as all.

"I come along, an' I just stopped an' looked at it, y' know. Never said nothin' t' nobody. I just stopped an' looked at it an' said, 'Doc, it's bleedin' pretty bad, ain't it?'

"Said, 'Yeah.'

"I said, 'Well, I'll stop it from bleedin' on y' if you'll bind it up.'

" 'Get away from here, Charley,' he said. 'You don't know nothin' about it.'

"I said, 'Hit's all right. I done doctored it.' I said, "It won't bleed n' more nohow. It's quittin' as fast as it can.' And it was. It 'as just slowin' up 'cause I doctored it quick as I saw it. And in just a few minutes, it just come t' a slow drip, just in a short few minutes.

"An' Doc, he looked at me, an' he quarreled. Th' old man, Doc, was always quarrelin' t' me about ever'thin'. An' he said, 'You believe you actually stopped that blood?'

"I said, 'Well, *you* didn't.'

"I says, 'Who did?' An' he'd laugh about it, but he argued all th' time. Wudn't nothin' to it."

—Charley Tyler, March 1968 and Spring/Summer 1996

"I can cure the thrash, I can stop blood, and I can take off warts. I can do most anything, but if I was to tell you'uns, I never could do it no more. It's a secret. If I take off warts, you'll know how I took 'em off, but you won't know what I done with 'em. If I tell you, I might not have no more luck. I can stop blood. I've stopped nosebleeds. And they was a man come by here. He was drunk, and he stabbed his hoss with a big knife. That hoss was a-bleedin' to death nearly. And my uncle happened to be here, and he said, 'You go out there and stop that blood on that hoss.' I just went out there and said somethin', and the hoss was all right. That man gave me five dollars. He just pulled out five dollars and throwed it down: 'Just take that and use it.' "

—Carrie McCurry, Summer 1977

DRAWING FIRE

When I draw the fire out, I leave that skin, when it's well, just like it was before it was burnt. —Charley Tyler

In the old days, doctors were few and far. Therefore, when emergencies arose, folks in the community sought help from nearby healers. Burns were common—burns from washpot fires, lanterns, carbide lights, woodstoves, etc. Not only were the burns painful, but they left scars that disfigured. There was often no ice, and running to the river to bathe the afflicted area in cold water would, to the minds of the healers, do harm. In fact they believe that the cold water "drives 'at [burn] further. It just keeps burnin' deeper and makes it worse to sore." Like other healers, these men and women would not share the secret for fear of losing their special "gift": "talking out fire" in Jesus's name.

—Angie Cheek

"My grandson burnt his arm on th' power saw—it 'as hot. And he burnt his arm. He come up hyere night before last night, I believe it was, and I blowed th' fire out of it. He said it hurt awful bad. I told him t' come back if it didn't quit burnin', but he didn't come back. I reckon it's all right.

"I don't have t' be alone. I can be right in a crowd an' do that. They don't hear me. They don't know what I say. I just talk t' th' Lord, and that's all."

—Mrs. Andy (Bashie) Webb, March 1968 and Spring/Summer 1996

"I've seen my wife doctor lots o' times. They was a fella over here on th' creek. His wife, she got burnt s' bad. I don't know how she did get burnt myself. And they doctored and doctored and doctored, and some woman told 'em about my wife. She went t' see 'er, and she begun doctorin' her. Just a few days, she could turn over in her bed and roll back."

—Andy Webb, March 1968 and Spring/Summer 1996

"You know a burn—how it hurts. There's fire in th' place where y' get burnt. You know that. You blow your breath on that, and the fire's gone out. . . . I believe in th' healin' power because the Lord has helped me. I know He has. That's the greatest thing they is—th' healin' power of th' Savior." [Her method for drawing the fire is to pass her hand over the burn three times, blow her breath gently over it, following the hand each time, and repeat the verse silently each time. Thus, unlike stopping blood, she must be present to draw fire.]

—Aunt Nora Garland, March 1968 and Spring/Summer 1996

"Well, you start off, 'Blessed was th' day an' holy was thou when our Savior, Lord Jesus Christ, first come inta th' world.' That's all I'm gonna tell y' because they ain't but about six more words to it."

—Charley Tyler

"Now that burnin', I wouldn't want t' push it too fer because it does come out o' the Bible, y' know. It takes good faith with it.

"Why did fire have to be drawn? Well, now, I'll tell y' why. When you're burnt, up here on top, and lot o' folks will, when they're burnt—a hand or anything—they'll pour cold water. Well, that drives 'at further. It just keeps burnin' deeper and makes it worse to sore. An' if you c'n draw that fire out, you don't have no sore. It just peels off. But if you don't get that fire out o' there, they leave a scar. Ain't you see'd folks, face burnt, where they hurt, they's a slick place? I don't leave that. When I draw the fire out, I leave that skin, when it's well, just like it was before it was burnt . . . I tell y', if it's bad burnt—y' know, it's cooked and peeled it right off where the clothes sticks to it—why, then y' have to do somethin' t' keep that from stickin', and y' can't tie a burn up 'cause if you go t' bandage up a burn, you just drive it to the bone . . . I can cure one in, oh, a third as quick as a doctor can . . . Now they do make some kind o' medicines now that help t' draw that fire out, helps t' heal it. But it's not like as quick as I c'n get it out because if you c'n get burnt, ten minutes after you get burnt, you call the fire in your hand. I'll get it out. It is gone. It'll probably pain y' a little bit; naturally, it'll be sore but not enough t' amount t' anything. But if it's a pretty bad burn and I go t' draw th' fire out of it, it hurts worse 'n when it went in for a minute . . . It just heals . . . and never leaves a scar. They ain't a scar nowhere.

"How do y' do it? Well, you start off, 'Blessed was th' day an' holy was thou when our Savior, Lord Jesus Christ, first come inta th' world.' That's all I'm gonna tell y' because they ain't but about six more words to it. I just stan' there an' look at it. [He doesn't touch the burn.] Oh, a lot o' times I will pick up a hand, like you 'as burnt, y' know, just pick up a hand and look at it, turn it around an' look at it. But that's not . . . I just say that t' myself. Nobody's hearin' me say it. Fact, I'll be talkin' t' him over there and a-drawin' th' fire out o' your hand at the same time, and neither one o' y' don't know I'm doin' it. I usually say the verse one time if it's a small burn, but if it's a bad burn, why, I like t' go see 'em. I can get th' fire out an' me not there, but then, quick as I can, I will go an' git thar t' see how it was. But I don't have t' be there. You c'n be at your house 'n' get burnt. Pick up th' phone an' call me if I had a phone so's I could answer y'. Call me, an' th' first thing I'll ask y' is 'Have y' done anythin' to it?' An' if y've put anything on it, I'll tell y' t' get it off as much as y' can. But I'm a fire doctor, an' I don't wait for y' t' get it off. All I'll ask y' then is 'What's y'r name, which hand, which foot, which laig [leg],' or whatever that it is that's burnt, and that's all I have t' know. An' I actually don't have t' know which hand or foot, really. I do like t' get th' name. I like t' have your name, an' then after y' tell me your name, I get th' rest of it.

"How to do that kind of work was a man teach a woman and a woman teach a man. I just never did try t' teach a man. [I'd teach a woman] to write the verse down on a little piece of paper so she could learn it by heart. Then you take that thing an' burn it—get rid of it. 'Course, anybody's t' find it, they wouldn't know what it meant nohow. I don't put on it what it's fer. I just write it down. An' if y' need it and haven't learned by heart, carry it with y' an' just read it over, an' it'll draw that fire out or stop blood. Then y' wind up askin' th' Lord t' . . . just like anybody else when they sayin' a prayer an' closin' it . . . 'In Jesus's Name, Amen'—you know, at the end of it."

—Charley Tyler, March 1968 and Spring/Summer 1996

CURING THRASH

There's three kinds of thrash. And th' yaller thrash is the one that's s' hard t' cure. It just comes up in clear blisters, and they can't eat, ner they can't drink. I can cure all three kinds. —*Mrs. Andy (Bashie) Webb*

Thrush, known as "thrash" to some folks in Appalachia, is a not-so-uncommon problem with babies and even their moms. Babies not only cry incessantly from the pain, but, with the blisters in their mouths and throats, they can neither eat nor drink. According to healer Charley Tyler, "Thrash is a thing that just works in y'r mouth . . . It'll go all the way through you. It'll kill y', an' a doctor can't do anything about it too much."

Dissatisfied with the treatment received from medical professionals, some mothers took their babies to a thrash healer for "doctorin'." In discussing the actual process of curing thrash, we learned from one source that you "don't blow in th' child's mouth. You do like you was tryin' t' suck th' breath away from th' child. You do that three times, and then that's th' motion." Though more than one method exists, they all seem to work for those who have "the power." Mr. Tyler told us, "Most of th' time I can doctor it, and tomorrer that kid'll never know it's ever had th' thrash." Though many skeptics pooh-pooh this art, many mothers with sick babies will give passionate testimony about the cures.

—*Angie Cheek*

"Thrash [thrush] is in a child's mouth, and it [the child] can't eat. And if it's a-nursin' th' breast, it gets all in th' breast, and they [the mothers] can't stand fer 'em t' nurse. It just comes up in yaller [yellow] blisters. There's three kinds of thrash, and th' yaller thrash is the one that's s' hard t' cure. It just comes up in clear blisters; they can't eat, ner they can't drink. I can cure all three kinds.

"My goddaughter brung her two twin babies up hyere, an' they had th' thrash. I doctored them and got them well, and here she come back. It was in her breast, an' I doctored it and cured it.

"Doctors tell everybody goes to 'em with a baby with th' thrash t' go hunt 'em up a thrash doctor. One man who lives in th' Flats [Scaly Mountain, North Carolina], his child had th' thrash, and they hunted ever'whar. They took it t' th' doctor, out yonder t' Clayton [Georgia] t' th' doctor, an' he said he couldn't do nothin' fer it. Says, 'If you know whar there's ary a thrash doctor, you better hunt it up and right now.' So they commenced huntin'. They come down here t' Mrs. Rogers, and she said she'd quit. So she told 'em t' come on up hyere. They fetched th' baby on up hyere, an' I doctored it. I told 'em t' bring it back th' next day. It had th' thrash bad. So they brung hit an' two more—they'd took th' thrash. I doctored them and cured 'em up; I had t' tell 'em t' bring 'em back they had it s' bad."

—Mrs. Andy (Bashie) Webb, March 1968 and Spring/Summer 1996

"You have t' watch. I come pretty near pullin' th' breath out of a little kid one time. Little too hard, an' he just quivered."

—Charley Tyler

"Thrash is a thing that just works in y'r mouth, you know. It'll go all the way through you. It'll kill y', an' a doctor can't do anything about it too much. You got t' have a different way o' doctorin' the thing . . . There's a yellow thrash, and they's what they call a 'red thrash.' That red thrash is not too much trouble t' cure. Hit'll cure pretty easy. Doctor can cure it. But that yaller thrash is a thing that's a blister. It blisters up in yaller blisters—looks like it'd have pus or somethin' under it, inside his mouth. And hit'll bust their lips up around here, y' know. I can cure one in a half a minute, and y' don't have t' bring it back a second time.

"Some of 'em cures it by th' faith they have, y' know. And they's some o' 'em that does it with a few words out o' the Bible 'at they use. And then some of 'em uses chemicals, y' know, like some kind o' weed they use t' doctor with. Some takes 'em t' a barn. My way of doctorin', though, if I met you out here in th' road, is you stand still, and I'll go behind th' car. If y' come t' my house, I'll just go through that door there an' just pull th' door to long enough t' doctor it, just so I'm out o' your sight. An' I don't never say a word. I just do somethin' t' it. It don't work, they claim, if y' don't stay out o' sight, without you're teachin' somebody—that don't make any difference, but they claim they are.

"I can teach all I want t', I guess. I guess I've taught five hundred. I've always taught women, and then th' womenfolks teaches th' men. A woman told me how. She was from over on Persimmon [outside Clayton, Georgia]. That 'as back in my young days—see, I got a lot o' people over 'ere and I used t' go there a lot. I picked up those things like that ever' time I got a chance.

"Well, y' use your hand. You get th' kid to cry or laugh and have it in your arms, and when it does, you set your hand over it thataway (cupping the fingers around the mouth); then you breathe. Don't *blow* in th' child's mouth. You do like you was tryin' t' suck th' breath away from th' child. You do that three times, and then that's th' motion. That's all y' got t' go through with. That's it. Don't breathe in. Just pull it to y'. Blow it away from him when y' blow your breath out. Blow it out of his face and then pull back t' do it but one time, without they're awful bad. I've never doctored one but once in all th' years I've been at it but one. That I had t' doctor actually twice to get it stopped. I had one that th' first time I doctored it, why it was some better, but it wadn't half well. It could eat a little. But I let 'em miss one day. Then I doctored it again, and then I never did doctor it anymore. It got all right. Most of th' time I can doctor it, and tomorrer that kid'll never know it's ever had th' thrash.

"You have t' watch. I come pretty near pullin' th' breath out of a little kid one time. Little too hard, an' he just quivered. You have t' watch about a lit-

PLATE 39 "You do like you was tryin' t' suck th' breath away from th' child." —Charley Tyler

tle one. You know, leetle beety [little bitty] ones is worse to have it, really, than bigger ones at one time of th' year; an' another time of th' year, th' big'uns has it, an' th' littluns won't."

—Charley Tyler, March 1968 and Spring /Summer 1996

CONJURING WARTS

Now, you don't cure *warts. You* conjure *them.* —*Varney Watson*

I don't like the word "wart." Caused by a virus (not by handling frogs or being unclean, contrary to the old wives' tale), a wart is a protuberance or an excrescence from the skin. I don't even like the words "protuberance" or "excrescence"!

In *The Canterbury Tales,* a work written around the frame of Middle English folks on a pilgrimage to the shrine of Thomas Beckett, Geoffrey

Chaucer describes the face of the crude Miller as having a huge wart with coarse red hairs protruding from it—ugh! Warts appear on toads, hags, ogres, witches, and various other practitioners of villainy. No wonder we humans find warts repulsive and seek ways to rid ourselves of them!

When most of us think of the word "conjuring," we think of magic, witchcraft, or the dark arts. I, like some of the healers, don't understand the power necessary to conjure warts. One conjurer told us that she says a verse from the Bible when she performs the ritual, but Oakley Justice told us, "It doesn't have anything to do with the Bible. I don't see why it works, but it does."

—*Angie Cheek*

"Maggie doesn't conjure warts when there are lots of people around because she doesn't want everyone to know how she does it."
—Gene Bingham

"My grandmother, Maggie Elliott, told us that the way she conjures warts is connected with the Bible. She learned the method when she was a small girl, and it was so long ago that she says she has forgotten who she learned it from. She lays two flint rocks on the wart and says a verse from the Bible. She would not explain the ritual to us, as this might cause her to lose her ability to conjure warts. She did say that the conjure would not work if medications have been added to the wart . . . She thinks that mountain people are probably the only people left who have the power to conjure warts because other people don't seem to believe in it anymore.

"She said that she wouldn't lose her power when she hands it down to someone else and that a person doesn't have to be a certain age before they can accept the power to conjure warts.

"Maggie doesn't conjure warts when there are lots of people around because she doesn't want everyone to know how she does it. She doesn't talk about it much." —**Gene Bingham, Fall 1977**

"The boy who told me about wart conjurin' was with me in the CCC [Civilian Conservation Corps] camps over at Hot Springs, North Carolina. We was out in the woods workin' on a girdling [making an encircling through the bark of a branch or tree] outfit. I had a wart about three-fourths of an inch high just above my left wrist. They would stop and let us eat or smoke, and I believe we had stopped just for a break; he told me to let him take that wart off me. I told him, 'All right,' but I can't tell you what he done.

If I was to, I might not be able to take them off anymore. But, anyhow, he told me just to forget about it. So first thing I know, the wart was gone. But he told me how he done it, and he showed me how he done it. But he said he could only tell one person, and that's all he could tell.

"I've done it after he told me, and I've took lots of them off. And I told Varney [Watson], but if I was to tell somebody else, it might not work.

"It don't matter if you pass it on from man to man or man to woman, I don't think. But I never have told no woman how to do it. That might be the way that it is supposed to go, but he never told me that. So that's all they are to it. I told Varney several years ago; he said he tried it, and it worked. And I never have told nobody else but him.

"Now I can't tell you how I do it, but I can tell you one thing of what I do. Take a knife, and on the wart you make a cross over the top. It works with the sap in the trees. If you do it before the sap comes up, it ain't as long gettin' gone. Or either when the sap is goin' down in the fall . . . if you do it pretty late in the fall, it ain't pretty long goin'. If you do it in the summer, it may be fall before it leaves; if you do it in the winter, it will be spring before it leaves. That's the way it works. But it does work with the sap. If you do it when the sap is rising, it ought to leave, and if you do it before, it leaves in the fall. But if you do it in the summer or winter, the wart will be a long time leavin'. The timber then ain't got no sap in it, and it'll not leave before the timber gets some sap in it.

"I took one off Bob Harrell's girl in Atlanta. He brought her over here one day. She didn't have no faith in it, but her mother and Bob both came and said they did. So I told her just to forget about it. Well, that was in the spring. I don't know how long it was a-goin', but it wasn't too long. So Bob's wife, I seen her; she said that girl would come in every evenin' and her wart was still there and said that she didn't believe in that. She told her *she* did. And one evenin' she came in, and her wart was gone.

"You know there are different ways of takin' them off. I guess some can take them off without seein' the person, but I can't. The one that taught me told me how to take 'em off, and that's the only way I've ever done it: Take a knife and make a cross on the wart, and I'll not tell you the rest because it might not work. He said not to tell but one.

"The way I take 'em off, it ain't hard to remember, and it doesn't have anything to do with the Bible. I don't see why it works, but it does."

—Oakley Justice, Fall 1977

"I am told that I can conjure warts. I have taken several off of people—at least they said I did. I know I did what I am supposed to do to take them off,

PLATE 40 "Take a knife, and on the wart you make a cross over the top. It works with the sap in the trees." —Oakley Justice

and it's worked on everybody I have tried it on. Sometimes it hasn't worked real fast. The longest took a year and a half. It depends on the time of year.

"Spring is the best time. In fall, the power is weakest. It has to do with the seasons. . . .

"My uncle Oakley Justice told me how to do it. I think the way it goes is that I can only tell one person myself, and so could my uncle . . . It has to be a blood relative. You can tell either the first son if there's no second son, or the second son who will have more power. It can't be through marriage. And this is how I got my power.

"If you notice, I said you had to be a blood relative. I am a unique case because my uncle is not a blood relative of mine. I am a second son, though, but my father was killed before I was born, so I never saw my father. You understand about as much of this stuff as I do, but Oakley said that me being the second son and never seeing my father would give me a lot of power. He said he could tell it to me, and he did—and it has worked so far.

"Now, you don't *cure* warts. You *conjure* them . . . Three months is the fastest curing time I've had so far. The worst case I ever had was when a friend of mine . . . her nephew came up from Atlanta. She had heard that I could conjure warts, so she told him. They came up, and really, he did have, I would say, around seventy-five warts. They were on his hands, on his arms, on his back, and really, that was the most warts I had seen on anybody. I did my conjuring. It was in the spring of the year, and it was when I was operating full force on this stuff. And I went out and did my conjurin' on him. He went back to Atlanta, and she got kind of rushed on the belief. In about three or four months, she had some warts taken off his hands or his back—I'm not sure. But before she had time to have the others taken off, they were cured. The ones they didn't take off were gone. The conjure was effective to them. . . .

"There are various ways of doin' it, and I think this maybe will give you kind of a hint. A lot of people don't know what a wart is. A lot of them say that it's a virus. Of course, it does have a seed in there, but where does that seed come from to get there to begin with? I think warts are probably ten percent virus and ninety percent mental anyhow. I think this is why my conjurin' works. I think my uncle gave me this power when I was fourteen, and I was eighteen before I tried it. I didn't believe it would work at first until I took one off.

"Back in the olden days, people didn't go to a doctor to have a wart frozen or cut off. They had to have some way of doin' it. I think, basically, this is where your conjurin' came up. This is not somethin' made up for Foxfire or made up just to sound good. This is somethin' people have been doing for years and years. It does work, and I'm probably as skeptical as anyone in the country. Don't ask me why it works because I certainly don't know. But it does work." —**Varney Watson, Fall 1977**

EVERYDAY MIRACLES

I could not read, and when I opened the Bible, it was the fourteenth chapter of St. John, and I read the first six verses. So God give it to me, and I didn't back up. I can't read anything but the Bible. I cannot even write my name or write a letter.

—Clarence Martin

During the three years of Jesus's earthly ministry, He performed many miracles. Most of us know the stories of calming the storm on the Sea of Galilee; walking on water; multiplying the loaves and fishes for the five thousand; turning water into wine for the wedding feast in Cana; healing the lame, blind, mute, deaf, unclean, and demon-possessed; raising Jairus's daughter and Lazarus from the dead.

Even though thousands were living witnesses of these miracles, many chose not to believe. "The light shines in the darkness, but the darkness has not understood it." (John 1:5). In attempting to identify Himself with the Father, Jesus wanted His chosen ones to have faith in Him and believe that He was one with the Father. He was going to the Father, and He would send the strength of the Holy Spirit to them from the Father so that they also would do great things.

The faithful in the so-called Bible Belt do not believe that God is a laissez-faire deity. They are confident that He is an omnipotent, omniscient, omnipresent Creator whose eye is even on the sparrow and whose hands dressed the lilies; how much more, then, is He watchful of man, into whom He blew the breath of life. Therefore, the faithful believe that "the Great I Am," Yahweh, is not a God of yesterday's miracles but a Lord who still moves stones today.

—*Angie Cheek*

"As I look back over my life, I see how everything fell into place and always worked out for our good." —*Claudine Palmer Cantrell*

"God has helped me in so many ways. One way is the time He helped me find my glasses. The time was mid-morning in early spring 1989. I had searched in vain for my eyeglasses that were misplaced a few days earlier. I felt so frustrated. I sat down in the living room where I could be alone. As I relaxed in my favorite easy chair, I found myself praying. As I became still and calm in prayer, a picture of a red coat came into my mind. I saw a human hand slide into the right pocket. I immediately remembered the red jacket I had worn to town a few days earlier. I joyously closed my prayer by praising God for hearing me. I thought of a favorite Bible verse—Philippians 4:19: 'But my God shall supply all your needs according to His riches in Glory by Jesus Christ.' Before I went to the closet for my coat, I was perfectly sure I would find my glasses. In addition, they were in the right-hand pocket of the red jacket I had worn a few days earlier. Praise God . . . God has brought our family through trials and performed many miracles in the lives of our loved ones. God is still blessing us daily. As I look back over my life, I see how everything fell into place and always worked out for our good."

—From the journals of Claudine Palmer Cantrell, Spring /Summer 2005

"I never went to school a day in my life except for a day or two. They was thirteen of us in the family, and we had to stay at home and work. There 'as days once in a while that I would get to go to school. I was so old that they let me go into two other grades, and I didn't finish a grade, not nary a grade, but I do thank God for what He has given me . . . I got to the third grade, and that is where I quit . . . I will tell you one thing for sure: I do the work that God wants me to do because God called me to preach the Word without education. I ran from it for six months, sayin' that I couldn't do it. I finally said, 'If you give it to me, I will preach it.' I woke up one Sunday mornin' readin' six verses from the fourteenth chapter of St. John, and I went right on to the church that night and asked the pastor to let me have the service on Wednesday night. He give it to me January 1, 1964. I have been preachin' ever since. I did not even know anything about the Bible. I didn't know what He had let me read. I could not read, and when I opened the Bible, it was the fourteenth chapter of St. John, and I read the first six verses. So God give it to me, and I didn't back up . . . I can't read anything but the Bible. I cannot even write my name or write a letter. I can read a little bit more than I used to, and I went through the Old Testament three times this year. I want to go through the old Bible because I want to know the Word of God. The Word of God is what sets us free, and I still say, 'Praise the Lord.' I don't see how lost people goes on and lives for the devil when they know Jesus suffered just for them. I didn't mean to go on preachin' there." **—Clarence Martin, Spring/Summer 2002**

PLATE 41 "I don't see how lost people goes on and lives for the devil when they know Jesus suffered just for them." —Clarence Martin and his wife, Lois

"After Brother died—he was buried at Clermont—I came on home, and that night I dreamed that Grandmother—my grandmother had been dead for seven years—and I dreamed that she was sitting in a chair right by that bed. It was so real. I thought I was holding her hand in my dream. She said. 'Eula, Berry never crossed the river.' She said, 'I couldn't find him.' And that just worried me.

"I said, 'Grandmother, you're not here. You're in heaven.'

"She said, 'Oh, no. I'm here. I come to tell you that Berry never crossed the river.'

"You know, that just worried me. It was so real. I thought I could feel her hand when I awakened. I said in my dream, 'Grandmother, Brother was a real good Christian. He was real good.'

"She said, 'I know he was good, and I know he should be here—but he is not. He's not here.' She said he didn't ever get across the river.

"I dreamed a lot of things.

"Papa said we could go to the circus in Gainesville. He was the mayor at that time, and we had tickets. We went in the afternoon. He said we had to get back before dark. We had a flat tire in Clermont—that's ten miles below Cleveland [Georgia]—on the way back.

"When we got home, it was just misting rain. Papa made me go to the barn and milk the cow. It was dark as pitch on across there from the house to the barn, and the barn opened with a big door. That was a 'livery stable,' they called it. They rented stalls, y' know, and it was court week. Well, it was dark. We had an old collie dog, and she was the sweetest thing. He wouldn't let me take that dog. He wouldn't let me take the lantern. I started down there. Brother always stood by me, and he got right in the first gate and had the dog and had the lantern. I didn't know he had it, though, 'til after. So I went on down there, and this hack that I was tellin' you about that carried Mama to the cemetery was sittin' there. I went on through that big hall, dark as it could be, on through there and opened the big door. And it screeched because it was a very big door. It opened goin' into the other pasture—the big pasture—and I opened that gate. The cow knew which way to go, and she came on. We got real close to that hack. Something said, 'Barn! Barn! Barn!' The cow stopped, and you know a cow or a horse either one will blow (whew, whew) like that when they're fighting or scared. She wouldn't move. I stood there, and in a minute it started again. I should have known that if somebody wanted to get me, they wouldn't have made that noise, and I was just sittin' there prayin'. I was so hot; I was just scared to death. I thought I was gonna die. The cow was just blowin'. She was really scared, too. It sounded like somebody was tryin' to get out of that big ol' hack. There was a big loft all the way across the barn. I went up to the steps and looked up, and somebody said, 'Eula, don't be afraid.' I recognized my mother's voice. Nobody believes me, but I know what I saw.

"Something says, 'Eula, don't be afraid. I'm here.' And I looked up there, and she was sitting in a straight chair. It was the most beautiful light I've ever seen in my life. It was just a halo of light. She had on a navy dress with white dots and white lace on it. She said, 'Don't be afraid. I'm here.' And you know, that cow just started walkin' into her stall. She knew where it was. I wasn't afraid. I started walkin' up the steps, and her hand was goin' down like she wanted to hold my hand. Of course it went away before I got to the steps.

"I went on and milked the cow and fixed the feed for in the mornin'. I went on up there, and poor ol' Brother was sittin' up there at the gate. He had somethin' over him and a lantern under a big raincoat, and he had the dog there with him. He was goin' to come a-runnin' if I called him over there.

"When I went over to him, he was cryin', and I said, 'Brother, don't cry.'

He said, 'Well, I was gonna go down there and getcha 'cause I was scared.' So I went into the house, and my stepmother and my daddy were in there. We hadn't had supper yet, and she was in there takin' some biscuits out of the stove. I said to Papa, 'Papa, I saw Mama.' He began to cry. He said, 'Oh, Eula! That was the wrong thing for me to send you down there. Somebody could a-been there in that barn.'

" 'Well, I saw Mama, and she told me not to be afraid.' He said that he believed every word I said 'cause I looked so happy when I came in. Brother was cryin', and he said that he wanted to see Mama, too. I never was afraid to go in that barn again, but he didn't send me anymore when it was dark. I was sixteen when that happened." —**Eula Carroll, Summer 1990**

"When people came to get saved, they'd get down on their knees and come weepin'. I believe that you've got to have a broken heart and a contrite spirit. The Gospel and the Holy Spirit convicts a man of sin, and when he's convicted, I've seen them come fallin' into the altar, cryin' for the mercy of God. Let them stay there until they get right with God. And when they get right with God, they'll endure the end.

"One night we had a meeting that had been goin' nine weeks. There were about fifteen or twenty in the altar and no one had been saved. A little boy, seven or eight years old, had been comin' to the altar every night; no one would invite him, but he'd come. Everyone thought he was too little to be saved, to be accountable. I didn't pay any attention to him, and I'd always go to the mountaintop and pray before I would come to preach on Sunday night. I was up there prayin', and all I could see was that little boy in that altar. And somethin' said to me, 'Have you ever instructed him?'

"I said, 'No, I haven't, and no one else has either.'

"So I went back that night, and old Uncle Abe Norman was the preacher. (It was his grandson.) I was prayin', and all I could see was this little boy. I said, 'I don't know. He might be closer to death than any of these men here.' You know, they all came up and got around that little boy, and he was saved. Then there was ten or fifteen saved just about as fast as they could come up—after he was saved. I baptized that little boy down there in the river, and that followin' week he was killed over there on the highway with a car.

"That taught me that God knows His business. I baptized him down there in the river, and that followin' week he was killed. I attended his funeral over there. God knows. That little boy was closer to death and closer to hell than these old men were. Things like that have helped me along life's way. You know, the Spirit will lead you if you let it. When it tells you to do a thing, it's right. I don't care—you don't need to argue with it."

—Preacher Ben Cook, Fall 1979

"I've seen God move, put broken bones back together, bring 'em off the bed when the doctors said there wasn't a chance for 'em. I went last Friday, prayed for a man that had cancer, and God healed . . . God healed him, praise the Lord, and I just thank my God for what He has done for me."

—Clarence Martin, Spring/Summer 2002

"I . . . asked God to spare my mother. I told Him that if He'd spare her, I'd obey her all the rest of my life. She lived, and I tried to do what I said I'd do." —*Addie Bleckley*

"When I was in my teens and while we were livin' at Eastanollee below Toccoa, Georgia, we thought Mother was near death one time. Eight of us children and Dad were out in the field. Dinnertime came, and Mother'd always ring the dinner bell when she got the food on the table. She'd rung the bell and then was taken sick suddenly. When we came in, she was lyin' on the bed and kickin'—didn't know anything—and frothin' at the mouth.

PLATE 42 "When we came in, she was lying on the bed and kickin'—didn't know anything—and frothin' at the mouth." —Addie Bleckley

Dad hollered, 'All you children that want to see your mother alive, come in here.'

"Of course, we all ran in to see how she was, and then we went on out. I went on the back porch and got down on the doorsteps and asked God to spare my mother. I told Him that if He'd spare her, I'd obey her all the rest of my life. She lived, and I tried to do what I said I'd do. She told me very often that I was more pleasure to her than any child she raised."

—Addie Bleckley, Summer 1978

> **"I can go out there and sit down, and I can just feel him. I can feel the Lord, like it was whenever I was out there with Daddy."**
>
> ***—Catherine Weaver***

"If Daddy [Charlie Bry Phillips] couldn't sleep, he'd get up prayin'. He'd sit with his Bible, and you could see the light on at two or three in the mornin'. Dad'd be readin' the Bible. He'd say, 'I'm awake for some reason. Maybe somebody that I don't even know about needs prayer.'

"Maybe three or four days later, somebody would say, 'Brother Charlie, I know that somebody was prayin' for me the other mornin' at three o'clock. I was so sick I thought I was gonna die.'

"He said, 'That's my answer.'

"People called him all times of the day and night and said, 'I want you to pray about this. I want you to pray about that.' He'd go out there to the prayin' rock; he'd put his little rocks up, and he'd pray about it. He'd stay until he got an answer. If some man was lost, someone might ask him, 'Look, this man's lost, and I want you to pray for him.' He'd put the rock for the lost man in the lost pile, and if the man got saved, he'd put his rock over there in the saved pile. If he backslid, he drawed him out of the saved pile: He was out of the will of the Lord. He wasn't *lost* again because if you're once saved, you can't be lost. Jesus would have to go back to the cross. So he took him *out* of the saved pile and put him down here out of the will of the Lord in neither pile. He wasn't livin' right, but when prayers were answered, he'd put it back into the saved pile.

"People would call requests in. Once he got 'My husband's run away with another woman. I want you to pray that God'll bring him back.'

"He said, 'Are you willin' for God to bring him back—any kind of shape that God brings him back, you'll take him back? He may come in a pine box.'

"She said, 'Well, yeah, I guess.'

"He said, 'You don't guess with God. You've gotta be sincere.'

"And then there'd be other people to call in and say, 'Somebody's sick. I want you to pray for them.'

"He didn't have a rock for everybody in the congregation, just special ones. He didn't pick out no special ones but just the ones that had problems and asked for help. He chose the rocks by just reachin' down to pick one up, but he knew which rock was . . . who it was. He could say, 'This is so-and-so.' He could tell you what pile they were in and why they were there. He could name every one of those rocks for you. I'm sure he had a rock up there for himself, but I don't know which one it was. That's probably somethin' nobody will ever know.

"Preachers from Habersham County [Georgia] would come up here and go out to the prayin' rock with Daddy. They would bring prayer requests of their own and go out there and pray about it. They wouldn't come back until they got an answer. It didn't matter if it was all night.

"A drunk man come to this preacher down there in Habersham, and he said, 'I need to talk to a preacher. I need to get saved. I need somebody to pray with me.' And that preacher said, 'Well, we'll pray, but I think we ought to go to Rabun County.'

"And the drunk man said, 'Whatever you think.' So they come up here and went with Daddy out to the prayin' rock. Daddy asked Joe, my husband, to go with him. They stayed out all night. It rained all night, and it didn't slack. They would pray and rejoice and cry, but they really prayed there until that man made it right with God. That drunk man put his head on that rock and didn't come up 'til next mornin'—daylight. When he came up, he came up a saved man.

"Now, a lot of the neighbors around here heard somebody out in the woods and questioned the noise that they heard. They thought somebody was out there hurt or somethin', and it was my daddy out there prayin'—at night and in the daytime. . . .

"There 'as this young man right up here that got out of the will of the Lord and quit goin' to church. Daddy pulled his rock out of the pile and went to talk to him. He said, 'You're out of the will of God. Your rock is in the wrong pile. You better get back where you're supposed to be.' He and Daddy went out to the prayin' rock, and that man got right again. Daddy put him right back where he was supposed to be. Now that man's . . . pastorin' a church.

"Since Daddy died in 1975, everything's just been left the way it was. All the rocks are there. I can go out there and sit down, and I can just feel him. I can feel the Lord, like it was whenever I was out there with Daddy. I can just get chill bumps all over me. I can just feel that there's someone there with me." —**Catherine Weaver, Spring 1984**

"In 1938, I was pregnant—seven months to the day—when I got hurt by a mule. It was an early Sunday mornin' before church, and I went to turn

PLATE 43 Mr. Phillips's prayin' rock

her out into the pasture. When I opened the stable door, she didn't come out. I said, 'Come out of there, Kate! What you doin'? Come on out!'

"Then I just stepped back for her to come out. Well, she just leaped up in my face. She took her foot and laid my leg plumb out. It didn't break the bone—just chopped the flesh up. She also bit me in the back and stomped me.

"After a while, Johnny woke up and looked out the window. He said a low voice woke him up, saying 'Johnny' real low. He saw me tryin' to crawl through a little place in the barn. The mule was still pawin' at me. Johnny jumped up and ran out and run the mule off and got me to the house. They got the doctor there and got me all done up. I came to enough to know somethin' had happened. I had false teeth—hadn't had 'em but a little while. Well, I missed 'em, an' I was a-beggin' them to get me my teeth. They hunted and hunted and finally found them up under the cow box where we fed the cows—the box was nailed off the ground. They weren't even broke. They was still clean.

"I stayed in the bed two months. I didn't lose the baby. It was a twelve-pound boy!" —**Flora Youngblood, Spring 1985**

THE HOLY LAND

From Bethany, we went to Jerusalem where we saw the place where Jesus was tried. It is believed the stones are the actual ones that Jesus walked on.

—Claudine Palmer Cantrell

When we look at the area that Jesus traversed when He became flesh, the area is really quite small, yet His life affected the entire world. His feet trod the sands and cities of His homeland. He played on Bethlehem's streets. He walked upon the cool stones of the temple in Jerusalem. He worked in Joseph's carpenter shop in Nazareth. He and His disciples, His fishers of men, walked through Cana of Galilee and Capernaum and Samaria. He knelt in Gethsemane; He stood before the Sanhedrin and Pilate and Herod; He endured a gruesome flogging; He carried His cross through the ways of the city up Golgotha's hill. They nailed Him to the cross, and He died there to ransom mankind from sin. Taken to a borrowed tomb, He, three days later, rose from the dead, talked with hundreds, ascended into heaven, and sits at the right hand of the Father. So are the beliefs of those who espouse Christianity.

To walk where Jesus walked is a dream of many believers. For Claudine Palmer Cantrell and her husband, Fred, the dream of going to the Holy Land, thanks to their son David and their daughter-in-law Barbara, became a reality, and Mrs. Cantrell's family, after her death, shared with Foxfire, through her journals, the thrill she felt in knowing that her Savior had left footprints there and that she was walking in His Way.

—*Angie Cheek*

"We left June 22, 1987. The following are some of my fondest memories of our trip, which highlighted and brought to life the teachings of the Bible, God's Holy Word, and the life of Jesus in that place. . . .

"We caught a boat across the Sea of Galilee. It is thirteen miles long and seven miles wide. The day was clear, and the water was as blue as the sky. I thought the water could get rough during a storm, and I remembered how

Christ calmed the waves and how Peter walked on the water. As we crossed the sea and saw the ruins of Capernaum, I was reminded of the fact that Jesus made His headquarters there. There, Jesus performed many miracles. Near here, He fed the five thousand and preached the Sermon on the Mount. We also saw the place where Christ cast the demons into the swine, and they were drowned in the sea.

"When we returned to the hotel, Fred and I gathered towels and a change of clothes and went to the River Jordan. We both were baptized. This was a special service. I shall never forget the joy and beauty of the service.

"The next place we saw was Cana of Galilee. This is where Jesus turned the water into wine. We visited Nazareth where the Angel Gabriel announced to Mary that she would bear the Christ Child. We went through the Valley of Armegiddo that is called the Breadbasket of Israel and passed Mount Tabor, the Mountain of Transfiguration. We went to the Garden of Gethsemane where Jesus often went to pray. This is located at the foot of the Mount of Olives.

"When we went to Bethlehem, we saw many small caves. The shepherds used the caves as stables for their sheep. It was there that we saw a manger symbolizing where the Christ Child lay. We toured the Mountain of Masada that is counted a great possession of the Jews today. From here, you could see some of the caves where the Dead Sea Scrolls were found. Just think how God used this arid area here to preserve His Holy Word. Then we went to Bethany and found a church that is built on the site of the home of Mary and Martha, and near here was the grave of Lazarus.

"From Bethany, we went to Jerusalem where we saw the place where

PLATE 44 Whoa! Claudine Palmer Cantrell and her husband, Fred

Jesus was tried. It is believed the stones are the actual ones that Jesus walked on. Now all of it is underground. We drove to the hills of Judea and saw Herod's stronghold. The dome of the rock is the most beautiful building I have ever seen, but just imagine what Solomon's temple must have been like.

"There is an old church still standing on the top of the Mount of Olives. As we stood looking up through the building, it was as though I could see Jesus rise up into heaven and could hear the two men in white apparel say, 'Why stand ye gazing up into heaven?' After we left this area, we went to the Wailing Wall. This is a very sacred place of worship for the Jews and the Muslims. . . . This trip really brought God's Word to life for me."

—From the journals of Claudine Palmer Cantrell, Spring/Summer 2005

HEAVEN

You're going to enjoy all the glories if you go there—see a rainbow about the throne and all those golden streets. Everything glorious! And there are pearly gates—such a coming and going through the pearly gates.

—Rural Georgia black folktale from
the Rose Thompson Collection

Is this world all there is? Viktor Frankl, in *Man's Search for Meaning,* asks, "Is it not conceivable that there is still another dimension, a world beyond man's world" (122)? Is heaven truly a perfect place with no weeping, no darkness, a place of complete happiness? Is St. Peter manning the pearly gates? Will he allow me to enter into the kingdom? Are the streets paved in gold? Is a mansion prepared for me? Will I see my loved ones who have gone on before me? Will they know me? With the transitoriness of this dimension of existence, all of us wonder about life after life. Some call it life after death, but do we actually die? I like the idea poet John Donne expressed in his "Holy Sonnet 10" of Death's not being "mighty and dreadful." Donne ended the sonnet with his assertion about the death of Death:

One short sleep past, we wake eternally,
And Death shall be no more; Death, thou shalt die.

In the millisecond I die, I live; therefore, not I but Death dies.

What is heaven like? This is a question for which we can ascertain no definitive answer—not now anyway, but someday. Christians, however, do not need to know now what heaven is like. Knowing that paradise exists and that by the grace and mercy of God through the death and resurrection of Christ they will live forever with Him is enough for the faithful. "The Lord is their inheritance" (Joshua 13:33), and "their inheritance will endure forever" (Psalm 37:18).

The following are examples of the steadfast conviction of the faithful that someday they will "join in and ring the gloryful bells."

—*Angie Cheek*

"Heaven is a happy and a holy place, and you're going to enjoy all the glories if you go there—see a rainbow about the throne and all those golden streets. Everything glorious! And there are pearly gates—such a coming and going through the pearly gates. There's a keeper of the gates, some of those old patriarchs. But the gates, the pearly gates, won't be shut at all by day, and there is no night. It's always day—bright, shiny day. And the stars in heaven shine so bright—beautiful, beautiful silver light. Oh, yes, stars in heaven. But that city has no need for the sun nor the stars nor the moon to brighten it. The glory of God shines all about. They rejoice and be happy in heaven. They sing and rejoice in that happy, holy place. And they ring those charming bells. Got crowns of glory, starry crowns . . . and harps. They play on the harps . . . and the bells, charming bells for to ring.

"You're going to meet the old Christians when you get to heaven. Don't know who they are, but they will be there just marching the golden streets. The ones who are there now are marching those golden streets. And when you get in heaven, Old Father Moses will be looking out for you—going to see Old Father Moses there watching out for you. And Old Father Gabriel is going to beckon you in. Oh, yes, there's glory in heaven, and you are going to ring the charming bells.

"There will be angels up there in white robes of righteousness . . . crowns on their heads, starry crowns! Angels with harps in hands, flying all around. Yes, child, they got wings. Yes, Lawd, heaven's a high and righteous place, and the chariot is going to take you home. When you get to heaven, the journey has done ended, and you're going to join in and ring the gloryful bells. You're going to ring the charming bells."

—Rural Georgia black folktale from the Rose Thompson Collection, Winter 1977

"I think a house with not a flower around it is the saddest-looking thing I've ever seen in my life. I can't stand it without some flowers. I work as hard, or harder, in my flower garden as I do in my vegetable garden.

"I cut them sometimes to take to the cemetery. I tell 'em, though, as good as I love flowers, I don't want people to spend a whole lot of money on me for flowers when I'm gone. I'd rather they give the money to some poor child somewhere that's not got anything much to wear. Use that money where it's needed.

"It's beautiful for people to give flowers so they can scatter them all over three or four graves in the graveyard. It's somethin' beautiful for people to do, but, nevertheless, it's such a waste. The cut flowers won't last but a day or two, and then they're gone. And you can't get a bunch of flowers anymore for less than ten or fifteen dollars. Well, a lot of poor folks will go ahead and buy them for people, and I think it'd be much better if they'd spend that for poor children or somethin' like that. That's the way I am. I've said just a rose will do me because I'm goin' to a country where there's goin' to be plenty of flowers, and so there's no use for people to waste 'em on me."

—Aunt Addie Norton, Fall 1976

"Well, my daddy was a preacher—preached all over Rabun County and Towns County [Georgia]. In North Carolina, he preached forty-somethin' years. He was ninety-one when he passed away. My mama, she was a housewife and loved the Lord. She always stayed at home. Papa'd go off an' run revival meetin's. He left us there with Mama. She always told us about the Lord. Jesus was always in our home. We 'as always told about His love, how we could always live for Jesus and be together in heaven; that's what I've always tried to do. I wanna meet 'em. They're gone, but I wanna meet 'em." **—Senia Southards, Spring/Summer 2003**

"Mom opened her eyes and smiled at us and told us to meet her in heaven; then she died." —*Claudine Palmer Cantrell*

"It was my job to sleep by Mom and to hand her water and medicine when she needed it. I could go right back to sleep, and Dad couldn't. One night I woke up, and Mama was singing. I lay still and didn't say anything. She was singing, 'Come, thou fount of every blessing; teach my heart to sing thy praise. Streams of mercy never ceasing, call for hymns of louder praise.' It seemed the room was bright, not the kind of light that showed the furniture but a radiance I can't explain. The room seemed to be filled with angels. I listened until Mom finished singing, and I went to sleep feeling very safe and happy. . . .

"Then [a few days later] about midnight, Mom opened her eyes and smiled at us and told us to meet her in heaven; then she died. I know my mother had the same faith as my grandmother that she would someday meet her little ones in heaven. I believe my mother and grandmother are together in heaven with all of their children gone on before us and that I shall go to be with them, Dad, and all of my loved ones."

—From the journals of Claudine Palmer Cantrell, Spring/Summer 2005

"Somebody called me the other day and asked me if I was happy. I said yeah. They asked me if I'd been happy all my life or if I'd been sad, and I told them, I said, 'Well, I've been happy.' When I was seventeen years old, I give my heart to the Lord, and I've been tryin' to live fer Him ever since. He's blessed me and give me strength fer almost eighty-three years . . . He promised us a mansion. When He went to prepare us a mansion, He said He'd come back and receive us unto Hisself. Where He was, we'd be also, and so I'm a-lookin' fer it. The Bible said to lay up our treasures in heaven where moths and rust won't corrupt and thieves won't break through to steal, so I just talk to the Lord. Ervin [her husband] goes to work at the Forest Service, but seems like I'm not alone. I can talk to the Lord, and seems like I've got company all the time. I just feel happy about it."

—Annie Chastain, Spring /Summer 1997

"I like one translation that I ran across a few years ago in a passage from Saint John's Gospel. The commentator gives us this translation: 'If any man observe my saying, he shall not notice this until eternity.' Then he goes on to explain: 'It's like a man sitting under a tree reading a book. As he reads, a leaf falls on the page of the book. And what does he do? Become disturbed? No, he brushes the leaf off and then goes on reading.' And he said that death is like that. It had no more significance for a Christian than that leaf which falls on the page." **—Rufus Morgan, Summer 1979**

PLATE 45 "I can talk to the Lord, and seems like I've got company all the time."
—Annie Chastain

"The Bible preaches that th' dead don't know anything at all. After any person dies, why, they don't know anything. They don't have any thoughts—don't know a thing in th' world.

"Well, they *couldn't* come back here. They couldn't come back and cause trouble and bother th' livin' because they can't *get* back. They're dead. They don't know anything.

"If you don't believe th' Bible, you just as well not believe nothin'. If it didn't teach that, y' might have somethin' t' base it on, y' see. But since they don't know anything, how could they come back 'cause they'd have t' be doin' a little thinkin' 'r somethin' 'r 'nother before they could get back and trouble anybody 'r anything.

"They's mediums that say they could talk t' th' dead and all that. I don't believe that. That's just a evil spirit. Really, I don't believe in 'em. They's nothin' t' base it on. They's no foundation. Cain't build a house without no foundation. Th' Bible destroys all th' foundation. If somethin' dies, it's gone—don't know a thing in th' world. You c'n find th' stories, but there ain't no foundation for 'em. That's what I call a myth—just not reality."

—Daniel Manous, Spring/Summer 1971

"Don't let this world get you. Think about where you want to spend eternity. Eternity is a long time, and I believe there *is* one. The most important decision that you will ever make in this life is to accept Jesus Christ."

—Sonja Stikeleather, Spring/Summer 2005

"There was one old lady who would scream and faint at everybody's funeral, regardless if they were anything to her or not."

—Opal Myers

"The old rule was that you couldn't bury anybody until they'd been dead three days. If you buried them under three days, they might come back. When somebody died, the neighbors usually went to someone's house to make the casket. They hardly ever made it at the home of the deceased because of the noise of hammerin'. The men would make the casket, and the womenfolk would cut and fix the linin' and trimmin' as soon as it was ready. . . .

"The people sat up all night with the body. They always had a wake. Everybody in the neighborhood would come. They'd bring food and sit up and sing. When my mother-in-law died, they sung all night—all kinds of church songs.

"Nowadays, most families take the bodies to the funeral home. There's not enough room at home now. Back then, they had a big sittin' room. I never brought my husband home. I just don't like to bring 'em home anymore.

"If it come a hard rain after somebody's been buried, they said he was goin' to heaven. That was just one of those sayin's. 'Course, it always rains after an old person dies. I've never seen it to fail.

"My daddy's duty was always to open the casket at the church. I can still hear him nailin' the nails down. There was one old lady who would scream and faint at everybody's funeral, regardless if they were anything to her or not, and I can see him get a-hold of all her skirts (they came to her ankles, you know) and stand her on her head until she came to."

—Opal Myers, Spring 1976

THE DEVIL

If you're servin' the devil, all of the clover leaves and rabbits' feet aren't goin' to help you any.

—Ethel Corn

Movies, television, and novels affect what many folks today think of the devil. Dressed in red long johns, he is merely a comic cartoon character with a forked tail and a pitchfork. Films depict him as a buffoon, a clownish character whom we humans defeat because of our innate resourcefulness.

C. S. Lewis wrote *The Screwtape Letters,* a supposed series of letters filled with advice from the elderly Screwtape, an important official and an experienced tempter, to Wormwood, his nephew and a junior devil on earth. The letters, instructions in temptation as to how to corrupt the faith of Wormwood's "patient" who is endangered by Christianity, refer to God as "the Enemy." When Wormwood asks his "affectionate uncle" and mentor whether or not he should inform people about the existence and activities of the devil and his helpers, Screwtape answers that the order from his supervisor was to keep humans "in the dark" concerning the existence of the devil: "I do not think you will have much difficulty in keeping the patient in the dark. The fact that 'devils' are predominantly *comic* figures in the modern imagination will help you" (40). And let's face it, many in our so-called modern age don't even believe in hell—no hell, no devil.

In the old days, the devil was a wicked demon out to get man's soul, a fiend manipulating, by any means necessary, unwary humans into a fiery pit of brimstone for all eternity. That's the devil of Revelation. For many believers today, the devil of the Bible is still a formidable foe: "Your enemy the devil prowls around like a roaring lion looking for someone to devour" (1 Peter 5:8). Knowing who our enemy is helps us prepare for his attack.

Flip Wilson, the television comedian, used to perform a skit about "doing bad things," and his famous line justifying his behavior was "The devil made me do it." The truth is that when we feel tempted, we need to reiterate what Christ said to Peter when the apostle tried to dissuade Him from the cross: "Get behind me, Satan" (Matthew 16:23). Our decision to sin against God is our own. Christopher Marlowe, a Renaissance poet and playwright, wrote

The Tragical History of Dr. Faustus. The play depicts a dabbler in the Black Arts who has made a pact with the devil for power on earth. At midnight on the last night of his life, the end of his contract with Satan, Faustus is in a frenzied panic as he realizes that the dark demons will come and take him to hell—no bargaining, no hiding. Though he calls on the earth and the mountains and the seas to cover him, he will receive no reprieve. He has no escape. The devil will have his due.

Many of the elders with whom we spoke feel that "th' devil's a-gettin' ahead of th' Master." They see Satan as a cunning adversary out to trap sinners, but they believe Christ has already defeated this demon adversary. They believe the truth of James 4:7: "Submit yourselves, then, to God. Resist the devil, and he will flee from you." Thus, not by their own power or good deeds but by the power of God's grace and the resurrected Lord, born-again Christians believe themselves saved. They pray for themselves, and they pray for others who seem to be serving the wrong master.

—*Angie Cheek*

"Behold! The great dragon is coming to take vengeance on our kingdom, all stained in hallowed blood." —*"Uncle Wright"*

"The devil was plenty smart back in the old days, and, bless your time, he was one of the greatest songsters in heaven. Surely was. He used to lead the singin' choir up there in heaven, and sometimes he would hop up on a pole and whistle just like a mockin'bird. There just wasn't any stoppin' him. He used to issue out the blessing three times a day amongst the other angels up there, and he named himself 'Champion Luther.' If ever there was a sight, he was one. Then he got to cuttin' up powerful bad; said if he didn't take that kingdom, he was goin' to build a kingdom to the north side of that one about a span above the stars. And that proves it was a starry heaven. Um-m-mhum!

"Well then, after he had done all that talkin', he up and banished himself. After a while, Michael was standin' by the Royal [throne] where God was seated, and he looked out and saw the devil comin' back. He said, 'Behold! The great dragon is coming to take vengeance on our kingdom, all stained in hallowed blood.' And when he got there, the devil raised a war. He fought and cut up scandalous and backed the angels up under the throne. God was sittin' there watchin' from the Royal.

"Then the devil disappeared again. And when he had come back, Michael looked out and saw him again. And he said, 'Be-ho-o-old! The great dragon is a-comin' again!'

"God didn't say anything to Michael the other time, but this time He said, 'Michael, you go out and meet him and put him out of here. If you have to reach back there in my wardrobe and take seven bolts of thunder and put against him, put him out of here, Michael! Put him out!'

"God was just sittin' on the Royal watchin' to see what was goin' to happen. Michael grabbed the devil, and the Lord told him to put him out. And so he threw the devil over the banister of time. Then he tipped over and peeped way down and saw the devil where he had dropped to, and he said, 'Lord, the great dragon fell way down to torment.'

"Then the Lord said, 'Michael, hurry right on down and beat the devil to earth and chain him tight and fast.' And that is what Michael did, and the devil has been chained ever since.

"You say you believe it. You might as well to, for it is written in the Bible for you to read."

—"Uncle Wright," rural Georgia black folktale from the Rose Thompson Collection, Winter 1977

PLATE 46 "Uncle Wright" weaves a story.

"They lived closer t' th' Lord than people's a-doin' today. Th' devil's a-gettin' ahead of th' Master. The' devil's a-gettin' along fast, y' know, and th' Master ain't a-gettin' all these folks t' do like they used t' do. That's my way a-lookin' at it. I think th' biggest thing in th' world a-sellin' more people t' th' devil, mebbe, is this pride, thinkin', well, I'm better 'n you are; I don't want nothin' t' do with you—all such stuff as that. Now that's th' foolishest thing 'at anybody can have in their mind."

—Thad "Happy" Dowdle, Spring /Summer 1971

"I think that the devil has got into people. There's so many distractions that's got into people out here. The devil is stronger than the Spirit. The people just can't convince themselves that they need Christ like they used to because there's so many other things that draw the people away. Christ doesn't change, and the Spirit doesn't change. But the devil is ever-present to convince people that they don't need Christ and that they don't need the Spirit, and he overpowers them. It takes a lot of prayer and a lot of meditation—a lot of Bible study—to be a true Christian."

—Esco Pitts, Spring 1978

PLATE 47 "The devil is ever-present."
—Esco Pitts

PLATE 48 “The only place you’re goin’ to get luck is by servin’ God.” —Ethel Corn

“I heard of people takin’ a rabbit’s foot for good luck. I don’t see where that can bring you any good luck. I have learned through life that the only place you’re goin’ to get luck is by servin’ God and bein’ close to Him. Good things will come your way. But if you’re servin’ the devil, all of the clover leaves and rabbits’ feet aren’t goin’ to help you any.”

—Ethel Corn, Summer 1979

THE END TIMES

Suddenly, there was this tremendous explosion. It was deafening, and then the entire sky turned blood red. Everybody jumped up and started screamin', and all of the bad people who stayed drunk in the community all ran and fell down where the altar had been and started prayin' . . . everyone got religion really quick when we heard that explosion!

—Vera Sawyer

The Apostle John wrote the Book of Revelation, the last book in the Bible, and warned believers: "Blessed is the one who reads the words of this prophecy, and blessed are those who hear it and take to heart what is written in it, because the time is near" (Revelation 1:3). John encouraged the faithful to stand firm, even unto death, because of the imminent final clash between God and the enemy: Satan.

This apocalyptic book, highly symbolic, is therefore difficult to interpret, but it is a prophecy of Armageddon, the scene of a great battle between the forces of good and the armies of evil, a battle that will occur at the end of the world. The four horsemen of the apocalypse—conquest, bloodshed, famine, and death, riding red, black, white, and dappled horses (Zechariah 6:1–8 and Revelation 6:1–8)—wreak havoc and destruction on humankind.

On Judgment Day, the day that earth and sky flee and the old order passes away, Christ will come victorious, and Satan will be "thrown into the lake of burning sulfur . . . [to] be tormented day and night for ever and ever" (Revelation 20:10). Christ will separate the sheep from the goats, and those whose names are written in the Book of Life will live forever in the Holy City. "But the cowardly, the unbelieving, the vile, the murderers, the sexually immoral, those who practice magic arts, the idolaters and all liars—their place will be in the fiery lake of burning sulfur. This is the second death" (Revelation 21:8).

Believers live the lives of victors, not victims. They look forward to the Second Coming. Jesus told His followers, "Behold, I am coming soon! My reward is with me, and I will give to everyone according to what he has done. I am the Alpha and the Omega, the First and the Last, the Beginning and the End" (Revelation 22:12–13). Though the Bible is clear that neither the angels nor the Son of Man knows when that time will come, the believers with whom we spoke take Jesus at His Word—the time *is* coming—and want to stand with the sheep, want their names recorded in the Book of Life.

—*Angie Cheek*

"For th' Bible says that th' world will be destroyed with fire an' brimstone. All man's work'll be burned up—all th' houses 'n' ever'thing. These stones'll be melted and all run back t'gether.

"And that moon you ain't supposed t' be on, that's th' second heaven

PLATE 49 "The Last Days is comin', all right."
—Hillard Green

accordin' t' th' Bible. It ain't natural. T' ain't no place we ought t' be 'til we die. It's a spiritual place. Ain't no place fer human flesh and blood. Th' air is heavy there all th' time.

"Th' Last Days is comin', all right—within thirty year. He'll be down here judgin' the' livin' whenever th' end comes—be judgin' th' people that's livin'. Don't have t' worry about them already dead.

"You know, you could live t' see that day come—th' day that th' Lord comes. You could live t' see it." —**Hillard Green, Fall 1970**

"In Possum Hollow [West Virginia], we grew up much like the young people here in Rabun County, with church and with a religious focal point. Sometimes we went to church every night. We also had big tent revivals that came around. Some would pitch a tent out in an open field, and evangelists would come and preach to us for about a week. Then they'd move on to other rural areas.

"One particular night, there was a little man preachin'. He was a tiny man, so, to impress all of us, he got on up on the altar to preach. He was jumpin' up and down really hard. The altar cracked in the middle, and he fell. A couple of guys took the pieces of the altar away, but the little man just kept jumpin' up and down, preachin' about the end of time.

"Suddenly, there was this tremendous explosion. It was deafening, and then the entire sky turned blood red. Everybody jumped up and started screamin', and all of the bad people who stayed drunk in the community all ran and fell down where the altar had been and started prayin'.

"This little man started shouting, 'It's the end of time! It's the end of time!' He was really impressed with himself because he thought he was preachin' right to the end of the world.

"What had really happened was an explosion at one of the chemical plants that surrounded us. West Virginia, at that time, was known as 'the chemical valley of the world' because all of the big chemical plants were there. Surrounding Possum Hollow was Nitro, where nitroglycerin is manufactured; Carbon and Carbide, where carbon and carbide are manufactured; and also the Goodyear Rubber Plant. That particular night, there was an explosion at the rubber plant, and the fire burned for days.

"I know that some of the people that got 'saved' that night went back to the beer joint and started doin' the same things they were doin' in the first place, but everyone got religion really quick when we heard that explosion!"

—Vera Sawyer, Summer 1992

"Well, then dawn came, an' people who hadn't killed theirselves was glad they didn't. But a lot of people did kill theirselves because

they thought it was th' end of th' world, and they didn't want to be here." —*Mary Carpenter*

"Well, they didn't know what Haley's comet was, an' they thought it was th' end of th' world. And a lotta people thought they didn't want to see it. They didn't want to be here when it come.

"They 'as just ignorant people; they didn't know. Y' see, back then, people didn't have a education. Well, I guess maybe they could go t' school a little bit if they 'as able, but, back then, people didn't have th' books. My mama couldn't write her name nor m' uncle. Neither one couldn't. They 'as lots of people that couldn't. So they didn't know what Haley's comet was. They wasn't idiots; they was just people who didn't understand what it was, an' they'd just go out and kill themselves. Mama said they 'as lots of people killed theirselves whenever th' day come. It was just a star with a long tail on it. Well, then dawn came, an' people who hadn't killed theirselves was glad they didn't. But a lot of people did kill theirselves because they thought it was th' end of th' world, and they didn't want to be here. An' I don't know what we seen . . . Just a big light a-goin'."

—Mary Carpenter, Summer 1973

"I knew I didn't come here to stay. The rich and the poor, the old and the young, all of us come to go. Just like a peach gets ripe and falls off the tree, you have got to move when your time come."

—Rural Georgia black folktale

PLATE 50 "They thought it was th' end of th' world." —Mary Carpenter

"Have you ever heard of a 'Dark Day' [eclipse of the sun]? I have seen one, and that was sad. That was sad.

I was in the field,
And I had my hoe.
I stood up and
Folded my arms.

"I said, 'Well, Lord, I have always heard of the Judgment Day, and I am ready to hover my brood just like a hen hovers her chickens.' When a child is twelve years old, the sins are on them; but all my children were little ones, and all their sins were on me. I haven't got one of 'the age.'

"I said, 'Yes, Lord, all of us are on the way together.' If our time was out, all of us were on the way together. All of us were going to cross the River of Jordan on the ship of Zion. I just stood there and folded my arms and looked for anything that might come. Law, yes, I have heard about the Dark Day and been qualified to go. Yes, Lord, I have prayed. All the folks said there wasn't going to be a Dark Day. They said that God hadn't told anybody that the Dark Day was coming.

"God hadn't even notified the angels in heaven, and that proved that man didn't know about it down here. They said that Dark Day wasn't going to be. But when that Dark Day did come, they all ran; they all cried out, 'It's the Judgment! It's the Judgment!'

"But, Lord, I just stood there and folded my arms, for I had been packing for it, for the Judgment. I knew I didn't come here to stay. The rich and the poor, the old and the young, all of us come to go. Just like a peach gets ripe and falls off the tree, you have got to move when your time come.

"Law, yes, honey, I saw that Dark Day,

I was in the field
And I had my hoe.
I just stood there
And folded my arms.

"For I had prayed, and, yes, Lord, I was qualified to go."

—Rural Georgia black folktale from the
Rose Thompson Collection, Winter 1977

"I've heard tales about people comin' back so many days and nights after they die. They come back after midnight and wander around where they had lived. I'd be so scared to go to bed, I didn't know what to do. If the spirits ever did come back, nobody I knew never seen none of 'em. It was just somethin' people talked about. When the spirits go back to our Father, that gives 'em death here on Earth. They'll be put in the spirit world until the day of Resurrection. Then the spirits will pick up their bodies, and we'll come forth to be judged by what we done in the flesh while we were here." **—Nola Campbell, Fall 1984**

"When they go just as far as the Lord wants them to go, honey, He'll zap them. That's what I believe." ***—Aunt Addie Norton***

"I think we should be gettin' ready for the last days. That's what I think it's all about. It's comin', children; it's not too long off. I'm not a prophet—but I've read my Bible a lot, and I've heard a lot of old people talk. These wars over there in Palestine . . . you know, the last battle that will ever be fought will be fought in Palestine. And I'm tellin' you, there's battles all around there now. They're closin' in there right now. And you know the Bible says that'll be the last battle that's fought. There'll be blood to the horses' bridles, to their necks, and it'll be a battle of Armageddon. That's the last one that's goin' to be fought. And the way that everything is goin' right now, the Bible is bein' fulfilled just as fast as it can be. And if people would be as anxious, honey, to prepare themselves to meet God as they are for preparin' themselves to have a big time and make lots of money, we'd be a whole lot better, I think. People will say, 'I've heard it all my life, and the Second Coming has never come yet. The Lord has never come again yet.'

"Well, He's comin'. And there'll be a comin' of the time before too long, I imagine. Now I'm no prophet, understand. I don't try to be because I know that nobody knows when the Lord is comin' again, but He's comin'. The Bible tells us He's comin', and He *is* comin'. I can't find much in the Bible that hasn't already been fulfilled. And when that Bible is fulfilled and the Word of God goes all over the world and everyone has heard about God, the end is goin' to come.

"Accordin' to my Bible, it's not too long, and the Lord will come again. People get so mean. When they go just as far as the Lord wants them to go, honey, He'll zap 'em. That's what I believe. I wouldn't be surprised any day that the Lord would come again."

—Aunt Addie Norton, Fall 1976

"I don't believe God will let any man and nation destroy the world. I believe He'll do it Hisself when He gits ready."

—Reverend Browning

"You know, we don't know what we gettin' into. We don't know if th' world's gonna stand for fifty years or twenty-five years, and it might be the shortest time.

"People don't know. He said when they say 'peace and safety,' then some destruction come upon mankind, and they shall not escape. You know, there's nations might think they're gettin' together, and all this time they're gettin' prepared t' take men's lives. And we just might be destroyed at any time. I don't believe God will let any man and nation destroy the world. I believe He'll do it Hisself when He gits ready. I believe He's gonna burn it up. I believe He's gonna burn it up with th' fire and brimstone that He's got in store. He's gonna do. Yeah. They may be a third part of th' people killed or just an awful lot of them, but when God gets ready, He's gonna destroy every man on earth." **—Reverend Browning, Spring 1973**

"If people'd get more normal and not get high up on one another and treat one another right and love one another and pray for each other, that'd be th' best thing could happen. But it'll never be, I'm afraid. I'm afraid that'll never be. I don't think it could happen.

"See, th' Lord made this world, and He put ever'thin' in it. And He 'as a-lookin' fer us all t' go to Him when we leave here. Our spirit goes back, and our body goes t' th' dust. And at Judgment Day, why, we'll be there with Him." **—Thad "Happy" Dowdle, Spring/Summer 1971**

"And we're livin' by his, man's, work instead of livin' by God's work, and that's where th' world's gon' be in th' end. They'll be no one saved accordin' to th' Bible. They 'as but a few saved in the Flood, and there ain't gon' be but a few saved in th' end this time neither." **—Hillard Green, Fall 1970**

"Some changes in the world are good, and some are not. Some of it has degraded people. They don't observe th' Sabbath as they should. They don't rely on nobody. They think they can rely on themselves. It gets 'em t' thinkin' that they can do anything within themselves, when you can't do that. They used to rely more on their Maker than they do now. They have learned so much that they think, I don't have to call on my Maker.

"Things won't get better, not th' way the world's goin'. I think Judgment Day is close at hand." **—Annie Perry, Summer/Fall 1975**

> **"What God has got me doin' is somethin' you better not monkey around with, or you'll be in trouble. Thousands on top of thousands of people will be turned away on the last day."**
>
> ***—Henry Harrison Mayes***

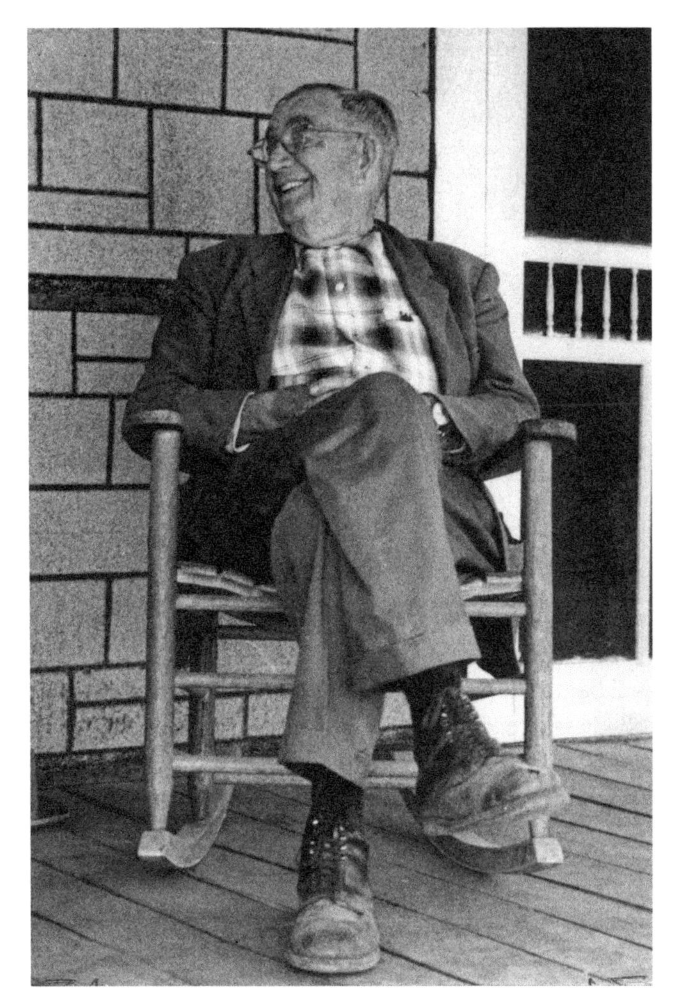

PLATE 51 "At Judgment Day, why, we'll be there with Him."
—Thad "Happy" Dowdle

"Now, the Lord don't have to give you a thousand warnin's. If He gives you a special warnin', that's enough. Sometimes you may get thousands of them before you leave, but one direct warnin' is enough . . . God has made me a universal watchman of the world. I am nothin' except what God has made me. You'll find that story in the Old Testament of the Bible in Ezekiel, chapter three. If the watchman posted on the wall to guard the city sees the enemy comin', he warns the people. If he don't do it, they'll be lost. He'll lose his own life, and the ones he should have warned will be lost with him. We must warn all people of the evils that surround them in this world. All church pastors are more or less watchmen of the world.

PLATE 52 Henry Harrison Mayes, "universal watchman"

"I ain't nothin'. What God has got me doin' is somethin' you better not monkey around with, or you'll be in trouble. Thousands on top of thousands of people will be turned away on the last day. The Bible says they'll come up and make all kinds of excuses, sayin', 'I done this. I done that.'

"God will say, 'Yes, but I had a little old man to warn you, and you didn't heed it.' " —**Henry Harrison Mayes, Fall 1984**

FAMILY

Back then, when people married,
a man's pride was in his family.
He didn't think about what it was
gonna cost to feed 'em, to clothe 'em,
and give them a chance to go
on their own in the world.

—Harriet Echols

Me and my parents spent a lot of time together because we were generally always around the farm. They were pretty strict—they tried to make a good man out o' me! We had to go to church, and of a nighttime we always had family prayer. They wouldn't let us get in the bed without that. There's a whole lot of difference in the way I was raised and the way kids are raised now, the way I see it.

—Lawton Brooks

In the past, "family" was a group of people—grandfather, grandmother, father, mother, children—who worked and worshiped together. Once the children were grown, they were not "gone." In fact, in the Southern Appalachians, family members lived in close proximity to one another. Outsiders called them "clans." They loved one another and each helped the others out.

In the old days, parents raised children differently. "Younguns" had chores they had to do—the well-being of the family depended on every family member's accepting responsibilities. Children worked in the fields; fed, milked, and rounded up cattle; gathered eggs; chopped wood—you get the picture. Many of those we interviewed told us about games they played and toys they shared, but they all admitted that because they had so many chores, they had little time for play. In truth, work often interfered with school; therefore, some related going through only a few grades.

Time to play was scarce, but money was even scarcer. People grew their own food and had to preserve it for winter. Their ingenuity in preparing and cooking what they had is amazing. Many related slaughtering hogs or cattle—families always had meat. In fireplaces or Dutch ovens or woodstoves, women and girls prepared recipes they invented or received from a friend or neighbor. Families bought very little at the store. Ladies told us about going to the store with their fathers to buy chicken feed, which came in large sacks. The sacks came in various prints, and the girls chose the print for homemade dresses.

Folks also doctored themselves or went to a neighbor who could help. We were stunned to read about a youngster who went to a neighbor who, though he was plowing his field, stopped long enough to get a pair of "tooth pullers" and extract the child's tooth! Others told us beauty secrets, and we are going to share some with you. You might want to try some yourselves.

Spoonin', sparkin', courtin'—dating—was usually a church affair. Almost all of our contacts told us about seeing others at church and walking home together. We heard about a-courtin' in a horse and buggy. A few told us about walk-in movie theaters. And marriage? It was forever.

How drastically family life has changed. To be honest, even defining what constitutes a family today is difficult. What happened to the family unit and to the parental figure, and why are children today being allowed the freedom to do as they please? Parents should be role models, and they should set boundaries for their children. The truth is, young people actually want rules. Furthermore, parents should spend more time with their children. If families became true families again, what changes would occur in today's society!

—Angie Cheek, Amanda Carpenter,
Diana Carpenter, and April Argoe

FAMILY TIMES

Hickory switches and whippings were the consequences for bad behavior. If parents caught their child lying, stealing, being rude to the teacher, or committing various and sundry other infractions, the miscreant would "get the dickens whipped out" of him or her. Parents enforced rules, and children minded their parents. If they didn't, those youngsters knew beyond a doubt that consequences would follow. Youngsters were also sure that if they got a whipping at school, another would follow at home. Behaving in church was another requirement. One mother told us that her children always sat quietly in church, not like children today. Parents would admonish their children to "remember their raisin'" or not to "get above their raisin'." What has happened to traditional child raising—the biblical idea of "spare the rod and spoil the child"? Even if you don't believe in whipping a child, what happened to "no" and "because I said so"?

American audiences have watched *Nanny 911* and *Supernanny* on television and are convinced that the atrocious behavior exhibited by the unruly delinquents on these shows would shock our elders. No outsiders would have been necessary to help discipline our elders' own children.

Unlike children of the past, today's youth have little responsibility to help maintain the household. Adults used to expect their children to work hard and to obey. In earlier times, if children did not obey, their parents disciplined them. In today's society, parents cannot even spank their children without having to answer to the authorities. Because many of today's parents either will not discipline their children or are afraid to do so, their children become involved in more and more mischief. Some youth are in dire trouble because of poor life choices.

Our elders' parents raised them "in the way they should go," and "the proof is in the puddin'," as they say. A look at our elders' code of ethics and their character reveals that they have "gone the right way."

—*Angie Cheek*

RAISIN'

"Children and their parents were together more then than they are now. There weren't many places to go and not much way to go. I mean, it took a long time. Most of the people had a horse or wagons. They could go, but they didn't go as much.

"There was a custom in the community—all communities throughout this section, I guess—whole families met at each other's homes, and they sang a lot. Very few had musical instruments. Some had banjos and violins and guitars, but not like they do now. They took the whole family."

—Ada Kelly, Summer 1974

"We got to play when we didn't have to work. My mother, if she'd caught us playin' with the ball on Sunday, I don't know if we'd have been able to sit down or not. They didn't believe in that. They believed in keepin' the Sabbath day holy. No, I never did allow my boys to play ball on Sundays. Why, there's so much difference between now and when I was raised, it's like night and day. People didn't allow their kids to play ball, and now that's all the adults think about—playin' ball and havin' their ball games on Sunday. You can see how the world is today, too. We're livin' in the awfullest time there ever has been!" **—Maude Sellars, Summer 1974**

"When the older people came, children weren't allowed to interfere much. We had to stay back out of the way. But we'd all eat together. We had a big table. The older people'd eat first, and then the kids would eat. But there wasn't any laughin' and talkin' and cuttin' up like kids do this day and time." **—Mary Cabe, Summer 1974**

"And people used to tell stories at night. Usually they'd sit around the fireside. I remember my great-grandfather telling stories, and I remember Nicodemus Thane. He was a widower, and he would come down to the house at night and tell ghost stories. Our eyes would get as big as saucers. We would be afraid to go to another room to get a drink of water: He would tell us such hair-raisin' ghost stories. They would also tell hunting and fishing experiences, and they always elaborated on them and told them bigger than they were!" **—Ellene Gowder, Summer 1986**

"When I was growing up, I was always using a lariat rope or some type of a rope. I was always flippin', lassoin' the horses, dogs, chickens, or somethin' with it all the time. One day, when we probably hadn't had television too long, my mother was sittin' watchin' television, and I was there sittin' around pretty close; she started to doze off to sleep. I tied her feet up. I was always practicin' tyin' somethin' up. I tied her up around the chair leg, and she fell asleep there. I kinda got my mind on somethin' else, and the phone rang. She jumped up to answer the phone with her feet tied and dropped in

PLATE 53 "She started to doze off to sleep. I tied her feet up." —Gary Davis

the middle of the floor, and, boy, did I catch it for that! I got in big trouble for that for sure." —**Gary Herman Davis, Fall/Winter 1999**

"Families used to be close when I was young. Jobs in these mills and plants have separated a lot of families. The father is comin' in as the mother goes out, and the children are left practically alone to rear themselves and don't know what to do. Children need their parents. When we lived in the country and came in from school in the afternoons, my mother was always there in a rockin' chair by the big fireplace, and if it was wintertime, my father was out huntin' or cuttin' wood. They'd always have somethin' cooked up. We'd go to the stove and look in the warmer and get somethin' to eat. Then we'd do our chores: bringin' in wood chips or firewood or goin' to the spring gettin' water for the night.

"Nowadays, when the children come home, Mama's nowhere to be seen, and Papa either, because they're on a job. I say the 'wants,' the material things of the world, have got it like this is now. That's why the children are like they are. We just came in automatically lookin' for our mama to be there, and if we didn't find her at home, we wondered what the matter was. We'd go huntin' for her.

"Our father passed when I was about nine years old. We children lived around with different relatives for a while. That wasn't a hardship then. If you were in the family, they would take you in. Then our mother married again, and we went to live with her in Grovetown [Florida]. She died when I was about fifteen. My grandmother had moved up here to Cornelia [Georgia] with some white people she had worked for in Appling [Georgia]. She said she had a dream that our father came and placed all of us with her; so she came and took us back with her, and that's the way we came up here."

—Anna Tutt, Spring 1978

"The snow would blow through sometimes, and there'd be three or four of us kids together sleepin' of a bed, you know. Mommy'd get up of a night, and there'd be snow over the top of our quilts. She'd take 'em off and shake the snow off and put 'em back on."

—Betty Crane

"Now, our homeplace—listen, I hate to tell you, but it was home. It was a one-room house with no loft—just one room. The snow would blow through sometimes, and there'd be three or four of us kids together sleepin' of a bed, you know. Mommy'd get up of a night, and there'd be snow over the top of our quilts. She'd take 'em off and shake the snow off and put 'em back on.

"There wasn't any glass in the windows—just two shutters. They opened from outside. And the door was white pine boards. He had nails for that driven into strips that went across the boards to hold the door together. There was a latch with a string. You just pulled it if you wanted to go out or come in.

"He hewed the chestnut oak logs to build it with, and Poppy made or built the house. He made the boards that covered the top. He split boards to line the cracks of the house, and he daubed them with mud, you know. And the floor was what people used to call 'puncheons.' You know what puncheons is? They're split out of poplar in big slabs, you know, and then hewed smooth. They're fitted onto the sills of the house, and they're pretty as they can be. When you would scrub 'em with sand and lye soap, they'd just be as pretty and white." **—Betty Crane, Summer 1978**

"One thing I remember from when I was young was that they didn't tell children where babies came from because they thought that was ugly. They just told us that they'd gotten us out of old stumps, and I've looked in many an old stump huntin' for babies. I kept huntin' 'til I was old enough to know better." **—Addie Bleckley, Summer 1978**

"It's not right what children are doin' out there. If they don't have somethin' to do at home, they're goin' to do somethin' out yonder."

—Addie Norton

"And lots of children are raised up this day and time that hardly know who their mama and daddy are. They're never with them. Their mother and daddy both work away from home all day and some at night. And I don't think that's good for the child. You know what I think a mother is for—to stay at home and raise her children 'til they get older and make them do what she wants them to until they get big enough to be on their own. I think a mother's place is in the home. I don't care who don't agree with me. That's the way I feel about it. That's the only time you ever get to love them up close. And they get to love you. When they're little, you can cuddle them up and love them, and they never forget it. And you don't do that if you work. You don't have time.

"Women have jobs now, and they have babysitters keepin' the children. And of course they don't make the children mind. The mothers go off every mornin' at daylight, and they're gone all day long; the children has got a babysitter, or they're big enough to stay by themselves. They do whatever they want to do. They've got no discipline whatsoever. That's the biggest mistake that a poor woman has ever had to make in her life—to work and leave her little babies at home alone or with someone else to take care of them—because I don't care how good that you might be to take care of my children. If they was little, you wouldn't take care of them and make them mind the way I will. I would because I'm their mother, and I want the best for my children. I've always felt that way. I wanted my children to mind, and they minded me. If they didn't, they got a lashin'—I mean, that counted. Some people will tell you you don't have to whip a child and that the worst thing you could ever do is to whip it. My Bible tells me not to spare the rod. It don't say it exactly the way people repeat it, but it's the same meanin'—not to spare the rod and spoil the child.

"Maybe I'm just old-fashioned, I don't know. I'm not hard on young people. I know that it's different now than it was when I was growin' up. There's so many temptations for the young people anymore. I feel sorry for them. It's an awful hard matter to live a good and godly life at this time. I don't understand all that the people go through—the way that people does you anymore.

"When your mother gave you a whippin' when you was young, she did it because she loved you. Well, you'd think, Mommy don't care nothin' for me, and I hate her because she whips. A lot of people feel that way—not everybody, but a lot of children do. But she never give you a lick where it hurt you worse than it hurt her. I've whipped mine many a time, and then I'd cry a whole lot longer than they would. I wouldn't let them see me, but I'd cry a lot worse than they would. I hated to whip them worse than anything in my life.

"It's not right what children are doin' out there. If they don't have somethin' to do at home, they're goin' to do somethin' out yonder. They need somethin' to do at home, some responsibility their parents have given them. Fact of the business is, the children are not to blame. The parents are to blame. There's nothin' for them to do around the house anymore. People's got gas or electricity or oil. There's no wood to get. There's no water to carry to the house. Now my children used to have to carry water from the spring down here in a bucket. One brought in wood one night, and another, the next night. They took it in rotation. Maybe one would cut wood and another bring water. Another would get the cows. That was the idea. My children had somethin' to do when they came in. That's the way to be. There's nothin' like that for children to do now.

"And a lot of mothers won't let their girls go on and help them to wash dishes, make beds, clean up—teach them how to do things like that. They won't let 'em in the kitchen because the children aggravate them and are in their way. It's the only thing the child has to do.

"If you bring that child up to work and to do things, it comes natural. They never forget that, and, really, they appreciate it when they get grown.

"A child is the responsibility of his parents. That's got to be started in the home, and then when he's big enough, he goes to church, and you teach him right." —**Addie Norton, Fall 1976**

"And they were polite. They didn't say 'Suzy.' They'd say 'Miss Suzy,' 'Miss Harriet,' or 'Miss Nancy.' We respected them in the same way. And they never met a lady that they didn't tip their hat and say, 'How do you do?' If they'd smoke in the house, they'd ask permission. You don't hear that much anymore. There are very few that ask. I can't hardly stand it, but I never object to anybody doin' it in my house. That's the way people were raised. That's the etiquette. That's the way they lived. I have a friend who lives over there near my old homeplace, and he's one of the most courteous men I've ever seen. When I see him, he comes over and bows so nice, reaches out and shakes hands; then he reaches around and gives me a big hug." —**Harriet Echols, Fall 1976**

PUNISHMENT

He had a hickory ready when we got there. We never did do that no more!—Addie Bleckley

"My parents were strict, and they weren't only strict at the house. If they let us off by ourselves, my daddy would say, 'Now, you better not do this—what I'm tellin' you not to do. If I get ahold of it, I'll whip you.'

"Well, we didn't do it because my daddy was a truthful man, and he'd whip me. He would've whipped us; he wouldn't have let us get by with it. When he let us go to the neighbor's house to play with the children, he'd say, 'If they're goin' somewhere, you come back. I want to know where you are.' If they were goin' somewhere, we came back home.

"He kept a real close eye. He just wanted to know where we were. He said he didn't want to turn us loose and let us be from here to the Chattooga River and not know where we were. We didn't have much freedom. Sometimes I thought we didn't have enough, but that was his way of thinkin'. There was one thing we were not allowed to do, and that was talk back. My daddy gave me one whippin'—one whippin'. Mama gave me so many whippin's I didn't keep count. But Daddy whipped me one time for tellin' him I'd not do it . . . if he wanted it done, to do it himself.

"What hurt me the worst was he made me come to him and made me come between his legs and let me sit on one leg, and he sat on a woodpile. He talked to me, and he said, 'Now, Annie, I'm your daddy, and you're not goin' to talk to me like that as long as you stay under my roof.'

"Dad taught me to be truthful, honest, and kind to everybody and not to speak ugly to any grown person. He taught me not to touch a thing that belonged to the other person without askin'. I know when we first started to school, there's a road that goes by this little bridge over here, and Miss Bleckley had an apple tree there. Apples fell in the road, and we didn't have any apples. Daddy said, 'Now, Annie, Miss Bleckley's got an apple tree right there on the side of the road. Don't you go pickin' up her apples.'

"I never did do any indoor work. I did outdoor work. I didn't like indoor work. I just helped my daddy. I was the only 'boy' he had for sixteen years. I was sixteen when Dennis was born.

"They treated us the same. Dennis didn't have more freedom because he was the only boy. He didn't get a bit more freedom than we did. After he was nineteen years old, he left home." —**Annie Perry, Summer 1974**

"My parents disciplined me with a hickory. They were strict, and I want you to know we asked our parents for permission to do anything. Our parents knew at all times where we were. They'd always tell us, 'If you get a whippin' at school, when you come home, I'm gonna give you another one. You've got to mind and respect your teacher. And don't you ever talk short or use any profanity. If I find out, you're gonna get a whippin'!'

"We always went to church and Sunday school when the weather was good. My father taught us, sayin', 'Pay your debts, if you die hard. If some-

PLATE 54 "My parents disciplined me with a hickory. They were strict." —Lelia Gibson

body's good enough to let you have somethin' on credit and you promise to pay them, you pay them! And tell the truth.'

"Yes, that's the way I was brought up. My mother was the same way."

—Lelia Gibson, Summer 1974

"Dust was flyin'! I was dancin', and he was whippin'!"

—Anna Tutt

"Daddy whipped me one time when he'd sent me to the spring for water. He was plowin', and it was about a mile to the spring. I went by the garden on the way, and oh, how I loved cucumbers. Instead of gettin' a cucumber and goin' along to the spring, I went to the spring first and got the water and came back and then got a cucumber and sat down in the shade to eat it. I forgot about my pa and just set the bucket down. I was eatin' my cucumber when I heard him call me, 'Anna, oh, Anna.'

"So I buried the cucumber and picked up the bucket and started to run to him with the water. He took one swallow and said, 'This water is hot!'

"He had a switch, and you'd a-thought it was an Indian dance down there. Dust was flyin'! I was dancin', and he was whippin'! Whenever I see a cucumber, I think of that time. I never will forget it.

"I remember my mother whippin' me one time. Sometimes she'd have two or three cows milkin' at one time, and we'd get lots of good, thick milk. I'd stay with the babies when everyone else went out to work. One time I got this little pan and got some of the clabbered milk with the rich cream. I went behind the smokehouse to drink the milk. I don't know why I was hidin'—they were all out in the field. I had a little ol' pet pig, and I had to give him some, too. When my mother came home, she said, 'Who broke the cream on this milk?'

"I said, 'I don't know, ma'am.'

"She said, 'Well, if you tell me the truth, I won't whip you.' So I said I did, and she just told me not to do it anymore.

"Well, I got hungry for milk again, and I did it again. When she came home, she wanted to know who had done it, and I told her. So she carried me to the buggy house and whipped me. That was another Indian dance out there in the buggy shed! I never did go in the milk after that. She said if you broke the cream, you wouldn't get much butter, and that's what we lived on then—butter, hot biscuits, and jam and jellies, stuff like that."

—Anna Tutt, Spring 1978

> **"When Dad got through with you, you were glad to get turned loose. When Mother did punish us, it didn't hurt much."**
>
> ***—Addie Bleckley***

"Our parents didn't punish us much. But we dreaded when Dad's time came. He put it on pretty heavy. When Dad got through with you, you were glad to get turned loose. When Mother did punish us, it didn't hurt much.

"One of the things I remember gettin' punished for was jumpin' over a pond just below our house. Anything they'd tell us not to do and we went and did, we'd get punished, and we sure wouldn't do it anymore.

"We had some neighbors that lived real close, and their children and all of us would meet down there. There was a little narrow space between two big ponds in the bottom near our house. We'd jump over that space. If we'd fallen in, we'd 've drowned. It was that deep.

"One Sunday, my dad decided to see what we were doin'. He came over to the garden and looked down. There we were—just runnin' and jumpin' over that little narrow, deep place. We knew we were forbidden to be there. When we saw him, the neighbors' children got scared and ran off, and we went to the house. He had a hickory ready when we got there. We never did do that no more!

"We had a big creek runnin' down through the farm. Mother'd send us off to pick blackberries. There were a lot of blackberry bushes out from the bank of the creek. We'd get in the creek and wade down it, pickin' whatever berries we could reach. Then we'd stay in the creek for a while. It'd take us a long time to get our buckets full, but Mother never did grumble. I didn't care too much to eat them then. I guess we'd fill up before we started puttin' them in our buckets. I enjoyed gettin' in that creek and wadin'.

"Used to, when preachers came for a meal at our house, we children had to wait to eat 'til after the grown-ups had finished. I didn't think that was right, but that was what they did then. They were afraid we'd cut up at the table.

"One time, while the grown-ups were eatin', when the preacher was there, we got into trouble about the ducks. We weren't livin' near a stream at that time, so we had a big ol' tub in the yard filled full of water. We caught those old ducks and put them in that tub, and we got soakin' wet. Mother had made us new dresses to wear while the preacher was there, and we got them wet all over. After he left, why, she had to take us in and strip us down and put dry clothes on us." —**Addie Bleckley, Summer 1978**

"I wore blue jeans all the time when I was growin' up 'til after I joined the church, but I wouldn't let the minister see me with my breeches on. And even though we had to work hard, we played lots of games, too. We played horse-shoe. We called 'em 'quates.' And Daddy and Mother'd take us to Sunday school Sunday mornin'; then they'd go up to see Granny. Daddy's mother. They'd leave us there, and we'd study up somethin' to do to laugh at. We'd apron the roosters and make them fight. Just cut a hole in a paper sack and stick their heads through it and set them down, and they'd go together and fight like everything. Daddy caught us one time about one of the roosters' heads a-bein' bloodied. He'd tell us we was gonna get a whippin', but he wouldn't whip us on Sunday—and he wouldn't forget about it. Monday mornin', he'd call us, and he'd give 'em to us!" —**Magline Webb Zoellner, Spring 1977**

"When we went to church or anywhere, we were supposed to be back at a certain time. They wouldn't let us go anywhere but to church by ourselves. Dad went with us to dances. We had to work, and whatever they told us to do, we did.

"If I did somethin' wrong, Dad would get a hickory and whip me. Dad never did give me many whippin's because I never did disobey him. Me and Mary would fight like cats and dogs, and I got a lot of whippin's for fightin'. Me and my first cousin got into a fight. Mama and Aunt Wally was gonna whip us and make us kiss each other. I wouldn't let Shirley kiss me, and I wasn't about to kiss her. Mama beat me and beat me, and I still wouldn't kiss her. Aunt Emma finally got to feelin' so sorry for me that she just picked me up and carried me off." —**Leona "Dink" Carver, Summer 1974**

"The other boy ran home, and his daddy whipped the dickens out of him and made him go back to the store and pay for the cigar. And that broke us. We never did take nothin' else." —***Lawton Brooks***

PLATE 55 Leona Carver tells former Foxfire student Kari Hughes about "whippin's."

"Me and my parents spent a lot of time together because we were generally always around the farm. They were pretty strict—they tried to make a good man out o' me! We had to go to church, and of a nighttime we always had family prayer. They wouldn't let us get in the bed without that. There's a whole lot of difference in the way I was raised and the way kids are raised now, the way I see it. You don't see much family prayer goin' on now.

"One time me and a boy went by the store after school, and he got some cigars. There was a big old showcase sittin' up there. In the corner was a hole that you could get your hand through, and there was a cigar box under it. We always stopped at the store to get us a piece of candy for a penny. He says to me, 'Let's get us a cigar.'

"I said, 'I ain't got no money.'

"He said, 'I ain't, but I'm gonna just reach down there and get one apiece. Will you smoke one?'

"I'd never smoked any, but I said, 'Yeah.' He reached down and got us one apiece. We stopped at a branch and lit those things and smoked a puff or two, and I began to get about half sick. And we smoked another round or two goin' up the road. And Lord have mercy! I kept gettin' sicker and sicker. I threw mine down, and I drank some water out of a mudhole. When I did, I commenced throwin' up. I got t' the house and laid down on the porch. I wasn't able to go on in the house. When my daddy came home from the mill, he said, 'Son, what's the matter with you?'

"I said, 'I'm sick, Poppy.' And he bent over me to see what was the matter with me, and he smelled that cigar.

"He said, 'You've been a-smokin'.'

"I told him, 'Yeah.' There wudn't no call to tell him not.

"He said, 'Where did you get it?'

"I said, 'Down at the store.'

"And he asked me where I got the money, and I told him I didn't have no money. I said that boy got it. So he said, 'Let's me and you go to the store.'

"Well, I wasn't able to go. I was about dead, but I had to go. I had to walk about a mile and a half down a hot river road, the sun just a-boilin' down. Honestly, I was draggin'. I'd never been as sick in my life, but my daddy made me go. He told me to tell the storekeeper just exactly what happened. Well, I had to tell him. I just told him that we got us a cigar, and that tickled him to death 'cause I was so sick. I was so weak—I was just tremblin' all over. Poppy gave me the money and says, 'Now you pay him for it.'

"The storekeeper wouldn't have it. He says, 'John, he's done learned his lesson. That boy had never done that before, and he'll never do it again.' Sure enough, I didn't.

"The other boy ran home, and his daddy whipped the dickens out of him and made him go back to the store and pay for the cigar. And that broke us. We never did take nothin' else. They tried to raise us children right back in them days." —**Lawton Brooks, Summer 1974**

CHORES

I was born in 1892. Just as soon as we got big enough to work, we all had a job. We had to work because that's how we made our livin'. Everybody had to work. They didn't know anything else.

—Esco Pitts

What is the problem with young folks today? If you ask someone who lived in the old days, they will tell you that the problem is that kids just don't have any responsibilities. Children today have no chores. Back then, every member of the family had a job as part of that family. Everyone had to help with the farming and other chores. How well you performed your jobs determined whether you had shoes, clothes, and food to last through the winter.

Nowadays, when the power goes out and our electric can opener or our dishwasher doesn't work or our curling iron won't heat up, we tend to moan and complain. We have become so used to having all of the modern conveniences that we think we can't survive without them. We forget that our elders lived their lives without electricity or indoor plumbing. Back then, a washer, dryer, or dishwasher was unheard of (as were cars)! Folks had to handwash their clothes and dishes. Imagine making your own lye soap and washing clothes when temperatures were in the teens and clothes froze on the clothesline!

Without having modern "helps," folks in Southern Appalachia became very resourceful. Chopping wood for winter warmth and for filling up the woodstove was a year-round job. Also, no running water meant that they had to haul water up to the house in buckets for drinking; cooking; and washing clothes, dishes, and bodies. With all of the chores that they had to do, folks had little time left for anything else, especially for getting into trouble.

—*Amanda Carpenter*

My chores at home consist of loading the washing machine and dryer, loading the dishwasher, and vacuuming the floor, but I've discovered from talking to my friends that many young people these days don't even do that. If you asked our contacts what was wrong with children today, most of them would say that children just don't have responsibilities anymore. Parents no longer give children chores; children are spoiled.

In the old days, everyone had a job to do. Some of the children would help in the garden—plant, plow, hoe, and weed. Then came the chore of canning the food grown in the garden. Other children would help out in the house by watching the babies, cooking, cleaning, washing clothes, and doing dishes. Most had to milk the cows and tend to the other animals. The boys had to bring in the wood, but in order to bring in the wood, they had to chop down a tree, cut it into logs, split the logs, stack the wood, and haul it to the porch.

People today take our luxuries for granted. We even complain about them. Young people today gripe about making their beds or emptying the dishwasher. Perhaps we need to be transported into the past for a day or two. Then I'll bet we would appreciate having all of our modern conveniences! Would having more chores and participating more in family work help children be more responsible? When our elders were children, they worked hard, and, as they would say, "it didn't hurt them none." Perhaps all play and no work has been detrimental to today's Jack—and Jill.

—April Argoe

"There was no limit to the time that we had to play if we got our work done. But we had our chores when we came home from school. First thing, our little school dresses were taken off, and a faded dress was put on. In the fall, we'd pick peas and beans off the cornstalks, and we had a dirt front yard that had to be swept with a brushbroom. We had to take up ashes out of the fireplace, sweep and dust the house, and wash the clothes.

"My brothers took care of the animals—horses and cows."

—Lelia Gibson, Summer 1974

"We didn't have spare time. Even when it was a-rainin', we had to pick off peanuts, and we had to shuck corn. There was somethin' we had to do all the time. We didn't have no slack time to play like children do this day and time. We were raised to work from the cradle on up. . . .

"Back then, we didn't have televisions or nothin', so we didn't know about things happenin' in the world like what's happenin' today. I bought our first television in the 1950s." **—Fannie Ruth Martin, Fall/Winter 2002**

"I can remember when my brother and I would get up every mornin'. I'd sit and hold the coffee mill between my legs, and he'd grind the coffee. My sister, Maggie, would fry the fat meat and make the cornbread, and we'd set the table. That's the way we three got breakfast all the time. And everybody had fat meat because we had plenty of hogs. We'd just slice that meat real thin. I like it now, but I didn't then. You'd take some of that grease and put it in the molasses and stir it up like butter and eat that with cornbread all the time." —**Opal Myers, Spring 1976**

FARMING

Back then, when people married, a man's pride was in his family. He didn't think about what it was gonna cost to feed 'em, to clothe 'em, and give them a chance to go on their own in the world.

—Harriet Echols

"Life was much harder. There was hardly any work to do but farmwork. Of course, some boys around town worked in the stores. My brothers farmed and cut wood—firewood and pulpwood. We raised everything, and we was busy the year round on the farm. They's always ditches to fix and terraces to repair and so on. But we had our recreation. We'd gather at neighbor houses at night durin' the week, after our work was done. I had to milk, feed the cows and pigs, and take care of the chickens, cats, and puppies from when I was big enough to do it. I never did much work in the house 'til I was sixteen, seventeen years old. I made biscuits once that you could have knocked a cow down with!

"The families were so big the parents couldn't do it all, and, back then, country people didn't have the money to hire help like they do now. Now a person can plow in a day with a tractor what it took two weeks to plow with the horses. Back then, when people married, a man's pride was in his family. He didn't think about what it was gonna cost to feed 'em, to clothe 'em, and give them a chance to go on their own in the world."

—Harriet Echols, Fall 1976

"Before starting to milk into the bucket, I'd scoot a stream into my mouth and a couple into the cat's mouth. . . ." *—James Still*

"I was born in 1906, on Double Branch Farm just outside of LaFayette [Kentucky]. Sometimes I tell people I was born in a cotton patch. Anyhow, I came to consciousness there. One of my first memories is of runnin' about with a small sack on my back Mama had sewed up for me. I'd pick a boll [seed-pod of flax or cotton] here and yonder and everywhere. Along about the time I was eight, I took on the job of milkin' the cow. I recollect goin' barefoot on cold mornin's and the cow steppin' on my foot. Before startin' to milk into the bucket, I'd scoot a stream into my mouth and a couple into the cat's mouth. . . .

"We children worked alongside our parents, hoein' and choppin' and pickin' and pullin'. Fodder is not thought much of now as stock feed, but, back then, we pulled every blade, tied it in bundles, and hung it on the stripped stalks. My sisters wouldn't work within sight of the road, and to keep from gettin' a suntan and freckles, they rubbed their faces with cream and wore stockin's on their arms and wide-brimmed hats on their heads. By the age of twelve, I could pick a hundred pounds of cotton a day."

—James Still, Fall 1988

"I had a great childhood. I was born before electricity, so we had a lot of chores. We had to cut wood and carry in water. I had one younger brother and one older brother growin' up. We didn't go to town much, but we made our own wagons and stuff like that to play with. We had chores to do like milkin' the cows and hogs to feed. I was raised on the farm and cut wood year-round so that in the wintertime we could have wood."

—Horace Justus, Spring/Summer 2000

"Back then, when it snowed, they wasn't cars to get out of it like they are now. We wrapped our shoes in tow sacks to keep the snow from goin' through and gettin' our feet wet. Most of the people didn't have to get out and go to the store and places. They had what they had at the house. They just ate whatever they had, and they didn't have to get out and go. Mostly what they had to go to the store for was salt, sugar, flour, and coffee. Most of people didn't go to the store after [corn]meal 'cause they had these mills around through the country, and they'd take their corn and grind their meal at them. You did have to go to the store for coffee most of the time. Then you'd get coffee. It was in them grains, and you'd put it in the coffee mill and grind it and make your coffee that way."

—Oza Coffee Kilby, Spring/Summer 1994

> **"It seemed like it [the snake] would go between the cow's knees and tie her up some way so she couldn't move. It'd be there gettin' the milk just like someone milkin' the cow, but she couldn't move."**
>
> ***—Anna Tutt***

"We children had chores to do; one of them was gettin' the cows to and from the pasture. That was fun! We'd have a row of cows goin' down the

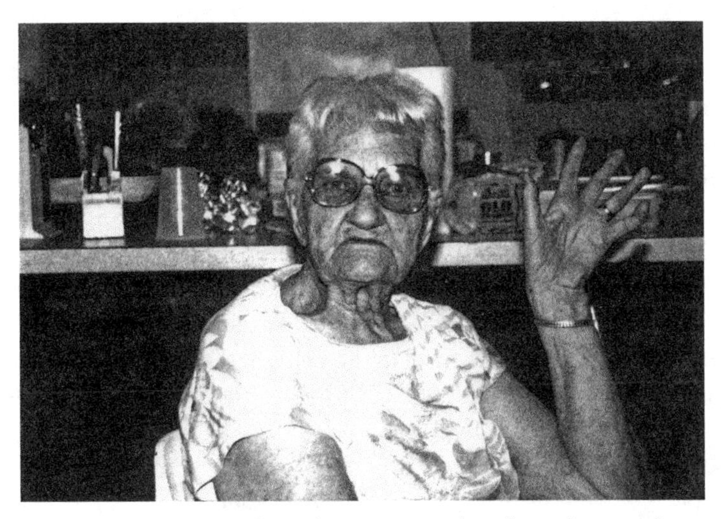

PLATE 56 "We wrapped our shoes in tow sacks to keep the snow from goin' through and gettin' our feet wet." —Oza Coffee Kilby

road toward the pasture, and sometimes they'd get on the other side of the creek that ran through the pasture when it had been rainin'. And the water would get up, and they couldn't get back across until the water subsided.

"Each cow had a different bell, and we knew which cow was which by the sound of its bell. We'd call the different cows when we went to let the bars down across the pasture gate. All of them would usually come, but sometimes when one didn't, we'd say, 'Uh-oh, a snake must've got her.' So we would go lookin' for her. I can't describe exactly how the snake was there, but it seemed like it would go between the cow's knees and tie her up some way so she couldn't move. It'd be there gettin' the milk just like someone milkin' the cow, but she couldn't move. We'd go get our daddy, and he had to go and kill the snake—get it off with a stick or somethin'—and then bring the cow home. I don't know for sure what kind of snake it was—maybe a black snake. Our grandmother lived nearby, and she would always tell us that the milk was poisoned and not to drink any from that cow for a few days. It would be muddy-lookin', you know—not clear and white.

"They grew corn, cotton, peanuts, wheat, oats, and cane on the farm. We children worked in the field, but I tried to get out of it as much as I could. I always had to go to the spring to get water or do somethin' to keep from workin'. We children had to keep our row on up with our parents, pickin' cotton or whatever. I'd see my daddy had his row out, and he'd come back and meet me with mine. I'd think, 'Oh, Pa loves me. He's goin' to help me.'

"But he had a switch in his hand, and he met me about halfway and said, 'Young lady, I told you to bring that row on up here.' I don't think he ever whipped me but once or twice, though." —**Anna Tutt, Spring 1978**

"When I was little, we had to get up early every mornin', about four o'clock. We had to get ready to go to the fields. We had to milk the cows, help Mama cook, and wash the dishes. We also had to feed the hogs and the chickens and cut wood with a crosscut saw. Anything on the farm, we had to do it. I plowed and done it all. Papa, he was a farmer. We were always workin' in the fields. We had to go to the fields in the mornin', and just as we got done milkin' and feedin', we had to go to the hogs and feed 'em. We always had a lot of hogs to feed and horses and ever'thing. Then we'd all go to the fields and work to twelve o'clock. We'd work 'til they told us to go home. We'd go home for dinner; then we'd go back an' milk and take care of ever'thing." —**Senia Southards, Spring/Summer 2003**

PLATE 57 "Anything on the farm, we had to do it."
—Senia Southards
Miss Senia's granddaughter Stacy Ammons works alongside her.

"I was born in 1892. Just as soon as we got big enough to work, we all had a job. We had to work because that's how we made our livin'. Everybody had to work. They didn't know anything else. You see, there wasn't any TV or radio or telephone. All the heat we had was one big ol' fireplace. You could lay a three-foot log in there, and that's how we kept warm in the wintertime. We cooked on it. Oh, I reckon I was fourteen years old before we even had a cookstove. We cooked on the fireplace in the old black pot. Your cornbread and biscuits baked in the [Dutch] oven in front of the fire. There is nothin' to compare to it. I wish I had it today.

"We had to do chores. We knew to do it and do it right! My daddy'd go before us when we were little and show us how, and then we were depended on to do it—whatever it was.

"We had to get all of our chores done before we could do any playin'. We didn't have any neighbors within two miles of the house where we were raised, but we'd get together and play on Sunday evenin'; if we had time on Saturday evenin', we'd play some. But we had to cut our own wood and bring it in from the mountains, and then we had stock. The first thing I had to do in the mornin's after I got big enough was to drive the cattle to our pasture about a mile and a half and come back and then go to school. Then I'd have to go get the cattle and bring them in for the night—do the milkin' and the feedin' of the stock, takin' care of them. That was about the last thing before we had our evenin' meal. And we didn't have any light but a little brass . . . a kerosene lamp, and it furnished the light. Of course we'd go to the woods and get a lot of lighter pine knots and bring them in, and we'd use that for light to study by. And that's the way I learned all my first studyin'. Get our lessons right there in front of the fire—be ready for the next day at school to recite." —**Esco Pitts, Spring 1978**

"We had to start workin' when we were very young. We worked in the field hoein' corn and anything else there was to do. We liked to tend to the chickens and feed 'em. And of course we liked to play a lot, especially if we had little calves. We liked to get out and play with 'em once in a while. We had to start milkin' the cows when we were pretty small. I would milk, but I was always afraid of the cow. I never did get kicked, though.

"We didn't have any crops for sale much. We just grew enough stuff for ourselves—corn, beans, other vegetables like that. We would keep a few chickens and have a few eggs to sell. We'd get a little money that way, but we didn't have much money." —**Amanda Turpin, Summer 1981**

"Children now don't have to work like [when] I was growin' up. Soon as you was big enough to hold a hoe handle in your hand, you'd have to go after it. And, Lord, I've plowed many a day." —***Betty Crane***

"We didn't have no wagon at all when we lived in Lickskillet [North Carolina]. We just had a horse that we'd ride sometimes—go to mill or somethin' like that, you know. When Poppy came home on weekends, they must have come in wagonloads from out at Toxaway to Highlands [North Carolina]; then he'd walk from Highlands on home and then go back on Sunday evenin'.

"With him gone most of the time, we had to work. We ain't like children now. John has to work—I'll excuse him. But children now don't have to work like [when] I was growin' up. Soon as you was big enough to hold a hoe handle in your hand, you'd have to go after it. And, Lord, I've plowed many a day. Had a yoke of oxen and a turnin' plow after we moved to lower Tessentee [North Carolina]. I'd plow all day with a turnin' plow. Used a single plow first, but after they got a turnin' plow, we used that—did most of it with a mule or oxen. I used two oxen. They'd just creep along slow. I knowed how to do it. I had a whip. I didn't whip 'em much, but they was afraid I might. I had reins—pulled 'em whichever way you wanted 'em to go. Then you would just plow one steer when you was cultivatin' with a single plow. Then they got later on they had those sweeps you could use. That would get the whole balk at once. Have to run three times with a single plow. What we called a 'balk' was the space between the rows—just the ground.

"But I was a 'boy' when I was growin' up—didn't know much about housekeepin'. Still don't know too much. I liked the outside. I still get out here every day and split the wood 'cause I just can't stand it without splittin' it. . . .

"There were peach trees all around the house. We had to clear all our land—fence it with split rails. We'd carry rails. Poppy'd split 'em. It tickles me to see people makin' a fence now. They don't know a thing about it. They don't put a stake in the corner—a post in the corner. What they do is put it in the wrong side. It just tickles me to see people tryin'. Our fences were ten rails high, and there were stakes in the corner on the outside to keep them from gettin' pushed over. We'd fence in the gardens.

"For milkin', you'd have to go and hunt 'em. We'd keep the milk and butter right in the spring—no springhouse. Sometimes have to go for miles huntin' for the cow or the calves—have to go maybe two or three miles to find the cow, but we had bells on them. Never lost one."

—Betty Crane, Summer 1978

"I had several chores at Tallulah Falls School [a private boarding school in Tallulah Falls, Georgia] . . . Every six weeks they gave us different chores. We never got paid for anything, but I didn't have to pay nothin' to stay down there either. Chores changed from sweepin' sidewalks to washin' dishes to

PLATE 58 Granny [Ethel Runion] tells her granddaughter April about life at the boarding school.

cookin' and waitin' tables. All the chores were all right. The boys did all the farmwork such as farmin', milkin' the cows, and gatherin' the crops. We had an apple orchard, and they picked the apples, too."

—**Ethel Runion, Spring/Summer 2003**

"My dad would do all kinds of things. He used to make us wagons to haul wood and haul the corn in out of the fields. We would pull it by hand. Two of them pulled, and the other one pushed. I was the pusher. T.J. and Horace [his brothers] pulled the wagon." —**Frank Hollifield, Fall/Winter 2003**

"I drove oxen and steers. One winter, my daddy had took a piece of land his brother was wantin' to have cleared. They'd give him the wood if he'd cut. I done the haulin'. Him and my sister just younger than me, they sawed and cut, and I hauled. I'd haul big ol' sticks. It took us all three t' load, and then I unloaded it. I just 'ended up' the side of the wagon and then let it fall off. We took it to the house, and then he busted it at the house. Oh, we had a mountain of wood! We needed it.

"We lived about two miles out from Blairsville [Georgia]. I can't remember back when I was too young, just small. We just lived in a farm home. We had most all farm animals. When I got old enough to help do the farmwork, I hired with a yoke of steers, oxens, whatever. Some people don't know what I'm talkin' about. I used them to plant our crops."

—**Julia Stephens Watkins, Fall/Winter 2004**

"We picked cotton to earn money. . . . We got two cents per pound, and we took that money to buy our shoes to go back to school with that fall." —***Mary Grace Speed***

"As children, we had to take the cows out and let them eat on the side of the road. I had to help work in the field and the garden. We had to help cut wood and get it in. My grandma cooked on a woodstove. That was part of my job: to help get the wood in. We picked cotton to earn money. We picked by the pound. We got so much per pound for pickin' it. We got two cents per pound, and we took that money to buy our shoes to go back to school with that fall. We didn't have shoes to wear while we were pickin' cotton. They was bolls that the cotton come out of. They would stick y' finger, and it hurt real bad. They was sandspurs in the dirt; we didn't have shoes to wear while we were doin' that, and the sandspurs really hurt when y' stepped on them."

—Mary Grace Speed, Fall/Winter 2004

"When I was nine years old, I stayed some with the Sam Woods family . . . I just helped clean the house and wash the dishes, things like that. They didn't pay me nothin' much—a dollar a week."

—Minnie Dailey

"Before I was big enough to hoe corn—the children had to hoe the weeds out of the corn back then, you see—they put us on the creek bank cuttin' grass for the horses. We had to help out in the fields, too. Other chores I had to do were to feed the chickens and cows, wash the clothes, and we'd take turns a-cleanin' the house.

"I was cookin' when I was seven years old. I would help out my brother and his wife. I had to get me a chair and climb up to the woodstove to put my bread on.

"When I was nine years old, I stayed some with the Sam Woods family who lived at Hiawassee [Georgia]. I just helped clean the house and wash the dishes, things like that. They didn't pay me nothin' much—a dollar a week. I gave it to my family. There weren't many jobs; people might hire you to stay with 'em or clean their yards. Workin' was about all we did, even as young children.

"For money, I'd hoe corn, pull fodder, cut tops off the corn, and lay the cornstalks down in piles. Then someone would have to go and tie 'em up in big bundles.

"We used to keep ducks and geese, and we'd pluck 'em to make feather beds and pillows. We also made quilts a long time, put cotton in them, and we had blankets that were warmer than the ones now.

"We used straw ticks on our beds under the feather mattresses. When wheat was thrashed and the grain taken out for makin' flour, we'd get the straw and stuff it into the tick, two big pieces of cloth—one for the top and one for the bottom—sewed together on three sides. We changed the straw every fall at thrashin' time." —**Minnie Dailey, Summer 1985**

"We worked in the field and hoed corn, helped to work the crop, and helped to gather it. The young children could pull weeds out of the rows. I can't remember the first time I ever worked, but I can remember pullin' weeds. By the time I was twelve years old, I was plowin'. I plowed—there was only one boy in the family and eight of us girls. It always hurt Papa to plow. He would let me plow, and he would hoe.

"I could take the plow and lay off a row as good as any man could by the time I was twelve. And from about then on up, I did just about any kind of work there was to do. I helped cut many a ditch and helped cover it. I've gathered crops, I've helped peel tan bark and hew ties, and I've helped cut pulpwood and [tannic] acid wood and helped snake them out."

—**Ethel Corn, Summer 1974**

"We went to the field and hoed corn. We milked cows and fed chickens and hogs." —**Margaret Wilson, Spring/Summer 2001**

"My daddy liked to farm. We went to the field and helped even when we were small. There were some things we could do. He'd start plowin', and we'd have to pick up all the old chunks and things like that that were in the way of the plow and pile them up to be burned.

"We used to carry water from the spring. It was way down a big, steep hill, and we had two big buckets to fill. My brothers' job was to bring in wood for the fire. We always had cows, and Mother milked them 'til my sister and I got big enough. Then that was our job." —**Addie Bleckley, Summer 1978**

"There are pine trees still there in Georgia that will never grow straight. We'd bend over the little saplin's and just have the most fun!"

—Harriet Echols

"We'd always have a bunch of calves. We'd take the calves out and let them graze. We didn't dare let them get down in the cotton or corn. Mother always had a bunch of chickens, and we took care of her chickens. Dad raised pigs, and it was my delight to get out and take care of and feed the little pigs. . . .

"Daddy had cattle, and we had to go to that pasture four times a day. Brother Wesley and I had to go; we had to walk it, and we were scared to death—afraid of rattlesnakes. When the mules weren't bein' worked—we

PLATE 59 "It was the longest time before Dad ever caught us. We'd ride calves." —Harriet Echols

had two mules and a horse at that time—we would get grapevines and make halters. I'd ride the horse, and he'd ride a mule. After we left the open meadow, we'd go down the creek and ride around that pasture to see that the cattle wouldn't cross the creek. Places where they could cross, Dad fenced off, but cattle'd break out sometimes. We'd ride around the pasture; after we checked, we'd turn our horse and mule loose, and we'd go on. It was the longest time before Dad ever caught us. We'd ride calves. There are pine trees still there in Georgia that will never grow straight. We'd bend over the little saplin's and just have the most fun! We did all those things and did our work, too." —**Harriet Echols, Summer 1974**

"I didn't have any specific jobs that I had to do. Everyone had to help out. You had to carry water, milk the cow, churn butter, cut the cane when it was ready to cut, cut cornstalks, cut wood, and to do all kinds of work. You didn't stand around and whine, boy—uh-uh. If you ever gave one excuse, you got whipped with a razor strap. I did not like that. But I liked work."

—**Clara Mae Ramey, Fall/Winter 1996**

"We worked all the time. Even in the winter, we fixed the fence around the farm and done clearin' around, and when the ground was dry enough, we'd plow in the winter. I had t' feed the chickens, ducks, hogs, sheep, but I went to school every minute that we had school. My daddy never kept us out

PLATE 60 "You didn't stand around and whine, boy—uh-uh." —Clara Mae Ramey

a minute from goin' t' school, no matter how much work he had to do that we could help him do. He said he didn't want us to grow up like he did."
—Annie Perry, Summer/Fall 1975

"We had to cut up feed with a pocketknife. The only way that we had to sort of keep the land built up was by sowin' rye when we got through with the fodder toppin' and everything. We had to take a hoe and go over and dig that ground up and do what we called 'choppin' that rye in,' and you just about hoed that whole field.

"There was a lot to do when I was growin' up. When I got up to where I could, I did a whole lot of the tendin' to the cattle in the summertime. We had to feed the hogs and things in the mountains and tend to 'em, and we'd take them a little corn and salt and stuff every week or two to keep them gentle. If we just let the hogs go all year long, they just went wild; then you'd have to dog 'em and tie 'em and drive 'em in, but, the other way, we kept 'em gentle." **—Jake Waldroop, Summer 1977**

"My daddy worked on public work when they was a-buildin' dams, but Mama sewed for a livin'. She made garments for people, and that kept her busy all the time. She was the seamstress for everyone in the community, so she didn't have much time. She sewed for everyone. She even made suits. Then she had all of us to sew for, too. She made all of our clothes—even made our blankets. She had sheep and sheared the wool, and she made the thread to make our socks and our blankets and everything else.

"Well, I had to sit up on the bench while my papa was cutting the wool off, and I watched 'em. Sometimes he'd let me hold the leg of the sheep or somethin' when he was workin' on it. And he cut the wool all off, and we took it to the house in a big old tub or basket or somethin' like that. Then mother had three or four big washtubs out there on the bench, and we'd put water in 'em and put the wool in there. He'd pick me up—oh, I was just a little feller—and he picked me up and stood me over in that tub and told me to wash that wool with my feet.

"Mama would take that wool in and spin it. She had a spinnin' wheel, and she took the loom upstairs. I remember that was where the loom was. I didn't get taught much about that until I come to Clayton [Georgia]. It was then I started school up there on the hill in the high school. I learned later on how to sew.

"Mama did teach me to sew before I got married. I bought my own sewin' machine before I got married and did my own sewin'. I couldn't make suits like Mama. I did make my own clothes—dresses and things like that. I learned to knit. I knit my own sweaters and socks and everything like that. We had plenty to do, I'll tell you that right now.

"I had to go to work most evenin's when I went home from school. I had to work a while gardenin' or diggin' taters or somethin'. We grew corn and potatoes and tomatoes and peas and everything everybody else did except cotton. I never did have to chop no cotton. You know cotton don't grow up in North Georgia too well." —**Varina Ritchie, Spring 1990**

COOKING

The girls did not do woodworkin' with us. They would stay around the house, cookin' and a-washin' with Mom.—Frank Hollifield

"When we got big enough to split stovewood, we'd saw it up with a crosscut saw. We'd have to carry it in the house, even before we got big enough to use the ax well. We had a little saw, and we'd get out there and saw the poles; then our dad would split them up, and we'd carry them in the kitchen for our mother to keep stovewood. We had an open fireplace in the living room. We'd build the fire up in the fireplace and sit around that at night. We'd take the ashes up and rake hot coals and maybe a chunk of wood and cover it up with the ashes, called banking. The next morning, whoever got up first, usually my daddy, would rake them out. He'd put some kindlin' in there and build up a fire. We didn't depend on matches then like we do now, so we'd have to keep the fire covered up. If your fire went out and you didn't have any coals to build the fire, you'd have to go down to the first neighbor and borrow some coals. You'd take a bucket or somethin' down there and get the bucket full of coals and bring them back to the house and put them in and get your fire started." —**R. M. (Mack) Dickerson, Summer 1976**

"Papa would go to the woods and catch a possum. He'd catch them at night. He had possum dogs, and he'd go and catch 'em and sometimes bring in two or three. In the mornin' Papa would kill them and put on a big pot of hot water, dip 'em down in that hot water, and scrape the hairs off them. It'd come off nicely. Then you take the insides out and parboil them a little bit. I know you've heard about possum and sweet potatoes. When the possum got about done, you take and put some sweet potatoes around it.

"When I was a kid, the possum head was my favorite. Mother would always pay me to do things, and she says, 'Now, Beulah, if you do so-and-so, I'll leave the possum head on.' When it got done, she'd cut that head off and give it to me.

"It's so different now from what it was then. I didn't like pickin' cotton. I don't know what it was about it. It was different. I had it to do and a lot of it, but I never did like to do it. My father had a great big three-horse farm—something like that. We had between twelve and fifteen bales of cotton a year. . . .

"It's so different from now—back when I was a girl. I wouldn't hardly know how to start tellin' you—it's just that much different . . . I think the parents are partly the blame for the problem so many young people have . . . I do know people were happier then than they are now."

—Beulah Perry, Summer 1974

"We baked in a Dutch oven with a lid that looked like it was upside down. You could put the coals on top of it and underneath it, and every time we went to stir the fire up, we would look about the cornbread and put new coals on it. It wasn't any trouble at all, but it took a long time to bake—about five hours." —**Lyndall "Granny" Toothman, Fall/Winter 1991**

"The best sweet potatoes I ever ate was cooked in a Dutch oven."

—Addie Norton

"I was born and raised over on Persimmon [in Rabun County, Georgia]. My mother died when I was twelve years old. My daddy looked after my brother and me. I kept house. I did the milkin', washin', ironin', cookin'—everything—just like I do now.

"After my mother died, my daddy said, 'Do you think you can keep up the house and do the cookin' and things like that?'

"I said, 'Daddy, I can try. I guess I can.' And I did.

"But my paw waited several years after my mother died before he got married again. He stayed home with me until I was grown. He got married one year, and I got married the next. They had five children.

"I had to get up pretty early. My daddy was always up early, and my brother and I got up early. And of course I had my work to do, but I enjoyed it.

"I cooked on a fireplace for a long time. The best sweet potatoes I ever ate was cooked in a Dutch oven—just pour in the pie and put some sweet potatoes in there and a little grease. Build a fire under the Dutch oven and shut that lid down. Anything cooked on a fireplace is best. . . .

"After I started keepin' house for my daddy, I'd find recipes in papers a lot of times. I'd try to make them, and sometimes I'd make a good one. I was young—fifteen or sixteen. I'd waste things, but Daddy'd never know. If it wasn't exactly right, I'd throw it in the slop bucket and feed it to the hogs before he got home." —**Addie Norton, Fall 1976**

"We didn't have to cut grass, but we had to dig taters and pick cotton. We used to dig up our taters, and when we baked the taters, we baked them in the ashes from our open fireplace. We'd warsh our p'taters and put 'em down there nice and clean and then cover 'em up with hot ashes, and they'd bake. They were just as juicy." —**Fannie Ruth Martin, Fall/Winter 2002**

COOKERS

The following is the result of student research.

FIREPLACE

Today most people have fireplaces in the homes as a luxury rather than as a necessity. Once used not only for warmth but also for cooking, the fireplace was at the very center of the home's life.

Cooking over a fireplace requires a great deal more time and effort than using a stove. Folks used dry kindling and wood to start the fire, and they cut green hardwoods—oak and hickory, for example—and brought them in to burn, since seasoned wood burns too quickly and gives off much less heat. Cooking required a bed of coals, which takes a full hour for a new fire to produce. Then, as the coals died down, folks added more wood slowly to maintain the temperature.

Many fireplaces had a fixed horizontal iron bar built in and running from side to side about three feet above the fireplace floor. Others had a bar that was bolted to the side wall of the fireplace on a hinge so it could be swung in and out. On these bars, pots and kettles that had a handle (bale) were hung by means of an S-shaped hook. Cooks used pots with a small bale on either side. With a pair of tongs that hooked into the bales and then into the S-hook, they hung the pot.

People used these pots suspended over the fire for heating soups and stews, boiling meats and vegetables, and heating large quantities of water. If the fire got too hot, or if something needed to be kept warm, not hot, the pot could be slid along the bar to the side or swung partly out of the fireplace.

For frying, cooks raked the coals out onto the hearth and set the frying pan directly on them. When boiling a small amount of water or making coffee, people would set the kettle on a few coals right up against the fire. An even quicker method was to place the kettle right on top of the burning wood.

Meat could be broiled simply by spearing it on the end of a long, sturdy fork with a wooden handle and holding it over a bed of hot coals or shaking it directly over the fire.

Unpeeled, unhusked, or unshelled foods such as potatoes, corn, onions, and nuts could be roasted by burying them in hot ashes for insulation and then placing live coals on top of the ashes. Ash cakes were baked by wrapping the dough in cloth, placing them in a cleaned-out corner of fireplace, and covering them with ashes and coals. They were supposed to have a delicious flavor when baked this way, but it was difficult to control the heat and keep the bread clean.

People often dried fruit and vegetables by the fire for several days to preserve them for the winter. The food would be placed on trays on the hearth away from the direct heat or would be strung and suspended from the mantel.

During the winter, the fire was kept going all day. At night, ashes were heaped over the coals to keep them hot until morning. A fire would start up again, "just like y' poured kerosene oil on it," when fresh wood was added in the morning. In the warmer months, the fire would be started up only when it was time to cook, and ashes would be raked over the coals to save them when no fire was needed.

DUTCH OVEN

One of the most useful cooking utensils was the Dutch oven. This is a heavy, round iron pot with a handle and an iron lid that has a half-inch lip all the way around the edge. One variation looks like a large frying pan with four small legs. It is usually called an old-timey oven or an old bread oven.

The Dutch oven was sometimes used outdoors, but folks most commonly used it inside by the fireplace. It was placed on hot coals raked directly onto the hearth. The lid and oven were preheated before using. The oven was preheated on the coals themselves, and the lid, directly on the fire.

When the oven and lid were hot, whatever was to be baked was placed or poured inside, the lid was set in place with a pair of tongs, and coals were piled on top of the lid. The lip around its edge kept them from rolling off.

Cooks had to be careful that the coals under the oven were not too hot, or the food would burn. The lid could be much hotter than the bottom, as it was not directly touching what was being baked.

Dutch ovens were usually used for baking bread and biscuits, but they could also be used for baking cakes, potatoes, and sweet potatoes, as well as roasting meat and heating soups and stews.

THE WOODSTOVE

Woodstoves are a great improvement over fireplaces for cooking, but they also require a lot of attention. As is true with a fireplace, dry kindling and green wood have to be cut to fit the firebox. Open the damper beneath the firebox, add wads of paper and kindling to the firebox, light, and then add green hardwood sticks as the fire catches. You should be ready to cook in ten minutes.

At the bottom of the firebox is a coarse iron grate through which the ashes fall into the ash box. The soot that rises into the pipe behind the stove later falls back down into the soot tray, which is directly underneath the oven. Both ash box and soot tray are drawers that must be cleaned out once a week if the stove is used regularly.

The cooking surface of a woodstove usually has six eyes or caps. Sometimes they are all the same size; sometimes they are of varying sizes. The one at the center in the back of the stove is the hottest, the two over the firebox are the next hottest, and the other three are the cooler ones. The heat under the eyes cannot be regulated individually, so pots have to be moved from one to the other according to how much heat something requires. Sometimes, when people want to heat something in a hurry, they remove an eye and place the pot or frying pan directly over the flames in the firebox.

Most of the stoves are fairly simple affairs. Some get quite elaborate, though. One larger variety even had a flat griddle on top for frying pancakes, eggs, and bacon.

The oven is usually located on the right-hand side of the stove beneath the cooking surface, and it is heated from the left and top by the circulation of heat from the firebox. The heat flows from the firebox through a four-inch high airspace directly under the cooking surface to the other side. It heats more evenly than one might imagine, but items being baked may have to be rotated inside the oven at regular intervals.

The main problem with the oven is that it is difficult to keep the temperature constant. Many varieties have a temperature gauge on the door, but this acts as a warning signal rather than a regulator. If the oven gets too cool, more wood has to be added. If the oven gets too hot, all that can be done is to open the door slightly or put a pan of cold water on one of the racks. If the water boils and the oven is still too hot, replace the hot water with a fresh pan of cold.

For something that takes an hour to bake, the fire has to be tended three or four times to maintain the temperature.

In addition to the damper directly underneath the firebox, which is left open the whole time the stove is being used for cooking, there is also a draft at the back of the stove directly under the two back eyes at the base of the stovepipe. This is left open for maximum draft when the cooking surface is the only surface in use. For baking, however, this draft is usually slid shut to force maximum heat to the oven.

In the oven the top rack is the hottest. Biscuits and cornbread are usually baked on the bottom shelf and then moved to the top shelf, if necessary, to brown them quickly. Cakes, pies, and roasts are usually kept on the bottom shelf the entire time. The top rack is used primarily for broiling meat, frying sausage, or toasting. Since woodstoves tend to heat rather unevenly, it would be dangerous for us to give you any cooking times here. You'll just have to experiment yourself and check frequently to see when the food is done. About all we can tell you, if you intend to begin using a woodstove, is that bread in Aunt Arie's oven took about fifteen minutes—sometimes less. The breads are done if, when you grab the pan firmly and shake it back and forth, it slides easily in the pan.

About two feet above the cooking surface, most woodstoves have two warming closets. These are metal boxes about six inches deep, each having a door that pulls down. They are used to keep food warm until it is ready to be served.

THE FIRELESS COOKER

In the old days, fireless cookers were very popular. People used them instead of stoves because they were safer. This fireless cooker had three openings big enough for pots to sit into. It got its name because it cooked food with hot iron wafers instead of fire. Other fireless cookers used soapstone because it held more heat and stayed hot longer than iron. Sometimes there were six iron wafers: two for each opening and one for under the pot, as well as one for the top of the pot so that the food cooked thoroughly.

The iron wafers were heated by placing them in the fireplace. The box was insulated with woodpulp. There were insulated lids for each opening.

The fireless cooker worked like an early version of a Crock-Pot.

PLATE 61 The fireless cooker worked like an early version of a Crock-Pot.

"People don't can like they used to. Nowadays, you can just run to the store and pick up canned vegetables cheap. It is really cheaper to go to the store and buy the vegetables, but you don't get fresh, preservative-free food. Cannin' gives you a sense of pride because you know that you have worked hard for your food, and it is hard work!

"If some of today's generation knew what it was like to have to can foods to survive, they might appreciate the cannin' tradition and teach it to their kids. We should learn to use what natural wonders the Creator has given us because you never know when times could get hard again, and we might have to feed ourselves." **—Gladys Addis, Spring/Summer 1999**

WASHING

CLOTHES

I can remember it bein' so cold that as she hung the diapers and clothes, they'd freeze.—Bob Justus

"We would start the fire with rich pine stumps. We took baths in a big tub. We also had to do laundry in the washhouse in these big washtubs. To wash

our clothes, we put them in a pot and boiled them. My mother made lye soap. Mom bought lye, grease, and other ingredients to make the soap."
—Thomas Coy Cheek, Fall/Winter 2003

> **"The clothes were real strong then, not like what we got now."**
> ***—Annie Perry***

"We had a hard time a-washin' th' clothes. We had a big old pot (I've still got that washpot) of iron, and y' gather up your dirty clothes; take 'em to th' branch; fill up your tubs with water, lye soap, and a big stick about so long, trimmed off like a bat. You'd have a big stump, piece of wood, settin' up that way, and put your clothes on there and beat 'em with that stick and then put 'em in th' pot and put a fire around the pot and some soap in the pot and parboil 'em. Then y' rinse your clothes and get all the soap out. You didn't have a wringer. You wrung this way [Annie makes a wringing motion] with your hands. And then hang 'em out on th' line and let 'em dry, and they'd be pretty and white. We'd hang 'em on th' grapevine and go to th' woods and get long, slim poles and get one with a fork and set it in there and hang your clothes on that. The clothes were real strong then, not like what we got now. The clothes today wouldn't last long, would they? You get after 'em with a battlin' stick like I used t' have t' get after Dad's old breeches—it would get 'em clean." **—Annie Perry, Summer/Fall 1975**

> **"I've helped make lye soap many a time—sassafras stick a-stirrin' it. Make it get to the right consistency. We'd drip it off our sassafras stick to see if it was thick enough or not."** ***—Betty Crane***

"To wash the clothes, we had a battlin' bench. We battled it on a block, and then we boiled our clothes in a washpot until they was clean. After they was rinsed good, we'd hang 'em out. We just toted 'em to the creek and rinsed them after we got them washed. The order was wash 'em first, battle 'em good, and then you put them in with some soap and boil them good for about thirty minutes after they got boilin' good. They was all sterilized good then. Then you take 'em out and battle on that block and then rinse them with that rinse water. But you wash 'em in soapy water and then you battle in soapy water, too, and then you put 'em in the tub and boil 'em. You'd battle 'em 'til you thought you had all the dirt knocked out of them.

"I've helped make lye soap many a time—sassafras stick a-stirrin' it. Make it get to the right consistency. We'd drip it off our sassafras stick to see if it was thick enough or not. Then we would put it out in a lid or somethin' and test it. You put grease in it to make it, and if it don't eat up all the grease, you know it's

PLATE 62 "The clothes today wouldn't last long, would they?"
— Annie Perry

not too strong. I don't know why they always used sassafras—adds a little flavor. We didn't have nothin' to put in it to give it a smell or anything except that. They do now. And when they make it, they make it where they have a store-bought lye now, and I don't know how to make that. But we'd keep ours in an old jar or jug or somethin'. We didn't have much that got hard like they do with store-bought lye. They can make it in squares or thin. But we always had a jug with lye soap. We didn't have no fancy soap then. We'd wash the clothes with it, and we'd wash the dishes with it." —**Betty Crane, Summer 1978**

"If we had to go back over that, there's some things like I couldn't take—like washin'. I washed out on the creek bank with my hands. I couldn't do that now. We made soap. We'd have barrels full o' soap. We killed our hogs for our own use, and we saved the entrails and cleaned them and made soap from the fat. My mother had a barrel, and she just made soap. Nowadays, they make it with Red Devil lye and make it hard like what you buy. But, back then, it didn't seem so hard." —**Mrs. Grover Bradley**

"They didn't nobody have any money back then. That's the reason we couldn't go to school—because we didn't have any money. We didn't go hungry, though. We had to help tote water to wash with and had to tote wood. Back in them days, we had to get a board and beat the clothes clean down by the creek. It would have been nice to have a washin' machine then. We had to sleep on straw ticks [mattresses]. We grew some of that rye, and every fall we'd empty our sacks and fill 'em with that straw. Every now and then, we'd kill us a duck and pluck feathers for a feather pillow. We had to farm all the time, and we had to get up corn."

—Ed Wilson, Fall/Winter 2001

"At a young age we would go with our mother to the wash place. We would carry the water, dip the water, and help hang out the clothes. We had a good life. I would like to see children in this day 'n' time go back and have to live the life that I did. Havin' fun really wasn't thought of much."

—Rose Ester Shirley Barnes, Fall/Winter 1997

"I can remember helping Mother. She was tryin' to make a girl out of me, too, I think. I'd wash dishes and do stuff like that, and my brothers and sister, Virginia, would not admit it now, but I would have to change diapers and hold one kid in my arm and churn butter. Mother claimed she'd come in and find both of us sleepin', and I'd be holdin' on to that kid. Virginia came late, and I had grown up and left home when she was born. That was life. 'Course, all of the chores, some of 'em, I didn't like. You know, it's like anything in life. But one of our main chores all of our life, 'til runnin' water came in, was carryin' water, carryin' water. You had to carry water to take a bath, and you can understand why people don't take but two a week. You have to fill up the tub. If it's summertime, we'd let the sun warm it up, and you'd just jump in and hang your feet over and take a bath. In the wintertime, you put it behind the stove. Mother was always after us to wash our feet before we went to bed. I guess we felt like we was clean if we'd washed our feet. Anyway, I had to help with all the chores—being the oldest—and take care of the kids and wash 'em. It was somethin'. How women coped is beyond me. I can remember bitter, cold days when Mother would be washin' clothes right below the stream. There'd be a big ol' black pot boilin', and kids would have to 'feed' it. I'd help hang out clothes and stuff like that. I can remember it bein' so cold that as she hung the diapers and clothes, they'd freeze. Mother would be washin' 'em in that boilin' water and then cold water. We used lye soap, and it made her hands raw. That used to get to me even though I was a kid."

—Bob Justus, Fall/Winter 2001

"When we washed clothes, we had a little branch, and I'd sit my tub down under that and wash my clothes. We had a big iron pot that you could boil the clothes in. You could boil 'em in that pot and then take 'em back over to the spigot and rinse and hang 'em out. It was rough washin' then. It was bad in the summertime, but when it was wintertime, it was really rough. It would get so cold the clothes would freeze on the line, but the sunshine would thaw 'em out." —**Oza Coffee Kilby, Spring/Summer 1994**

"Washin' was done usually at a creek near the house. The people searched out a spot that would be near a good spring or a good creek and built their house there. We usually washed at the creek with a big iron pot to boil the clothes in. The men searched the woods for hollow logs and would saw them off in six-foot lengths or more, then hollow them on out into a smooth, hard surface. And that was your tub for scrubbin'.

"My sister and I had washed a quilt and carried it down to the edge of the creek where there were some rocks. We were rinsin' the quilt, havin' fun with it, holdin' it out and lettin' the water catch in it. Finally, we got it up. I twisted one end, and she twisted the other. We got tickled about it and dropped the quilt in the creek. I had to run down the creek after it."

—**Aunt Lola Cannon, Summer/Fall 1975**

"Sometimes there'd be bugs in our house. They called them chinches [bedbugs]. They'd eat the blood out of you if you didn't get rid of 'em. We'd take the beds down and pour boilin' water on them and on the floors. We used kerosene oil, too. Those were the stingin'est things! Used to, everybody had 'em, but I ain't seen any in Lord knows when!"

—**Minnie Dailey, Summer 1985**

DISHES

"See, we didn't have runnin' water, so one of my jobs was to carry water. We had a couple o' buckets; we'd go up on the hill above the house where the spring was, and we'd carry water. At night you had to get up water. Then when Mama washed, you had to carry a whole lot o' water. She had a big black pot out where you filled it up, and I washed dishes. And, bein' oldest, I had to care for the little ones." —**Lois Duncan, Spring/Summer 2000**

"My chores at home were to wash the dishes every night. Back in those days, people didn't have electricity, so my job every day was to wash the lamp chimney of the lamps and polish them. My brother was supposed to bring in the kindlin' and the coal. Sometimes he didn't, so I had to do that, too." —**Hazel Killebrew, Spring 1991**

"We had the dishpans to wash the dishes in. We had a iron kettle that we boiled our water in for washin' dishes. And we didn't have but one dishpan, but we needed two. So we'd have to wash 'em and set 'em out on the table and then put 'em back in the dishpan when we throwed the water out and scald 'em, you know. We used the table for a cook table and an eating table, too.

"The dishes was store-bought—most of them. They was kind of delft [a style of glazed earthenware, usually blue and white, originally made in Delft, Netherlands]. What do you call it? Delft? Heavy.

"To get the water, we had a gourd out there, and we would dip it up from the spring and put it in a wooden bucket. We had wooden buckets then, you know. And we'd carry it to the house—wasn't any runnin' water in the house. Poppy had a spring all rocked up pretty."

—Betty Crane, Summer 1978

"Before starting to school, I recall sitting on our long bench washing dishes and placing them in another dishpan for Mama to scald with a kettle of hot water. When they were cooler, I dried them with a flour sack and placed them in a corner cabinet in our long dining room."

—Ruby Mae Miller Cheek, Spring/Summer 2005

MAKING BROOMS

I love a homemade broom 'cause you can get down under anything with one hand and sweep it out.—Flora Youngblood

"We children would cut broomstraw. It would be as high as your head. We'd take what we always called tater forks because we used to dig taters with 'em and get the husks off the straw with them forks. We'd clean it real good. We'd carry big bundles of that broomstraw to the Sautee Store [in Sautee, Georgia] and trade it for goods. We'd have to carry it walkin' because we didn't have any other way of goin' much except footin' it. The Sautee store owners would buy every bit of it. They'd just take the bundle of straw from us children, and they'd make it into brooms. They'd sell them for about seventy-five cents for the broom—gave us about ten cents to the bundle. We could've made it into brooms, but they said, 'Just bring it on.'

"We made our own brooms for use at home. We'd cut out about that much straw [about four inches in diameter] and wash it real good. Then we'd take a potato fork and strip all that husk off. Then take a good, stout cord—not too big around, something like a fishin' cord—and make a loop.

We'd run that cord down a little more than halfway of the straw and then just wind it up to the top. You wouldn't tie the cord but just stick it back down in the straw as far as you could. Then we'd cut the ends off the straw as far as you could. Then we'd cut the ends off the straw at the bottom and just sweep the floor. I love a homemade broom 'cause you can get down under anything with one hand and sweep it out."

—Flora Youngblood, Spring 1985

"We had to make our own brooms and scrub brushes, and sometimes we made shuck brushes, you know—have a board with a hole bored in it, and then you pull them shucks through there and make a shuck mop. And for brooms we'd go to old fields and bring broom sage in to make our brooms to sweep with—just sage. Gather it together and put a loop in our string and pull it tight and then wrap it around to the top; then you pull the string through the stalk up there, and then it'd hold. I got some down in Franklin [North Carolina] one time and made me one that lasted for years. That's since I've been here—finally wore it out." —**Betty Crane, Summer 1978**

CLOTHES

Everybody was sort of alike—no one had hand-me-downs to give away. We wore our clothes out. We didn't wear the new off and throw them away. We'd wear them just about as long as they would hang on us.

—Amanda Turpin

When God first created man, man was naked, and until man and woman ate that apple, they were fine with being unclothed. Then came the fig leaf. Today no one except nudists would consider socializing while naked. In fact, the brand name of the clothes a person wears matters a great deal.

If we lived in the old days, brand-name clothing would not concern us. Many people made their own clothes and clothes for their families from cloth they bought for a dime a yard, or if they didn't have the money to buy cloth, they used printed feedsacks. Males we interviewed told us about having two pairs of "overhauls" [overalls] and two pairs of shoes—one pair for everyday wear and a better pair for church. Ladies told us about having two dresses—and no makeup!

I am not saying that we should go back to making clothes out of feedsacks. (You wouldn't be able to find feedsacks from which to make clothes now anyway!) I do think, however, that we should be less concerned with what other people are wearing and more concerned with other aspects of our lives. Wouldn't it be nice to live in a society where children were not ridiculed because they could not afford expensive clothing? Our emphasis on brands of clothing causes us to "brand" people. How sad.

—Amanda Carpenter

Abercrombie & Fitch, American Eagle, Old Navy, and Hollister are all brands of clothing worn by teens today. If a teen wears clothes marketed under such labels, others consider him or her cool. If teens don't wear the popular brands, others think them to be people who simply don't measure up.

Ideas about clothing were different in the old days. Can you imagine having to make your own clothes? That is what our elders had to do because they were unable to go to a store and buy clothes. Sometimes women bought cloth at the mercantile for ten cents a yard and made clothes for every member of the family. Sometimes they couldn't afford to purchase cloth, so they made their clothes with printed sugar sacks or feedsacks that they saved after they fed the animals. Not only did women sew, but some helped shear the sheep. Then they carded the wool, spun it, knit with it, and turned it into socks, hats, and scarves for their families. Clothes were a necessity, not a status marker.

The truth is that clothes do not make the man (or woman). I know how it is to wear homemade garments because my Aunt Ruthie used to make dresses for my sisters and me and mail them to us. I felt proud to wear them, and I still do not judge others by the clothes they wear. Material things are a part of our worldly life, and someday they will all be gone.

—April Argoe

"When I first started to school, I had one sister and one brother going at the same time. We wore anything we could get, except I never wore pants to school. We didn't have much of anything, and there wasn't much money. Everybody was sort of alike—no one had hand-me-downs to give away. We wore our clothes out. We didn't wear the new off and throw them away. We'd wear them just about as long as they would hang on us."

—Amanda Turpin, Summer 1981

"Suddenly I realized I was a girl—terrible thing! I had to quit wearing all those boy clothes and get into some frilly things. I grew up with a family of people who were very self-reliant, and nothing was ever thrown away. We utilized everything. Feed came in feedsacks, and a lot of them were printed. I made a few things with feedsacks, but they're hard to get now because they stopped making them, I think in the fifties. The feedsacks came in many different patterns. I remember going with Daddy when he went to get feed on Saturday so that I could pick out the ones I wanted. Mama made many things with those sacks. Believe me, you find it in an old quilt, and it will be the fabric that is still there. It just wears forever. It's pretty tough, and it has a linen-like weave. My daddy's mother was constantly making things, too. She wove hats from palmetto fronds." **—Sonja Stikeleather, Spring/Summer 2005**

"Back in them days, it was rough goin'. They wasn't much goin' on then. We'd raise cattle out on Seed Lake [Rabun County, Georgia]. Right there where Wycle's Store was, we'd turn them loose. They'd go up to Trey Mountain. We'd have about twenty-five or thirty head of cattle durin' the summer. We'd have to go and walk them mountains about every two weeks. Daddy would sell them in the fall, and that's where we got all our clothes and food for winter." —**Ed Wilson, Fall/Winter 2001**

"Before my mother married my daddy, my daddy rode by one morning and invited her to a party. It was the day of the party. Mama, like women today, declared she had nothing to wear. There was no time to go for material, so she gathered up several empty flour sacks and dyed them with pokeberries, dried and pressed the sacks, and cut and made the blouse in time to wear to the party. She said, 'I got more compliments on that blouse than almost anything I ever wore.' That was typical of Mother's ingenuity and thrift. It was the spirit she showed all the years she was raising her [thirteen] children." —**Ruby Mae Miller Cheek, Spring/Summer 2005**

"When I was about four years old, I had went to my uncle's for dinner. My cousin and I slipped off to play, and we had to take care of my little Sunday dress. Mother told me if I got it dirty, she'd whip me. Well, I wanted to play. We went to the mill and played around the edge of the millpond. Well, I tried to jump across the creek where it came into the pond. The bank caved, and I went into the pond. But she caught me by the dress and pulled me out, or I'da drowned. I was almost scared to death. If she hadn't been bigger than I was, she couldn't have done it. She undressed me and pulled off her dress and put her dress on me, just keeping her petticoats on. She washed the mud out of my clothes, and we spread 'em on the bushes. It was hot, so they dried quickly. We hid in the bushes all evenin', each one of us half dressed until my clothes dried. My mother never did notice that my clothes were wrinkled or they'd been wet. And when we got home, she told me to pull off my dress so it wouldn't get torn or dirty. She said, 'Aunt Harriet won't make you another one that pretty.' Aunt Harriet made all our clothes with her fingers. . . .

"Back in the twenties and thirties, the young people, the girls, wore long hair and braided it and put it up. Then they had the longer dresses with ruffles, lace, sashes, and pretty things. And the young men were just the nicest bunch of young men. I don't mean they were any better than the boys today, but they worked and had their work clothes and their good clothes. If they went to town during the week, they dressed with an everyday shirt and pants. But on Sundays, they dressed. Their hair was cut, parted, and placed to perfection. Boys now do a lot of work to their hair, and boys go to the beauty parlor and have all this hairdo to put on. But then, they kept their hair trimmed above their ears. They were clean-shaven—there were a few old men who had beards." —**Harriet Echols, Fall 1976**

"It's so much cheaper to make your own clothes. You can have so many more clothes for th' same price. I still make my own clothes unless somebody gives me a dress 'r somethin' ready-made. I never buy no clothes—ready-made dresses—hardly ever. And no tellin' what a homemade pair of stockin's would bring now—it's such a rarity.

"I've been makin' things ever since I can remember. I've been makin' my own clothin' since I was fourteen, and I'm learnin' t' do new things ever' year, every day, nearly." —**Ada Kelly, Summer/Fall 1972**

"Now, I had a cousin that made shoes. He tanned the leather and made just as good-lookin' shoes as you nearly ever saw. And he never did use no tacks in 'em. He used wooden pegs—made his pegs out of maple. He would punch a hole in the leather and drive them pegs in there, and there would be no comin' apart. But they would be so slick that you couldn't stand up in leaves and all. You would break your neck in 'em, but they would really last." —**Richard Norton, Spring/Summer 1975**

"Our clothes had patch on top of patch."

—J. D. Martin

"We got two pair of overalls for school. When we got home, we put them old, patched ones on. We took care of them; that's what we wore. Usually, stuff was a lot better in them days than it is today, material-wise. They would still have good color when the spring come and school was out. We'd wore them all winter. We had to wash them in a washpot, boil them in there to get them clean, and you'd run them through clean water to get all that soap out of 'em because you used lye soap. I never did know that much about that.

"We didn't wear our overalls to church. Our shoes that we wore to school were just brogans, lace-ups. Then we had what we called slippers back in them days. They were just low-top shoes that you wore to church. We had two pair of shoes.

"Our clothes had patch on top of patch. A lot of my clothes, my mama made. Most of my shirts, she made." —**J. D. Martin, Fall/Winter 2004**

"I decided I wanted to sew while she [Mama] was gone to town. I wanted to make somethin', and I didn't have no material to make anything out of. Mama had some pretty window curtains."

—Oza Coffee Kilby

"Back then, when it snowed, they wasn't cars to get out in like they are now. We wrapped our shoes in towsacks to keep the snow from goin' through and gettin' our feet wet.

"When my daddy died, my mama said, 'That's it. I'm not goin' to stay here any longer.' So we moved away . . . After several years, my mother married again. She married Melvin Bray, and we come back to Rabun County. Mama would buy me pretty clothes, and we wore knitted blouses. I had a blouse that had stripes and stars on it, and when we come back to this area, I was the only one that I knew of that had silk hose . . . Mama had a sewin' machine, and she did a lot of sewin'. She was a good hand at sewin'. She'd make clothes. She made my dresses and things, and she was really good at sewin'. One day she left to go to town, and it took all day to go to town and back—you know, the old roads was rough back then. Well, I decided I wanted to sew while she was gone to town. I wanted to make somethin', and I didn't have no material to make anything out of. Mama had some pretty window curtains. The girls back then wore little smocks. They was made of a light material. I decided I would make me a smock. I took her curtains down, and I made me one. Mama had a fit! I had looked at a smock, and I could see how to do them. It done pretty good. I made it just by lookin', and that's how I do my clothing now. I don't go by a book, but if I see somethin', I can copy it. . . .

"When I married, I didn't have the money to buy clothes back then. I made the children's clothes out of sugar sacks. Ferd made liquor, and he'd get sugar in big ol' sacks. They had great big ol' letters on 'em. The letters were hard to get out. You'd have to boil 'em in potash [potassium carbonate] to get the letters out. They had dye powders that you could color 'em and make 'em whatever color you wanted." —**Oza Coffee Kilby, Spring/Summer 1994**

OMIE: When I was little, my mom and dad lived on a farm. They had eleven children. There were three brothers older than me, and we all worked. Mostly I helped my mother in the house and carried water to the farm. We all worked together. I'd make a pie or sit down and work on some quilts. We made our own covers to keep warm with. The only things we ever bought were just little things. We didn't even buy much to make our quilts out of. We'd take our flour sacks and put them together to make our linings and covers to keep warm.

When I was younger, we made our clothes. After I got big enough to sew, I made mine myself. I generally got one pair of shoes a year.

HARLEY: You just got one pair of shoes a year. I remember wearin' brogans. My uncle made shoes and called them brogan shoes. We'd wear them; you could wear them from now on. I don't know why they wouldn't wear out. They just wouldn't.—**Omie and Harley Gragg, Spring 1989**

SCHOOL

We'd help my daddy in th' fields. Then we'd have nothin' t' do, and th' teacher would say, "If you've got nothin' t' do, well, come on then. Maybe you'll learn somethin'."

—Annie Perry

We've all heard the stories about one-room schoolhouses and walking miles to school in the snow; no buses traversed the back roads of rural areas in those days. Our grandparents often embellish the story, adding, "And I was barefoot!" Youngsters would rush into the school to warm their frozen bodies by the heat of the potbellied stove. Either the teacher or a designated student had to arrive at the school early to ready the fire in the stove and heat up the cold classroom. Children wore their everyday brogans with their overalls or feedsack dresses. They brought lunch to school in pails, and their families had to purchase their books.

Schools sometimes were located in the church, and only one or two teachers taught all seven grades in one or two rooms. Some of our contacts confided to us that they were unable to learn much because teachers could not devote enough time to them or to any given grade and because children were needed at home on the farm for sowing and harvesting. Most told us, however, that they have fond memories of their teachers and their time at school.

In some schools the teacher would call one grade up to her at a time. While the instructor was teaching that grade, the other students would do their homework or work on a subject that didn't require a teacher's help. Today's teachers generally have a master's degree, but in the past most teachers completed their education only through the seventh grade. Flora Youngblood recounted her memories of her teacher: "I don't know how old our teacher was, but she was young. She didn't have any formal education that I knew of." Moreover, female teachers "way back when" could not marry. If a female teacher married, the board of education would terminate her contract immediately.

Children in one-room schoolhouses used a slate and slate pencils. Today's schools provide free and reduced breakfasts and lunches, books, graphing calculators, counseling, and nursing care. Schools have their own libraries and gymnasiums. Our schools have computers with Internet capability, but some of our elders are unsure about the benefit of modern technology. Bob Justus told us his concern: "I don't think a kid in a classroom ought to see a computer for about three years—use his head." Today's courts prosecute parents who don't send their children to school. Most dads and moms today want their children to finish high school and go on to further their education at a university, two-year college, or technical school. Our elders believe that having common sense might be more important than accumulating degrees!

—*Amanda Carpenter*

"Mama taught us our ABCs on the mantel rock. We already knew the figures when we started to school. She taught us on the arch rock. She would write on that with a piece of charcoal.

"We had to hike to school, and school took up about eight o'clock and let out at four o'clock. And in the wintertime, we had to take our lantern with us to the top of the mountain and hide it in an old burnt stump until we came back from school, and then we'd get it. We didn't have but two months' school then, and later on we had three. Mr. John Arnold was our first teacher, and he was a good one. He was from down around Franklin [North Carolina]. School was just in the wintertime. I went through six grades, I guess.

"We used slates and slate pencils back then, you know. We had spellin' matches and such as that. They did have Sunday school in this schoolhouse, too. It was up on 'Broadway'—what they called it then. There's no building there now. It's gone. Had a little bell they rung to come in to books or come in from recess. It was a frame building, the best I remember. We had a wood heater. We brought our lunch in a syrup pail. We had beans or whatever we could get for dinner . . . cornbread.

"I was in intermediate arithmetic, language, history, and geography. I guess there was around nineteen or twenty students. It was a one-room school and one teacher. Our grades usually set in one place, graded like that, and when the teacher would call on us to recite, we'd all have to go up front. We had to write stories ever' once in a while for our English—things like that. We had books then, and we got to keep our books then. I think they ought to get to keep them now. I think they like to review them. The state furnished them, and later on you had to buy them.

"I had to walk about four miles to school. We come up from the head of Tessentee [North Carolina] across Fork Mountain and down to the lower end of Fork Mountain—you know, where Broadway is. Now, that's where we come to school." —**Betty Crane, Summer 1978**

PLATE 63 "[I]n the wintertime, we had to take our lantern with us to the top of the mountain and hide it in an old burnt stump until we came back from school." —Betty Crane

"They built a college. It was a wooden structure. The name was Providence College. Well, it burned down. So they rebuilt it, and it burned again. They taught Latin, Greek, calculus and pre-med. It was very good for that time. I suspect I'm the only one who knows anything about that college. The Batesville [Georgia] people don't know anything about it now because that's been a long time ago. The only reason I know about it now is because my family was connected with it, and it was on our property. I know where it stood. But there are no documents or anything left. Everything burned. But Dr. John Jackson and his brother, Dr. Walton Jackson, both got their pre-med education there. They aren't alive now. When the college burned the third time, about 1884, they built Piedmont College. It's not the same site. This college was sponsored by people from the New England states, and they came down. I don't know how Great-Grandpa got in touch with them, but he did.

"He was a peculiar man. If someone from Elberton [Georgia] wanted to come up from there and go to school at Providence and didn't have a place to stay or didn't have any money, he'd build him a one-room cabin and let him live out in it. When he graduated, someone else got to stay in it. So he tried to see that the young people were educated. That old house was even used as a dormitory. I remember my grandmother telling me one time there was one boy there who was kinda timid and, oh, just not one of the boys, so to speak, and they were always picking on him. She says, 'I'll tell you what you do, David. You go down to the cornfield. We're going out to get even with these boys.' So she said, 'Now here. You cut up some of these cornstalks just exactly such and such a length'—the length of a bed slat—and made up this other boy's bed beautifully. They had feather beds, and oh boy, they were fluffy and nice. The boys roughhoused a lot at night. So they were running and jumping on the beds and doing everything boys do to entertain themselves to let steam off. So this boy, who was the leader of the roughhousing, decided he would jump up on this other guy's bed. Well, he did. He jumped and *kerplunk!* He hit the floor and said, 'Now, what have I done!' David just kept a straight face as if he didn't know a thing about any of it, but that put an end to this roughhousing and picking on him. . . .

"I never went to a nine-month school in my life—never heard of such a thing. No, four- and five-month-term—that was it. And that was split. You had a term of six weeks, which was called the layin'-by season. That is where you have finished up plowing, hoeing, fertilizing, and all you have to do is wait for the crop to grow. . . .

"Finally, I got to go to grade school, but when I was ready for high school, we didn't have one around here. So I had to go away to a boarding academy called Hiawassee Academy. I had to borrow one hundred and fifty dollars to go, but I went ahead. And in 1928, I finished and had an A-1 teacher's certificate, which at that time qualified you to teach in rural communities. And I did feel qualified to teach because my mother, my uncle, my aunt, my grandfather, my great-grandfather were all teachers, and I naturally inherited something from them. . . .

"At that time there were almost no schools available in the county. Mrs. Green from Helen, Georgia, who lived in the Nacoochee Valley, had been up at Moccasin Creek to a lumber camp, and she saw what a deplorable situation it was. I think she was the person who decided to do something about it. She talked to the men in the office at Helen who owned the camp about getting a teacher up there. They said the best they could do would be to pay room and board.

"Then Mrs. Green heard that I was wanting a position as a teacher somewhere, and along about the first of August, she came to my house. She said, 'You have a teacher's certificate, don't you?' I said, 'Yes, I do.' She said, 'We're looking for a teacher to teach school up on Moccasin Creek.' Well, I was desperate for a job, and I looked forward to a great adventure. Barely eighteen and just out of high school, I said, 'Yes, I'll go.' I didn't have any experience, but I guess even a poor teacher was better than none. . . .

"It was rather amusing when I first went up to the camp. I had no way of getting up there. There were not as many automobiles then as there are today, and they were not as good-looking either! And I didn't have one because I was too young to have saved up the money to buy one. Well, I didn't know how in the world I was going to get to camp. It was just beyond me. But I had a friend who lived about three miles down the road. I said, 'Jeff, would you by any means have enough time to carry me back to Camp Moccasin?' He says, 'Yes, when do you want to go?' It was an old '23 model long-bedded truck. I got in that old truck; we huffed and we puffed. The road wasn't paved. We'd bump, and we'd bounce to this side and to that side and the other.

"Finally, we arrived at camp. I didn't know what to do going into a place like that. There I was standing there with my suitcase, not knowing a soul—not one—and then the sheriff, Mr. Sullivan, came up and asked me what I wanted. I told him I was supposed to open up a school. He looked me up and down like 'I'll give you two weeks, and that will be the end of you.'

"But anyway, he said, 'Where are you going to live?' I said, 'I don't know! The company said they'd furnish room and board.' He said, 'I know there is no place at all for you to live.' That's when the sheriff took pity on me and said, 'Well, I'll tell you, the school is very important, so I'll just move out of my boxcar and move into this building over here where you'll be teaching.' Well, he moved, and I moved in. That boxcar had one bed in it, a potbellied stove, and two chairs. Someone brought a dynamite keg in, and I had a thirty-five-cent mirror—that's what I had for my dressing table. My closet was an army blanket stretched across one corner. There were two little windows up near the top and no curtains, no electric lights, no running water or facilities. I burned coal in the heater, and at least someone would always bring coal to me so I didn't have to go and get the coal. . . .

"The schoolroom was heated with a fireplace that burned logs, and, of course, there were no lights in it. We used oil lamps. Someone up there could do very good carpentry work, and he made me six or eight long benches where three people could sit on the same bench. I took a sheet of linoleum and painted it black with enamel paint like a chalkboard, which worked very well. I had a word rack, I guess you would call it, where you could put the word 'Baby Rae' and 'Spot' and 'cat' and what-have-you.

"That's the equipment I had for teaching. There was not a book, a library. There was nothing. So the next day I hired someone to carry me to Hiawassee to a schoolbook depository, where I bought some books. I had to buy all of the books myself. Sometimes I would get paid for them, and sometimes I wouldn't. Most of them were on the first-, second-, or third-grade level. I found that I might need one set of books on the sixth-grade level because one child could do sixth-grade work. As they progressed, I would get books that they could feel comfortable working with.

"The children were from many different backgrounds, financial and otherwise, but most of them had some connection with the camp. Before the camp moved in, there were some native Rabun County people living in there, and their children walked three to five miles into school. I remember there were some Rogers and some Ellers, some Thompsons, and it seems like some Powells. Their descendants still live up there. Then there were six or eight families who had children and who were camp-connected and were from Helen [Georgia] and Robertstown [Georgia] and would live right there at the logging camp. Some of them had never gone to school a day. I had children from fourteen, fifteen, and sixteen years of age who had never gone to school one day. They were very smart. They were culturally deprived, but they were very anxious to learn.

"The first day of school, I had books and chalk and a chalkboard and everything pretty well ready. The majority of them, as I said, had never been to school, and they didn't know what school was all about. The children began drifting in one by one, and they would look around the corner, not knowing whether they were supposed to come in or not. They would come to the door and look and look and look. I would have to go outside and say, 'Come on in. This is the school. Come on in.' They got around twenty-four of them. They were awed; they were stunned. They stood around with their eyes glaring and their mouths open. And they waited for directions, but they were very, very nice in every respect. They waited for you to tell them what to do and where to sit. They were not students who were headstrong and would go into anything without some forethought or someone telling them what to do. Finally, we just sat there and talked a while, talked about school, how many people were at home, if they had any pets, and all that stuff. You have to do things like that sometimes. I gave them their books and tried to tell them what I expected out of them. Some of them could understand; some didn't. But the children always looked forward to their classes, and the chalk seemed to fascinate them. They didn't know whether to pick it up or what to do with it. They had to become adjusted to a lot of things.

"We started class at eight o'clock and stayed until three-thirty. We had three recesses: forty-five minutes of a morning, one hour at noon, and thirty-five minutes in the afternoon. During recess we had games to play. We played tag, drop the handkerchief, anty over, blindman's bluff, and little white daisy. Little white daisy was a singing game where you formed a circle and would go around and around and sing this song. I've forgotten it, but I remember the name of the game. The boys liked to play with slingshots. That wasn't a good idea, but they did. I let them because I didn't know any better. They were also interested in guns and fishing. Sometimes they would go fishing during recess. They brought their own lunch and ate it at noon. They wouldn't eat at the camp mess hall where I did.

"We had one room for all the grades, and in some grades we had only one or two pupils. I had to do the best I could. I had no help whatsoever, and it was good that I had no discipline problems. It was trial and error for me to determine what grade they were in. I would start out with the Baby Rae series of books. If they could read that and do simple math—addition and subtraction and so forth—I gave them the Zaner method writing books, which was like the Palmer method. I got primers. I made a card chart, and I had cards with one, two, or three words on them. I would put words on the chart for them to recognize, and I would teach phonics at the same time. The fact that I was so inexperienced myself made it hard, but you'd be surprised at the amount of education they got. . . .

"We used cursive writing only. I did not teach printing. That came years later. I still think maybe there is a mistake there, too, because high school children can't write as well as they once did when they were required to study the Palmer method of writing from the time they were in the first grade. I think it has affected their handwriting considerably.

"The children really learned a lot since they had never been to school. If I assigned them anything, they'd memorize it. We did have spelling bees, and that was usually Friday afternoon. We would more or less go over everything we had during the week. I'd say, 'How many of you can spell so-and-so?' Hands would go up. And 'How much are three plus four?' And they were good at it, considering the time they had been at school. It was amazing the progress they made because they really wanted to learn, and the parents were well pleased because they had no earthly way of sending their children to school. One of the boys I taught went on to finish school at Georgia Tech, and I was proud of him. The others mostly settled down in other areas, and they sent their children to school and believed in education. They got along fine.

"The next job I got was down at Turnerville, Georgia, where I taught for three years. I was paid fifty-five dollars a month and had to pay for room and board out of that. Then they raised their standards and said, 'A teacher has to have two years of college training before she or he teaches.' I went to Piedmont College [in Demorest, Georgia] and the University of Tennessee then. I made my two years. I taught with a two-year certificate for four or five to six years; and then they said, 'Well, you have to have a degree.' So I went back to night school and summer school. I carried my children with me. I guess the Lord was pretty good to me in that I didn't have to hire a babysitter at college because the students took my children and kept them for me. So I finished college, and then I taught several years longer at Robertstown." —**Ellene Gowder, Summer 1986**

PLATE 64 "The majority of them . . . had never been to school, and they didn't know what school was all about." —Ellene Gowder

"There were a few teachers that enjoyed switchin' certain children. I was always glad I wasn't one them." —***Hazel Killebrew***

"I went to school at Roundbottom [North Carolina] for four years. We had two classes, and each classroom had one teacher. The classes had kids from the first grade up to the seventh grades back then. Even though the older kids were in the same classroom with the younger ones, they never picked on them. We knew if we did, we would've gotten popped.

"We were taught to behave in school. I learned very early the consequences of not minding. I got one paddlin' in school when I was little, in the second or third grade. On the way to school in Roundbottom, you had to go across the railroad tracks and across this wooden walkway that covered a gully. We were all supposed to walk on the walkway, but I had a habit of jumpin' down into the gully. One day, when it snowed, the gully got full of snow. The teacher told me that the next time I jumped into it, she was goin' to switch me. And of course, I didn't believe her, so I went right back over there and did it again. She switched me! I was real surprised. After that, I broke my habit real quick!

"There were a few teachers that enjoyed switchin' [whipping or spanking] certain children. I was always glad I wasn't one them. I always stayed a distance away from those teachers. We had some good teachers, too. The best teacher I ever had I was in the sixth grade. She didn't have any uproar in her class. She had no trouble at all with controlling the classroom. Everybody always minded. The book *Good Morning, Miss Dove* reminded me of my teacher. She would give us a look out of the corner of her eyes, and then we would know to sit down and shut up.

"We would go to school four to six months because of the weather or just because of bad times.

"I graduated from high school in Highlands, North Carolina. We had pretty much the same subjects you have in school today. We didn't have computers or anything like that, but we had English, history, geography. I particularly remember algebra and geometry. I started algebra in the seventh, and I had it for about two years after that. Then I had geometry. I also took Latin. It was the only foreign language offered when I was in school." —**Hazel Killebrew, Spring 1991**

"We used to salute the flag every morning. Kids were chosen to carry the flag up there in the front when we was pledging allegiance to the flag. That was a great honor. It's funny, isn't it? We would almost fight over who got that and also who cleaned the chalkboard with those old erasers. Boy, we'd volunteer to do that job, and we got picked. We'd go out there and beat them things, get powder all over us. Now, they don't use stuff like that. Most kids got computers now. That's another thing. I don't think a kid in a classroom ought to see a computer for about three years—use his head. That's why I skipped a year. Too, they had to have discipline."

—Bob Justus, Fall/Winter 2001

GOING TO SCHOOL

I had to walk a mile and a half through the mud, rain, snow, ice, sleet, and everything else. I'd have to wade up to my knees, and ice would freeze on my hair.—Lyndall "Granny" Toothman

"I had to walk a mile to school. We did not have buses back then. I would either ride a bicycle or something else. By the time I got home, I had several chores I had to do." —**Thomas Coy Cheek, Fall/Winter 2003**

"We missed a good many days on account of the weather because we had no transportation. We had to walk. We'd put on a raincoat if it was rainin' and go to school, just so's it wasn't real freezin' cold.

"I didn't get to go when I was six years old. I had to wait a while 'til I got old enough to where I could walk that far. It was a pretty good little piece, about a couple or three miles." —**Flora Youngblood, Spring 1985**

"I first went when I was five, and I had a bad experience. The teacher scolded us, and so I went home that evening and put my dinner bucket and my books down. I said, 'I'm through with school.' I never went back until I was eight, and I had to walk a mile and a half through the mud, rain, snow, ice, sleet, and everything else. I'd have to wade up to my knees, and ice would freeze on my hair. I had seven gates to open because there were farms. My parents and I lived on the farm against the mountain, the last farm on the dirt road, so I had longer to walk than anyone."

—Lyndall "Granny" Toothman, Fall/Winter 1991

"I went to school on Little Germany [Rabun County, Georgia] for one year; then we moved to the valley, an' I went to Rabun Gap-Nacoochee School [in Rabun Gap, Georgia] for a year. I rode the school bus, first school bus I ever rode, only one I ever rode. I went there for a year. Then we moved up here on the head of Black's Creek."

—Senia Southards, Spring/Summer 2003

"My first year of school, I went to Midway School [near Carnesville, Georgia], a two-room schoolhouse. I did not get to attend at times: Bad weather and sickness hindered my first year. We had to walk some three miles. When I started to Red Hill [near Carnesville, Georgia], Mama had me to start in the first grade again. School buses started running when I went to Red Hill. It had two benches on each side covered with leather; a bench also ran down the middle. You could straddle it or sit sidesaddle. The windows were covered in roll-up curtains. They had a rod running through the bottom of it."

—Ruby Mae Miller Cheek, Spring/Summer 2005

"I started goin' to Clayton, and we had an old bus. It was a homemade bus from a back of a pickup the first year. We all rode back there. The next year, Neil Justus, he bought a bus. It had seats runnin' long ways, just like a bench. We sat on them; then in the summertime he'd take the whole body off and use it to haul hay on it. They'd still be hay in the bus that fall when we started school, but I guess that was some of the good ol' days. We didn't know what a heater was in the bus. We left before daylight and got in nearly after dark. Sometimes we would get stuck on a road and have to walk home. We're lucky we made it. All in all, we had a good childhood."

—Horace Justus, Spring/Summer 2000

"I went to school about two miles and a half from here, toward the east. I went for thirteen years. One of my nieces said, 'Why, Annie, I wouldn'ta went that long.' I went 'til I was twenty-two years old. Yes, and I didn't get farther than th' seventh grade. But that was all right—I went to school. I wasn't dumb, but there wasn't nothin' else t' do from July to December. We'd help my daddy in th' fields. Then we'd have nothin' t' do, and th' teacher would say, 'If you've got nothin' t' do, well, come on then. Maybe you'll learn somethin'.' I never went a year but what I learned somethin'."

—Annie Perry, Summer/Fall 1975

"Sometimes in the wintertime, the snow would be on the ground, and sometimes it'd be a foot deep or deeper. But my daddy would help us to get to school. Many a time at the close of school when we started home, we'd meet him partway shovelin' the snow in the road so that we could come through—get back home without havin' to wade in a snow too deep."

—Esco Pitts, Spring 1978

"Before I was old enough to be enrolled in school, I'd sometimes go with my sisters. It was a two-mile walk, and they often had to carry me part of the way, usually on the way back. I was very small for my age—the only child who had to stand on a box to reach the blackboard. The teacher once asked me why I didn't come to school more often, and they tell me I replied, 'I wish Mama would let me.' " **—James Still, Fall 1988**

"When I started school, if I went through the black section of town, I could cut off about a mile or two. I had me a little black girl for a friend. I wish I could remember her name, but I don't remember her name. I passed by her school goin' to my school." **—Daisy Justice, Spring/Summer 2004**

THE SCHOOLHOUSE

We had a big potbellied stove that would heat the whole school during the winter. It was all the heat we had.—Thomas Coy Cheek

"School was fun then, really. We'd sit on benches, and there was a big old stove in the center of the room to keep us warm. It took me the longest time to learn my ABCs. I could say them by heart, but I didn't know what they looked like. And I used to read by the pictures. If I saw a picture of a bird or a kite in the primer, I'd just say 'bird' or 'kite' when the teacher asked me. I couldn't spell either. If they told me to spell cake, I'd spell it K-A-K-E and get it wrong.

"We could look out the windows at school and see men diggin' ditches for water lines, and our teacher said, 'You see those men out there? It takes ten or fifteen men two or three weeks to dig that ditch now, but one day they'll have a machine that will dig it in so many minutes with one man operating the machine.'

"We said, 'Oh, he doesn't know what he's talkin' about.' We couldn't see it back then, but it's here now. Everything's push-button."

—Anna Tutt, Spring 1978

"It was a one-room schoolhouse, and we had little benches, not desks. They had a primer, first grade. And then they had second and third grade and fourth grade and on up through the seventh. But there wasn't very many in either grade, just maybe two or three. Now when I got in the fourth grade, it was me and one other girl. We was in the fourth and fifth grades for two years by ourself." **—Flora Youngblood, Spring 1985**

"We all went to a school, a one-room school down six miles east of Clayton, an' you only could go through six grades there. I lived too far from Clayton to get to go to any high school, so I didn't go to any high school at all. I wanted to go but could not walk the ten miles to get to go to high school. So my daddy told me, said, 'You're gonna have to help me make a crop so we'll have somethin' to eat.' He teached me how to milk a cow, an' he teached me how to plow mules." **—Harold Houck, Spring/Summer 2000**

"The schoolhouse was big and divided off into rooms with curtains, so classes could be held together or apart."

—Willie Elliott, Fall/Winter 1991

"The first school I ever went to was a one-room schoolhouse. They had all the grades in the same room over in Little Germany . . . Then we moved up here on the head of Black's Creek. I went to Mountain City School [in Rabun County, Georgia]. We had separate rooms down there. The third and fourth was in the same room, and first and second were together."

—Senia Southards, Spring/Summer 2003

PLATE 65 "He [my daddy] teached me how to plow mules." —Harold Houck

"I started school at age four. Back then, you could start any time you wanted to—in a one-room school. It was from the first grade to the seventh all in one room. It ran ages four to eighteen. Some of 'em were my uncles, my aunts. I went to school with them. I went to school there for three years." —**Lois Duncan, Spring/Summer 2000**

"The schoolhouse was a good building. It was built in plank. The first school building I ever went to was about a mile from here. I went there 'til I was ten or twelve years old. And then they consolidated the schools together; there was two schools. One couldn't get along through the winter by itself, so they put 'em together. Then I went from this side of the Baptist Church to a slab-blocked building with a roof on it. When it rained, it leaked at th' top of the door. We'd go start up to class, go up right through that water." —**Annie Perry, Summer/Fall 1975**

"We had a stove in the schoolhouse. They had a plank fixed here. They put a plank in here, and they put sand on it—you know . . . the floor. Then they put us a stove in, and the pipe ran out. We fired it with wood. Whoever got there first built the fire. If two or three boys got there before I did, they would wait for me to get there and we would go in; they would help me build the fire." —**Varina Ritchie, Spring 1990**

"I don't know how to tell y' how the school was, but the grammar school and the junior high were right next to each other. They had the fifth, sixth, and seventh grade. Through the grammar school, we had first, second, third, fourth." —**Daisy Justice, Spring/Summer 2004**

"There's every difference in the world now than when I was in school. We went to a little one-room church that was used as a schoolhouse. It was located at Bethel, about halfway between Tiger [Georgia] and new Highway 441. We had little long, straight benches in a row with one teacher. . . .

"When we first went to Tiger, the little schoolhouse was down by the Methodist church, and we still had the straight benches. I guess that was about 1906 or 1907. They built the new schoolhouse, as we called it, over here where it stands now, and they made desks for us. . . .

"Our classes were all in the same room. There were seven grades then, I reckon." —**Amanda Turpin, Summer 1981**

SCHOOL TERM/DAY

We'd start in and go 'til it came time to pull the fodder, and then we'd have to stop out then and cut them tops and pull the fodder.
—Jake Waldroop, Summer 1977

"We had school only about three months a year. That's all they gave the colored folks. I think the white folks had six and up to nine months later on. Our school would get up to fifth grade or maybe eighth—I don't remember." —**Harley Penland, Winter 1977**

"Mother had three daughters that needed to be in school, and then our little school just run for three months a year, y' know, over there. Clayton High School ran for nine months. That's why Mother's brother got her to move us children—so we could finish high school. That's how come we went to Clayton." —**Varina Ritchie, Spring 1990**

"We didn't have a long-term school. We used to all have to get out of school and work in the fields. When that was over, we were ready to go back to school!" —**Amanda Turpin, Summer 1981**

TEACHERS

[B]ack in those days, the teacher did more whippin'. Disciplinin' was considered just teachers' work—keep the children quiet and make them behave themselves.—William Freeman Alley

"When I went to school, we had only one teacher and had maybe three grades in one room. She would talk to one group and then go to the next group and teach them for a while."

—Thomas Coy Cheek, Fall / Winter 2003

"I don't know how old our teacher was, but she was young. She didn't have any formal teacher education that I knew of."

—Flora Youngblood, Spring 1985

"We had three teachers, all women, and they lived in the dorm with us." **—Mary Pitts, Fall 1987**

"I began school in a little one-teacher school for the first three years in Betty's Creek [Rabun County, Georgia] where the church is now. That land was given by my grandparents for school and church services. I went there for three years—had one teacher, and we had six grades."

—Floss Sitton, Spring / Summer 2001

"My first teacher was just a little bitty lady, and she taught us seven or eight years. I still remember her. She kept a bunch of hickories, round as that walkin' stick, sittin' in the corner, and, back in those days, the teacher did more whippin'. Disciplinin' was considered just teachers' work—keep the children quiet and make them behave themselves."

—William Freeman Alley, Winter 1983

"I was about five or six years old when I started to school. That was down at Eastanollee near Toccoa [Georgia]. It was just a one-room, one-teacher school. Our teacher was an old, gray-headed man named Mr. Gain. He started off teachin' the ABCs, and that's all I learned that whole term—one-room school and no other teachers helpin' him. The schoolhouse was plumb full, and the children were not divided into grades. That's just the way it was. We didn't have too long a term of school, about five months. We had to walk about three miles to get there." **—Addie Bleckley, Summer 1978**

"I had a wonderful teacher in the first grade, a Miss Porterfield. The first day of school, she wrote my name in chalk on my desk and handed me an ear of corn and told me to shell the kernels and make an outline of my name. We did this many times over, and by the end of the day, I had learned its shape and could write it on paper." —**James Still, Fall 1988**

"We didn't have enough clothes back then to keep us warm. Me an' my brother, Randolph, went one day to school an' liked to froze to death. Mrs. Cathey kept us by the heater all day to get us warm enough to come home that evenin'." —*Senia Southards*

"They had all the grades in the same room over in Little Germany [in Rabun County, Georgia]. All the classes was in one room. We had one teacher that taught all of us. Then we moved up here on the head of Black's Creek [Rabun County]. I went to Mountain City School [Rabun County]. We had separate rooms down there . . . But the teachers had more time to teach the children a lot better than they did all in one room. I had a good teacher. Mrs. Beulah Cathey was one of my teachers. Mrs. Prater was another one of 'em. I liked all of 'em. They 'as all good to me. In the winter sometimes it would get so cold we didn't get to go to school. We didn't have enough clothes back then to keep us warm. Me an' my brother, Randolph, went one day to school an' liked to froze to death. Mrs. Cathey kept us by the heater all day to get us warm enough to come home that evenin'." —**Senia Southards, Spring/Summer 2003**

"But the teachers didn't get but thirty-five dollars a month, and that was the one that got the most—from twenty to thirty-five dollars. They had what they called Teachers' Institute. They'd go, and they'd train 'em. Then they'd give 'em their papers and have 'em go to work at them. And then they'd grade their papers, and they had one, two, and three grades: first, second, third. I never had a schoolteacher in my life, honey, that had a high school education. They generally went through the seventh grade and went to this Teachers' Institute. A good scholar that had just finished the seventh grade could teach school. I'm not foolin' you."

—**Annie Perry, Summer/Fall 1975**

"School is a lot different now than when I went. You see, we only had one teacher, and all the kids were in one room. They had a stage in the schoolhouse, and she would get one grade to go up on the stage. When she got through with them, the next class went up there—first, second, third, right on to the seventh. That's the way it worked—one class, then the next." —**Oakley Justice, Summer 1979**

"Our folks kept us in school while it was a-goin', and we went every day. There was one year I went and never missed a day. The schoolteacher give me a little present for not missin' a day, and I was so proud of that. It was a little teacup and saucer, and I've got it in yonder now."

—**Bessie Miller, Winter 1983**

"We had one teacher and seven grades. My teacher was Avery Watts, the lady that lived there at Liberty [Rabun County, Georgia]. She would tell you what your assignments were for the next day, or that day, and you had to get it. If you didn't get it, your mama and daddy made you wish you had."

—**J. D. Holcomb, Summer 1992**

"Dr. J. A. Green was my first teacher, and Colonel Thad Bynum was my second teacher. After that, we went to Tiger School [in Tiger, Georgia]. We had women teachers, too, but my first three teachers were all men. . . .

"When a teacher worked with a specific group, everyone went to sit in the back except the ones in the class that was called to go up to the teacher's desk. Everybody could sit there and listen if they wanted to, though."

—**Amanda Turpin, Summer 1981**

"We had five or six grades. It could have been seven grades. It depends on your age, see? You'd fluctuate. I might be in a class with just three or four kids, and we would have our assignment—teacher'd work with us. The other grades'd be working on homework or working on their spelling, and that's another thing, see? You would maybe be learning to write, and you'd have these sheets of paper, ruled paper. They don't do that anymore, I'm sure." —**Bob Justus, Fall/Winter 2001**

"The teachers were required to visit in the home of every child at least once during the year. At the end of our monthly report, they asked how many home visits we made during that month. We tried the best we could to follow those guidelines set by the Virginia State Board of Education. We had a supervisor that came by once or twice a month and worked with us."

—**Henrietta Reynolds, Spring/Summer 1993**

LUNCH

If we had fried rabbit in our lunch pail, we'd sit so everybody could see it. That was a big treat.—Anna Tutt

"They would go to the classroom and then, around noon, get out for lunch. Some students went home for lunch, but others brought their lunches." —**Willie Elliott, Fall/Winter 1991**

"We brought our lunch in a bucket. We used to mix up syrup and butter and put it in a little bowl. We'd put that in the bucket and have our bread to put it on. Sometimes that was all we ate." —**Addie Bleckley, Summer 1978**

"They brought their lunches. They brought some milk in a bottle, and I brought milk in my own bottle. And they brought a box or a basket—or whatever they had—with their sandwiches and things in it. We turned them out at twelve, and they went to the spring and got them some water if they wanted to. They'd eat their lunch on the outside of the schoolhouse. Most of the time I ate mine at the desk, but I let them go outside most of the time. When they got their lunch eat, they could play ball or whatever they wanted to do 'til I rung the bell. When I rung the bell, they lined up out there like soldiers." —**Varina Ritchie, Spring 1990**

"The school did not furnish our lunch. We would bring our own—biscuits, jelly and jams, meat, or whatever we wanted."

—**Leona "Dink" Carver, Fall/Winter 1995**

"We used to go to school through pine thickets and broom sage because it was a bit of a ways there. If we had fried rabbit in our lunch pail, we'd sit so everybody could see it. That was a big treat. But if we had peas and cornbread, or somethin' like that, we'd always turn our backs and sit on a log to eat because that wadn't very special." —**Anna Tutt, Spring 1978**

SUBJECTS

We had a green-back speller. It had the ABCs in it and some words for spellin'. Then they'd lead you on up to where you could read the words. That was the only book I had for two years.—Addie Bleckley

"I didn't enjoy school too much, but I liked to read. I read, I reckon, more than any other person. To give book reports, the teacher generally assigned you so many a month. I read far more than she assigned. Sometimes I would read five or six, maybe ten in a month. I read every book we had over, sometimes two or three times. Then we got a library at the school, and I was permitted to bring books home. My biggest pleasure was reading. But I never could spell; I still can't spell today. They gave us a spelling class when I was in high school. I could give the definition of each word, but I couldn't spell it."

—Lyndall "Granny" Toothman, Fall/Winter 1991

"That first year, I took wood carving, mechanical drawing, a little surveying, and then I took the dancing. We'd dance at least two or three times a week there in the daytime, as well as regular evening dances on Tuesday and Friday nights.

"There'd been a lot of problems with the dancing because old people here connected any kind of dancing with the old hoedowns where everybody got drunk in a big square dance and tore the place up. So the Folk School [John C. Campbell Folk School in Brasstown, Georgia] called it singing games, and they concentrated a lot on the traditional folk dances from England and Denmark, as well as America. But it was years and years before they ever dared to do any of the mountain old-time square dancing."

—Fred Smith, Fall 1987

"At school, we had eight subjects. We took a spellin' class, geography, and home ec [economics] back then. I had two years of algebra. I was good in math, and that was what I planned to major in in college."

—Mary Pitts, Fall 1987

"We learned our ABCs the first thing and the basics—readin', writin', and arithmetic. . . .

"We studied readin', writin', arithmetic, spellin', geography, American history, English, agriculture, and physiology. I guess that was about all. We didn't read much except our schoolbooks when we were children. We read other books sometimes after we got up big enough. . . .

"I guess I was the best in spellin' of most any subject. I got the prize for the most head marks at the end of one year. We just had two classes in spellin'. The little ones were all together, and I got to help with them. See, we would stand up and have oral spellin'. We had a lot of spellin' words. We spelled in the old blue-back speller, and I spelled the school down then. I guess spellin' was my best subject." **—Amanda Turpin, Summer 1981**

"On Friday we would have spelling matches. All of the smaller children would come into the next room where the bigger children were. They had two captains, and they would give each captain the same number of team members. The whole schoolroom was lined up on each side. Of course with the little fellows, they would start with small words they could spell, you know, until, like in the fourth, fifth, sixth, seventh grade—then it was bigger words. And I would always go to the end of the line because I knew I was comin' up as far as nearly the head because I was a pretty good speller.

"I remember workin' the long division in arithmetic; that was real hard, and it was complicated. But once I did get into it, I went on. I remember I used to make marks on the paper, draw lines. That was the way I had to count. We didn't have a computer, and those little calculators, we didn't have those. I had my fingers and those marks on the paper.

"We were graded by our report cards: A, B, C, D, E, and F. F was failure, and E was almost right at failure. And of course A was perfect, I guess; B was good, and C was fair. I stayed kind of between B and A. I might have got a few Cs. But I don't think there were many because I tried real hard, and I would make As." —**Selma Mosley, Spring 1989**

"We had a green-back speller. It had the ABCs in it and some words for spellin'. Then they'd lead you on up to where you could read the words. That was the only book I had for two years. Then we went through a blue-back speller. When we got through with that, we were pretty far up on the education level. We didn't learn to count or cipher for a long time.

"I remember some pictures in one of my books. There was a picture of a boy who had run away from home and had climbed up in an apple tree. The picture showed him in the apple tree, and they were tryin' to get him down. I had almost forgotten that little story." —**Addie Bleckley, Summer 1978**

MISCHIEF AT SCHOOL

She was drinkin' that water, and up came the school bully and jerked that dipper out and broke one of her front teeth.

—Walker Word

"There was always a bully in school. We didn't have waterworks when I was a kid in school. Before recess, the teacher would send a few boys out to draw water. I was selected one day to do just that. I had just had me a drink, and up walked this pretty little girl named Dixie Holloway. I put about half a dipper full of water and handed it to Dixie. She was drinkin' that water, and up came the school bully and jerked that dipper out and broke one of her front teeth. Well, I knocked the h— out of him. Blood flew everywhere. I looked up, and here was the school principal. He was a nice fellow. His name was Preacher Cook. He took us back to his office and made us bend over his desk. He really gave us a whippin'. Well, I didn't think I needed a whippin'. Anyway, that afternoon, after leavin' school, I saw the preacher. I picked up a rock and threw it at him. I knew that if I'd hit him solid that it would have killed him. It just grazed his ear. I shouldn't have done it. He went and had a little talk with my dad. He said to Dad, 'Mr. Word, Walker threw a rock at me today.'

"Preacher Cook wanted me to make a public apology the next Monday mornin' at the assembly. Well, it came Monday, and the auditorium was filled because everyone wanted to hear me apologize. When the time came, I got up and said, 'I threw a rock at Preacher Cook. I missed him, and I'm sorry.' So I never did really apologize to him because I said that I was sorry that I missed him." —**Walker Word, Spring 1990**

"I got in some trouble. Once, I slipped out the window and played in the snow when it had snowed down there. When I got caught, I got a D on

PLATE 66 "I threw a rock at Preacher Cook. I missed him and I'm sorry." —Walker Word

deportment, and they [the staff at Tallulah Falls Boarding School in Tallulah Falls, Georgia] took my free Sundays away from me. I had to go and apologize to the teacher in front of the class . . . I never really got in bad trouble, but I did get a lick on the back one time. The teacher was mad at the whole room and just came down the row and gave each one of us a lick. It hurt because it was a hickory. I got a paddlin' in the second grade for talkin' once. I don't remember too much. I got four or five licks. It scared me more than it hurt me." **—Ethel Runion, Spring/Summer 2003**

"We had pretty good teachers, and we were kind o' bashful. We were too bashful to try to cut up much. We pulled a prank on the teacher the first day of April. We'd run off and leave her. Most of the students thought that was fun. I never got a whippin' in school. It wasn't because I was good: I was sneaky, so I never got caught." **—Amanda Turpin, Summer 1981**

"When we started a new term, the teacher didn't know the children. They would send a certain boy to go out to cut them a switch. Them boys got to wringin' 'em before they brought 'em in. So the teacher would give a strike and it'd fly all into pieces. The teacher, she come to me one day and asked if I'd go and cut her some ironwood switches. She said, 'Now, I don't believe you'll do what they been a-doin.' I went and found some good ones and brought them in. Talk about some boys gettin' it—they did!

"But the teachers didn't keep order much. It was pretty noisy in there. That hurts about studyin'. They didn't keep much order. Some did, but about all of them was women teachers, and them ol' big boys, you know, wouldn't mind.

"About the biggest thing we got punished for was writin' letters—like a boy would write a girl a letter. One time me and a boy was sittin' together. We oughtn't to have done it, but we did. We didn't like a certain boy; we wrote a love letter. That boy I was sittin' with said, 'You write it. Write a good love letter, and when we are out, I'll slip in and put it in a girl's book.'

"I wrote it. When we come back in, we kept watchin', and we seen her read and read. She took it up there and give it to the teacher. She read it and looked everywhere. And when we had another recess, she told that boy, said, 'I want you to stay in here.'

"He stayed, you know, and she shut the door. Boy, that boy told me that he was gonna get it now. He come out, and he said, 'Boy, somebody played a trick on me.' He said, 'I never wrote her no letter. Somebody played a trick.' He said, 'She beat me to death about it. I couldn't tell her.' He said, 'She don't like me nohow.' She had had trouble with him. He was pretty rowdy.

"I told that boy I was sittin' with that we done wrong there. He said, 'Don't ever tell that boy, or we will have a fight with him.' I never would pull a trick like that again." —**Harvey J. Miller, Spring 1978**

"I never did get a whippin' in school, I don't believe. Some of the older boys didn't like the teacher much, and they used to tease him a lot. He was so old, you know, it was easy to tease him. He never did whip much, but when he did, he'd get a hickory and really whip 'em."

—Addie Bleckley, Summer 1978

"Before starting the eighth grade in Clayton, I went to Tallulah Falls Boarding School [in Tallulah Falls, Georgia] for three months. Even though we had moved from Clayton, I came back and boarded at the Bleckley House to go to high school. I stayed at the Bleckley House. Then another girl, older than I was, and I decided that we might want to stay the night at the Nicholson House. When we went there, I was about thirteen or fourteen, and the other girl was about sixteen or seventeen. There were some nice, young men that wanted us to go to Hiawassee [Georgia] with them, but Mrs. Nicholson wouldn't let us go. So what we did was slip out the window! I shouldn't tell you this because nothing bad happened, but thank goodness it didn't. They were such nice young men. They'd take us out to ride—go over toward Hiawassee on the dirt road and to other events. We had another little girl in the room with us from Chechero [a community outside of Clayton, Georgia]. We thought that she was asleep, but she was watching us go out and come in, so she told Mrs. Nicholson.

"Well, Mrs. Nicholson kicked us out, so we had to go back to the Bleckley House. She told my mother she didn't want to; she said she thought I was led by the older girl. I said to my mother, 'I was not! I wanted to go as much as she did; we couldn't have any fun or dates, and so that's why we went.' My mother said, 'When this school term is up (my father, in the meantime, had died in July 1924), you're going down to Madison, Georgia, and stay with your aunt and uncle and finish high school there.' "

—Jo Kinman Brewer, Fall/Winter 1993

> **"Next day he come to school—he could just see a little out of one of his eyes, and he had big lips. They was just turned wrong side out. He said he'd give five dollars to find out who did it."**
>
> ***—Kimsey Hampton***

"When I was in school, in the fifth grade, it was in a one-room schoolhouse with one teacher. Along in the early fall, we was all playin' anty over

over the schoolhouse, havin' a cuttin'-up time. The teacher rang the bell for us to come in. All the students on the back side of the house just stepped in through a low window instead of goin' around front. Me and a husky boy was the last two steppin' in the window. The teacher turned around from the door and seen us, and then he really gave us a lickin'. He didn't say nothin' to the rest of the students. Well, me and him got together an' talked a little bit about it. The teacher was a grown man about forty-four years old. We had to walk back an' forth to school. He'd always wait 'til we'd all left school before he left, and he'd come on over later. There was a big hornets' nest beside the road—great big hornets' nest. We decided to stir up that nest for the teacher when he come by. One of us stayed at the nest, and the other got up on the hill to watch for the teacher. When he come around the bend, the one on the hill hit the nest and ran. He ran as fast as he could. Then we both got up on the hill behind some bushes where we could see.

"The teacher come walkin' up with his head down. Them hornets all just ZZZZZZZZZZZ in his face. God! That hat went up in the air and he went to stompin' his big feet—he had about number twelve shoes! And then he run just as hard as he could go.

"Next day he come to school—he could just see a little out of one of his eyes, and he had big lips. They was just turned wrong side out. He said he'd give five dollars to find out who did it, but me an' that other feller didn't say nothin' to nobody. He'd a-eat us up again. We got even with 'im."

—Kimsey Hampton, Summer/Fall 1975

"I remember back when I was in boarding school, about 1919. Somebody got some rope. There was a hallway with doors all the way up and down each side of the hall. They tied this rope tightly to all the doors, criss-

PLATE 67 "They tied this rope tightly to all the doors, crisscrossing the hall." —Marinda Brown

crossing the hall. We never found out who did it. The girls couldn't get their doors open. It would just pull the next one tighter. My room was at the end of the hall; they didn't tie up my door, so I saw what was goin' on. We tried and tried to find out who did it but never could."

—Marinda Brown, Summer/Fall 1975

GAMES AND TOYS

I don't suppose many of these things that we did when we grew up are common today because people can go off on car rides and things like that. They don't usually get together on Sunday afternoons or Saturday afternoons and have a ballgame or horseshoe pitchin' or playin' Tag or somethin' like that that we used to do when we grew up.

—Margaret Norton

Are today's parents plagued by the wants of their children? Bombarded by commercial advertising, young people feel they *need* the latest computer, PlayStation, Nintendo, cell phone, plasma television . . . car! After all, newer is better, right? We have become a nation of consumers. Many baby boomers have maxed out their credit cards, taken a second mortgage on their homes, and generally lived above their means. Sadly, children mimic their parents. Modern society seems obsessed with acquiring *things.*

Furthermore, calculators, computers, and television have changed the lives of our children. No longer is a vivid imagination necessary. America's young people park themselves in front of a technological toy and zone out. Even with all these "toys," most children today whine to their parents: "I'm bored!" Unlike children of former generations, our children are not developing their imaginations. Ruby Cheek, one of our contacts, told us about making a ball: "We'd take a bladder from a hog when it was killed, and before it got dry, we'd wash it, usually in lye soap, and take an oat straw and blow it up tight. That was our basketball." Buck Carver told us about playing townball with a homemade ball made out of twine. Our elders played with toys they or their parents created. They hopped and skipped and jumped and ran. They played with their siblings and cousins, mainly on Sunday afternoons because the rest of the week they were working on the farm, and they worked hard.

Studies today report that our nation's children are not getting enough exercise, and many of them are overweight. Though we enjoy all the conveniences that our modern world offers, perhaps we should revive some aspects of the past.

—*Amanda Carpenter*

Children have always played games, but unlike children a generation ago, today's youth don't seem to be playing old-timey games. Perhaps the demise of games is not only because of the advent of computers, television, DVDs, MP3 players, and the like but also because children today seem to be too busy: piano and dance lessons, gymnastics, clubs, football, soccer, cheerleading, church activities, and on and on. You're probably thinking that sports are games, but what happened to all the games—crack-the-whip, anty over, hide-and-seek, townball, green man's garden, fox and dogs—our parents and grandparents used to play? Those outdoor games were not only fun but also helped young people be physically fit.

Younger children, in the old days, played games with their neighbors and cousins at school, after their chores were done, or on Sunday afternoons after church. Children used their imaginations. They played with slingshots, marbles, balls, rocks, sticks, or broken dishes. Parents often made toys for their children. Mothers made dolls from rags, cornshucks, apples, and even cucumbers! Dads built wagons, tops, dumbbulls [a wooden toy that makes a loud noise when you whirl it around], sleds.

Are children indeed too busy today to play games? Are parents too busy to play with their children? Although most of us would not want to return to those "good ol' days," perhaps playing together is a good idea for the well-being and survival of families today.

—April Argoe

GAMES

"Some of the games we played were marbles and hide-and-seek and other kid games, I guess you'd say. We played in playhouses a lot. We'd get out in the woods and make us a playhouse—rake up leaves and make beds and find pretty green moss to decorate the furniture."

—Amanda Turpin, Summer 1981

"When we were little, we played games for our entertainment. We had some playmates that would come and play with us. The games I remember playin' the most are that game anty over—where you throw balls across the house—and catch and hide-and-go-seek and crack-the-whip.

"Crack-the-whip is a game where you line up a whole bunch of kids and put the smallest one on the end of it. They make motions, and the little one on the end gets tossed all over the place. I was the one that always got tossed all over the place.

"We also played ball. We played what we called townball. It was not like baseball. Instead of havin' a diamond, we had four bases straight in a row, and we played it with a baseball and a bat." —**Hazel Killebrew, Spring 1995**

ANVIL SHOOTING

When the smoke and dust cleared, they were standing there, black and dazed. Their clothes were all tattered. Their hands and arms were full of gravel.—Jim W. Clark

"When the children weren't in school, they walked the railroad. When I was in Turnerville [Georgia], in 1932–1933, the only recreation we had Sunday afternoon was walkin' the railroads. You and your boyfriend would get together and walk alongside the railroad tracks. We walked the trestles, too—that was fun. We actually didn't know anything about gettin' in a car and goin' because it was something we'd never done. In other words, when I grew up, people knew how to entertain themselves. You'd be surprised! We had horseshoe games. We'd shoot anvils. To shoot anvils, you'd empty out six or eight shotgun shells and get the powder out (not the shot—just the powder). You'd wrap that powder up in an old cloth or something so it wouldn't spill and put it in the hole of an anvil. You'd put you a fuse to light it and get a good piece away, too! The anvil would shoot straight into the air. It makes a terrible noise. The boys used to do that, especially on the holidays." —**Ellene Gowder, Summer 1986**

"My background is not with an anvil shootin'. I guess I always liked explosives. I worked for the Georgia Power Company for several years as a dynamite man. They were digging holes and would hit rock. I would go there and blow the rock up. I don't know if I was the only crazy one or what, but I done it. It doesn't take a lot of know-how. It's mostly common sense, really. An explosion is nothin' but controlled force. That's what you got to keep in mind.

"They used anvil shoots to open a celebration in the past. I've read where they closed celebrations with it much like on a Fourth of July. I don't know the earliest known shootin' of the anvil. The earliest in documented cases was when David Crockett was elected to Congress. The occasion was celebrated by anvil shootin'. I know it pre-dates that, but how far before that I don't know. It was real common. It was done in New England, out West, and in the far South. I talked to a man one time who told me that he remembered his grandfather talking about it bein' done in Andersonville [Georgia] a hundred years ago, so it definitely was in this area. In talkin' to people, I've never heard of anybody that could tell me it's been done in the last fifty or sixty years.

"It was competitive. The competitive part of it was tryin' to level and straighten the bottom of the anvil—in other words, so you would have your projection go straight up and straight down. The competitive part of it would also be the height that you could blow the anvil and how close you could get the anvil to land near the area that you blowed it. If you take your time and level it correctly, your projection will go straight up, and everything will be as perfect as possible. I've done it before. That anvil will go straight up and not even turn over and come straight back down. It's almost unreal, but people seem to like it more if you tilt it a little bit, which causes the anvil to flip end over end. The anvil won't land as close, but even doin' that, you can see the holes in the ground at seven or eight feet. I've never had it land over ten feet. . . .

"John Rice Irwin actually read about it first. He called me one night, and he knew what he was talkin' about. We just got to talkin' about it. You know that John's purpose in life is to revive and maintain things like this [at the Museum of Appalachia in Norris, Tennessee]. We started checkin' around to find somebody that knew how. We talked to one guy that was from Alabama. He traveled through here every now and then, so I got to talk to him. He told me a little bit about it. John had plenty of anvils. I had a few, so we just started out. We come up on this bottom anvil first because it was the right size to shoot from. We thought this concave effect would cause a problem, but, like I said, it won't work without it. We got an anvil that was flat. We shot, and we shot and shot. I thought, well, this would allow us to put more powder. We accidentally came across the concave on the top anvil. Sure enough, the first shot went eighty feet. So with a little luck and a lot of digging, we came up with a method that actually works.

"What you are striving for is to get that powder burning. If you seal that anvil, it tends to come up in the air slow. You lose all the things you need to get that pressure buildup. . . .

"The bottom anvil is sitting upside down with this concave effect. That is where we put the powder. Then we use an iron plate. To be honest, I don't know what part this plate plays, but it won't work without it. We use just a plain old cannon fuse, approximately one pound of powder, dependin'. The bottom anvil is 250 pounds, and the top anvil that goes up in the air weighs 148 pounds.

"I use 4L with black powder to shoot the anvil. When I first found out about this, I didn't have anybody to come up and say, 'Gene, this is how you do this, step by step.' We read about it and heard about it, but nobody knew how to do it. We experimented with it.

"You know, I've often wanted to go out in the middle of a field somewhere and just see what you could do. I believe you could put the anvil in orbit! I think it is a lot of show. Smokeless powder would burn faster and blow the anvil higher, but you wouldn't get that black ball of smoke and a ball of fire. I would sometime like to do one at night to see what it would look like at night.

"Sure, it's dangerous, but if you use your head, it's not. The most dangerous thing is setting the other anvil on top of it. I tried to get a bronze plate, but the bronze is too soft. What I have is a low-tempered piece of iron.

"If you was bent over the anvil, it would take your head off. It really would. There's no doubt in my mind that your head would go right with that anvil.

"When the explosion goes off, people with their trigger cameras never get it. It's a loud noise for those who try to take pictures. The noise is so loud that they can't hold their cameras steady. For a person who has never seen it before, it's a real surprise. We'd blow an anvil straight up! That's a lot of energy. It makes some kick!" —**Gene Purcell, Spring 1991**

PLATE 68 "The competitive part of it would also be the height that you could blow the anvil and how close you could get the anvil to land near the area that you blowed it." —Gene Purcell

"We lived next to the courthouse in Vernon [Alabama]. On the Fourth of July, and sometimes at Christmas, people would bring anvils and shoot them on the courthouse square. There would be dozens of people. Various people would bring their own anvils. I remember doing this for several years.

"One time two men were preparing to shoot their anvil, and they had used all of their fuse. They had been nipping a good bit all day, and they decided to make a fuse. They took a newspaper, put black powder on it, and they rolled it tightly. They thought it would burn slowly. But when they put one end in the powdered anvil and lit the other end, the explosion was instantaneous. They didn't have a second to move away. When the smoke

PLATE 69 "People would bring anvils and shoot them on the courthouse square." —Jim W. Clark

and dust cleared, they were standing there, black and dazed. Their clothes were all tattered. Their hands and arms were full of gravel."

—Jim W. Clark, Spring 1991

ANTY OVER

"For anty over, you divided the people, half on one side of the house and half on the other. They'd throw the ball over the house, and if you caught it and they caught you, then you'd have to go on their side. Then whoever was left on that side, well then, they lost. You'd say, 'Anty over, anty over, send so-and-so over.' " **—Ethel Runion, Spring / Summer 2003**

"We played anty over ball, too. Someone would throw the ball over the house and run around to see who caught it. If it didn't get caught, they'd have to toss it around and let us throw it back over the house again."

—Martha Roane, Winter 1983

"We played what they called anty over—throw a ball over the house, a bunch of children on one side and a bunch on the other side. One, if he'd caught the ball, he'd slip around and strike some of us, and that knocked us out of the game. We played games like that." **—Mrs. E. H. Brown, Summer 1974**

"You see, if you threw the ball over the roof—one team on one side and one on the other—whoever caught it would run around the other side of the house and hit a person with it. That person was out if you could slip around and hit him with it before he could get out of sight of you. And we always had to play with old yarn balls. They wouldn't hurt you. If you got hit on the head with one, it wouldn't hurt—just bounce off."

—Lawton Brooks, Summer 1974

"When I was in school—along when I was about sixteen—our main game was anty over. We'd throw the ball across the schoolhouse. We'd divide up the crowd—part would be on one side and part on the other. We'd throw the ball back and forth, and if anyone on one side caught the ball, they'd all run around and try to tag the ones coming from the other side. Everyone they tagged had to join that side. Sometimes they'd play 'til maybe just one was left, and sometimes not any was left on that side. They just kept workin' like that way. That was a lot of fun. We spent all of our time as far back as I can remember doin' that.

"I got my nose hurt one time. We had a new boy come to school. His first day, it was kind of a cold, bad day, and we were playin' anty over. We ran into each other, and, oh, it just smashed my mouth and nose! I was sick for about a week." **—Marinda Brown, Summer 1974**

"We played anty over. You stay on this side, me on that side. I'd throw the ball over. Whoever catches it wins. I liked to got killed playin' one time. I threw the ball over, and a girl hollered. She ought not to have done that. I started around the corner of the schoolhouse, and we met. I'm tellin' you the truth, I bet I went ten feet out through those rocks—like to killed her, too. We just run face to face. Teacher didn't whip us, though. We said it was just an accident. I never played no more ball."

—Kenny Runion, Summer 1974

"We played anty over. We had a small school, and so we'd throw a ball over to the other side. The other bunch was over there, and they'd try to catch it. Then they'd throw it back, and they'd holler, 'Anty over!' before the ball'd come over." **—Lois Duncan, Spring/Summer 2000**

"We had games even in that one-room school. I think they called it anty over. I don't even know what it meant, but we'd bounce something like a tennis ball over the school or the church—same thing. Some'd be on one side and some on the other and just bounce it back and forth."

—Bob Justus, Fall/Winter 2001

BALL

"The boys played a game similar to baseball in the flat area of the yard. The ball was made of cloth of many colors and sewn together with lots of stitching." **—Willie Elliott, Fall/Winter 1991**

"I can never understand how they play baseball now. We just had one that threw and then one that hit the ball. If he hit it far enough and he went around the bases, he scored. The men and boys used to play baseball. Baseball was *in* then. We never heard of basketball nor football—just baseball. A lot of times girls would get out and play baseball, too."

—Bertha Dockins, Summer 1974

"Everyone played ball together. We raveled up socks and made our own balls. We'd take a rag and ball it up in the center. Some people used rocks for the center. And sometimes we'd make them out of pure yarn and then sew them good after we got them wound up. It was balled up just like you would ball up yarn to knit.

"For the bat, you'd get a common-sized little hickory and trim it down, but generally we'd get a plank about five inches and gauge it down to make a handle for it." **—Ethel Corn, Summer 1974**

"The neighborhood used to play softball all the time. I used to play softball, and I could outrun my brothers and sisters. I could outrun all of 'em. I would hit the ball—and I can hit the ball—and it would just go everywhere. We'd play softball in different places. We usually played down in this pasture down here below my house. We used to have the best time. A lot of times before the road got like it is now, we'd get out in the middle of the road and play ball. I mean, we'd hit the ball. And sometimes we'd be at school, and we would play ball. I used to love to play ball. I mean, I'd hit and get on the base every time. We had one girl that went to school with us. She would always get up there, and we'd have a rock for bases. She'd take the bat, and she'd hit the rock and beat up the base. She'd break the base! We didn't have no base to run to! We had a lot of fun, and there was a lot of kids back then. At school you had a good time playin' 'cause you was playin' ball for recess. It was so much fun you did not want to stop and eat. You just wanted to play. We got in fights and everything. But still, it was all over in a matter of minutes. Everybody would forgive each other, and we'd be right back where we started. We played in the woods, and we used to go pick up apples, grapes, potatoes, and stuff like that." —**Sadie Owens, Fall/Winter 2001**

"Townball was our biggest sport. We played it with a bat. Take the bat—somebody on the opponent's side pitched the bat and you caught it. Then you stacked hands. Whoever came out on top—you had to leave about one-half to one inch at the top—had to be able to throw that bat so far before it was called a legal hold. Then they'd choose their players for each side; the one that had the top hold on the bat chose first. Each side could have as few as three or as many as three or four dozen, if they had that many. And of course you have your three bases, a pitcher, and sometimes a catcher if there's enough. If you caught a ball on the bounce or if the catcher or fielder caught it on a fly, the batter was out. Usually, in runnin' the bases, there was nobody holdin' base, and they just threw the ball *at* you. It was usually a homemade ball made out of twine. When you were between bases, if you were hit, you were out. I've been burnt with them things pretty bad. The ball's center was made from an inner tube when you could get the darn stuff, and the rubber gave it life. That was the main thing to play at school for us boys." —**Buck Carver, Summer 1974**

"We'd play base- and townball. A lot of people back then would play townball. You didn't have to tag anybody—just throw the ball in between them and the base. We did that a lot. We'd called it cow pasture ball. On Sunday evenin', we'd play townball out in the pasture, and we'd have a great crowd of people from different communities come in and play with us. We were a very close and happy family. I had six brothers and five sisters—a dozen. We enjoyed the things we did. We had a real good time playin'."

—J. D. Holcomb, Summer 1992

"We played townball. We had a firm rubber ball and would use the battlin' paddle [a paddle used in washing clothes] to hit the ball with. Usually, we had to whittle another one if we broke it. We made our things that we enjoyed playing with. We'd take a bladder from a hog when it was killed, and, before it got dry, we'd wash it, usually in lye soap, and take an oat straw and blow it up and tie it tight. That was our basketball. We had a goal made out of a hoop that went around a barrel. We tacked it onto the house and another one on the wellhouse about twelve feet opposite."

—Ruby Mae Miller Cheek, Spring/Summer 2005

"We had us a ballground laid off—kept it cleaned off good and everything—and schools would come play baseball with us up here—different schools. And, man, we had a tough bunch—about as mean as they get!"

—Richard Norton, Summer 1974

FOX AND DOGS

"We'd play fox an' dogs. Get an old Sears and Roebuck catalog, tear it to pieces, go off a-strewin' it through th' woods. We'd let him get started about thirty minutes, an' then a whole bunch of 'em trail that, y' know. He'd be th' fox, y' know, an' the whole bunch of us 'ud be th' dogs. Sometimes he'd take us five or ten miles over them mountains, in those rabbit places, briar patches." **—Florence Brooks, Fall 1973**

"We was also bad t' play fox and dogs and holler. One would be a fox, and the others would be a pack of dogs—some of the dogs barkin' at him, you know. We'd tree 'the fox' and then chop him down. Sometimes we'd hurt him a little." **—Buck Carver, Summer 1974**

"I guess we kept in shape 'cause we'd play fox and dogs. You know, one'd be the fox, and one, the dog. 'Course, we really made bows and arrows and spears. I mean we made bows and arrows. We didn't fool around. Luckily, evidently, we didn't shoot at one another much 'cause if we had, we'd a-hurt one another, but we would do this and play all afternoon on Sunday afternoons. Sometimes we'd do things—'course it wasn't safe—like we'd climb Big Face Mountain, they called it, when we got a little older, and it had rock cliffs on it. We'd climb around those things and do all kind of crazy things. One time we was playin' down on another slope. We was playin' on this rock, and one of my good friends, Ted Parker, fell. It was wet for some reason, water seepin' down the rock. He slid all the way down the face of this huge rock. It just scalped the back of his head—scared us to death. Blood was just a-pourin'. Life was great, boys, I'll tell you what. We'd go swimmin' in what we called an old swimmin' hole. It was the baptizin' place, too." —**Bob Justus, Fall/Winter 2001**

"Then during recess our biggest game was dogs and fox. We had somebody appoint somebody to be the fox. The rest of us was dogs. See, we was right in the woods—get up there in them woods. Sometimes we would get way back in the mountains there and makin' so much noise barkin' like dogs, you know, that we couldn't hear that bell ring, and we'd come in late. But the dogs would have to catch the fox and bring him in. When they caught him, they'd have a dog fight. You could hear them. Somebody would catch him—you could tell. You could hear them and go see what was takin' place."

—Harvey J. Miller, Spring 1978

FOX AND GEESE

"Twenty-two pieces of white corn represent the geese. Two pieces of red corn represent the foxes. Foxes may catch the geese, but the geese may not at any time capture the foxes—only use their greater numbers to corner them. The object of the game is to be able to stop the foxes so that they have no other place to move.

"Geese are set on each corner and intersection. The two lower corners on the right and left sides of the foxes (points B, C) are left open. The first move is always made by one fox. He has two choices: (1) capture one of the geese by jumping into an empty space, or (2) move to the centerline (at point A).

"The fox may, at any time, move into an adjacent, empty space or jump over one goose (in any direction) into an empty space beyond, thus capturing that goose. A fox may also move or jump into a space occupied by the other fox.

"Geese may move in any direction into an adjacent, empty space but cannot jump other geese or foxes.

"The small end of the board belongs to the foxes, and they cannot move back down into it; nor can the geese move down there. The line separating the foxes' end of the board from the main playin' surface is called the fence.

"Again, the object of the game is to stop the foxes so that they cannot make another move. It is very difficult to corner the foxes after ten to twelve geese have been captured, so the geese must act quickly to block the foxes."

—Kenny Runion, Spring 1973

PLATE 70 The object of the game is to stop the foxes

"We played fox and geese. We'd just have a board and have it marked off and just played it with corn. Part of the corn would be red, and part would be yellow or white so you could tell whose men were whose. There'd be two players, and you'd just see which one could beat—get the most players off the board. It was a little like playin' checkers." —**Mary Cabe, Summer 1974**

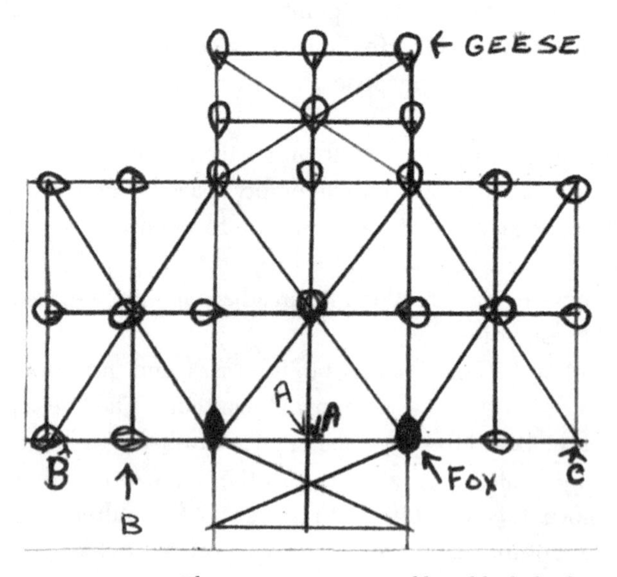

PLATE 71 The geese must act quickly to block the foxes.

TAP HAND

"When we played tap hand, we'd get in a circle facin' the middle. The person who was 'it' would walk around the outside of the circle and tap a person on the head and start runnin' around the circle. The person tapped would chase the one that was 'it,' and if he caught that person before he got back to the empty space in the circle, that person remained 'it.' If the one who was 'it' got into the space in the circle before bein' caught, the one tapped became 'it,' and the game continued." —**Minnie Dailey, Summer 1985**

"Occasionally, we'd have a Saturday night to play. We'd get out and hold hands and make a big ring and play what we call tap hand. One would stay out of the ring and walk around and tap someone, and that one was supposed to run and try to catch the one that tapped him. If he didn't, he had to run around the circle and get back to the place that he left."

—Julia Smith, Summer 1974

"We formed a ring. One stayed on the outside and went around and chose a person to tap, and that person tried to catch the tapper. If he didn't catch the tapper by the time he came back to his place in the circle, he got back in the circle. If he did catch the tapper, then the tapper went around and tapped somebody else." —**Leona "Dink" Carver, Summer 1974**

"We joined hands in a circle, and one would be out. He'd go around and tap someone. The one who was tapped tried to catch the one who tapped. If he did, the one who tapped was out of the game. The person who was tapped went once around the circle to catch the one who tapped him. If he couldn't catch the one who tapped him, they both went back into the game. If the person who was tapped didn't catch the one who tapped him, the person to the right in the circle of the person who was tapped gets to tap next."

—Lelia Gibson, Summer 1974

"We played marbles. We played ring-around-the-rosy, go in and out the windas (that's a singin' game), and we played tappin'. The way you did that was the one that'd be 'out' was gonna do the tappin', and they'd run around the ring and tap somebody and then take off. Then you'd run after 'em, and if you caught 'em, then they had to stay out or get in the middle or some'n. That was tappin'." —**Lois Duncan, Spring/Summer 2000**

DROP THE HANDKERCHIEF

"One of the games we played was drop the handkerchief. Everybody gets around in a ring, and one has a handkerchief. We called the handkerchief 'it' back then. You go around and drop that handkerchief behind somebody; then they grabbed the handkerchief and ran around the ring to see if they could catch you before you got back around to that spot."

—Ethel Runion, Spring / Summer 2003

"We played drop the handkerchief. You get in a circle, and you drop the handkerchief. One would see it, and the other would run around and get it. The one who gets it has to get in the middle."

—Naomi Welborn McClain, Spring / Summer 2004

OTHER GAMES

"I've played marbles, but they were bought marbles. We'd make a square in the dirt and put a marble in each corner and one in the center. You first tried to shoot one corner marble to the center marble. Then you tried the next corner, and so on, 'til you got all of them together. That was pretty hard to do. Maybe we'd play with three, four, or five other children. One person got to continue shooting as long as he got the marbles to the center. And then the next person got to go. Whoever had the most of his own in the center won the game and won the marbles that were in the center."

—Lelia Gibson, Summer 1974

"Now a lot of times we made our own marbles with packed clay. You see, the only heat we had was fireplaces. If you lived next to a patch of clay, you got a bunch of that and made it up in a stiff wad. You worked out your marbles—rolled them in your hands 'til you got them perfectly round—and you got some hot ashes on a shovel and buried a row of marbles and then covered them with more hot ashes. Let them bake 'til they were good and hard. It didn't take too awful long. Change the top ashes two to three times. It'd take an hour maybe. We'd always make one bigger than the others—we used that for the middle man." **—Buck Carver, Summer 1974**

"We used to play games. We'd have candy drawin's when we'd all get together. It was planned ahead of time. We'd buy two or three boxes of stick candy, different colors. We'd break it up, put it in a dishpan, and mix it all together. Somebody'd sit in here with a cloth over the dishpan. You'd have to run your hand in there, and you couldn't see what you was gettin'. We were all coupled up. We'd always let the girls draw, and then we boys would try to match our girlfriend's. If you got one like hers, you got to keep it. If you didn't, you had to put it back and go on. We'd just keep doin' that until we'd get that candy all drawed out of there. Sometimes we'd put in two or three hours. It was fun. We enjoyed it." **—Billy and Annie Long, *A Foxfire Christmas***

"We'd play pleased or displeased, and we'd play crossed questions or crooked answers. That's so funny. You line up a bunch of girls on one side and a bunch of boys on the other; three people tell them separately what they're supposed to ask and answer. Neither one of those three know what the others said. We usually got a man to tell the boys somethin'. They might ask, 'Will you marry me?' Well, no one else knew what the boy was going to ask the girl, and the girls had answers they were supposed to give like 'Come see me sometime,' or 'I'll meet you at the washplace [the creek or branch where the clothes were washed]." —**Burma Patterson, Fall 1985**

"We played a game called the devil and the promised land. A big branch went down through our pasture. Some places it was wide, and some places were narrow enough to jump across pretty good. There'd be about eight or ten of us on one side. We'd put one on the other side, and he was the devil. Now we had to cross the branch and go around him and jump the branch back. Now if he caught us before we made the run around him, we had to go on to the devil's side." —**Lawton Brooks, Summer 1974**

"We had a game that we call green man's garden. We'd play two sides and have one crowd over here and one over there. They said some little somethin' like 'Where are you?'; and the other group would say, 'In the green man's garden.' The first would say, 'What are you doin' in the green man's garden?'

" 'Eating the green man's grapes.'

"Then the reply came back somethin' like 'The green man will get you.'

"The ones over here would run over to the other side, and the ones over there try to catch the ones that have been in the green man's garden. And as many of them as they could catch, they'd put in the soup pot.

"One time they had a water tap out in the yard, and one of them was goin' to tap him. Instead of just runnin' right around the ring, she was goin' to the water tap. One of the other girls was supposed to help her, and they were goin' to get him, put him under that tap, and wet him good. It turned out the other way. He wasn't a very big boy, but he was strong enough to outdo the girls." —**Julia Smith, Summer 1974**

"Miss Jinks, our first woman teacher, taught us green grass. She had us sittin' around on seats in one corner at the wall. She sat back on one of the desks and told us how to play green grass. You start off with 'Here's a crooked crab tree.' And the one that had it said to him had to say it to the next one. And that one would have to turn around quickly and say it to the next one. Each person added something on—like 'the crooked grass that grows under the crooked crab tree,' and we had to say it every bit every time. One would say it to the next one, and he'd say, 'Yes, it's the crooked crab tree.'

"Here's how I think it went:

Person 1: Here's the crooked crab tree.
Person 2: Is it the crooked crab tree?
Person 1: Yes.
Person 2: Here's the crooked grass that grows under the crooked crab tree.
Person 3: Is it the crooked grass that grows under the crooked crab tree?
Person 2: Yes.
Person 3: Here's the crooked [something] on the crooked grass that grows under the crooked crab tree.
Person 4: Is it the . . . etc.

"And they'd make it up as they went along." —**Julia Smith, Summer 1974**

"We used to play hide-and-seek a lot. It's been a long time since I thought of that. We'd all hid, and the person who was 'it' would holler. He used to yell, 'Bushel of wheat, bushel of rye, those ain't hid, holler *I!*' Then any person who wasn't hidden yet would holler 'I!' and the person who was 'it' would wait a little longer before he began hunting for the others."

—Bertha Dockins, Summer 1974

"We played hide the thimble. One person gives out the thimble—pretends to give it to everyone, but only one person gets it . . . just drops it in her hand with everybody sittin' there. Everybody closes their hands and makes like they have it. The person who gives out the thimble asks everyone who has the thimble. If no one guesses who got it, then the person who gave it out that first time has to give it out again. But if they guess who got it, the one who did get it gets to give it out. If nobody can guess it, the person who gave it out says, 'Rise up, thimble,' and the one that has it rises up. Then they have to give it out." —**Florence Brooks, Summer 1974**

"We played thimble, huntin' a thimble [hide the thimble]. You have a thimble in your hand, and you go around and act like you're puttin' it in everybody's hand. But you put the thimble in one person's hand. Then they have to guess which one has the thimble. If they don't guess it, then they have to pay a penalty. They either had to kiss somebody, let somebody kiss them, sing a song, or do a dance. We played spin the bottle, and the one it was pointing at had to pay a penalty like that." —**Louise Tabor, Winter 1986**

"A great bunch of us would get out and pitch horseshoes all day on Saturday and Sunday. That's two days we got to rest. We had a lot of fun. It was a long, sandy place where we'd drive up stobs [stakes]. Four of us would pitch, and if you got close to the stob, you got one point. If you rung it with your horseshoe, you got five points. If you leant the horseshoe up against the stob, you got three points. Two people were on each team; whichever team lost would set down, and two more would get up and pitch against the winners. If they lost, they'd set down. That's the only way you could tell the champions, pitching against each other." —**D. B. Dayton, Summer 1980**

"Jackstraw was one of the first games I learned. I learned to play it with Daddy before I even went to school. That was our amusement on rainy days or Sunday.

"We had little straws that were probably six inches long. They were all colors. We also had two little wire hooks. We would shuffle the straws out in a big heap on the table. Then each player, with his hook, would try to pull out as many straws as he could without disturbing all the others; he couldn't let any of them shake or fall, or his turn was up. The person with the most straws won." —**Lola Cannon, Summer 1974**

"Kitty walks a corner, that's a game we used to play a lot. One person is kitty, and he goes around to everybody in a circle. He moves and pats you and tries to get you to laugh. If someone can't control their emotions and smiles or laughs, he has to become the kitty." —**Marinda Brown, Summer 1974**

"Daddy'd play with us—blindfold in th' house when we were young. And on Christmas when th' children would come in—th' neighbors always visited one another then—he would play a finger game. He'd make us put our four fingers down thataway [hanging]. I forget just this minute what he called it. And he'd count 'em, y' know, and whichever it came out on, he had somethin' to do with it. We'd have t' go and do it. Apparently, there was some sort of rhyme or verse that went along with the countin', and the person's finger that the verse ended on would have to go and do some little thing. Then the counting would start again until all the players had had to do somethin'.

"Then he'd play club first stack up, and he had a great ceremony. He'd say he'd knock it off or take it off. The person who starts makes a fist with the thumb of that stickin' up. The next person makes a fist around that thumb, stickin' his own thumb up for the next person to lock onto, and so on until there is a vertical stack of fists all interlocked. Then the person whose fist is on the bottom removes it and says, 'You want me to knock it off, take it off, or let the crows pick it off?' The person whose fist is on the top grips the thumb beneath it tightly, tells how he wants the other to try to remove his fist, and then tries to keep him from doin' it. If he said, 'Knock it off,' you bet he knocked it off!

"And there was another game called slap, hug, and kiss. One player would sit in a chair blindfolded. Another player would stand behind him, and the rest of the players would be in a line in front of the blindfolded person. The one standin' behind would make a silent signal that meant a slap, a hug, or a kiss. Then he would ask the blindfolded person to call out the name of one of the players in the line. The blindfold would be removed, and that person would have to go to the player whose name he had called out and do to him whatever the silent signal had indicated.

"And he just played with us and enjoyed playin' with us like that."

—Anna Howard, Spring 1972

"We used to play marching around eleven. We'd catch hands and go 'round and 'round and sing a little song. I don't remember what it was now!"

—Minnie Dailey, Summer 1985

"We had a game we played called marchin' around the level. We'd all catch hands, and we'd sing:

We're marchin' around the level,
We're marchin' around the level,
For we have gained today.
Good-bye, I hate to leave you,
Good-bye, I hate to leave you,
For we have gained today.
One kiss and I will leave you,
One kiss and I will leave you,
For we have gained the way.

"While we sang that, we'd march. We'd catch hands and go in pairs and march like soldiers. We'd always get on level ground to do it because that went with the song. We'd march 'in the level.' " **—Lelia Gibson, Summer 1974**

"One game we played I called peggy. I've asked people around the country if they've ever heard of it. I said that they ought to market peggy or somethin', but it's a game that could be dangerous because you have to have enough room to play it. You go out here in the woods somewhere and cut a long stick. You would probably hunt all day tryin' to find a stick in the size that you wanted. You'd cut little pieces of wood about a foot long or less, usually out of persimmon. You had a peg in the ground, and you'd tap that peg. When it bounced up in the air, you tried to hit it. We would get down in the park and play there nearly half a day. Sometimes you'd have ten, twelve, or fifteen players, and you could play partners. If you lost, you had to wait your turn. A lot of times, a peggy would break in two. If a peggy broke in two, the longest part of it was the one that counted. I guess I played peggy when I was twelve, thirteen, fourteen, or fifteen years old."

—Johnny Mize, Summer 1989

"We'd play blindfold and pleased an' displeased—it 'as a little ol' thing—a gang of us 'ud be sittin' around, and one of us would be up all th' time. Well, if I was th' one that 'as up, I'd ask you if you were pleased or displeased. If you'd say you're pleased, I asked, 'What pleased y'?' An' you could say, 'A-settin' with so-an'-so, I'm pleased.' If you're displeased, I'd say, 'What will it take t' please you?' Well now, you might say you'd be pleased if so-an'-so would get up an' go over an' set with a certain person, or for that person to get up an' set with another. Whatever you put on 'em, they had t' do. If they didn't do that, why, they'd black that person's face. If y' played it, y' had t' play it out, but it just goes on around like that. Sometimes we'd make a person get out an' walk plumb around th' house in th' coldest time in the weather." **—Lawton Brooks, Fall 1973**

"Sue and Hansel made a tennis court in back of the big barn with backstops. I usually ran after stray balls. When they both went to college, I was thirteen, and I had to start all over again, as grass had taken over the court. I was playin' with Sue's racket by myself against the front of the barn. I got the idea I could make my court in the horse lot. With our ax, I cut down four slender pine trees about twelve feet tall, scaled them with a drawing knife, dragged them to the house, dug four holes for the posts, laid them down in front of the holes, and nailed some old chicken wire across. Here was a time to have some help. Luther was the only brother there, so with the help of cousins next door, we tied ropes from the mules' gear to the top of the posts and pulled the posts upright into the holes. So I was ready to lay off my tennis court. There was always something to make white lines out of when outhouses were cleaned. Using a large funnel, I went to work. I had to cut it [the court] short two feet. We enjoyed this court lots of days, playin' with relatives nearby. The only one I could not beat was Aunt Retta's son. He was left-handed and was so quick!" **—Ruby Mae Miller Cheek, Spring / Summer 2005**

"We'd also play William Trembletoe. Put your fingers down and count 'em off while sayin' a little rhyme:

William Trembletoe, he's a good fisherman—
Catches his hens and puts 'em in the pan.
Some lays eggs; some none—
Wire, briar, limberlock,
Three geese found in a flock—
O-U-T spells out*!*

"Now that's all I know." —**Minnie Dailey, Summer 1985**

"Sometimes we'd carry the ducks up to the top of the high hill, and we'd fly them ducks back to see them light [land] in the lake. We'd carry them way up on the side of the mountain and throw them and watch them fly back to the pond.

"And we used to play William Shinfull:

William Shinfull, he's a good fisherman—
Catches 'em at hand; put 'em in a pan.
Some lay eggs; some lay none—
War [wire], brar [briar], limberlock,
Three geese in the flock.
Flock fell down; the mouse run around—
O-U-T spells out on a rock dish cloud.

"Whichever one it spelled 'out' on, they did go hide. And then we'd hunt them. We used to play all kinds of little ol' games. We'd get out of a night and play hide-and-seek 'til midnight." —**Magline Webb Zoellner, Spring 1977**

TOYS

"Whenever you saw me, you saw that slingshot . . . When my brother would do something I did not like, he would run to get away from me. If he did not get away, then . . . flip!" —**Thomas Coy Cheek**

"Yeah, the summer of '42, it was just under way. We were much more interested in comic books. We didn't have the G.I. Joes or any toys like that, but we did have battles with spitwads. We would fold up paper and put 'em on a rubberband. And sometimes we'd drive two nails into a board, and we'd get all these huge rubberbands like you would use with model airplanes. We'd stretch 'em across the board, and, boy, you could really pop somebody with those things! 'Course, the camp leader frowned on all this, so what we'd do is we'd have our metal can with tennis balls in it—you'd buy these cans, and they had three tennis balls in them. You'd take the tennis balls out, and you'd fill 'em up with all your ammunition and your rubberbands and everything, and you'd just put one tennis ball on the top so everybody would think it was nothing but tennis balls. Then when the battles would start, like after dark, we would get the ammunition out, and we'd usually bombard the next cabin 'cause the cabins were real close together. In fact, between cabins 18 and 19, where I was, there was just a walkway. There was just that short distance between each of those cabins, so you could easily bombard the guy in the next cabin with things. One of our favorite pranks was to make what we called a coat hanger bed. We would sneak some coat hangers in under the mattress and prop the end of it so that it was just barely supported by the coat hanger. So when somebody jumped up on it, the coat hangers would bend, and the bed would collapse."

—Rutherford ("Ruddy") Ellis, Jr., Spring / Summer 1997

DOLLS

"I never did have but one doll. Uncle Jepp's wife made it, and I was so proud of it. I was as proud of that doll as somebody now would be if it cost $2,500. She made me that doll for lookin' after the kids so she could hoe corn . . . She made me that one, and it had a black dress. We didn't have any toys, you know." **—Blanche Harkins, Spring 1975**

"Mama used to make dolls. You could also get rag dolls in the stores. Then they went to makin' dolls with just their heads filled and then sleepy dolls. I was a pretty good-sized youngun before I ever saw any sleepy dolls. There weren't many toys back when I was growin' up.

"I can remember my first doll. They had just come out with what they called the Dutch doll. Their body would be stuffed with straw, but their arms and legs and faces would be delft. My sister and I had sleepy dolls, and mine wouldn't go to sleep. Mel [her brother] was always doin' somethin'. He told me to take my doll and hit it over the plow handle, and it would go to sleep. I did, and it broke that doll's head all to pieces. It was made out of the same thing that cups and saucers were made of.

"We'd cut doll clothes like we'd cut dresses for a baby, and after I got older, that was the way I learned to cut and sew."

—Ethel Corn, Summer 1974

PLATE 72 "I never did have but one doll. Uncle Jepp's wife made it." —Blanche Harkins

"There's the only toy I ever owned in my life. [She shows us a small, old doll.] I wouldn't take a nickel for that thing. The dress is old, but not as old as the head. I've played with that thing, y' know. I've worn out several dresses, and it had to have more dresses made. I expect it would be at least seventy years old, maybe seventy-five.

"You had to make the body and fit it to that little head. That's all there was. Now that's Pard—that's her name. That was my partner, y' know, and I called her Pard." —**Mrs. E. H. Brown, Summer 1974**

"Most times, when we made rag dolls, we took a little knob of cotton and packed it tightly in a cloth and wound it around for its neck. Then we rolled another roll and fastened it to that for arms. Sometimes we made legs the same way, but most times we just made heads and arms and let them have a long dress.

"I had one doll that was big enough to wear my baby clothes. It was too big for me really, but they wanted me to have it. I didn't have china dolls. Some of the neighbors' children did. They were more expensive. Later on, I had bought dolls with papier-mâché heads and legs and everything, but they weren't the commercial toys made in those days that there are today.

"We didn't make the cornshuck dolls then. I don't remember seein' them until some years later when they got to sellin' them in craft shops. We didn't know about that. And I didn't know about apple-head dolls either."

—Lola Cannon, Summer 1974

"Mama made me a rag doll on a forked stick and put a head on it. I forgot what she made the hair out of now, but that was my doll. We didn't have no bought toys then. She made me a doll out o' that forked stick and made the head and arms out o' rags and legs out o' that forked stick. We'd play with corncobs and build pigpens. Dishes that had been broke, we had to play with them. We'd ride sticks like it was our horse."

—Effie Mae Speed Bleckley, Spring/Summer 2004

"I was told that after I was born, Mama and Papa decided they were not going to have any more children. My parents ordered a diaphragm from my father's half brother, Dr. Oscar Miller. They had to order it from another country since diaphragms were not legal here. One day when our parents were visiting someone, my two oldest sisters got into Mother's trunk where she kept her best things: lace, material, etc. Sue, the oldest, was going to make some doll clothes for Betty—she had a bisque doll she received from Santa. Lizzie (later called Betty) found the diaphragm and said, 'This will make a good doll's hat.' She stretched it over the curly hair of the doll and stuck a beautiful hatpin in it to hold it on. Some years later, after Anna and Lois were born, Sue told Mama she should not have any more children. Mother found out about the hatpin and told Sue it was her fault. Then came Lucy and George."

—Ruby Mae Miller Cheek, Spring/Summer 2005

Cornshuck Doll

The materials needed to make a cornshuck doll are a ball of twine or crocheting thread (not nylon, as it stretches); scissors; a bowl of water to dampen the shucks; clean shucks—white, or any available colors (mildewed or dark shucks may be used for bottom layers of skirt and inside parts of dolls); and corn silks—blond, red, and brown—for hair.

Different people have told us varied lengths of time to wet the shucks before using. It seems the best formula to follow for dolls is to trim a few shucks, dip in water for three to five minutes, then drain and use. The shucks seem easier to use when dampened for a short time rather than soaked. As the shucks dry on the newly made doll, they will fluff out. The sashes will tighten up so that they don't come untied when dry.

There are many variations of the cornshuck dolls. Some wear dyed dresses—the shucks are dyed just like fabric before making the dolls. There are boy dolls with pants; there are various sizes from three to four inches high to those about twelve inches high.

The pattern is a basic style, and once you get the gist of making a cornshuck doll, you will develop your own techniques and try out various methods of your own.

The following are steps to make the various parts of a cornshuck doll:

Head "Cut a cornshuck two inches wide and six inches long. Fold over lengthwise, making it one inch wide. Fold this down several times to make the filling for the head. Cover with another shuck. This shuck will extend below the neck to form the upper body of the doll. Tie this at the neck to hold it tight.

Arms "Take two shucks about the same size for the arms. Twist the shucks. (One shuck is used for each arm.) Bend each twisted shuck in half and tie them on—one on either side of the body at the neck—with string. Take another shuck and wrap one arm—forming a sleeve beginning about one-fourth inch from the folded end (hand) and wrap back toward the head. Bring the end of the shuck across the back of the doll diagonally to the waist. Do the same for the other arm. The diagonal strips crisscross in the back and are tied with a piece of string at the waist. Now cover the body with two shucks—one goes across each shoulder. They crisscross in back and front. Tie these at the waist with string.

Skirt "Place shucks lengthwise, one at a time, around the waist to form the full, long skirt. Use as many shucks as needed for desired fullness. Tie at the waist with string. Trim the skirt to make it even so that the doll will stand straight.

Bodice "Crisscross two shucks over the shoulders and bring down below the waist in front and back and arms. Fold another shuck into a long, narrow strip. Put around the waist and tie as a sash in back to hold the bodice secure. An apron may be added before the sash is tied by cutting a shuck into a heart shape and placing it around the waist—narrow end of shuck at the waist.

Hair "Use corn silks. Dampen the silks and put over the doll's face. Tie silks with string around the forehead. Flip the hair to the back, exposing the face. The hair will completely cover the string.

Hat "Take a one-and-a-half-inch-wide strip of shuck about six inches long. Place over the head, leaving hair exposed right above the face. Fold the hat down over the back of the head. Then fold in the sides to the middle, bunching in back. Tie with string and cover with narrow shuck for the hat tie. You may draw a face on with a pen and ink.

Broom "Take several shucks about three inches long and tie with string about a third of the way down. Take a straight pin and shred the lower two-thirds. Stick a toothpick or small stick in the top for the handle. Touch a little glue to the end of the stick to make it stay. The doll may also hold a bucket or a bunch of small, dried flowers. Any small, deep container (as a plastic cup) may be used for a bucket. Punch holes in each side of the 'bucket' and run a twisted shuck through the doll's hand and then through the holes of the bucket to form a handle." —**Daisy Justice, Spring 1974**

Cucumber Doll

"I'm going to make a cucumber doll like me an' my sister, Beulah, used t' play with. You need a knife, a cucumber, scissors, some cloth, a needle, and a safety pin. We'd pin a diaper on them and make a 'dress' out of a square cloth—fold a hem, gather it with a needle and thread, and tie it around its neck. We used t' have a lot o' fun playin' with those things. We used t' make 'em and feed 'em. The doll is hollowed out, so the 'food' goes right through.

PLATE 73 "[O]nce you get the gist of making a cornshuck doll, you will develop your own techniques." —Daisy Justice

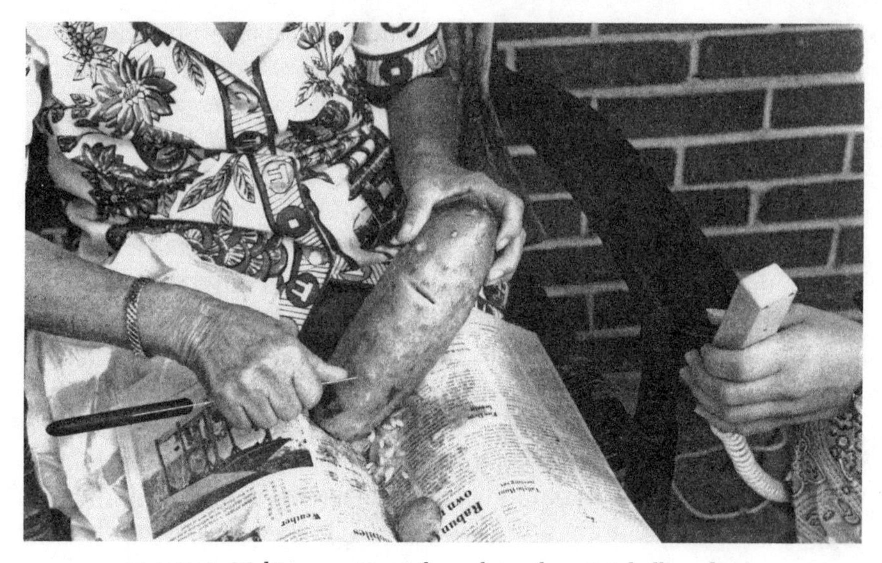

PLATE 74 Making sure to cut through to where it is hollowed out, cut a notch where you want the mouth.

We made clay mud with water, poured it in 'em, and then the diaper was in a mess. We'd take it off and change it. We never fed it anything else. Milk would have gone down it, but we was in a Depression—we didn't have enough of that. We'd get mountain moss off a log, make 'em a bed, put 'em in th' bed. We didn't put hair on it, but, you know, if we'd thought of it, we could o' got corn silks and made 'em some hair. The doll wouldn't last more than a day or two because 'drunkards' [fruit flies] would get after it.

"I don't know of anybody ever doin' that but me and my sister, Beulah. She was four years older than me, but she had to play with me or else."

The following are Florence Brooks's steps in making a cucumber doll [See Winter 1975]:

- Any cucumber will do, but Florence prefers to use a long one—ten inches or more. The greener it is, the better.
- Cut about an inch off the bottom end of the cucumber.
- Using a knife, scrape out the seeds and pulp to the point where you plan to cut the mouth.
- Cut a notch where you want the mouth, making sure you cut through to where it is hollowed out.
- Using the point of the knife, cut out the eyes and nose and stick small pebbles in the eyeholes to make them stand out more.
- To make the diaper, take a piece of cloth about six inches square and fold in half diagonally and pin it on as you would a diaper.

- To fashion the dress (really a skirt), use a piece of material about ten inches square.
- Fold down the waistband and gather it with a needle and thread.
- Using the ends of the thread with which you gathered the waistband, tie the dress around the "neck" of the doll.

Potato Head Doll

"We had Raggedy Ann dolls, and my older sister made dolls—my father wouldn't buy dolls. Back then, people had to work for a livin'. Dad didn't believe in foolishness, so we didn't have any toys. My older sister made my first doll, and I guess I was eight or ten years old. We made rag dolls and cornshuck dolls, and then we learned to do potato heads—you take potatoes and make a doll. You get one big potato and get sticks and make its legs.

PLATE 75 For the diaper, take a piece of cloth about six inches square, fold it in half diagonally, and pin it on.

Then you get a smaller potato and make its head and find sticks for his arms. A potato will last a long time." —**Harriet Echols, Summer 1974**

Apple Doll

To make an apple doll, Miss Francis likes to use Rome Beauty, which is a tart apple. She prefers apples picked in the fall, as the earlier apples are more prone to rot.

"Peel the apple but do not core it. Scrape it smooth. Cut out slight hollows for the eyes—make a diagonal cut on each side for the nose. Cut a slit for the mouth; then scrape off more around the nose shape. The stem of the apple is at the top of the head. Soak in salt water for thirty-six hours. This preserves the apple and keeps it white. Some people also use lemon juice to keep the apples from discoloring.

"After the apple is taken out of the salt water, insert beads for the eyes. These can be bought at a dime store or through a doll supply house. Run an eighteen-inch piece of floral wire through the apple. A one-inch loop should extend from the top. The wire left at the bottom is used to form the body.

"Dry in a 200-degree oven from six to eight hours. Attach a drapery hook to the loop at the top of the apple and hang this from the rack in the oven. After this, let the head stand in a dry place at room temperature for another twelve to fourteen days to completely dry out. It will shrink and form the facial features in this time. Use watercolor or embroidery paint to paint color into the face. Then spray with varnish spray plastic to further preserve the head.

"Next, measure the body. The length of the body is determined by the size of the head. Figure that the body should be seven times as long as the head. If the head is one and a half inches, the body should be at least ten to eleven inches long. For the arms, take another wire. The length is determined by the total length of the body from head to toe. The arms should be the same length. Fold in half and hang around the neck by twisting through the shoulders so the arms will extend from the shoulders.

"Cotton batting is used to pad the body and neck. Narrow strips of cloth—T-shirt material works well—are wrapped around the neck. Wrap the body down to the waist. Tack the ends with needle and thread. Go from waist to crotch. Then pad and wrap the legs separately, starting at the feet and working up to the crotch.

"Apple hands are shaped and dried the same way as the heads. Toothpicks are inserted in them so that they may be tied to the arms with thread. Pad the arms with cotton going from the hands to the shoulders, crossing cloth strips in back and front. Tack the ends.

PLATE 76 "Make whatever type character you feel the face fits." —Hilda Francis

"Put on shoes and socks ordered from a doll supply house. Dress in regular doll-sized clothes. Make whatever type character you feel the face fits." **—Hilda Francis, Summer/Fall 1975**

"For an apple-head doll, you peel an apple, and while the apple is fresh, you shape features on it with a teaspoon. And then the best part is to string them up with a string through the center. In a dry, airy place, hang them up and let them shrivel. When they shrivel, the features you have made are still there. You put in tiny sequins or somethin' for the eyes and little pearl beads for the teeth. The texture of the dried apple looks like a real old person's skin. They're really interesting. I expect they'd last a long time. If you got one wet, I imagine it'd lose its shape. You see a lot of them in the craft shops and such places." **—Lola Cannon, Summer 1974**

WAGONS

"We used to make wagons. We'd saw the wheels out of old black gum trees—saw them about three inches thick. I had a big old auger to bore a hole through the wheels, and we'd take soap and grease them things with old homemade soap. We'd get them slick, and they'd stay slick. We had to push the wagons to the top of the hill to ride down.

"We'd tie a rope to the front axle and have our seat over the back wheels, and we'd guide it with the ropes. You get started down the mountain, and you could just fly!" **—Lawton Brooks, Summer 1974**

"My daddy used to make little wooden wagons for us. He always made the boys one. You cut the wheels out of slices of big logs like Claude's [her son] got out here. They would bore a hole in the center of each one for the wheels, and then make the axles. It wouldn't take more than about a week to make the wagons if he'd get at it. He'd get on there and just ride. We would have the best time on them little ol' wagons! All of us played—the girls and the boys. We loved that.

"My daddy would also make sleds, and he would go and try to find a piece of timber, you know, that was kindly bowed up to make the runners. He'd get another piece and kindly nail it on the runner. If he couldn't, he'd hew it down, and then he'd put a bed in it, floor it, and then the sides. He'd put two little nails there up front and put us a chain there, you know. You could either pull it or get in it and sit and get pulled. You could also use staples in place of the nails. The sled was about three feet wide by three and a half feet long.

"You would also steer it with that chain or rope. Like if you was goin' to get in at the top of that hill and come down, see, you've got a rope in each hand, and you can kindly guide it. If you didn't have that, you'd go every which way, or you'd run in the ditch. Boy, we'd use our little sleds 'til the runners would be just as slick as it could be. The more you use it, the slicker it'd be." —**Icie Rickman, Fall 1989**

"We made our toys back then, son! We'd go to the woods and cut down a pine tree and saw us some wheels off of it, bore a hole in that wheel, and make our wagons that we would play with. Whatever we wanted to play with, we made it." —**Lois Ann Martin, Spring/Summer 2002**

"Lots has changed. My boys didn't have any toys or games, only somethin' that they made. Their daddy would make wheels off a tree trunk for them to put on a wagon. The older ones never had nothin' bought. The last two had more than the first two because the older boys would buy them things. They'd make them a wheel and get 'em a little stick and put a piece across there and roll that thing in front of them. They'd get up there on the hill and come down there just a-flyin'.

"It seems to me like they enjoyed it a whole lot more than the children do now with all the toys and things they've got. Now they have so many toys. They play with them a day or two, and that's it. Then they throw them around." —**Addie Norton, Fall 1976**

"Most of what we played with, we made ourself. The boys would saw black gum logs and get wheels off of it and make wagons. A lot of times, they'd get out in the woods and cut down a young tree and leave the stump up high. Then they would split the tree and mount it on the stump and make a merry-go-round—get one on each end and ride around, you know. We had to make what we had to play with mostly."

—Amanda Turpin, Summer 1981

"My brothers would get out and cut some wheels and make an old-fashioned wagon. I mean, just put sticks in and put wheels on it. They'd take a saw and saw the logs about two inches thick for the wheels, and then they'd nail them to hold them in there. They took some axles, and then they'd put these wheels on. Then they'd pull them around, and if it come a snow or anything, they'd get on it and run down the mountain. That was a lot of fun! They'd put a rope on it, and it worked kind of like a steerin' wheel." **—Bertha Dockins, Summer 1974**

"We made wagons. We made the wheels out of old black gum—made many of them. Used to haul wood on them. We'd make the darn things and get up on a mountain—you steered 'em with your feet. And to pull them, you tied a rope on each end of the front axle. We kept those wheels greased with axle grease 'til they rolled pretty easy. We'd get on that mountain, and sometimes the thing would get goin' so fast where we'd see we couldn't make the curve. We'd bail off and leave the thing and let her go. I guess we got up to twenty mile an hour, maybe more." **—Buck Carver, Summer 1974**

SNOW SLEDS

"Oh, the children had sleds, but these were made just about like the big ones, which were used for haulin' loads. Whenever it'd snow, they'd get out their sleds, and they did have a time with them! Why, even my children did that! They'd go up on a mountain and turn those sleds loose. Two or three of them would get on and come down the mountain."

—Bertha Dockins, Summer 1974

"We made sleds to ride when the snow was on the ground. We made the runners out of sourwood. They often grow with the proper crook in them for runners. One time we didn't have a sled. There come a big ol' snow, and we had a big ladder. We drug it and started back down the hill, and the thing left the road and run aground a stump. It swapped ends—liked to have killed both of us! It was my daddy's ladder. It tore the ladder up and tore us up, too. My brother, he was hurt pretty bad for quite a while."

—Lawton Brooks, Summer 1974

PLAYHOUSES

"When we moved to Georgia, my father bought land with lots of pine trees on it, and he was clearin' it. He left a piece just behind the barn so the cows would have shade, and there were a lot of little poles. Our brother cut us poles and built us a little log house, and each of us girls had a room. He whittled us out all kinds of cooking utensils, and I learned to do it, too. It was as long as across this house. We just played house."

—Harriet Echols, Summer 1974

"The children took leaves and pinned them together with little sticks, and fenced in a place for the house. They'd make straw brooms and sweep the house out. They'd take pieces of dishes and anything they could find for their playhouses.

"All little girls had a playhouse, and they'd just play there hours at a time. They'd take their dolls—I don't believe they made dollhouses—I think they just played with their dolls in the playhouse. They'd set up rocks for tables and chairs and make their little doll a chair to sit in. The boys in the family would make little doll beds out of cornstalks." **—Ada Kelly, Summer 1974**

"We'd make our playhouse out in the woods. We used broken dishes. We'd get green moss for carpet and get flat rocks to make beds. We'd fix us a table and eat off our broken dishes. We just had the best time."

—Lelia Gibson, Summer 1974

"I used to play dolls—made a few, not many. My mother and aunt did most of the makin'. I've made a dollhouse all by myself, and I had a good time just like I do now.

"I had two cousins, and we stayed together a lot. We made playhouses—didn't have anything much to put in them like children do anymore, but we had playhouses. We'd get a box for the house and make little beds to go in there.

"In the fall of the year, we'd get green leaves, red leaves, and yellow leaves and pin them all together and make big ribbons. We'd put them all over our playhouses. We decorated them up right pretty. One time me and one of my neighbors was playin' together in the playhouse, and we pinned some leaves together. We happened to get ahold of a white summate [sumac] tree that had pretty yellow leaves on it. We pinned those together and put them in our playhouse, and it was just a little while until I was poisoned from the toe to the head and all over my feet. I couldn't even turn over in the bed. My daddy had to turn me. I was poisoned all over."

—Addie Norton, Fall 1976

GUNS

"We had just what they made us—nothin' but popguns and squirt guns. You'd chew up paper for this ol' popgun, pull it back, and it'd spit. We had 'em. I reckon there's still such a thing now as that. We made 'em out of elder tree branches." **—Kenny Runion, Summer, 1974**

"We had another toy we made with big spools—it had a big opening that would hold a grain of corn or a pea or bean. Well, we'd take a little carpet tack or a sprig, tack this rubberband around—tack them both with one tack. We had a plunger in back; it went back a ways, and this rubberband came around it. We had a little slot in the plunger so it'd hold in that slot—put a pea or a grain of corn in there, and it'd send a pretty good ways. We had a kind of corn with little old slick and hard kernels. That stuff would whack pretty good in those little ol' corn guns.

"But nearly anything we had those days was homemade. To tell you the truth, there was very few toys on the market, and what few there were, we couldn't afford. We just didn't have the money.

"We had our popguns. We'd get an elder—that's pithy [soft, sponge-like substance in the center of the stem]. First thing, it had to be good and straight. We'd hew us out a stick to punch that pith out with. Sometimes that pith would pack up in that and maybe jump out three to four feet when it did pop out. You get all that pith out, and then you loaded them with spitballs. They'd make a pretty crackin' racket. We always had one load in front and another one in the other side with a ramrod. 'Course, that's compressed air in there. Lots of time we'd blow in the barrel, but that didn't help any, I don't think. When you pushed the back spitball up with the ramrod, it threw the front ball out. Some of them shoot pretty doggone hard. I've nearly had blisters on me from those." **—Buck Carver, Summer 1974**

HOOPS/BANDS AND WIRE

"We'd get small steel bands—like those that go around a wheel—and we'd get two sticks and put them together in the shape of a T. You go along and guide the band—we got a lot of kick out of runnin' them things. Just had old dirt roads to run them in. There weren't any cars to run you out of the road, so then you had the whole road." **—Lawton Brooks, Summer 1974**

"We'd get a hoop off a wooden barrel, a wooden hoop. Then we'd get a stick with a bend in it. We'd start off and roll the hoop with the bent stick—just run and roll 'til we gave out. The stick had to have a little bend in it—you couldn't stabilize the hoop just standin' still. The crook in the hoop would stabilize it." **—Lelia Gibson, Summer 1974**

PLATE 77 "Whenever you saw me, you saw that slingshot." —Thomas Coy Cheek

SLINGSHOTS

"The boys made slingshots. They'd cut them a forked stick—had to be about seven to eight inches long. And on the ends of the forks, they used rubber and wrapped it around those forks. They used string to hold it secure. Then they'd put a rock in the center of the rubberband, pull it back, and let it go."

—Lelia Gibson, Summer 1974

"My brothers are all older, and most of them were gone before I got along too far. I was the baby of four boys. I had one bad habit, I guess you might call it. Whenever you saw me, you saw that slingshot, which is a forked stick with two rubberbands that were fixed to hold a rock. I kept one of them in my pocket all the time. I would shoot just to shoot, and I would not shoot anything in particular. When my brother would do something I did not like, he would run to get away from me. If he did not get away, then . . . flip! I was pretty good with it." **—Thomas Coy Cheek, Fall/Winter 2003**

OTHER TOYS

Tom Walkers

"We made Tom Walkers. Me and Marie has made a many a one. They are things like crutches, only you put steps on 'em and get on them steps. Yeah,

PLATE 78 Roy Roberts on a pair of Tom Walkers he made for the children who stay at his cabins.

that's what we used to play with, and that was as famous back then, son, as it is if you was to get a new car. Back then, we'd be just as happy with such as that as you would be with a new car today."

—Lois Ann Martin, Spring/Summer 2002

Tops

"We had homemade tops. They usually consisted of a spinner. You take a spool and whittle it to a sharp point. Then take out a round peg and plug it in the hole of the spool and slope it to a sharp point. Take that in your fingers and spin it on the floor." —**Buck Carver, Summer 1974**

Dumbbulls

"Bill Lamb, my uncle, was bad to make things—he'd make what they called the dumbbull. It was made in a way that when you whizzed it around, it would make an awful racket. He'd take a plank and whittle it down thin—about ten inches long by three inches wide—and sharpen the edges in some way and bore a hole in one end. You'd attach a string to it—about five feet long—and whirl it around, and it'd make the awfullest racket you ever heard!" [We've been told this toy was also called a bull-roarer and that it sounds like a bull's bellowing.] **—Ethel Corn, Summer 1974**

Bubble Blowers

"We used to get an old sewing thread spool, take some soap, and make a lather in water. We'd dip one end of the spool in the lather and blow through the other end and make bubbles. They'd be different colors—they'd be red, pink, blue, all colors." **—Lelia Gibson, Summer 1974**

Bow and Arrow

"We used to use mulberry roots for a string. They're real yellow. Dig up a root, and the bark will peel off just like nothin'. And there ain't no way you can break that.

"You could use that mulberry root for the string for a bow and arrow, and we used to take a stick and make an arrow out of it. Usually we could whittle it down and drive a tack or somethin' in the tip to shoot at birds. I've killed lots of birds, and I'm sorry to say it. That's one of the things I've regretted in my life. There was all sorts of birds back then. Now there's none. I try to keep them fed all the time now." **—Arch Bishop, Winter 1989**

Crossbows

"I used to make an old wooden crossbow—made somethin' like a gun. I'd get a plank and saw it out like the stock of a gun; made a bow like for a plain bow and arrows and mount the bow crosswise to the gun stock at the front. Then I'd string the bow and make a trigger in the gun stock t' hold the string back, set my arrow in the bow, and pull the string back ready to shoot the arrow. The trigger'd hold the arrow ready to shoot 'til I pulled it, and it'd slip up the string and shoot the arrow." **—Lawton Brooks, Summer 1974**

PARTIES

A boy and a girl would draw a piece of candy, and if they got two sticks just alike, they could keep it; if they didn't, they put it back. I had lots of boyfriends.

—Oza Coffee Kilby

Corn shuckin's? Candy pullin'? Most horrified teens today would ask, "What kind of party is *that*?" Parties in the old days were neighborhood events. Strict parents let their children attend these supervised gatherings, which were held in the church, at the school, or at a neighbor's—no "sex, lies, or videotape" to corrupt . . . just good, clean fun.

The purpose of some gatherings was to help a neighbor. When the time came for harvesting corn, the whole neighborhood would come together and help one another by holding cornshucking parties. They would have one at one house one night, and the next night they would go to someone else's house. To make the parties more fun, they even gave prizes to people who found red ears of corn hidden in those gigantic heaps of yellow ears. Upon shucking all of the corn for the day, folks would have supper and then a dance. Other parties they held that grew from necessity were pea thrashings and quiltings.

Although some of the parties were to aid friends and neighbors, other parties were strictly for fun. Socializing was the point of these get-togethers. Many a girl's heart fluttered at the thought of a special beau's walking her home and holding her hand. That kind of innocence is refreshing when compared with the worldliness of folks today and with the decadent lifestyle of many of today's teens (and adults). Perhaps we do need to return to the good, clean living and good, clean fun of days gone by. I, for one, would welcome that change.

—Amanda Carpenter

BIRTHDAY PARTIES

Our parents would always make us a cake and invite some of our friends in. An' we'd always get some kind of little present, like clothes t' wear, socks, maybe a rag doll. —Florence Brooks

"The family always did somethin', baked a cake or somethin' for the birthday—just not too much difference in that . . . about like they do now, I guess. Only now, children have lots more toys—too many. Don't know how to appreciate them. I really do think that's true."

—Ada Kelly, Winter 1973

"I generally got a good whippin'. Well, all they'd do . . . they'd just say, 'Well, it's your birthday.' An' that 'as it." **—Kenny Runion, Winter 1973**

"For th' birthday—just a good dinner an' always Mommy (we thought she 'as the best cook ever—she loved to cook) would bake party cakes, an' they wasn't only pretty, they 'as good. An' they wasn't no bought cake mix."

—Lucy Lamb, Winter 1973

ICE CREAM PARTIES

"We had ice cream parties, too—usually on Saturday night. See, most ever'body had four 'r five cows, and we'd make boiled custards—you know, that's fixed with milk and eggs and sugar and flavorin'. It's delicious, but where y' put a lot o' eggs in it, it's s' rich y' can't eat much of it. We'd get about five ice cream freezers and invite th' youngsters in. And we'd get in th' parlor and get around th' organ 'r piano and sing and play games. See, we didn't have anywhere t' go. And that's what we did for our recreation was our parties." **—Harriet Echols, Spring/Summer 1971**

CANDY DRAWIN'S

"When they had a candy drawin', they took a dishpan and got two boxes of stick candy. Then two partners would come in at one door and go out another one. They had the pan covered over with a towel; then they'd stick their hand in and get out a piece, and the other one would do the same. If it matched, you got to keep it, but if it didn't, then you had to put it back. I remember the last one of them that we had on Betty's Creek [in Dillard, Georgia] was when Mrs. Wright, down at the school . . . she'd heard tell of candy drawins', but she never had been to one. So (I don't know what Sunday school class she was teachin') we had a candy drawin' for 'em so she'd know what a candy drawin' was."

—Daisy Justice, Spring/Summer 2004

"We used to have dances at people's homes. We used to have barn dances out there in that big old barn. We'd go out there and dance in that barn. It was a new barn. People would gather their corn, and then they would have a corn shuckin' and get everybody to come in and shuck their corn for 'em; then after they'd shucked the corn, they'd have a candy drawin', and they'd get this different-colored stick candy and put it in a pot. A boy and a girl would draw a piece of candy, and if they got two sticks just alike, they could keep it; if they didn't, they put it back. I had lots of boyfriends."

—Oza Coffee Kilby, Spring/Summer 1994

CANDY PULLIN'S

"Well, we had a candy pulling, too. We'd make up the syrup. We always had a big cane patch, and we'd make the syrup . . . A crowd would gather around, and we'd have a circle candy pull. This was sort of dating, too. The boy would choose the girl that he wanted to pull candy with, and he'd pull candy with her." **—Nora Garland, Winter 1973**

"When they made syrup—th' last run of th' syrup—they'd cook it down 'til it got real thick. And just along toward th' last before it got ready t' take up, they'd put some [baking] soda in it. I really don't know what that did to it, but it seemed t' make it get whiter or somethin'.

"And a boy and a girl would usually butter a dish and cool it off some and then get it up in their hands, y' know, and work it 'til they could get it in a ball. Then th' boy would get at one end an' th' girl at th' other, and they'd pull backwards and forwards 'til they got it so it'd pull out in great, long pieces.

"Then they'd divide some of it and pull it out in long pieces sort of like stick candy and lay that out on the platter 'r somethin'. When it got cold, you could just take a knife and crack it all, and it'd be sort o' like yellow stick candy. It was real good.

"And they always had boys and girls doin' it together. That was all th' fun there was in it. Just invite th' young folks in t' make syrup candy."

—Mrs. Ada Kelly, Winter 1973

"Y' grease yer hands with lard so it don't stick on yer hands. If y' ain't got no lard on yer hands, it gets all over yer hands and gets warm. And y' go out there and get yer partner and cut that syrup out in big pieces, and then y' pull that and keep a-pullin' around and around 'til it gets plumb yella."

—Will Zoellner, Winter 1973

"We had 'pound suppers' where usually all of the younger people of the community would get together and bring a pound of food. We had candy drawings and cakewalks. We grew our own popcorn and our own sorghum syrup, and we had candy pullin's. We'd take that sorghum syrup and boil it down 'til it was very stiff and put a tablespoon of soda in it to kind of whiten it up a little bit. When it would get cool enough, we'd put a boy over here, and he'd pull that sorghum candy with his girl. We stretched it to make it white, and the more you pulled it, the whiter it got. Then you laid it down on an enamel pan. You could pick up one of those sticks as a whole and take a knife and hit it, and it would chip off into little pieces."

—Ellene Gowder, Summer 1986

CORN SHUCKIN'S

"We'd have a corn shuckin', and after that we'd have a candy drawin'. You had a lot of corn. People gathered the corn then, and they'd go around the evenin' before and invite them to the corn shuckin' the next day. Two or three women would come help get dinner, and we'd kill the hogs and have plenty of backbone and ribs, a big pot full. Mother had a big pot. She cooked that mess of backbones and ribs, and she cooked chicken, you know, and made dumplin's, a sweet potato pie, and things to eat—I guess things that people wouldn't notice now. That would go on for about six to eight weeks—but switchin' to other people's houses. If we didn't get done—and sometimes we didn't—then we'd have two corn shuckin's, but y' know, it didn't cost a thing. We'd just have to fix dinner, and if it was late when we got through, we'd fix supper. We never thought about chargin' for anything like that." **—Nora Garland, Winter 1973**

"And they'd always bury a drink right in the middle o' that pile and pile their corn on top o' it. Then we'd have t' shuck all th' corn t' find it. We'd shuck all night t' get t' that half gallon o' liquor."

—Florence and Lawton Brooks

"We used t' have them old shuckin's. They'd just pile up their corn in their barnyard, y' know, instead o' puttin' it in their crib. And then they'd ask all their neighbors around t' come in. And they'd always bury a drink right in the middle o' that pile and pile their corn on top o' it. Then we'd have t' shuck all th' corn t' find it. We'd shuck all night t' get t' that half gallon o' liquor. Then we'd all have a drink and probably have a dancin' th' rest o' th' night, if we got done in time.

"God, you never seen such shuckin' corn!

"Then sometimes they'd have it where th' man that found th' first red ear got t' kiss th' prettiest girl, and sometimes he'd shuck like th' devil tryin' t' find a red ear o' corn. Somebody'd find one generally ever' time. It was funny because back then 'at was th' worst thing a boy and girl could do would be caught kissin'. That's th' worst thing you could do!

"Ever'body 'as invited—wasn't nobody skipped. They invited th' young and old. They all come together. And you never seen such cornshucks in your life! And if we got done at midnight 'r somethin' like that, why we'd have a big dance from then on to towards daylight. We never counted none on sleepin' that night—no way when we was havin' them big corn shuckin's 'cause we knowed it'd take th' biggest part o' th' night.

"'Bout all th' way we had o' havin' fun was at them shuckin's. But I thought it was mighty nice o' them t' have things like that. I wish they'd have 'em now back like they used to. There 'as lots o' fun in that."

—Florence and Lawton Brooks, Spring/Summer 1971

"And they used t' have corn shuckin's all the time, y' know. You'd go t' maybe a dozen different corn shuckin's in one fall. Them old people, y'

PLATE 79 "We never counted none on sleepin' that night—no way when we was havin' them big corn shuckin's 'cause we knowed it'd take th' biggest part o' th' night."
—Florence and Lawton Brooks

know, they used to, when they went gatherin' their corn, have a big ol' tin t' put it in so they could shuck it and throw it in th' crib. Lots of times they'd set 'em a gallon jug of good ol' corn liquor right in th' middle of it down in there; they'd see who could shuck fastest—get t' that jug in there first. Let me tell y', it was *liquor* back in them days—it wasn't just ol' potash stuff that'd make y' sick. What they made, it was made right. If you had a gallon like they did back then, you could make most any kinda medicine you wanted to now. All 'liquorish' medicine we have is made with alcohol in it. But it ain't good like it used t' be—I can tell you that!"

—Hillard Green, Fall 1970

"Sometimes th' first one that got a red ear 'ud get a ten-dollar prize. That's what they called pokeberry corn—looked like poke come in it. And ever' once in a while, you'd get a plumb red ear. And th' girl that got th' red ear, she chose her partner t' dance with later.

"One I went to—was about fifteen families lived over there (Ledfords and Penlands and Duncans)—whoever got th' first red ear got a Jersey cow. Nicest thing you ever looked at. Well, we got t' shuckin' around there and finally got in a fight throwin' corn east and west. Somebody socked me with a ear down th' side o' th' head. I caught th' thing, and it 'as a blood-red ear! When it hit my head, I seen th' red corn fly. I cracked it right quick—pulled th' shuck off—and says, 'Look what y' done! Gimme good luck!'

"So I got that—'bout a two-year Jersey heifer. I sold it—got about a hundred dollars fer 't." **—Will Zoellner, Spring/Summer 1971**

"Used t' be all these areas in here was big farms. Mr. Cabe would haul up wagonloads of pumpkins, watermelons, and corn. Well, they and all their neighbors'd get their corn gathered in; then they'd start, 'n' they'd go from place t' place—maybe twice a week they'd have a corn shuckin' at a different place. And all th' men'd get in th' barn and shuck, and if there was too many [to shuck], women, they'd go help shuck, too. And then th' others 'ud cook supper—have a big supper just like we have goin' t' a church supper 'r somethin' like that.

"And then they'd put th' corn in log cribs made where th' air could go through and finish dryin' th' corn they'd gathered in from th' fields. And they'd store th' pumpkins in a barn and cover 'em with th' shucks and th' leavin's from th' corn t' keep them through the winter.

"And, well, it's just fascinatin' how they did."

—Harriet Echols, Spring/Summer 1971

"Sometimes they'd shuck 'til twelve at night before they'd ever get up and sing and holler and 'hoop and all th' devil!"

—*Aunt Arie Carpenter*

"Well, Poppy'd raise a big crop o' corn—maybe two hundred bushels—and put it in a crib shed. On a certain day, they'd have a corn shuckin' and get all th' neighbors from ever'wheres t' come in here. If we had 'em like we used to, we'd have ever'one o' you younguns come down here, and we'd have th' best time.

"They'd always come at dinnertime—some of 'em before dinner. Well, they'd go on t' shuckin'. Sometimes they'd shuck 'til twelve at night before they'd ever get up and sing and holler and 'hoop and all th' devil! And they'd take th' shucks and hide people in 'em and do ever'thing. Why, they had ever' kind o' fun in th' world. That made people love t' go to 'em. If you'd been contrary or hateful, wouldn't o' been nobody'd wanted t' go.

"When they got th' corn shucked, they'd put th' man of th' house on a rail and carry him t' th' house and set 'im down and comb his head—comb th' lice off his head down on th' floor and stomp 'em with their feet. You know, that wadn't so, but they just done that fer th' devilment and fun!"

—Aunt Arie Carpenter, Spring/Summer 1971

"I always got th' biggest thrill out o' that—just th' children and me. Just th' very smallest children would get in and shuck corn and always look for th' red ears. Ever'body that found a red ear had t' be kissed. I didn't like that too much, though!

"They'd come all day and just spend th' day, y' know, and go up into th' night. And then they'd have a dance. We'd have our lanterns and lights around, y' know, and we'd shuck up into th' night and have a big feast with tables loaded with all sorts of good foods."

—Marinda Brown, Spring/Summer 1971

"That was just a good time for us all. We enjoyed bein' together and doin' somethin' t' help somebody, too." —Mrs. E. H. Brown, Spring/Summer 1971

"We had corn shuckin's. People farmed in those days, and they lived on the farm. They'd gather their corn in the fall of the year and pile it under the shed in the crib. Then they'd go out in the community and invite all their neighbors to come in and help husk the corn. They'd come in, and the womenfolks, a lot of them would help at the corn pile. A lot of the older women would gather in and prepare the meal for the people—have a big dinner.

They'd have a great spread of somethin' to eat. So they did that, and they had a good time. After the corn shuckin' was over in the evenin'—if they got it all shucked and put up in the barn and had everything cleaned up—lots of times there was plenty left over from the midday meal for the evenin' meal. After they'd eat supper, they'd have a party, and we'd have a candy drawin'."
—Esco Pitts, Spring 1978

"They shucked, and they shucked; every time they found a red ear, the boy would get to kiss his sweetheart."

—Ellene Gowder

"One time I was real small—I guess I was about four years of age. They wanted to see who had the best team of oxen, and they hitched them to some logs they had put together with hooks. The team of oxen that could move those logs so many feet always won the contest. I also remember corn shuckin's were a very important thing back then. The last one I went to was about sixty-five years ago. There was a young lady lived just above us in school. My brother was going to school, but I wasn't. They let me carry my lunch to school with him. After school we went out to Mrs. Smith's house where the men had been shucking corn all morning long. They shucked, and they shucked; every time they found a red ear, the boy would get to kiss his sweetheart. Anyway, they shucked until they got pretty well into the center of the pile and found a jug of whiskey. Well, that had to be passed around. Everybody had to have a drink of that whiskey, and they finished up that corn." **—Ellene Gowder, Summer 1986**

QUILTIN'S

"People'd work all fall piecin' quilt tops, and when they got 'em all pieced, they'd invite in all th' neighbors and have a quiltin', and that quilt 'ud be for th' person that invited 'em in. And whoever they had th' quiltin' for furnished all of 'em dinner. If it 'as at your house and it 'as for you, you'd furnish th' whole dinner—even if there 'as twenty women there.

"They could quilt one out in a day, easy. Lots o' times we've had quilts out at breakfast and quilted two." **—Margaret Norton, Spring/Summer 1971**

"People used t' get t'gether, and they'd just put up one. They could make as many days out of it as they wanted to. They'd piece one fer one family, set in, and draw another one fer another family, y' know—just kind o' kept it goin'." **—Marinda Brown, Spring/Summer 1971**

"They had quiltin's, but I never could quilt. My stitches were s' long you'd have t' keep your toenails broke off t' keep from gettin' 'em hung!

"People were neighbors. They all helped each other t' do things. If you got anything t' do now, y' do it yourself, or you let it go undone—whichever y' want to." —**Annie Perry, Spring/Summer 1971**

SINGIN'S

"When you'd have a singin', you'd usually have a group of people get together and sing and have refreshments like tea and coffee and ice cream, y' know. They'd gather at different persons' houses or at th' church—whoever had a pianer 'r organ—and they'd play and sing just like any other get-t'gether.

"Usually y' sung religious songs, but sometimes they'd have like a sports party where you'd just sing sports songs. But usually it was religious songs, and we'd sing for two 'r three hours and have a few refreshments and go home.

"And then, sometimes, they had 'em all night long. You'd start at eleven o'clock and then go th' rest of th' night. As fer me, I'm not a good hand t' set up 'til all hours. I'd go t' sleep!" —**Margaret Norton, Spring/Summer 1971**

"They'd have 'em in their houses, and then sometimes they have 'em up there at Andy Cope's fish farm [in Dillard, Georgia]. He's a great singer, and this feller from Lakemont [Georgia], Horace Page—all them go up there, and sometimes they sing all night.

"I'd just go t' listen t' it. I never did sing. They used t' have old-time songs, y' know, like 'Walkin' in th' King's Highway,' but they don't sing anymore—oh, and 'They're Namin' th' Prophet,' 'That Honorable Man,' and 'On Down t' th' River Jordan.' But th' songs they sing now is different from when I 'as growin' up.

"And sometimes at th' church we'd have what they called an all-day singin' an' dinner on th' grounds. That was good, too."

—**Harry Brown, Sr., Spring/Summer 1971**

"Lord, yeah. People used t' have singin's at their houses. Sometimes we'd walk ten miles t' one. They'd have songbooks, y' know, with Gospel songs, and th' house 'ud be so full o' people. They used t' do that lots—move all over the settlement. When me an' Florence was married, we done 'at fer a long time. Fer years after we 'as married, we went nearly ever' night. Lots o' times people'd have t' walk four 'r five miles, but they'd go. They'd be there. They'd all go.

"That was about th' only thing that went on durin' th' week. That'd give the young people a place t' go, and they'd always go. If a ol' boy got him a girl, he'd have her come t' th' singin', y' know. Had a nice time. Always had a nice time. No joke about it, it was nice. I think there ought t' be lots more—wouldn't be half as much meanness done.

"But they quit all that now, I reckon. Don't hear tell o' that no more."

—Florence and Lawton Brooks, Spring/Summer 1971

"Gettin' together for a singin' was our way of dating and socializin' when I was a boy. If anybody had a wagon and mules, we'd load up on that and go to someone's home in the settlement. If we didn't go in the wagon, we'd all get together and walk. We all had our sweethearts, and we'd each get with our girl and march down the road. We didn't have electric lights, so we sang by kerosene lamps. And most of the homes didn't have any musical instruments, so we sang without music. And lots of times we would have a candy drawin' at the singin'." **—Esco Pitts, Spring 1978**

"We'd go to the neighbor houses and have singin's; we'd study our Bible and church/school work. But I can't sing anymore—I don't have the breath. There was always someone to make music. We had the organ, and somebody'd play the banjo and the violin; my father played the harmonica, and my brother could play anything on the jew's-harp. We'd always do somethin' like that, and we took it different times at different houses. The houses were fairly thickly settled on the farms and plantations. In the winter, we had parties where we'd make syrup candy and parched peanuts and peanut candy. Sometimes the parents would join in on these parties. And some nights when the hunting season was on, the older boys would go huntin', and we girls would piece and quilt until the boys come back to gather up their sisters or girlfriends. We were never bored and lonely because people had big families, and I bet there were twenty-five young people almost in hollerin' distance to where we lived. That was the type of recreation people had. They'd get t'gether—big families. Most had at least four children, sometimes up to sixteen children." **—Harriet Echols, Fall 1976**

HOLIDAYS

My sister finally saw it: two watches. They were hung on the little reindeer—a lady's watch and a man's watch. Dad and Mama had got their watches fixed and gave them to us for Christmas.

—G. A. Nasworthy, Jr.

Holidays are for spending time with loved ones, both family and friends, and celebrating. Although some families have forgotten the spirit and joy of the holidays, others still carry on their traditions year after year.

One Southern tradition is to eat black-eyed peas and turnip greens on New Year's Day, a ritual to guarantee prosperity in the new year. Unfortunately, you have to eat a mountain of them because the belief is that you will receive a penny for every pea you eat and a dollar for every turnip green! Better come hungry! Today, we can hardly get the menfolks to the table for peas or anything else because of the day-into-night football games on television.

Do you remember decorating brown paper sacks and trading valentines with classmates when you were in grammar school? How exciting to receive one from that special someone! One contact with whom we spoke told us that "you had to be careful about doin' that b'cause the teacher might catch you passin' somethin'." Mary Cabe told us that they didn't get to "make no cards or anything like that." In the past, school supplies were nonexistent. Parents had to purchase school supplies, and some teachers bought materials for their classes out of their meager paychecks. Perhaps, sadly, making valentines was a luxury no one could afford.

Many children today still go on Easter egg hunts; however, often, today's eggs are plastic. In the old days, many children used beet juice, walnut hulls, or wheat straw to color real eggs; others could afford store-bought dyes. Mothers made new dresses for the girls out of gingham or calico, and boys wore "little old knee pants." Lawton Brooks told us, "I wouldn't be caught on top o' Rabun Bald with a pair of them [knee pants] on!"

Fireworks and anvil shooting punctuated the Fourth of July. Gene Purcell told us, "We'd blow an anvil straight up!" Folks remembered parades in town, big dinners, and Confederate reunions. Lelia Gibson told us Confederate veterans were still alive when she went to a Fourth of July celebration in Franklin, North Carolina, and they would stage reenactments of battles.

Halloween was a time for pumpkins and pranks. Mischievous boys put a man's brand-new buggy in the top of his barn, "cow-swapped," rubbed soap on store windows, and performed various other acts of mayhem.

And then came Thanksgiving and Christmas. Our contacts described their decorations and special memories. We heard about cutting down trees and dragging them home to decorate with strung popcorn and crepe paper. Our elders did not receive name-brand clothes, jewelry, MP3 players, or cars. Almost all told us about receiving an apple and a piece of candy. Some received a pencil, and some received gifts handmade by their mothers and fathers. I'm certain that today those gifts would be cherished heirlooms. Those of us today know about caroling and serenading. Who would ever have thought that "serenading" meant banging pots, shooting guns, ringing bells, and creating as much clamor as possible? Nora Garland shares with us her "serenading" experience: "We went up to one place, and the man told his wife, 'Lula, just carry the bed out and give 'em some room.' The couple cleared their great big room out for dancing and playing games."

Folks in Southern Appalachia played games and sang. They enjoyed the moments spent together, for holidays were a respite from their lives of hard work. Holidays are special days, days to celebrate, and these special days are times to be spent with the ones we love. They are days to carry on (or begin) traditions. The past allowed less time for leisure, less money, fewer conveniences, fewer gifts. Perhaps less used to be—and still is—more.

—Angie Cheek and April Argoe

NEW YEAR'S

"Didn't pay no 'tention. Some of 'em would eat hog jowls, turnip greens, an' black-eyed peas. Somebody once said t' me on New Year's, 'Whatever you do today, you've got to do every day this year.' "

—Harry Brown, Sr., Winter 1973

"We had a good time at New Year's. We generally had turnip greens. It's good luck for you. That's what they said." **—Annie Perry, Winter 1973**

"Oh, yes, the church bells would ring a half hour before twelve o'clock midnight. They would ring the old year out, and a half hour after twelve o'clock, they'd ring the new year in. They had fireworks—Roman candles—and the boys would have cap holsters with caps. We also ate peas and hog jowls and backbones and ribs. Old people'd save all their hog jowls 'til New Year's." **—Lelia Gibson, Winter 1973**

Margaret: We didn't pay much attention t' New Year's then. We had certain things that we wouldn't do on New Year's, like not wash. You wouldn't wash an' hang up no wet clothes on New Year's. If y' did, you'd wash for sickness all year. But you'd just work an' you'd clean house an' you'd sew an' you'd patch an' you'd churn an' you'd cook, cook a big dinner an' have hogs' jaw an' peas—black-eyed peas—so you'd have a lot of money, y' see.

Richard: That's what the old folks claim—if you have hogs' jaw an' peas. I think we have peas th' year round. They ain't nothin new t' me on New Year's. I think it's ever' day here.

Margaret: No, not ever' day—we haven't had any this week.

Richard: Well, we had butter beans, an' that's just as bad!

—Richard and Margaret Norton, Winter 1973

NEW YEAR'S SUPERSTITIONS

"If you sweep the trash out the door on New Year's, you will sweep your luck away."

"If a man is the first one to come into your house on New Year's, your chickens will be roosters; but if a woman is the first, your chickens will be pullets."

"Whatever you do on New Year's Day is what you will be doin' for the rest of the year."

"On New Year's Day, eat turnip greens and black-eyed peas. Every turnip green you eat is every dollar you will make the next year, and every black-eyed pea you eat is every penny you will make the next year."

"If you leave your Christmas lights up past New Year's, you will have bad luck." **—Spring/Summer 1996**

VALENTINE'S DAY

"We never did pay much attention to it back in my young days. We never did make no cards or anything like that." **—Mary Cabe, Winter 1973**

"We maybe made a few valentines—we were careful about doin' anything like that, b'cause th' teacher might catch you passin' somethin'."

—Harry Brown, Sr., Winter 1973

EASTER

"Oh, yes, we always celebrated Easter. We always had a big ol' chicken. Mama cooked an' boiled up some eggs, an' maybe she'd cook a cake. I got all dressed up on Easter. We always got us a new dress on Easter; then we always went t' Sunday school, an' we'd have an egg hunt. We lived up only a right smart little way from th' church." **—Annie Perry, Winter 1973**

"We couldn't eat eggs except on Easter Sunday. About two weeks before Easter, we'd steal the eggs. When the old hen laid, we'd go get them eggs, and we'd hide 'em. By the time Easter come, we'd have a pretty good bunch. We'd boil 'em, and we'd color 'em with a broomstraw. It'd just color 'em yellow-lookin'. That's all the coloring we had."

—D. B. Dayton, Summer 1980

"Now that's when we always had th' eggs—dyed them, colored 'em up all colors—an' you know what we used? They's a weed in th' woods come up at Eastertime—grows up kinda spindly. We'd get that an' wrap it around the eggs an' boil 'em an' make 'em pretty an' yellow. We usually always had a big, fat hen fer Easter, maybe baked. Maybe we'd boil it an' make dumplin's. All th' fathers an' mothers hid th' eggs out in th' woods an' pasture. It used t' be we'd have it at th' church an' there'd be a prize egg. You'd turn it in an' get your prize . . . usually a box of candy 'r somethin' special that 'as different.

"We had a special service Easter an' ever'body'd always wear their new clothes—new dresses, shoes, an' ever'thing. Our mother made us new clothes for th' summer around Eastertime. You couldn't go to th' store an' get 'em all ready-made. Even th' little babies—they used t' make long dresses that'd come plumb over their feet—looked like gowns—an' they'd put on all this trimmin'. They 'as sweet little ol' things.

"Lotta times th' families'd get together for Easter."

—Bertha Dockins, Winter 1973

"They'd make new dresses out o' gingham and calico. They pretty much quit wearin' winter clothes an' shoes after Easter. Yep, went t' goin' barefoot an' go barefoot as long as you could." **—Florence Brooks, Winter 1973**

"Sometimes we'd dig up roots of plants to color eggs for Easter. When we pickled beets, we'd take the juice and boil it and color the eggs red. Usually, some of the bigger children would hide the eggs for us. They'd go where they was a lot of grass. They'd have some extra eggs fixed for the ones that found the most eggs or the prize egg. I don't remember what we put the eggs in. I don't reckon I ever had an Easter basket."

—Minnie Dailey, Summer 1985

> **"Mom got to wonderin' what was goin' on with her eggs. She wasn't gettin' many because we were slippin' and gettin' 'em and hidin' 'em."** *—Amanda Turpin*

"Just before Easter, we children liked to gather the eggs. Every time a hen would cackle, we'd be listenin' for them, and we'd go get the eggs and hide them. By the time Easter came, we'd have a lot of eggs ready. Mom got to wonderin' what was goin' on with her eggs. She wasn't gettin' many because we were slippin' and gettin' 'em and hidin' 'em. We had a potato house, and there was a lot of sawdust in there. We'd get the eggs and hide them in the sawdust. Some got uncovered one day, and my daddy found 'em. He went to scratchin' and found a half bushel of eggs. He told Mama, 'Come out here, and I'll show you what's been a-goin' on with your eggs.'

"We wanted to be sure we had lots of eggs for Easter. We'd get out and find a kind of weed that we colored the eggs with."

—Amanda Turpin, Summer 1981

"We had more fun about Easter than any other holiday they was. We'd hide eggs, an' we'd color 'em. We'd fight eggs [hit the eggs together]—if I had an egg that whipped yourun, I got yourun. We'd all try t' get a guinea egg somewhere because they's the hardest you can get, an' they'd break ever'body's egg. If you had one, you was lucky 'cause you could whip ever'-body an' get their eggs. Everybody'd have a big bunch of colored eggs—their pockets just full—an' we'd fight 'em. We'd eat the broken eggs an' eat eggs all day. We had t' steal our eggs most of th' time because people sold their eggs t' buy other stuff. They was only worth ten, fifteen, twenty cents a dozen, but they'd just give the kids just so many eggs t' color, an' we had t' steal the rest. They wasn't no ifs, ands, or buts about it—everybody in the neighborhood stole eggs just wherever they could find 'em. Me 'n' m' brother one time had stoled up a big ol' bunch, an' we 'as a-puttin 'em in a stovepipe in a brushpile. We'd slip around to th' nests 'fore Mommy told us t' gather up th' eggs. We'd slip around an' take one 'r two out of ever' nest. We'd get us three or four ever' day an' run stick 'em in that stovepipe. It come a cold snap an' froze our eggs. We went t' boil 'em, an' they just spewed out all over everything. They'd busted an' thawed. We didn't have no eggs at all for that Easter.

"Most of th' time we'd color 'em with walnut hulls—color 'em a dark brown. Most of th' time that's all they had. Seems like we had more fun on Easter than ever' other time.

"They made 'em new clothes. They'd make little old dresses for th' little girls, an' for boys they'd make little old knee pants that ride down over th' knee an' things such as that—made a big ol' ring around your leg. I wouldn't be caught on top o' Rabun Bald with a pair of them on!"

—Lawton Brooks, Winter 1973

"We always had a big egg hunt on Easter. That was when I was young. Now you see white worn th' year round, but back then you never seen nobody with white on 'til Easter. An' then they'd go t' wearin' white. They followed it back then.

"We didn't believe in the Easter Bunny, not when I was a young child. Long after I was married was the first time I heard of the Easter Bunny."

—Ethel Corn, Winter 1973

"Our mothers wanted us to wear our capes to keep warm, but we didn't want them to cover up our new Easter outfits; so we didn't. We was fine goin' t' church, but when we came out, about a half a mile from the church, it began to snow." ***—Lelia Gibson***

"We would have egg hunts and color eggs. We had one egg that we'd call th' golden egg, and whoever found the golden egg got a prize. Sometimes it would be money, maybe a quarter or fifty cents. Sometimes it'd be a box of candy, stick candy. The children colored our own eggs, and some older woman hid the eggs while we children stayed at the house. They'd call us when they were done; then we'd go ahead and hunt the eggs. We'd dye the eggs with store-bought dye, but some people did it by boilin' the eggs with wheat straw t' make 'em yellow. People also used faded cloths—put them in the water and boiled it and added a little vinegar to set the dye.

"We'd go to church on Easter when we could get there. Sometimes the weather would be too bad. In those days you had to have your Easter bonnets and Easter outfits. Our hats had artificial flowers on 'em. One Easter Sunday, Kitty Conley and I went to church. Our mothers wanted us to wear our capes to keep warm, but we didn't want them to cover up our new Easter outfits; so we didn't. We was fine goin' t' church, but when we came out, about a half a mile from the church, it began to snow. Well, our clothes got wet. We was worried about our hats, so we took our hats off and ran 'til we got to our homes. Then we went to a neighbor's for dinner. They had baked ham, cakes, beans, jellies, pickles, cornbread, biscuit bread, and we ate like pigs!" —**Lelia Gibson, Winter 1973**

"Every Easter we went up to Yonah Mountain [Tallulah Falls, Georgia]. They had the Devil's Pulpit. It was a rock that came over, and you could get on it. Right up under that, they had the Tight Squeeze. It was two rocks, and if you just went in right, you could go through that. If you got caught in there, it was too bad.

"The top of the mountain had Lovers' Leap. That's where those two Indians run away and jumped off that mountain. One Easter my grandmother had bought me a hat. I wore it up there. I was standin' there pretty close to the edge, and a big wind came up and just blew it off Lovers' Leap. I was afraid to tell Papa, but we had a real good time." —**Eula Carroll, Summer 1990**

FOURTH OF JULY

"It was always fireworks, an' they'd have log burnin' an' rollin'. They'd take a cat hook [a large tool, hinged like scissors, to clamp onto a log] an' roll 'em. They had footraces in sacks an' the fat man's race an' the greased pig—floured an' greased, just as slick as it could be. An' then whoever caught that pig, got it an' won a prize. I'll tell you, that's a hard thing t' do.

"Back then, the girls didn't join in nothin' like that. They'd have been talked about if they had, but I don't see no harm in it. I don't see no harm in a lot o' things people wants t' cut 'em down for. I said I never could see no harm in good, clean fun, an' I'm proud t' have my fun." —**J. M. Parker, Winter 1973**

"They used t' have parades in town, but we didn't do much at home. It was a day off work, and we'd just sit around, have a good time—go fishin', go campin'." —**Bertha Dockins, Winter 1973**

"Yeah, they had a big day then. They had a big dinner an' all kinds of music an' marches—had a big day. They done it down there about th' Methodist church. Bring their piccolo an' bugle an' play an' march, an' they'd make talks; them old fellows could talk." —**Kenny Runion, Winter 1973**

"On the Fourth of July, when I was a child, they was several Confederate veterans that was yet alive. On July 4, they had old soldiers' reunion in the town of Franklin [North Carolina]. They'd set up tents where the Confederate monument is, and they'd have barbwire entanglements on both sides. Old Captain Bill McDowell was captain in the War between the States.

They had their old musket loaders with powder in a cow horn, and they'd wad up newspaper in tiny wads and pour powder in the barrel of the gun and punch the paper wad down with a ramrod to where it would fire. The Confederates was on one side, and the Federals, on the other. Old Captain McDowell would come along and bid all his men farewell for the battle. Then they'd have false battles. They had a man playin' the fife and another beatin' the drum as they marched with Captain McDowell leading. He'd lope up an' down the street with these guns a-goin' on, this firin', and he'd say, 'My Lord, I wished it 'as true. I wish this was real!' He was so enthused. He was excited t' death. An' I looked at him, an' I said t' myself, 'The idee of wishin' this was th' truth again!'

"Mrs. Madeline Trotter, an old lady, baked gingerbread. She baked it in cakes, and she had it out at her front yard at the gate. She had a table out there, and she'd slice and sell this bread and a pint tin cup full of apple cider for five cents.

"One of the old Confederate veterans, I don't remember which one,

PLATE 80 "They had a big band, music, and dances, too." —Minnie Dailey

would sing out to his wife, 'Hey, Patty, don't you want some good old cider, good old cider?'

"We got all dressed up for the Fourth of July. The girls'd dress up in calico, what you'd call print. The town wasn't decorated special, except the town marshal would go along and clean the town streetlights—kerosene lights. People just gathered and had this Confederate reunion."

—Lelia Gibson, Winter 1973

"On the Fourth of July, we'd have a big dinner up at Hiawassee [Georgia]. They used to have carnivals, too. They had a big band, music, and dances, too. Back then, my uncle, who lived in Tate, Georgia, had some boys that had a band, and they'd come up to Hiawassee and play. They played fiddles, banjos, guitars, and everything!" **—Minnie Dailey, Summer 1985**

"They used to have fiddlers' conventions around the Fourth of July. That was always something the country people had to look forward to. Franklin [North Carolina] was the area. Of course people from all around, even Highlands [North Carolina], would go. This wasn't really called the Fiddlers' Convention, I don't reckon, because it was mostly local people. I don't ever remember a street dance, but of course there'd be private dances."

—Marinda Brown, Winter 1973

HALLOWEEN

Jack took his hatchet and carved a cross on the bottom of the apple tree. I don't know if you know about the devil and crosses, but the devil couldn't get by the cross because it was on the tree trunk. So he was stuck up there for something like forty years. —Pat Cotter

"This is a 'Jack Tale' that my grandfather told me about—how the jack-o'-lantern got its name.

"There was an old Irish farmer that lived very close to him, and he was very, very mean. He didn't go to church on Sunday. He didn't go to PTA meetings. He didn't pay his paperboy. He was just all in all a bad character. He did have one attribute that made him famous in East Tennessee. He grew some of the best apples in the state. On his farm there, he had fine apple trees, and he grew the best, biggest, and sweetest apples in the state. Even the governor would come in and buy his apples. They were just great.

"The devil heard about Jack's apples. It don't happen so often now, but the devil used to drop in and see people every now and then. So the devil dropped in at Jack's house one day and said, 'Jack, I hear you've got the best apples in the state.'

"And Jack said, 'I have. I've probably got the best apples in the Eastern United States.'

"And the devil said, 'Well, I'd like to have some of 'em.'

"And Jack said, 'Well, you'll have to go to the very back part of my farm on the highest hill, in the tallest tree, on the very top limb. That's where you'll find the sweetest apples.'

"So the devil said, 'Well, I think I'll go get some of 'em.' So he left and started to climb the apple tree. Jack followed him with a hatchet. And the devil clumb to the top limb. He set down, picked an apple, and sure enough, it was the sweetest, best-tasting apple he'd ever eaten. While he was up there partaking of the apples, Jack took his hatchet and carved a cross on the bottom of the apple tree. I don't know if you know about the devil and crosses, but the devil couldn't get by the cross because it was on the tree trunk. So he was stuck up there for something like forty years. He couldn't get down; of course, he was hopping mad all this time. Well, Jack eventually died of meanness and old age.

"His first stop was heaven, and St. Peter said, 'You've been so mean and bad, you can't stay here.' He said, 'You'll have to go to hell.'

"When Jack died, the spell was broken, so the devil came down out of the apple tree and had to walk all the way back to hell. He was mad and thirsty. He had been up there a long time with nothing to drink. He and Jack got to hell about the same time, and they had an awful fight. The devil was mad, and he was ripped. Jack was ripped because he'd gotten kicked out of heaven. The devil said, 'You can't stay here in hell after what you've done to me.'

"And Jack said, 'I've got to. I hadn't any other place to go.'

"And the devil said, 'No, you can't,' and they fought some more. The devil gets the best of a lot of us from time to time, you know. Well, the devil started getting the best of Jack, and Jack lit out runnin'. The devil hadn't had enough, so he picked up a hot coal out of hell and flung it at Jack. It come bouncing along and Jack saw it and he said, 'You know, I've been condemned to wander through eternity in darkness. I can't go to heaven, and I can't go to hell. I might be able to use that coal.' He started to reach down and pick it up to use it for a light, and he realized it was hot. So he looked over in a field, an' sure enough, there was a pumpkin. He took his pocketknife out, and he hollowed out the pumpkin, cut a hole in it, and put the hot coal in there. Halloween night now, you can still see him going up through Union County [Georgia] and some of the other places with his light. That's how my grandfather told me the jack-o'-lantern got its name." —**Pat Cotter, Fall/Winter 1990**

"Now one Halloween . . . we 'as bad t' do mean things. Old Uncle Tommy Vinson, he was the preacher—lived right across th' river over here. An' Mel an' Curt an' Max [her brothers], they went and pulled up cabbage by the roots an' loaded his buggy full o' cabbage an' rolled it up t' his front door an' on th' porch. An' now they'll talk that teenagers are s' mean. Well, if you study back, what they do isn't s' different from what we did. We'd get out an' rock people. We was pretty mean. We'd just slip around an' do things—just tricks. There 'as no treats.

"We didn't dress up because we didn't want nobody to see us. We 'as afraid t' be seen." —**Ethel Corn, Winter 1973**

"They used to get out an' play pranks. One man had a brand-new buggy, an' some old boys got that buggy an' set it right top of his barn an' tied it there. There must have been a whole bunch of them—th' owner had t' get a bunch of neighbors t' get it down.

"One time some boys went to a fellow's house, knocked on th' door, an' when he come out, they threw a bucket of water on 'im. People didn't go in for celebrations like they do today. You had t' work t' keep a-goin'. They didn't know all this business." —**Harry Brown, Sr., Winter 1973**

"Trick-or-treating was about the worst mischief we got into. We would go get somebody's cow and take it to somebody else's barn and take their cow to another barn—swap all the cows around. The owners didn't know we was doin' it because they'd be in the bed asleep. They'd go out to milk the next mornin', and they would have a different cow standin' in the stable."

—D. B. Dayton, Summer 1980

"On Halloween, they just went around to the houses an' done meanness. They slipped around and didn't make no racket. They'd wire their door shut from the outside, put their buggies on their porches, fill the buggy up with cabbage. I never did get into that. Poppy'd have skinned me alive. I was afraid, too! But I knowed a lot of 'em that did. It didn't ruin the cabbage. It was th' time o' year cabbage should be took up. They'd pull 'em up by the roots, so then all the people had to do to store their cabbage was to bury 'em.

"On Halloween, people would also take soap an' go around to the stores an' other places of business and soap 'em good—just wet the soap and rub it all over the windows. They just messed up the windows of stores and such. They never did people's houses—they's afraid they'd get caught and get shot!" —**Ethel Corn, Fall 1975**

PLATE 81 "They'd go out to milk the next mornin', and they would have a different cow standin' in the stable." —D. B. Dayton

THANKSGIVING

"We just had one day out for Thanksgivin', and we had Thanksgiving dinner at school. We made dressing, cranberry sauce, candied potatoes, green beans, baked hens, pumpkin pies, and cakes. Some of the students lived so far away they couldn't get home and were happy to stay there [at Rabun Gap-Nacoochee School]. A lot of them didn't have homes to go to. Also, Mrs. Ritchie saw that we always had a Christmas tree. People would send in boxes of things, and we had apples, oranges, nuts, and candy.

"If I could call back time, I'd call back the three years that I was in the dormitory at Rabun Gap with the same people. They were all good, and we just loved one another. Mrs. Ritchie was just a mother to us. Mr. Ritchie was away most of the time raising money for the school, but when he'd come home, he'd get up in the dining hall after breakfast and talk to us about his

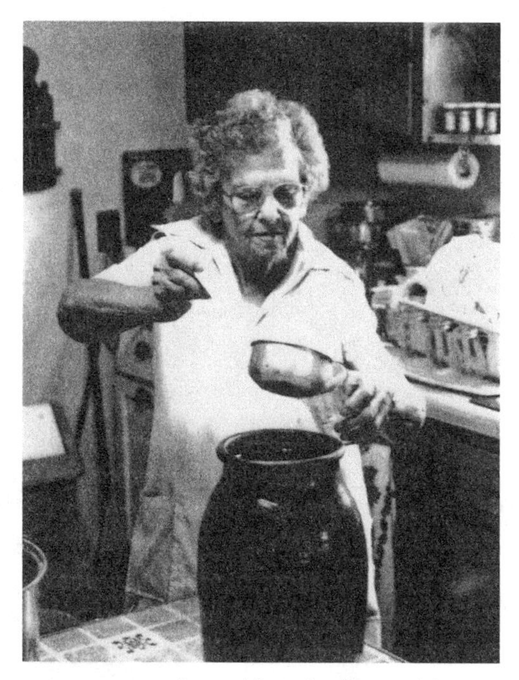

PLATE 82 "People would send in boxes of things, and we had apples, oranges, nuts, and candy." —Mary Pitts

trip up North. He kept us in there at times until it was time for us to start dinner. Why, it was just one big family.

"There were visitors from up North, people Mr. Ritchie had called on, who would come down to see the school. They were rich, and they'd help our school. They'd eat in the dinin' hall, and we'd get to see them."

—Mary Pitts, Fall 1987

"We usually cooked a good dinner for Thanksgivin', and usually some of th' neighbors would get together—maybe two, three families in a home—have dinner, an' just have a good day together." **—Ada Kelly, Winter 1973**

"We'd get together and have a big dinner, lots of chicken and dumplin's, and sit around and talk an' play games, maybe. And of th' night, th' old people'd make kerosene balls—make a big ball of old cloth and yarn—an' soak 'em in kerosene an' light 'em an' get out in th' meadows an' play—fireball, they called it. They'd stand around an' throw 'em to each other, just like they was a-playin' ball. You'd have to get shed of it pretty quick—they'd burn you t' death, but nobody ever got burned or hurt." **—Mary Cabe, Winter 1973**

PLATE 83 Mary Cabe poses on her front porch.

CHRISTMAS

I was only three or so, but I remember this distinctly: Santa Claus left a sooty footprint on the hearth where he had come down the chimney. —Clyde English

"When night come, we always went t' the chimney corner, pulled our stockin's off, an' hung 'em up . . . Put up a dirty sock. It's just as good in a dirty sock as it was in a clean sock." ***—Annie Perry***

"We always celebrated Christmas, ever since I've been big enough t' remember. When night come, we always went t' the chimney corner, pulled our stockin's off, an' hung 'em up. An' Santa Claus come while we was in bed asleep. Put up a dirty sock. It's just as good in a dirty sock as it was in a clean sock. We'd stick a stick in the chimney and hang them stockin's up on the stick, an' when we woke up next mornin', it'd be full of apples an' oranges and two or three sticks o' candy.

"We decorated our tree with popcorn. We popped a lot o' popcorn an' strung 'em on a string, an' that made just as pretty a decoration as you ever seen up on a small Christmas tree. It was a job—sometimes they wouldn't string. Sometimes they popped in two. We put on stars made of white paper—tinsel, if we could get it. We had holly. We generally had a holly tree for a Christmas tree. But anything else makes a better Christmas tree than a holly tree. Phew-wee! We had mistletoe—put mistletoe up on th' tree. We had to climb up in a tree an' knock it down. We had special food. Old, cold food ain't fit t' feed a pig. I don't like cold food at all. We had hog meat. We didn't never have any turkey because nobody liked turkey. It 'as too dry. We had chicken." —**Annie Perry, Winter 1973**

"How we enjoyed our Christmas tree, which was made up entirely of old-fashioned ornaments. Before each Christmas, each child received one toy,

PLATE 84 "I begged and wanted a tricycle and a bicycle. But little girls had to have dolls." —Iris Daniel Engel Barnes

and I begged and wanted a tricycle and a bicycle. But little girls had to have dolls. So I had my dolls, but I never had a bicycle until I was grown. I got one then, and that was the first one that I had."

—Iris Daniel Engel Barnes, Fall/Winter 2003

"My parents had Christmas trees, an' when we children was big enough t' work, we'd always go somewhere on Christmas—go to a dance 'r somethin'. An' my mother used t' have us each a stockin'. She'd put candy an' apples an' oranges in it—that's about all there was t' put in it. We didn't get no more presents 'cause it took all we could raise and scrape t' keep somethin' t' eat an' somethin' t' wear. Now, we never had no Santie Claus, but they had us a-thinkin' that they was a Santie Claus.

"They did have programs, but back before I 'as married. At th' schoolhouse at Christmastime, they'd have a Christmas tree in th' playground. It was a holly tree, an' ever'body put Christmas ribbons an' such as that on th' tree. I'll never forget one time we had a dance at one of our friend's up on a mountain. There 'as a boy down there had a big ol' ribbon up at his lapel—went to th' bottom of his coat—an' he was a-dancin'."

—J. M. Parker, Winter 1973

"Us kids, we took a big cardboard box, cut a little Christmas tree out of it, propped it up on our library table in the livin' room, made little ornament things for it, put it on the tree, and had the best little tree." ***—Josephine Miller***

"When I was ten years old, my stepfather broke his arm just before Christmas. We was goin' to have nothin' for Christmas. Us kids, we took a big cardboard box, cut a little Christmas tree out of it, propped it up on our library table in the livin' room, made little ornament things for it, put it on the tree, and had the best little tree. Uncle Earl, who was in the war, came to our house on Christmas Eve and brought us a Christmas tree. He had come home on leave. He was still in the Army. He made a career of it. We had a little box of ornaments and tinsel. We had a new family in our neighborhood. Their mother and daddy was dead, and they was livin' with their sister and her husband. There was three of those brothers, and they were the nicest boys. They had little nieces and nephews of their sisters, so it was a pretty big family. They had just moved into our neighborhood. Us kids said, 'Mother, can we give our Christmas tree and things that Uncle Earl brought us to them?' She said, 'Oh, I don't know.' People were proud, so proud. I said, 'They won't care. Let us kids take it over there and give it to them.' We walked through

PLATE 85 Jo Miller and her husband, Jim, a toymaker

the fields, and there was a big snow on. My brother and my little sister and I walked and carried this to where they lived. We gave them the Christmas tree, and they were so proud of it. We recycled a cardboard box, and we colored it with green crayons to make us a Christmas tree. We loved that tree so much that we wanted to give our real tree away. We did, and then they had Christmas, too. I was ten years old."

—Josephine Miller, Spring/Summer 1999

"My parents told me about ol' Santa Claus comin' down the chimney, and we had a big ol' chimney—said he come down and delivered our presents into our stockin's. I never did see his tracks—you know, where he had left any sign—and when I was about five or six years old, I was beginnin' to doubt Santa. Next mornin' when I got up—Christmas mornin'—I found a gun in my stockin', one of those little ol' cap busters, cap gun. Didn't have rolls of caps with it—just stick one cap in there at a time, pull back the trigger, and BANG! I got that gun outta that stocking. It was the first one I'd ever seen, and the caps was just loose in a little box. I shot all the caps up that were in the stockin', and I got to wonderin' where I could get some more. We lived in a two-story house. There was rooms upstairs, and I remembered seein' some of the caps on the steps. It looked like instead of

Santa Claus comin' down the chimney, he came down the stairs. I just tracked him back on up there in one of the upstairs rooms, where they'd dropped some of them there caps. Right then, I was beginnin' to doubt ol' Santa Claus. I knowed he didn't come down the chimney.

"Mother knit our stockin's from wool. We had lots of sheep and grew our own wool. It was just one of our regular stockings that we used for Christmas, for Santa Claus. Sometimes we'd get candy and apples and oranges. The first orange I'd ever see'd was in my sock. I didn't know what they was. I liked it. I've liked oranges ever since.

"I remember my daddy givin' me a shotgun. He give that to me, the first real gun I ever had in my life, at Christmastime."

—Minyard Conner, Fall 1985

"We had more snow back then than we have now. I remember one Christmas we had a big snow on the ground. We were just kids, and we just could not understand how Santa Claus was gonna come see us. We all wrote letters and put 'em in the back window on the outside ledge with a rock on 'em to hold 'em down. Somebody got out there and made some big tracks coming up to the letters. They acted like they came up from the road. Whether it was Dad or D.J. our uncle, I don't know, but somebody came and got our letters. We had an orange, a couple of nuts, and a big pillow of peppermint candy. We were happy because Santa Claus came to see us."

—Susie Smith, Summer 1990

"When Christmas came, we had nothin' to do but go rabbit huntin'. School was usually vacated, and the teachers got a week off as far back as I can remember. . . .

"We'd decorate the house with holly and mistletoe and homemade things like that. We'd put mistletoe over the door, but we never did kiss under it when we were small. I guess maybe the older folks did, but I don't know.

"The only Christmas tree we would have was the one at school. They would have a tree just as high as they could get it in there on the stage. I've known 'em to have a great big ol' sticky holly for the Christmas tree. All the gifts were tied on the tree.

"We always hung our stockings up for Santa Claus on Christmas Eve night. We used bought stockings—my mama never knit our stockings. I remember one Christmas we begged Mama to hang her stocking up, and the next morning there was great big ol' sweet potato in it. Oh! Us kids thought that was so funny! We got some oranges and apples, candy. Maybe the girls got a little doll, and the boys got firecrackers or something like that. And that was it.

PLATE 86 "The only way I knew we were celebrating Christmas when I was a kid was that Mama always cooked up an extra batch of cakes and pies." —Clarence Lusk

"For Christmas dinner, if we killed a chicken, why, that was enough. It was just more or less another day. The only way I knew we were celebrating Christmas when I was a kid was that Mama always cooked up an extra batch of cakes and pies. Now we have our family all together and have a Christmas dinner of turkey and dressin' and all the trimmin's, but we didn't do that when I was growin' up." —**Clarence and Alma Lusk, Fall 1985**

"She opened the stove door, and here came my cat. Its paws were scorched and its hair was singed just a little bit, but the cat really wasn't hurt. But it sure never went back in that stove!"

—Lyndall "Granny" Toothman

"My dad's birthday was December 27, and that's when we had the more traditional—what other people had for Christmas—dinner. We either had a couple of big Plymouth Rock hens, or if we'd raised enough turkeys that year and not sold them all but saved one back for Christmas, we had turkey. We didn't like cornbread dressing, so Mother made a good biscuit dressing out of biscuits about two days old, crumbled up, and celery we raised ourselves and onions and so on. She took broth off the hen or the turkey and put pure broth over the bread crumbs until it was gooey-like, and she stuffed the bird with dressing. Whatever we had left over, we put in a little bake pan and baked separately—all on that wood cookstove. It had a big oven with two doors that swung both ways.

"I'll tell you a little story about that oven. It was a cold, cold day, and Mother had left both oven doors open so the heat could come out. We had a big ol' cat there, and the cat crawled up in the oven and went to sleep. Mother got ready to get dinner. Why, she shut both doors and built a fire! [Laughter.] And we heard this cat a-screamin'. We was runnin' around the house, but we couldn't find it. We came back in, and we could still hear that cat a-screamin'. All of a sudden, Mother thought, it must be in the stove. She opened the stove door, and here came my cat. Its paws were scorched and its hair was singed just a little bit, but the cat really wasn't hurt. But it sure never went back in that stove!"

—Lyndall "Granny" Toothman, *A Foxfire Christmas*

"Now on Christmas Day, we didn't have the traditional Christmas dinner that the neighbors did. We had a special dinner that all of us looked forward to all year round. And sometimes we would have to begin preparing for three months before. The dinner consisted of fried country ham—we always cured our own meat—and red-eye gravy. I guess you all know what country ham and red-eye gravy is. *[After you remove the ham slices from the frying pan, add flour to the grease that's left in the pan. Let it brown. Add water or coffee and continue to stir. You may leave off the flour and just add coffee and stir.]* Then we baked Irish potatoes and baked sweet potatoes and a pot of leather breeches beans, potato salad, dandelion salad, and deviled eggs—we always had deviled eggs—or raised biscuits, corn pone, jellies, jams, and preserves and three or four different kinds of homemade pickles, and we always had plenty of milk and butter.

"We also had either strawberry or dandelion wine. Then for dessert, it was always boiled custard and Lady Baltimore white cake, and for the children they also had chestnuts." **—Lyndall "Granny" Toothman, Fall 1985**

"You cooked a big dinner, and the relatives came in t' eat—just sort of like they do now. Maybe they'd come an' stay three, four days. They had t' walk. We had a aunt that lived up here on Patterson Creek, an' she'd always come stay a week with us through Christmas. We'd decorate our house an' hang up our stockin'. We always hung up our stockin' an' decorated with holly an' the kind of greenery we had. We didn't have bought decorations or things like that unless we had some paper an' could make a chain, y' know, colored paper—an' ivy, whatever we could find. We had a Christmas tree an' hung up our stockin's. We'd get a orange an' a apple an' three, four pieces o' candy an' maybe a harp [harmonica] 'r a pencil 'r a monkey a-climbin' a string or somethin' like that. An' our mother's an' daddy's shoes, they'd always be oranges in their shoes." —**Margaret Norton, Winter 1973**

"It was 1957; I was about twelve years old. Dad, G. A. Nasworthy, Sr., was a meat cutter with Winn-Dixie. In the summertime, he'd be in and out of the freezers; then he'd come home to the farm, and he'd work all night on the farm. He seemed to have a cold all the time. He just shrugged it off, but it kept getting worse and worse. Finally Mama got him to the doctor, and after tests and all, they found out that he had cancer of his larynx. He had to have his larynx removed. He could not talk, but he could write notes and things like that. He just couldn't talk when they took his voice box out. He never had the 'speakers,' though. He learned to talk without 'em. He'd have him a five-gallon bucket while he was out plowin' at night, and if he wanted somethin', usually a cup of coffee, he'd beat on that bucket. When I heard that bucket, I knew he wanted somethin'. As he learned to talk—they taught him to talk using air—you had to really listen to him. His voice was real raspy and low, but it got to the point that I could be way on the other side of the room, and I could understand everything he said.

"My dad had had a laryngectomy. He had insurance, enough that could take care of his speech and for what he had been through with his surgery, but that was all. He was not working.

"This Christmas, somehow or 'nother, Mom and Dad had got across to us that we didn't really have money to do much of a Christmas. So my sister, who was about three years older than me, we were pretty well resolved. You know, we were owed nothin'.

"And so Christmas mornin' we had a little bitty tree on top of the TV. Christmas mornin', we go ahead and get up, and we come in the middle of the room. My mom and dad were sittin' at the kitchen table havin' coffee. My dad was a big coffee drinker. He 'saucered' the coffee. He'd boil it hot as he could, and he'd pour it in a saucer and blow it, so we always called it 'saucered' coffee. But he had already had his coffee when we came in. We'd glanced at the little tree. We were thinkin', well, maybe there was somethin', but we didn't see anything—just the little tree there and the two little sleighs. And so we headed into the kitchen to eat breakfast.

"We started eating, and I think Mama . . . no, I believe it was Daddy said somethin' about 'Well, did you check the Christmas tree?' And we said, 'Yes, sir, we saw it when we came by it.' And he said, 'Well, you didn't see anything on it?' We hadn't seen nothin'. He said, 'Maybe you oughta go back and look again.' So we jumped up and ran back in there to see if there was somethin'. We looked; we didn't see nothin'. So we go back to eat breakfast 'cause we didn't see nothin' there. So Mama said, 'Well, you need to go back and look . . . look a little more.' So we went back and started lookin' again.

"My sister finally saw it: two watches. They were hung on the little reindeer—a lady's watch and a man's watch. Dad and Mama had got their watches fixed and gave them to us for Christmas." **—G. A. Nasworthy, Jr., 2005**

"At Christmastime, most every girl on the street got one doll. One year I got a thing full of fruit. Mama and Daddy, they didn't have the money. I looked forward to Christmas because of the new doll . . . Christmas was celebrated when we went to my grandmother's, which was my mother's mother, in Dillard [Georgia]. Everybody come, and we fellowshipped all day long. We had a big dinner—no gifts. Our gifts were being a family. That was our Christmas: a doll and family." **—Loraine Corbin, Fall/Winter 2004**

"Well, one special gift I got was a toothbrush made out of birch or black gum twigs. It was about eight inches long, and one end was chewed to make it like a brush. We'd dip it in a snuffbox and brush our teeth with that. It was so special 'cause it's the first one I'd ever gotten."

—Lara Coggins, *A Foxfire Christmas*

"My daddy had a little country store, and at Christmas he'd have oranges shipped in on the train and candy and little toys. I remember he had little toy lamps that would light up. We'd get real loud noise. He'd have firecrackers. We children would get up early and go shoot caps and firecrackers.

"We'd get little store-bought dolls. I remember getting the prettiest one. It was a little china doll. She had on a little gold necklace. It was painted on. That was the most special present I ever got." **—Lucy Hyatt, Fall 1986**

"I remember wakin' up one mornin' and findin' a box of goodies under the bed. There was a big school tablet about two inches thick, rough paper, and it had a big 5 on the cover. And there were penny pencils that were made out of cedar. They were regular pencil length and round, but they were slimmer. The erasers was glued in the end—no metal, just the cedar wood." **—Lucille Ponder, *A Foxfire Christmas***

"Some of the gifts we got were dolls, maybe one or two times, and if we were lucky, some of the kinfolk would bring us chewin' gum and toys. My favorite present was a doll that my mama made out of cornshucks. We would make some of the toys we played with. We would make a ball out of thread and bat it back and forwards on the weekends. Sometimes you would find an old puzzle at school, and they might have let you have it or put it together." —**Essie Ritchie, Spring/Summer 2004**

> **"There was nothin' under the tree, not one thing. . . . All the other children at school had told us about the great Christmas dinner they had last year. Dinnertime arrived, and, to my surprise, it was not special but the same water gravy and biscuits that we had every day."**
>
> —***Clyde Hodge***

"I just knew this year Santa would make it to my house! This Christmas mornin', I woke up before anyone else did. I said to myself, 'I want to see what I got. I've been so good this year.'

"To my amazement, there was nothin' under the tree, not one thing! I checked all nine trees, and there was nothin'. I was so sad, I cried again. All the other children at school had told us about the great Christmas dinner they had last year. Dinnertime arrived, and, to my surprise, it was not special but the same water gravy and biscuits that we had every day. Christmas was a big disappointment. I couldn't understand. Everybody else was makin' such a big deal over Christmas.

"I went next door to see little Susie. I wanted to know if Santa had stopped at her house again this year.

"Susie answered the door and said, 'Oh, Clyde, look what I got for Christmas.'

"She had the most beautiful blondheaded doll I had ever seen. I stammered, 'It is a beautiful doll, Susie.' But my thought flashed, why had Susie got something for Christmas, and I never got anything? I made up my mind that it was not fair that Susie got a doll, and I didn't get anything. I waited patiently for Susie to lay down her new doll. We played for an hour. Then Susie's mother called her to dinner.

"I said, 'Let me hold your baby while you eat.'

"Susie said, 'You can hold her until I get back.'

"Quick as Susie went to the house, I took off with the dollie. I thought if I couldn't get anything from Santa, Susie would have to forfeit her doll, too. I climbed up on this big rock cliff in the backyard. I found a hole under this boulder. I took her doll and hid it and then piled rocks over the hole to cover it up. I sneaked down from the cliff and went in the house. I sat down on the floor appearing to be busy.

"Susie began hollerin', 'Clyde, where's my dollie? Clyde, where's my dollie? Where's my dollie?'

"I said, 'Somebody must have stolen your dollie.'

"She ran home crying, 'Mama, Mama, someone stole my dollie.'

"Well, you probably guessed, her mama marched over and asked, 'Where's Susie's dollie?'

"I said, 'I don't know where Susie's dollie is.'

"But when Dad came home and took me out back to the shed and used his belt, I confessed to burying her doll."

—Clyde Hodge, *A Foxfire Christmas*

"For Christmas we'd get some candy, oranges, apples, maybe a doll, colorin' book, and crayons. I guess that's about all—I mean for the girls. Boys would get 'em a little ol' car and candy and oranges, an apple, maybe a colorin' book for them. It sure was exciting for us." **—Ada Crone, Summer 1980**

"It was hard times back when I was a child, and when Christmas came, people enjoyed it. They really loved to see Christmas come. I'd get a new pair of shoes every Christmas, and I'd sleep with 'em on the first night. Since we didn't get but one pair a year, they had to do us. We could tear 'em up if we wanted to, but if we did, we went barefooted. If we took care of 'em, they lasted us all winter. When the first day of May came, I was tickled because Mama'd let us go barefooted." **—Nola Campbell, *A Foxfire Christmas***

PLATE 87 "For Christmas we'd get some candy, oranges, apples, maybe a doll, colorin' book, and crayons." —Ada Crone

"My mom and dad got along best you've ever seen 'til Christmas. Daddy'd get drunk ever' Christmas. He worked like a slave through all the rest of time. When Christmas come, we'd have two peppermint sticks of candy, a orange, and a apple in our sock. We hung our socks up then, all of us. That's what we'd have. My daddy went off to the store one time. He got our Christmas that day, and he got him a new pair of overalls. Somebody gave him some liquor—he couldn't buy it, but somebody gave him enough to get him drunk. He walked home. It's four miles from town to where we lived, and when we seen him comin', Mommy says, 'He's drunk.' She could tell just as well when he got drunk. We went out to meet him. He had a box of candy and one leg of those new overalls under his arm. The other leg of 'em he was a-draggin' in the dirt. He had that candy strowed everywhere. We went back down the road and picked up the sticks of candy where he had spilt it—them long, hard sticks of peppermint candy. Then they wasn't no sugar sticks.

"When he got home, Mommy got on him. Just as sure as he got drunk, she'd get on him right then and make it worse. If she'd just a-waited 'til he'd got sober, it'd been a whole lot better. But she'd get on him, and they'd quarrel. They'd have a cuss fight just as sure as he'd get drunk. They wasn't a Christmas that passed hardly that he didn't get drunk, but through the other times, he hardly ever did."

—D. B. Dayton, Summer 1980

"That made me think of where Santa Claus started. I forgot I have that tradition. I remember when we used to hang our stockin's up Christmas Eve night, and a friend of mine—he's dead now—put up a switch in my stockin'. Lord, I just cried!

"Way back there, we didn't have oranges like they do now, so we wouldn't each get one in our stockin'. There was three or four of us children, and Grandmother would cut an orange and give me a piece and her a piece. One child didn't get a whole orange. Oranges were high then because they didn't have much then. They'd divide 'em and give us each a section of rind."

—Carrie Stewart, Fall 1981

"We used t' always go a-serenadin' on Christmas Eve. That's when we got our biggest fun. It was children that went. I really thought there 'as a Santa Claus. We always had our stockin's. We felt there was a Santa Claus. An' back then, that's the onliest time that children got toys 'r candy an' stuff. They didn't get it like they do now ever' time they go to th' store right where there is somethin' t' buy. I believe that's why children don't take as much as they did back then because they didn't have all this.

"We'd have a tree. We decorated it mostly with crepe paper. Sometimes they'd buy stuff an' take these sycamore balls an' paint 'em different colors an' popcorn, and then it was lit with a candle. And when my younguns was little, we'd put up a great big tree an' candles, an', boy, the first thing we knowed, that the tree was a-catchin' fire! I never did put a candle on a tree an' light it no more. That gave me a scare.

"The children all got presents—th' parents'd get 'em for the children. An' at school, why, they was presents for all younguns. The younguns didn't buy none, but they'd have a Christmas tree there." —**Ethel Corn, Winter 1973**

> **"We would sing and have the ol' shotgun a-shoot, shoot, shootin'. We would ring bells and beat dishpans and anything else we could find to make a noise. Everybody'd have a bell."** ***—Bass Hyatt***

"They'd have big serenades some Christmas Eve nights. A crowd would get together and go serenadin', serenade everybody's house around. We would go to the houses and shoot and ring bells until they let us come in, and they treated us. They would give us candy, apples, or just anything. I know a family that treated us real good with corn whiskey [laughter]. We

PLATE 88 "When my younguns was little, we'd put up a great big tree an' candles, an' boy, the first thing we knowed, that tree was a-catchin' fire!" —Ethel Corn

would sing and have the ol' shotgun a-shoot, shoot, shootin'. We would ring bells and beat dishpans and anything else we could find to make a noise. Everybody'd have a bell. The boys would have guns. When it got so cold, we used to wear big ol' wool coats to go serenadin'.

"Christmas didn't used to be as big and drawn-out like now. We would get candy and an orange or two for Christmas and sometimes a toy. One of the kids got three little owls carved on a log one time. We would get little tin horns back then, some kind of little toy, you know. The boys and girls would have firecrackers shootin' all over the country.

"We never did have a Christmas tree at home when I was a kid. We always hung our stockin's above the fireplace so that Santa Claus could fill them up. We believed that Santa Claus would come down the chimney. We believed in him for a little while—never very long, though: The older kids would tell us who Santa was. Kids found out pretty quick. They never did believe in it long.

"We always had a big Christmas Day dinner. We had a chicken or a turkey, and we'd always have lots of pork. We killed hogs just before Christmas, and we'd have sausage and backbones and ribs and all such as that.

"We always got a little something on Christmas. We put up a big tree in the church for the settlement. The only type of Christmas tree I ever saw back then was a holly bush. They'd have all them berries on there. They'd tie the top of the tree to the church ceiling, and you could grab ahold of a limb and turn it, pull the presents off, and see the kid's name. We'd trim the tree with popcorn. Then we'd take the gifts that we were giving and just spread them out—hang 'em up on the tree. They'd be somethin' people made—aprons and things.

"I remember goin' to a little gatherin' back up here on one Christmas Eve. They had a Christmas tree and a box supper, and some of the children would recite little speeches about Christmas.

"There was one little girl who got up and told the one about 'Twas the night before Christmas, and all through the house, not a creature was stirring, not even a mouse.' Well, it came to the part about when Santa Claus laughed, 'his little round belly shook like a bowl full of jelly'—and they thought that was the funniest thing. They'd never heared that one before. They laughed an hour about it. I never did have no hand in those recitations myself.

"The school never did have a Christmas tree, but the schoolteachers would turn out and treat the kids a little before Christmas, bring the kids candy or apples." —**Bass Hyatt, Fall 1986**

"We celebrated Christmas at our house by having most of the family in. Back then, the folks met up on Christmas—the brothers and sisters and their children. We would start celebrating on Christmas Eve, and by Christmas night all of us children would be real tired. I think the parents stayed up and visited and told tales.

"But on Christmas Eve and Christmas night, we were celebrating—all of us together. My three brothers would be right along with my sisters and me. I had two older brothers and a smaller one. We had big families back then. Everybody knowed each other, and we had the most of fun. I do think we had more fun than kids do now. We didn't have wheels, but we had our legs. We walked, serenadin'. We didn't ride in a car. We all wanted to be together. There wasn't nothin' but just a road wide enough for one wagon or car to pass. . . .

"If we didn't yell and whoop, why we'd go to singin' Christmas songs—'Jingle Bells' and 'Santa Claus Is Coming to Town.' We'd go serenadin' whether it was warm, sleetin', rainin', or snowin'. We didn't let nothin' stop us from doin' that. That was our yearly thing. We enjoyed it. I think they ought to now, but so many lights so close together, you'd know if anybody was comin'. You couldn't slip up on them unless you lived out in the country. That was fun!" —**Burma Patterson, Fall 1985**

> **"One time, they got a wagon and tied it up in a tree, an' that old man never could find it. They had t' go show it to him a month or so later."**
>
> —***Bertha Dockins***

PLATE 89 "We'd go serenadin' whether it was warm, sleetin', rainin', or snowin'." —Burma Patterson

"Christmas was th' big thing. They'd go serenadin' on Christmas Eve, an' they'd go to a house an' turn out their cattle an' pick up some of their things an' hide 'em. Maybe it'd be a month b'fore they'd tell th' folks where they were. That was th' young people—teenagers. Old people didn't do that! One time they got a wagon and tied it up in a tree, an' that old man never could find it. They had t' go show it to him a month or so later. An' they'd bring their guns an' their bells with 'em serenadin' an' shoot th' guns and ring th' bells. They'd sing Christmas songs, shoot firecrackers. It was wild! But, you know, they don't do that no more—they got t' where they'd do so much damage. My husband told me about one time where he grew up: Somebody shot under th' floor, an' th' otherun shot higher; it went in an' hit th' man's bed where he lay. An' they said they quit after that. People was gettin' too mean.

"Always had a big meal—had pies an' cakes, ham 'r beef, dried apple pie, berry pies, sweet potato pie. Usually a lot of th' family'd get together—not all dressed up. They just went on th' way they was an' had a big celebration.

"We had stockin's—just th' children did—an' they'd hang 'em by the fireplace. An' if they didn't have stockin's, they'd put it out there with their shoes 'r their boots. An th' parents'd fill 'em with candy apples. Now, in my time, oranges were scarce, an' our parents'd get us maybe one apiece. As far as toys, I've got one little doll I got long ago—a little bought doll."

—Bertha Dockins, Winter 1973

"We'd get together and go serenadin' the people in the community on Christmas Eve or maybe Christmas night. I didn't get to go 'til I was twelve or thirteen. That was about 1927 because I was born in 1915. Some of the men and boys would have guns and just shoot for the noise. We'd have bells and take pans and beat on them with a stick—anything to make a racket with. We'd go around somebody's house and holler. If they was sociable, they'd let us in. They might serve us some juice or other refreshments. It seemed a funny way to celebrate Christmas, but then we didn't have as many things as young people do now for entertainment. We just had to make up our own.

"If we had snow during Christmas, we'd get out and run around in it barefooted—get out and run a short distance—and then back to the house. We'd run so fast our feet didn't get cold.

"I guess lookin' forward to Santa Claus and what we might get was my favorite part of Christmas. It was very simple—a little toy, an apple or orange, a stick or two of candy. Why, if that's all we got, we were satisfied because there wasn't anything else.

"We had a fireplace, and we used to say Santa Claus came down the chimney. Some of the older children got curious about Santa Claus, so they put ashes around the hearth to see if they could get Santa Claus's footprints! Well, the next mornin', there'd be a footprint there. I can remember my daddy would get up on Christmas mornin' as early as we'd get up or before and get a big fire goin' in the fireplace so we'd be warm. Then he'd sit there and enjoy the children seein' that footprint and everyone openin' their stockin's as much as we did.

"One present stands out in my mind that I got when I was just a young girl. My older sister got me a little Red Cross doll all dressed up in a Red Cross uniform, like a nurse. It had a china head and wasn't very big, really, not over eight or ten inches high, but that was a special gift."

—Anne Thurmond, Fall 1985

> **"Now kids get so many toys they don't enjoy Christmas because every time they go to the store, it's Christmas. They won't get out of there 'til you buy them a toy. The only time we got a toy was at Christmas."** ***—Lawton Brooks***

"Back then, there wasn't much Christmas, to tell you the truth, because there wasn't nothin' for you to have like they is now. We didn't know what a firecracker was. Never heard tell of a firecracker. All the noise we made for Christmas—serenadin' people on Christmas Eve—we done with a shotgun. We'd get shotgun shells fifty cents a box, and we'd get out there and shoot up in the air—serenadin' people. Them shotgun barrels would get so hot we'd have to set 'em down and wait a while and then start again.

"Just gettin' out and goin' around, sneakin' up to someone's house, was our entertainment at Christmastime. That's what we called serenading. They didn't know nothin' about it, and we'd just come up shootin', ringin' bells, and makin' the durndest noise you ever heard. If they was in bed, they'd just have to get up and ask us in. They'd always invite us in and feed us—they were lookin' for a bunch anyway. They'd have somethin' for us to eat and sometimes give us a present or somethin'.

"There'd be about twenty-five or thirty of us. The girls would join us, too, and we'd all go. Everybody would make some kind of noise, one way or another. We were just serenadin' the people that lived around in the settlement. They wasn't thick settled, though, like they are here. There might be somebody lived here, and it might be half a mile out there to the next house, maybe a mile. But we'd go and just keep a-goin' 'til we gave 'em all a good round. We had to walk, and sometimes we go for five or six miles—take us half the night to get back after we got through serenadin' people. 'Course, we'd never get in 'til way along up in the mornin'. We'd be goin' all night nearly.

"We'd do tricks to people, too. That was part of serenadin'. People in them days would have a cow and a horse at least, in the stalls in the barn. While the people were asleep that night, we'd take the horse out of one stall and put it in the cow's stall and move the cows into the horse's stall. They'd go in there to milk the next mornin'—we liked to be there to watch—and there'd stand the horse in the cow stall. Boy! They could get mad! They'd throw their milk bucket down on the ground. They'd be mad enough to kill somebody, but they didn't know who done it. Us kids got a lot o' kick out of that. We'd do all kinds of tricks like that. We'd move people's stuff and hide their stuff, hide their axes or somethin' else. Whatever we could find loose, layin' out, we'd hide it—wouldn't put it where he couldn't find it, but he'd maybe have to hunt for two or three days for it.

"Oh, yes, we had gag gifts. I'd always fix up somethin' that nobody wouldn't have—wrap it up mighty nice—and send it. Had a lot of fun with that. I don't remember what any of them was—we done so much of that. In fact, we done more of that than anything else. . . .

"I was a pretty good-sized boy before we ever had a Christmas tree. We always thought Santa Claus came down the durned chimney all the time. We hung up our stockings, but we didn't put up no Christmas tree. Santa Claus would bring us all kinds of candy and oranges, things like that, but they wasn't no toys. I'd rather have a tricycle back then than have a Cadillac today.

"We had to make our own wagons. We always had us a wagon, kept us a good wagon. If ours got to wearin' out, our daddy would make us another one. Now he'd have us one for Christmas.

"We didn't have no little ol' toy pistols, cap busters, to play with. Didn't know what they was. All the guns that we ever had was made out of wood. Somebody would just whittle 'em out. We couldn't buy things at the store for Christmas like you can now. I have an idea that was really better. Now kids get so many toys they don't enjoy Christmas because every time they go to the store, it's Christmas. They won't get out of there 'til you buy them a toy. The only time we got a toy was at Christmas. And that was a year apart. But then it just wasn't there to buy.

"We'd get up about two o'clock Christmas mornin'. As soon as we heard Daddy start grindin' the coffee, we knew we'd better get up. (I've still got that ol' coffee grinder.) We was all early risers because my daddy always got us out at five o'clock in the mornin'. I don't care if it was pourin' rain, snowin' knee-deep, you come out of there. If it was too bad to get out in the field and work, we'd go to the barn—clean up. He always found us somethin' to do. So we was used to gettin' up early.

"Christmas Day was a huntin' day. All of us boys went a-huntin' that day. Our parents would let us have about two days at Christmas to hunt in, and I always had me about five or six good dogs. . . .

"We always had a big Christmas dinner, all kinds of pies and things. We raised our own turkeys and all kinds of chicken, so we had our own turkey for Christmas dinner. I'd say coconut cake and lemon pie are my favorites at Christmas. I never get tired of those things. I'll eat 'em 'til they make me sick, and I'll still love the dadblame things. I just love 'em.

"We always had church, Christmas or not, and that's one thing we had to go to. . . .

"Some of our folks would come down from below town and spend Christmas with us—about five or six of them would. There was always somethin' goin' on at Christmastime. We was at their house, or they was at ours. We'd have a good time, enjoy a few days durin' Christmastime. The family gets scattered out, but they always come back home for Christmas, always did come back for Christmas to see us. We always looked forward to Christmas, had a lot of fun." —**Lawton Brooks, Fall 1985**

"On Christmas Eve night, we'd all go a-serenadin'. We went from house to house. We'd put on different old clothes, you know, and carry things to beat on and cowbells to ring—all things to make noise. We went up to one place, and the man told his wife, 'Lula, just carry the bed out and give 'em some room.' It was a great big room, and they cleared it out for dancin' and playin' games. And some of 'em did dance. I didn't, though. It was against my religion, but my brother would play the harmonica. They'd turn the big room over to us. We'd all play games like go in and out the windows and spin the bottle, and I can't remember what all. We'd be there 'til midnight.

"We'd play tricks on people, too, and my brother helped do that. One place where we went to dance and play games had two big horses with white faces. Those boys took shoe polish and painted them black! They painted those horses' faces! Those folks never said a word about it.

"We had a big dinner on Christmas Day but not on Christmas Eve. We didn't have no cakes then because we cooked over a fireplace. But Mother made a great big stack of apple pies out of dried apples and a great big, high stack of pumpkin custards." —**Nora Garland, Fall 1985**

"I remember about the first thing I ever got besides candy and oranges. I was six or seven. Santa Claus brought it. It was a monkey made out of a piece of tin climbin' a string, and that thing would go plumb to the top of it. Then you could let it back down. That's about the first present I remember gettin'. . . .

"My favorite present was a little cap pistol I got from Santa Claus. Santa Claus was about the same as he is today, but he didn't have red clothes like he's got today. We thought he came down the chimney usually. But one time he brought us some candy and came in the front door. I was about six years old. He asked me what I wanted for Christmas. Then he jumped up directly and said, 'Oh, Lord! Them deers are leavin' me. I got to go.' He went to hollerin', 'Ho, ho!' and went out the door after 'em. I knew who it was, but I played ignorant, you know. To him, I didn't know who it was. He didn't come in until after dark. Every Christmas we kept listenin' for him, but we never seen him but that one time.

"We would get up in the mornin' and open presents; then we went out and played in the snow. It almost always snowed on Christmas when I was growin' up. We always went and played in it and went sleddin' in the sleds we made.

PLATE 90 "Santa Claus brought it. It was a monkey made out of a piece of tin climbin' a string, and that thing would go plumb to the top of it." —Billy Long

"We went serenadin' on Christmas Eve. We'd go to somebody's house and make a racket singin', shootin' guns, ringin' cowbells, and runnin' around the house until they'd let us in and give us somethin' to eat. There were about twenty of us kids that would go. We stayed out one Christmas Eve all night long." —**Billy Long, Fall 1986**

"I was only three or so, but I remember this distinctly: Santa Claus left a sooty footprint on the hearth where he had come down the chimney. Of course, my daddy had taken his shoe and pushed it on the back of the fireplace and then set it on the hearth, but I was sure that Santa Claus had come down there and that was his footprint.

"Santa Claus always came and filled our stockings. There was a tradition that a Brazil nut was in the toe of the stocking. We would get an apple and, later on, oranges (they weren't very common when I was little) and candy raisins, which were a special treat, and, generally, one present.

"I know I got a book one time, and another time, I wanted a necklace so bad that I cut a picture of one out of the Sears and Roebuck catalog and hung that picture around my neck to hint that's what I wanted—and I got a necklace . . . One year he put a pretty ribbon for my hair in my stocking.

"It was traditional to have a Lady Baltimore cake for Christmas. That's a white cake, and it has a filling of nuts and raisins.

"I don't think Christmas was any better back then, but it was different. We just didn't have the material things that people have now. And we were taught the meaning of Christmas. That was the good thing about it."

—Clyde English, Fall 1985

"We'd decorate the house with holly and cedar and mistletoe. We always had a Christmas tree, but we made our own ornaments then. We grew our popcorn. We'd shell it and pop it over the fire coals in a wire popper. We'd string the popcorn with a needle and thread. We didn't put butter on it if we were gonna use it for the tree—just dry popcorn.

"We would make roping—weave crepe paper together for the tree. Sometimes we'd use solid red, sometimes solid green, sometimes weave two colors together. We'd put that on the tree, just like you use tinsel now. We'd cut out shapes in construction paper and make ornaments. We'd put a string through a little hole in the ornament and hang it on the tree.

"Someone would usually dress up as Santa Claus and come around by the house on Christmas Eve night, and a lot of the young people would go serenading that night. They'd just go from house to house. Maybe they would go in and sing, or maybe they'd pull tricks on somebody. They might move somethin'—like if a hay rake was sittin' there, they'd take it and move it somewhere else.

"They'd shoot off fireworks at Christmastime, usually on Christmas Eve. We had hickory wood; my brothers would take the hickory coals while they were red hot and pour water on 'em and then hit 'em with the back of a poleax or somethin' like that, and those coals would shoot and sound just like firecrackers shooting. My brothers have done that a lot of times.

"We'd always hang our stockings up across the mantle. We'd get raisins and candies and oranges and apples—sometimes a doll. The present I remember the best was a sleepy doll, a doll that would shut its eyes when you would lay it down. And it had pretty hair—looked real. I was nine, I think, when I got that doll.

"Christmas dinner would usually be a baked chicken and dressing, sometimes ham, and then biscuits and cornbread and vegetables—and, of course, pies and cakes. My mother always made a raisin cake. That was very special because we didn't have it many other times. She would put a raisin filling between the regular yellow cake layers and then put a white icing—what we call now a seven-minute icing—on the outside of it. The filling was made with sugar and water and raisins. She always made a coconut cake and a chocolate cake, too, but the raisin cake was the special one."

—Bessie Kelly, Fall 1985

"At Christmas there were five of us: Mom and Dad, Bernice, Lloyd, and myself. We enjoyed our Christmases very much. It was just the inward family. I imagine Christmas was my favorite time of year because that was when we got a lot of food and cake. You know a kid loves that.

"We would sit around the fire at night, of course. The fireplace was the only heat we had for the house, and we would sit around it. We would get a lot of rich pine, you know, and then get the fire blazin'. Then my mom and dad would tell us stories about Christmas and Christ's birthday and why we had it.

"We got the tree in the woods where there were holly trees. We would just walk and hunt until we found us one. They were three or four feet tall or somethin' like that. They wouldn't be big. Our houses weren't big then, you know.

"I guess decoratin' the tree, which was a holly, was the most fun to me. We put popcorn on it and such as that. We always had what decorations we made at home, you know, out of holly and mistletoe, and we would make loops out of paper and make chains."

—Leonard Hollifield, Spring 1989

PLATE 91 "I imagine Christmas was my favorite time of year because that was when we got a lot of food and cake. You know a kid loves that." —Leonard Hollifield

"We had a Christmas tree at school. Every Christmas tree back then was a holly. You didn't see any other kind. Our teacher would order us pencils with our names on them. Oh, that was somethin'—with our names engraved on them. Then she'd give us an orange and about three sticks of candy rolled up in white tissue paper. That was a wonderful treat to us, an' we appreciated that more than you would ever think children would now. They get so much.

"'Til later years, we'd raise our own meats for Christmas. We'd kill hogs in November an' save the backbones an' ribs, and my mama'd cook a big pot of them at Christmas. They'd kill roosters and hens and make chicken and dumplin's. She'd bake hams, and we'd have our own homegrown meats and vegetables—Irish potatoes and sweet potatoes. We didn't have to go to the store for very much.

"She'd cook a big pan of cornbread and biscuits and put clean white cloths over them, and that'd keep 'em just as moist and good.

"She'd start cookin' about December 22 or 23, so she already had the cakes and pies cooked before Christmas—sweet potato pies and pumpkin pies. She cooked on a woodstove at that. It was good food! She didn't go out and buy anything.

"She cooked food to decorate our Christmas tree, too. She'd make gingerbread men and women and little boys and girls and tie strings around their necks and put them on the Christmas tree. Our Christmas tree was always a holly with red berries, and holly trees are stout. You can tie about anything on them. We didn't have much sweet stuff, and that was our treat.

She sweetened the gingerbread with sorghum syrup from the cane my daddy had grown.

"We were farmers. My daddy grew our popcorn an' we popped our own popcorn. We would thread it into popcorn strands and put those all over the tree. Mama would get big holly berries, and we'd string those into a strand for the tree. And I'm not kidding—those were the prettiest decorations to me of anything nearly you could put on a Christmas tree.

"Then she'd pop a BIG dishpan full of popcorn with a lot of butter, pure country butter. She'd cook sorghum syrup into a candy 'til it'd spin a thread, and she'd start pourin' that over the popcorn 'til she got as much as she wanted. Then she'd grease her hands and make popcorn balls. She'd even let us help make the popcorn balls. That was a big Christmas treat for all of us.

"They wouldn't get the tree 'til about December 22 or 23, a few days before Christmas Eve. Now Christmas Eve night was when we'd put stuff on it that'd spoil, like the gingerbread people. You couldn't let them stay too long. We'd decorate it Christmas Eve night for Christmas mornin'.

"We would go out in the forest and get the prettiest pine burrs [cones] to decorate our house at Christmas. They're beautiful yet! My mother would take snow-white lime and paint those pinecones. Well, she left some natural—white and natural. She fixed the pinecones 'til we had decorations galore just out of pinecones. We'd get all kinds of cedar and make flowerpots out of them. My mother would take crepe paper and make roses—pink, blue, yellow (yellow was my daddy's favorite) and tie those roses on that cedar. She would get a coat hanger and bend it round and tie pine greenery around it and then attach pine burrs and also tie some of those different-colored roses on it and hang that wreath up on the door.

"My parents didn't go to the store and buy any gifts. My mother would have a pair of socks she had knit for my daddy. We had sheep, and she spun the wool. She knitted all the girls' stockin's. She might knit a scarf for some of us. Then my daddy was good at takin' his little ol' handsaw and knife and makin' things. I remember one year him makin' a big ol' dough pan. My mama would roll out dough for biscuits and cookies in that wooden dough pan.

"We didn't have wrappin' paper and ribbons. A lot of times, my mother would just put our presents under a tree or in our stockin'. She might drop them in a brown paper bag. In later years, she did have tissue paper.

"We had a fireplace and a mantel, and Dad would drive nails in to hang our stockin's on. We had stockin's with garters, and we'd take that garter and put it 'round our stockin' and hang it up on that nail; that's where Santa Claus would put our Christmas gifts.

"About the only things we'd get in our stockin's were peppermint candy and oranges and little Kewpie dolls for us girls and maybe some pencils, and the boys would get a knife.

"We were brought up to believe in Santa Claus, and there's still a Santa Claus for me. There always will be. The longest day I live, there'll be a Santa Claus. I think the spirit of Christmas is Santa Claus—is giving."

—Burma Patterson, Fall 1985

"Christmas was the main holiday of the year. Everybody took Christmas off. We wouldn't have to work around the farm. Usually, our dad would especially get some wood up, ready for good, big fires. He would always get what he called a backstick, a big log to put in the fireplace, and it would last about three days. I guess it was called a yule log in England. Dad just called it a backstick.

"We would always cook a lot of things—plenty to do for several days—so if company came in, we'd have somethin' sweet. Mother didn't make cakes. She made gingerbread and pies, fruit pies. Oh, she might make those pies maybe two days before Christmas. Of course we were tempted to eat them. [Laughter] She'd serve part of that before Christmastime, so we had somethin' beforehand. . . .

"Now our Christmases when I was a child were very simple. Of course, we didn't expect much at Christmas because we lived on the farm, and about all the extra cash would be from what we called peddling. Dad would take some cabbage and produce down in the country—that would be Toccoa, Lavonia, Hartwell [Georgia], and those towns—and he'd bring back supplies we needed.

"Instead of going to the store, Mother made our decorations, and she'd get everything from the woods. We decorated the windows and doors and got some mistletoe to hang over the doors.

"We didn't bring in a Christmas tree when we were children, just the evergreens from the woods to decorate with. Mother used flour to make snow to put on the evergreen boughs, and then she sprinkled salt for the crystals to look like ice. She made a paste of flour and water and then put it on the leaves and sprinkled on regular salt, and it glistened. It stayed on, too. I know Mother didn't have any glue of any kind.

"We didn't have special stockings to hang up for Santa Claus, just clean ones that we wore that mother had knit for us. We'd hang them up, but we didn't have very much in those stockings, maybe an orange and some stick candy. I remember one time we had little dolls, and that's about all the toys we had.

"I can still remember how much I loved Santa Claus! When I was about seven or eight years old, my parents told us there wasn't a Santa Claus. I was so depressed because I had thought he was real."

—Lassie McCall, Fall 1986

"I can well remember they got my sister Pearl a sleepy doll, and mine wouldn't close his eyes like that and go to sleep. My brother told me if I'd hit it with a hoe handle, it would go to sleep, and I give it a lick with that hoe and it broke!" ***—Ethel Corn***

"I can't hardly tell you my favorite part of Christmas when I was a child. I loved every minute because that was the day our Savior was borned on.

"We'd decorate the house with cedar and holly, and my daddy would generally get the Christmas tree. We've had trees here that would touch the ceiling. We'd make decorations with different-colored paper—link chains—and with popcorn and pinecones. Back then, there was no electrical power, and we used candles with clamps on the bottom to decorate the tree. One tree, one of those candles got too hot, and then needles caught on fire. I never did put another candle up on a tree.

"We would get these sycamore balls and paint them all different colors, and they made pretty decorations for somethin' that was free for the asking. For snow, I'd take wash powders and add some water and beat them with an eggbeater—just beat a foam out of it—and put that all over the Christmas tree like snow. It would stay there for three or four days.

"On Christmas Eve night, they'd have a play at the church, a Bible play, and we'd go caroling and sing and have fun. Then we'd have candy drawings. Someone would buy stick candy and break it up, mix it all up—all different colors—and we young people would choose up partners. If you and your partner didn't draw the same color candy, you'd put it back. If we did draw the same color, we'd keep it. We'd do that until all the candy was gone.

"I never knowed Dad to work on Christmas Day. He'd just take that one day off from the farm. The family was always together at Christmas.

"My favorite Christmas gift was a Dutch delft doll, made of china, you know. I can well remember they got my sister, Pearl, a sleepy doll, and mine wouldn't close its eyes like that and go to sleep. My brother told me if I'd hit it with a hoe handle, it would go to sleep, and I give it a lick with that hoe and it broke!

"As I got older, I hated to see a white Christmas because the old people always said, 'A white Christmas for a fat graveyard.' I don't know if there was anything to this, but there'd be a lot of deaths during the year following a white Christmas. It seemed like it worked out that way. I don't like to see a white Christmas.

"People buys toys for their children every week nearly, nowadays. Every time they go to the store, a youngun gets a toy, but they don't enjoy it. They just play with it for a few weeks, and then it's all tore up. But when Christmas came, if they didn't get toys all year round, they'd like it a whole lot better. They get so many they don't hardly enjoy it. Christmastime was the only time we got toys and all things like that. There's a lot of difference in the way it was then and the way it is now." —**Ethel Corn, Fall 1985**

"When I was a child, at Christmastime we never had a Christmas tree in our home. My mother set th' table with plates, an' each of us had our name written on a slip of paper and put in this plate. Then we received stick candy; chocolate drops; and chestnuts, black walnuts, hazelnuts; and then we'd get raisins in the bunch. The girls got dolls, and the boys would get Barlow pocketknives and toy pistols. All this was on the table. And we never decorated for Christmas. We just cleaned house. The neighbors would come in and see what we'd gotten for Christmas. And every Christmas mornin', Jule Grissom would come down to our house with a large paper bag with apples and oranges and bananas. And of course, my mother always had a cake and cookies for Jule and his family. They were the best of neighbors.

"My mother would bake five or six cakes a day or two before Christmas. Then we'd have a big cured country ham. She'd put that on to boil a day before Christmas. This ham, when it got tender and done, was skinned; then my mother'd put black pepper, cayenne pepper, and she dotted it all over the ham. Then we'd have a turkey with all the trimmings. Then we'd have green beans, jellies, preserves, biscuits, and cornbread. The neighbors would come in. Us children would play outside, and the old folks would sit in the house, swappin' recipes and talkin' about the weather and home chores they had to get done.

"If we couldn't get to church, the neighbors would come, and we'd gather around the organ and play and sing Gospel music and Christmas carols."

—**Lelia Gibson, Winter 1973**

"Seeing what we got from Santa Claus was my favorite part of Christmas. I had a team of goats. One year my daddy made me a wagon and a harness for the goats. We got a sled he made, too. It'd snow, and we'd get out and sleigh-ride! I remember one time when I was pretty small, we got a little red wagon. It was about the same size as wagons little children have now. I guess that was my favorite gift.

"We didn't have a Christmas tree back then. We always hung a stocking, or we set out a basket. We'd get some candy and nuts and oranges. Oranges were a treat. And Brazil nuts used to be a favorite. Our stockings were just homemade, but they were not the ones we wore every day. They were bigger!

"Mother used to start baking two weeks or more before Christmas: pound cakes, layer cakes, fruitcakes. We didn't dare come in the house and stomp the floor when she had a pound cake in the oven! My favorite uncle, Noah Randolph, was a good cook! He'd always bring a cake or something when we'd get together. It would be just the family and Grandmother and Grandfather. We'd go to their house for dinner in a buggy or a covered wagon, and we'd have a heated stone in the wagon to keep our feet warm. It was just two miles." **—Margaret Bulgin, Fall 1985**

"At home, we would put up our trees two or three days before Christmas. We never would take it down until after New Year's. I still don't take my tree down 'til after New Year's. They say it's bad luck. That would make a pretty decoration for your tree. We would loop the plaited crepe paper through the tree, like you do tinsel now. We'd get out a lot and hunt hollies, too. They had those pretty red berries.

"We'd do serenadin' a little bit before Christmas Eve. A lot of people shot guns while serenadin', and we'd shoot firecrackers if we had them. The people would come out, and they'd give you stick candy, nuts, oranges, and things, and, if they didn't, the serenadin' would begin. They would put their horses in the cows' stalls and the cows in the horses' stalls. They would hide axes and things like that, hiding their tools, you know. . . .

"We did believe in Santa Claus. We'd get up on Christmas mornin'; the first thing we'd do was look in the fireplace, and there'd be two tracks where he went up. Our daddy had put those in the ashes with his shoe mark, you know. . . .

"On Christmas, our biggest meal was dinner. That tradition has held out through the years. But instead of having turkey, like we do today, we'd have chicken and gravy, dressing, and potatoes. My daddy was bad to hunt. Sometimes we would have squirrel or somethin' like that, wild meat."

—Icie Rickman, Fall 1989

"We made homemade candy, and my mother made cookies and cakes. At Christmastime she didn't get to go to town too often, but she always ordered our Christmastime candy from Sears Roebuck. We had a little mail carrier, and Mama would always order a bucket. The bucket had about five or six different kinds of candy: Some of it was hard, some of it was chocolate cream drops, just various kinds, but she always ordered our Christmas candy from there.

PLATE 92 "The first thing we'd do was look in the fireplace and there'd be two tracks where he went up." —Icie Rickman

"I always looked forward to Christmas. We always had candy and oranges. That was a treat for us. My daddy had an apple orchard, you know, just a home orchard, and we always had apples. We always had those, but we seldom had oranges and candy. We looked forward to having that special treat of more candy and oranges. . . .

"There was one gift that I remember that I got at Christmastime, and I still have it. It was a New Testament that my Sunday school teacher gave me. Then I had my own Bible. I thought that it was great.

"We had a Christmas tree. Most of the time we had a holly bush, and we always tried to get one with berries on it because that gave us some more color. We went out and got our Christmas trees. I was raised on Persimmon [in Rabun County, Georgia]. We lived very close to the woods, so there were a lot of hollies in that area. We would always go out and cut us down one and bring it in, but we always had a Christmas tree.

"We made some of the decorations. We used holly, and I remember there used to be a beautiful vine that grew wild on our land. We would get Dad to help, and we would drape the vine on the tree. It looked real pretty. Sometimes we would string popcorn and make a rope of popcorn."

—Mary Ann Hollifield, Spring 1989

"Usually there would be eight to ten throwing these fireballs with an audience sitting away up in the small lot near the barn. Sometimes the thread would peel off that ball, and it would just be so pretty, like a star falling." ***—Ruby Mae Miller Cheek***

"Usually we had 'fireworks' before Santa came. We enjoyed raveling out old work socks that Papa wore out. We'd ravel 'em and make them into a ball. We'd take a handful of cotton and pack it and then wind the unraveled yarn around it into a firm ball. The ball would be larger than a baseball. Once they were wound real tight, we'd soak them in kerosene in a bucket for several days. Then at Christmastime, we, along with our nearby cousins, would go down into the pasture at night and light them and throw them high up in the air and see our fireworks. Usually there would be eight to ten throwing these fireballs with an audience sitting away up in the small lot near the barn. Sometimes the thread would peel off that ball, and it would just be so pretty, like a star falling. The object was to catch the fireball and throw it again to someone near or a good catcher. We thoroughly enjoyed that. Sometimes we set the pasture on fire! We had to stomp it out, or we cut off some green pine limbs to brush out the fire. When we'd come in, we'd have kerosene-black hands we'd have to wash."

—Ruby Mae Miller Cheek, Spring/Summer 2005

"There was an old man who lived out in the country from Burnsville [Mississippi] by the name of Tom Coke. Every Christmas mornin' he would shoot the anvil. We lived about three miles away, but it sounded like it was right in our backyard. It had a ring to it that I'll never forget. I never did see him do the actual shootin', but every Christmas, everybody in the whole area would be listenin' for that anvil blast early in the mornin'. He never failed to fire it. My great-uncle knew old man Coke, and he told me about how he did it. He'd lay down a heavy timber and put a pile of black powder on it. He'd set the anvil on this, and then he'd scatter a little stream of powder for a few feet. He'd light that line of powder; the fire would run to the powder underneath the anvil, and that would make the explosion."

—Bob Lowery, Spring 1991

"One particular Christmas—I guess I was about eleven or twelve—I had been by myself. Daddy was down here in the city with his friends, and Eldon [her brother] was away. I had got a Christmas tree, and at school we'd colored little strips of paper and glued them into chains for Christmas decorations. It was Christmas Day, but I felt very much alone. I really did. So I thought, 'Well, it's Christmas Day, and there's gonna be good spirit and good cheer at the preacher's house.' I walked across the field, crossed the creek on a foot log, and then back up through another field to his house. When I went in, I didn't feel any kind of uncomfortableness. Their house was so nice and warm, and I was cold. I didn't have a fire at my house that day, and I was wet. On my way over, I'd slipped off the footlog and fallen down into the creek—just like a kid will. The smells of turkey and dressing and all that food had my mouth watering. You've got to look at an eleven-year-old kid to see what I'm saying. Anyway, I went in, and the only thing I could think was, Oh, boy! I'm gonna get somethin' to eat because they wouldn't dare ask me to leave on Christmas Day. There's just no way.

"And then all the family went in to eat. I stood back because I would never go into anyone's kitchen without being asked. Then the pastor came out and pulled me aside, and he told me, 'Carolyn, I don't get to spend much time with my family alone, and I would prefer to have this time alone. I would appreciate it if you could come back later.' See, he had been working in Atlanta some and preaching on Sundays up in Youngcane [Georgia]. He didn't say, 'Would you leave?' He said, 'Come back later,' but I knew what he meant. I'll tell you what, that was probably the only man I've ever hated in my life. That man was an A-number-one hypocrite. I disliked him then, and I dislike him today—and he's dead. I still dislike anyone who even looks like him. I've had drunk guys in Atlanta come and try and rape me, and I've fought them off with a butcher knife. I don't hate them the way I hate this preacher because they never professed to be loving and gentle and kind and then turn around and turn away someone for just something to eat."

—Carolyn Stradley, Fall 1984

Making a Christmas Wreath

"Well, you start with wire or a coat hanger. I don't remember when we didn't have coat hangers, and I can't see they've improved them either! I am going to use this linen string, just a twine, but it's good and strong. This is just greenery out of the yard: Norway spruce and cedar cypress. Now, if you are going out in the woods to get it, you might look for white pine. The twigs and tips are what you want to use. When we were little, we would have used white pine or native cedar that you find in the woods or white hemlock. Sometimes I use sprigs of holly with berries on them. And I always put a red bow at the top!

"First of all, bend the coat hanger with your hands into a circle. Leave the hook at the top to hang the wreath up by and to tie the red ribbon on. [Mrs. Bulgin lays the branches of greenery around the coat hanger and begins to tie them to the wire with the string.]

"Now this first time around is really your starter. Then go back and stick in twigs and the holly. You may want to cut little pieces of string and tie on these smaller twigs. If you plan to tack the wreath on a glass door, you would need to fill in the back side of the wreath also.

"Now tie on a pretty red bow and presto chango! You've got a Christmas wreath. They're not hard to make, and it's just part of getting ready for Christmas with us. It's just one of the things we do." **—Margaret Bulgin, Fall 1985**

PLATE 93 "This is just greenery out of the yard: Norway spruce and cedar cypress." —Margaret Bulgin

PLATE 94 "Presto!" —Margaret Bulgin

RECIPES

To people of the Appalachian area, no food is better than a home-cooked meal. Folks always gathered at mealtimes. Families still gather around a common table on Sunday after church to fellowship and enjoy down-home cooking. I love my mom's and my grandmother's cooking. As a little girl, I loved going to my grandmother's home. I especially liked breakfast at her house. Most of the time my twin sister, Diana, and I would ask for oatmeal. My grandmother would make our special oatmeal with white sugar, brown sugar, and cinnamon, and we would add raisins. Not a day went by that my grandmother did not make her homemade buttermilk biscuits. At lunch we often talked her into cooking her specialty: kind of like vegetable soup, which we called mess. She never used a recipe to make the mess: She just added whatever she had in the house or garden.

Almost every family has a recipe like my grandmother's mess that has been passed down from generation to generation. Many folks have recipe boxes filled with formulas for dishes, recipes from moms and aunts and grandmas and friends. Everyone loves to have an overflowing recipe box of food memorabilia. So in this section we pass down a few recipes to you, our loyal readers. We chose these recipes because they seemed special. We hope you and your family enjoy them.

—*Amanda Carpenter*

A great home-cooked meal is the best food to eat because it is made with love and care. Andrea Watts Williams told Diana Carpenter, a former Foxfire student, that the secret to cooking is love. The most educated culinary artist in the world cannot be the greatest chef without love. In our fast-paced world, people have forgotten what a home-cooked meal tastes like because nowadays it's all fast-food restaurants and eating on the run. Sitting down with your family to enjoy a meal and discuss the day is history. Jokingly, many ladies have told me that their stove has been inoperative for years!

Cooking and trying new recipes can be fun and interesting, especially with our modern stoves! Imagine cooking in a fireplace or on a woodstove. What if preparing meals were an event? In truth, in the old days, all household chores—washing clothes, making brooms, cleaning the house, making clothes, and cooking—were events! Still, our elders inventively created imaginative recipes for meats and vegetables and bread, as well as drinks, cakes, cookies, and pies.

We hope you will be brave enough to try making sassafras tea, cabbage casserole, syrup sweet bread, old-fashioned vinegar taffy, chocolate buckeyes, or tame gooseberry pie. Though you might not actually want to prepare some of the recipes (hog's head stew, groundhog, possum, squirrel dumplings), we do hope you enjoy reading about some of the delicacies our Appalachian mothers and grandmothers prepared. And you might want to consider passing some of your favorite recipes on to your loved ones and friends. After all, recipes are legacies.

—*April Argoe*

[Editor's Note: In the interview below, Lamar Alley, who runs a mom-and-pop grocery store in Lakemont, Georgia, told us no one cooks anymore. Modern folks don't cook from scratch anymore. Perhaps some of you will want to challenge his theory.]

> **"Now people just pull up in their cars and come in and out and leave in a cloud of smoke. They got to get home and put those TV dinners on."** —***Lamar Alley***

"Daddy built the store [Alley's Grocery in Lakemont, Georgia] in 1925. That's the year the road was paved up through here . . . Back when I can first remember, you'd walk on the porch and in the front door. Over here on the left was the post office. Down the left-hand side, Daddy had a wooden counter with two glass showcases on it. The heater was over here in the post office, and then on the right-hand side, he had a candy counter. Daddy got a phone in about the middle thirties. It was on the back wall. None of this electrical refrigeration was here. We didn't have any refrigeration at all. I didn't have anything I needed to keep cold except for the Co-Colas. . . .

"Lots of my customers walked, but there were a few automobiles; some of them had horses and wagons and buggies. Some of 'em even had sleds pulled behind cattle and steers. They'd do their tradin' and get their staples of life.

"Now people just pull up in their cars and come in and out and leave in a cloud of smoke. They got to get home and put those TV dinners on, you know—didn't have time to get in the freezer and get anything out this mornin'.

PLATE 95 "Daddy built the store in 1925. That's the year the road was paved up through here." —Lamar Alley

"I can't compete with large groceries like Bi-Lo and Winn-Dixie. It is difficult to be small. You got to hang in there and do the best you can."

—Lamar Alley, Spring/Summer 1994

DRINKS

SASSAFRAS TEA

Pearl Martin scrapes off the thin layer of bark on the sassafras root. Bring the roots to a boil in water. One can use either the roots or the bark in the boiling process, but Pearl prefers to use the roots. The longer the roots stay in the water, the stronger the tea will be. One can also dry the roots out before boiling or use them green. To make a gallon of tea, Pearl boils four average-sized roots in a gallon of water for fifteen to twenty minutes. After the tea is strained, it is ready to drink. It can be sweetened with either sugar or honey. The tea can be made strong, then diluted before it is drunk, as Pearl prefers, or made to suit one's taste without diluting. The tea can be served either hot or iced and can be refrigerated indefinitely for future use. **—Spring/Summer 1996**

In the spring, gather roots and tender twigs of red sassafras. There is also a white variety, but one woman told us it would make a person go blind if he drank a tea made from it.

Pound the roots to a pulp if they are very big and wash them with the twigs. Boil them, strain, and sweeten. **—Winter 1970**

CIDER

8 pounds dried apples
2 pounds raisins
16 pounds sugar
10 ounces tartaric acid
2 teaspoons salicylic acid
1 nutmeg (optional)

"Cook apples thoroughly done in five gallons water. Cook raisins separately and mash them up in one-half gallon water. Mix with the apples and strain. Dissolve tartaric acid in one quart boiling water and pour in juice. Dissolve sugar in one gallon of boiling water and pour in juice of apples and raisins. About the third day, put in the salicylic acid dissolved in a cup of boiling water. Six gallons of water may be added to all of this. Put all in 16-gallon keg. Can be flavored with one nutmeg." **—Reverend R.O. Smith, Winter 1971**

CHEESE AND BUTTER

CHEESE

Mrs. Thelma Earp makes her cheese from raw cow's milk. First she strains the fresh milk and allows the cream to rise so she can skim it off and make butter. Next she clabbered the skimmed milk by adding two or three tablespoons of buttermilk per gallon of skim milk and letting it sit for two days. After the milk has clabbered, it can be refrigerated until you are ready to use it. She then puts the clabbered milk on the stove and heats it to a little more than lukewarm. She said that it should be pretty hot, but not boiling—not so hot that it would burn your hands.

Once the clabbered milk is thoroughly heated, she pours it into a strainer made with a cotton cloth pinned over a bucket with clothespins. She then gathers up the corners of the cloth and squeezes the whey through the cloth, leaving the curds.

Mrs. Earp then puts the curds in a bowl and adds one and one-half teaspoons of salt and a raw egg. She prefers barnyard eggs to store-bought eggs because they make the cheese yellower. She mixes it all in with her hands, and it is ready for cooking.

She puts a lump of butter about the size of a large hen egg in a big iron frying pan and melts it. Mrs. Earp prefers a wood cookstove because it heats more evenly and slowly. The electric stove browned the butter, and some burned flakes of butter got mixed in with the cheese. When the butter is melted, she adds the curds and keeps turning them in the pan over a

PLATE 96 Curds, salt, and a raw egg

medium heat. When all the curds are melted enough to run together into a cake, she puts them out into a dish to cool. —**Winter 1975**

BUTTER

Mrs. Thelma Earp uses an electric churn to make her butter, then works the butter up with a ladle. Throughout the entire butter-making procedure, her dainty fingers never touch the butter. She uses the ladle through every step.

After the churning is completed, she skims the butter off the top of the milk and puts it into a bowl. Using the ladle, she squeezes as much of the remaining milk out of the butter as she can. She then pours ice water over the butter to wash all the milk out. She drains off the milky water, adds more ice water, and pours this off the butter. She does this a third time, and the butter is noticeably stiffer. She then washes it a fourth time and adds a little salt—"Have to salt. I don't know why. That's what Mama told me."

PLATE 97 Butter in the iron frying pan

She then drains it the fourth time and presses the butter into the mold with the ladle. The butter is pushed out of the mold onto cellophane wrap. She wraps the cakes of butter individually and shows them off to us.

—Winter 1975

COTTAGE CHEESE

To begin the process of making cottage cheese, pour about a gallon of raw (unpasteurized) whole milk into an enamel or other metal pan. [Any amount of milk may be used. The amount used here is what is preferred by Harriet Echols for her family.] Mrs. Echols lets her pan of milk sit on the back of the woodstove in the winter or just out on a kitchen table during warm weather so that it can sour slowly. This process may take only one day, or perhaps two, according to the temperature. Mrs. Echols does not heat the milk at all before it clabbers. When on the stove, it is not over direct heat—only in a warm place.

After the milk clabbers, the cream is lifted off and refrigerated. The cream may be used later as sour cream in any recipe where it may be called for, or it may be mixed in with the cottage cheese after it is made to make the cheese creamier.

The skimmed, clabbered milk is then heated over a low fire until it curdles. It is removed from the heat and poured into a colander or cheesecloth to drain all the water out. This usually takes a couple of hours. It may also be hung in a cloth overnight. Mrs. Nora Garland remembers that she put the curdled milk into a clean flour sack and let it drain overnight outside.

PLATE 98 Mrs. Earp shows off her individually wrapped cakes of butter.

Then both Mrs. Garland and Mrs. Echols told us that they would work up the cheese by putting it back into a pan or bowl and squeezing it with their hands or a spoon or spatula, getting out any remaining water. Mrs. Echols warned us not to work the cheese too vigorously or get the curds too fine. Then a little salt may be sprinkled in to taste, and to make the cheese creamier, some of the sour cream may be mixed in with it. The cottage cheese is then packaged in small containers and refrigerated. It will keep several weeks in the refrigerator. **—Winter 1975**

How to Churn Butter and Make Buttermilk

- First you have to milk the cow—about two milkings (two different days of getting milk from the cow or one from two different cows).
- You need to save both and do not do anything to them 'til you add 'em together and let it set 'til the cream rises to the top of your bucket.
- Pour everything into the churn.

- The cream will make the butter in the churn.
- Tie a cloth around the top of your churn—you will have to use a churning barrel. Set it by the fireplace and leave it there overnight to sit and sour—you have to wait 'til it sours before you start to churn it.
- Put the lid on it and make sure that the lid won't move when you start. Then use your stick to beat the soured milk. Beat the stick in an up-and-down circular motion until it turns to butter and buttermilk. You can press the butter into a butter mold if you want to get fancy.

—Effie Mae Speed Bleckley, Spring / Summer 2004

PICKLING

The following is a note from Mama Daisy [Daisy Justice] concerning pickling:

"Be sure that the signs are not in the bowels. [For an explanation of signs, see *The Foxfire Book,* pages 212–227.] When the moon is new is the best time to make kraut or pickle beans, corn, or green tomatoes. If the signs are in the bowels, they will be slimy or soft and not fit to eat. Do not use iodized salt for pickling."

PICKLED PEACHES OR APPLES

Peel apples or peaches, quarter, and put in a pot. Make enough brine of two parts vinegar, two parts sugar, and one part water to cover the fruit. Add ground cinnamon, nutmeg, and allspice to taste and cook until tender. When done, lift the fruit out and pack into jars. Keep brine simmering and pour into jars over the fruit, leaving one-half inch at the top. Seal immediately. **—Spring / Summer 1996**

SAUERKRAUT

"Select firm cabbage heads and chop. Have a clean churn jar—usually five-gallon—and pack the jar with alternating layers of chopped cabbage and a sprinkling of salt—usually a half cup of salt per gallon of cabbage. You need not add water, as the cabbage will produce its own.

"When the jar is filled, cover the cabbage with a clean, white cloth, large cabbage leaves, or a saucer. Then place a flat flint rock or other weight on top of this to hold the cabbage under the brine. Let this stand for ten days—or as long as necessary to get it as sour as you want.

"When this is completed, take the kraut out and pack it in canning jars. Then put the jars in a pot of water and bring it to a boil to both seal the jars and cook the cabbage.

"Old-timers used to leave the cabbage in the churn jars, omitting this last step, but it turns dark. Jars keep it in serving-sized portions, and they keep it fresh.

"Some add a pod of hot pepper to the churn at the beginning of the whole process for additional flavoring." **—Daisy Justice, June 1968**

"Measure one gallon of chopped cabbage and place in large churn. Spread three-fourths to one cup salt over the cabbage and pack the cabbage down firmly. Do not add any water to the cabbage in the churn. There will be an accumulation of water from the cabbage itself.

"Add a second gallon of chopped cabbage, spread three-fourths to one cup salt over it, and pack it down. After two to three gallons of cabbage have been packed down in the churn, water will rise above the level of the cabbage. Keep adding a gallon of cabbage and three-fourths to one cup salt until the level of the water is at the mouth of the churn. At this point, put clean cabbage leaves over the chopped cabbage in the churn. Clean and scrub a smooth stone and lay on top of the cabbage leaves. This will prevent the chopped cabbage from floating to the top. Cover the top of the churn with a clean, white cloth and tie securely with a string.

"Let the churn set seven to ten days in the kitchen. The higher the temperature at which the cabbage stays, the faster it will ferment. The kraut may remain in the churn indefinitely with the amount needed to eat being taken out and the churn recovered with the cabbage leaves and stone. It will become saltier as it gets older if left in the churn, but it will still be suitable to eat throughout the winter."

[The Underwoods pack their kraut in clean canning jars after it has fermented as much as they want it to and heat the jars in a boiling water bath on the stove for ten minutes to seal them. They store the jars of kraut in a dark, cool place.]

—Willie and Bessie Underwood, *Foxfire's Book of Wood Stove Cookery*

"Chop up your cabbage fine. I've always judged how much salt to put in by the size of the container I'm using. If it's a gallon container, I put two tablespoons of salt. Fill the container with water and weight the top down carefully. Then I watch 'til it ferments. You can tell by the bubbles coming up in the jar. The time it takes to ferment depends on the heat. In cool weather, it will take quite a bit of time. I can't judge how long it'll take. I just have to watch it." **—Lola Cannon, *Foxfire's Book of Wood Stove Cookery***

"You make your kraut when your cabbage is tender. You wash and trim your cabbage and chop them up. I've got a little chopper that my husband made for me that looks like a little hoe. I've got a small churn jar that's great big around and holds about four gallons. It's good to chop in. I put my cabbage in there and chop it up. Then I pack it in a big jar and put a layer of cabbage and a little salt, more cabbage and more salt. Usually cabbage will hold its own water. The salt draws it out. Then you may need to add a little water to cover the cabbage and let it set in there nine days. Then you put it in your cannin' jars and set the jars in a pan of water on the stove. Let it come to a boil and can the kraut. It gets too sour if you leave it in that big churn jar and don't can it. You taste your kraut along while it's in the churn, and when it gets just right, like you want it, you put it in cannin' jars. Then just set them out in the can house."

—Margaret Norton, *Foxfire's Book of Wood Stove Cookery*

CHOWCHOW

5 pounds apples, peeled and cored
5 pounds sweet peppers, seeded
1 pound hot peppers
2 chopped onions
4 ounces (½ box) pickling spices
½ gallon vinegar
1 cup water
3 pounds sugar
3 tablespoons cinnamon
Salt to taste

"Grind apples, peppers, and onions in food chopper. (Cabbage and pears can also be used.) Tie pickling spices in small cloth bag. Place them and all remaining ingredients with the chopped apples, onions, and peppers in large container on the stove. Cook until the mixture is hot through and through. Remove spice bag. Pour chowchow into sterilized canning jars, filling to the top of each jar with some of the liquid. Place freshly boiled canning tops and rings on the jars to seal."

—Addie Norton, *Foxfire's Book of Wood Stove Cookery*

"My chowchow has green tomatoes, peppers, onion, and cabbage in it. It's made like kraut. It isn't cooked. You just chop up all your vegetables and put them in your jar. It sets in there 'til it gets as sour as you want it. Then you can it. Some people put hot pepper in it, but I use sweet peppers."

—Margaret Norton, *Foxfire's Book of Wood Stove Cookery*

PEPPER RELISH

"Grind up twelve pods of red pepper, twelve pods of green pepper, and twelve onions together. Make up a vinegar-sugar mixture to pour over them. Use about a pint of vinegar for that many peppers and onions. I don't add any other spices because you'd be chewing on them when you eat the relish." **—Margaret Norton, *Foxfire's Book of Wood Stove Cookery***

PLATE 99 Margaret Norton is famous for her woodstove cookery.

VEGETABLES

POKE SALAD

Poke is probably eaten more frequently than any other wild food in this area. It must be picked in the early spring when the leaves are still yellow-green and the asparagus-like stalks no higher than four to six inches. The purple-red berries that appear later, if used at all (in wine, for example), must be used very sparingly, as they can be extremely poisonous.

The greens are usually washed well, parboiled for about ten minutes, rinsed three or four times, and then fried in plenty of fatback grease until tender. They can then be seasoned with salt and pepper. Many scramble eggs in the pan along with the greens just before they are done. Another woman said she served the greens along with sliced hard-boiled eggs and chopped onions. Pepper sauce or apple vinegar also adds a nice flavor.

The stalks are also eaten, but only when young are they truly good. They can be sliced, peeled first if desired, rolled in cornmeal or flour, and fried until tender.

To pickle the stalks, slice and scald until tender and then add warm vinegar and spices.

Fried poke is believed to be a fine spring tonic. Old stalks, leaves, berries, and the white root should be avoided, as they can be harmful.

—Spring/Summer 1996

CABBAGE CASSEROLE

1 large head of cabbage
1 teaspoon salt
½ stick butter or margarine
2 cups grated cheddar cheese
1½ cups buttered bread crumbs
3 cups Basic White Sauce (below)

Shred cabbage. Cook five to eight minutes in boiling water with one teaspoon of salt. Don't overcook—cabbage should remain crisp. Drain well. Layer in buttered two-quart casserole: cabbage, enough sauce to cover, second layer of cabbage, remaining sauce, then cheese. Top with buttered bread crumbs and bake at 300° for fifteen to twenty minutes. Yield: 8 to 10 servings.

BASIC WHITE SAUCE

1 cup margarine
3 tablespoons all-purpose flour
Salt and pepper
1 quart milk

Melt margarine in a saucepot and add flour, salt, and pepper to make a paste. Add milk and cook until thick, stirring constantly.

—Recipes from the Dillard House, Fall/Winter 1997

CORN PRODUCTS

GRANNY'S GRITS

1 cup grits
2 cups water
½ teaspoon salt (if desired)
Butter or margarine as desired

"Sift and wash grits (to wash, pour water over grits and let the chaff and fine meal float to the top). Drain water off grits. Repeat three times. Put one cup grits, two cups water, and salt in a medium-sized boiler. Bring to a boil over medium heat. Simmer over low heat about twenty-five minutes or until done (thickened)." **—Mary Grace Speed, Fall/Winter 2004**

HOMINY

"You use old field corn, white corn. Before you start, you have to gather your corn and shuck it and then shell it, and I always blow the silks out of mine; then I put it in the pot. I put more water in it and more lye. You have to boil it an' get the husk off it, an' then you cook it. You put soda in it an' lye, an' when it boils low enough, it skins itself. Then you take it out an' wash it—I don't know, about a dozen times or more! Then you put it back in a pot, an' you put water up over it an' boil it 'til it's tender. If you want to, you can fry it in bacon grease. It's really good! You put salt in it. It's better if you cook it outside in a big, black iron washpot. You can't cook it in aluminum pots because of the soda. The weather doesn't matter except that it has to be clear weather. Yeah, it has to be a beautiful day outside so you can wash it a bunch of times. To me, the white hominy is lots better than the yellow hominy. It just tastes better." —**Belle Wilburn Henslee, Spring/Summer 1997**

BREAD

GRANNY'S CORNBREAD

1½ cup self-rising flour
1¾ cup sifted cornmeal
1 tablespoon salt
¾ to 1 teaspoon baking soda
1 cup whole milk
1¼ cup water

"Preheat oven to 400°. Mix all the above. Grease a large iron skillet; sprinkle with a little cornmeal. Pour meal mixture into skillet. Bake for fifty minutes or until golden brown and firm to the touch."

—**Mary Grace Speed, Fall/Winter 2004**

CORN PONES

1 pint cornmeal
1 teaspoon baking powder
½ teaspoon salt
1 tablespoon lard
Milk

Mix together meal, baking powder, and salt. Cut in lard and add enough milk to make a stiff batter. Form into pones with hands or add some milk and drop from the end of a spoon. Place in a greased pan.

Bake in a hot oven for about half an hour. —**Winter 1970**

SYRUP SWEET BREAD

2 eggs
3 tablespoons butter
1 cup syrup or molasses
2 cups self-rising flour

"Preheat oven to 350°. Cream eggs and butter. Add syrup. Fold in flour and mix good. Bake in lightly greased pan until brown. This usually takes about twenty minutes." —**Ruth Holcomb, *Foxfire's Book of Wood Stove Cookery***

OLD-FASHIONED GINGERBREAD

½ cup sugar
½ cup butter
1 cup molasses
1 cup flour
½ teaspoon soda
1½ teaspoons ginger
½ teaspoon cinnamon
½ cup sour milk
Nuts and/or raisins if desired

Mix all ingredients together. Put into a large loaf pan and bake for about an hour. This recipe is at least 100 years old. —**Winter 1970**

JELLIES/JAMS/PRESERVES

GRANNY'S MUSCADINE [GRAPE] JELLY

About a half-gallon of muscadines
1 package Sure-Jell
6 cups granulated sugar
Clean jars and lids

Directions:

- Pick about a half gallon of muscadines. (You might need more.) Get the darkest purple ones that you can find.
- Wash them; get off all spray if there is any; make sure that you throw out all of the bad ones that you find.
- Remove the peel by gently squeezing the grapes one at a time; place the insides in a bowl.
- Mash the peeled grapes through a colander and catch the juice in a bowl or pot. (You should now have about five cups of juice.) Get out any extra seeds that might have gotten through the colander.
- In a pot, on the stovetop, bring the five cups of juice to a boil.
- Stir in the Sure-Jell and six cups of sugar.
- When the foam-looking gel rises to the top of the juice, let the mixture boil for one minute.
- Pour into the jars (whatever size you prefer).
- Tighten the lids as tightly as possible.
- Let set until it cools and seals: When the jar seals, you will hear a pop, and the lid will have changed—it looks sunken.
- Store the jars of jelly away until you need them. (It is better to leave jelly away for a while and let it settle. It will taste better.)

—Effie Mae Speed Bleckley, Spring/Summer 2004

PLATE 100 "This jelly recipe is one we all can do!"

DAMSON PLUM JELLY

"Pick over the fruit. Wash and drain. With a fork, prick each damson several times. Bring fruit very slowly to the boiling point and mash with a potato masher as soon as the fruit is soft. Put through a sieve. To each quart of this liquid, add one and one-half pints of sugar—heated sugar. Bring to the boiling point. Boil five minutes. Skim and fill your glass jar. Seal with paraffin."

—JoAnn Jarrio, Summer 1987

DAMSON PLUM PRESERVES

16 pounds damson plums
12 pounds sugar
3 quarts water

"Wash, dry, and weigh the fruit. Prick each plum a number of times with a coarse needle.

"Put the sugar and water into the kettle and bring slowly to a boil; then skim. Add the plums a few at a time so the fruit will keep its shape. Cook until soft. Pack into scalded jars and seal with paraffin. Two kettles will speed the work." **—JoAnn Jarrio, Summer 1987**

DAMSON PLUM JAM

4 quarts damson plums
1 quart cold water
Sugar

"Wash plums, remove the pits, add water, and cook the fruit until soft. Measure and add two-thirds as much sugar as fruit. Stir mixture over low flame until sugar is dissolved. Boil rapidly until mixture is thick and clear. The flavor of the plums should be practically unchanged and the color a rich, sparkling red. Pour into sterilized jars and seal while hot."

—JoAnn Jarrio, Summer 1987

MEAT

HOG'S HEAD STEW

Recently, we came across a recipe for stew so interesting that we had to share it with you. The recipe comes from the Joanne Carver family, the members of which plunge in each harvest time in a cooking-canning spree that goes for days and leaves them more than ready for the winter. The measurements given below yielded sixty-three quarts last time around. If you can't handle quite that much, cut proportionally, subtracting or adding other ingredients according to preference.

1½ hogs' heads
2 shoulders or hams venison
4 chickens
1 peck onions
1 gallon Irish potatoes
5 half gallons each tomatoes, corn, peas, carrots
6 large cans tomato juice to thin
1 package poultry seasoning
Bay leaves (to taste)
5 pounds salt (or to taste)
Worcestershire sauce (to taste)
Pepper to taste [Both Worcestershire sauce and pepper may be substituted for, or added to, the tomato juice.]

"Cook the meat until it comes easily off the bones. Cool. Remove the meat from the bones and grind it up—or run through a food chopper—together with the other ingredients. Place the mixture in quart jars, seal, and cook in a pressure cooker for sixty minutes at ten pounds pressure. Then store away for the lean months." **—Joanne Carver family, Spring 1969**

The mother's [Leona "Dink" Carver] recipe for the same stew, provided to us by Brenda Carver, varies somewhat:

"Use one hog's head, two chickens, four pounds ground beef, one gallon tomatoes, four No. 2 cans [fifteen ounces] each of peas, corn, and carrots. Chop and blend ingredients, can, and cook in pressure cooker for thirty minutes." —**Brenda Carver, Spring 1969**

SOUSE MEAT

"I'll soak this [hog's head] now and soak all th' blood out of it until in th' mornin' it's just as white. Then I'll take an' grind it on that sausage grinder an' take th' juice that this is cooked in, part of it, and put some sage 'n' black pepper 'n' red pepper and stir it all up until it's so good 'n' fine as it can be, and then put it in them cannin' jars 'n' seal it—then open it in th' winter. I love it better'n anything in th' world. Why, lot o' people eats it cold."

—Aunt Arie, Spring/Summer 1970

RACCOON

[Editor's note: Begin the cooking process with skinned, gutted, washed meats.]

The most common way of cookin' coon is to put it in a pot of salted water (one spoon of salt per pound). Add one or two pods of red peppers or one tablespoon of black pepper and let it boil in a pot with no lid until the meat is tender. Remove, put in a greased baking pan, and bake until golden brown. **—Spring/Summer 1970**

POSSUM

The most common way of cooking possum is to parboil it in water containing salt and red or black pepper (to taste). Boil until tender and then put in a greased pan surrounded or filled with sweet potatoes. Then bake until golden brown—about two hours if you're usin' a woodstove.

—Spring/Summer 1970

GROUNDHOG

Parboil with spicewood [*Betula lenta*] twigs (to take the wild taste out) until tender. Pepper it an' put it in a greased pan to bake until brown.

—Spring/Summer 1970

SQUIRREL

After soaking the squirrel long enough to get all the blood out, cut it into pieces and roll the pieces in flour, salt, and pepper. Fry until tender and brown. If the squirrel is old, you may want to parboil it in water containing sage to take out the wild taste. **—Spring/Summer 1970**

SQUIRREL DUMPLINGS

Cut the squirrel up and parboil the pieces for five minutes. Then remove the meat and cook it in fresh water until tender. Add to the broth one-fourth teaspoon of pepper, one tablespoon of butter or cooking fat, and some milk. Prepare the dumpling dough.

To prepare the dough, combine 1 cup flour, baking powder, and ½ teaspoon salt in a medium bowl. Combine milk and melted shortening. Add to the dry ingredients, along with the chopped fresh parsley. Stir just to moisten dry ingredients and drop by tablespoon directly into the boiling broth mixture. Cover and return to boil. Reduce heat without lifting cover. Cook for ten to fifteen minutes and serve hot. **—Spring/Summer 1970**

RABBIT

Cut the rabbit into sections. Remove the legs and separate the ribs and back section by cutting up the rabbit's sides vertically.

Parboil the pieces in a covered pot in salted (two tablespoons salt) water to make it tender—if it's not young and tender already. For frying, put the parboiled pieces in a greased pan and fry until brown on all sides, seasoning with a half teaspoon pepper. Some roll the pieces in meal or flour before frying. For baking, dip the parboiled pieces in a breaded solution consisting of two eggs, four tablespoons of flour, one-fourth cup milk, and a half teaspoon pepper. Put pieces in an oven and bake until brown (about 30 minutes).

—Spring/Summer 1970

DEER

Cure

Sometimes hunters salt the entire carcass with about twenty-five pounds of salt, let it dry, and hang it in the smokehouse. When they need pieces, they simply strip them off and cook them. Others cut the deer into pieces very similar to those that a beef is cut into (legs, ribs, rump, loin, etc.). These pieces, dried in the sun until all the moisture was out, were then put in the smokehouse. Put into a fairly thick salt brine and leave or salt down (about one inch thick) and put in the smokehouse to cure in the same manner as pork.

Soak

Before cooking meat from the smokehouse, soak the pieces overnight in clear water. If you kept them in brine, simply cook without adding salt.

Cook

- For steaks from the smokehouse or brine, slice into pieces one-half inch thick, four inches long, and three inches wide. In a skillet, brown in butter and simmer until tender, depending on the toughness of the meat. Salt is not needed since the meat was salted during curing.
- For fresh steaks, roll in flour, pepper, and salt until covered and then put in a frying pan with one-half cup of shortening and fry slowly until tender or until both sides are browned.
- For fresh roasts, some put a four-pound roast and one pod of red pepper (to kill the wild taste) in water and parboil, leaving the lid off, until tender. The meat should be completely covered with water. When tender, take out, wipe dry, sprinkle salt and pepper to taste, and then brown in an oven.
- For stews, cut two pounds of meat into one-inch cubes and brown on all sides in a small amount of fat. Then in a stewing pot add the meat, two cups water, four potatoes, six large carrots, four medium onions, one quart of tomatoes, one tablespoon salt, and one teaspoon pepper. Bring to a boil and simmer for three hours. After three hours, thicken with three tablespoons flour and one-half cup water. Then eat or store in a cool place and heat as needed. **—Spring /Summer 1970**

BEAR

Many of our contacts cooked bear roasts and steaks in the same fashion as beef or venison. One suggested parboiling the fresh meat until tender and adding several large apples to the water. When the apples fall apart, the meat is ready to be taken out, seasoned, and baked. **—Spring /Summer 1970**

TURKEY

After cleaning, some then cut off the legs and breast (saving them for frying like chicken) and stewed the rest. Others rubbed the outside with lard, sprinkled it with two tablespoons of salt and one teaspoon of pepper, replaced the liver and gizzard, and baked it for about three hours on low heat. After baking, two cups of the resulting liquid were sometimes mixed in a saucepan with two tablespoons flour and one-fourth cup water and heated to make gravy. Chopped liver and gizzard could be added.

—Spring /Summer 1970

TURTLE

The meat was soaked overnight in salty water (some with a little soda also) to remove the wild, strong taste. It was cooked according to any of the following directions:

Parboil (if desired) and roll in flour. Put three tablespoons of flour, one tablespoon salt, and one teaspoon pepper in a covered skillet and fry the meat until brown on all sides.

Or, after parboiling (with salt and hot pepper if desired), cool and dip meat into a batter made of one cup plain, sifted flour, one-half teaspoon salt, one teaspoon baking powder, two beaten eggs, and one-half cup milk. Fry in deep fat until golden brown.

Or, stew in sweet milk and butter, pepper, and salt just like oyster stew.

—Spring/Summer 1970

FROGS

"First, after y' get 'em dressed [cut the legs off and clean them and throw the rest away], get your grease not too awfully hot—if y' get it too hot, when y' put 'cher legs in, they'll jump out.

"Roll 'em in flour an' salt an' pepper like chicken, an' fry 'em; or either y' can take buttermilk 'n' an' egg an' whip it t'gether and roll th' legs in either bread crumbs or cracker crumbs an' fry it."

—Lake Stiles, Spring/Summer 1970

FISH

"There are a lot of ways you can cook trout—bake 'em, fry 'em, or stew 'em. First you cut their heads off and clean 'em. Now these stockards [stocked fish], I'd stew 'em and take the bones out and make fish patties out of them because their meat's too tender to hold together to fry.

"To bake fish, you coat them with a little grease and lemon juice. Heat your oven to about 350° and cook 'em about thirty minutes.

"You can fix any kind of fish the way you want 'em, but, to me, trout's the best." **—Minyard Conner, Spring 1981**

"Best way to cook fish is to roll them in cornmeal and put 'em in a good, hot pan of grease. Sometimes fry some good salt meat [pork fatback] and cook 'em in that grease." **—Melvin Taylor, Spring 1981**

"Mama used to fry fish for us for breakfast. Nowadays, I usually give away what I catch because we don't eat fish. When I do cook them, I just roll the fish in cornmeal and a little salt and fry them in grease on the stove. Some people can't eat fried fish, but my kids just likes them fried brown. They eat them that way with hush puppies." **—Florence Brooks, Spring 1981**

"Have a little grease in your pan. We would always roll them in cornmeal and lay them in a pan with a little grease in it. Fry 'em on one side and then

PLATE 101 "You can fix any kind of fish the way you want 'em, but to me, trout's the best." —Minyard Conner

turn them over and brown the other side. When you get done, go to eatin' on 'em." —**Jake Waldroop, Spring 1981**

"About the only way I like fish is to fry them in Crisco 'til they're good and brown." —**L. E. Craig, Spring 1981**

"First, I salt the fish. Then I roll 'em good with cracker crumbs or cornmeal. I think cornmeal makes a better flavor. Then I put them in the shortening to fry. It's important to have your shortenin' pretty hot. Then turn them over and let them brown on the other side. I always turn my heat down and cook 'em slow so they get really cooked all the way through. One thing I don't do is to put a top on the skillet. The reason is because it makes the cornmeal soft and easy to come off. Leave the skillet open after you've turned your heat down. I cook stocked fish about twenty-five to thirty minutes because they're not usually tough or hard to cook.

"If a fish is real wide [thick], I slice it in two down the back. If you like crisp fish, just slice them and cook 'em quickly." —**Leonard Jones, Spring 1981**

"You can fry most of the fish we catch around here. Roll them in meal or flour and put salt and pepper on them and fry them in grease or vegetable oil. I like speckled trout the best." **—Willie Underwood, Spring 1981**

"I roll 'em in meal, lay them in a pan of grease, and turn them over and over. It don't take but a minute or so to cook a fish. They'll cook before you can say 'scat.' All you want is enough to get him brown. It don't take no time." **—Lawton Brooks, Spring 1981**

"Trout are easy to cook. I scrub them with a scrub pad or dishrag gourd to get the slime off. Then I cut their heads off and cut their stomachs open to take their innards out. I never have tried to take the bones out. I fry them with the bones in. Then I wash 'em again and roll them in cornmeal.

"I have a big, black fryin' pan that I put Crisco in and get it hot enough to smoke. I turn the heat down some and brown them about ten minutes on either side, and they're ready to eat.

"We might have hush puppies to go with them and slaw and french fries. You could also serve cornbread or french bread and some iced tea."

—Blanche Harkins, Spring 1981

FRUIT

DRYING APPLES

"I would peel my apples and slice them and put them in the oven when I finished cooking a meal. I'd slip the trays in there and leave the oven door open. It would take several days for them to dry because I would leave them in there only until the oven cooled down.

"Now I dry them over my hot water heater because it's a low heat, yet it dries the apples out. I can stack three trays of apples up on the heater by putting pieces of wood across and separating trays."

—Lucy York, *Foxfire's Book of Wood Stove Cookery*

"I've always dried apples out in the sunshine. Then I put them in the stove and heat them, get them hot all the way through. I pack them in gallon jugs while they're real hot, and they just keep real good. We didn't have gallon jugs years back, and we used large crocks."

—Lettie Chastain, *Foxfire's Book of Wood Stove Cookery*

APPLE BUTTER

"Use tart apples . . . as they cook up more quickly than sweet apples. Peel and core; cook until tender in a small amount of water. Mash. Add crushed gingerroot or cinnamon, if available. Sweeten with sorghum syrup. It will be the consistency of thick applesauce.

"The Dickersons called this apple marmalade if it was cooked down to jelly." —**Lucy York, *Foxfire's Book of Wood Stove Cookery***

"It takes three bushels of apples to make a stir. You can keep the apples for three or four days before using them in the apple butter. I wouldn't have nothin' but the Winesaps. That's the only kind that makes good butter. The other kind won't cook up good. Sour apples do. An apple that has a sweet taste to it won't make good butter . . . First you peel the apples and cook them on a stove for fifteen or twenty minutes. Then run them through a colander. Clean the kettle with a solution of vinegar and baking soda. Some people use wood ashes. Brass is the only kind of kettle I would have. It just makes better butter somehow. I don't like a copper kettle because it affects the butter taste, I think.

"You can use any kind of wood for the fire except pine. It would affect the butter taste. Don't let the wood touch the bottom of the kettle, or the butter will burn. Pour applesauce in the twenty-gallon brass kettle heated by an open furnace.

"When you stir [Pat made the butter-stirring stick himself out of cypress], you go once on one side and once in the middle. You see, the bottom is 'marrow,' and that way it won't stick. Constantly stir the applesauce until it's hot enough to melt sugar. Then, using one five-pound bag at a time, at regular intervals gradually pour fifty pounds of sugar in. Let it cook for about two hours and keep stirring.

PLATE 102 "I wouldn't have nothin' but the Winesaps."
—Mr. and Mrs. Pat Brooks

"After it is taken off the fire, add four fluid ounces of imitation oil of cinnamon or desired flavor. Then pour into jars. Each stir yields about seventy-five jars [varied sizes]." —**Mr. and Mrs. Pat Brooks, Winter 1973**

CROCK GRAPES

Collect dry, sound fox grapes. Pack them in a churn and pour boiling hot fresh molasses or syrup over them. Then take two clean cloths. Dip the first in hot beeswax and the second in hot tallow and tie each cloth separately around the top of the churn.

Make this in the fall when the grapes are fresh and ripe. Then set the churn in a cool place until winter. They can be eaten during the winter after they get mildly fermented. —**Winter 1969**

PIES

SWEET POTATO PIE

2 sweet potatoes, about fist size
2 teacups milk (about 12 ounces)
½ stick butter
2 cups sugar
½ teaspoon cinnamon
Dash of salt

"Peel sweet potatoes, slice, and put in pan of water. Boil until tender. Leave the water in them. Add milk, butter, and sugar to the potatoes. Heat to boiling. Add cinnamon and salt.

"Roll out a thin biscuit dough and place on top of the sweet potato mixture. Allow juice to boil through dough until dough is thoroughly cooked. Sprinkle sugar on top of the pie and set the pan in the bottom of the oven to brown on top."

—**Ruth Holcomb, *Foxfire's Book of Wood Stove Cookery***

"I used to make the best sweet potato pie you ever put your tooth on. Sweet potato pie is wonderful!

"You just peel your potatoes and cut them up raw. Cook them 'til tender. Add a teaspoonful of cinnamon. I don't want but a dash of nutmeg—quarter of a teaspoonful—in mine. Put a tablespoon of butter and a cup of cream and a cup of sugar in your pan. The sweeter you make your sweet potato pie, the better it is!" —**Addie Norton, *Foxfire's Book of Wood Stove Cookery***

"To make sweet potato pies, peel raw sweet potatoes. Cook the cut-up potatoes until tender. Add one teaspoon cinnamon, one cup sugar, one-fourth teaspoon nutmeg. Mix together one tablespoon butter and one-fourth cup cream and stir into the potato mixture. Pour into a baked pie shell and heat in a moderate oven."

—Margaret Norton, *Foxfire's Book of Wood Stove Cookery*

TAME GOOSEBERRY PIE

Mix two cups berries with three-fourths cup sugar and cook, stirring to mash the berries, until it's thick. Make some plain biscuit dough, roll it out, and cut into one-inch-wide strips.

Pour berries into a pie plate, place the strips of dough crosswise on the berries, and bake at about 450° until the crust is brown. **—Winter 1970**

FRIED APPLE PIE

To make the apple pies—they are really tarts—Blanche Harkins uses either dried red or yellow apples. She really prefers yellow apples, as she feels they make tastier pies.

To dry the apples, Mrs. Harkins first peels and cores them and then cuts them into thin slices, soaks them in salt water, drains them, and lays them out in a single layer either on a flat board or in a pan on a white cloth. She puts them outside for several days in the sunshine to dry. They shrink to about half their original size, and when they are completely dried, she stores them in sacks in a dry place until she's ready to cook with them.

To prepare fried pies, she adds a small amount of water to the dried apples, cooks them until they are tender, and then mashes them up with a fork. She says, "Add enough sugar and cinnamon or allspice for your own taste. For four small pies or tarts, use one quart of dried apples." **—Spring 1976**

"Use one quart dried apples cooked in a little water until tender. Add one-half cup sugar and a little allspice. The dough for two large pies requires four cups self-rising flour, lots of lard, and a little water. Knead the dough and roll it out thin. Put the cooked apples on the dough, fold over, and fry in a iron skillet in lard until brown." **—Mrs. Jake (Bertha) Waldroop, Spring 1976**

COBBLERS

"A deep-dish pie, or cobbler, is one that has no crust on the bottom. It has fruit on the bottom. Some people put fruit, a layer of pie dough, a layer of fruit, then their crust on top. They started cooking on top of the stove because when they put it in the oven, the crust on top would get done before the layer of dough in the middle. By cooking it for a few minutes on top of the stove first and then finishing it in the oven, it would cook evenly."

—**Ruth Cabe, *Foxfire's Book of Wood Stove Cookery***

"Put your fruit in a pan with a little juice or water. Get it to boiling on top of the stove. Add sugar and butter. I like to use a biscuit dough, but some people use pie pastry just as well. Just roll it out good and thin and make enough for two layers. Dip half of your fruit and juice out and save. Put a layer of the dough on the fruit remaining in the pan and boil that a few minutes. Pour that reserved fruit and juice back in and place the second layer of dough in the pan. Let this boil up. Then put it in the oven to brown."

—**Bessie Underwood, *Foxfire's Book of Wood Stove Cookery***

"I make cobbler out of peaches or blackberries or cherries. I cut up the cherries and get the seeds out. Use any fruit you want to. I use a square aluminum pan now and make up a biscuit dough. I put the cherries, or whatever fruit I'm using, in the pan, usually a quart of fruit, and put some sugar on them—it takes a lot of sugar. And I use margarine now 'cause we don't have the butter like we used to have. For a quart of berries, I use about two

PLATE 103 Bertha Waldroop explains the art of pie and cobbler making.

tablespoons of butter. Stir it around in the fruit and cover the fruit with the dough. I do just like I was gonna make biscuits—roll the dough out right thin, cut it in strips, and put it on top of the fruit.

"Then I put it in the oven and pour water about halfway up in the pan with the fruit. Bake it at 350° about thirty minutes, and when it browns on top, I take it out. If you wish to, it does make it awful good if you put some margarine on top of it—that makes it real good—and it's ready to eat.

"Way back years ago, we didn't have a deep freeze, and we'd can our berries, cherries, and other fruit."

—Bertha Waldroop, *Foxfire's Book of Wood Stove Cookery*

CAKES

APPLESAUCE CAKE

2 teaspoons soda
2 cups applesauce
2 cups sugar
1½ sticks butter
2 eggs
3 cups plain flour
1 teaspoon baking powder
1 teaspoon ground cloves
½ teaspoon salt
1½ teaspoon nutmeg
1 tablespoon cinnamon
1 cup chopped pecans
1 cup raisins

"Preheat oven to 300°. Add soda to applesauce and set aside. Combine sugar, butter, and eggs and mix well. Beat in dry ingredients. Add applesauce, nuts, and raisins and mix well. Pour into a tube pan and bake at 300° an hour and a half. Cool before removing from pan."

—Arizona Dickerson, *Foxfire's Book of Wood Stove Cookery*

WALNUT CAKE

½ cup butter
2 cups brown sugar
3 eggs, separated
2 cups plain or cake flour
3 teaspoons baking powder
⅔ cup milk
1 teaspoon vanilla
½ teaspoon salt
1 cup ground walnuts

"Cream butter and sugar together. Add beaten egg yolks. Sift dry ingredients into the cream. Add milk, vanilla, salt, and walnuts. Fold in whipped egg whites. Bake in a tube pan at 325° for seventy minutes."

—Aunt Addie Norton, *Foxfire's Book of Wood Stove Cookery*

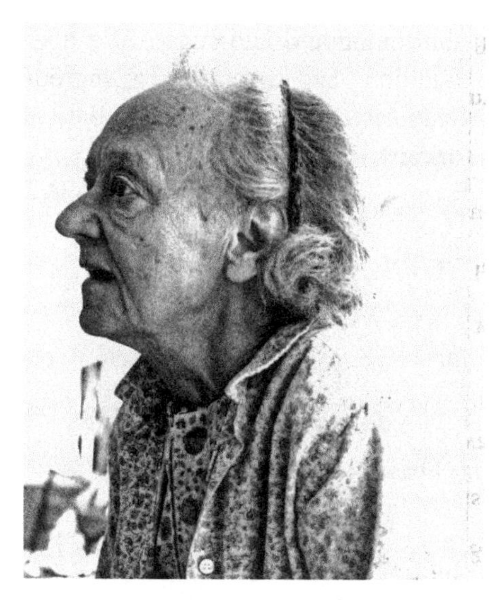

PLATE 104 Arizona Dickerson's applesauce cake is hard to beat!

CARROT PUDDING CAKE

⅔ cup sifted flour
⅔ cup sugar
1 teaspoon baking powder
¾ teaspoon baking soda
¾ teaspoon salt
½ teaspoon cinnamon
¼ teaspoon cloves
¼ teaspoon nutmeg
⅔ cup currants
⅔ cup raisins
⅔ cup grated raw potatoes
1 cup grated raw carrots
⅓ cup milk

"Mix and sift dry ingredients. Add the fruits. Stir until well coated; stir in potatoes, carrots, and milk. Pour into a greased pan and cover with lid and steam in a large pan of hot water for two and a half hours.

"Serve with Carrot Pudding Sauce—made as follows:

"Mix one cup powdered sugar, one large teaspoon vanilla or wine, the yolks of two eggs, beaten. When ready to serve, add one-half pint cream, whipped." —**Margaret Norton, Fall 1967**

MINCEMEAT CAKE

4 cups shortening
6 cups sugar
1 dozen eggs
13 cups flour
2 teaspoons salt
4 teaspoons baking soda
8 cups mincemeat
5 cups chopped apples

"Cream together shortening and add sugar. Add eggs a few at a time, beating after each addition. Sift together dry ingredients and add to creamed mixture. Mix in mincemeat and apples. Bake in two 16½" × 26" pans in a 350° oven for thirty-five to forty minutes."

—Christine Wigington, *A Foxfire Christmas*

COOKIES

OLD-FASHIONED TEA CAKES

1 stick butter or margarine
1 egg
1 cup sugar
2 tablespoons milk
½ teaspoon vanilla
1¾ cup flour (leave out salt and baking powder if self-rising flour is used.)
½ teaspoon salt
2 teaspoons baking powder

"Cream butter, egg, sugar, and vanilla. Sift flour, salt, and baking powder. Alternating, add dry ingredients and milk. [Begin and end with dry ingredients.] Blend well. Chill the dough for several hours. Remove from refrigerator and roll out into half-inch thickness. Cut out with a biscuit or cookie cutter. Bake in a 375° oven for eight to ten minutes.

"More flour may be added to make the dough stiffer, and cookies may be cut out immediately instead of waiting for the dough to cool."

—Bertha Waldroop, *Foxfire's Book of Wood Stove Cookery*

TOP-OF-THE-STOVE COOKIES

4 tablespoons cocoa
2 cups sugar
1 stick margarine
½ cup milk
½ cup peanut butter
3 cups quick cook oatmeal
Pinch of salt
Vanilla

"Put cocoa, sugar, margarine, and milk into pan on top of stove. Heat two minutes. Add peanut butter, oatmeal, salt, and vanilla. Lay a sheet of waxed paper on the counter and drop cookie mix by spoonfuls onto the paper. As the mixture cools, the cookies will harden and be ready to eat."

—Arizona Dickerson, *Foxfire's Book of Wood Stove Cookery*

SORGHUM MOLASSES COOKIES

1 egg
1 cup brown sugar
1 cup sorghum molasses
¾ cup melted butter
¼ cup boiling water
Salt
Flour [see below]

"Slightly beat egg. Add sugar, sorghum molasses, butter, water, and salt. Add just enough flour to knead into a medium-stiff dough. Roll out and cut with a cookie cutter. Bake at 400° for eight to ten minutes. Makes thirty-six small cookies." —**Louise Coldren, *A Foxfire Christmas***

CANDY

CHOCOLATE BUCKEYES

2 cups of smooth peanut butter
1 stick of margarine softened to room temperature
2 cups of Rice Krispies [optional]
½ teaspoon vanilla [optional]
One-pound box of confectioners' sugar
12-ounce package of chocolate chips
½ block of paraffin

"To make buckeyes, mix together peanut butter, margarine, Rice Krispies, vanilla, and sugar. Mix well. Make into small balls and chill overnight. The next day, melt chocolate chips and paraffin together in a double boiler over hot water. Stick toothpicks in balls and dip into chocolate mix. Do not completely cover. Place on waxed paper." —**Edith Cannon, Spring 1992**

OLD-FASHIONED VINEGAR TAFFY

2 tablespoons butter
1 cup brown sugar
2 cups molasses
1 tablespoon vinegar
⅓ cup water
Pinch of baking soda

Combine ingredients and boil until a small amount cracks when dropped in cold water. Pour in buttered pan to cool. Butter hands and pull, when cool, until it becomes light in color.

This can also be used as a covering for popcorn balls.

—**Spring/Summer 1996**

PLATE 105 Edith Cannon and her "Ma-ma" doll

POTATO CANDY

Peel and boil one large white potato. When done, mash up with a fork, add a little salt, and pour in a box of confectioners' sugar. This makes a stiff dough.

Roll out on a dough board that has been well floured in a layer ¼ inch thick. Spread peanut butter all over the top. Roll up like a jellyroll (make two rolls if you like). Put this in the refrigerator.

Cut with knife. Serve. Good any time. **—March 1968**

- Cook and mash a homegrown potato. You can mash it with a fork or the back of a spoon.
- Add enough sugar to make it sweet. You should use powdered sugar—if you do not have any powdered sugar, use real fine white sugar mixed with a little flour. It sets up pretty fast, so work quickly.
- Put on a shiny tabletop or waxed paper and mash down with a rolling pin or a canning jar laying on its side and rolling.
- Spread homemade peanut butter, hickory butter, or pecan butter across the flattened-out potato mixture. Start at one side and roll it into a long roll.

- Let it lay around until it starts to look dry. If you have a refrigerator or icebox, put it in there. If you don't, put in a cool place where flies don't see it.
- Cut off in circles and place on a glass plate for your friends. Kids eat it too fast, and the sugar is bad for their teeth. **—Vera Sawyer, Summer 1992**

POPCORN BALLS

YIELDS 30 TO 35

1 quart sorghum
2 gallons cooled, unsalted popcorn
1 teaspoon baking soda
Butter, margarine, or other shortening

Utensils:

1 large iron skillet
2 large dishpans or bowls (one for the popped corn and one for the finished popcorn balls)
1 mixing bowl (for the cooked syrup) and several kitchen spoons

"Put about half a quart of sorghum in the large skillet to heat on the stove. It needs to be large because the syrup boils up and iron because it heats easily and will not burn the syrup. The syrup is ready when it will not form a 'hair' when dripped down from the spoon. This takes roughly five minutes to cook. Pour the syrup into the mixing bowl and let it cool for several minutes. Put butter on hands to keep the syrup from sticking to them when forming the balls. It is better to use cold popcorn than warm popcorn because the syrup will stick better. With the first batch, place a small amount of popcorn into the palm of one hand and carefully spoon about a tablespoon of syrup on top of it. The syrup will still be hot. Pack the popcorn and syrup mixture together with hands. Put more butter on hands after making a couple of balls because the syrup is sticky.

"In the second batch, while boiling the other half of the syrup, add a teaspoon of baking soda to it. (Soda will make the syrup boil up, and it will be easier to work with.) Pour the syrup into the mixing bowl and pour the remaining popcorn on top of it. Stir up with a wooden spoon and scoop out with hands to form balls. When each ball has been completed, place it into a large dishpan to cool." **—Lessie Conner, Spring/Summer 1996**

RELATIONSHIPS

When I was sixteen, I thought I was in love, and it made me sick—sicker than a dog. My pap tuck [took] me to the doctor, and, come to find out, it wasn't love—it was worms.

—The Wolfpen Notebooks, *Fall 1988*

[**Editor's Note:** *The Wolfpen Notebooks* are twenty-three six-by-four-inch wire-hinged notebooks. All entries are written in ink in what used to be called "library hand." The first were recorded some sixty-two years ago. Most of the participants are now dead, but the notebooks give voice to their laughter and tears. Author James Still wrote down various quips and comments told to him and recorded them in what became known as *The Wolfpen Notebooks.*]

Parents today debate about the proper age for their child to begin dating: fourteen? fifteen? sixteen? thirty-two? Some parents allow their teen to group- and double-date before tackling single dating. In the old days, if you asked a schoolgirl if she had a boyfriend, the answer would probably have been "Oooo, no! I hate boys!" Third-graders today say they are going with someone. Of course, they're not going anywhere, but they do have a steady.

Dating, as we know it, is a privilege that our elders did not have. In the old days, so-called courting occurred at church or walking home from church. A few did go to "walk-in" theaters to see such classics as *Gone With the Wind,* but coming up with the dime for a ticket was difficult for some. When a young woman did actually begin dating, a chaperone—many times an older brother—went on the date, too. Sitting among the family members, many young men and women did their courting in the family living room.

Back then, dating seems to have been more exciting. The opposite sex remained a mystery. The first time a couple held hands or kissed was special, an event that made a young guy's or gal's heart palpitate faster. Perhaps folks called courting "sparking" because the sparks truly flew!

Nowadays, many young couples do not enter into relationships as innocents. The opposite sex is no longer a mystery.

Perhaps young folks should spend more time listening to the wisdom of their elders. Perhaps we could actually learn something from couples who have been together in holy wedlock fifty, sixty, and even seventy years!

—*Amanda Carpenter*

Today's teen's idea of dating would be completely foreign to our elders. We interviewed Henrietta Reynolds, who told us that her parents knew who, what, when, and where: "If we went out on a date with anybody, we were closely supervised as to what time we got home, where we were, and how we behaved." All those with whom we spoke had similar stories.

Many parents today do not know exactly where their teens are at any given time, whom they are with, what their children are doing, or what time to expect them home. Times have certainly changed.

Dating should be a time to get to know each other. Our elders' parents had rules about relationships and gave their children some wise advice about dating and marriage: "You can't date him if I don't like him." "Don't date someone you wouldn't marry." "You'd better behave." "If you want t' git married, he'll hafta ask my permission."

Many folks married people they had known all their lives: neighbors, friends, schoolmates. Their relationships grew at church. They held hands and stole kisses. Sometimes they went to the movies or dances, but some parents didn't allow dancing. One of our contacts went to a square dance, and when her father questioned her, she told him they weren't dancing—it was a game: "twistification"!

Angie Cheek, our former Foxfire Magazine facilitator, has shared with me how she met her husband: a blind date. She and Bobby, after dating for six years, have been married thirty-seven years. She told us her husband had good role models: Bobby's parents, Coy and Ruby Cheek, were married for seventy years May 31, 2005. We have met many couples who have had "forever" relationships. Perhaps in reading about O.S. and Olene, Minyard and Lessie, Harley and Omie, Lawton and Florence, and so many others, we will learn their secret to a lasting relationship.

—*April Argoe*

DATING

"We couldn't go to dances or parties. They'd have house raisin's, but they'd have to go with us if we got to go, and then we couldn't dance. Daddy

PLATE 106 1997—Dressed for the celebration of the 125th year of the founding of Toccoa First Baptist Church where Ruby and Thomas Coy Cheek have been members since 1941.

didn't believe in dancin'. He was very religious—Mama, too. They'd let us go to any revivals or anything like that, but that was our social life. If I wanted to see a boy, they had to see him, too, if I was to see one. They'd let him come to the house, but sometimes they wouldn't like him. I couldn't go with him no more if they didn't like him." —**Betty Crane, Summer 1978**

"We'd take in all the movie houses, all the vaudeville shows. They had two vaudeville houses that opened up on the side street. Then they had another place where there was traveling music shows. Then later on they opened up the Paramount Theater [California]; that was a big first-class movie house. They had seven shows that would come by every week. That's where I first saw Ginger Rogers. We'd go and see all those travelin' musicals—they'd travel the country. They put on some good musicals. Lordy, they were good!" —**Paul Power, Spring/Summer 2003**

"Dating was much, much different back then also. You did not start going out with boys when you were thirteen or fourteen years old. You got on up

PLATE 107 Paul Power and his wife, Bernice, on their last trip to Florida

fifteen, sixteen, maybe seventeen to go out with boys. Then you had a strict curfew, and you had to be home when your curfew was up. If you wasn't there, you better have an extra-good explanation of why you wasn't there. If you were not there, you would not leave again. A lot of time was spent at your boyfriend's, or your boyfriend would spend time at your house with your family—more than goin' places an' all." —**Donna Bailey, Fall/Winter 2003**

"There's a lot of difference now in dating than when I was a girl. There's been many a change. We dated altogether in bunches. We weren't allowed to be somewhere out by ourselves with a boy. I never was allowed to be out away when someone wasn't with me and knew somethin' about me. And we walked to do our courtin'. We walked along the road. We'd go to church in great big bunches, and we'd stay together. We had our dates, and we talked together. We'd tease each other and have a race down the road, one after the other—things like that. If I'd done things like I know of some boys and girls are doin' now, my daddy wouldn't have left any skin on me, from the top of my head to the bottom of my feet." —**Aunt Addie Norton, Fall 1976**

PLATE 108 Angela (Lina) dell'Arciprete, from Milan, Italy, became the bride of John Gurley Davis from Clayton, Georgia, in 1946.

"Dating was a no-no. You had to be at the end of high school before you could go out to date—that was age sixteen because we didn't have twelve grades. And for a few months, several months, until Mama and Daddy got to know the boy, we had to have a chaperone. But, you know, we didn't think anything about that. The boys knew that they had to go through the 'exam' from the adults. We knew, and we were satisfied.

"We cheated sometimes—well . . . a lot! I had my oldest brothers that helped me. Boys would invite me to go to the movies or something; then we all would meet at the corner, and my brothers would say, 'Now, you be here right on time,' the time they set. And so I did. And we met there and went home together, and Mama was satisfied that I was out with my brothers. I had three brothers and a sister. The sister, I used to get mad at her because—I called her the witch—she was the one that really followed me and checked on me. My brothers never cared about it. They trusted me. But my sister was always like a policeman, and I resented her. She was five years older, but when we had to live together, we got along fine. There was very much affection between the two of us, except she was just like a policeman."

—Angela (Lina) dell'Arciprete Davis, Spring/Summer 1994

"If we went out on a date with anybody, we were closely supervised as to what time we got home, where we were, and how we behaved. We were more closely chaperoned than a lot of the teenagers today, but it was just normal. We didn't think too much about it."

—Henrietta Reynolds, Spring/Summer 1993

"When I dated, the boy had a rubber-tired buggy with a fine horse. That's the first I remember ridin'. I was sixteen years old."

—Eula Carroll, Summer 1990

OLENE: We first met at the Holiness Church in Mountain City [Georgia]. It's the Mountain City Church of God now. I lived at Mountain City, and he lived here at Wolffork [in Rabun Gap, Georgia], where we live now. When I first met him, I thought he was nice-looking. He's still nice-lookin'. At that age you don't think about what's he gonna be or how good of a livin' he's gonna make you. I was just thinkin' about what he looked like and how he was.

O.S.: I liked her looks. She was a pretty girl back then. Well, she still is now. I used to walk three nights a week to Mountain City to see her. . . .

OLENE: On our first date he just walked me home from church; that's all. There wasn't much to do back then. We went to the movies once in a while but not often because money wasn't very plentiful.

—Olene and O. S. Garland, Fall/Winter 1995

> **"Back then, that hair was just as black as a crow. Her eyes were just as brown as a chinquapin. It made my heart just flutter like a motorboat."** ***—Carl Henry***

CARL: We met goin' to the same school on Persimmon [a community in Rabun County, Georgia]. We knew each other for a good long while before we started datin' because we lived in the community together. Our houses wasn't too close to start with, but later on they was. We were friends before we started dating. In school days, we went to school together about two or three years. We were in different grades at the same school. Back then, you just had the seventh grade over there. When we were goin' to school, I stayed with Uncle Jim Keener. She was with her granddaddy. I'd take her them sweet buck apples. I'd put that in her desk and bring her trinket pins and things like that. That's all there was to do. She had black hair back then, but it's sort of a white now. She's not colored it. Back then, that hair was just as black as a crow. Her eyes were just as brown as a chinquapin. It made my heart just flutter like a motorboat. That's the love affair that we had.

BUREL: On our first date, we walked to the church. Back then, you just went to church on Sundays and prayer meetin' through the week. That was all. So we went to prayer meetin' and to church together when we were courtin'.

CARL: And I'd walk her home and wherever she'd go. If it was an all-day service or somethin' at the Persimmon Baptist Church, we'd walk back up on the upper end of Persimmon, about four miles backwards or forwards.

Every once in a while, we'd borrow the A-model Ford of the man that I was workin' with. Then we'd go places like Rainbow Springs to see some of her people—things like that. We went to Scaly [Mountain, North Carolina] to the Miller's. We went different places.

BUREL: It was fun when you didn't have a vehicle of your own. The man he worked for loaned him his. We enjoyed it.

—Reverend Carl and Burel Henry, Fall/Winter 1995

JUANITA: We met in high school. I was in the tenth grade, and Jimmie was in the eleventh. We were high school sweethearts. Jimmie stood out to me because he was different. I noticed him in the library. Instead of just cuttin' up, he'd go get the newspaper and read it. That's the first time I ever remember really seein' him. He'd get up from the table, go up to the newspaper rack, get the newspaper, and read it. I just thought that must be a pretty smart boy, or he wouldn't be reading the newspaper. We knew each other and were friends about six months before we started dating. I liked him a lot, but that was back when girls didn't pick boys. Boys chose the girls. So I was really tickled when he asked me to date. I wasn't real sure my daddy would let me either. I liked him. He was a good ballplayer. I liked ball. I just liked him because he was him.

JIMMIE: Juanita was somewhat different from the other girls. She was pretty much of a one-person type girl. She wasn't a partygoer. In the early fifties, it was a different world from the way it is now, but there was still a distinction between all the popular and the unpopular. We had some like interests. Juanita was a good basketball player. Sports and activities were limited then. It was all school affairs. There wasn't the programs and activities that we have today. We had a lot of things together and got to know each other because of sports. I played football, and she played basketball. She was interested in the things I was interested in. The first date was just riding home from school to Juanita's home in Mountain City, just comin' to the house or takin' her home from ball practice. It was a while before regular dating started. We didn't have a lot to do.

JUANITA: Jimmie and me would go skating or square dancin'. Square dancin' was the thing because back then, in the fifties, the school sponsored the square dances, and that was their means of makin' money. They had them on

PLATE 109 Jimmie and Juanita Kilby celebrated their fiftieth wedding anniversary in 2004.

Wednesday nights and Saturday nights. We'd go skating and to the drive-in theater. That was what we liked to do. We dated for two years before we married. —**Reverend Jimmie and Juanita Kilby, Fall/Winter 1995**

> **"I didn't make any advances to her. I'd just hold her hand or somethin', but that was all. I misled her, I think."** —*L. M. Keef*

Mary Olive: Before we were married, Lee and I worked near each other. We ate lunch together a lot of the times, and that's where we got acquainted. He had a storage garage, and I worked in a big apartment hotel at the switchboard.

L.M.: It was the storage for this apartment that Mary Olive worked for. The people in those apartments had no other place to store their cars because they had a very small storage garage, and it wasn't big enough. So I had the overflow. What they couldn't handle, I did. I went over there lots of times. I thought she was pretty. That was mostly the reason. I thought everything of her.

Mary Olive: I was twenty-five or twenty-six when we started dating. Lee and I were friends for a while before we started dating. We had known each other about a year and a half. I thought he was real nice. That was the main thing when I first met him. He was real nice-looking, too.

L.M.: That was her mistake number one. We didn't do much on our first date—we just rode around. I didn't dare get near her. I thought that she'd

PLATE 110 "I didn't dare get near her. I thought that she'd reject me, see." —L. M. Keef

reject me, see. So I didn't make any advances to her. I'd just hold her hand or somethin', but that was all. I misled her, I think.

—L. M. and Mary Olive Keef, Fall/Winter 1995

"Have y'all heard of a 'box supper'? When I was growin', they used to have 'em when they raised money for anything. The young girls would get a candy box or somethin'. They'd decorate it up, wrap it in crepe paper, and fix it to look pretty. They'd fix a meal (sandwiches and cake or somethin') and put it in that box. The boxes were sold, and the men did the biddin' on the box. He didn't know whose box he was buyin'. The highest bidder got the box, and he had to eat supper with the girl that fixed it."

—Frances Harbin, Fall / Winter 2004

"Sometimes they'd have a box supper—a cake sale. And the young folks would bring in cakes, and they would auction them off. Whoever bought this cake got to court the girl that made it. That's the way they got their money out of it. The money was taken up for different purposes. They had different interests that they would raise a little money for. I think most of it went to the church. They'd say, 'Now here's a cake baked by a certain young girl in the audience.' And the young men would go to biddin' on that, and if she had a special friend there, he'd bid just as long as he had any money. And the other boys tried to keep him from winnin' it because they wanted to make him pay for it. They did, too!"

—Esco Pitts, Spring 1978

"We walked down to the Luftee River [North Carolina] and started to cross when he said, 'Give me your paw.' I didn't know whether to give him my hand or my foot!" —*Lessie Conner*

LESSIE: We courted on and off for pert' near five years. We'd court awhile, then fight awhile, and we'd git back together.

MINYARD: I remember the first time I kissed your granny. She jumped like a bull.

LESSIE: The first time we met, before we really started courtin' was when they was a-havin' a box supper at school. They'd take a box and put in a piece or two of fried chicken and some cake and tie a piece of red crepe paper around the box, makin' it real pretty. Then they'd hold them boxes up with the gals' names on 'em and auction 'em off to the boys. They held up my box, and Minyard won the bid. I think he paid a quarter fer it. That was the first time that I ever went with him. We walked down to the Luftee River [North Carolina] and started to cross when he said, "Give me your paw." I didn't know whether to give him my hand or my foot! When I give him my hand, he pulled me up to him and kissed me, and then he kissed me good night again when we got to my daddy's house.

MINYARD: We got married on a set of railroad tracks. . . .

LESSIE: Now, Minyard, there you go again with them tales. We did no such of a thing. We was married in John Freeman's backyard, next to the railroad tracks. John was the justice of the peace, and he run a little country store down at the foot of the hill.

MINYARD: There was me and your maw, Ben Fisher, Charlie Conner, and my brother, Lee. They was our witnesses. I was twenty-three, and your granny was eighteen and a pretty thing!

LESSIE: He tried to get me to marry him three or four times before that, but I wouldn't hear of it. Then I finally figured he was the best I could do, so I give in. Right after we got married, we moved in with Minyard's mama fer a year or two. Then her [Minyard's mama] courtin' got in the way of everything, so we moved out. **—Minyard and Lessie Conner, Spring/Summer 1996**

"When couples went courtin', they usually just walked on the road, probably meetin' each other somewhere and talkin' a while. There wasn't that

PLATE 111 "He tried to get me to marry him three or four times before that, but I wouldn't hear of it." —Lessie Conner

much to do back then except to go to church. We didn't have any picture shows or anything like that to go to. There wasn't much to do back then like there is today. Most people went courtin' on Sunday because that was the only time they had to get out and do anything.

"We used to have a lot of box suppers. The girls would cook the lunch and put it in a box, and they would decorate the box pretty with crepe paper and ribbons and different things. The boxes would be put up for auction, and the boys would bid the boxes off. They was a lot of fun, especially if some boy had a special girl and he would want her box. Naturally, the other boys would keep runnin' the bid up and make that boy pay a big price for the box. After they got all the boxes sold, each girl would match up with the boy who bought her box.

"At some box suppers, boxes would bring in as much as twenty-five dollars, and twenty-five dollars was a good price back then. My sister's box brought twelve dollars one time, and that's about the most that one ever sold for at our school. The money from the box suppers was usually used for buyin' somethin' we needed at school or in the community. We'd sit around and talk with one another before time for the boxes to be bid on. Then we'd pair off and eat." —**Amanda Turpin, Summer 1981**

> **"We had the last box supper I went to before I got married. I guess Jess Shirley found out from somebody what my box looked like, and he just kept bidding and bidding."** —***Varina Ritchie***

"You had a horse and a buggy. That's the way we went a-courtin' when we went to all doin's. We went in the buggy. He had the prettiest horse in Clayton. Nobody had a prettier horse than he did. And he kept her so fat and pretty.

"I've been to box suppers several times down here about Tiger [Georgia]. They used to have box suppers pretty often before I was married. I've been to box suppers—hear about the boys' fightin' and a-wrestlin' and doin' this, that, and the other because if someone got their sweetheart's box, they didn't like it.

"All the girls would take a box, and if that boy was smart, he'd get around and find out what his girl's box looked like. So when they went to biddin' on 'em, he'd bid higher. If someone would bid ten dollars, he'd bid a little bit more, you know, like that. He'd get the girl he wanted to eat supper with, the girl whose box he bought.

"They bid against him 'cause they knew what he was doin'. Henry was the one who bought my box that night. He got to take me home.

"The box suppers were lots of fun, and they made up money for the church for good things. After someone bought the box, we'd open that and sit down. Somebody would play the banjo and fiddle and the guitar, and some of 'em would dance." **—Varina Ritchie, Spring 1990**

"My parents wanted us to socialize with other boys and girls because they wanted us to grow up together and to know each other. They also wanted us to be around each other.

"We went a-courtin' instead of on dates, as you call them today. I went to the movies sometimes. There wasn't anything except a walk-in theater in Clayton at the time. Sometimes we would go to the neighbor's house and listen to records on an old record machine."

—Naomi Welborn McClain, Spring/Summer 2004

"Social life? [Chuckles] Back when I was growin' up, they had a movie theater in Clayton. We didn't do regular, you know. Like when *Gone With the Wind* come out, they's a whole truckload of us loaded up and went to Clayton t' the movie. Then we had candy drawins', and like when people's gon' can beans, they'd pick a bunch o' beans—like two or three bushels—and they'd have bean stringin's or pea shellin's. I never did go to a corn shuckin'. I've heard of it all my life, but I never did go to one. It was probably before my time. They was held once a week."

—Daisy Justice, Spring/Summer 2004

"Most times, the way you'd meet some boy was he might come home with your brother, or you would meet him at a church and revival meetings. It's

PLATE 112 "When *Gone With the Wind* come out, they's a whole truckload of us loaded up and went to Clayton t' the movie." —Daisy Justice

real funny—the young boys would never go inside the church, but they'd be there. They'd be out in the yard lookin' in the windas, winkin' at the girls. We'd wink back at 'em. Then when you came out the church, if a boy wanted to take you home, he'd come up and take you by the arm, and if you didn't like him, you'd just push his arm off or, most times, kick him. He realized you didn't want him. If you went home with him, he had that arm 'til you got home." —**Lois Duncan, Spring / Summer 2000**

"Back then, if a boy come to see a girl, they had to sit around among the family and talk. And they couldn't get out—the daddy just wouldn't let the girl go out with the boy. They had to sit around among the family and talk and do their courtin' there, right in the house. Well, sometimes they let 'em go to the movie. They had one movie here in town then—'theater,' they called it. They went there once in a while, and they'd get out and ride around maybe. But they didn't do that very often 'cause their family wouldn't let the boy take the girl out that way. They didn't trust 'em." —**Ada Crone, Summer 1980**

"Oh, and my husband, bless his heart . . . I got to tell y' how I met my husband . . . I was eighteen years old. No, I guess I was seventeen, and this friend of ours was goin' to take some young people fishin'. We were real good friends, so she asked me to go fishin' with her. So I went over to go a-fishin'. They all got in the cars and left to go down the river except this boy and girl. I knew the girl. She was sittin' in the car with this boy, so we got in

PLATE 113 Lois Duncan (here seen in her younger years) told us about winkin' at the boys.

the car with them. She told me who the boy was on the way down to the river. Well, he wound up to be my husband! The first time he saw me, he told the girl he was with, he said, 'That'll be my wife someday!' We went to the river; none of the girls would go out and help with settin' the hooks and things, and he said, 'Who's goin' with me?' I said, 'I'll go with y'!' We went down to the creek and back, and he wound up to be my husband. Now that's how I met my husband. Yeah, this is what I tell everybody: 'I went a-fishin' and caught a sucker!' We were married forty-three and a half years. When we were datin', you couldn't go by yourself, so my brother had to go with me. Every time I had a date, he had to go with me. He was my bodyguard." —**Fannie Ruth Martin, Fall/Winter 2002**

"I met my husband in South Carolina. I was workin' in a town called Ware Shoals. A bunch of the girls that I worked with and I had gone to a drive-in one night. He, my husband, came in and started talkin' to me. I was real flippant with my answers to him because I had a boyfriend, but we saw each other for about five weeks before we married." —**Donna Bailey, Fall/Winter 2003**

"After that, I thought havin' a date could be a very dangerous thing. Later on, I found out that the statement I just made can be true throughout life! The older you get, the more dangerous havin' a date becomes!" ***—Walker Word***

"Naomi had a daughter, my cousin Mabel. She was a sweet, pretty girl who was ten years older than me. She was sixteen, and I was six. I saw her, and I said, 'Mabel, I want to date. Will you date me?'

"She said, 'When do you want to date?'

"I said, 'If they will hitch a horse up for me on Sunday afternoon, let's go for a buggy ride.'

"She agreed to that. We got that buggy and she said, 'Where are we goin'?'

"I said, 'Let's go to Bush's Mill [near Waco, Georgia].' It was two or three miles away. It was a beautiful place. Mabel and I had got almost there at Bush's Mill and came to a railroad track. We crossed that track. Right after that, a train came along. The train blew its whistle. Our horse, Bob, was frisky. That whistle scared him half to death. He took off runnin'. Mabel got hold of the reins because I was too little. My feet wouldn't even touch the floorboard. I held on for dear life. Bob ran down a gully, up a bank, and across a big cotton patch. After a bit he stopped. That ended our date. We went home as soon as we could. After that, I thought havin' a date could be a very dangerous thing. Later on, I found out that the statement I just made can be true throughout life! The older you get, the more dangerous havin' a date becomes!" —**Walker Word, Summer 1991**

"So after a while, that white thing crawled up the bank of the road and across the road and on up the other bank and climbed a tree. I seen that thing, and I just knowed it was a booger. I was ashamed to go back to my girlfriend's house." ***—Kimsey Hampton***

"When I was a little feller and just big enough to start a-courtin', I was afraid of the dark. I'd see somethin' along the road and think it was a booger, and I'd run. So one night I was a-takin' this girl home; this bunch of boys decided they'd give me a scare. They took some old chicken wire and kinda doubled it up around a great big thing and put a sheet over it and tied a wire to it and put the wire across the road up in the forks of a bush. Up above this, they put a wire from one over to the other. Well, I looked, and I could see that thing. It would weave. They'd pull that wire up on the hill, and I didn't know it.

"So after a while, that white thing crawled up the bank of the road and across the road and on up the other bank and climbed a tree. I seen that thing, and I just knowed it was a booger. I was ashamed to go back to my girlfriend's house, and I knowed good and well if I could get even with it, I could outrun it. I got up just about even with that thing, and I broke to run just as hard as I could go. 'Bout the time I made two or three big steps, my big toe got hung in that wire and both sacks of leaves hit me right in the face. I hollered 'til you could hear me for two miles. I just knowed that thing had me." —**Kimsey Hampton, Summer/Fall 1975**

"In 1909, I had a date with a young man who lived four or five miles from me. He came Sunday mornin' to spend the day. He had a brand-new buggy that he had driven over in. I had a brother about eleven or twelve, and he had a friend visiting him. While we ate dinner—my brother and his friend didn't eat—they filled my date's buggy with pumpkins and switched the back and front wheels. He didn't know about it 'til time to leave that afternoon. The pumpkins were in the space where the top folded down. He saw the boys watchin' him from a hill, and he drove off as if nothin' happened. When he got out of sight, he changed the wheels again. But he didn't find the pumpkins until a good while later. They were hidden under the folded-down buggy top and started to rot." —**Ada Kelly, Summer/Fall 1975**

"When I was sixteen, I thought I was in love, and it made me sick—sicker than a dog. My pap tuck [took] me to the doctor, and, come to find out, it wasn't love—it was worms." —***The Wolfpen Notebooks*, Fall 1988**

"The first girl I ever kissed, or tried to kiss, here's what happened: she didn't know how, and I didn't know how. We bumped teeth, and that's all that happened." —***The Wolfpen Notebooks*, Fall 1988**

MARRIAGE

My wedding dress . . . I went to the store an' bought me a pretty piece o' blue material and made me a coatsuit—made it myself. Back then, people mostly wore blue. It was a medium-blue.

—Julia Alice Stephens Watkins

"I was twenty when I met him. I was twenty-one when we got married. I guess I was twenty-one in April, and we got married that December—the eighth of December. He asked me to marry him just out. At first he'd get back and write me, but I kept on 'til I made him ask me. I wouldn't give him an answer 'til he asked me in person. He 'as kinda backward. He'd be a-comin' to see me on Sunday evenin', and then he'd go back home and write me a letter and ask me to marry him. I kept tellin' him, 'Well, we'll talk about that.' Now I made him talk 'fore I'd tell him yes.

"My wedding—there wadn't much to it. We just got married at home—my home. I married at home, and my husband done come for us to marry. The preacher come—my old uncle Tom Coker Hughes (he 'as a Methodist preacher)—and he thought my husband-to-be hadn't come, and he said, 'Wonder when that boy's a-comin'?' My husband had got there. He kep' a-waitin' and a-waitin' in another room. Uncle Tom said, 'Well, it looks like that boy 'ud come on.' And someone said, 'Well, he's done here.' He'd been there a purty good while. Mr. and Mrs. Miller was thar, and his sister and two of his nieces was thar. Just a few people from the settlement was thar.

"My wedding dress . . . I went to the store an' bought me a pretty piece o' blue material and made me a coatsuit—made it myself. Back then, people mostly wore blue. It was a medium-blue. Lord, I don't know what my husband wore. I forgot. No music. No flowers. We just got married and left. No honeymoon. That wasn't in style back then."

—Julia Alice Stephens Watkins, Fall/Winter 2004

"I dated Ruby while she was in school because she was a year behind me. I dated her until the next year, and fourteen months later, we got married. When I asked her, we had been dating for over a year, and we decided that was what we wanted to do. I asked Ruby Mae Miller to marry me her last year of school. My marriage has lasted for seventy years. I think that is because we were willing to say we are sorry and were not trying to have our way all the time." **—Thomas Coy Cheek, Fall/Winter 2003**

"I met my husband at a party, a young people's party. I had been in and out of love and in and out of engagements a number of times. We were starting to get into World War II. Boys were being drafted, so people were getting down to business and deciding to get married. I married right at the beginning of the war, just at the time he would have been drafted. I met him at a young people's party, and we went together for a few months. Then the draft came. When he then realized his number was about to be called in the next few days, we went ahead and got married. The wedding was scheduled, and the invitations were out. The music was planned. The flowers were ordered for a certain date. It was a home wedding in my school. It was a private wedding: Just family was invited." **—Iris Daniel Engel Barnes, Fall/Winter 2003**

HARLEY: We got married in 1924, on the twenty-fourth day of February. We have been married sixty-five years. The day before we got married, I caught the train from Lakemont [Georgia] and rode it to Clayton [Georgia, about six miles from Lakemont]. I went over to the courthouse and got the marriage license. Then I went back and caught the train back to Wiley [between Lakemont and Clayton]. I got off at Wiley and walked way over to a field about a mile from where Jeff Taylor lived. I got him to meet us the next day at Flat Creek [on Lake Rabun] to marry us. The next day we had to walk down there. We had no other way to get there. We got married right in the middle of the road.

OMIE: It was cold that day. It was blowing snow. It was hard, but I'd do it again. **—Harley and Omie Gragg, Spring 1989**

"He [a man named John who looked after horses behind the mercantile store] said, 'Let me tell you somethin' about your daddy and his horses. A long time before your daddy married your mother, he and I went one Sunday to Salem campground [near Waco, Georgia]. I handled his horses. We went to a preachin' service, ate a meal, and was sittin' down on a bench by a spring. All of a sudden, your daddy-to-be jumped up and said, "There goes my wife."

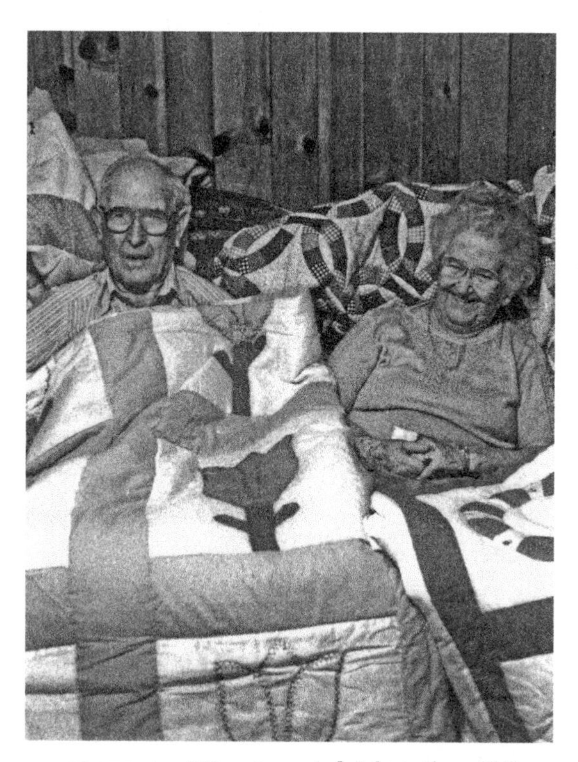

PLATE 114 "We got married right in the middle of the road." —Harley Gragg

There were two ladies that we had never seen before ridin' in a buggy. I asked him which one was his wife, and he said, "The one under the umbrella." ' My mother-to-be and her sister were there attending the preachin' service.

"Well, Daddy didn't meet her that day, but he sure found out who she was. She lived in Bowdon, Georgia. The next day he told John to hitch up his horses and ride to Bowdon and tell his wife-to-be that he was busy buyin' cotton, and that after cotton season was over, he'd like to come courtin'.

"I think it took my daddy three years to convince my mother to marry him. I think she was also goin' to college at that time. They finally married."

—Walker Word, Spring 1990

> **"He said they had people strung up here—horses, wagons, buggies; said they'd never seen th' like just all up an' down th' road, waitin' 'til we come. But we went th' old dirt road."** ***—Lawton Brooks***

LAWTON: I was twenty-three, an' Florence was nearly sixteen, when we got married. I had t' tell a lie an' get two more fellows t' tell a lie.

FLORENCE: I was just a few days lackin' of bein' sixteen.

LAWTON: I took two boys with me—had t' have witnesses with me—t' get m' [marriage] license. Had t' go t' Hiawassee an' get it. I lived in North Carolina but had t' get m' license in Georgia an' went to Georgia t' get married. See, in North Carolina—they're tight on y' in North Carolina—had t' go through a whole lot of this ol' red tape up there, an' in Georgia you didn't have t' do nothin', only get with it. I got these old boys t' go wi' me. My first cousin, he was a-sellin' licenses up there, clerk of th' court 'r somethin'. So he knowed me, an' he says, "Now, Lawton, I don't believe that" [that Florence was eighteen]. He just told me what he thought.

I says, "Well, I do. She's eighteen years old."

An these two ol' boys with me said, "Yeah, yeah." One of 'em said, "Well, I knowed her ever since she 'as a baby. She's eighteen years old." An' they'd never even seen her then. So we fooled around, and I finally paid m' license. Eighteen was the age, but I got m' license just the same.

Well, ever'body wanted to see us married. I knowed ever'body, y' know, an' ever'body knowed me. An' they always ganged around with me all th' time. I told 'em I 'as goin' to th' Georgia–North Carolina line [at Hiawassee, Georgia] to get married—just across th' line. We had to be in Georgia t' do it. So they thought I was goin' up to ol' man Pendle's. He lived just across th' line here at th' main highway. So ever'body thought that was th' place. He said they had people strung up here—horses, wag-

PLATE 115 "I was twenty-three, an' Florence was nearly sixteen, when we got married." —Lawton Brooks

ons, buggies—said they'd never seen th' like just all up an' down th' road, waitin' 'til we come. But we went th' old dirt road an' went up t' th' other Georgia line an' got in th' preacher's house right over the line. He married us, an' we 'as out. We'd been back an' forth in no time, an' they spent all day waitin' over there.

—Lawton and Florence Brooks, Fall 1973

"A couple would generally court about five years. People didn't get married so early back then, you know. They used to say if you married in blue, you'll always be true; if you married in red, you'll wish you were dead. I imagine people married in just anything they had. Most people married at home. You didn't kiss your bride back then. The usual marriage age was about eighteen to twenty. Usually a man had some sort of livin' he could offer his bride.

"Ral and I went to school together. You know the first time I ever did see Ral, he was just big enough to think about goin' with the girl he loved; I just fell in love with him then, right from the beginnin'—seemed like I was maryin' my folks. He always called my folks uncle and aunt, and we called his folks uncle and aunt. I love him very much—better and better every day. By the time we were through courtin', we knew each other pretty good.

"We had honeymoons, and Ral and I went to Anderson, South Carolina, on our honeymoon and spent a week. That was a big trip back then. There's my ring. My other ring was white gold. It got too little, and my daughter wears it around her neck on a chain." **—Nora Garland, Winter 1973**

> **"Olene started to school early one mornin', and I picked her up about a mile and a half from her home. We sent a telegram to her mother to tell her what we had done."** ***—O. S. Garland***

OLENE: We dated for nine months before we got married. I was fifteen, and he was twenty-one when we married. We got married in a civil ceremony in Walhalla, South Carolina. We went there because they didn't have a waiting period. We didn't have any kind of a reception or honeymoon afterwards. We didn't ask my father if we could get married.

O.S.: Her mother didn't want us to go together, so we slipped around together and got married. I wanted to ask her father's permission to marry her, but I reckon she must've been scared that they wouldn't give her to me because she wouldn't let me ask them. So we run away to Walhalla, South Carolina, and got married. Olene started to school early one mornin', and I picked her up about a mile and a half from her home. We sent a telegram to her mother to tell her what we had done. We were afraid she wouldn't get the telegram, so Olene wrote her a note and left it with one of her first cousins. My dad saw her mother in town after she had gone down to the depot to get the telegram, and he said, "Did you get that telegram?" She said, "Yes, I got it." She was so mad. Her mother didn't want us to go together because she said I was too rough, and she didn't want me to go with her. I was—I drank some back then. After we got married, she thought the world of me. I didn't blame her. I wasn't mad at her at all. I wouldn't have wanted my girls to go with a boy like that. And she wasn't mad at me either after we got married. She stayed with us in her old age. **—O. S. and Olene Garland, Fall/Winter 1995**

CARL: I had to ask her mother's permission to marry her. She had a good mother. I was twenty, and she was sixteen when we got married. We were married at the Rabun County courthouse on December 22, 1933. Will Smith was the ordinary. We didn't know nothin' about receptions then. We just got married and went to work. We didn't have no honeymoon either. We didn't have enough money to go on one.

—Reverend Carl and Burel Henry, Fall/Winter 1995

> "I had my ring on, and Daddy come in the kitchen where we was washin' dishes. My sister took my hand up out of the dishwasher and showed my daddy the ring." —*Juanita Kilby*

JIMMIE: I left it up to Juanita to tell her parents that I had proposed. I think I was afraid of her daddy. In the beginnin', her parents wasn't especially fond of me. I had somewhat of an unwarranted bad reputation. But after I met them and came to the house, we had no problems. Juanita's mother and daddy was fond of me. They was real good to me.

JUANITA: The way it happened is when Jimmie gave me the engagement ring, I was afraid to show my daddy. I was wearing it, and my sister and me was washin' dishes in the kitchen. That was when we didn't have hot runnin' water in the sink, and we had to do our dishes in two dishpans. I had my ring on, and Daddy come in the kitchen where we was washin' dishes. My sister took my hand up out of the dishwasher and showed my daddy the ring. It liked to have scared me half to death because I didn't know what he was goin' to say. He said, "You'd better keep that thing out of the water, or it'll turn." He didn't realize that it was a real diamond.

JIMMIE: My family liked Juanita. They picked at her a little bit, and she wasn't used to that because it was such a big family.

JUANITA: Right off, our friends realized that Jimmie and me cared a lot about each other. It was just assumed from the very onset that we'd be partners for life.

JIMMIE: We were married at the Baptist church in Clarkesville, Georgia. I was livin' in Atlanta, so what I did is I told Juanita to be prepared, and we'd get married on the way as we moved back to Atlanta. So we had a preacher standin' by at the Baptist church in Clarkesville, and we went down the road with all our things that we had loaded up in the car, stopped at the church, had the wedding, and went on to Atlanta to our apartment. That was our church wedding—just me and Juanita and the preacher.

JUANITA: I was eighteen and Jimmie was nineteen when we got married.

—Reverend Jimmie and Juanita Kilby, Fall/Winter 1995

"I remember when I told her [Grandmother Pinson] that I was goin' to get married, she said, 'Now, Amy, you just be hushin' up your mouth. You don't know any more about gettin' married than a goose knows when Sunday comes.' " —**Amy Trammell, Summer 1978**

"We always heard the rhyme that tells you what color to wear when you get married:

"Married in pink, your spirits will sink.
Married in blue, you'll always be true.
Married in black, you'll wish you were back.
Married in yellow, you're ashamed of your fellow.
Married in white, you've chosen right.
Married in green, you're ashamed to be seen.

"I don't guess too many people went by that back then. They'd just wear what they had. I just wore my suit, and we just went to the preacher and got married. As my daddy used to say, 'Wasn't no ceremony about it.' "

—Christine Wigington, Summer 1985

PLATE 116 Amy Trammell pans for gold.

"I think it's all right for a woman to live by herself if she wants to. But then again, if you think about it this way, when you get old and you've lived alone all your life, you've got nobody to live for."

—Aunt Addie Norton

"When you get married, they've really got a responsibility. If you're single, you can do as you please, go where you want to go, do what you want to do. And I think you can have the happiest life in the world.

"I feel some people get married before they know somebody well enough, and before long, they're quarrelin'. I don't think divorce is right. I don't like it. Sometimes it can't be avoided, but it's such a tragedy.

"I think a woman should be at least twenty-one or -two years old—maybe older than that—before they marry. But these little fifteen-, sixteen-year-old girls—they don't know the world for nothin'. I believe in people marryin' their own kind—not a wealthy man marryin' a poor girl or a mountain girl who didn't have much.

"I was eighteen when I was married. I was eighteen in December and married in February. I feel like I married too young—in a way I do. My husband and I lived together for sixty-one years, but sometimes I wonder if I'd stayed single, maybe I would have accomplished a lot more things.

"I think it's all right for a woman to live by herself if she wants to. But then again, if you think about it this way, when you get old and you've lived alone all your life, you've got nobody to live for. You've got no children to live for, and you've got nothin'. I don't know what in the world I'd do if it wasn't for my children." —**Aunt Addie Norton, Fall 1976**

"We was married very young. I had always known him and liked him. He didn't ask Daddy if he could marry me. I think I just told Daddy I was gonna marry him.

"Then we went to Walhalla, South Carolina, to get married. We took Paul Beck and Helen Beck, Paul's wife. They carried us over there. I was only sixteen. I've been married most all my life. I borrowed my mama's overcoat 'cause we was married in December, on the twelfth. It was cold, and I borrowed her coat. When I left the house, she told me not to lose her coat. We come back to her house and spent the night. I didn't know what I was a-gettin' into." —**Effie Mae Speed Bleckley, Spring/Summer 2004**

"We got married in the North Clayton Baptist Church. It's above the shirt factory. I had a very, very small wedding. My wedding, the whole thing, didn't cost but a little bit over a hundred and a few dollars. My dress was the one I wore to the junior-senior prom. The girls always wore white dresses, you know. My dress was white lace, and Mom took satin material and covered it for my train and my veil. That's about all. My sister and his brother was in the wedding, and that was it. His dad, his brother, and my brother were ushers. We got the ushers to light candles and all that. My wedding lasted about two minutes; then it was over. That's about it. I don't regret it. I'd do it again. We didn't have a honeymoon. The reason we got married July 2 is because that's the week he was off work. We couldn't afford a honeymoon, so we left Rabun County and went to Anderson, South Carolina. We spent one night there. We were back home by eight o'clock the next mornin', and I cooked breakfast." **—Eunice Hunter, Spring/Summer 2004**

"I met my husband at a restaurant. I 'as runnin' my own restaurant above the sawmill, an' he come up there an' eat with us. He liked my cookin', an' that's the way I met him. He come up there to eat with me—said he married me to cook for 'im. We've been married forty years. My grandpa told me we wouldn't stay together six months, but we fooled him—been married forty years and still got life to go." **—Senia Southards, Spring/Summer 2003**

"I don't believe in divorcin'. I'm against it foursquare. Now, you girls know who you're marryin' before you marry, and don't ever let me hear of you havin' a divorce. There's not many things you can have a divorce for, according to the Bible. But now don't ever marry somebody that you'll have to get a divorce from. Know who you're marryin' and what kind of family you're gettin' yourself into, and it'll work out. Then be good." **—Addie Bleckley, Summer 1978**

"May 31 of this year [2005], Coy and I will have been married for seventy years. We have had a wonderful life together. Always be fair with your mate. There were times we had differences, but we usually settled our differences behind closed doors and made up before the day was over. Also, I believe you can do anything if you set your mind to it and work toward it."

—Ruby Mae Miller Cheek, Spring/Summer 2005

"I had never went to a movie theater until I was fifteen. We had a walk-in theater. I think the first movie I saw was a Western, and being [that they were] young, it scared the other kids. I think it was Uncle Troy that had taken us.

"I quit school when I was in the eighth grade to get married. I had got married at the age of fifteen and was a mother at sixteen. Back then, you were not considered young when you were fifteen and sixteen. I have three sister-in-laws that got married at the age of fifteen, so it was not counted as bein' too young to get married in my family."

—Roberta Hicks, Spring/Summer 1994

PLATE 117 "I had got married at the age of fifteen and was a mother at sixteen." —Roberta Hicks

"When I got married, I did not know how to do anything except make french fries. I could not cook. I had never washed clothes. I did not know anything about keepin' house because I had never done it. I had to struggle. I did not particularly like children, so I had never bothered with them. I had to take care of my children on my own. It was a quite a dramatic thing for me to even go to the grocery store and buy groceries 'cause I did not know what to buy." —**Donna Bailey, Fall/Winter 2003**

PLATE 118 "Today's kids have a lot more to worry about than I did as a child." —Rose Ester Holcomb Shirley Barnes

"Young people today have got a hard life. Today's kids have a lot more to worry about than I did as a child. All I had to worry about was how I was goin' to tell my mother that I got married. I couldn't imagine havin' to tell them that I was goin' to die from AIDS."

—Rose Ester Holcomb Shirley Barnes, Fall/Winter 1997

"I wish we could swap wives like we do horses. I've got one I'd like to give somebody a ding-busted good cheating with."

—*The Wolfpen Notebooks,* Fall 1988

"I know positive your woman rules you. Mine will have her way even if she has to burn the waters of the creek. The woman is the boss in this country." **—*The Wolfpen Notebooks,* Fall 1988**

"I'll tell you about wives. After a while, they stop being sweethearts, and the husband just becomes one of the children."

—*The Wolfpen Notebooks,* Fall 1988

"You can always find yourself a wife if you're willing to take your equals."

—*The Wolfpen Notebooks,* Fall 1988

DOCTORING

[**Editor's Note:** Foxfire does not espouse any of the following as remedies for certain ailments. We are simply reporting what the folks around these parts avouch as treatments and cures.]

I never did take much doctor medicine. I don't guess I've took a tablespoon of doctor medicine in my life. Whatever was ailin', we took home remedies for it. And if we didn't know, we'd get to the old people and learn how, learn what the remedies are.

—Gertrude Mull

Many children today are afraid of going to the doctor or the dentist, but if they knew what doctoring was like in the old days, they would appreciate modern medicine more. Many adults died in what we today consider middle age. Women died in childbirth, and the infant mortality rate was astronomical. In fact, in perusing the old articles from *The Foxfire Magazines,* we read story after sad story of the untimely death of infants and children. Furthermore, with no antibiotics or vaccines, many folks died from illnesses easily prevented or cured today.

Though they made house calls, doctors were miles away and made the trip by horse and buggy, so the time was long between the hour doctors received a summons and their arrival at the home of the patient. Also, the crude methods of "curing" folks seem unbelievable by modern standards: Folks talked about sitting in a kitchen chair and having their tonsils removed—with no anesthesia! Imagine lying on the ground and having the local tooth puller put his knee on your chest and yank your tooth out with what amounted to a pair of pliers!

Medicine today is miraculous. Physicians specialize, and the pharmaceutical industry has produced a wide variety of drugs. Moreover, over the years, researchers have discovered cures and vaccines for diseases that once killed thousands: tuberculosis (once called consumption), typhoid, typhus, smallpox, polio—the list is long. We are very fortunate to be living now, when medical professionals have the knowledge and technology to help patients survive and live healthy, long lives.

—April Argoe

"To treat a cold, we used boneset [*Eupatorium perfoliatum*] tea or tea from feverweed [feverfew, *Chrysanthemum parthenium*]. Boneset's got blue blossoms on it. The tea is made out of the leaves. You pour boiling water over the leaves, let it set, and drink the tea off of it. Pennyroyal [*Hedeoma pulegioides*] is really good, too. Do it the same way. Or you might use a rag with turpentine and grease in it. You drop some turpentine right on your dressing and add grease to it. Put that on the chest and put a warm rag over it. That'll fix 'em up, too.

"Take the powder out of goldenrod [*Solidago*] flowers. It's good for cuts—keeps down infection. You just break the blossoms off, put 'em over paper, and let 'em drop. Sift that to get all the crumbs out of it to where it'll just be pure stuff—the powder out of the blossoms.

"Yellowroot [*Xanthorhiza simplicissima*] is good for infection, too. That's the best thing in the world for ulcerated stomach. A lot of people used to come to Grandpaw—wanted him to fix them up a tea from yellowroot.

"Trailing arbutus [*Epigaea repens*] and coltsfoot [*Tussilago farfara*] are both something that you couldn't get over for coughing. Just take the leaves of coltsfoot and make tea out of it. You get lady's-slipper [*Cypripedium*] root or sweet gum [*Liquidambar styraciflua*] bark for nerve trouble.

"I never did take much doctor medicine. I don't guess I've took a tablespoon of doctor medicine in my life. Whatever was ailin', we took home remedies for it. And if we didn't know, we'd get to the old people and learn how, learn what the remedies are.

"My husband used to be a herb doctor and was a clergyman, too. You'd go to him and tell him, say, 'A friend way down the road is bad cut.' (Maybe he'd cut his arm or leg or somethin'.) The blood 'ud stop right then when he was told about it. Right then, it'd stop and never bleed another drop. My grandpaw was a clergyman, too, and had a gift to stop blood."

—Gertrude Mull, Summer 1983

"The doctor would come when we needed him, whether we had money or not. Dr. Paul Killian was a good ol' doctor. He'd go anywhere and doctor anybody. He was good to the poor people. . . .

"We used home remedies quite a bit. For a cold, we used to have what they called British Oil. They'd get it at the store. They'd drop it in with some sugar and give it to the sick person. I gave it to my younguns, but I hadn't seen none in a long time. . . .

"The best thing for the croup was possum oil. When you killed a possum, you'd take the fat and render out the grease and put it in a bottle. I'd give my children a teaspoonful. . . .

PLATE 119 Yellowroot (*Xanthorhiza simplicissima*)

"And I used to chew an orange peel for colic. We'd peel the orange and lay the peels up and let them kindly dry and then chew them. . . .

"Castor oil was what I used for constipation. Now people have quit takin' that stuff. I don't know why. We used to put it in our ears when we had an earache, too. Pour that castor oil in there and put some cotton in. Sometimes we'd put a sourwood stick or a persimmon stick in the fire and let it get hot enough for the sap to run out. It looked like soapsuds. We'd catch that in a spoon and pour it in the ear. . . .

"Kerosene oil's what I used for leg cramps. That's the only thing that would stop it for my husband, Ben. I'd just rub it on the bottoms of his feet and on his legs. He'd holler and take on like he was dyin' with those cramps. He couldn't even get out of his bed. I'd have to get ahold of his feet and pull him out. I'd rub that kerosene on him, and that stopped it. . . .

"Now for vomiting, I'd break off a peach tree limb and scrape the bark off. I'd boil that part that was under the bark and make a tea out of that and let the sick person drink that. . . .

"I hardly ever took my kids to the doctor for a fever. I'd fry onions in grease and rub that grease all over their chest and put a wool flannel cloth over it. That also works for pneumonia." **—Minnie Dailey, Summer 1985**

"In those days, if you needed a doctor, the doctor would call on you at home. You wouldn't go to a hospital—never heard of a hospital. If you needed a doctor, you'd have to send someone to get him. It'd be eight or ten miles away. Take you half a day to go and get him, so you better not get sick. It ain't like it is now.

"Since it was so hard to get a doctor in there, my grandfather and my father and all of the other men of the community went ahead and made a horse path across the mountain and called it the Doc Woody Trail because the doctor was Burnett Woody.

"When somethin' serious happened, the doctor would come. One time a horse threw me, and I fell on my shoulder. We were in a field near the road, and a Dr. Guffey came by and looked at my shoulder but didn't treat it. He told my mom and dad, 'He'll never use that arm no more.' He said I'd never be able to put it behind me, but I did.

"The way we did our teeth, there was a fella that had a pair of forceps—or tooth pullers, they called it. If you had a bad tooth, you'd go up to his house, and he'd get you down and take your tooth out. That's what we did in the dentist business. The last'n he pulled for me, he got me down. I went to his house, and he was hoein' corn in the field. He sent one of his children to the house to get his pullers. He got me down between the corn rows and took my tooth out.

"We took care of a lot of our own problems. One time we was peelin' tanbark, and somethin' stung me on the foot. I thought it was a bumblebee sting. After a while, it wouldn't quit hurtin'. I looked down, and there was two marks. I told my dad I believed that I was snakebit. He looked at it and said, 'I believe you are.' So I went down there where the snake had bit me. I looked, and there was a copperhead layin' there. 'Well,' he said, 'you go to the house, but you take your time and don't get hot.' The house was down the hill, and in about five minutes, I was there. I told Momma a snake bit me. She went and got the turpentine and held the bottle to that place. Then she got a gallon of kerosene and set my foot down in it and soaked it for a while. Then she made a poultice out of a soggy paste of hot water, meal, and salt. She mixed it up and got it real hot and put it on there with a cloth around it. She left it there 'til the next mornin'. That was it. My foot swelled up, but I never did get sick. The doctor never came."

—Roy Roberts, Spring 1985

"He'd put one of 'em homemade pullers in there and give 'er 'at yank . . . He'd have one knee on your chest—caught y' with his left hand and got in yer mouth. Take his pocketknife and cut around it 'bout a half-inch deep—little blade of a knife. You could just hear that a-squrshin' in there." ***—Kenny Runion***

"Ever'thin's different. Ain't nothin' now like it was then. You didn't go ever' time you sneezed then to a hospital. There wadn't nary 'un. Back yonder, th' doctor made a twenty-four-mile trip. He'd come here and stay with y' about an hour, doctor y', and give y' ever what you needed. And when he got ready t' go and give y' ever what y' owed him, said, 'Five dollar. Five dollar'—and what would that cost now? Cold or hot, he'd come. He'd come cold or hot. He'd have a big gray horse, and a big bird dog 'ud come lopin' right in with him.

"And sometimes if y' got sick, they'd have old granny doctors 'at 'ud come see y'—doctor y' up. If y' had th' flu—they called it th' grip then—they'd go out and get some boneset [*Eupatorium perfoliatum*], some pennyroyal [*Hedeoma pulegioides*], and put a big ol' pot on. Had fireplaces. They'd fill 'er about half full, boil 'er down, give y' a teacup full of it, and put y' in th' bed. You'd just wet a sweat up. Few minutes and you'd be knocked out. You've took quinine, ain't y'? 'At ol' boneset's as bitter as it. Those olduns would come and doctor y'. Wouldn't cost you a dime. They'd stay all night with y'.

"And I never heard tell of 'pendicitis 'til I was growed. I watched ol' Doc Lyons operate on a woman in Towns County [Georgia] fer one. I didn't know there was such a thing. People called it th' cramp colic. They'd lay down just as close t' that fire as they could get and bake that place, almost burn it.

"Biggest thing they had was what they called dropsy. Yer feet go t' swellin' down here, and it just goes up. Other words, yer blood just goes t' water is th' best way I can explain it t' y'. But la-a-a-aw, there's ten t' heal y' now when there wasn't nary 'un then.

"If y' got yer leg broke, they'd know just what t' do. They 'as a feller ridin' on a wagon, and he 'as settin' down on th' couplin' pole—don't know what he meant 'less he 'as drunk. And his feet was just about 'at fer from th' ground—about a foot. And he hung his foot there agin' [against] a stump and broke his leg square in two—just broke it. Way they done when 'at happened, they just rolled his breeches leg up and go out there and split some wood pieces and commence right here around yer leg. They'd place it back th' best they could and go plumb around yer leg with them little pieces. Then they'd tie it with a rope or a good stout string, and there'd you'd set fer about twelve month. And that's what y' got—no doctor medicine. Didn't have no doctor medicine at all. It 'as just pull and take it. No dopes. No dopes at all. No shots. No nothin'! You 'as just there in the chair. . . .

"If y' had t' have a tooth pulled, you come in to a feller name of J. Garrett. He'd say, 'Lay down on 'at floor, feller.' You'd stretch out there on th' floor. He'd put one knee here on your chest and catch you just like 'at around your head. He 'as stout, too. He'd put one of 'em homemade pullers in there and give 'er 'at yank. If it broke off, 'at's all it wrote. If it broke off, he couldn't get it. But if it didn't break, he'd bring it. You couldn't get up. He'd have one knee on your chest—caught y' with his left hand and got in yer mouth. Take his pocket-knife and cut around it 'bout a half inch deep—little blade of a knife. You could just hear that a-squrshin' in there. Sometimes his pullers 'ud slip off. Great goodness! You'd hear all kinda racket in your head—just like bustin'. He'd say, 'Oh, my pullers slipped off.' They 'as old, homemade 'uns from th' shop. Sometimes they'd get slick and slip off. Great goodness! Might'n ye bust yer head. He'd go back again. Keep on 'til he got it, unless it busted off.

"But now when all 'at was over, you didn't owe him a dime—didn't owe him a thing, didn't charge a dime. He'd pull half a dozen fer each one of us—not a cent. You had t' hold yer mouth wide or prop it open with a stick. After it 'as pulled, you'd fill your mouth full o' salt. You know how 'at hurt now—washed yer mouth out—and th' next day it 'as feelin' good. You didn't go around with yer lip swellin' down here with 'at old poison, y' know. Just looked like y' always did—if he didn't bust it. If he busted it in yer mouth, then he'd have t' pull it out by pieces. You didn't have shots either. Now, boys, you had t' have nerve!" **—Kenny Runion, Fall 1971**

PLATE 120 "Now, boys, you had t' have nerve!" —Kenny Runion

"Mama, from her experience living in a doctor's home, knew how to take care of most any illness or hurt. If we stuck a nail in our foot or cut ourselves with a piece of tin or anything like that, we would sit on the wood steps, and she'd build a little fire. She put wool rags over the fire, and we'd sit there and smoke our foot. I remember one time I got so tired of sitting there. I wanted to go play, and I said, 'Mama, I think I'm done.' She said, 'Let me see that foot,' and I held it up for her. She said, 'It's not black enough.' So I had to sit and smoke it some more. She would gather herbs and plants for medicine and knew exactly where the yellowroot and other plants were located. She parched and ground up senna [*Cassia*] leaves. A small dose of this tea would help settle a stomach, and a large dose was used as a laxative. Mama was not a registered midwife, but if the doctor could not make it in time, she would go to deliver the baby. She said if she could save their lives, she'd do anything she could. Mama contributed so much, not only to her family but also to others."

—Ruby Mae Miller Cheek, Spring/Summer 2005

"There was only one doctor that was employed by the loggin' company. They took a couple of dollars out of everyone's salary in order to pay him. I remember when I was little, one time, the doctor came up to the house because I was feelin' dizzy and sick. The doctor gave me a dose of calomel [a white compound used as a purgative], and I just thought I was goin' to die. It was awful! It made me sick in the stomach, and it gave me diarrhea! Gosh, it was awful! Back in those days, they didn't have much medicine, and calomel was one of the standard things they gave you. For a while after the incident, every time I saw the doctor comin', I would run and hide in the woods. He sure wadn't goin' to doctor *me* anymore!"

—Hazel Killebrew, Spring 1991

"There was no such thing as aspirin, but they did sell pills. They also sold liniments for anybody that thought they had rheumatism, what they call now arthritis. There was a Rosebud Salve. You could order it, but you couldn't buy it in stores. We'd order that salve and went around and sold it.

"Then there were peddlers who came through with all kinds of stuff. They would have just bags full of patent medicines, and they'd sell a lot of that." **—Martha Roane, Summer 1983**

The following are home remedies for various illnesses. Again, Foxfire does not attest to the effectiveness of these purported remedies.

ARTHRITIS AND RHEUMATISM

- Make a tea out of the bark of the witch hazel [*Hamamelis virginiana*] tree and drink that. It'll cure rheumatism.
- Let rattlesnake master [*Eryngium yuccifolium*] root, wild cherry [*Prunus serotina*] bark, and goldenseal [*Hydrastis canadensis*] root sit in one gallon of white whiskey and then drink.
- Rub some wildcat oil on the affected parts.
- Drink a tea made from the seeds or leaves of alfalfa [*Medicago sativa*].
- Cook garlic in your food to ease it.
- Carry a buckeye [glossy brown nut of the *Aesculus*] in your pocket.
- Carry an Irish potato in your pocket until it gets hard.
- Carry a raw potato in the pocket to prevent it.
- Drink powdered rhubarb dissolved in white whiskey.
- A magnet draws it out of the body.

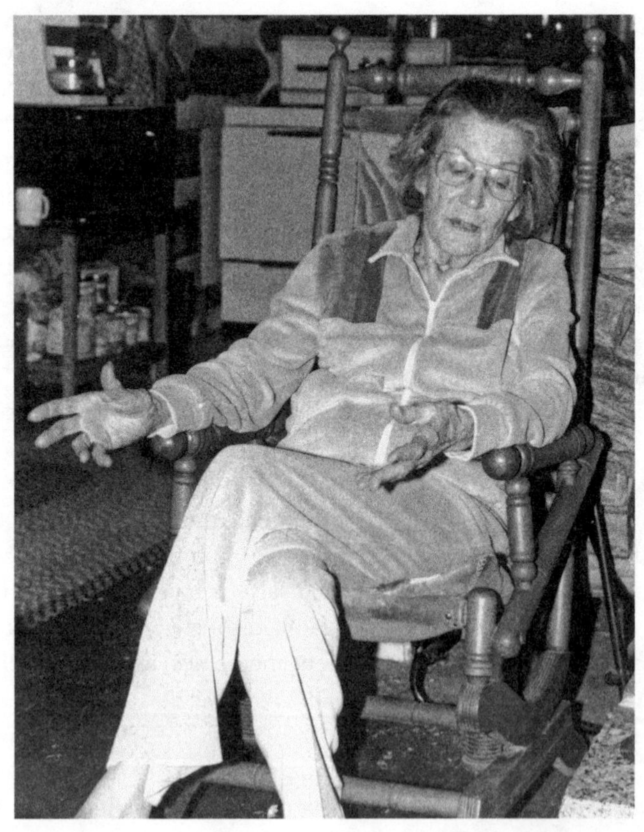

PLATE 121 "The doctor gave me a dose of calomel, and I just thought I was goin' to die." —Hazel Killebrew

PLATE 122 Rattlesnake master [*Eryngium yuccifolium*]

ASTHMA/HAY FEVER

- Take twenty-five peach kernels and cook or steep them in a gallon of water. Dose is one tablespoonful three or four times a day.
- You walk up to a black gum tree and have someone drill a hole right above your head. Cut off some hair from your head and put it in the hole; then put a cork in it, and you won't have the asthma again.
- Stand a child up against a sourwood tree and bore a hole in the tree right at the place the child's head comes. Put some of the child's hair in the hole, and when he grows taller than the hole, the asthma will be gone.
- Take a sourwood stick the size [height] of the child when he's two or three years old. Put it in the top of the house where it won't get wet. When the child outgrows the stick, the asthma will be gone.
- Swallow a handful of spiderwebs rolled into a ball.
- Keep a Chihuahua around the house.
- Smoke strong tobacco until you choke.
- Put a dry stick under the doorstep, and when you reach that height you will be cured.
- For all infections of the lungs, take one quart of tar and two quarts of pure rainwater. Put them in an earthen vessel. Steep them together as hot as can be without boiling for eight hours. When cold, pour the liquid off and strain it through a cloth and add to it one pint of the best brandy or whiskey and a pound and a half of loaf sugar.

ATHLETE'S FOOT

- Soak your feet in bleach and water.

BED SORES

- Brown and pulverize eggshells. Take a teaspoonful three times a day.
- Make a tea of clover blossoms, dry or green, and drink at mealtime.

BLOOD PROBLEMS

- Blood pressure: Drink sarsaparilla (sasparilla) [*Smilax*] tea.
- Blood purifier: Make a tea of burdock [*Arctium*].
- Blood tonic: Make a tea of bloodroot [*Sanguinaria canadensis*].
- Stop bleeding:
    - Put kerosene oil on the cut.
    - Take soot from the back of fireplace in an old chimney and press it against the cut.
    - Put lamp oil or turpentine on the cut.
    - Apply powdered alumroot [*Heuchera*] to the wound.

BRAIN DISEASE

- Use walnuts—the kernel resembles the brain, and the shell resembles the skull.

BROKEN ARM

- Put a splint on the arm and wrap a cloth around it. Leave it like that until the arm gets well.

BRUISES AND SPRAINS

- Apply crushed hyssop [*Hyssopus officinalis*] leaves directly to bruises.
- Apply Saint-John wort [*Hypericum*] or parsley [*Petroselinum crispum*] leaves directly on sprains.

BURNS

- Cut an Irish potato in two at the middle and lay it on a cloth. A handkerchief is a good thing. Bind that handkerchief with that potato in it around the burned place. In ten minutes, you can't even tell you've been burned. That's the truth. You can't tell it—the heat is gone. Let that potato stay there until it turns black. Then the place where the burn was will be as white as cotton because you got that fire out of there. If you get that heat out of there fast enough, it won't even blister.
- Put baking soda on the burn.
- If the person has never seen his father, he can cure it by blowin' on it.
- Put a mixture of lard and flour on it.
- Make an infusion from the dried rootstocks of bloodroot [*Sanguinaria canadensis*] to relieve the pain of burns.

CHEST CONGESTION

- Mix some lard and turpentine together. Put it on a cloth and put that on your chest.

CHILBLAINS [A painful, inflamed area on the hands or feet due to exposure to cold]

- Mix one pint of water, one ounce acetate of zinc. Apply. [Very highly recommended by George Gillource, M.D., Louisville, Kentucky]

CHINCHES OR BEDBUGS

- Burn sulfur in a closed house.

COLDS

- Break some boneset [*Eupatorium perfoliatum*] leaves and stems into a pot and boil it; then set it off and let it cool just enough to be able to drink it. Drink about half a cup and go to bed. Put about four blankets on you. In about thirty minutes, you're just as wet from sweat as if you

were thrown in a creek. Your cold's gone. But you better be careful about getting out quick because the pores of your skin are really open.
- Boil some boneset in water. Strain and drink.
- Put ginger and sugar in hot water. Drink this and go to bed.
- Drink hot lemonade before going to bed.
- Drink boneset tea or lady's-slipper [*Cypripedium*] tea.
- Use goose grease salve.
- Drink whiskey and honey.
- Drink onions roasted in ashes (good for babies).
- Drink castor oil.

CONSTIPATION

- Take about two teaspoonfuls of turpentine.
- Eat prunes or drink prune juice.

COUGH

- Mix honey and soda together. Take a teaspoonful before you go to bed and a teaspoonful when you get up.
- Take the leaves of coltsfoot [*Tussilago farfara*] and make a tea.

CRACKED OR CHAPPED HANDS

- Rub pine resin on them.
- Rub petroleum jelly on your hands at bedtime and then wear gloves to bed.
- For chapped hands, the old-timers used mutton tallow. When they killed a sheep, they rendered the grease out like you do hog lard. When it got cold, they'd have big ol' pieces of it. It'd just be hard. Then they'd take that stuff and grease their hands real good.

CROUP

- Make a little ball up of a half teaspoon of sugar, a drop of kerosene oil, and about a half teaspoon of Vick's salve. Swallow this.
- Swallow groundhog oil.

CUTS

- Apply camphor, sugar, and turpentine.
- Apply kerosene oil.
- Take the powder out of goldenseal [*Hydrastis canadensis*] blossoms and sift. Apply the pure powder to the cut. It helps keep down infection.
- Apply to the weapon that caused the cut instead of the wound.

DYSENTERY/DIARRHEA

- Take one tablespoonful of Epsom salts and one teaspoonful of paregoric [camphorated tincture of opium] in a tumbler of water and take a swallow after each paroxysm [spasm]. Relief is certain.
- Boil plantain [*Plantago*] leaves (not the roots) and drink the tea often. This will cure dysentery. Also a tea made from dried strawberry [*Fragaria virginiana*] or blackberry [*Rubus allegheniensis*] leaves will stop dysentery.
- Drink blackberry juice.
- Boil shavings from the inner part of white oak [*Quercus alba*] bark (tannic acid).
- Drink the juice or the inner part of persimmon [*Diospyros virginiana*] limbs.
- Drink burned whiskey.
- Pull up some blackberry roots and boil them. Strain and drink the water.
- Boil a lady's-slipper [*Cypripedium*] in water. Strain the water and drink.
- Brew tea from the leaves of alumroot [*Heuchera*] and drink.

EARACHE

- Take hot ashes from the stove and make a poultice of that and apply to the tooth or ear.
- Take the goody out of the inside of a walnut and boil it in a teaspoon of water. Put a few drops of this in the ear.
- Pour fried onion juice in the ear.

FEVER

- Teas made from boneset [*Eupatorium perfoliatum*] or the roots of butterfly weed [*Asclepias tuberosa*] or wild horsemint [*Monarda punc-*

tata] or feverweed [feverfew, *Chrysanthemum parthenium*] that grows flat on the ground are all good for colds, flu, and fevers.
- Tie a bag containing the sufferer's nail parings to a live eel. He will carry the fever away.

FLU

- Make a tea of rabbit tobacco [*Gnaphalium obtusifolium*] and pennyroyal [*Hedeoma pulegioides*]. Boil them together 'til the tea is black as tar. Give the children that tea. They'll sweat that night and sweat that flu out.
- Make a tea from the leaves of catnip [*Nepeta cataria*]. It is good for helping the ill person to sleep (also good for colds).

FOOT CRAMPS

- When you start to bed, pull off your shoe. Take it over there and lean it against the wall, bottom side up. See if you have that cramp anymore.

HEADACHE

- Dissolve and drink two teaspoonfuls of finely powdered charcoal in half a tumbler of water. It will relieve a headache in fifteen minutes. Take a Seidlitz powder [a cathartic with laxative properties] one hour afterward.
- When you get your hair cut, put the hair under a rock, and you won't have the headache.
- Wet brown paper in apple vinegar and lay on the forehead.
- Make a poultice of horseradish [*Armoracia rusticana*] leaves.
- Rub camphor and white whiskey on the head.

HEART

- Dandelion [*Taraxacum officinale*] tea is a heart stimulant.

HEARTBURN

- Stir a teaspoon of baking soda in a glass of water and drink.

HICCUPS

- If you can remember the last place you seen a frog that had been run over by a car on the road, it would cure the hiccups.
- Take nine sups of water, and you will quit the hiccuping.
- Put vinegar on sugar and eat.
- Drink about a half glass of water.
- Eat a teaspoon of peanut butter.
- Put half a teacup of dried apples in a teacup of water and bring to a boil, stirring occasionally. Strain out the remains of apples and drink the juice while hot.

HIVES

- When a child has the hives, let him or her chew a little catnip.
- Boil a bunch of catnip [*Nepeta cataria*] in water. Strain and drink.
- Boil ground ivy [*Glechoma hederacea*] in water. Strain and drink the tea.
- Use catnip leaves and put them in a pot. Pour boiling water over them and wait a few minutes. Remove the leaves, sweeten the liquid, and drink.

"Use ground ivy [*Glechoma hederacea*]. If babies had the hives, we'd give them a tea made from ground ivy. That's a vine that grows all around here. Just pour some boilin' water over the leaves in a teacup. Let it cool, sweeten it a little, and give a little to the baby."

—Minnie Dailey, Summer 1985

INFLAMMATION

- Boil a beet leaf. Then put it on the inflamed spot and tie a cloth around it.

INGROWN NAILS

- Mix together "perfectly fresh tannic acid (one ounce) and six drachmas [unit of weight; a dram—0.125 ounce] of pure water. Dissolve with gentle heat. Paint the soft parts around the nail twice a day."

INSOMNIA

- Drink lady's-slipper tea [*Cypripedium*].
- Drink catnip [*Nepeta cataria*] tea.

ITCH

- Put a mixture of lard and sulfur on the itch.
- Mix gunpowder and sulfur and apply the mixture to the itch.
- Boil a bunch of poke [*Phytolacca americana*] salad roots in a big wash-pot. Let it cool enough and then wash them all over just like a regular bath. (You might jump up and down like you were on fire, but it will kill that itch.) Some people use sulfur and mix it up with the lard from killing hogs. Apply that concoction on the itch. (Some folks don't like the latter cure because of the scent of sulfur.)
- Make a salve of balm of Gilead [*Populus candicans*] buds fried in mutton tallow. Add petroleum jelly if you wish and apply to the affected area.

KIDNEYS

- Make a tea from boiling mullein [*Verbascum*] roots.
- Get the dead silks off an ear of corn. Boil in water. Then drink the water.
- For treating kidney stones, gather a handful of trailing arbutus [*Epigaea repens*]—both leaves and roots. Boil it at least an hour in a half gallon of water. Drink two or three cups a day if you have a kidney stone bothering you. To prevent a recurrence of kidney stones, drink a quart or so a month.

MASTITIS

- Apply cabbage leaves to the breast(s) and leave them there for a while.

MEASLES

- Spicewood [*Betula lenta*] tea will make them break out.
- Drink sassafras [*Sassafras albidum*] tea.

- Drink sheep waste tea—make a tea of sheep dung.
- Any herb tea will help break them out.
- Make a poultice of eggs, cream, and Epsom salts and spread on them. Take it off after it dries.

"Lemon tea's what I gave my children if they didn't break out with the measles. You had to get 'em broke out, or those measles would kill you. I made the lemon tea just like you make lemonade, only I boiled it."

—Minnie Dailey, Summer 1985

"When we had the measles—and nearly every child had 'em—my father would move a big bed in the livin' room in front of the big fireplace and make us lay there. He made a tea, and he wanted us to drink that tea. I'd put it in my mouth, and when he got gone, I would raise up and spit it in the fireplace. I don't know what kind it was, some kind of tea that would make us break out with measles faster. My sister got so sick. She finally broke out with them measles, and it was bad. We had to blind the windows because they said it would hurt her eyes for the light to come in. I said, 'Oh, no, I don't want to be sick like her,' so I finally drank that tea. My sister couldn't eat, but I could. I never was that sick." **—Martha Roane, Summer 1983**

MOUTH SORES AND FEVER BLISTERS

"We'd chew a little yellowroot [*Xanthorhiza simplicissima*] for upset stomach or for sore mouth, like sores in the corner of your mouth or fever blisters." **—Minnie Dailey, Summer 1985**

NERVES

- Drink spicewood [*Betula lenta*] tea and sassafras [*Sassafras albidum*] tea. To make sassafras tea, gather the roots and tender twigs of red sassafras in the spring. Pound the roots to a pulp if they are very big and wash them with the twigs. Boil them, strain, sweeten, and drink.

NOSEBLEED

- Let your nose bleed on a knife blade and stick the knife in the ground. Your nose will stop bleeding. Or take a pair of scissors and run them down the back of your neck. That will stop the nosebleed.

- Put cold cloths on the neck and forehead.
- Place a nickel directly under the nose between the upper lip and gum and press tightly.
- Take a small piece of lead and bore a hole in it. Put a string through the hole, tie it, and wear it around your neck. Your nose won't bleed again.
- Lie down and put a dime on your heart.
- Sniff the powder from puffballs, and it will stop.
- Hang a pair of pothooks around your neck.
- Place scissors, points up, on your back.

"When my sister's nose used to bleed, my mother hooked a pothook, like they used to cook over the fireplace with, around her neck. Then Mama would pull a hair out of the top of my sister's head, and the nosebleed would stop." **—Minnie Dailey, Summer 1985**

PAIN

- Roast some poke [*Phytolacca americana*] roots by the fire. Scrape them clean with a knife and grind them up. Make a poultice out of the powder and apply it to the bottom of the foot. It will draw pain out of anywhere in the body.

PLEURISY AND PNEUMONIA

- Spread dry lobelia on a greasy cloth. Spread over as large an area as possible.
- To bring down the fever, put some quinine and hog lard on a cloth and put it on your chest.
- Give the person two teaspoonfuls of oil rendered from a skunk (polecat).
- Make an onion poultice to make the fever break. Then give the person whiskey and hot water.
- Make a tea of butterfly weed [*Asclepias tuberosa*], add a little whiskey, and drink. *[This can be toxic in large quantities.]*

POISON IVY

- Use a mixture of buttermilk or vinegar and salt. Put on the rash.
- Make a strong brown tea by boiling willow [*Salix*] leaves and put the liquid on the affected areas.

- Take some witch hazel [*Hamamelis virginiana*] and add all the boric acid that will dissolve in it. Apply to affected parts.
- Rub wild touch-me-nots [*Impatiens*] on the areas.
- Boil milkweed [*Asclepias syriaca*] leaves in water. Rub this water on the poisoned skin.
- Snap the stem of the jewelweed [*Impatiens capensis*]. The juice of this plant is a natural cortisone.

POISON OAK

- Rub some leaves from a touch-me-not [*Impatiens*] plant on the place where you got it. It'll cure it.
- Dab bleach on the rash with some cotton. Do this several times a day.
- Snap the stem of the jewelweed [*Impatiens capensis*]. The juice of this plant is a natural cortisone.

PULLING TEETH

Eva: And pullin' teeth—don't pull 'em when the signs is in the heart. Pull 'em when the signs is in the knees, and they won't bleed so bad. 'Course, they'll bleed a little.

Frank: I know about that heart business. They's a woman down here had her tooth pulled when the signs was in the heart, and it liked to bled her to death. And she sent down for my uncle down here at this white bridge to stop the blood, and whenever they told him, it stopped. But it liked to killed her. **—Eva and Frank Vinson, Spring 1980**

RISINGS OR BOILS

- Mash a rotten apple around the rising and tie a cloth around it.
- Make a plaster for it out of wilted mullein [*Verbascum*], poplar, or cabbage leaves.
- Take the skin out of eggshells and place it on the area.
- Put a wilted briar leaf on it, wrap with a cloth, and leave it on overnight.
- For boils, put salt meat on the spot to bring the boil to a head.
- For corns and risings, eat sulfur and honey mixed.

- Make a poultice out of the dried roots (gathered during the summer) of jack-in-the-pulpit [*Arisaema triphyllum*]. Apply to affected area.
- Use the inside surface of the bark of a linden tree [*Tilia americana*] to draw the boil to a head.

SNAKEBITE

- Make a poultice out of the dried roots (gathered during the summer) of jack-in-the-pulpit [*Arisaema triphyllum*]. Apply to affected area. It will help reduce the swelling.

"I don't mind a snakebite if you ain't bit on the vein or above the waist. If you are bit above the waist, they ain't nothin' in the world you can do because in fifteen minutes you are dead. And if you are bit below the waist and not on the vein, you'll last for a while. Of course it'll hurt. Now if you get snakebit and you're no more than fifty feet from the house, you better get in. When that poison goes up there to your head, you'll be sick. I've been bit. I know. Talkin' about sick, you're sick—and scared; that's what kills people. They get scared to death. They say, 'Oh, I'm snakebit! What am I gonna do?' I just sat down like that and said, 'Well, I'm snakebit.' I got about the length of this room, and I had to lay down—like to have killed me. For three days I felt like bustin', but after three days, the swellin' went down. It got all right." —**Kenny Runion, Fall 1977**

SORE THROAT

- Make a poultice of kerosene or mutton tallow and tie it around your neck.
- Boil the inner part of some red oak bark. Strain and drink the water.
- Eat honey; mix honey with moonshine and drink it.
- Tie a dirty sock around the neck.
- Gargle with kerosene oil.
- Swab the throat with iodine.
- Put some asafetida [resinous material from the roots of plants of the genus *Ferula*] in a cloth bag and tie it around the neck.
- Gargle with a half cup of water, two tablespoons of vinegar, and a half teaspoon of salt.
- Take a sock you have worn inside a boot for a week; tie it around your neck.

SORES

- Don't ever burn the cloth bandage from a sore. You must bury it in order for the sore to heal.
- Mash up yellowroot [*Xanthorhiza simplicissima*] and put it on the sores.
- Chew yellowroot for mouth ulcers or sores.
- Use a salve made from mutton tallow, balm of Gilead [*Populus candicans*] buds, and fresh turpentine from pine trees.

"Make a salve of heart leaves gotten out of the ground in the woods. Boil the leaves. Add lard and turpentine and continue to boil until the mixture gets thick. Put the salve on sores as needed."

—Florence Carpenter, Spring 1979

STINGS

- Cure that sting in three minutes. Use table salt. Just lay a cloth down and put about four tablespoons of salt on there. Then pull it tight around the sting, and in ten minutes you can't even tell you've been stung.
- Put tobacco or snuff on a sting. Homemade tobacco is the best of all. Take a leaf of homemade tobacco and wrap it around anything to take the swelling out.
- Mud or tobacco juice will stop the itching and pain.
- Make a poultice of goat's-beard [*Aruncus dioicus*] root to treat bee stings.
- Snap the stem of the jewelweed [*Impatiens capensis*]. The juice of this plant is a natural cortisone.

STOMACH

- Castor oil is good for the stomach. Just drink a dose, and it heals as good as it goes down.
- Boil some yellowroot [*Xanthorhiza simplicissima*] and strain it. Add honey to it and take two tablespoons before meals.
- Get some yellowroot off the creek bank. Soak it in water. Then drink the water.
- Drink a tea of wild peppermint [*Mentha piperita*].
- Drink some blackberry [*Rubus allegheniensis*] juice or wine.

- Drink a tea made from the lining of a chicken gizzard.
- Drink the juice left over after cooking kraut.
- Chew calamus or yellowroot and swallow the juice.
- Drink a tea made from goldenseal [*Hydrastis canadensis*] roots.
- To stop vomiting, grind up some peach [*Prunus persica*] tree leaves in a rag. Put the rag with the ground leaves in it on the person's stomach.
- To settle the stomach, place five small flint rocks in a glass of water. Let it sit for a few minutes and drink the water.
- Boil or chew yellowroot.
- Boil two or three whole ratsbane [*Chimaphila umbellata*] plants in about a pint of water. Strain, sweeten, and drink.
- Make a tea from the root of wild ginger [*Asarum canadense*] to relieve a stomachache.

"Wine's good for you! You drink just a little bit for your stomach. If you get sick at your stomach, take a little bit of wine. It ain't gonna hurt nobody! It's good medicine if you use it right. I went down to see my daughter when she was in the hospital in Atlanta. She had blood clots in her legs. They tried everything nearly. Finally, that doctor said, 'Your blood's too thick. I'm gonna put you on some wine.' And they did. She drunk wine. She'd just pour her out a glassful and drink it every once in a while. She ain't went back now in several years for blood clots." **—Lawton Brooks, Summer 1985**

SWEATY FEET

- Boil dried chestnut [*Castanea dentata*] leaves until you have an ooze. Apply this to the feet.

TEETHING

"When a baby starts to cuttin' teeth, you can take a mole's foot—his left front paw—and tie that around the baby's neck. You won't hear a sound out of it. I didn't do that to mine, though. I used a dime with a hole in it. I put that on a chain around their neck." **—Annie Mae Henry, Winter 1977**

THRASH [THRUSH]

- Burn an old leather shoe and make a tea from the ashes. Give the child a few sips often.

- In the spring, drink water from a creek bed just after it has rained.
- Place a sage leaf over the child's mouth and blow through it.

TONSILS

- Gargle with tanbark tea made from chestnut [*Castanea*] leaves.
- Gargle with salt water.
- Smear balm of Gilead [*Populus candicans*] salve all over the person's chest.
- To burn out the tonsils, scrub them several times a day for several weeks with iodine and turpentine.

TOOTHACHE

- Make a small amount of wine from pokeberries [blackish-red berries of pokeweed, *Phytolacca americana*] and mix one part of the wine with eight parts of white whiskey. Take a small spoonful a couple of times a day. This is also good for rheumatism and muscle cramps.
- Hold whiskey on the tooth.
- Put some damp ashes in a cloth and hold it against the sore tooth.
- Put baking soda on the tooth.

"We used a tea from chinquapin roots for the toothache. We'd dig up the roots, wash them, and boil them. Then we'd hold that water on the tooth. When I had a toothache, I felt like it was goin' to bust everything in my mouth out. It hurt so bad. That tea killed the nerve, though. You just hold that tea in your mouth until the pain stops or put a little on cotton and stick that down in the tooth." **—Minnie Dailey, Summer 1985**

WHOOPING COUGH

- Mix alum powder and honey together in a bowl. Take a teaspoonful when you start coughing.

WORMS

- Get the seeds out of Jerusalem oak [*Chenopodium botrys*] and boil them in syrup until it makes a candy. Give the person with the worms a piece of the candy every other day.

- Take garlic.
- Boil Jerusalem oak seed [*Chenopodium anthelminticum*] in molasses and sulfur and take a spoonful.
- Boil Jerusalem oak seed [*Chenopodium anthelminticum*] with sugar added. Let it thicken, but don't let it boil too hard. Take a spoonful.
- Make a tea from black-eyed Susan [*Rudbeckia*] roots and drink.

MONEY

We didn't have any electricity. We had oil lamps just like these you see now that people keep for emergencies and decoration. We had to buy the oil at the store, ten cents a gallon, and now it's about a dollar a gallon. We cooked on a fireplace and a wood cookstove . . . Back then, there wasn't no money much.

—Minnie Dailey

Can you imagine going into a store and buying a loaf of bread for a nickel or spending ten cents for a gallon of kerosene that would last a month? Although the cost of everyday necessities was much less back then, so was the amount of money that a person made. Many of the people we interviewed told us about working hard all day in the fields for a dime, a quarter, fifty cents, or a dollar. Money was definitely hard to come by. Folks didn't buy much from stores—just coffee, salt, and sometimes sugar. Many times they bought what they needed on credit, and then, when they were able, paid the bill. Most of the time, however, money did not change hands: People bartered eggs, milk, broom sage, and other items for needed goods. Many told us that they went through the Depression without the suffering that city folks endured. They made their own clothes, grew and canned their own vegetables, and raised their own livestock.

In the old days in Southern Appalachia, no one had much in the way of material possessions. What they valued was their faith, their families, and their land. Folks who fell on hard times could depend on their neighbors for help. In fact, if folks fell ill, the whole neighborhood would bring food, chop wood, plant or harvest crops, or do whatever needed doing. They were indeed their brother's keeper.

Yes, money was hard to come by, but these industrious, inventive people did fairly well without it and helped others, too.

—*Amanda Carpenter*

Money is important in our time. Of course we need money to provide food, clothing, and shelter for our children, but we want more than necessities.

We want luxuries. Our elders struggled to provide the basics for their families. They worked hard on their own farms and were still strapped for money to purchase store-bought items.

Many of you can remember buying a soft drink for a nickel or a gallon of gasoline at the pump for twenty-five cents. Why, a mother could buy a week's worth of groceries for a family of five for twenty dollars. Our elders bought goods for less than that. Have you gone to the store with an elderly person lately? Elders are shocked by the prices of food and clothing and goods today.

Times have changed. Now it seems everyone wants to be wealthy. Accumulating wealth and power was simply not an issue in the good ol' days. Folks were grateful for their blessings and shared what they had with their neighbors. They believed in the old adages "You can't take it with you" and "Do unto others as you would have them do unto you."

In fact, Anna Howard, one of our contacts, said, "If you're gonna lay it away and worship it, you just as well go down there and pick up as many rocks as you have dollars and lay them away—they'd do you just as much good. If you worship your money, you're not worshipin' God." People and relationships, not money, are what's important in life. Our elders knew this truth and lived it every day.

—April Argoe

"We sold gas for twenty-one cents a gallon. Kerosene was ten cents a gallon. All our drinks were seventy-five cents a case—ten cents for the crate and sixty-five cents for the drinks. Later, we started haulin' our own drinks instead of havin' them delivered, and we got another fifteen cents off of that." **—Roy Roberts, Spring 1985**

"If a fellow needed a loan—twenty, fifty, or five hundred dollars—instead of goin' to the bank, he might come and borrow that money from me. If I knew his father was a good man, a businessman from the country, I never took a note on it, but I never lost a dollar. I wouldn't charge nothin' for interest—just told them to take the money and use it. My wife, Martha, knows for the last twenty years I was in business, I never hardly lost a dollar."

—Ed Roane, Winter 1983

"My daddy didn't have no money to pay his tax. We had to pay a poll tax back then. He wasn't worth much, but he wanted to vote. You couldn't vote if you didn't pay your poll tax. If he got ahold of one dollar from one year to the next, he would pin it up in his overall pocket with a safety pin. It'd stay right there 'til taxpayin' time. He'd keep it a whole year in that there bib pocket. He'd go pay his poll tax, and then he could vote like my granddaddy for a while. He told me, 'Son, if I'd knowed you'd be a Republican, I wouldn't a-fed you another bite.' He's told me that a many a time and just about that strong, too." **—D. B. Dayton, Summer 1980**

"Since money was scarce and little cash was ever actually exchanged, there were several other ways of paying up one's account. Trading goods between store owner and customer was one option. Items traded included hogs, bottom chairs, wool, manure, syrup, rye, lumber, loads of wood, and coffee. Coffee was bought at the store green. If one's account needed paying, one could resell green coffee to the store owner. Peaberry was the most popular coffee then." **—Winter 1983**

"The welfare inspector came a few months ago and found out that someone had given the family a box of clothes for the winter; the welfare check was cut by twenty dollars after that. When the woman has eighty-eight dollars, she can get one hundred and twenty dollars worth of food stamps. If she doesn't have the eighty-eight dollars, she gets no food at all. For a year the entire family had nothin' but a quart of green beans each night. Breakfast was fried flour and coffee for nine children and their mom."

—Spring 1969

"I cooked up there at Mountain City Colonial Lodge, and we had to work on Sundays. We worked seven days a week, really. We'd go into work at 'bout six-thirty in the mornin'. We had to fix breakfast, we made lunch, and then we got off 'bout two o'clock. Then we had to be back at work at five o'clock to do supper. So that was some pretty long hours. We got ten dollars a week, plus our tips. That's what we made, but that wasn't much money. My grandkids have that in a day, 'bout it."

—Eunice Hunter, Spring / Summer 2004

"There was money enough to get along. I had a uncle over here in th' Patton Settlement. If y' had a few dollars, you could raise you some yearlings and stuff. I'd gather up a bunch like that—go t' a neighbor's house, and if he had one t' sell, I'd buy it if I could, y' know. And I'd bring it in and put 'em together. My uncle would come over there and buy th' whole bunch, and I'd make a little on it. . . .

"Way it happened, they 'as an old gentleman come and bought this lot here, and he started t' put up a little house. Well, he put up a little shack. Just this room was just about what he had up. And he 'as an ol' bach', y' know—never had been married—and his folks all lived over yonder on th' other branch. He got homesick and wanted t' sell it t' me.

"So he come in one night when I come in. I talked with 'im awhile. Said, 'I'll tell y' what I come out here for, Mr. Dowdle.'

"I said, 'What's that?'

"Said, 'I want t' sell you my little place out there.'

"Well, I 'as hardly able t' buy that and run m' business, too. But we talked on a little bit, and I asked him then what he wanted for it. Said he wanted eight hundred dollars. 'Well,' I said, 'I wouldn't be interested.'

"So he went on back t' his cabin, and he stayed gone a couple o' nights. When I come in again, he was at th' house again. We talked there t'gether, and he said, 'Uh, have y' thought any more about buyin' m' place?'

"I said, 'No, I never give it a thought.'

"He said, 'I want eight hundred fer it.'

"I said, 'I wouldn't be interested at all.'

"And he went off that time. And th' next night, here he was out there again. He said, 'Uh, you never did make me no offer.'

"I said, 'Well, I always make a man an offer, and if he can't take it, it don't make me mad.'

" 'Well,' he said, 'what would y' do?'

"I said, 'I'll give you six hundred fer yer place.'

"He says, 'That's awful little.'

" 'Well,' I says, 'it ain't much. No, but six hundred dollars—you don't just roll it up ever'where.'

" 'Well,' he said, 'I'm gonna go back over yonder t' m' folks. When could we make the deed?'

"I said, 'Make th' deed? Right in th' mornin' if y' want to. I've got yer money. When you make th' deed, yer money is ready.'

" 'Well,' he said, 'we'll just go t' town in th' mornin then and get it all done.'

"I said, 'Suits me fine.' So I moved out here—sold off part of it, and that fer way more money than I give fer th' whole thing. So I've still got this, and I'm gonna keep it long as I'm here."

—Thad "Happy" Dowdle, Spring / Summer 1971

"I was makin' twenty-five cents a day for ten hours, and the rest of 'em was makin' ten cents a day." ***—Paul Power***

"Our uncle was the superintendent of the tannery, but there was no jobs to be filled. Most everybody was just makin' laborers' pay, so he got out of it. My uncle, he must have thought that I was the best thing that had come down the pipe. He never told me to stay away from the factory because it was dangerous. He would let me roam around anywhere I wanted to, and when I was old enough to fill a water bucket, he made me a waterboy in the summertimes. I would go to the spring and dip my two pails in there. They had a big ol' pipe where the water spit up. I would reach down there and fill one bucket and then the other bucket. Then I'd take 'em back to the factory, and the men would always tease me. They'd say, 'Waterboy, waterboy, let your name be found. If you don't like the job, just throw your bucket down.' They would tease me all the time, so the next year Uncle gave me and a bunch of us kids jobs. They got their tannin' bark from Rabun County. It was red oak and chestnut bark they get off the trees here in the summertime. They would ship it down to Buford [Georgia], and us kids would unload it. I was makin' twenty-five cents a day for ten hours, and the rest of 'em was makin' ten cents a day. We'd unload the cars and stack the bark where they would have a year-round supply."

—Paul Power, Spring / Summer 2003

"I was a sawmiller for a long time. I started when I was sixteen. I worked for Homer Trotter. I got paid ten cents an hour, so for ten hours a day, you made ten dollars a week. That was some hard work for that amount of money. They weren't many jobs back then except farmin'."

—Ed Wilson, Fall / Winter 2001

"When I was fourteen, I was a housekeeper. The work was not really all that hard, but the money we made back then was pocket change compared to what young people make now. Nowadays, what some people make in an hour is what I was makin' in a week. I thought I was doin' good if I made five or ten dollars a week." **—Dorothy Welborn, Fall / Winter 1997**

"We were raised on the farm. We done a lot of cannin' and things like that. There were five of us in school at one time. Of course we didn't have a lot of money. So we'd go to the cannery, and Mama would can food; then we would take it to the school, and they would give us lunch tickets in exchange. Of course they wouldn't give us money, and that's how we paid for our lunches. I guess all through grammar school we canned green beans and applesauce. We had a small orchard on the farm. It had all kinds of fruit, so we canned just dozens of cases of applesauce. We would give it to the school for lunch tickets. That really helped in those days when there wasn't a lot of money, and they gave us good lunches at school."

—Horace Justus, Spring / Summer 2000

"Daddy fished with people on the lake, and they paid him good. Durin' the war and when times was real bad, we didn't get commodities. Daddy wouldn't have any extras. He worked, and people paid him good if they caught a lot of fish. Durin' that time, when the lake was full of fish, he got paid good every week. Daddy always had money. We didn't have a car, and we didn't have no electricity."

—Margaret Wilson, Spring / Summer 2001

"To show you how poor people was, you know how we got our brass kettle? My mother bought it. People would go broke and sell out. They would put the word out they were sellin' out. When people moved off, they'd sell things. So these people moved down in Crossville, Tennessee—went on a train. They sold their things for what they could get for them. People didn't have much money, so that kettle didn't cost us over three or four dollars. We was offered forty dollars for it. Then another man said that he'd give me a hundred. I said, 'I've been offered forty already, but I won't sell it.'

"And now them balm buds [balm of Gilead buds]. You know about that, don't you? Boil them down and use that for a salve. They went one year for a dollar a pound. They're eighty-five cents now down here at North Wilkesboro [Tennessee]. And there's a man that took a load of hides down there Monday. He took eighty-five. He called 'em rat hides—muskrat hides. He said, 'Hides this year, it just ain't been cold enough, so their fur's not thick.' He said they was bringin' in a good price, though. He made money by takin' them down there. He just called 'em rat hides.

"Now we just got one pair of shoes a year, and we went barefoot except for Sunday. Mother would make soup [pinto] beans. Back then, soup beans brought a good price. You've heard talk of what they called brogans? Buy those—sell them soup beans. Take a big sack full—a bushel; go and buy shoes and other things. Fall of the year, they would thrash those beans out—set them a cloth on the porch or a bedsheet or somethin' and thrash them out when they got dry—took them and beat them out with a frail [flail]. They didn't bring the price they bring now. Now two pounds of beans are a dollar-forty!

"Some people made their own shoes, since there wasn't much money. We didn't, but we made our own cloth." **—Harvey J. Miller, Spring 1978**

"My father ran a store on Scaly [Mountain, North Carolina], and people would go all over just to get the cider he sold. It was just a flavored-up drink. You could get peach and apple, and it sold for five cents a glass."

—Harry Brown, Sr., Spring 1976

"The first 'horse' I ever owned was a jack [male donkey]. I was eight years old, and I bought him with money that I got together from tradin'. I started tradin'—I'd say five years old or six—pencils, knives, what have you. So I saved my money 'til I had fifteen dollars, and I bought me a jack. But my father, a Baptist preacher, didn't want me to have this jack, so I carried him off to a barn quite a ways from where we lived. When he got out Sunday morning to start his circuit—four churches—the jack started brayin', and he wanted to know whose that was. Finally, I had to say it was mine. Well, he said, 'If you'll go to church and be a good boy and go to school, I'll let you keep him.' The temptation was so great for me to get to ride that jack and drive him to a little old two-wheel cart that Sunday I put in the whole day with him. When my father come home Sunday night, naturally, my mother told him what all had happened. He said, 'Take that back.' That's the only time I've ever went back on a real bargain. It like to have killed me to have to take that jack back. This ol' boy wouldn't give me my money back, so he kept the money and the jack, too." **—E. H. "Hob" Duvall, Spring 1976**

"One time a man gave us two goats. Dr. Robinson said, 'Walker, you take the goats.' I turned them in our large pasture, and soon I had thirty-seven goats." ***—Walker Word***

"As a youngster, I would ride in a buggy with our Dr. Robinson to make calls. People would send for him from all directions. I would drive the horse and let him rest. Sometimes it might be midnight and miles away when we would head home. We would wrap ourselves in a blanket and both go to sleep. The horse would take us home. Dr. Robinson was a wonderful man and did great things with what he had to work with.

"Dr. Robinson would travel just about the whole country administering to the sick. People would come from all around to Dr. Robinson. He would get so worn out that he would ask me to drive him in the buggy and let him rest. He was overworked and would ask me to go with him at night.

"Most people did not have any money. They would give him a ham or a pig or most anything. We had a cage built on the rear of the buggy to handle such things. One time a man gave us two goats. Dr. Robinson said, 'Walker, you take the goats.' I turned them in our large pasture, and soon I had thirty-seven goats. . . .

"My father was very affluent. He was president of a bank. My uncle Grady Word ran the Waco Mercantile Company [in Waco, Georgia]. He and his brothers had a cotton gin and a sawmill. My father was chairman of the board of deacons for years and years. He was chairman of the school board. His name was on a plaque as one of the builders of the high school. We had everything that anybody could want. I remember when we had the only car in town. I remember when we got the first radio in Waco.

"When I needed money, all I had to do was tell Uncle Grady. He would take it out of the cash register and charge it to my daddy as apples. Daddy loved apples and did not care how many apples I charged."

—Walker Word, Spring 1990

"Dad [Varina's husband] came up here and bid on a house. It was put up for sale by the administrator. The children's parents had died, and they wanted to sell. It was put up for sale in front of the courthouse—for public sale. Daddy came and bid on it. I don't remember what we paid for it. We paid four dollars or somethin' like that a month. We got a money order. We didn't have no bank, but we mailed it in. We had to do some things to get that four dollars a month to pay for that place." **—Varina Ritchie, Spring 1990**

"Near everythin' has changed. There is such a difference in people. Back when I was growin' up, anybody that was sick, why, people had time to go see them, and now they haven't. People would go to see the sick and help them out, and if people get sick now . . . well, it just seems they don't care. I feel that's where people are missin' a whole lot. I believe people should help people in need. . . .

"People didn't have the money t' help out, so they'd go and do somethin' for others. When Grandpa Dills was sick, people'd go in and plant his corn and work in hit. Then they'd get in wood and things like that. People would help do things that had to be done. Most people now has got jobs, and they don't help out like they did back then. And people don't go see the sick like they use t' either. They don't have time, I reckon." **—Belle Dryman, Winter 1976**

"Well, back then, the most worry we had was clothes and shoes and taxes. I guess it was in my grandfather's generation that they started taxin' land. I guess they paid taxes. It had to be money, I think. Back as far as I can remember, it did. But it didn't amount to anything. Most of th' time, this place here didn't amount to more 'n about four or five dollars. Now there're different things to worry about. The only thing . . . they made their clothes, a lot of them back then. And they'd knit socks and sweaters and stuff like that. Shoes was a bother—had to get shoes. It's changed so much from the way it was then." **—Richard Norton, Spring 1975**

> **"We sold butter, potatoes, pigs, and chickens. We'd trade vegetables. Eggs would bring ten cents a dozen, but you had to trade 'em for groceries or somethin' to get a due bill. They wasn't no money back then."**
> ***—Clarence Lusk***

"I had bought a new T-model truck in 1925, and I run that truck almost day and night at times, takin' people to the doctor or haulin' whatever they had to haul. People cut crossties way back then and sold 'em in town, and I'd haul crossties into town and bring back a load of fertilizer or other supplies those folks had ordered. Sometimes when I got back, somebody'd be sittin' here waitin' on me, and I'd have to go again. That's the way I made money. I didn't do that free of charge.

"We growed all we eat, and we made a livin' farmin'. We had two or three cows, two or three hogs, mules, and I don't know what else. I think my wife had about three hundred chickens at one time. We sold butter, potatoes, pigs, and chickens. We'd trade vegetables. Eggs would bring ten cents a dozen, but you had to trade 'em for groceries or somethin' to get a due bill. They wasn't no money back then." **—Clarence Lusk, Summer 1985**

"We used to keep ducks and geese, and we'd pluck 'em to make feather beds and pillows. We also made quilts a long time—put cotton in them. And we had blankets that were warmer than the ones now.

"We didn't have any electricity. We had oil lamps just like these you see now people keep for emergencies and decoration. We had to buy the oil at the store, ten cents a gallon, and now it's about a dollar a gallon. We cooked on a fireplace and a wood cookstove.

"Back then, there wasn't no money much, and we had to grow what we had to eat. We grew beans, cabbage, tomatoes, everything like that in our garden. We canned everything we grew. We dried fruit, too. My mother dried blackberries. She just put 'em on a cloth and let 'em dry. After she dried 'em, she cooked 'em with a little water. Then she'd sweeten 'em. You could make pies out of 'em or anything you wanted to! Why, they was good! They aren't as good dried as they was canned, but back then they didn't have too many cans to can in.

"When we didn't have cash to pay for groceries, we'd get 'em on the credit. Then when my father got a payday, he'd go pay the bill. When I was a youngun at home, my mother had a bunch of chickens, and when they'd lay eggs, we'd take the eggs to the store and swap 'em for a nickel or dime's worth of brown sugar. We'd get a great big pile—more than you'd get now for a dollar, I guess.

"We raised cows and milked 'em. We had steers to work in the fields and to haul with. My father used the steers most of the time because he loved them more than he did the horses. I could catch those steers by the horns 'cause they was gentle. We could take a rope and tie it around their necks, and they'd lead like a cow.

"We killed the cows and pigs in the winter. They'd build a big fire under a big washpot. Then they'd take a one-blade ax to hit the hog in the head to kill it. Then they'd put it in that pot of hot water to scrape all that hair off of it. It would come off as clean as anything.

"When they killed a cow, they would skin its hide just like skinnin' a rabbit. They would sell the hide. It used to bring a right pretty good price.

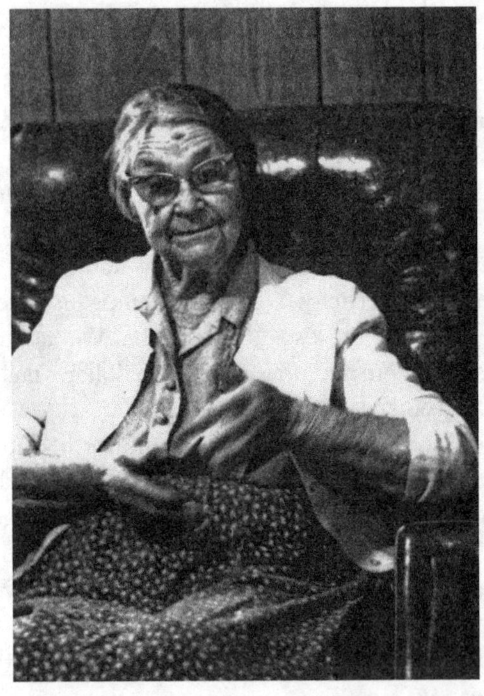

PLATE 123 "We didn't have any electricity. We had oil lamps just like these you see now people keep for emergencies and decoration." —Minnie Dailey

"When we cured the meat out, we just took a whole lot of salt and let it soak in. When it got cured out, we'd hang it up in the smokehouse. In March, we always took our meat down and washed it and then hung it back so the wild animals wouldn't get in it. We'd put black and red pepper on it to keep the flies off. We did this in March because of an old sayin' that the meat should always be washed in March so the bugs and such wouldn't get in it. I don't reckon I ever ate but one bite of beef in my life. I watched 'em kill a cow one time, and I couldn't stand it."

—Minnie Dailey, Summer 1985

"Yes, times has changed. I'd have to say times was better then. They was better. People was better, too, a whole lot. If you had a job to do, you just put the word out, and the next mornin' the hill'd be covered up with people. They'd come and help ya. Wouldn't want no pay to do it either. They wouldn't want no pay.

"There used to be people would come right around just like they come to your patch and make it and go on to the next patch and make it and right on around 'til they got done—same way by thrashin' your rye and your oats and your wheat and whatnot. People come and thrash it. Went right around to the next man and stay all night over where dark come on. Why, today you could start down the road here and ask a man to come and help you do something for nothin', and he'd say, 'Well, that 'scallion's a-goin' crazy.' "

—Grover Bradley, Spring 1975

"I've wondered myself how we made a livin'. That time was different than it is now. Everybody tended these hills and made their own corn. There were corn mills that they could take their corn to and grind it. They made their own vegetables. They canned those vegetables. Maybe they had a tobacco crop. And we used horsepower to plow our gardens. They had their own cows to milk. They had their own hogs. They made their feed to feed those hogs. They sold one hog, and maybe they sold a calf from that cow.

"We didn't have gasoline. We didn't have no telephones. We didn't have no televisions. A gallon of kerosene would last you a month and cost you ten cents. What did you have to buy in the first place? All you had to buy was your clothes—maybe thread—and your coffee. If you had any cereal, oatmeal, or rice, you bought that, or sugar. A few things like that you had to buy. Besides that, all you had to do was pay your taxes. You can see what I'm talkin' about. Everybody got by. We were poor, but we never did go without somethin' to eat—always had plenty to live on.

"One time my dad bought a farm on credit. I believe it was eighty acres. It had a house on it, and we had to finish up the house and clear the land. We just fixed it up so we could live in it. We had to go out, and we had to peel chestnut oak bark; we paid for that place cuttin' chestnut oak bark.

"We'd peel around the tree. We'd cut the tree down, and we'd stack the bark with the sap down—lean the strips of bark up against the tree. In the fall we'd come back and carry that bark out. If we couldn't get our sled up to where the bark was, we would pile it on top of brush and pull it down the mountain with horses to our wagon. Then we'd haul it to Barnard [North Carolina], which was ten miles, and pile it up there until we got a railroad-car load. Then we would load that car up and ship it on. We paid for that place like that.

"Though we didn't make much, we didn't miss things because we didn't have them and didn't know about them. I'm goin' to say that it brought your family closer together because of the fact that you stayed together and talked your problems over. You loved each other better, and so, when you got to thinkin' about that, I think it's a better livin' than it is right now."

—Roy Roberts, Spring 1985

"The hardest time I ever lived through was when I was a child. The river got out and ruined our crops. Now we really did hit it hard that time.

"Mama always put up a lot of canned stuff. We had enough food. It was rough stuff, but we had to make do. They was a lot of people starvin'. But people who had food would chip in. People who lived in the country had it a whole lot better than them in the city." **—Ethel Corn, Summer 1974**

> **"We didn't have any money to pay the doctor. I came near dyin', and the doctor said, 'That's all right. I know how times are, and probably you have things that we don't have.' We had plenty of corn, nice fat hogs to kill, and plenty of meat, so we gave him hams and corn in the place of money."** ***—Harriet Echols***

"We went through the Depression when my first baby was still livin'. It was hard. We just didn't have any money, and there was nothin' t' make any—there was no work. You couldn't get but just so much flour. Each person was allowed just a few pounds of all these commodities that you'd have to buy.

"The people that had a farm and raised their own food could live, but you didn't have anything to buy clothes. It was hard, and I had my oldest daughter and son in school. People got together—like someone was larger than

PLATE 124 "The river got out and ruined our crops. Now we really did hit it hard that time." —Ethel Corn

you, and she handed down her clothes to help you out. Mabel, still today, won't wear hand-me-downs because she got so tired of other people's old clothes.

"We didn't have any money to buy anything, and my first baby died that was born durin' that time. My second baby died; then my oldest daughter came along, but we didn't have any money to pay the doctor. I came near dyin', and the doctor said, 'That's all right. I know how times are, and probably you have things that we don't have.' We had plenty of corn, nice fat hogs to kill, and plenty of meat, so we gave him hams and corn in the place of money.

"That's the way people got along—they just exchanged with each other. The colored woman that helped me when I was feelin' poorly was the sweetest thing. She'd say, 'Mrs. Harriet, I don't have any chickens and eggs.' We had plenty of chickens and eggs. And we had a lot of syrup that year, and milk and butter, so I shared these things with her. She'd wash and fold our clothes, and she'd come and hoe the garden. When I got able to get up and sew—I wasn't able to do anything for a long time—I'd sew for her, and she'd do my washin' to help pay her bills. I worked with them

PLATE 125 "In times of need, we just helped each other out 'cause you just didn't have money to hire it done." —Harriet Echols

and helped them, and they helped me. I'd never have been able to raise my first children if it hadn't been for the good Negro woman that lived close to me.

"That's the way people lived back then. They shared with each other. I quilted for people for the money to buy cloth to make clothes for the children and for me and shirts for my husband. In times of need, we just helped each other out 'cause you just didn't have money to hire it done.

"We had to use our own homegrown honey and syrup—we couldn't buy sugar—and made gingerbread and sweetened the fruits and things and lots of times made jam with syrup or honey. It wasn't only us. It wasn't only the country people. Our ministers, they didn't have money because we couldn't afford to pay our tithes at church; we shared our food with our ministers, and they were just as happy to get it.

"My husband's father set up a sawmill, and my husband worked there—then at the shingle mills. Then we got to where we could have a little money. Then the Depression eased up, and then it hit hard times a few years later. My husband had several different jobs; then his father got sick, and we moved back to the farm. My son and I worked the farm, and that's how we lived.

"Then my oldest son was killed at Pearl Harbor, and my oldest daughter was trainin' for a nurse. I raised the two next ones by myself. I just moved up here with 'em. I raised them and got my oldest daughter through college, and Leonard worked durin' the day and went to school at night. They made it on their own.

"Of course it was hard times durin' the Depression and the world wars, but it's been hard on me all the way through." **—Harriet Echols, Summer 1974**

"Money is th' root of all evil, and it rules th' world right now."
—Hillard Green

"It was awful back then. Everybody had t' work then. Everybody worked on th' farm. There wasn't no factories or nothin' hardly . . . I had to work all th' time then, Lord, yeah. Take a man on th' farm, he has t' be goin' 'fore daylight 'til after dark. Keeps him a-goin' just like these people up in th' chicken business, y' know. . . .

"People nowadays don't live right. It's just how long they're gonna live and how soon they're gonna die—just what they can get in their hands now. Always wantin'. They just reach an' take ever'thing they can, seems like. Ain't got no mercy on no one else. If I didn't depend on Him, I wouldn't have anybody t' depend on. You can't depend on a neighbor these days. Ever'body is for themselves. Ever'body's lookin' out for money. They're not lookin' out for th' humans. We've got t' look out for ourselves. If we don't look out for ourselves, what are we goin' t' do?

"We had freedom back then. We was free. We went anywhere and did kinda as we pleased. But now we can't do it. Money is th' root of all evil, and it rules th' world right now. Ever'thing is goin' for money. They'll do anything. They'll kill, rob, steal, and ever'thing else all over th' world now. You hear tell of it anywhere y' go now.

"It's fast times now, y'know. Ever'thing's flyin'. These automobiles runnin' to and fro from ever' corner of the world. Well, ain't they goin' from ever' corner? You can't hardly travel fer 'em. You can't walk along th' highways 'r nothin'. You ain't got no freedom 'r nothin'. You've got t' be in under some kind of control." **—Hillard Green, Fall 1970**

"Soup and crackers was a nickel. I mean, you'd get a good bowl of soup, too. Nowadays, they won't give you an empty bowl for a nickel. . . . Used to be, all the shoppin' was done in one day. They'd work through the week; then you'd go to town on Saturday. An' y' know, the biggest part of the time you stayed all day 'cause it took you too long to go up there, and you either had to walk back or drive the horse and wagon or mule and wagon. In fact,

PLATE 126 Hillard Green, drawing water from his spring, says, "Take a man on th' farm, he has t' be goin' 'fore daylight 'til after dark."

that's the way you traveled back then. There was very few automobiles and trucks at that time whenever I was growin' up as a youngun. We used to walk it a whole lot. They finally paved to Warwoman Dell [outside Clayton, Georgia] in the 1950s, and we thought that was the greatest thing in the world. About the middle to late fifties, they paved Warwoman Road on out.

"People nowadays, they go to the store and buy everything, just about, to eat, and lots of people don't know how to grow anything or where it comes from. Like a feller told me one time, he said, 'Children think milk comes from the store. They don't realize it comes from a cow.' A person could get back to that kind of life one day if things get bad enough."

—J. P. Speed, Spring / Summer 2005

"But now almost everybody's got to where it's dog eat dog. That's the one trouble we have now. If a man's got a dollar's worth of stuff to sell, he ought to sell it for a dollar instead of askin' five dollars for it . . . People have just gone crazy. We've got a situation that's got to get worse or better, one."

—Charlie Ross Hartley, Spring 1976

BEAUTY SECRETS

[**Editor's Note:** Foxfire does not vouch for the effectiveness or worth of the following beauty "secrets." Some individuals may, in fact, have adverse effects due to allergies or sensitive skin. Use these "cures" at your own risk.]

> *Tie five little flint rocks up in a rag. Throw them away at the forks of a road. When someone picks up the rag to see what's in it, your corn will go away, and they'll get one.*
>
> —Annie Henry

Today's woman can go to any department store, drugstore, or discount store and be overwhelmed by the choices in makeup, perfume, cleansers, and all kinds of products to enhance beauty. Magazine covers and advertisements bombard society with the "perfect look." Sales in age-defying products, all touting miraculous results, have soared in the last decade. Women search for the miracle elixir that will remedy wrinkles.

The idea of beauty used to be the clean, fresh, natural look. People did not wear much makeup. For one thing, beauty products were simply unavailable for purchase. Women and girls looked to plants for makeup and beauty treatments. They used elderflowers, chamomile, parsley, rosemary, thyme, yarrow, watercress, lemons, and hundreds of other plants. They smeared their lips with pokeberries, they defined their eyelashes with charcoal, and they rinsed their hair in southernwood.

Today's society is obsessed with skin-deep beauty, but our elders didn't seem to be overly concerned with outer beauty. To them, neither clothes nor beauty products make the man or woman. Inner beauty is true beauty.

—Amanda Carpenter

Beauty seems to be an important aspect of every woman's life. Most women quip, "I won't even go to the garbage can without makeup." Women simply feel undressed without makeup.

People also enjoy soaking in a Jacuzzi filled with scented oils, bath beads, and moisturizing crystals. Shaving gels, hair removal creams, lipstick that won't smudge or wear off, waterproof mascara, exfoliating scrubs, tooth whiteners, and on and on, fill store shelves. The shopper's problem today is not finding a product but deciding which product to purchase. Imagine having to be creative enough to invent your own makeup and beauty aids from plants and other items found around the farm.

Many women of the past did not wear makeup. Ruby Cheek told us, "Back then, we just washed our face, and that was it." However, they did soften their chapped hands, remove corns and calluses, wash their hair, and brush their teeth. They bathed at least once a week, and one contact told us his mother made all the children wash their feet every night before going to bed.

Following are many beauty secrets our elders shared with us.

—April Argoe

TERMS

Infusion Pouring water over an herb to extract its active qualities.
Decoction An extract of an herb obtained by boiling.
Compress A folded cloth moistened with an herbal infusion.
Poultice Crushed or chopped herbs, heated and enclosed in cloth.

HAIR

- Wash your hair in ice-cold beer and then rinse it clean for strong, shiny hair.
- To lighten hair, while basking in the sunshine, take pure lemon juice and run it through your hair. To distribute the lemon juice evenly, squeeze it into a bowl and dip a comb into it; then comb it through your hair.
- Rinse freshly washed hair with a solution of one tablespoon vinegar to one cup of water. This rids your scalp of extra buildup and gives it shine.
- Beat an egg. Wet hair, work the beaten egg into the scalp, and leave it for five minutes. Rinse.
- Use southernwood [*Artemisia abrotanum*]. Its slender hairlike leaves are gray-green, and when crushed, have a strong scent of lemon. An old remedy claimed southernwood cured baldness, and it is still used in some hair products. To use it as a rinse for soft, shiny hair, cut some of the tender shoots off, boil them in water, cool, and use the liquid as a rinse. Do not rinse it out. Dry hair and style as usual.

- To encourage hair growth, use an infusion or decoction of rosemary [*Rosmarinus officinalis*], chamomile [*Anthemis*], southernwood, or yarrow [*Achillea millefolium*] rubbed daily into scalp or used as a rinse after shampooing.
- An infusion of rosemary is a good rinse for brunettes.
- As a shampoo or wash, use "four ounces powdered borax [sodium borate], one ounce gum benzoin [*Styrax*], one ounce white wax, one ounce paraffin, one ounce white sugar. Mix ingredients by melting. While warm, make into sticks and wrap in paper."
- For dandruff, use one tablespoonful of tar to a teacup of rainwater. Dampen hair with the water, avoiding the tar. Or make a pomade [perfumed ointment] of one part pine tar to three parts hog lard.
- To curl hair, take a Prince Albert (tobacco) container and cut it up, roll some paper around it, and, once it is rolled, twist it into hair. You can also take strips of cloth and tightly tie them into clean hair. For best results, do this before bed, and in the morning, voilà!
- For lice, wash the affected hair in kerosene—it may make your hair reddish-looking. Lice will lay eggs. The eggs make nits [lice eggs]. The nits will hatch out. If this happens, you might have to wash it in kerosene again.
- For head lice (cooties), shingle [cut] hair close and use kerosene.

"I never used makeup or lipstick, but I used to curl my hair with curlers that I heated on the fire. The curlers had handles that were made kind of like scissors. I'd stick 'em in the fire but not get 'em too hot or they'd scorch my hair. Then I'd hold 'em open and stick some of my hair on them. I'd curl it around the curlers and hold it there long enough for the heat to curl my hair." **—Minnie Dailey, Summer 1985**

DEODORANT

- Pour baking soda in your bathwater. Powder underarms with baking soda; use this as a general body powder.

HANDS AND NAILS

- Use chamomile [*Anthemis*] flowers to make an infusion. Soak your nails in the infusion for ten minutes three or four times a week. On alternate

days, dip your hands and nails in warm olive oil and wear gloves for ten minutes.
- Women of the Appalachians spent their time with their children or in the garden with their husbands or fathers, and their nails were constantly in water. This strengthened their nails and helped to shed old cuticles. Plus, farming—having their hands in the earth—is nourishing for the skin.
- For chapped hands, use mutton tallow. When the sheep are killed, the fat is taken out and fried. The tallow is taken from the grease.
- Women, when they went to functions of a social nature, wore gloves, hiding their wrists and upper arms. Wearing gloves protects the hands from the sun and unsightly dark sun spots.

For chapped hands, "rub hands in a mixture of homemade soap and cornmeal. Bring the soap and meal to a good lather." **—Amanda Turpin, Fall 1976**

SKIN

- To heal rough, itchy skin and smooth out skin texture, rub lemons on knees and elbows. Loofah pads could also be used to soften rough, calloused skin. Use pure lavender [*Lavandula*] oil in your bathwater to both soften and add a light scent.

WARTS

- To remove warts, take a small Irish potato and rub it over all the warts you've got. Don't let nobody know much about your business. Go out of the house and bury that potato where the water runs off from the eave of the house. When the potato rots, your warts will be gone. The potato does not have to be peeled, and even if it sprouts, the potato itself will rot. Then the warts will be gone.
- Rub the wart with a penny and give it to someone. They will then get the wart.
- Keep the wart painted with castor oil, and eventually it will disappear.
- Count the warts. Tie as many pebbles as there are warts in a bag and throw this bundle down in the fork of a road. They will soon go away.
- Put some cow manure on them.

- Steal a dishrag and hide it under a rock. The warts will go away.
- Steal your neighbor's dishrag and throw it away and never think of it for at least two weeks.
- Wash hands in stump water [rainwater collected in a hollowed-out stump] and don't look back.

"Another way to remove warts is to take a stick about a foot long and rub it over all your warts. Cut a notch for every wart and go to where there is a swamp branch. Walk backwards, stick it in the ground, and don't look where you put it. Just leave it there." **—Kenny Runion, Fall 1977**

"Count the number of warts you want removed and write that number on a piece of paper. Give that to the person who is goin' to take them off. They'll go away. That works. I've had that done." **—Annie Henry, Winter 1977**

CORNS AND CALLUSES

For corns or calluses on your toes, "tie five little flint rocks up in a rag. Throw them away at the forks of a road. When someone picks up the rag to see what's in it, your corn will go away, and they'll get one."

—Annie Henry, Winter 1977

FACE

- To cure acne, dab rubbing alcohol on the infected area to dry out pimples. Also, use compresses made from warm infusions of elderberry [*Sambucus canadensis*] flowers, lady's mantle [*Alchemilla vulgaris*], or thyme leaves. You can make an ointment out of the thyme leaves. You can also use the juice from the leaves and stems of watercress [*Nasturtium officinale*]. Apply directly on the pimple.
- For a clear complexion, make a steam bath of peppermint [*Mentha piperita*] leaves.
- To reduce the appearance of large pores and freckles, make an infusion of lady's mantle. Parsley [*Petroselinum crispum*] also helps to fade freckles. Wipe the infusion on your face with a cotton pad.
- For freckles, wash your face with stump water that is three days old and don't think of a possum.
- For freckles, put sap from a grapevine on them.

- Put stump water on freckles to lighten them.
- To lighten freckles, make a poultice of eggs, cream, and Epsom salts and spread on freckles. Take it off after it dries.
- Buttermilk and lemon juice mixed together and put on the freckles will remove them.
- For petechiae (small veins appearing on the face), make an infusion of yarrow. Wipe the infusion on your face with a cotton pad.
- To make toilet lotion for the face, use one tablespoon pure olive oil and one tablespoonful rose water. Bathe hands and face in warm, soft water; work lotion in skin with fingertips. Apply at night before retiring.

To remove pimples, mix and apply "1 ounce benzoated lard, ½ ounce almond oil. Perfume with jockey club extract and oil of orange."
—Reverend R. O. Smith, Winter 1970

"To keep from getting a suntan and freckles, they rubbed their faces with cream and wore stockings on their arms and wide-brimmed hats on their heads." **—James Still, Fall 1988**

FACIAL MASKS

- To make a facial mask for dry skin, peel one peach and remove the pit. Mash the peach and mix it with two teaspoons of unflavored yogurt and one tablespoon of strong marigold [*Tagetes*] infusion. To make this infusion, pour one cup of boiling water onto one tablespoon of crushed marigold petals and leaves. Then apply to the skin and leave for fifteen minutes. Wash with warm water and pat dry. Apply a moisturizer.
- To make a facial mask for oily skin, mix together one finely grated carrot, one beaten egg white, and two tablespoons of a strong infusion of chamomile flowers and yarrow leaves or flowers. To make this infusion, pour one cup of boiling water and three teaspoons of each of the chamomile and yarrow. Then let it cool. Apply to the face and leave for fifteen minutes. Wipe it off with a soft cloth or tissue and rinse with warm water; then splash with cold water and pat dry.
- For another facial mask for oily skin, in a blender, puree one egg white; one small peeled, chopped cucumber; one teaspoon of lemon juice; and one-fourth cup of freshly picked peppermint [*Mentha piperita*] leaves. Apply to the skin and rinse your face in lukewarm water. Then pat your face dry.

ODORS

- If your hands smell from handling fish or onions, wash them in apple cider vinegar to remove the odor.

BODY

- For stretch marks, use bee balm [Oswego tea]. Bee balm was usually used on the farm to soften a cow's udders. Women noticed its healing effects, and they used the cream to heal cracks and spots in their skin.
- Also, Ivory soap, which could be found at a local mercantile, was commonly used to wash the face. It softens the skin and leaves it feeling clean and fresh.
- Women spent a lot of time outdoors, so their complexions were extremely healthy and radiant.

MAKEUP

- Makeup was extremely limited for women in the Appalachians. What they used was usually found in their gardens or at the local mercantile.
- To make eyebrows darker, light a match, blow it out, let it cool, and then wet the black tip and pencil in the eyebrows.
- For darker eyelashes, take a piece of charcoal and wet it; take a small brush and apply to lashes.
- For longer-lasting lipstick, take pokeberries from pokeweed [*Phytolacca americana*] and smear the juice on your lips. This acts as a stain and usually lasted all day because it was highly staining. Don't get the juice on any clothing or skin.

"Back then, we just washed our face, and that was it, 'bout it."

—**Ruby Mae Miller Cheek**

LOTIONS

- One of the oldest lotions used by women in the Appalachians is Corn Huskers Lotion. It was found at the local mercantile.
- The following are steps to make your own lotion: "To start, you need to do a lot of researching. Research the different ingredients. The

> ingredients we're using today is twelve ounces of distilled water, two ounces of glycerin, one ounce emulsifying wax, and one-half ounce of stearic acid. You will also need two ounces of mango butter, one ounce coconut oil, one ounce meadow-foam oil, one and a half ounces of emu oil, one teaspoon fragrance oil, and one-eighth ounce preservative.

"First, you need to measure the ingredients as carefully as possible. Everything is done in weight. Then we need to melt the emulsifying wax, the stearic acid, the mango butter, and the coconut oil in a big pot. Then mix really well with the other ingredients. When it starts to cool, we need to mix the one-eighth ounce of preservatives with the other ingredients.

"Unfortunately, I have to buy most of the supplies I want over the Internet because I cannot find them locally. They just come from all over the world. I use only premium ingredients, top-grade ingredients.

"The varieties are endless. It is just as far as your imagination can go. You can make as many different varieties as you want. Right now, I think the most popular ones are the fruit fragrances. Pear, mangoes, raspberry, and things like that are real popular right now. My favorite fragrance changes. Usually it is whatever I am working on. I like patchouli a lot. Maybe that says something about my age. Lavender is a favorite. I like bland sandalwood. I like musky smells, I guess.

"Most of my products are sold wholesale. I sell to stores, and then they resell them. I also have a website where I sell products over the Internet. My website is www.scsoap.com, and I have them in stores all up and down the East Coast. My lotions are in three stores around here. They are in Hillside Orchard, Old Clayton Inn, and Andy's Trout Farm gift shop.

"Just do some research and decide what you need for your skin because each of the different ingredients do different things, depending on what skin type you have. . . .

"I do not have any horror stories in making lotion. Making lotion is a lot simpler than making soap, and it is not as dangerous as making soap because you do not have any caustic ingredients. There is nothing in there that can hurt you. When you are making soap, you have to deal with lye. You do not have to be near as cautious with making lotion.

"The only thing you could go wrong with lotion is if you made it too greasy and you just were not happy with it or it just smelled horrible. It is just trial and error. I made some I just was not happy with, but that happens to everybody, regardless what they make.

"This is the only place I make lotion. This is the reason my house looks like it does—because I do everything right here.

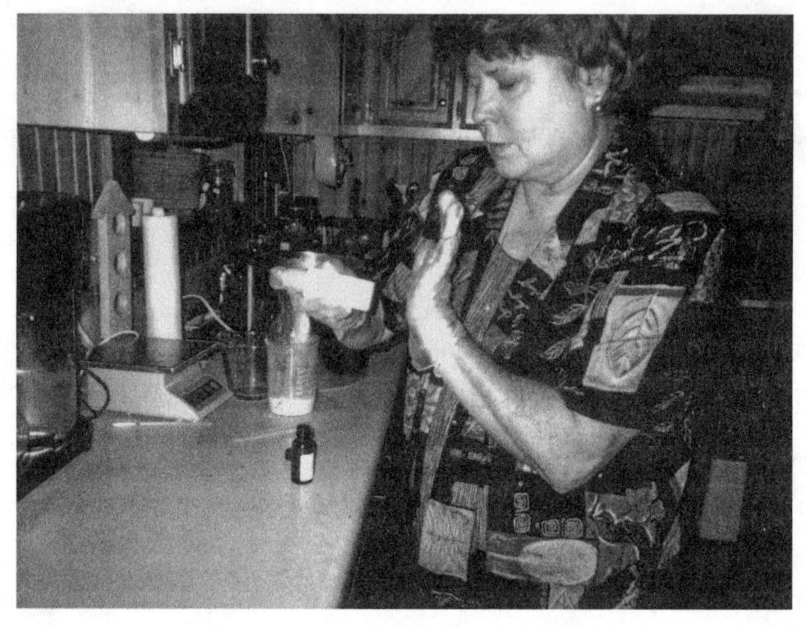

PLATE 127 You can make your own hand lotion.

"Okay, we have got everything. You have to pour it into the bottles while it is hot because once it gets cool, it is hard to pour it. Put one teaspoon of fragrance oil in there, and then you just shake it real well, but carefully, because it is real hot. Once it cools off, it is gonna be nice and creamy. A small bottle would sell for about four dollars. This time of year, lotion does not sell as good as it does in the wintertime. I think we use a lot more lotion of a winter because our skin gets so dry. In lotion you try to use ingredients that will absorb into your skin. In the wintertime, if you want, you can put a beeswax in it to stay on top of your skin to protect it. In the winter, if you are going to be out in the cold, your skin won't absorb the beeswax. It will stay on top of your skin and keep your skin from drying out. I do not like to use beeswax in lotion in the summer because it feels greasy, but of a winter, it needs it. It is great on your legs, too, in the wintertime when they get itchy and dry." **—Gwen Oglesby, Spring/Summer 2002**

TEETH

- There is a tree called the black gum (sour gum) [*Nyssa sylvatica*] tree. People used the limbs of this tree to brush their teeth. They would chew the tip of the limb until it became a bristle, and then they would soak it in baking soda. They would then brush their teeth with it.

- Cut a twig off a sweet birch tree and fray one end by chewing or with a knife. The twig, when the bark is peeled, has a “minty” fragrance and taste. Use the frayed twig to brush your teeth or chew on it to freshen your breath.

ADVICE

Advice is worthwhile if it's accepted.
—Garland Willis

Creon, the king in the famous Greek tragedy *Antigone,* by Sophocles, pontificates about the wisdom of seeking advice and the dangers in not heeding it: "He who is unwilling to seek advice is damned." Ironically, later in the drama, Creon refuses to listen to the wise advice of others; therefore, he has already predicted his own doom.

Advice can be helpful to all of us *if* we are willing to listen and accept it. Many adults we've grown up around have shared with us their life stories and have counseled us. As Ode Reeves tells Foxfire, "A lot of times, people go into somethin' without stoppin' and studyin' about it." Malcolm Dillard, another Foxfire friend, told us, "We have to spend some time thinking what the end results are going to be . . . what are our actions going to lead to?" So true! Many people jump into decisions and situations without thinking; they must then deal with the consequences. Unfortunately, though, the words of wisdom of our elders often go in one ear and out the other. Garland Willis shared a truism: "Counsel unheeded, it is a worthless thing."

Confounded, our elders shake their heads at the hedonism and the what-can-you-do-for-me approach of the boomer generation, and today's teens are certainly a mystery to them. Though some call today's teens Generation X, some young people have set worthwhile goals and are committed to excellence. We do know, however, that many teens have taken the wrong path in spite of counseling by others. Thomas Coy Cheek, one of our contacts who is over ninety years old, has some good advice for society today: "If they will let God lead them and try to be a good Christian, then they will leave the drugs and other stuff alone."

Though having knowledge is good, having wisdom is better. Few of us are wise when we are young. Wisdom and discernment are spiritual gifts, and *most* of the time, these gifts seem to come with age. Creon's son Haemon, however, seems to be the wise one as he counsels his father: "Since wisdom is rarely found, the next best thing is to be willing to listen to wise advice." Perhaps Haemon's words provide good advice for us all.

—*Angie Cheek and April Argoe*

TO YOUNG PEOPLE

Be really content with the state that the Lord has you in at the time you're in it. —Andy Hunter

"My advice to the younger, upcoming generation would be to listen to your mother and father. Try to be truthful, not only with everybody else but yourself also. We have to spend some time thinking what the end results are going to be. We need to always think about that. Also, what are our actions going to lead to?

"It's unfortunate that every generation has to learn over and over again. Some people are wise enough to heed their instructions and listen to the older people. We really want to set you people of today on the right track. Some people are wise enough to do that."

—Malcolm Dillard, Spring / Summer 2003

"The advice I would give the youth today is to learn how to cook, learn how to do housework, and learn how to plan meals. To me, when you cook a meal and you sit down with your family, that's family time."

—Eunice Hunter, Spring / Summer 2004

"Teenagers today want to get out and go. They can't go without going and having a drink or be on a drug. If you do drugs, that can impair your mind. You do things you would not do otherwise. If they will let God lead them and try to be a good Christian, then they will leave the drugs and other stuff alone. I drank a half a can of beer one time in my life, and that was sixty-eight years ago. I have not tasted of it since, and I have got along all right. I do not even take the drugs the doctor gives me all the time. I went to the dentist. He gave me a prescription. The next time I went to him, I told him, 'This prescription you gave me was not worth a flip.' He said, 'I don't understand,' so I pulled out the prescription and gave it to him. He said, 'No wonder': I did not have it filled. I do not believe in drugs. Of course there are times you have to take them. Leave them alone if you can because they can get you in trouble. You are a lot better off without them."

—Thomas Coy Cheek, Fall / Winter 2003

"The main thing now is fer the young people to turn to God an' serve God an' love one another. We're supposed to love one another, an' my advice to 'em is try to love one another but shun any bad company, unless you treat 'em nice and try to pull 'em over. Nobody don't stoop too low but what reach out a hand and try an' pull them up. An' be somebody if you can, but when you can't, don't let them pull you down with 'em. You're supposed to turn back and not let 'em drag you down, too." **—Ethel Corn, Winter 1973**

"I have some advice for younguns—I sure do—if they'd do it. If all you young people would get y'self in a church somewhere and turn y'self over to the Lord—I'm talkin' about get saved, start servin' God—we'd have a good country to live in everywhere. That's the only hope we have. If they don't turn to God, it's gonna get worser, and time is gonna get worser than what we see right now if people don't come back to God and do their first work. You can't get that across to people today. God will always be with you through good and rough times." **—Lois Martin, Spring/Summer 2002**

"I guess we can say that back in the old days it was much harder than it is today. Most kids don't have to work. They only work if they want to, and we didn't have any of them nice cars or airplanes. Yeah, you kids sure have it

PLATE 128 "Time is gonna get worser than what we see right now if people don't come back to God." —Lois Martin

PLATE 129 "Yeah, you kids sure have it easy." —Vaughn Billingsley

easy. One thing I can tell y', though—get a job and a good education, or y' ain't gonna be nothin' in life." **—Vaughn Billingsley, Spring / Summer 2003**

"All in all, I wouldn't change places with any man on earth. If they drove up to my house right now and said I won the lottery, I'd say, 'I've already won it, boys. Give it to someone that hasn't.' I have a great life now and enough memories of a fun childhood to live on forever. I think young people now are missing out a lot—not enough gettin' outside, gettin' dirty, and playin' pranks." **—Gary Davis, Fall / Winter 1999**

"To the teenagers of today, I would pray most earnestly that you, any of you, would find something to be your job in life or your goal in life that would give you as much pleasure and as much of accomplishment as my teaching has done for me." **—Bettie Sellers, Spring / Summer 2002**

"I would tell children of today not to lie. Of all the trouble I ever got into, I wouldn't lie. The school even said that to my mother once: 'Paul will not lie.' If you lie, you have to tell more lies to cover up the first thing, and then it's out of control. Another thing I'd tell them is not to gossip. If you tell things that you hear other people say, and you don't know for a fact that they are true, then it gets spread further and further. I'll tell you, you'll tell your friend, and it'll just spread, spread. The bad thing about that is you can't put

PLATE 130 Gary Davis and his wife, Dawn, on an elk hunt in Wyoming

it back in the bottle. Do not gossip, do not lie, and do not be afraid to work. I always had a job in the summertime. Even though it didn't pay much, it at least kept me off the streets." **—Paul Power, Spring / Summer 2003**

"I would advise the young people to just be sweet children, honor their mother and dad, go to church and Sunday school, and, by all means, go by that blessed Bible. Then you won't make a mistake. Just try to do right. You know if you want to do right and try to do right, you've got lots of help. Our heavenly Father is standin' there waitin' with a mendin', helpin' hand—He's right there to help. Young people today are different from the way we were, and my heart goes out for the youths. I just live with them in my mind. I love young people, and so many people now don't give the young people credit for lots of their goodness." **—Beulah Perry, Summer 1974**

> **"Oftentimes, when you meet somebody else's need, you'll find your own needs met."** ***—Bob Thomason***

"I don't have much advice to give. I'm not much of an advice giver. What I try to do is reach out to the young people as much as possible, and I try to

PLATE 131 Aunt Arie shows Beulah Perry how to make a basket.

give 'em a positive role model to work from. I want to be able to let them know that they can be different from everybody else. You don't have to follow along with the crowd. That's what I taught my own children. I gave 'em freedom to make their own decisions, too. I feel like that was part of our bringin' 'em up in the church.

"I think the best thing you can do for anybody is love 'em, whoever they are. Some people, it's hard to love. It's hard for me to do at times. But everybody wants attention at some time, and they're gonna do what it takes to get it. If you can give 'em some positive attention, sometimes that'll make a difference. It did for me. People took time out to help me when I couldn't help myself or didn't have sense enough to help myself.

"That's the advice I'd give people, especially young people: Reach out to people; don't think about yourself so much all the time. Oftentimes, when you meet somebody else's need, you'll find your own needs met. That's pretty simple, but it's hard to do. I think in this world we get so wrapped up in ourselves so much—and I'm guilty like everybody else—that we don't see what's goin' on around us—all the hurt. That's my advice. Try to be there for other people and be there for yourself."

—Bob Thomason, Spring / Summer 2004

"The youth today have the best opportunity to do and learn for God, the best I've ever seen it. Teenagers are different. People have just growed up quicker. People used to not let their children hear nothin' or not let them do nothin' much else. Now they do as they want to, I reckon—most of them does. If I could, I would tell them to never drink. Don't ever drink strong drinks. I would tell them to certainly watch their company the way they should." **—Furman Chastain, Fall/Winter 2003**

"The advice I'd give to young people is to stop, look, and listen and make sure they're right before they do somethin'. A lot of times, people go into somethin' without stoppin' and studyin' about it. I've done it myself—made some good trades and made some bad trades, done some things I shouldn't have done. If somebody would stop and study it a little, they wouldn't do some of the things they do." **—Ode Reeves, Spring 1982**

"Well, I'll tell you what my best advice to anyone comin' into the world would be: Start in the church. When you're real young, grow up in the church. Also, be honest. I believe in bein' honest. I'll tell you, never tell a lie. If you tell a lie, you got to tell another. I tried to teach my children to be honest. They should serve the Lord. Another thing would be to have a lot of respect for older people. I believe in startin' them when they are real young." **—Eula Carroll, Summer 1990**

"Advice that I think would be very important to give young people today is to be honest and sincere in whatever you do and seek Christ in your life, 'cause life's nothin' without Him." **—Frances Harbin, Fall/Winter 2004**

"If I could say anything to our young people today, it is if you've got a dream, don't think it is too far off. Be content and just kind of let the Lord work His way in your life. Don't be impatient. The biggest thing I can advise someone is to be really content with the state that the Lord has you in at the time you're in it. If your dream is to be something, don't let people laugh at you. Use your weakness as your strength. I have always been that kind of person. I'm an underdog, and I love bein' an underdog. I let being an underdog be my strength. If you are an underdog, let it be your strength."

—Andy Hunter, Spring/Summer 2002

"We have lots o' long-tongued people, lots of 'em. And you can just sit and listen, and you can catch 'em. I just wait and never say a word about it. I just wait, and sometimes it ain't no time 'til they're caught."

—Anna Howard

PLATE 132 "If your dream is to be something, don't let people laugh at you." —Andy Hunter

"Live close to the Lord and let Him put it on your heart. And don't tattle. I don't say you do, but you asked me for my opinion. Live and be truthful and honest, whatever comes. Tell th' truth. Sometimes it hurts, but let 'er pop. I'd tell th' truth on my daddy just as quick as I would on a rank stranger that I've never seen. Some people would do some other way—besides tellin' the truth—to save 'em if it was just their own kin, and if it was somebody else, they'd tear 'em all to pieces. Now, that's just exactly th' nature. And my advice t' any young person is to take th' Lord first, be honest and truthful, and never lose your confidence in nobody or cause them to lose confidence in you. You'll never get it back.

"I try my best to learn just what th' Bible said. You can't be perfect all the time. You'll maybe do a little somethin' that don't please God, but you don't get forgiveness for that, all th' same. And be friendly and good to ever'body and especially to old people—folks you love.

"God can put on your heart or mind anything He wants you t' do, and I know He can. He has mine. It'll come to you just as plain.

"And I try t' be all th' same alike. I don't talk about people. I don't say no harm about nobody and all they do. It says in th' Bible t' do unto others as we wish t' be done by, and I feel that way about that. And I feel like if you're in earnest and you got your faith in th' Lord and ask Him for anything, He'll put it right on your mind.

"But if you're bad and slip and hide and steal somethin' from somebody and don't want them t' see you, well, now, that's against God. You'll be caught up with sooner 'r later. You can talk with people and from their talk tell that lots of 'em are tattlers. We have lots o' long-tongued people, lots of 'em. And you can just sit and listen, and you can catch 'em. I just wait and never say a word about it. I just wait, and sometimes it ain't no time 'til they're caught.

"Kindness and love is th' main thing. Now that's my advice. It's good t' know you've got a friend. It's love—just like I made a friend out of you. I see people that their looks and their ways just a-gives t' you and you love 'em. And th' next time you see 'em, you love 'em better." —**Anna Howard, Spring 1972**

"I would not advise young people to work in a sawmill these days because there are a lot of better jobs out there. It might be okay if you were to work in one of the modern mills, but there are better ways of makin' a livin'. I would definitely advise them to find better jobs so that they could build a better life." —**Milton Speed, Spring/Summer 2005**

PLATE 133 "Kindness and love is th' main thing." —Anna Howard

TO PEOPLE IN GENERAL

"I think I've lived the best that I can. I don't think there is anything I would go back and change about it. My preacher, Nelson Price, was preaching one Sunday, and he was telling us what to do to live a long and happy life. He told us that there are four things in life you need to make a happy life: The first one was work, second was religion, third was play, and the last one was love. I have had all four of them since I was a young man [Lee Garner was ninety October 1998] and would not give any of them up."

—**Lee Garner, Fall 1999**

"You just as well laugh as to cry 'cause nobody don't care nohow. That cryin' don't do no good. Don't do no good."

—**Thad "Happy" Dowdle, Spring/Summer 1996**

"I've learned what's important in life. It's not power, wealth, or popularity. It's actually having somebody there to love you, being able to work and contribute to the welfare of other people." —**Ben Purcell, Spring/Summer 1994**

"Advice is worthwhile if it's accepted. It means somethin'. But counsel unheeded, it is a worthless thing, you see. It's not worth anything if it's not accepted. . . .

PLATE 134 Ben Purcell spent almost sixty-two months as a prisoner of war in Vietnam, fifty-eight of those months in solitary confinement.

"I'd start at home if I was gonna set in to counsel a child. I'd first say that parents ought to be Christian parents. The Bible requires that. Then I would advise the children to always have a listening ear to what the parents told them and accept the good counsel. Older people are gonna pass on, and the younger is comin' in, don't you see? And they're gonna have to take our stand for tomorrow." —**Garland Willis, Spring 1973**

"Once a woman decides to be a wife, she has to stick to it. A divorce will not help matters any. It only breaks the family up. Once a wife, a woman has to get it in her head that she can't get out of it without hurting herself and other people. . . .

"That was what I was trying to say all along, when I was writing about women trying to wear the pants. Being a wife is a career in itself."

—"Annie," Summer 1974

"Love is the thing that's missin' today. That's the main thing. If people loved one another, they wouldn't want to harm each other but would want to help each other like they did back in my childhood days."

—Lillie Nix, Spring/Summer 1996

"I see older people who seem kind of soured on life, and they feel they haven't had a chance in life. I feel we make a lot of our chances."

—Lola Cannon, Spring/Summer 1996

PLATE 135 "Set a goal for yourself and try not to follow everybody else." —Ada Kelly

"Set a goal for yourself and try not to follow everybody else. There's a tendency to be just like the others, but don't do wrong things because you see others doin' them. Set a goal and try to keep your life clean and pure—you'll never be sorry." —**Ada Kelly, Summer 1979**

"Once the money's gone, it's all gone, and what is there left? . . . Money just isn't worth anything. But if you've got the land, you can make it."
—**Furman Arvey, Spring / Summer 1996**

"They want me t' sell and move away from here. But I won't do it. It's just home—'at's all. I spent my happiest days here."
—**Aunt Arie Carpenter, Spring / Summer 1996**

"Advice that I would give to other people is that to think of another as a friend, you have to be a friend. I guess the most important thing that I have ever learned is that I am not always right. There are a few sides to every situation. If I see that I made a mistake, then I will say that I am sorry. If you are selfish and say that you are always right, then you are always going to fight. The first thing is to grow up with God. Let Him lead you. Ask Him to do it and do not decide to do it your way and forget about God. Treat your fellow man the way you want to be treated, not thinking everything you do is

PLATE 136 Thomas Coy and Ruby Cheek in their younger years in front of their home in Toccoa, Georgia

right and everything he does is wrong. Be considerate of other people and treat them like you want them to treat you."

—Thomas Coy Cheek, Fall/Winter 2003

"And ever'body's in a hurry. Where they goin'? Back then, you could meet an ol' feller with an ol' ox wagon, and he'd stand there half a day if you wanted t' talk, stand as long as you'd talk. You meet a feller now, he'd run over y'. Where's he goin'? Just ain't got no patience."

—Kenny Runion, Spring/Summer 1996

"People used to go see one another, and they didn't have no way to go but walk or ride a horse. Now they're livin' a lot faster than we did back then. Nowadays, they ain't got no time to go see anybody. They're goin' all the time, and they don't go nowhere either."

—Claude Darnell, Spring/Summer 1996

"Most everyone has an eerie feeling about funerals or about the dead person. The dead person is not goin' to bother you. It's the live one you got to be worried about. The dead person will make you hurt yourself, but he won't bother you." **—Walter Stancil, Spring/Summer 2003**

"There was one thing my daddy always told me. He taught me from the time I could remember that you were always on time. You could not go anywhere late—you were always on time. Then, on top of that, he always told me and my brother that you did not lie, you did not steal, and that if you would lie, then you would steal because it was all the same thing. Those values have stayed with me all my life. Two things I have never liked was lyin' and stealin'.

"If I could go back in time, I would make families closer like they used to be. Television would not be a part of my household like it is at this point. There's a lot of changes I'm sure most everybody would make in their life if they could go back. I think I would strive to be a better person, not that I've been that bad. I've tried my best to be the best I could be at everything I did. I would be a whole lot more interested in school and doin' my lessons and learnin' all I could." **—Donna Bailey, Fall/Winter 2003**

"I just know my life's been a rough road, but I got over it. I'd tell people always try to be good and be honest—I don't want no liars. An' try to trust in the Lord and do what you think the Lord would want you to do."

—Julia Alice Stephens Watkins, Fall/Winter 2004

PLATE 137 "[My father] always told me and my brother that you did not lie, you did not steal, and that if you would lie, then you would steal because it was all the same thing." —Donna Bailey

"People should be open to the unlikely things that they never thought that they would do." —*Priscilla Wilson*

"We have this phrase that we use: 'the gourd life.' Gourds have all these really cute puns that just work perfectly. We used to have a little car that said, 'Have you driven a gourd lately?' When we talk about 'the gourd life,' it is just a takeoff on 'the good life.' The gourd life is not really 'the good life,' or at least not the way most people perceive 'the gourd life.' What it means to us is to invent it and just go along, and I would encourage people to do this. People should be open to the unlikely things that they never thought that they would do. You have to do what you want to do. You cannot go through life doin' things because they are what you are supposed to do. The real 'gourd life' is not about how much money you can make or what kind of car you drive. It is what your life is really like every day. Artists and craftspeople seem to get a lot of attention for our creativity, but that can happen in any field or walk of life. You just have to do what is right for you. You just have to make sure you are happy about who you are and what you are doing with your life. Live your life for yourself." —**Priscilla Wilson, Spring / Summer 2002**

PLATE 138 Priscilla Wilson shows us what makes hers a "gourd life."

"Treat people right . . . an' be honest with 'em in ever' way in dealings and help 'em out. If they need help, help 'em out. If somebody needs help, why not go and help 'em?" —**Robert Arvey, Fall 1971**

"My advice is don't tell stories [lies] and be good to everybody. Always respect somebody older than you and go to church. Believe in God, honey, and always tell the truth. I still believe that all that stuff is true, and I hope God sees it that way and will take me home when it's time to go."

—Effie Mae Speed Bleckley, Spring / Summer 2004

LONGEVITY

Many have searched for the fountain of youth, the magic elixir, the potion that would help us humans remain young and vibrant. Fantasy and science fiction writers have woven plots depicting this discovery; ironically, the plots often include murder, even the killing of friends and family, in order to gain control of the secret. Modern-day geneticists claim to be on the verge of halting and even reversing the aging process. Researchers recently touted that in the not-so-distant future humans may live five hundred years. It's almost inconceivable! Today, senior citizenship begins around the age of sixty, but this fact may change in the future.

All of us have read reports of cultures in which many individuals live past ninety or even a hundred years old. We all know elderly folks who are still active and sharp. Do they have a secret? A few of our contacts have their own theories about living long, and who are we to argue? Their long lives are proof!

—Angie Cheek

"But I'll tell you what I think. People lived better than they do today. Back then they put up ever'thing they had to eat. Raised about ever'thing, like we do now, but they didn't have things like we do now. Back then, all the old people lived to be old. My grandpa was ninety-four when he died. You know, not many people of this younger generation will ever see that age. Of course, well, they took care of themselves better then. Well, they worked harder, but they was tougher. It seems to me the ones that worked the hardest was the toughest and the strongest and stood up the longest. People is just not a-workin' like they used to work. They are makin' an easier way, and they are goin' to run into a wall some of these days, too, because somebody is gonna have to do the work or somebody is gonna starve, one."

—Richard Norton, Spring 1975

"Why have I lived this long? [Mrs. Watkins was one hundred and seven years old April 12, 2004. She was born in 1897.] Well now, that's up to the good Lord why I've lived this long, but I may have done somethin' durin'

PLATE 139 "I ain't no knickknack eater."
—Julia Alice Stephens Watkins

my life that has holped [helped]. For instance, in eatin', I ain't no knick-knack eater. I just eat common vegetables, mostly vegetables. I don't eat a lot o' meat, and I eat a lot o' wild greens in growin' up. I think that adds to y' life. Mostly, I drink water—clear, cold water. I don't drink nothin' else much. I will drink a little milk along. I used t' drink a lot o' milk, but I've got to where I don't drink much milk."

—Julia Alice Stephens Watkins, Fall/Winter 2004

"I think one reason I lived so long [Mr. Cheek was ninety-three years old April 2, 2006] is I tried to put God first. I also have a sweet tooth, so I eat honey. I usually eat it once a day. Sometimes I will eat it two to three times a day. It is not just a half a spoonful neither. I think that has helped me to keep my health what it should be. I had seven hives of bees; now I only have two. I have not had any honey since eight o'clock this mornin'. What I contribute my health to at this age is the Lord blesses a clean life."

—Thomas Coy Cheek, Fall/Winter 2003

PLATE 140 "What I contribute my health to at this age is the Lord blesses a clean life." —Thomas Coy Cheek

"I guess all of us Dickersons have lived so long because of the way we live. We had an old clock on the mantel, and we got up by it and went to bed by it. We never stayed up real late. We had to get up early and get ready to go to the field for work. Just eat regular, get up regular, and sleep regular."

—Terry Dickerson, Winter 1986

PLATE 141 "Just eat regular, get up regular, and sleep regular." —Terry Dickerson

THE LAND

Once the money's gone, it's all gone,

and what is there left? . . . Money

just isn't worth anything. But if

you've got the land, you can make it.

—*Furman Arvey*

Now "home," by the way, when I say it, is always Rabun County. I mean, really this [house] is my home with my wife and the children nearby, but what I mean is, to me, the ancestral home, the childhood home. That's always there.

—*Bob Justus*

The word "home" conjures up many emotions and has been the subject of many sayings: "Be it ever so humble, there's no place like home." "Home is where the heart is." "There's no place like home; there's no place like home; there's no place like home." Though for some people, home refers to the house where they live, and for others, home is the house in which they were raised, for many people of the Southern Appalachians, home is the land, the mountains. Generations of mountain pioneers made their living from the land, as towns were few and far between in the mountains in those days, and jobs were almost nonexistent.

Working with nature and against all odds, those courageous mountain folk carved out a place in history even as they toiled to make a living from the land. As the property they homesteaded and claimed from the wilderness was passed down from generation to generation, the struggle for survival left an indelible impression on the people of the mountains. Because of the realities of mountain life, independence, self-sufficiency, and stoicism were common traits.

The people who settled this area passed on to their children a love for the mountains and a devotion to home uncommon in our era of mobility and isolation. As those generations of family members worked their farms, land ceased to be simply a place to live and work and became a heritage to be preserved and passed on to the next generation.

As time passed, the mountains began to change. Years of hard use led to erosion and the disappearance of forests, and people from other areas began to come to the Appalachians. Many of those outsiders were looking for second homes or country getaways. As the population increased and time passed, the cost of land inevitably rose. These issues created a conflict for many mountain families: Should we sell and give our children money or keep the land and give them the farm? Another controversy near to the hearts of mountain families is the one concerning environmental laws. Whose rights are more important: those of the landowners wanting to change (or in their own view, improve) their property or those of the community at large, who think certain protections should remain in place no matter who owns the lot?

Though the land is changing, much about the mountains remains the same. The air at the top of Black Rock Mountain, located above Foxfire's offices in Mountain City, Georgia, still feels much cooler than that at the bottom. Even during the hottest days of summer, a cool morning breeze still blows in the mountains. The birds still sing, the woods are still dark, and the mountains still bear a blue haze in the evenings. Like the old mountaineers to whom we spoke, I cannot foresee what changes the future will bring to my beloved mountains. I can only hope that my generation will preserve and protect these precious hills for our children's children.

—Lacy Hunter Nix

ACQUIRING LAND

Barak Norton, my grandfather, he had a Indian name. He was a little bit Indian . . . He liked the Cherokee, kept about nine chiefs and nine boys here and took food to 'em up in the mountains after they [the government] run 'em out. He carried bread and stayed with them lots of times. He didn't like it—none o' these old fellows didn't like it—when they took th' Indians' land.

—Richard Norton

For many of the folks we interviewed, land is not merely a commodity. Rather, it is an inheritance, something to be passed down from one generation to the next. Many of our contacts could trace the ownership of their land to the time when no one owned the land—when the Cherokee Indians lived there and when some of the original residents of this area homesteaded there. Still others could remember when land sold for only a few dollars per acre.

Most people we interviewed inherited their land from a close relative, usually parents or grandparents. In fact, parents often viewed retaining the land for their children and grandchildren as their duty, just as many parents and grandparents in today's world want to provide financing for their children's education.

While many mountain folk welcome their neighbors and feel an obligation to work together with them for the well-being of the community, you may notice resentment from some as to the issue of outsiders acquiring local land. Many people felt they had been duped when, after having sold their land for the going rate—which was quite low—they realized that the money was actually very little, and their land was gone. The lesson was a hard one, and one many other families took to heart. Still others saw some of their neighbors being forced to sell off large tracts of land simply because they could no longer afford to pay the property taxes. And the issue of eminent domain has recently made national headlines. Perhaps eminent domain will also have an impact on folks whose families have owned their land for generations. Hear what the local elders have to say about acquiring land and the changes they have experienced.

—Lacy Hunter Nix

BUYING LAND

"Back when I was growin' up, you could buy an acre of land for three and four and five dollars. Well, land got to goin' up a little and a little at a time. When the first Florida people began buyin' it here, land wasn't no more than twenty-five to thirty dollars an acre. But that's what made people sell—because they thought that was a terrible [high] price, you see. And so they thought they could make some money, and they thought these people comin' in here were rich people who could help them out. And it did help some people about a job—help them out a little bit and all—but now it's just goin' right the other way, you know." —**Furman Arvey, Spring 1980**

"Way back in them early years, land wadn't very valuable, and you could buy land for two or three dollars an acre most anywhere you wanted. And people started comin' in here—tourists—and they'd buy fifteen or twenty acres here and there, and the first thing you know, these people was out of land. They didn't have no land, and very few of them had any money.

"Most of them had enough land that their house set on, and a few acres to farm on, but they'd actually sold all the rest of it off to different people. They had a place to live on, but the rest they actually sold to get money to survive on. They sold it off just for money. Maybe they had to sell it. I don't know about that.

"And then the government bought up a lot of the land. All these mountains you see back in here? I'd say they ain't got over a dollar an acre in all that." —**Ellison Wall, Spring 1980**

INHERITING LAND

> **"We built this house right here in the woods. We cut the timber, and my neighbor here, my daddy's cousin, said he'd saw the lumber and plane it for me."**
> ***—Clarence Lusk***

"My daddy told me he'd give me this place here if I wanted to stay on with it. See, my great-granddaddy owned a lot of land in here. This is what they call the Smeltzer Creek Community. So we built this house right here in the woods. We cut the timber, and my neighbor here, my daddy's cousin, said he'd saw the lumber and plane it for me if I'd bring the logs up there. That was about 1927–28. They come up here and cut the timber, loaded it out with mules and hauled it up the creek here to a sawmill and had the lumber cut and run it through the planer. Me and Alma married in '26, and we moved up here to this house in '28. 'Course we've added some to it since then.

"We cleared the land up here. Had new ground, we called it back then. We started to farmin'. We had a lot of cleared land, and we just eventually made our land fields bigger. That's about the way we started out.

"We have only one child, a boy. He lives up here beyond us just a short distance. He's about like I was; he'd stay on with us. And our granddaughter's livin' right over across the way. Our grandson's buildin' him a new house right down on a section of our land near this house. So I reckon they plan on stayin' here, too. I've also got one great-grandbaby. She's nearly two years old." —**Clarence Lusk, Summer 1985**

> **"This was a Indian camp right here and across the [North Carolina state] line, too. I guess the Hoppers got the land after the Cherokee Indians moved off it. They cleared it. They didn't buy it; they just homesteaded. Yeah, I think that is the way they got it."**
>
> —***Richard Norton***

"Barak Norton, my grandfather, he had a Indian name. He was a little bit Indian. More like them than they was theirselfs. He liked the Cherokee, kept about nine chiefs and nine boys here and took food to 'em up in the mountains after they [the government] run 'em out. He carried bread and stayed with them lots of times. He didn't like it—none o' these old fellows didn't like it—when they took th' Indians' land. Them old fellows then, well, I'd rather a-had their word than a note from these today. They believed in right, an' you couldn't change 'em much.

"This was a Indian camp right here and across the line too. I guess the Hoppers got the land after the Cherokee Indians moved off it. They cleared it. They didn't buy it; they just homesteaded. Yeah, I think that is the way they got it. Uncle Tom Hopper, he's the one that is as far back as any record I've got. Tom Hopper divided it. They was four of the Hopper boys. Jepp Hopper, he owned part of it down here on Mrs. Hambidge's, the Rock House. They owned practically what the Hambidge Foundation [Betty's Creek Community, Dillard, Georgia] owns now, all of the boys did.

"My mother and uncle bought two tracts. They bought the tract where the Martins live. They got this place below the mill on this side of the creek, thirty-five acres of that. That's what my mother give my sister over there. It run from the left-hand side of the creek up to the mill, you know, where the gristmill is.

"Now my grandfather's first wife was a Hopper, and she heired [inherited] this on this side of the line [in North Carolina]. And her name was Florie

Hopper. My mother was named after her. After that, it was just passed down to my mother an' then I got it from my mother. It was just me and her until I got married.

"I have got about fifty acres up on a mountain up there, and the government tried to get part of it. I wouldn't let them have it. There is so much of this land been sold to the government now. That is what is makin' it hard on people. Some people could be workin' this land and payin' tax on this land and be cultivatin' the land. But the government ain't payin' tax on it, and the people can't get it. You go up on Pickens' Nose up there [a mountain at the head of Betty's Creek] and look down there and see what we own down here. It's just a little spot. And the government owns all the rest of it. I don't think it's right for them to hold that off of it. It can't make 'em much. They sell a little timber off of it. But think how much better it would be if somebody was farmin' it and a-livin' off it. Think how much better the people would be." —**Richard Norton, Spring 1975**

> **"I've lived here on Betty's Creek [Rabun County, Georgia] all my life. I was borned in that house on the left-hand side of the road as you go down."**
> ***—Margaret Norton***

PLATE 142 Richard and Margaret Norton of the Betty's Creek Community in Dillard, Georgia

"My grandfather was named Doc Burrell, and he come here from over about South Carolina or somewhere over in there. His wife was a Carter, Sally Carter, and he used to own this land that's right here [the Rock House on the Hambidge land]. Before Carroll Latimer owned it, Grandpa Burrell owned it. That was on my daddy's side. My daddy's name was Rom Burrell. Rom owned some land up the road from here. He didn't own this up here because his daddy sold it before he was big enough to own land. You know that old house that's up on the left-hand side of the road as you go down? Well, that's ours. That's where we was born and raised. Now the way he got a-hold of it is he married . . . well, my mother was born there. He married Love Beavert and he inherited half of the land and him and her bought the other half. There was just two heirs in to it, which was Love and Faye. Faye was my mother's niece. And my daddy bought her part of the land, so . . . it all belonged to him.

"Now Rom Sr., my daddy was brother to Decatur, and he owned what is now Moon Valley. Now my grandmother Burrell had a sister by the name of Lou Lindsay. He took care of Lou Lindsay, and she gave him what she had. She had that land up there, and she was a Carter before she married Mr. Lindsay. And he didn't live very long. She was Sally's sister, and they come from Towns County, Georgia.

"I've lived here on Betty's Creek all my life. I was borned in that house on the left-hand side of the road as you go down. The only place I've ever moved was from down there up to where Richard is. I've seen all the changes as they come along up here on Betty's Creek."

—Margaret Norton, Spring 1975

"I was born right where I live today. My people pioneered this area. They were here since 1818, and then they got their papers and deeds in 1823, I believe, through the land lottery. So we've been here ever since. The way the land lottery worked, the best I remember, was you had to go out and stake a territory and live on it so many years before you could apply for a deed. It was practically free. I think some of them paid as little as twenty cents an acre for the land. And they would camp, cut logs, and build a log house to live in until they decided they wanted to move permanently.

"Well, my great-grandfather Joshua Sutton first built a little log cabin and decided he liked living up there pretty well. So then he built that sawed plank house that's just below me and brought his bride there. He reared a big family of children. He had slaves, too. They took his name after they were freed. He gave the land for the church and the cemetery, and the first person buried in the cemetery was one of his little slave boys."

—Ellene Gowder, Summer 1986

SELLING THE LAND

Things are goin' too high, and money just isn't worth anything. But if you've got the land, you can make it."

—Furman Arvey

My husband and I, as with most of the other couples I know, make land and home purchases with an eye toward market gain and resale value. We feel no guilt about selling one piece of property for profit and then buying another, and we have little emotional attachment to a lot or any building on that lot. The issue of whether to sell or keep a piece of land has never become an emotional issue for us. So far, most of our decisions on properties have had a purely financial basis.

For the people you'll meet in the following section, however, the decision to sell land is often an emotional one. For most of them, money is of little use, and the idea of selling their children's "heritage" is foreign to their value system. Time after time, they told us money was no use to them if the land was gone. They have lived without money and material goods, but they know how to use the land to make a life for themselves.

Still, others made the decision to sell with little or no regret. Some saw that their children's lives were no longer in the country and wanted to be able to give to their children financially. Others saw the potential for conflict over the land after they were gone, and they sold it in order to avoid feuding among family members. The question of whether to stay or to sell has long been a subject of contention in this area and will most likely continue to be, not just in this community but in rural communities all across America.

—Lacy Hunter Nix

"I wish everybody could keep their land. Things would be a lot better off."

—Furman Arvey

"Well, after my daddy and my mother both died, we sold off the homeplace and divided the money. There was ten of us children, and there was just some thirty-seven acres up there in that tract and no chance in the world to divide it up fairly. So we sold it. I wish everybody could keep their land. Things would be a lot better off. The demand has run the prices up, run the taxes up and everything. Now it's gettin' nearly impossible for a boy raised here on a farm or around here to buy him a farm and a house 'cause you take four or five thousand dollars an acre for land, and then to build a house, it's somethin' else. These Florida people are doin' all the buyin' now, and we don't know what it's goin' to turn to, you know.

"I think everybody around here made a mistake to ever sell their land. There's some good people comin' in here, but lots of people here left themselves with nothin'. We made a mistake sellin' our land. Once the money's gone, it's all gone, and what is there left? Just like the little heifer out yonder. A fellow offered me $500 for her. I said, 'I can see the heifer, but if I had the money, I wouldn't see it very long. I'll just keep her a while.' Money ain't worth nothin'. A man's gotta have some of it, ain't he? But when you sell off all you have to get it, you have made a mistake. It don't last long. It sure don't.

"Take that homeplace up there. When we sold it, I think we sold it for a thousand dollars an acre. I thought that was a great price. But it ain't now for a place like that.

"Things are goin' too high, and money just isn't worth anything. But if you've got the land, you can make it. I remember when people switched from wood heat and wood cookstoves to oil. I figured then it was the wrong thing to do. So I never have made a switch—still cut my own wood off my own land and use it for heatin', cookin', everything. Now people are comin' back to me. I'm afraid we're gonna have to go back to some of that old-time stuff." —**Furman Arvey, Spring 1980**

> **"I knew neither my son-in-law nor any of my grandchildren would ever be interested in farming. They never will be. Their lives are in the business world. By selling my land, I can give them financial aid in the future, and I can see them have things that I can enjoy seeing them have while I'm living."** ***—Mabel Kitchens***

"I think [that selling the land] was a wise thing to do because we were reaching the time that Jack [the man leasing her farm] was not going to be able to farm. It would have cost me about six thousand dollars a year to pay the taxes and to keep it bush-hogged [mowed down] and in shape. I said that was foolish—I didn't have the money to do that. People don't realize how much a farm can cost you. What would be the point of holding it when eventually it would have grown up again? Another reason for selling the land was that I knew neither my son-in-law nor any of my grandchildren would ever be interested in farming. They never will be. Their lives are in the business world. By selling my land, I can give them financial aid in the future, and I can see them have things that I can enjoy seeing them have while I'm living. . . .

"I think that under the conditions, Neal [Mabel's late husband] would have realized that it would have been the right thing for me to do. He would have understood, I'm sure.

"But I kept the house and three acres here. There is just no way I would have moved. Neal and I had so many good years together in this house. As you get older, when you live in a place for almost forty years, your roots become deep. There is no way that I would have sold my house. They couldn't have offered me a price that I would have taken to start over again.

"I still have another tract of land of about twenty-six acres. I also have about forty or forty-five acres down here on the main highway, so I still have seventy acres of land altogether. I'm not without land, but I don't expect to sell any of the land I have left before I die. I'm going to leave that to my family." —**Mabel Kitchens, Winter 1989**

> **"I learned a long time ago that you can do without the money. You can do without it, but if you got a home, you can't do without that. You'd better stay with your home."** —***Lawrence Ellis***

"I intend to run my sawmill until I get to be eighty-eight or eighty-nine years old. Then I think I might retire. When I finally retire, I'm not goin' to sell my sawmill. I'll just leave it settin' here. I don't think any of my children will take up the business. They got better sense. They all got better sense than I had.

"If anyone finds a legal way to make me move, they'll have to haul me out. I'm goin' to put up stiff resistance. The Good Lord is the only one that I'll move for. If He tells me to go, now I'm goin' to have to go. I ain't goin' to put no argument on Him!

"The only advice I'd have for other people in a situation like mine is 'Don't sell!' People ought to be as stubborn as I am and not let them have it! If somebody wants me to do somethin' that I don't want to do, I just tell them one time, and I'll never change my mind! I've got a one-track mind, I reckon.

"I just like livin' here. I could have sold out lots of times, but I won't sell it. I don't own too much land, but I wouldn't sell it for no price! I do not even put a value on my land because I don't want to sell it. I'm here to stay. I've been asked to put a value on my land. They don't never make me no offer; they just say, 'How much do you want?'

"And I say, 'I don't want it.'

"A feller come out here the other day. Said, 'I heard a man told you that he wanted to make you a rich man, and you wouldn't have it.'

"I said, 'You're always hearin' somethin' about me. What little I got ain't for sale, and I wouldn't even price it even if you did offer to make me a rich man!'

"This land here is my home. I learned a long time ago that you can do without the money. You can do without it, but if you got a home, you can't do without that. You'd better stay with your home. You need it. I don't never plan to sell my land or my home as long as I live. My wife, she's just like me. 'Course she's not as big a fool as I am, but she don't want to move. My kids don't say nothin'. They learned a long time ago that Dad was the boss.

"But after I'm gone, my children will get the land. I guess they'll sell it. I guess, then, if somebody would offer them a good price, it'd be gone!"

—Lawrence Ellis, Winter 1989

"There is too much land a-growin' up, and the population is gettin' bigger all the time. I don't know just how long it's gonna last. It is just a shame that the old people is a-lettin' the people talk 'em out of their land, sellin' it and all. We ain't goin' to on Betty's Creek. We are goin' to set down on it. I could have sold this place for a thousand dollars a acre, but I figure that such fellows as that right there [points to his nine-year-old grandson Tony] has got to have a place to live. And if we sell it, you can't get it back. It is gone."

—Richard Norton, Spring 1975

> **"Somebody comes nearly every day to buy land. But we got four children and seven grandchildren. They all got to have a place to live. Richard won't sell an acre of land . . . The money would soon be gone, and you wouldn't have nothin'."** ***—Margaret Norton***

"Before the pavin' of the road, this was just a small settlement, and all the families and the farmers owned their land. Now lots of the land has been sold out, and now they have new families moved in here or they are in the process of movin'. They have bought land up here and are buildin' houses. If people sell their land, the mountains might get overcrowded. They don't sell it for the money. They sell it because the tax is so high that they are not able to pay it. So many people are wantin' land, I don't know why now. You know, Rabun County was established on land at fifty cents an acre, and back in them days people didn't have no problem over [survey] lines. They would say, 'Your land is here, and my land is here.' You didn't hear no fussin' and fightin' over lines like they do now.

"In other places, people are sellin' out their land even to where their children wouldn't have anywhere to live. But now, not so up on Betty's Creek.

People on Betty's Creek won't sell their land. Somebody comes nearly every day to buy land. But we got four children and seven grandchildren. They all got to have a place to live. Richard won't sell an acre of land for $2,000. He's been offered $2,500 for one acre. But what would he do with his $2,500 and his land gone? Well, the money would soon be gone, and you wouldn't have nothin'.

"Sometimes people that are gettin' old and their grandchildren have inherited it. Maybe the grandchildren haven't lived here—lived somewhere off from here—and they decide to sell their land. That is the only kind of land that has been sold. They have moved off to the city or somethin', and they say, 'Well, we had rather have the money as to have the land.' They sell ten acres of land for $10,000. That's all the land that has been sold here on Betty's Creek.

"People are gettin' so crowded now. Everybody needs land. Everybody needs somewhere t' live. Well, we haven't got any but good people that come in th' last few years. They come up here from Atlanta and Florida, and they say their idea is to bring money into a section, not to come take it away. There's people that works for 'em 'at wouldn't have those jobs. They could have got a job, but they'd a-had to a-left Betty's Creek. They'd a-had to went somewheres else, back'ards an' for'ards each day. 'Course, when I grew up, they wasn't no place to work. They wasn't no factories or no place to work."

—Margaret Norton, Spring 1975

MILLS

GRISTMILLS

Back then, it took a lot of cornmeal to feed a family. It was cornmeal for dinner and supper. It's an amazin' thing that back then when we didn't have a God-blessed thing, we had all that good stuff to eat. —*Arch Bishop*

In order to survive, early mountain folk had to derive the maximum benefit from every resource available. Our "modern" concept of conservation is actually quite old, born not of good intentions or concern for the future, but rather of necessity. Like the Native Americans, early pioneers of the Appalachian Mountains used every part of plants and animals to make what they needed to live. Unlike modern families who sometimes landscape with plants ill suited to the area, mountain families had to find hardy and prolific plants, those that could not only survive the Appalachian climate but thrive here.

Corn was just such a plant. Farm families could plant and tend acres of corn during the summer and produce in the fall a delicious and useful addition to the family's diet. Several different ways existed to prepare corn for family meals: corn on the cob, cornbread, corn pones, creamed corn, and popcorn, to name but a few. When the summer was over, farmers could then dry the stalks on which the corn had grown and save them to feed livestock through the winter.

As corn was such a common crop, gristmills became a common fixture in Appalachia. Gristmills were of necessity located close to creeks, or branches (a word for creek in the local dialect). The water from the creek would power the waterwheel, which would then turn, by means of several gears, the two enormous stones inside the mill to grind the corn. Today, we visit specialty foods stores and pay a premium for stone-ground meal. To our pioneer forefathers, stone-ground meal was merely a staple in the typical diet.

The gristmill was also a gathering place for community members. Waiting on corn to be ground provided a welcome respite from the near-constant hard work required to maintain a farm and an opportunity to socialize with neighbors. Money payments were neither required nor expected. Instead, millers used a barter system, taking specific quantities of meal in exchange for bushels of ground corn. After the grinding was complete, families took the meal home and used their creativity in the kitchen to turn simple cornmeal into many of the country dishes we know and love to this day.

—Lacy Hunter Nix

"My daddy had a little gristmill—corn mill—and it was the only one in the district. Everybody come to mill from the whole district here. Some kids would ride a mule. Some would carry their corn—half a bushel, peck, or bushel—and we'd grind about a bushel an hour. The people who came to mill had a mill sack. They kept their mill sacks washed nice and clean, and they'd bring their corn in it to mill and take it back home full of cornmeal. We'd play all the time while the mill was a-grindin'. We had lots of friends, too." —**Virgil Ledford, Fall 1982**

> **"When Dixie ground the corn, he took a toll for payment for grindin' the corn. . . . They wudn't no money exchanged. That's just the way it was done in those days."** ***—J. P. Speed***

"The mill I am usin' belonged to Dixie Wilbanks. He operated the mill over on Warwoman Creek [outside Clayton, Georgia] for years. When Dixie passed away, his grandson, Ricky Darnell, inherited it. Ricky, he let me use the mill up 'til this time.

"We always took the corn to Dixie to get him to grind it for us. We just watched it and observed how he done it. Then later on, after Dixie passed away, my oldest son got interested in the mill. He rebuilt the raceway and the wheels with family and friends; from then on, we just operated it, and we learned by doin' how to do it. The mill has two standin' stones: One of 'em rotates; the other one sets still, and the grain feeds in from the top. You set the stones coarse, medium, or fine. It makes fine cornmeal for cornbread or coarser for grits. And it turns it, rolls it out into a box. This mill was run by a waterwheel when Dixie Wilbanks operated it. After the years went by, the waterwheel rotted, and the raceway rotted away; so they moved that mill out, and I pulled it with a Ford tractor belt and pulley off the power takeoff [the Ford tractor motor powers the belt and pulley, which then powers the mill and makes the grinding stones turn].

"The corn I use is the open-pollinated Kenner corn and Prolific. We believe it makes better cornmeal, and I was just raised up to the kind we use. This corn has been in the county for years.

"Usually we plant it the later part of April, first of May, so it'll get mature and hard by the time the first frost comes. We pick it by hand after it has two or three frosts on it in the fall and it gets semi-dry; then we pick it and throw it in the trailer behind the tractor. We haul it home and put it in the crib to dry. After we gather it, we bring it and put it in the crib. We try to pick after the sun shines on it at mornin'. That gets a head start on it, and y' keep checkin' it along and along to see how dry it's gettin'. Then finally y' shuck it, and y' pile it in a bin so the air can circulate through it for so long. You can feel of it and see when it shells off the cob easy; then y' run it through the corn sheller. Then put it in sacks and dry it again to get it to where it'll run easily through the mill. If you try to grind the corn before it gets good and dry, it wads up, and it don't make good, fine meal. The corn has to dry for different times—it's accordin' to how well it dries in the crib—before you shuck it and shell it and stuff. Sometimes I lay it out in the sun in the sack. I got some in front of the heater right now dryin'. Otherwise, it's no certain date. You just kinda feel of it and go by feel and touch.

"I have a large Deerborn corn sheller that shells easily. All y' have to do is turn the handle and feed the corn into it. Usually, they's some damaged grains and little 'uns on the end that don't grind good. Well, next you set the mill up, and the way I do it is I run the stones up tight so they won't turn and let it off 'til it's runnin' free. Y' could probably stick a paper between the stones down in there. Then from there you start feedin' the corn into it, and y' adjust the rocks 'til it gets the fineness or coarseness that you want it ground. Some people like it fine; some, coarse. Thataway, y' can get it the

PLATE 143 J. P. Speed demonstrates the use of his corn sheller.

right texture. If y' get it too fine, it don't make good cornbread. Some people like grits; y' have to really open it back up to get grits out of it [to get it coarse enough for grits]. By feelin' of it by hand, that's the only way to tell. Lots of times it takes a sifter if we're makin' meal, and we sift it and see how much bran is left over.

"People tell me that this here open-pollinated corn makes better cornmeal. It's ground slower and kept cool. Otherwise, it never does heat up. It's got a different texture. Y' add bakin' soda and salt or bakin' powder—whatever y' want—to it.

"When Dixie ground the corn, he took a toll for payment for grindin' the corn. Beginnin' with, Dixie would take one full box [of cornmeal], and years later he would take two of the little boxfuls for grindin' a bushel of corn. They wudn't no money exchanged. That's just the way it was done in those days." **—J. P. Speed, Fall/Winter 2004**

"The mill is an important icon of America's life and history."
—Laurence Holden

"I began volunteer work at the mill in March of 1990, and I have worked there ever since. I enjoy working at the mill. The setting is the great, high ridges of the Nantahalas. You are able to see them just outside the mill door. I enjoy meeting the old fellas who bring their corn to be ground and listening to their stories of old times. They tell when they were youngsters of walking to school and coming back afterwards to pick the meal up.

"The Hambidge Center is a center near the mill that owns places such as Betty's Creek Mill, and it is listed on the National Register of Historic Places. The reason I decided to work at the mill is because the Hambidge Center is one of the most important cultural assets in this region. There is an old Native saying that says 'What is good is given back.' Native Americans used to distinguish between gifts and capital. You may keep your Christmas present, but it ceases to be a gift unless you have given something else away of similar value. It is where the term 'Indian giver' comes from (which was a misunderstanding of the colonists). This is because Native Americans gave them gifts; they expected the receiver to pass it along, and when they kept it, the gift giver would be insulted and come to retrieve it.

"The first thing you have to do when building a mill is to find a place on a creek where the water falls a lot in a short distance. They did this at the mill a long time ago. Next, you build a race or a sluice that the water runs down in order to turn a waterwheel. You must have a constant fall of water to turn the wheel. Connected to the waterwheel are four wheels. The waterwheel has a shaft that comes in through the basement of the mill. On this shaft is a chain that connects the other three wheels. Every time the wheel on the shaft turns once, the small wheel turns thirty-five times. The small wheel connects to two sprockets by a pulley and one more at the very top inside the mill. The small wheel connects at the top and actually turns the stone which grinds the corn, but it all begins with the water flowing down the race and turning all the wheels in the process. When this process happens, you get about seven horsepower.

"Up in the mill attached to all the wheels and sprockets is a box. Inside the box are two buhrstones that grind corn into either meal, grits, or flour. You can control how fine you want to grind by a screw that moves the stones either closer or farther apart. One of the stones inside the box turns; it is called a 'running' stone. The other is called a bed stone, and it has a hole in the middle of it; it is called an eye. The stone surfaces have lines in them called furrows and are approximately five-eighths of an inch deep. They shallow out to nothing at the edge, and the corn will come through the middle. This process is how the mill basically works.

"My work at the mill is just my little attempt to give back something to the Hambidge Center. I am an artist and have been going to the Hambidge Center most summers to work on my art. I paint collages. While there, in 1990, I was told the mill was no longer operational, so I worked on it to get it running again. Since they could find no one to run it locally, I agreed to volunteer my time to keep it going. The mill itself is an overshot of a waterwheel-powered gristmill at the Hambidge Center. The wheel is twelve feet in diameter, and the stones are sixteen-inch pebble buhrstones. A buhrstone is a flat stone representing the edges of the grain in the stone, like a tree when sawed off. Pebble refers to the flint in the particular kind of granite stone we have at Betty's Creek Mill.

"The mill was rebuilt by the Hambidge Center. It was originally built between 1830 and 1860 by the Hopper family. It was built at a place called Old Hopper Mill Shoals. A shoal is a shallow place in a river or sea. The shoal is why the mill is located where it is. It was the Old Hopper Mill Shoals because of the Hopper family who built the first mill there. It was built there because this was the place where the water fell the farthest in the shortest distance along Betty's Creek. The original mill fell into disrepair in the mid-1930s; in the early 1940s the site was deeded to the Hambidge Center. Mary Hambidge had the mill entirely rebuilt. The construction was then completed in 1944.

"We run it exactly the way it was run in 1944. Sometimes people come and volunteer their time to help out. Up through the 1970s, local farmers brought their grain two or three days a week during the winter months to have it ground. Now fewer and fewer farmers exist in this area. Some still come, mostly in their seventies and eighties. They bring anything from a pillowcase full to five or six bushels of corn. People like their grain ground at the mill better because it was done on the stone and because it is so fresh.

"The mill is an important icon of America's life and history. The people in Betty's Creek Valley depended on local mills to provide meal and flour for their daily lives. Before the Second World War, Barker's Creek Mill was only one of several in the valley. Now it is the only one preserved. People like to come visit a symbol of the way life used to be that is now gone from these hills and from most places in America. They also come to enjoy the great meal and grits, which more modern methods cannot compare to in quality. The most interesting thing about the mill is that it is a living example of a

PLATE 144 Laurence Holden at Barker's Creek Mill

PLATE 145 The waterwheel at Barker's Creek Mill

way of life gone from these hills that we can still preserve. The skills involved in grinding grain well is a lost art; by keeping it open and running, I preserve some of those skills to pass on to the next generation."

—Laurence Holden, Spring/Summer 1999

"The old man shut the mill down to go to dinner every day. If anybody was there, he'd ask them to go to dinner with him. One fellow told him, 'No, your wife don't know I'm comin' for dinner. She wouldn't have nothin' cooked for me.' The old man said, 'H——, we have somethin' to eat whether you come to eat with us or not.' "

—Arch Bishop

"After the war, I would assume Rob McClure and the Palmers built the mill. It ran until, I would say, in the forties. It would have been seventy-five or eighty years old. They had to come from way up the creek there. They built a dam. Then the old-timers sighted their ditches with a plain carpenter level, figured out where they were goin' to come, and I'd say most of it was dug by mule and drag pan. They've had drag pans around for a long time. That scoop and mule was a wonderful machine. You could load that up and take a lot of dirt out in a little while. And lots of it was drug by hand around the rock cliff. It is about a half a mile up the creek where the head's at. Now where it stops at, they got a watershed dam up there.

"They used one-by-twelves fitted together with sides of them [for the sluice]. They had white oak timbers. They set it out, and it come right down through there. They had a spillway, and the overflow water run off to the right. It was just a big sheet of water pourin' all the time. When you wanted to run the mill and grind corn, you closed that gate, and then the water poured onto the wheel. You done it all from the mill. You had a wire runnin' to it, and when you pulled that wire, it closed the gate on the water. It was a pretty tall wheel. It was a good fifteen feet high. They just let the last wheel go [rot]. The wheel was rebuilt twice in my lifetime. He had a pretty good reservoir back there. You could grind several turns of corn and not have to worry about the water. Sometimes it would get low, and you had to wait until the mill got caught up, but like now, when the water's runnin' full, you could grind continually. It took about fifteen minutes to grind one bushel. At one time this was a two-story mill, and they cut it down to one-story. I believe it was a flour mill. They had a sawmill in the back of the mill to the waterwheel.

"In my days, a lot of people came here on Saturdays. All the bootleggers made whiskey, and they'd bring their corn in to be ground. Whiskey was a big business, especially in Dawson County [Georgia]. It was sure crowded around here gettin' three or four teams of mules and wagons and backin' them up and gettin' the meal out.

"We always had one fellow who always sharpened the millstones. They always said these rocks [millstones] came from England. Sometimes if a mill didn't grind in a good bit, you'd have mice. They'd get in there and build a nest. Then you'd have ground-up mouse in your bread! Every door has a cat hole.

"A lot of times when I was a kid, I'd have to tote a half a bushel of corn to the mill down here. The rest of them [Arch's family] would be in the field, and when I got home, I had to hit the fields, too; when you talk about havin' somethin' to ride in, it was always a wagon.

"Back then it took a lot of cornmeal to feed a family. It was cornmeal for dinner and supper. It's an amazin' thing that back then when we didn't have a God-blessed thing, we had all that good stuff to eat. We'd have ham, meat, biscuits, and gravy. And now what do we have? Toast and coffee. The old man [McClure] shut the mill down to go to dinner every day. If anybody was there, he'd ask them to go to dinner with him. One fellow told him, 'No, your wife don't know I'm comin' for dinner. She wouldn't have nothin' cooked for me.' The old man said, 'H——, we have somethin' to eat whether you come to eat with us or not.' "

—Arch Bishop, Winter 1989

"People don't pay money for havin' their meal ground—they pay corn. It's been like that ever since I can remember." ***—Pearl Martin***

In 1975, Claude Darnell and Pearl Martin described to Foxfire students the operation of the gristmill, including payment for services.

CLAUDE DARNELL: This mill was built in 1944 [by Mrs. Hambidge]. I done the rock work and worked some on the buildin', too. We grind one day a week, sometimes twice. They come from Franklin [North Carolina] and everywhere to have meal ground. They is one man that comes all the way over here from Asheville, North Carolina.

Oscar Martin, he used to grind. Alden Justice, he used to grind, and I'm just here when they can't find anybody else. I've been grindin' off and on for about thirty years. They get a miller, and he quits; I have to grind until they can find another. I don't mind it. I can't do hard work, and it's not too heavy work.

PEARL MARTIN: Now you take a person like Claude, it takes him most of the time to brush up and put the meal in sacks. Just about all the time keeps one person busy.

CLAUDE DARNELL: Sometimes there's a lot of people that come in, and then some days there's not s' many. They generally come in the mornin'. They mostly come in the wintertime. In the summertime, it's not too good because the water gets low; the lower the water, the less power.

The first thing I do when I get here of a mornin' is grease the whole thing inside and out. Then I go to grindin' if there is anybody here to grind for. Grover Bradley was here this mornin' before I got ready to grind. He generally brings about three or four times what he brought this mornin'. I have already ground about forty bags. Yeah, they come and bring their corn and have it ground.

People generally bring about ten bushels of corn. Grover brings about eight. We sell some corn for a dollar a bag, ten pounds in a bag. People don't pay us for grindin' it, not in money anyway.

PEARL MARTIN: Yeah, people don't pay money for havin' their meal ground—they pay corn. It's been like that ever since I can remember. We bring our corn down here all the time. When we was at home, before I married, we never did bring less than a bushel. Most of the people that lives around here now brings about a half-bushel. Just for a small family, it don't take much. **—Claude Darnell and Pearl Martin, Spring 1975**

SORGHUM MILLS

Boy! That was good stuff. It was good with hot biscuits! I wish I had some now. —*Jim Turpin*

In an era before supermarkets, convenience marts, and even Internet grocery services, families relied on country stores to provide them with the staples that they could not produce themselves: flour, sugar, salt, coffee, and cloth. Even when those items were available, they were often scarce, as was the money necessary to purchase them. That lack caused farm families to seek creative substitutions. One such substitution was in the choice of sweeteners. Appalachian families found and cultivated honey, sorghum, and sugarcane to take the place of sugar in their daily lives.

Old-timey farmers grew sugarcane and sorghum for making molasses and sorghum syrup. The time of year for grinding and making syrup was autumn, and these activities often became a framework for social activities.

To the elders with whom we spoke, no modern syrup available in plastic or glass jars in the supermarkets of today could compare in quality or taste to the sweet nectar produced by their own hard work.

—*Lacy Hunter Nix*

"And another thing my daddy had was a syrup mill, and everybody in the district came in and made syrup. We kids would play in the pummin's [a by-product of the syrup-making process] and cane while the adults were makin' syrup. We also sampled the syrup out of the boiler, and we had a fine time. We'd get out and play games—marbles, horseshoes—and fight and go on and have a good time." —**Virgil Ledford, Fall 1982**

"Daddy always greased the boiler pan with burnt motor oil to keep it from rustin' before he put it away each year. The next fall, it would take about two days to get it cleaned up before they could make the syrup. To clean the pan, they'd have to fill it full of water and take five or six boxes of soda and pour in it. They they'd take steel wool and scrub it 'til that boiler was perfectly shiny.

"The boiler sat right over the furnace. To keep from burnin' the woodwork on the boiler, they would paint it with mud and pack red clay under the edge. Finally, they'd pile the furnace full of wood slabs, ready to set it afire.

PLATE 146 This is the side view of a sorghum furnace. The smokestack is a fourteen-foot length of culvert.

"There was a one-inch metal pipe that was screwed into the barrel into which juice from the squeezed cane was caught. It ran all the way down to the boiler pan. Daddy would whittle out a wooden peg to plug that pipe when he got his boiler full. That boiler would hold about twenty gallons of syrup. It is made of solid copper because copper trays get the syrup the hottest. He had a plug in the lower end of the pan also; when the syrup was cooked, he'd pull that plug, and sorghum would run out. Nothin' was added to the juice. Just the cane juice was cooked. When it came out, it looked like honey—clear and pretty.

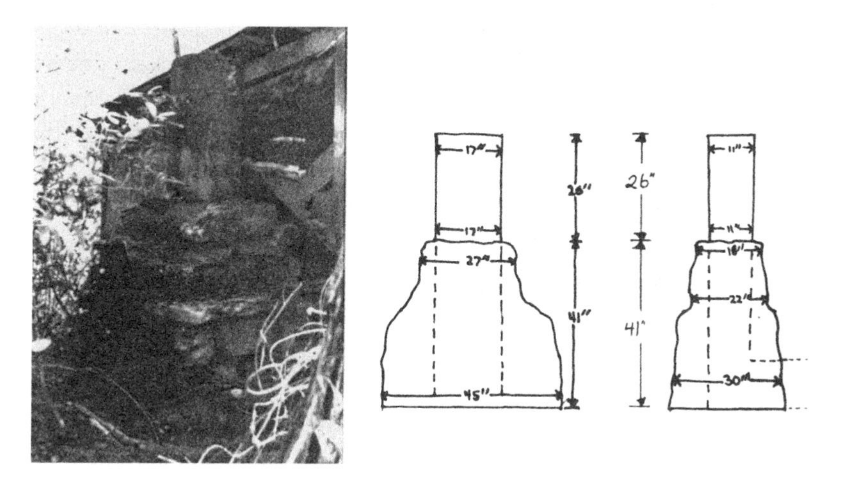

PLATE 147 Diagram of a sorghum furnace

"He'd make twenty-five or thirty gallons a year and sometimes even fifty. It depended on the cane crop. We'd store it in gallon mason jars. If we had enough, we'd sell it for seventy-five cents a gallon. A gallon of syrup wouldn't last long. Syrup and honey were the only sweeteners we had back then. We didn't have enough money to buy sugar. We had to either make our own stuff or do without.

"Boy! That was good stuff. It was good with hot biscuits! I wish I had some now." —**Jim Turpin, Summer 1985**

"We grew our own sugarcane for syrup and used that for our sweetenin'. My daddy took the cane to the syrup mill, and we'd go with him. They had a syrup mill over on Hog Creek up there on the other side of Hiawassee [Georgia]. We had to strip the fodder off and then cut the stalks down. We cut the heads off the cane, and then we'd haul it to the mill. They would grind the cane, boil the juice from it, skim the skimmin's off, and cook it 'til it was syrup. We would store the syrup in stone jugs and wooden barrels. We sold some of it but kept enough for us to cook and eat with." —**Minnie Dailey, Summer 1985**

SAWMILLS

I've been workin' with the sawmillin' for fifty-four years. I am satisfied with the salary or I'd have changed jobs about forty-somethin' years ago. —Lawrence Ellis

During the winters, when there were no crops to be planted or tended, local men would occasionally go to the woods to log out timber. Before state governments built roads and trails through the forests, many old-time loggers and logging outfits would take their sawmills into the woods with them rather than carry the logs out of the woods intact.

Sawmills, much like gristmills, used waterpower. Instead of a waterwheel, however, the sawmill made use of a boiler to produce the steam required to run the mill. When possible, logging outfits placed sawmills over streams so that the stream could carry away the sawdust produced.

Running a sawmill was not without risks. The following excerpt is a glimpse of the hazards of owning and living in close proximity to a sawmill. This excerpt describes the home of Bede Norton, the son of Barak Norton:

> A sawmill behind the home, on the location where Andy Cope's Recreation Area [in the Betty's Creek Community] is now, had a boiler fired by

wood, the sparks from which kept setting Bede Norton's house on fire. Discouraged, he moved in with Barak while building a new home farther away from the mill. [Winter 1977]

In spite of the hazards involved, owning and operating a sawmill proved a profitable way for generations of men to supplement their families' meager farm incomes.

—*Lacy Hunter Nix*

"Once in a while there'd be somebody haul some logs in on wagons wantin' it sawed to build a barn or a house. They'd come in and swap work instead of payin'. Most of the time, if they wanted lumber, they'd just come and work around the mill or work in the woods a few days, you see, and take their pay in lumber. And that was one of the ways they got their buildin' material back then."

—Millard Buchanan

"Back then you took your sawmill to the woods with you. You'd put it back in the mountains middleways of what territory you was goin' to log. Then you'd pull logs into it from all around, saw them up, and then move your lumber out. It would have cost too much to move the logs out if you had very many of them to move. You wagoned some, but you wouldn't wagon too many.

"You just took the mill to the woods, maybe saw a half-million feet or somethin' like that at the place, and then move the mill to the next place—just kept on movin' it back into the woods as you went so you could pull your logs to it on the ground. And the lumber, then it was all hauled out on wagons and took to a railroad.

"The sawmill had to be in kind of a flat place, a place where there was plenty of water on account of your boiler. You had to have plenty of steam. Had to have it on a good-sized branch [creek]. And then, too, they was a lot of wood moved by branches. See, they had flumes. I don't guess none of you's ever seen a flume. It's just a water trough made out of twelve-inch-wide oak boards, and two of them nailed together here in a trough—V-shaped. Or some of them be twenty-four inches wide and wouldn't be V-shaped. Then you turn water into them. Maybe go four or five miles back in on the head of that branch where it come out of the mountain and run good and build what you called a splash dam—just a dam that would fill up overnight, you know—hold several hundred gallons of water. Next mornin', then, turn the water into that flume trough and go to puttin' wood in it—just one stick of wood right against the other one. The water'd take it down. It'd maybe go three or four miles like that.

"Then somebody would be down there at the lower end where it leveled out pickin' it up and loadin' it on a wagon and takin' it to a railroad car. That was acid wood, mostly, and lumber, too. [**Editor's Note:** Acid wood is wood used in the making of tannic acid.] They'd pick up lumber the same way after it was sawed.

"See, that was a cheaper way of movin' it, and it saved a lot of time. Take a pretty good while to build one of them flumes, but they'd keep on lastin'. Wasn't too much repair to do on them either. If the water went to freezin', they'd take the water out of it so there wouldn't be nothin' to break it down. And then if it got a whole lot of frost on it, it'd run without water. It would run on that ice. But lots of times that was too fast. It'd run so fast it'd jump the trough 'cause there's places that'd have to be curved on it. And it wasn't easy to carry that wood back uphill to put back in. It shore wasn't!

"But a two-inch branch would carry that. You'd cut the acid wood and pile it up all along the flume, and then, when you'd turn the water into it from that splash dam, why, just put the wood in. Then that flume would be full all the time. You'd flume enough wood there to haul a dozen teams then, all day long on down to the railroad. Load it on a car.

"But now that sawmill, it took a big-inch pipe runnin' free about all the time runnin' water for the mill. And then the branch run through under the saw and carried the sawdust off. They used to put the sawdust in the creeks there if they was one close enough to where they could have that saw box right over the creek. Then you wouldn't have to have nobody to move no dust. The branch would wash it off—take it away.

"The mills was steam engines—steam boiler and steam engines. Fired him up and got a good head of steam up—enough to pull the engine—and you throwed the steam on the engine, and that's what done your sawin'. Had your saw just like they've got it now, but it was pulled with steam in place of gasoline engines.

"One of them steam boilers—one to pull a big mill—was a pretty good-sized thing, and the engines were just about twenty horsepower. Wasn't none of them over twenty horsepower.

"They was a little drive wheel—about an eight-inch wheel—on that engine, and it was cast iron—heavy son of a gun. And when that thing got started and picked up his speed, why, it took a lot to slow that old big cast-iron wheel down. Long as you kept a boiler with plenty of fire and water in it, you could have steam to saw on. Had a pop-off valve on it. They only got so hot, and then the steam pressure would open it up to keep it from blowin' up. When that pop-off valve opened, it was ready to go to sawin' then! If a man knowed how to fire one, he could just about keep that pop-off valve goin' all day long 'cause while they was changin' logs, his steam would build back up, and it would pop again. Back when timber was so heavy and so big, it took 'em a good while to saw a log up.

"The way they operated was somethin' similar to what they operate now. One outfit would saw—he'd do customer sawin', but the most of the time he logged his own mill and just sold the lumber—buy timber, you know, and sell the lumber. Once in a while there'd be somebody haul some logs in on wagons wantin' it sawed to build a barn or a house. They'd come in and swap work instead of payin'. Most of the time, if they wanted lumber, they'd just come and work around the mill or work in the woods a few days, you see, and take their pay in lumber. And that was one of the ways they got their buildin' material back then. Sometimes it was a problem gettin' men to work in the woods and the mill both 'cause the population was thin then. They wasn't too many people, so that was the way they'd do. They'd swap work for somethin' they needed.

"If they were goin' to be sawin' there for a while, they'd build a bunkhouse for the men workin' the mill. Shirley [Millard's wife] ran the bunkhouse sometimes and cooked for the men. We had our own little place to stay in, and the men stayed in the camp. Then, when the sawmill moved out, they left the camp behind. People comin' in gatherin' herbs could stay there, or hunters, sometimes moonshiners. They got used a lot, so they were kept up. Someone would come along and stay over a night or two and do a

PLATE 148 A working sawmill

repair here or there to keep it up, and the next man the same way. Some of them camps stayed there for years and years that way."

—Millard Buchanan, Summer/Fall 1975

"I've been workin' with the sawmillin' for fifty-four years. I am satisfied with the salary or I'd have changed jobs about forty-somethin' years ago.

"I learned how to run a sawmill when I was eighteen. I've never had any other jobs than sawmillin'. The only other thing I produce is my gardens and patches. I used to do my own loggin', my own timber cuttin', truckin'. I got sixty-two years old, and I thought I was old enough to retire. I sold it all. I sold my mill at that time. It got so borin' that I bought this one back.

"I have people comin' here and walkin' on a walkin' stick, and they'll say, 'I'm so old that I can't do nothin'! I'm just cripplin' around.' And I'd say, 'Well, how old are you?' They'd be about eight or ten years younger than I am. I ain't never stayed but one night in the hospital in my life. It was for kidney stones.

"My mill hasn't ever had a real name. I just call it Lawrence's Old Sawmill. The sawmill was made in 1934. It sold for $450 then, and now the same mill is worth $23,000 and some dollars. It's powered by a Yamaha engine, but it's almost wore out—got to where it wouldn't pull good.

"I get more business now that I used to. I saw more from Georgia than I do from North Carolina. When I raised my family, I worked to make a livin', but now I do it more as a hobby. I work just when I take a notion.

PLATE 149 "I worked to make a livin', but now . . . I work just when I take a notion." —Lawrence Ellis

"A guy came around—I don't know where he was from—wantin' to make a movie. That oak tree was green, and he said, 'If it wasn't for that big oak tree, we could get a plane in here. I'd love to make a movie!' I said, 'I ain't got time to make a movie.' I could have made some money then, but I'd rather make it from sawin' big logs." **—Lawrence Ellis, Winter 1989**

"My two brothers and I grew up around a sawmill, and then we started workin' in a sawmill in 1960. We still have the sawmill and work in it today. Our sawmill does not have all of the new things that the modern mills do. I always liked workin' around the sawmill because you are cuttin' lumber, and you can cut anything at any length you like, from a half-inch board to a quarter-inch board to any thickness you wish. To get four boards, you have to have five inches because you will lose a quarter of an inch to sawdust. The only thing is, when you pull one inch, a fourth of it turns to sawdust; so every time you need to saw an inch board, you will lose a good bit of the board—just like if you take a six-inch board, you will only get four inches out of it because you lose two inches to sawdust. The width of the log . . . you can make a two-by-four or whatever size you need. It's like makin' soup.

"Our sawmill has not always been in this location. The mill used to set over where my son, Ricky Speed, lives. It's not even a mile from here. We moved it over here because my brother owns this land. It was hard to get to, so we got it out here on the road where people could get the sawdust and get the trees in and out of here a lot easier. The sawmill is kind of like an antique today. You can tell we do a lot of work here from the sawdust we've got piled up.

"The mill has been in the Speed family since the 1940s. I used to work with my dad and my brother. After that, my two brothers and I were the only ones that worked here. Every once in a while we would get our grandchildren to help us. A few years back, my brother Neb retired from the fire service, and now it is just my oldest brother, Marlor, and I that work here in the sawmill.

"When we retire, I guess we will just keep the sawmill. The truth is, we are already retired. Last month my oldest brother turned eighty years old. I guess we are never really goin' to retire. We are just goin' to keep the sawmill to work in part-time.

"Most of the modern mills don't really have any hard work. Most of them have a log turner. Here we have to roll the logs down by hand. In the modern mills they lay the log up with a machine. If they want the logs to come down here instead of goin' over there, they just press a button, and it brings it down to here on a chain. In the modern mills, they have diesel or electric engines. Here we use a 400 Pontiac motor because we don't do that much

PLATE 150 The old sawmill on Warwoman Creek outside Clayton, Georgia

anyway. Most of the time we only work about four or five hours a day. We don't work many hours because of our health. It was really hot this last summer, and we could not hold out to do it.

"The sawmill was a way of life back in the forties, fifties, and sixties. It was just like someone goin' to work in a plant today. Back then, it was the only place to make some money. You could do that or cut jack pine, which for those of you who don't know, is pulpwood. You could cut pulpwood into five-foot lengths for seven bucks, and you would not make that anywhere else.

"I built my entire house usin' my own sawmill. We cut all the logs and split them ourselves. We let them air-dry, and then we ran them through the mill. We also did the paneling ourselves.

"All of the waste, we will pile up here in front of the sawmill, and people will come and get it. I had one person that came and got a piece of scrap wood and used it for a door sign. Different people get slabs for different things. My niece came up here and got a few slabs to paint and sell; it's a hobby of hers. The sawdust goes to a chicken farm or a chicken house, and they use it.

"The biggest log that I cut was four feet wide. We had to take the power saw to split it in half. Then we cut twenty-inch boards out of half of the log. That was a real chore. It took up half the day to cut up a log like that. After we split it, we took wedges to split the rest of it, but we don't do that anymore. The biggest ones we get now is around eighteen to twenty inches—probably one or two like that that are pretty good size.

"Most of the time, since we work by ourselves, we don't really have that many accidents here. We have had just minor cuts with the saw or the ax. My brother cut his foot one time, but, other than that, we have not really

PLATE 151 "I guess we are never really goin' to retire. We are just goin' to keep the sawmill to work in part-time." —Milton Speed

had any bad accidents. My brother was twenty-one when he got his foot cut. What made it really bad was that it was one of our own rigs, too.

"Used to, we would get the logs from the woods and load them up by hand. We would bring them out of the woods and into the yard. We could load them up and haul them in. Then we would go back and get another load of wood. My dad used to use horses and oxen to drag the logs, and he would use crossties. Finally, about two or three years ago, we bought a loader. We don't go to the woods anymore. It has been a couple of years since we have. It's just been piled up here, and, like I said, we are doin' contract work. We are workin' for someone else. I don't have logs here whatsoever. All of the logs I have here is for contract work.

"We did use the sawmill for a special project that we had. Before we cut the lumber for the house, we finished the log home kit. We planned to take them down to Franklin, North Carolina to try to sell them.

"I used to work in the Burlington Carpet Factory. I started in Burlington back in 1958 and stayed for thirty-two years. I continued to work in the sawmill part-time. We did not work for ourselves. We worked for other people that owned sawmills. Now we have our own sawmill.

"I would not advise young people to work in the sawmill these days because there are a lot of better jobs out there. It might be okay if you were to work in one of the modern mills, but there are better ways of makin' a livin'. I would definitely advise them to find better jobs so that they could build a better life." —**Milton Speed, Spring/Summer 2005**

LOGGING

It was hard work, but I'll tell you the reason I followed it: That's a thing they's fast money in. It's hard work, but it's fast money. Pays good money . . . That's the reason I fooled with it all the time and wouldn't fool with nothin' else.

—Millard Buchanan

Logging is difficult, demanding, and dangerous work. Imagine the physical strain and risk involved in going into the woods and felling a tree large enough to kill a man (or several) were it to fall in the wrong direction. Then, after the tree is on the ground, men must then load the tree into a vehicle and take it from the woods upon roads that are narrow, steep, and winding.

When Foxfire students interviewed local men about logging, the men were not talking about logging with our modern equipment and methods. These men remembered when loggers made their own roads through the woods and cut trees, not with gas-powered chain saws but with man-powered crosscut saws. Trucks to drive the logs out were not commonly available, so horses, oxen, steers, and mules had to perform the dangerous task.

Foxfire 4 includes a more comprehensive discussion of logging. Here we have included but a sampling of what we heard about this fascinating subject. Bill Lamb remembers watching loggers work with oxen. Millard Buchanan describes the gradual changeover from beasts to modern machinery.

—Lacy Hunter Nix

"Lord, the punishment they had. If there was ever a blessin' that come on anything, it was when they got the trucks and bulldozers to log with to take all of that burden off the old horses and oxen . . . They was some people that didn't have no mercy on themselves nor the cattle neither. That's what made it so bad." ***—Bill Lamb***

"They'd take them old log carts—I don't know to this day why they wouldn't trail up logs [place the logs in a line hooked together]—but they'd hook the oxen to them carts, and then they'd just have to scatter around to stay out of the way of that log pushin' that cart down the mountain. In the place of stringin' up four or five logs like people got to doin' finally in this country, why, they'd just have to outrun one log.

"I've seen poor old steers—and them with big yokes on—I've seen them have to run just as hard as they could run to stay out of the way of a log, and the log just runnin' them over. If it run out of the loggin' road and hit somethin', it was just about one's neck broke or his leg or somethin' 'r 'nother that way. Sometimes they'd try to J loose [run up and then to one side ahead of the logs; the motion makes the shape of a J] from one where it was on too bad a run. And if you hit a rock solid sometimes, just stall them just as dead as they could be until you pulled and twisted off.

"I'll tell you what I've seen. I've seen as high as five or six yoke of cattle to one log when they was in here loggin' out the old virgin timber. I've seen five or six yoke go through all the punishment that ever you see'd on anything. 'Course the ground wasn't level, you know. Just to get out, it was over a hump or in a holler. And I've seen steers picked plumb off of the ground by the head goin' through a low place in there, and then I've seen them goin' over the top with the old wheel cattle in back next to the log—maybe them pullin' over there—and them just havin' to slide their head right sideways in the ground to keep from catchin' their nose in the ground.

"And every once in a while an old steer'd get a foot cut off—catch it between a log and a rock or somethin' you know—and maybe just cut their foot just about off. Have to kill them.

"Why, it was a sight the punishment that was put on the old cattle. They was always short-legged nearly, you know, and couldn't get around good. People always used a whip as long as from here to that seat over yonder, and a man could make the hair fly off a steer with that. Them old whips a-poppin'—they'd go like rifles sometimes.

"And sometimes five or six yoke—and them all strung out—well, if the road wasn't straight, they'd go around a tree here and below a tree yonder—like people would do buildin' a road through the woods. They'd dig all the roads and put in a fender log and they'd come down through there and get at a tree and them old wheel cattle that was back next to the log—it was a sight to see how they'd goose them old cattle there with them whipstocks, you know, to make them wheel over to keep that log from bindin' against the tree here. And them other ones out yonder had lots of that load out yonder past that, you see. Well, they had to hold them cattle and their load, too. Well, that'd make the awfullest strain on them cattle ever you see'd. If it'd jerk them over and throw them over the fender log, then it was back up everything 'til you got them back up.

PLATE 152 Bill Lamb holds his ox yoke.

"Lord, the punishment they had. If there was ever a blessin' that come on anything, it was when they got the trucks and bulldozers to log with to take all of that burden off the old horses and oxen. Why, they'd have a great big barn full of cattle—maybe ten or twelve head of cattle. They was some people that didn't have no mercy on themselves nor the cattle neither. That's what made it so bad. A poor old steer doin' everything it could, and then a man just reach over and lift him off the ground. Why, I've heared them whips pop as big as a thirty-eight pistol—just 'Ka-bow! Ka-bow!' And if you was where you could see, lots of times the blood was tricklin' out of them steers where they was hit. They'd make a plait on a cracker as long as my arm out of thread; they'd beeswax that thread, and they'd plait it on the end of that whip, you see. And then they'd have a big, long whipstock on them.

Why, they could just stand here and whip one yonder at the edge of the porch and just make him bounce." —**Bill Lamb, Summer/Fall 1975**

> **"They'd [a pair of bay horses] stand there . . . and whenever I stopped over to get them lines, they'd hit that thing with everything they had in 'em. And if I happened to miss the lines, I wouldn't get 'em stopped for a hundred yards, a-hollerin' at 'em. But if I got a-hold of the lines, we went to the yard, my shirttail in the air!"**
>
> ***—Millard Buchanan***

"Loggin' with oxen—that's nasty. It's nasty when you're foolin' loggin' with them. The general field of loggin' is just hard work—work from before daylight 'til after dark. That's the general field—havin' to wade in mud hip-deep half the time and snow and ice the other half. That's like the kind of winters we used to have at that time. We've not had no rough winters in a long time. We ain't had no really rough winters since the early forties.

"We used oxen to drag the logs out of the woods with, and then we used horses to carry them to the mill and from the mill to the railroad sidin'. We used horses to wagons, and we used oxen to wagons. From the time the log started out of the woods 'til it got to the railroad sidin', it would take about three weeks.

"We had pullin' contests up until World War II—mules in their class, year-old fillies up to six-year-old—like that. They'd pull weights. You keep addin' on 'til they couldn't pull anymore. No money prize unless maybe you got two dollars and a half for havin' the best in the country. But everybody knowed you had the best! Or you'd get a ribbon—great big thing to hang up on the wall. Blue was first, yellow second, and pink was third. If you got that pink ribbon, that was somethin', you know. That was the startin' of breedin' up stock—cattle and horses—because from '30 until up about '33 was when they started bringin' this registered stock in here and breedin' up the size of them. See, that old-type Devon, they'd have to be seven or eight years old to get up around 1,400 to 1,600 pounds. It was somethin' unusual for one to get up to 1,800 or 2,000 pounds. He'd have to be ten or twelve year old. Well, you take the same cattle the way they got it bred up with that registered stuff, and by the time he's three years old, now, he'd weigh as much as he would whenever he was eight back then. Same way with horses and mules.

"I had a pair of bay horses. I reckon I kept them about three years and logged with them. And them confounded son of a guns would stand and listen at me drive them grabs [an L-shaped piece of metal that was driven into the log with a mallet in order to hook logs together]—and they could tell just as well when I got done drivin' the grabs as I could—and they was restless.

They'd just stand and paw the ground and look back at me. And they never would move as long as them lines was layin' on the ground. They'd stand there. When I went to hook the header—I'd just reach and get the header grab and hook onto the logs before I'd reach for the lines—and whenever I stopped over to get them lines, they'd hit that thing with everything they had in 'em. And if I happened to miss the lines, I wouldn't get 'em stopped for a hundred yards, a-hollerin' at 'em. But if I got a-hold of the lines, we went to the yard, my shirttail in the air!

"Boy, I pulled big logs with them! I've had eighteen sixteen-foot-long ones behind them at one time. Load three trucks with one load comin' off the mountain. That was over yonder above Cherokee [North Carolina] on Black Rock in that steep country in there. And that was virgin timber. We cut timber in there. We cut a lot in there that the four-foot scale stick wouldn't even reach across the end where you scaled it. We just cut all kinds of hemlock and chestnut in there that was bigger than the scale stick would scale. I pulled it with them little horses, too. I called them 'little' horses, but they was big.

"Regular teams, most of the time, was six cattle—three pairs for heavy work and heavy loggin'. As a usual thing, it was a six-head team. If you was on level ground, you wouldn't move too much in a day, but if you was on steep ground, you could take six head of cattle and in places trail as many as fifteen logs behind them—just looked like a freight train. And a lot of times, just one trip a day is all you'd make—bring in anywhere from fifteen to twenty logs at a time. Take half a day to go get 'em. Maybe be two o'clock before you got 'em all trailed together and ready to go out with 'em. And that one trip a day's all you'd make 'cause you might be pullin' two mile, two mile and a half—pull so far and stop and rest, you see.

"I've worked all day many a day and not even get one log to the mill—maybe take two days to get one log out pullin' him all the way. Flat ground, big logs was hard to move. Sometimes you'd walk up to one lyin' on the ground, and it was all you could do to see over the tip of it. They don't have nothin' like that no more . . . A few times I've had as high as twelve head of cattle to one log. Me and my buddy had three yokes apiece, and we'd pull all twelve to some of the big stuff to move it. It'd be so big they'd have to bore it and put powder guns in it to split it before it'd ever go on the saw carriage—quarter it up. You don't see nothin' like that no more, not in this country. It's all gone.

"Back then, they wadn't no roads. Roads was just what you made wherever you went through. If we was goin' to move a whole lot of logs, and a good distance, we used corduroy roads [see diagram]. You'd use that three, maybe six months—fix the road just for that. Them logs goin' over it would keep the dirt off the top of the poles for a while, and the logs would just slide across the poles—that would make them slip across easy. But you wouldn't hardly be able to snake on it for much more than three months because the poles would keep gettin' pressed down into the dirt from heavy logs goin' over them until the dirt would be level with the tops of the poles. And then you'd just have the road.

"Where the road had a dip in it, we put long poles in it we called bull poles to hold those logs up and get them over the dip. Them corduroys had to run just about the way they grade a highway now. What you chopped out with an ax was the road you had then—or what you dug with a mattock and shovel or one of those old scrapes or slip pans. Only way you ever used that wheel scrape would be buildin' a road to where a sawmill was goin' to be sittin' for three or four years.

"Now if it was to come a dry spell like this, you'd turn branches into the road to make it muddy and make it slicker to pull on. The rainier the weather was, and the harder the ground was froze, the more you could move, and the better you got along with it. Loggin' was better in the winter than it was in the summertime 'cause the ground froze. You really didn't have better weather—just better loggin' weather 'cause it was cold and the ground froze. You'd pull a few loads on the road, and it freezin' ice; that's when you could move a whole lot. When it would go to freezin' and gettin' icy, that would be the time to get the logs. When it was too rough for most people to get out of the house, well, that's when loggers worked and got a whole lot done. I never did quit on account of rough weather—that was the best time to move stuff.

"And you want to put your biggest log in front, your next biggest one behind, and so on down to the last. Leave about eight inches in between them to get slack . . . The cracker [the last log in the string] would go past, and he'd be a foot off the ground when he passed. He'd be goin' as fast as any of these cars that go down through here a-racin'. That gets your team out of the way so they don't get run over 'cause it's exactly like a freight train behind 'em, and I mean by the time they passed, they would really be flyin'. Over there in the Smokies, you turn some of them loose on some of them mountains, and it'd sound like a thunderstorm. You could hear them a-roarin' for miles.

"[Sometimes the team can't get out of the way.] They can't stay in front of the logs 'cause the logs run so fast they'll kill 'em—break their legs and kill 'em. We broke a few steers' legs and two or three necks. Actually, I didn't never kill none myself, but I've skint 'em all over. And I never was hurt myself—just skinned, get jerked down or knocked down, shins skint all over, elbows, knees, maybe a limb fly up and hit you across the back or shoulder or somethin'. You'd be sore for three, four days. But as long as I worked 'em, I never did get no broken bones.

"Now the team that was on the wheel—the ones that carried the wagon tongue—now they caught it rough. That front wheel would hit a rock, you know, and that tongue would hit that steer hard if they was makin' any speed—especially downhill. It'd just about knock 'em off their feet. I've seen 'em knocked plumb down to their knees. See, you've got that tongue right in that yoke, and if a front wheel hits rock or somethin' solid, the tongue slams over, and it hits that steer and jerks this other one's weight on him, too. Now that was rough on 'em, really hard on 'em. Wagonin' is hard work on 'em.

"Reason it took two men was one to drive and one to run the brake. You've got a brake on that wagon. The brakeman walked behind—had a steel guide with notches on it. You started goin' downhill, and he'd just mash down on that brake handle and hook it in one of them notches. If it got to goin' too fast, you just rare down on it and hook it in another one. Then when the wagon got down the hill and went to gettin' too hard to pull, why, he'd raise it a notch, you see? And he walked behind, and the driver walked up front—didn't have reins. He'd just talk to them, and they'd mind.

A Corduroy Road:

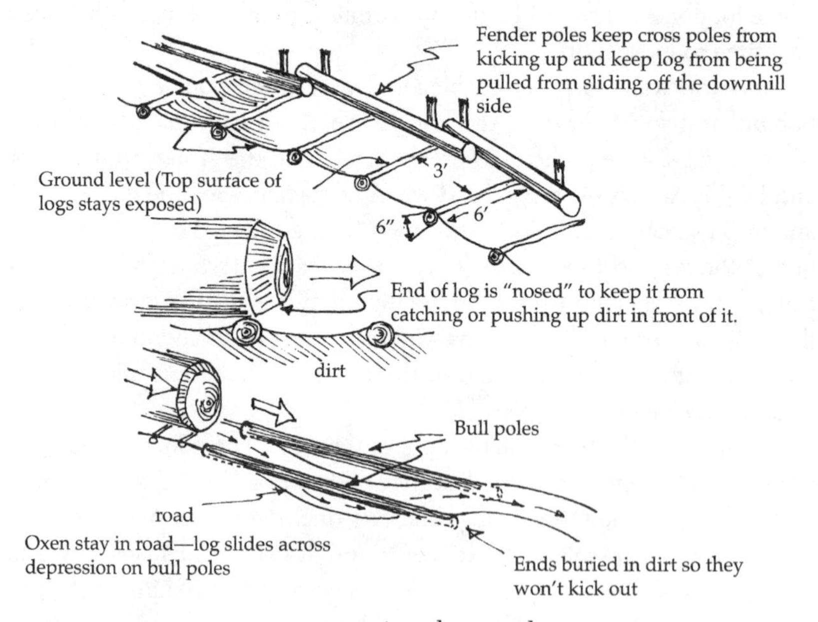
Fender poles keep cross poles from kicking up and keep log from being pulled from sliding off the downhill side
3'
6'
6"
Ground level (Top surface of logs stays exposed)
End of log is "nosed" to keep it from catching or pushing up dirt in front of it.
dirt
Bull poles
road
Oxen stay in road—log slides across depression on bull poles
Ends buried in dirt so they won't kick out

PLATE 153 A corduroy road

"They'd pull wagons more with mules back then than they did with horses 'cause a mule would go further and didn't take hardly as much to feed him, and he was much faster with a wagon than a horse was. You can feed a mule—just feed him of a night, put him in plenty to eat tonight and just get him used to that—and you won't have to feed him no more 'til tomorrow night. You've got to feed a horse three times a day to hold him up if you're workin' him hard, but a mule, you don't. So they'd use a mule—haul long distances with 'em and just feed 'em once a day.

"Now, steers were the same way. You don't have to feed them but once a day if you feed 'em good. You can take and feed 'em—like we fed 'em cottonseed meal and hulls—and feed 'em plenty of a night. They've got four stomachs, you know. What one eats tonight—he'll belch that up and chew his cud—and what he eats tonight don't do him no good until tomorrow. He's got to belch that up and chew it and let it go back into that other stomach tomorrow before it does him any good. And then they'd eat buds along the road, you know, and leaves and so forth and so on while you was workin' 'em. They'd be a-grazin' along while you was loadin' and restin' them. See, they'd fill that one stomach up there where they'd chewed that other out; then you'd lay the cottonseed meal and hulls to them that night, and that'd finish it. So that one big meal in a night was all they needed, and they'd stay fat all the time. That was another advantage of havin' 'em."

—Millard Buchanan, Summer/Fall 1975

> **"Hit wuz dangerous work, but I never did know of any of 'em gittin' drowned 'r gittin' hurt. They 'as pretty skillful men, an' they knew how to take care of themselves."** *—Jake Waldroop*

"I was born about seven miles from here goin' right on out Highway 64 [in North Carolina], but at that time they wasn't no good road. You went down through Wallace Gap, and a little old path went down and across Nantahala River and went off into an old cleared-off field where Sam Valentine had built a log house there. When my daddy went to loggin' after that house was vacated, he made a loggin' camp out of it, and that's where I was born, right there in the Roane Bottom, almost on the bank of the Nantahala River. I've spent most of my life through these mountains here.

"My daddy would take a contract of loggin'. He would put up a camp, and my mother would cook for the men. Daddy boarded the men, and he'd hire them to work. I was born there in the loggin' camp in the Roane Bottom on the Nantahala River where Daddy had a contract. . . .

"We had it pretty tough comin' up in the cabin where I was born. My father had a camp built out of logs and used poles for rafters. I don't think that cabin had any lumber in it at all. It had a big rock chimney, and they'd get up a lot of big wood and keep a big fire in there. Daddy had the kitchen partitioned off. All the rest of it was just a big livin' room; that's where we all stayed. Daddy had a little place built for the men to sleep, but we'd all eat at the same table. The workhands that he had hired a-workin'—cuttin' the timber and buildin' and helpin' him log—had them a little shack to itself.

"There was one section there that was a pretty big territory, and I guess it took him from two to three years to log that out. When he finished loggin', he just went off and left the camp. . . .

"That was virgin timber that we cut then, and they wouldn't fool with anything under twenty-four inches. They'd want it to be two foot or better. We wouldn't fool with it back then if it wasn't very fine timber. He'd have some logs that would have as much as seven or eight hundred feet to the log.

"He logged all out here all up 'n' down the Nantahala River. They logged with cattle-steers. And they built a big splash dam out there. The way they built them back in them days mostly, why, they built 'em with logs an' rock. They used some lumber in 'em, y' know, not a whole lot. See, they'd build them big pens an' fill 'em with rock an' sand an' dirt. They built 'em where they'd hold that water up. Then they had a gate—a splash gate to 'em—at the apron o' that dam where they could raise it or lower it. When they'd lower that, y' know, why, that shut the water off, an' that dam would fill up. Well, you got a big batch o' logs in the river. Why, they'd let the splash off 'n' hit'd come on down an' pick 'em up an' carry 'em on down through Nantahala Gorge an' on in there at Nantahala Station. There they had a mill, an' that's where they took 'em an' sawed 'em. They had a kindly a boom built out there surroundin' where, y' know, the river'd leveled off. They had cables 'n' things fixed t' stop them logs, catch the logs there.

"Well, my daddy, he put in a slide up at the Big Branch. They 'as a mile o' that slide. Well, they'd have landin's, y' know. They'd be a landin' here. See, the branch 'as comin' right through here. Well, here'd be a draw mouth of a cove 'r somethin'. They'd have a big landin' there. They'd land logs, an' on up th' branch there'd be another'n—then on both sides thataway. The mornin' that they got ready that they's gonna turn that dam loose, turn the splash loose, why, they'd grease that slide. And they'd be a crew o' men, an' they'd go up an' go t' dumpin' them logs, rollin' them logs off them skidways into that slide. An' they'd hit that slide, an hit 'as like a greased bullet, boys. Hit 'as goin' *Sh-ploog* into that river. An' they'd put thousands o' feet, an' the splash'd pick 'em up 'n' take 'em right on down to the station. An' there they got 'em out an' sawed 'em into lumber. I imagine it 'as shipped out from there to different points.

"Yeah, they had men. They 'as crews, when they turned these splashes

PLATE 154 "We had it pretty tough comin' up in the cabin where I was born." —Jake Waldroop

loose, that'd drive the river, y' know, an' hunt for logjams. I c'n remember some of 'em. They 'as Ed Cruse, John Winfrey, Lee Riddle, Swift McConnell, an' some Sawyers from over in Graham County. Yeah, they 'as several men that'd ride them logs right down through there, an' if they wuz a jam, why, they broke it loose. They'd just pick 'n' pries 'em loose with them peavies, them big hooks they'd have. Hit wuz dangerous work, but I never did know of any of 'em gittin' drowned 'r gittin' hurt. They 'as pretty skillful men, an' they knew how to take care of themselves.

"When the hired hands were workin' in the Roane Bottom where I was born, why, my father paid them fifty cents a day plus board. A day then was ten hours right out on the job." —**Jake Waldroop, Summer 1977**

"The roads were so bad then you couldn't get out in the truck much sometimes in the wintertime, so we'd pile up the wood, and when there was a pretty spell, we'd just load up, haul it down to Dil-

lard, and load it on the railroad. If we could get out of our road down there, we'd load it on a train car and ship it off. I done that until the acid wood was all gone."

—Billy Long

"There was quite a bit of timber here when my daddy came up here and bought this place. There was some sawmill sittin' right over there in that field. A lumber company came in, and they got this whole creek, Betty's Creek [Dillard, Georgia], and Barker's Creek. And he sold them his timber. They cut the majority of the timber that was cut then. They'd just cut out the mature timber. They didn't clear-cut nothin', just went through and got out the valuable timber. Seems like it was Genett's [Lumber Company]. I don't remember just who it was. That was before my time. They came in here and cut all that timber out. But, you know, there wasn't none cut for years after that, and the second growth came.

"I farmed mostly. I worked with wood a whole lot, too. Cut timber. Cut dogwood, telephone poles, crossties. I worked with my daddy and my nephew and my cousin. We'd just go up and cut the timber one day and get it out the next. We'd generally have two teams, and when we'd take the timber to Dillard, I'd take one wagon, and they'd take one.

"We used to take out telephone poles and haul them to Dillard. We'd go up in the woods, cut them, snake them out—pull 'em with a horse or a mule. They'd be thirty-five to forty feet long. I think maybe we cut chestnut timber for the poles—had to be so big, you know. We'd sometimes get out two telephone poles on a wagon. They'd bring five dollars and a half, I believe, per pole.

"I cut dogwood for shuttles after I got married. They used dogwood because it was firm, you know. We'd have to haul the dogwood up to Mountain City. They had a little shuttle mill there. They'd saw the dogwood up into two-inch-square lengths. The lengths varied, just ever how long the buyers wanted them to be.

"We cut chestnut oak for tanbark. We'd cut the trees down and peel the bark off in the spring of the year, and then just stand it up beside the log and let it dry. After it got so dry, we'd go back and sled it out. If we couldn't get to it with a sled, we'd carry it out. We got our tanbark here and hauled it down there to Dillard in the wagon. We made crossties out of those logs, too. We'd get most of the tree when we'd cut down one.

"This was government land we were cuttin' some of the timber off of. We had to buy the timber. You paid by however many cords you got, you see. For crossties, the government people would come and mark the trees. They'd walk through and tell you how many each tree had in it. Roscoe Nichols, with the Forest Service, used to come up here years ago. He'd sell

PLATE 155 Logging the old way

the timber. He'd figure out the boundaries in the National Forest he wanted worked. He'd come up here and walk up to a tree and say, 'That one's got two, three, four, or five crossties in it.' Sold the trees to the men who were loggin' for so much a crosstie. Seems like it was ten cents. That was about all the money we had. That's right.

"All the chestnut timber began to die from the blight sometime in the thirties. When World War II came along, they got to buyin' that dead chestnut. They'd make acid out of it and paper. That's after we had married—early forties. We went to cuttin' up that chestnut and gettin' it out of the woods. By then, you know, I had bought an old truck. Some other people was gettin' the timber out, and I was doin' most of the haulin'. We'd just get it out and haul it to Dillard on the truck. If it 'as pretty weather, I have loaded a train car load a day. Six truckloads will make a trainload. That was back in the early forties that I started that.

"The roads were so bad then you couldn't get out in the truck much sometimes in the wintertime, so we'd pile up the wood and, when there was a pretty spell, we'd just load up, haul it down to Dillard, and load it on the railroad. If we could get out of our road down there, we'd load it on a train car and ship it off. I done that until the acid wood was all gone."

—Billy Long, Fall 1986

The advent of automotive production and the ready availability of trucks made logging somewhat easier. As Millard Buchanan's description of log-

ging using trucks demonstrates, however, logging was still quite a hazardous occupation.

> **"I rolled a load of logs off on myself over yonder at Genett's one time . . . I was down in the millyard, and they shut the saw down; all run to me, and one of 'em run in and called the ambulance. They thought it'd killed me."**
> ***—Millard Buchanan***

"Back then, when we was workin' steers, they wasn't such a thing as a truck. You either skidded your logs to a sawmill or brought them to a wagon. They wasn't no trucks used in the woods up 'til '35, and they was very few then. See, you didn't even have a dual-wheel truck. The first one of them was made in '32. And the trucks that was first used back then was pulled with a one-wheel sprocket drive. They didn't even have a driveshaft on 'em. They was just one wheel that pulled.

"And they wasn't no roads to run 'em on because everything that was hauled was hauled with teams and wagons and steers and wagons, and it was just out of one mudhole into another one. They wasn't nowhere for 'em to go, so they wasn't no good, see?

"But the truck took the place of the wagon to start with. He [the truck] only delivered the lumber after it was ready to load on the railroad car. After he took the place of the wagon, why then, he gradually went to goin' back in the woods and takin' the place of the horses and steers. They got to buildin' roads and puttin' them back in the woods. But they wasn't too much of that done, now, until up in '37 and '38 when they started takin' them back into the woods.

"The first trucks was a very small rig. Well, they hauled an awful load for their time, but they didn't move too much because they was too small, and their motors was so small they didn't have much power. I know you know what an A-model Ford is. Well, you know about what you can move with a A-model motor. Well now, that's the size motor they had in them. Four-cylinder Chevrolet . . . it was the same size motor the A-model was. A-model was about as strong an order as they was, so you can tell by that how much you could move with it. That's the way it started out. If you had one you could haul three-quarters of a cord of wood on, you really had a good truck; but you could take a team and a wagon and haul a full cord! And you couldn't go much faster in a truck than you could with a team and wagon because they wasn't no roads. So if you wasn't haulin' somethin' but six or eight or ten miles, you could get along just as good with a good team and wagon as you could with a truck.

"Back then, you see, the state took the roads over, and they got to buildin' roads. Back then, they wasn't no road tax, and the way you built a road back in them days was with what they called a poll tax. You paid two dollars a year to vote—that was poll tax. Well, in place of payin' any taxes, you worked on the road one day out of the year for that poll tax. You either had to work a day yourself or hire a man to work in your place. And that's all the roadwork they was. They wasn't no state taxes or county taxes or nothin' on the roads, so the individuals kept them up with that one day of work. And then maybe goin' by somebody's house here along the edge of their field, it'd get real bad, and the field would be covered over in rock. They'd [the field's owner] want to get them rock out of the way where he was tendin' his field. So he'd haul them rock and pile them in the road and work it down so far. Well now, that's the kind of road work there was.

"And then the state, then, went to chargin' taxes and took the roads over and just went to buildin' strips here, yonder, and about. And the trucks then got to operatin' and cars got to operatin', and they got to raisin' the tax on gasoline and stuff, and that there's what made the whole thing go to buildin'.

"But, see, all durin' that time they wasn't no way for it to build because they wasn't takin' no taxes in. It was just like . . . if you started to go somewhere, they was half the time it'd just be like hittin' that field out there—gettin' out there and pickin' out a hard place in the field to drive on and hopin' it would hold up a few days for you to haul over. Keep somebody busy fillin' up the potholes where you'd mire down. Somebody was haulin' rock all the time fillin' up ruts. That's the only way you went.

"When it rained, you done work wherever you had teams and wagons, but you didn't do nothin' when you first started off with trucks. When it set in to rainin', they stayed parked 'cause you couldn't get nowhere with 'em. If you was haulin' downhill where it was fairly steep, you could take a good team and hook it in front of one of the trucks and pull him up the mountain and load him. He'd come down all right! But he sure wouldn't go up. Every time he went up there, you had to pull him up—pull him up there and get him pulled around—and then you could load him and come on out. But that was the way you done it and the only way you could do it then.

"Even when the first dual-wheel trucks came in, it was hard. You could haul the logs to the truck with a dozer and load it or drive on in, and if you got stuck, get the dozer to pull you out. Or put a twenty-foot pole in between the dual wheels and run the truck on that pole until you got out of the mud. I've poled out of many a mudhole like that—that, or pull out with a pair of horses or a skidder if you were close to one. Or if you was haulin' downhill, put on a set of chains and go in and then take 'em off when you brought him out.

"You know, you could outrun one of them old trucks anywhere 'cause that drive sprocket wouldn't let it go but so fast—it wouldn't turn but so fast. You could turn one down a forty-five percent grade and outrun it if you wanted to 'cause it wouldn't get no faster. It just had one speed, and when it got up that far, that's as fast as it would go!

"I rolled a load of logs off on myself . . . one time. I was about half asleep. They'd filled up a hole—I guess it was about five feet deep where we'd wallered [wallowed] it out with the trucks. They'd filled it up with sawdust. It was soft, and I pulled up to the edge of it and went to unload a load and chopped my standards out to roll 'em off. They was five of them logs rolled over me. Mashed me 'til my eyes swelled shut. I didn't even know when my kidneys acted or my bowels moved for a week. And you know, it never broke a bone. But now it shore messed my muscles up! But I was in the sawdust, see? They'd just filled the hole up with the dozer and smoothed it over, and them logs just rolled over me and buried me in that sawdust. 'Course the sawdust was hard. Hard enough that, God, I'll tell you, it give me a mashin'! I was in the millyard, and they shut the saw down; all run to me, and one of 'em run in and called the ambulance. They thought it'd killed me. I told 'em to cancel the ambulance call 'cause they wasn't nothin' wrong with me. Rolled around on the ground there a few minutes and finally made it up and got up and got in the truck and thought I'd go back to the woods and get another load. But time I got to the foot of the mountain, I seen I couldn't load when I got there. So I drove on to the house, and when I got to the house, I couldn't get on to the house, and they took me to the doctor. I was out about two weeks, I think, before I went back. Went right back at it again. Didn't have enough sense to quit." —**Millard Buchanan, Summer/Fall 1975**

Millard Buchanan also explained to Foxfire students the economics of logging.

> **"And back in them old dark coves in the Smokies, they used to be a lot of sugar maple that would go up six foot across the stump, and it was just as curly as it could be—what they called bird's-eye back then. Lord have mercy, if a man had it now, what would it be worth?"**
>
> ***—Millard Buchanan***

"We just cut the best back then—the biggest and smoothest. If you want to saw out good lumber, you've got to have good trees. Back whenever we was loggin' with oxen, we didn't cut nothin' but the best because there wasn't no sale for nothin' else, hardly, and even what we got out didn't bring much. We hauled many of a load of number one timber—oak boards that was eighteen to twenty inches wide and sixteen foot long, wide enough to almost make a tabletop, and it was clear all the way through. And we hauled it from the mill to a railroad sidin' and loaded it inside a railroad car and shipped it to Chicago for twelve dollars a thousand [feet]. The same lumber now [1975] would run at least eight hundred dollars for the same amount. We got twelve out of it. And it had to be good to sell at all. If it wasn't the best, you just didn't sell any of it. Cherry and walnut and oak sold better than any of it did. And we sold curly walnut, curly birch, curly cherry, and curly maple. And it wouldn't bring but twelve or fifteen dollars a thousand!

"And there was big chestnut. I've cut chestnut trees that had twenty-one cord of wood in them—load a full railroad car load of wood out of one tree. I've cut a lot of it six and seven foot across the stump. And chestnut wasn't worth nothin' 'til Champion Fibre Company went to makin' a lot of paper. And even then it was $1.25 a cord—that's 160 foot. A cord and a quarter is actually what you sold. And that was to cut it and take it to the mill! And a lot of chestnut sold for light poles and phone poles for a long time. Back years ago, young chestnut was about the straightest thing growed in the woods. We used to get them out and load 'em on a car fifty foot long and them be ten inches at the little end—put them on flat cars. We loaded them with a block and tackle and a team of horses.

"And back in them old, dark coves in the Smokies, they used to be a lot of sugar maple that would go up six foot across the stump, and it was just as curly as it could be—what they called bird's-eye back then. Lord have mercy, if a man had it now, what would it be worth? And they made floorin' out of it, now. And then a lot of it went to Chicago where they made furniture out of it. And some got gunstocks made out of it. And a lot of it was exported to Finland and Sweden. It was precut here to where it could be handled and put on the boat—four-by-twelves, six-by-sixes, six-by-eights—and then they recut it down to smaller sizes over there. What they done with it, I don't know. And then black walnut went to Sweden, too.

"But we'd start loggin' wherever the kind of trees we wanted were. We'd cut one kind one time and another kind the next. Maybe be maple one time, maybe poplar one time, and maybe walnut or oak. We cut more oak than anything 'cause there was more of it than anything else.

"So we'd just go where the most of it was and the best. A lot of times we'd get orders, and whatever they'd order, you'd cut. A car would hold about twelve or fifteen thousand feet, so we'd get orders for a [train] car load at a time, you see—mostly oak—and then we got a whole lot for hickory, see, to make wagons out of.

"Then after World War II, they [the government] had everything took over, and if you logged any at all, you had to have an OPA card to do it. [**Editor's note:** The OPA card was a card issued by the Office of Price Administration, a former government agency (1941–1946) charged with regulating rents and the distribution and prices of goods.] You had to take it to the

PLATE 156 Narrow-gauge railroad brings chestnut wood to the storage yard.

rationin' board and get them to approve it to your card. I know, because there was one time durin' all that that I had over 250,000 feet layin' on the ground ahead of me, and me loggin' with three pair of horses.

"It was all stamps then. You had to have that stamp before you could buy anything. The stamp wouldn't buy you nothin', and your money wouldn't buy nothin' if you didn't have the stamp. On lumber, if you didn't have that stamp, you couldn't buy it. They was tryin' to allot it out to where everybody'd get a equal share. Lumber was still goin' that way 'til plumb up after '46. And, see, there was a ceilin' price on it—they couldn't sell it but for only so much. Seems to me like it was sellin' for forty-five and fifty dollars a thousand then. See, there was a ceilin' price on the lumber, a ceilin' price on cattle, a ceilin' price on hogs—there was a ceilin' price on everything regardless of what someone would give you for it. That set price was all you was allowed to sell it for. The millionaire couldn't buy no more than the poor man could. You were allowed so muc h at such a price, and that's all you could get. If you wanted to build a new house, they would allot you so much lumber for it. You couldn't get but so much. You couldn't get out here and build any kind of house you wanted. You built accordin' to the size of your family, and then you got so much lumber to do that with, you see?

"And now that about takes us up to the more modern loggin' with trucks and all that." —**Millard Buchanan, Summer/Fall 1975**

FREE RANGE OR OPEN RANGE

Back then we had lots of hogs because you let 'em run in the mountains. You didn't have to keep everything in a pen then. Almost everybody in the family had a few hogs of their own. And you'd go out and feed 'em. It was a pleasure to feed 'em. You go out and hunt 'em up and feed 'em; it might take all day to find 'em. I enjoyed that a whole lot, goin' into the mountains.

—Mrs. Grover Bradley

When most people think of farms and farm animals, they think of lush, green, rolling pastures; big, red barns, and cows with bells around their necks munching grass contentedly. When many of the mountain folk we interviewed were young, however, such a scene was more fantasy than reality. The reality was that before the 1930s, most Appalachian folks kept farm animals in what was called free range or open range. That is, farmers turned their cattle, sheep, and hogs out into the woods to forage for food during the summer months. Only during the winter months did the farmers find their animals and bring them to the farm to feed. In those days, farmers fenced in their gardens and allowed their animals to roam free, quite the opposite from our modern gardens and pastures.

Many of our contacts spoke of going into the woods to hunt for their cattle or hogs (to bring them home either to be butchered, to go to the market for sale, or to be kept and fed for the winter). Milk cows wore a bell around their necks, and farmers brought them in regularly for milking. Farmers marked their animals with patterns of slits and holes in their ears and most did not worry that the thieves would steal the animals; in those days, people considered honesty and integrity more valuable than any cow or hog. Besides, if a member of the community was in need, neighbors would simply pitch in to help that person or family.

Several of the people with whom we spoke thought the days of free range were better than today. Some of them thought the diet of chestnuts, acorns, and other plants found in the woods, as well as the exercise the animals received, made for better meat. Others remembered those days as a time when the food was better and more plentiful. Most remembered that era fondly.

—*Lacy Hunter Nix*

The Basic Alphabet:

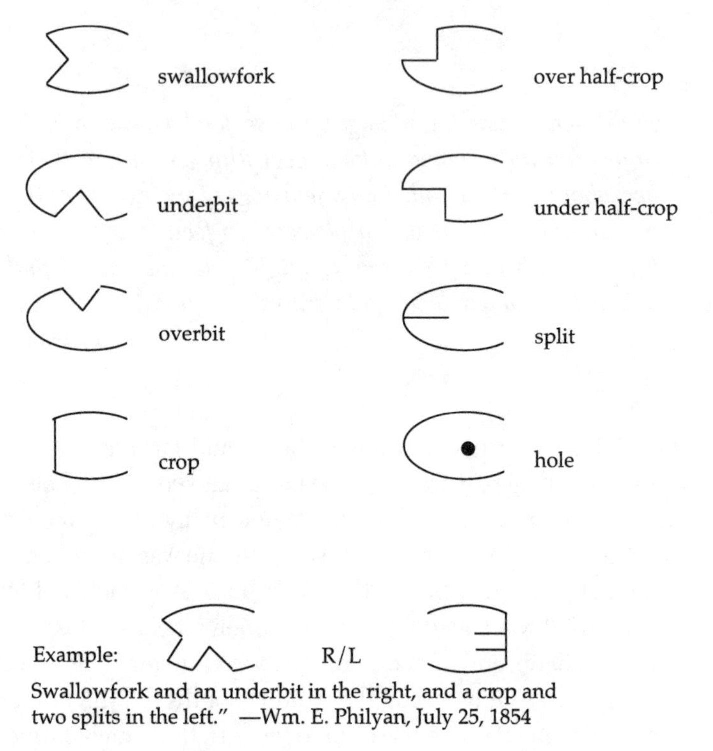

PLATE 157 Farmers used "ear crops" [cutting into the ear] to identify their animals.

"Up until the time the stock laws were passed that required all stock to be fenced in at the farm itself, most stock ran loose in the woods and grazed on what they could find. Dairy cows were kept close to the farm for daily milkin', but the others were taken out in the spring, turned loose to range, and then gathered back up to be fed at home through the winter.

"There was no pastures. Our cows were turned out—lay around in the bushes—had to chase them in to milk them. Get wet all over in them wet bushes. We didn't make hay—just corn and fodder.

"And we kept hogs. I let them run in the woods and eat the acorns. We'd lose a few back in the woods—never know what come of them. They'd die, some of them would—get that milk sick. Couldn't get home. It'd kill them. Or some were stolen by them too lazy to work—but not many.

"We'd mark the stock's ears. [**Editor's Note:** See the diagram for an explanation of the marks.] Everyone had his own mark so he could tell whose was whose. Our mark was two swallowforks and a hole in the right.

There was lots of combinations. Some had some of the awfullest darn marks I ever heard tell of. Swallowfork and underbit in the right and split in the left. Always marked the right and left. I saw a bunch of cattle in Atlanta down at a calf show way back in 1930, I guess—somewhere back in there. They said they come from Mexico. They had them cut all to pieces. I couldn't even read their mark.

"We used to range our cattle in the mountains. Had an old sow here one time, and she was heavy with calf. I was wantin' to take the rest of my cows to the woods in the spring of the year. So I decided I'd just leave her here, and when her calf got up about a week or two old, why, I'd take her on out there, too. Chase them up in the woods. They don't ramble off much in the spring—stay around pretty good. Thought I'd put a bell on her.

"Well, I went up there to Tate City [Georgia] and backed up and turned my cow out and put the bell on her—she never had a bell on before in her life. They got out of the truck, and away she went t' runnin'. That bell scared the calf, too. Man, had a heck of a time. Calf got away from the mother. I stayed around there and worried with her for about two or three hours, and that little old calf wouldn't come out to her. Finally I believed I heard the other cows a way up there on the mountain. I went out to my other cattle. Come back down there, and he'd got with her then; I drove her on up the creek, and she got in there with them. But boy, that scared me. I couldn't find the calf nor the dog either. He'd run off and hid somewhere 'r 'nother and just left her there, you know. But she wouldn't leave at all with that calf gone.

"Then the first black cow I had here—half Durham and half black—decided to take her to the mountains. She'd run one summer in the mountains as a heifer. Next spring I decided I'd put a bell on her. There was a great big ol' ditch out there from the barn, and I put a bell on her a few days before I took them out, you know. Boy, I never heard such jumpin' up and down and bellerin' in my life! She got down in that big ol' ditch and stayed all day. She'd happen to sling her head and wouldn't think; that bell'd ring, and she'd take another trip! They just have to get used to it.

"You could get out in the woods, though, and salt them, and they'd hear you go to callin', and, boy, you never heard the like comin' down off of them mountains just a-flyin' to get that salt. And if they was anybody else's with them, they'd come, too!

"Sometimes I'd team up with four others on Persimmon [a community in Rabun County, Georgia], and we'd put all of our cattle in together. Then we'd bring them in and separate them out. We done that up there in at Big Bald one time, and I never did get as mad in my life. Grady Ledford went with me up there, and Eddie. I'd been the day before, and I knew where one bunch was up there—couldn't find the other. We pulled up over at the mountain, and Grady was goin' to drive them down the Coleman River. Me and Eddie was goin' over on what we called between the Bald and Shootin' Creek in there and separate all them out and bring them down there. Pick him up.

"Well, we got them all separated out and walked down there—we was gone three or four hours, I guess—and he was goin' t' meet us at what we called the Wheeler Fields. And we come down through there and the bells a-rattlin' and goin' on and couldn't hear no tell of Grady nowhere. And we got down there and stopped, and, after a while, he got t' hollerin' a way up there on the side of Little Bald and it about dark then—him mad, too.

"Got up there, and he had a bunch of them in there. They was a lot of acorns that fall and they was just goin' through them cliffs a-huntin' acorns, you know. He couldn't do a thing in the world with them by hisself—had them here and here and there, and they was just a-goin' around them rock cliffs and over logs. We finally got them all surrounded up, and—I always used a walkin' stick up there—and I flew in there tryin' to run them downhill. And we had them all hemmed up there, and I was a-usin' my walkin' stick on them, and some of them pulled down the rock cliff there and slid plumb from here to that fence out yonder! We finally got them all separated in and got them all down there and had to leave them and go back the next day to get them.

"But he'd been all that evenin' tryin' to run them out and never had got them down. It was five hours, I guess, six. I could hear him hollerin'. He'd lost his dinner. And he had a rope, and he'd lost it! We had some terrible times with this cow business.

"Sometimes they'd get over on the Shootin' Creek side [North Carolina] and go as far as Highway 64—and that's a long ways—head of Buck Creek. And they was bad to get down on Nantahala.

"I had two, and Kate [Decatur] Burrell had two up there the year the war ended in 19 and 45. You know, we never got those cattle in 'til the sixth day of February! That was the year them forest [Forest Service] fellers had the little deer over there—they'd brought the deer in here. But they was there and had a little place fenced out and it sowed in rye for the deer. And they had some field glasses with them and saw some cattle up there on the side of the mountain—said one of them had a hole in its ear. I'd been over there inquirin' to him about them, and he sent me word that they was over there. We pulled over there and couldn't find them! They'd been three or four snowstorms that winter up in there. We'd find their sign all around there. Finally that forest feller put them up down there. He was a-campin' there lookin' after the deer, and he'd go home every weekend. Finally, he got ahold of them and put them in a stall over there. Didn't have nobody over

PLATE 158 Mack Dickerson tells us about the chaos that erupted when he put a bell on his cow and turned her loose.

there to help him water them or nothin', so he finally turned them out. We went back one Sunday mornin' over there and tracked them. He'd had to turn them out that night since we didn't come—we were a long time about gettin' the word or somethin'—so he'd turned them out, and we took their tracks out up what they called Curtis Branch. Found them up there and drove them home. Sanford Garland was at the post office lookin' for mail from some of his boys in the service and saw us go by and asked us what we were doin' drivin' cattle. I said, 'We're just gettin' them in from takin' them out last spring.'

"He went up there and looked at them. Said, 'Them's fatter 'n them I got at home, and me feedin' them all the time! Wonder what that [Forest Service] feller'd take to run mine over there!'

"You know them old big ferns? You ever see them out here in the woods? Ones that stay green all winter? That's what they lived on. And they'd get up under those cliffs out of rain and sleet.

"But you could trust people then. I lost a few over there, but not many. People would send you word, and you'd do the same. Them old folks is all dead and gone now. All of them honest. They'd tell you where your cattle was at—just worked through each other, you know. You can't trust nobody nowadays or believe nothin' they say, hardly. Ain't like them old-timers."

—R. M. "Mack" Dickerson, Spring 1974

"We used to range our hogs up here. The old hogs just ran anywhere they wanted to 'cause there weren't no fences. They'd get fat on chestnuts. Why, you could go out on a mornin' like this when it's just drizzlin' rain, and they would really be fallin'. You could go out and pick up a bushelful in no time at all. Some kind o' blight killed the chestnuts. They ain't no wild chestnuts in the woods at all now.

"I don't know, it ain't as good now as it was then because here the stock get out of the fences, and you have to watch the garden and put a fence around the garden and keep the stock run off." —**Edith Darnell, Spring 1975**

> **"Well, back when I was a boy, they didn't care how much you hunted or how much you fished. And there was more game then than there is now."** ***—Claude Darnell***

"Back when they had the open range, back when we had our cattle up in the woods, we didn't have to worry about our garden. We used to have twelve or thirteen cows all the time. We just turned them loose, and they would just run out all over this whole country. We would have to get out and hunt for them.

"I don't remember what year it was that the open range went out. I guess it was around '28 or '30. The people around here voted for fencin' in the land. There was more voted for it than there was against it. Well, back when I was a boy, they didn't care how much you hunted or how much you fished. And there was more game then than there is now. I don't know that it helps to stop the burnin' or not. I've seen these woods afire plumb around here—just a ring all the way around the mountains. They used to burn them—not all the trees, just the underbrush—so the cattle could have somethin' to eat." —**Claude Darnell, Spring 1975**

"I would like to see the mountains like they was when they had the open range. I sure as h—— would like to see that. We had hogs, and we turned 'em in the woods. There was plenty of mast [the nuts of forest trees accumulated on the ground], and the hogs would get fat. You put 'em up and fed 'em somethin' like a week, and they'd run all that. They had a better meat than the ones that are corn-fed. People lived better—had more to eat than they do now." —**Alex Justice, Spring 1975**

"It hasn't been too long ago that they had open range. People took out their cattle to th' mountains in th' summertime, an' you'd go once in a while an' salt 'em an' see how they was gettin' along. An' they'd stay all summer, you know, the cows that would calve in September, your dry cattle, an' hogs. When they put the refuge in, they just said, 'You're gonna have t' fence up your place now an' take your cattle an' hogs out of th' mountains or sell 'em'—'cause the stock law came into effect."

—Margaret Norton, Spring 1975

"We had free range back when I was young. All of these mountains were free range, and you had to fence your crops in. Everybody had sheep, and that called for fetchin' them from the mountains. Brother Jim and I had to fetch sheep when we were boys. Then when I was thirteen years old, my dad died, and we had to take on a lot more chores.

"Brother Jim and I built a sheep pen, and we had a black sheep over there that wore a bell. We would go over there to feed her and one of us would get on that sheep's back while she was eatin' her corn, and she'd just twist around and try to shake us off. She'd leave her head in that trough, still eatin', just as intelligent as a pet dog.

"A lot of time in the fall of the year, we would go out and hunt the sheep. Sometimes, though, they'd come on in by themselves. The black sheep wore the bell, and I remember I woke up early one mornin', and I heard the bell ringin' right up there on that ridge. She brought all the sheep in. We had twelve or fifteen of them then; that old mother sheep—when grass or stuff was bit down in the woods—she'd come home for feed, and the others would follow that bell just like people will go to a bell now. That sheep lived 'til the black wool on her back had turned white and the wool around her head was white.

"Brother Jim and I would feed the sheep, and we would help shear the sheep. When Mother had to take over after Dad died, she sheared the sheep and carded the wool, and she rolled it up in rolls about the size around of a broom handle. She'd spin that wool and knit socks and sweaters and winter caps for us children. She'd work 'til ten or eleven o'clock after we went to bed at night spinnin' that old spinnin' wheel. It's still upstairs right now. I can hear hit now. When she'd pull that wool out, she'd get a long thread just as true as it is today. The only way people will stay up that late now is to watch TV.

"We had bells on the cows, too. When we'd hunt a milk cow, we'd listen for that bell. You could hear it for half a mile. We knew right where to go. When that bell began to rattle, and she'd leave out, the rest of the cows would follow. They had learned. Animal life is sensible. It was interestin' to us back then to watch how the animals took care of themselves.

"All of the cows were out in the mountains together. They had marks on them, and we used to check the brands and bring ours home. I've walked from here up behind Taylor's Chapel Church to drive down milk cows—

quite a walk. That would take just about a solid hour. Mother would milk them and put that milk in that concrete trough in there. We'd churn every day. I'd set down and churn milk with a wooden dasher and a three-gallon jar, and that was real butter." —**Terry Dickerson, Winter 1986**

"I remember goin' back in the mountains with my daddy cow huntin'. The woods was just full of cows and hogs." —***Clarence Lusk***

"I'd just love for you to see that mountain country when I can first remember it to what it is now. They was people lived from here plumb on back through them mountains in my daddy's young days. People would hit the mountains for makin' a livin'. You see, they could range their cattle, grow hogs and sheep, and fence in their little field. They'd build a fence around their gardens and just turn the cattle and hogs out in the woods and the mountains to graze. That's the way they made their livin'.

"I remember goin' back in the mountains with my daddy cow huntin'. The woods was just full of cows and hogs. We'd mark our animals in the ear with so many splits. Some people would brand 'em, but all I ever knowed was croppin' them—cuttin' certain notches out of the ears. I know some people who had as high as three hundred head of hogs up there, and every one of 'em marked. They'd have big gangs of cattle, too."

—**Clarence Lusk, Summer 1985**

"If I was the boss of the mountains, I would put it back there like it was when it was a wild country—fill that mountain full o' hogs an' cattle. You take that mountain the way it was when the government took it over, they wasn't no tellin' how many thousand of cattle and hogs that was raised up in there. Back when they made me take my hogs out of there, we had seventy-five head up in there. Well, I guess there was a lot of them that would have run $170 apiece. Then we had all the meat we wanted to eat year-round. I raised more hogs than anybody up here. I didn't worry about that then because I had so much that I couldn't use it all anyway. Now I can't even buy a good mess of meat, and it costs me $11 to go deer huntin'." —**Richard Norton, Spring 1975**

"Mama's people were farmers. Granddaddy Johnson was an absolutely wonderful farmer. I grew up in a very rural area with a great big extended family around me, and we utilized everything. Cannin' and all that stuff, we were all pretty much self-sufficient because everyone raised their own vegetables and had their own cattle and pork. Believe it or not, hogs were runnin' wild in those days, and you could go out and get a hog and butcher it."

—**Sonja Stikeleather, Spring/Summer 2005**

"Used t' be open range. You fenced in your gardens instead of fencin' in th' stock. Lots of times cows would push over th' rail fences and turn th' whole herd into your corn—or hogs would slip in. Dogs would grab 'em. He'd squeal like he'd not come back for a year after they turned him loose, and then he'd be back th' next day. I've been awful aggravated in my time at stock in my fields." —**Bill Lamb, Spring/Summer 1970**

> **"Ninety cents a head if you want to graze 'em on the open range. I couldn't pay ninety cents for six hundred head of hogs with the rogues and rascals stealin' half of 'em."** —***Will Zoellner***

"Then here come the stock law in there, and when it came I had so much cattle, so many hogs, I couldn't put them on my land and keep 'em alive. I had to have that mast—the big mountains in there was covered in mast and white clover, and the hogs were doin' fine. But then, ninety cents a head if you want to graze 'em on the open range. I couldn't pay ninety cents for six hundred head of hogs with the rogues and rascals stealin' half of 'em. I was just gettin' enough out of them to do for meat. The cattle, the government wouldn't let them go at all. They said that the cows would browse the timber down—wouldn't let it grow.

"It had been burned every year. What was there was great big, and the ground was clean. You could see five hundred yards in that forest. When you burn the mountains, that sterilizes the country, and every tree that was alive was loaded with acorns. That's what them old settlers wanted—acorns for the hogs.

"They was hogs in the woods—you'd never miss 'em. Everybody'd go and get him what he wanted. I marked mine, but it didn't do no good. If anybody else wanted one, he'd go get him. They'd pick the best ones, of course. I'd lose about twenty-five out of a hundred. We stayed there 'til the government closed us out." —**Will Zoellner, Spring 1977**

FARMING

And we raised corn and everything. We would always have a pretty good crop of corn, have eight or ten acres in corn. Well, Margaret would work in the garden and leave the field to me. And the kids would work in the garden and the cornfield, too. I would work in the field when it was dry and do somethin' like gettin' out that bark when it was wet.

—Richard Norton

Farming as a way of life has disappeared all across America. Without vast tracts of land and commercial crops, a farmer can make little money working a farm. Our society emphasizes monetary transactions and accumulation rather than the production of physical goods. For early Appalachian people, however, subsistence farming was not a choice—it was a necessity.

Our culture idealizes life on a farm, much as it has many other aspects of rural life. Realistically, farming was and is a difficult, physically demanding, never-ending job. A drought, an ill-timed hailstorm, a fire—a variety of uncontrollable factors could destroy a family's means of existence almost overnight. Still, families clung to the land and the way of life. They made what they could and did without when they couldn't. With hard work, ingenuity, creativity, and faith in their Creator, Appalachian farm folks made a way of life centered around family.

The people with whom we spoke described for us a way of life that is difficult to imagine for most of us today. They told us about typical days and shared a few anecdotes. In 1975, Foxfire students spoke with Wilbur Maney, a county extension agent, who shared with us his insights on why farming was disappearing as a way of life. The factors that he mentioned are still prevalent in this area today. While the days of subsistence farming may have come to an end in Southern Appalachia, the stories of this time remain alive in the memory of local folks to this day.

—*Lacy Hunter Nix*

"My parents had old-time ways of farmin' that people don't use very much anymore. We always saved different kinds of seeds: bean seeds, potatoes, and corn. You wanted to kinda pick the best. In corn, you always picked a good, straight grain. You could see it when you shucked it. My daddy always wanted to plant that kind. When he was shuckin', he would lay them out.

"With beans, he'd let some of them go to seed. They'd turn yellow; then he'd pick 'em, let them dry, and hull them out. We used to make all of our soup beans that way.

"With sweet potatoes, you usually just take so many, bed them down in a tub or somethin', and they'd sprout out and get big enough to set out. We'd slip them eyes off and reset them.

"We just planted ever how much we wanted. We started at our garden here on the side and put a couple of onion beds in there—not too long, about as wide as this table—and mound it up. We called them beds—from one end of the garden to the other. We made two of them about two feet apart. Then we'd go from there with cabbage and tomatoes. We just dusted the vegetables very little. We never were bothered that bad with bugs. You know my beans this time—I never did dust a one of them. I've heard them talk about plantin' garlic beside of beans to keep the bugs off of them. Plant a row of garlic about every three or four rows of beans.

"We always grew popcorn and broomcorn. We made our own brooms. We made sorghum every year. We used to grow rye. Daddy never did grow

PLATE 159 Billy Long breaks up the new ground with one horse and a single-foot plow.

wheat. It 'as a little too much trouble. We had to go to Franklin [North Carolina] to get flour. I can remember when we'd have flour once a week, Sunday mornin's, for biscuits.

"I don't know much about mole beans bein' used to repel moles. Daddy always kept a mole trap. You could just set that mole trap and catch those moles. You'd just press the trap down into the ground, and it had jaggers on the side of it. The mole would mash the trap down as he was diggin' the ground up. He'd throw that spring, and the thing would catch him. The jaggers on each side would stick right through him. It always got him. My daddy would make and buy traps, both. I never did know him to keep but one trap at a time, but he'd keep it set and keep catchin' moles with it.

"We never grew any herbs. We got our herbs out of the woods—ginseng, lady's-slipper, yellowroot." —**Billy Long, Fall 1986**

"All the farms in Wolffork [in Rabun County, Georgia] were small acreage. The farmers couldn't afford to buy fertilizer and didn't have many cows for manure, so they learned to rotate the crops. They'd plant this here place in corn this year and sow it in wheat or rye in the fall and let that grain grow up. Then they'd rotate the crops instead of havin' to pay for the fertilize. They couldn't buy it—you can't hardly buy it now, $160 to $170 a ton, and it won't pay for itself. It just won't pay out now. A ton of fertilize won't increase the crop production enough to pay for it."

—Terry Dickerson, Winter 1986

"Back then, a day would be I would get up about six, and then I generally always went and fed the horse an' cows. I had about three or four. I kept Durham cattle all the time. They were milk cows, and we raised calves from 'em. Margaret has done th' milkin' all the time since we been married. I never could milk much to do any good, so I never did like to. And my mother, she done the milkin' on up 'til we 'as married. Margaret can beat anybody milkin' now that I ever seen. I bet you she has had twenty-five or thirty people out there in the last year tryin' to learn to milk.

"We had chickens, too. We had lots o' chickens, these big, red Rhode Island chickens. I wish we had some now, but you can't get any. And I had to cut up some wood or somethin' or other like that. I guess we ate breakfast around six-thirty or seven o'clock.

"And we raised corn and everything. We would always have a pretty good crop of corn, have eight or ten acres in corn. Well, Margaret would work in the garden and leave the field to me. And the kids would work in the garden and the cornfield, too. I would work in the field when it was dry and do somethin' like gettin' out that bark when it was wet.

"I was gettin' out tanbark [bark gathered by mountain people that was sold for use in the making of tannic acid] up on top of that mountain. And we generally started about eight o'clock in the mornin'. We would work about ten hours. We was gettin' it out with the horses, and when I got there, we had to harness them. And after we got 'em fed, we had to up the sled on them and ever'thing.

"We had two mules and two little old horses. They was small, but they was good 'uns. I would take an ax and trim the road, and the one I drove, she would come right along behind me. She would keep right up with me, and I never had to touch her. I never had no lines on her at all. I would just talk to her. She would hook the sled against a tree, and she would back up and swing around and come right on plumb to the top of this mountain, and it 'as steep as it could be.

"We hauled it to Dillard on the sled and up on a train car. We would get out a load about every day. It just depended when we got our last load of tanbark in as to when we got off work. Sometimes it would be five-thirty or six o'clock.

"We didn't get out the tanbark in the winter. You see, you can't get it out in the winter. You commence right now in May, the new moon in May. That's when the sap starts risin', and it'll start peelin'. We cut down the trees and peel it up until the first of July. They used it for tannin' leather all the time. I wish I could get some shoes tanned with it now. They would be a lot better shoes. It made a lot better leather when it was tanned with bark.

"Well, when we got in, we would unharness the horses and feed 'em and water 'em and bed 'em down and come in an' eat supper and set around. We would always, when we fed the horses, we would feed the cows and all before we ate. An' hogs, I always had a few hogs to feed, and I would do that of the mornin' and night.

"Well, in the evenin', I would just do one thing and another. We would work to dark and then come in. I used to do a lot of woodwork, and a lot of times I would do that at night. I made shuttles for them to weave with . . . I just done a little of about ever'thin'. I would get my leather from my neighbors, and we used it to make bell collars for cattle. I made my plowin' harness and lines; then it got to where you couldn't get that homemade leather, so we had to buy everything.

"A lot of times in the wintertime, I was huntin' when I ought have been in bed asleep. I would take the hound dogs of mine, and we would get out of the night and fox hunt. And we would stay out the biggest part of the night."

—Richard Norton, Spring 1975

"I don't hardly tend any corn here now—about a acre. You know, when Dad died, we divided up the property. Well, I got about eight or ten acres in cultivation. I got most of it in grass—just a garden and a tater patch and a few roastin' ears. I can't make corn and work, too." *—Billy Long*

"We've used horses all m' life. My daddy raised horses, and he had a horse and buggy all the time. I was drivin' horses when I was ten years old, I guess. My daddy would do the plowin', and when it come harrowin' time, you know, we had a disk harrow, and Dad, he never would turn me loose with the horse by myself, you know. And he would just work around the edges of the field to keep an eye on me. So he would let me do the harrowin'. See, he needed a little weight on the harrow, and he was too much. He just put me on and put me to draggin' the horse.

"After he would plow it, we would drag the harrow over it, smooth it down, and then plant it. Then we would have to work it—worked it four times with a horse and hoein'. We tended about twelve to thirteen acres in corn then. We used the corn to feed the hogs, cows. Sometimes we would sell a little, but most of the time we would feed it.

"Don't do much farmin' with a horse no more. I like a horse to lay off and plant with. A tractor is good to harrow with, but outside o' that, I had rather have a horse. I don't hardly tend any corn here now—about a acre. You know, when Dad died, we divided up the property. Well, I got about eight or ten acres in cultivation. I got most of it in grass—just a garden and a tater patch and a few roastin' ears. I can't make corn and work, too." **—Billy Long, Spring 1975**

"We butchered our cows and hogs in the wintertime. We generally dried our beef. We'd hang up the meat and let it drain, and we'd put it in something like a cheesecloth to protect it from the flies and gnats. We'd hang it over the big wood range in the kitchen to dry. That stove would heat the whole room, and we hung the beef in there. It wasn't too bad to keep. It was all the way we had. There wasn't many people who dried beef. It took quite a bit of work to take care of it, and it was pretty small stuff in those days. They didn't butcher an animal after it got over five hundred pounds. It was too big. Now they butcher some of them weighin' nine hundred and even eleven hundred pounds. Animals like that were too big for us to handle. It had to be small stuff—somethin' we could handle. Somethin' that big, you couldn't dry it all out. There'd be moisture around the bones for months.

"We salted the pork out in a tight wooden box and laid it up with salt, and it'd keep for months. We had a smokehouse right out there, and that's where we'd keep the salt pork and the beef when it was dry."

—Terry Dickerson, Winter 1986

PLATE 160 "They didn't butcher an animal after it got over five hundred pounds. It was too big. Now they butcher some of them weighin' nine hundred and even eleven hundred pounds." —Terry Dickerson

"Up here we just, m' dad 'n' m' grandpa, they just put in about ever'thing then, you know . . . about ever' field they had t' put in corn. We'd stay in the field just about 'til we got it laid by then. We didn't have nothin' t' do to it 'til the cuttin' tops and pullin' fodder off the corn. Tried to lay it by by the Fourth of July.

"They kept us in the field hoein' corn 'til it was a-silkenin' and tasselin'. We had t' hoe it at least four times. That's what they'd call 'a-layin' it by'—you know, 'til it was made. Then after corn got ripe, matured, why, they'd go back then and cut tops off it and pull blades off the stalk and tie it in a little bunch an' hang it off a stalk 'til it dried and then go back and stack it. That's the way they done up in here." —**Oakley Justice, Spring 1975**

"If you've got your own hogs and sheep and your cattle and your chickens and ever'thing, why, you can have your own meat an' eggs, your own cornbread." —***Hillard Green***

"All I got back when I 'as young was what I sold in th' fall. They'd come from Asheville over here and buy sheep and cattle and things like that. Always had a bunch o' sheep t' sell. I used t' keep about forty ewes all th' time and a bunch o' cows and yearlin's—yoke steers when I farmed all th' time for a livin'. I never could make a livin' without farmin'. With a family that way, you can't hardly make it.

"If you've got your own hogs and sheep and your cattle and your chickens and ever'thing, why, you can have your own meat an' eggs, your own cornbread; and we always raised about one hundred bushels o' wheat. And we never went t' th' store for nothin'—only just a little sugar and salt and sody [soda] and stuff like that. We'd get enough money out of what we sold that way. We'd sell our sheep—a bunch of 'em—and we'd get about seventy-five cents a head for sheep. When you got a dollar, it would go somewhere at th' store. You'd go t' th' store with a couple o' dollars and get more stuff than you could carry back home. You go t' th' store now, and it costs about fifty dollars, looks like, to get as much stuff as we used t' get that way. I've seen my uncle buy coffee at three cents a pound." —**Hillard Green, Fall 1970**

"Pauline was ten, Raymond was one, Mabel was five, and Tommy 'as just a baby when my husband died. He 'as a plowin' and had the lines around his shoulders; they hit a solid rock and broke 'em loose from the plow, and the animals pulled him up over the plow stock, hurt him, an' it set up pneumonia and side pleurisy—killed him. He had the check lines around his shoulders, and the team hit a rock and jerked him with the plow. Now that happened in 1930, and I raised the kids all by myself. I never did marry anymore. I didn't want to." —**Julia Alice Stephens Watkins, Fall/Winter 2004**

> **"We've had cattle all my life. I turn them into the cornfield and graze them in the mornin'. I stay out there with them. Sometimes I piece quilts when I'm with them."** —***Belle Dryman***

"Tops and fodder is what we used t' feed cattle, long back. And then we'd plant corn and wheat in the same field. Wheat growed in the fall of the year, and hit was ready in June. We'd cut it in stacks. The thrashers would come and thrash the wheat. Then we'd take hit to the mill and grind it. Then we'd take the straw and feed that t' the cattle. Hit's good feed. As long as we lived on the river, I never knowed my daddy t' buy corn—only one year. We only made enough to last one year. Sometimes bugs would get in the corn and tomatoes, but they weren't no blight like they is now. No animals, either, ever bothered our garden. They was never no coons or groundhogs around here, but there are now.

"Hit takes a lot of hay when you go to feedin' cattle. I still pitch hay. Hit's harder for me now. I didn't have no brothers—the women had t' do the work. Now they ain't nobody that you can get t' do nothin' much. That's the reason that I help Foy [her son]. He stacks hay lots of times, and I have went up on the cab of the truck to pitch hay.

PLATE 161 “I didn’t have no brothers—the women had t’ do the work.” —Belle Dryman

“If you tend t’ cattle like I do, I guess they will come when you call ’em. Mine do. I think I’ll keep that white one over there, just t’ see what kind of cow hit’ll make. I don’t git much milk. We sell three or four calves a year, and when the cows get older, we sell them, too.

“We’ve had cattle all my life. I turn them into the cornfield and graze them in the mornin’. I stay out there with them. Sometimes I piece quilts when I’m with them.

“People used t’ clear their land mostly with an ax, ’course the bushes and stumps with a mattock. But back then people didn’t have tools like they do now. Just horses and mules, that’s all they had to plow with. Now we ain’t had no horses lately. The way Foy works, why, he don’t have time t’ work ’em. We just have a tractor.” —**Belle Dryman, Winter 1976**

In the Spring 1975 issue of The Foxfire Magazine, *students asked Wilbur Maney, who was then the agricultural extension agent for Rabun County, to identify some of the factors causing farming to pass out of favor as a way of life. Following is his opinion on the subject, beginning with an answer to the question of what was the biggest problem a farmer in Rabun County had to face.*

“Rabun County rain. With a slow horse, you can turn an acre . . . well, it takes quite a while . . . and we get eighty or ninety inches of rain, most of it coming around April and May, and you got to have your corn in by May 15 to let it grow good. Even though they had all the time they needed, the weather didn't always cooperate with them. That's it: getting the corn in the ground in the spring and, once it is made, gettin' it out in the fall of the year. You can't go in the field with a mule and a wagon when the wheel goes down a foot deep in the ground in the mud.

"When they stopped the open range, that stopped a lot of agriculture. Two things that had an effect on that were the railroad trains and the highway. The train was killin' a lot of the animals, and as the insurance companies found out, the animals that the train hit were the best ones in the herd. So the railroad people said, 'Let all these people put these animals in a fence.' And there was no insurance on cars, and the motorists said, 'We are tired of hittin' these animals. If a farmer wants to keep an animal, let him build a fence.'

"Most of the land on Betty's Creek is in grass now—not much farmin'. Once it was all in corn and small grain. Corn is too expensive to grow now. People can make more money doin' other things. Now it costs $110 an acre to grow. That includes fertilizer, seed, labor, and machinery. You get anywhere from 140 to 150 bushels to the acre. Right now, corn is sellin' for $3 a bushel, which would bring you $300 clear profit, but this is the highest corn has been in my lifetime. Usually, corn sold anywhere from $1 to $1.50 a bushel. Back durin' the Depression, I guess a lot of people worked all day for a peck of corn, and it was at one time, the main crop. They fed it to their hogs, give the shucks to the cows. They used every bit.

"And when there was open range and the hogs could make it on berries and chestnuts and acorns, they could get really fat in the fall of the year 'cause there was a tremendous food supply from the chestnuts alone. But I don't guess there is a dozen hogs on Betty's Creek now. You have to feed 'em corn, and it isn't worth it. Most people don't like to feed hogs—don't like that odor. And then hog cholera killed most of 'em out in the late thirties.

"Back in those days, they weren't the same type of cattle we've got today. That has all changed, too, over the years. Cattle then could survive on a small amount of feed. The cattle now would starve to death on the open range. Today's cattle are not bred for such. They are raised up to put the feed to 'em, and if they don't get it, they starve.

"People quit keepin' cows because their families aren't so big anymore. As the times changed, people started sellin' the milk they didn't need. Okay, the laws began to change, and they put their milk into five-gallon containers, set it along the side of a road, and a man would come along and haul it to a creamery. Then people began to say, 'Well, this is not the most sanitary thing.' The law said that you've got to keep this in a milk house, keep it cool.

PLATE 162 Wilbur Maney talked to Foxfire about how new laws changed farming.

Then with electricity came the bulk tank, and they are very expensive. Now only a few people own a cow." —**Wilbur Maney, Spring 1975**

"People used to stay at home and work—made what they had and done without what they didn't make . . . I think people were happier then than they are now. They appreciated what they did get."

—**Belle Dryman, Winter 1976**

THE MOUNTAINS

If I was in charge of the mountains, I'd just let 'em be natural. I think once in a while the timber should be cut off of 'em because when it gets big, it just falls down and knocks others over. But so far as to puttin' houses on top of 'em and big highways on top of 'em, I don't agree with that. Of course it don't look fair for some people to own ever'thing and some people not to have anything. But you could start out and divide everything equally with ever'-body, and how long would it be before somebody would be out? That is what the people here say.

—Margaret Norton

For many of us raised in the mountains, our identity is tied to this wonderful place that we call our home. Sure, we are humans; we are Americans; we are even Southerners; but most important of all, we are mountain folk, born of great pioneers who survived almost insurmountable odds. Those old mountaineers left us a legacy of independence of spirit, yet interdependence with our community; courage in the face of great challenge, yet humility in the face of our Maker's mighty creation.

For many of our contacts, these mountains are a gift, a heritage, to be preserved and passed on to the next generation. We may disagree on the method of preservation. We may disagree on the best use of the land. We may even disagree on whether those outsiders are helping or hurting our precious home, but we all agree that these mountains and this place are a gift that we must treasure and protect.

—Lacy Hunter Nix

"The mountains were more precious than ever when I got back from those wars—not only the mountains but the whole United States."

—Bob Justus

"I got to Korea, and one bitter cold winter day, there was a group of us walking around the side of this snowy hillside above a little village, and I heard this whistle way off. We turned around and looked: Coming out of the valley into the mountains was this steam engine, and it sounded just like the one that used to run in Rabun County. I'll never forget how that old, mournful whistle just brought tears to my eyes 'cause I'd never been away from home before. I was just young—eighteen, nineteen years old. There I was in Korea, and it sounded like home.

"The mountains were more precious than ever when I got back from those wars—not only the mountains but the whole United States. When I came back on the ship was early one mornin', and the fog was on the water outside the California coast there; then the sun broke through. We were approaching the Golden Gate Bridge, and the sun was shining on that golden color, that Golden Gate. And not just me, but several on that ship, tears were flowing down their face . . . Each time I come back, actually, I start drivin' and climbing these mountains, and it all comes back to me—you know, the way I was raised and the life I lived, and it was just a rush of a great feelin'.

"I believe in the integrity of keeping our own sovereignty. I don't believe in selling out to the United Nations. I don't believe in one-world government, is what I'm tryin' to say. I believe that if we become a one-world government, we're gonna lose our freedom and gonna lose our identity. I don't care. That's why I was opposed to that World Trade Organization.

"These people you'll never see in these back rooms are gonna be making decisions about what we buy and sell; and eventually it will drag down just like the school systems have done, in my opinion, and drag down everybody to a lower level, and we're gonna be turned into a third-rate country like some others. See, I've been over in other countries, and American people'd better wake up. There's never been on the face of the Earth a nation blessed with more than we've got, includin' freedom, even the poorest . . . Almost anyone in America can make a livin' and have decent shelter. I mean, look at what a lot of us lived in when I was a kid and the hard, hard work we used to have to do.

"So you ask me, and I tell you: I really believe it was an honor to serve the United States. See, it goes back to—it was still being taught when I was in school—patriotism. It wasn't what the government owes you or the country owes you, but it taught us to appreciate our country and to do what we could for it. I don't agree with everything in Kennedy's life, but you know what his statement was: 'Don't ask what your country can do for you but what you can do for your country.' That's what makes countries great. But it boils down to fighting, and I think what carries most all men in war is your home, your family, and America is your home, your family. You think about that.

"I used to have dreams about these beautiful mountains. I've written an article about this dream I had in Korea. More than once that dream'd pop up. And I'd walk down out of the cove—and this is a true story—I'd walk down out of the cove on the Big Face Mountain, and there a little stream came out of that cove and flattened out, went among these great oak trees, and I think near the creek was poplar. There was an open kind of glade there surrounded by trees, and there were ferns, high as my head, ferns growing along the stream. And I walked out. I'd been squirrel hunting. All along the sandbar there among those ferns were thousands, I guess, of beautiful white butterflies. And when I'd walk, they'd all come up in a great swarm, and the sun was shining down. It's just like a picture of paradise, and I would dream that in Korea. So when I got back home, I went back up there. 'Course, it wasn't the same time o' year, but, you know, it was still there. That beautiful little glade was still there. And so help me, I never dreamed that again 'til I went to Vietnam years later—over a decade later. I had the same dream two or three times. Anyways, I was back home, and it was some time 'fore I got around to gettin' back up there. Used to go up there hunting. At the headwaters, we'd catch a lot of brook trout. So I went up there, and—I'm not sayin' this to resent 'em; in fact, I think they're a nice couple from Florida—this couple had the back part of this land and built 'em a house there. Right where that glade used to be with all those marvelous butterflies and ferns growin' up high as your head was this house, and they'd cut those trees and made a pond." —**Bob Justus, Fall/Winter 2001**

"I think we're the luckiest people in the world right here. I've been many places. I've been all across the United States. I've been to Washington and to most of the states close to home. I've traveled a lot, and I've not found anywhere yet that I love more than these mountains. I wouldn't want to live anywhere else but Rabun County or Macon County [North Carolina] because I was born and raised here, and it's a pretty country. I don't like the city—you don't have room.

"I don't know about Georgia anymore, but the Florida folks and the folks from other places, they're goin' to take over North Carolina after a while. There's houses stuck up on every little mountaintop. I've not got nothin' against the people because I think there's some nice folks that comes from other places here and settles down, but I don't think they ought to just come in and take over.

"What kind of a country are we goin' to have after a while if we let everybody from all over the world come in and settle in our mountains? What are we goin' to have after a while? It's serious to me. Of course, I don't mind it for myself because I know I'll not be here, but my children will be here and my grandchildren.

"These people [from outside] are speculatin'. They're makin' big money. They go back and make fun of the people up here. They call us hillbillies. They don't think we have any sense. They get everything off of us for little or nothin', and then they sell it for a big price.

"I think they've ruined our peaceful country. They come in here. They buy land. They won't let you walk on it. They put out a sign sayin' 'No trespassing' and put up gates and fences, and what benefit are they to North Carolina or Georgia? They come and stay about two or three months. They never buy a car tag up here. They run you off the streets, and they crowd you in town. They swirl all over the road gazin' at everything instead of stoppin' and lookin'. I think they're more harm to us than good. Maybe I ought not, but I believe that. The only way to do is for mountain people to quit sellin' their land to them. I don't know what else to do.

"Sometimes I think if these people had to go back and live about fifty, sixty years ago, just turn back time from 1910 thereon up to 1920, and let 'em share just what people had at that time, I wonder what this world would be. I wonder what people would be anyhow. The people, I wonder what they would do." —**Addie Norton, Fall 1976**

> **"I'd just like to see more people wake up and see what they're doing. It's amazing what you can do with just common sense. Maintain a border on all your streams; keep your land from erosion whether you got a farm or whether you just got a lot."** —***Bob Justus***

"These mountains [Habersham County, Georgia] are just not the way they were when I was a kid, though. It's been trashed. I don't understand. My grandparents, my dad, when I began high school, they were teaching us in school to preserve the land: row cropping and the terracing and maintaining trees and foliage along streams and all that good stuff. And years before that, they had farmed badly. That erosion ruined a lot of the land, and the early cutting of the forest ruined a lot of the streams early on. But anyway, we're doing worse today than we did fifty years ago.

"If you talk to an individual, they say they care. I was never much of a joiner, but I've joined the Smart Growth Coalition and the Soque River Watershed Association. Now 'home,' by the way, when I say it, is always Rabun County. I mean, really this house is my home with my wife and the children nearby, but what I mean is, to me, the ancestral home, the childhood home. That's always there.

"Now it grieves me. Like that lovely valley where I was raised—it's been trashed. Those beautiful mountainsides have been scalped—and the beautiful, wonderful trout stream we had with the deep, dark holes and the grapevines growing over the stream and the ferns along the banks and snakes and frogs and turtles, all the insect life in the summertime just swarming with all this different kinds of water life, see. Now you walk down there, and it's full of sand and mud and the banks caving in and cattle everywhere. A recent report I read was where they took a test somewhere on the creek. It had too much *E. coli* and very few fish anymore and very few frogs. It's that way on the lakes, too.

"We used to go to Lake Burton. 'Course, there 'as very few houses then—mostly woods. I have fished over there as a boy and met a moonshiner with a boatload of moonshine in the daylight. Jumped out on the bank to get a plug loose from a tree, and there at my feet would be moonshine behind a log. That's how remote it was, you know. Then the lake was full of fish, and sometimes we'd cook 'em for breakfast or midnight or whenever we got done. And we began to cook all the little frog legs and whatever we had to go with it. Fifteen years before Dad died, we was over there fishin', and I said, 'I don't hear no frogs.'

"He said, 'They're gone.' He said, 'They're almost all gone.'

"That's the way it is now. 'Course, it's probably pollution and too much wave action. Frog eggs and most fish are in shallow water, and that's where they lay their eggs.

"But that's life now. There's just too many people livin' that close to the lake, but it's a nationwide, and even gettin' to be a worldwide, problem. The frogs and lizards, spring lizards are the first ones to be affected by poison. I don't know. I'd just like to see more people wake up and see what they're doin'. It's amazing what you can do with just common sense. Maintain a border on all your streams; keep your land from erosion whether you got a farm or whether you just got a lot. I tried here on this place to keep every tree I could possibly keep and had to cut some 'cause every time I had a ice storm, there'd be limbs on top of the house. But that's the way we was raised. I'm not saying we were perfect. We were far from perfect, but, overall, we took care of the land. I remember that time when the government came along and said, 'Well, there's too much erosion. We're goin' to spend millions of dollars and bring rock in here and put 'em on the stream banks to stop this erosion.'

"My dad and grandfather, Neal and Jesse Justus, told 'em, 'We don't need any.'

" 'What do you mean?'

" 'We're takin' care of our land,' and they were. They had all that growth along the stream banks. They didn't need no rocks, and they didn't take any. I read not long ago that most of that was a failure. You just cannot dump a bunch of rocks, especially if the cause is continuing on. I just believe that I learned a lot of respect about it, and I think it's common sense. I don't care what anybody says.

"I've got friends in the Forest Service, but I never, and Dad didn't either, agreed with the clear cut, not on the scale that they're doin' it. Here's what I believe: Nature or God or whatever had the right things growin' where they should be growin'. And for man to come along and say, 'Ah, we don't need none of this,' and whack it all out, you know, especially with many, many acres over steep hillsides, is just not necessary. So, as a result, I think it's caused a lot of harm.

"But now the great harm is development. Everybody wants to come to these lovely mountains. If they keep developing, they won't be lovely, see? Here's the thing: A lot of the people that appreciate it the most—the mountains and what we have here, and join like the Smart Growth Coalition, or like up in Rabun County, I guess it's the Chatooga River Coalition or whatever you call it—is the people who move here from somewhere else and see what's still here and what is gonna happen. There's no question in my mind. These four-lanes, see, they're gonna build another one east to west. Habersham County is fixin' to turn into a giant bedroom community of Atlanta. Just in one year, a hundred new subdivisions was approved, last twelve months. It just eats my heart out.

"There's so many people that's shortsighted. They just don't think ahead. A lot of people that mean well, they don't want no kind of rules or no kind of laws to govern what they do with their land, but it's all bein' destroyed. I don't know the answer. I just hope that they can work out some things, save some things for guys like your age, your family. I mean, where you gonna go? I just hope and pray that people will wake up.

"During and after the Great Depression, they began to use CCC [Civilian Conservation Corps] camps. They corrected a lot of things like that. They began to bring the land back then. They restored watersheds; they began to practice terracing so all the water doesn't rush downhill at one time in great force. I notice a lot of farms now. They're bulldozing away those terraces. They want it all smooth, see. They don't think. You got grass, thick enough sod; they hold most of your land together, but on these slopes, the water's gonna shoot off. It's not gonna stay, and it's gonna hit down there on the stream with a great force and undermine it. Trees are gonna topple in. That's why anywhere you go, any of these streams and rivers, you'll see trees toppling in on great bodies of water." —**Bob Justus, Fall/Winter 2001**

ETTA: You take, for instance, as you go toward Blowin' Rock, they have bulldozed that hill off, and that's an ugly sight. Oh, it's ugly. And that was a beautiful place. I hate to see these places done that way. I think it should be left like Nature intended it to be.

CHARLIE: Everybody from away from here wants a place in the mountains now. I could just walk out here and stick a little note up "for sale" and sell this place maybe that day. But there's a lot of us don't want to do that. Others, whenever stuff goes to gettin' up in value, we all get excited. We want to bore with a bigger auger. But me and Etta, we're not goin' to do that. We never have. **—Etta and Charley Ross Hartley, Spring 1976**

> **"The beauty that is in this earth is something that folks appreciate and enjoy, and it doesn't get out of style. There may not be that big hoopla over it like there is over the Internet, Cabbage Patch dolls, or Disney World and that kind of stuff, but I think when all of that's gone, we'll still have Tallulah Gorge, and we'll have the Rocky Mountains and the Appalachian Mountains."** ***—Bill Tanner***

"Tallulah Gorge [in Tallulah Falls, Georgia] was formed hundreds of thousands of years ago through a combination of several geological actions. Upheaval of the plates and the surfaces below the actual surface of the earth moving around allowed weaker areas to be exposed right next to harder areas. What you had was a river flowing and being allowed to dig deeper right here at the gorge. Then the surrounding area, along with several other geological principles, also helped form the gorge. One of the interesting things is that it's a relatively new formation. The Appalachian Mountains and the folks that study the stuff realize that millions of years ago the Appalachians were taller than the Rockies. The gorge was formed when the Appalachians were already fairly old and weathered, so the gorge—even though it's hundreds of thousands of years old in the scheme of things—is a relatively young formation. The depth of the gorge is a little over nine hundred feet, the length of the gorge is a little over two miles, and the width of the gorge is a little less than half a mile.

"When Tallulah Falls first became a tourist attraction, it was a real rugged, remote area. In the early days, before it became a tourist attraction, there were just a few farmers around. People were doing a lot of hunting. On into the creek bottoms, there was good farming, but right here around the gorge, it was a little more difficult. The folks had to be a little more hardy than their neighbors a few miles north or east or west of them. As it grew into a tourist attraction, it got kind of unusual . . . There were hotels and restaurants and businesses around that were just here to cater to the tourists, so it was a different place than it is today.

"The Tallulah Gorge first became a tourist attraction in the late 1800s . . . I think the gorge has remained successful all these years because it's natural; it's not something man has done. I think with a large segment of the population, the beauty that is in this earth is something that folks appreciate and enjoy, and it doesn't get out of style. There may not be that big hoopla over it like there is over the Internet, Cabbage Patch dolls, or Disney World and that kind of stuff, but I think when all of that's gone, we'll still have Tallulah Gorge, and we'll have the Rocky Mountains and the Appalachian Mountains." **—Bill Tanner, Fall/Winter 1998**

"We moved [relocated] sixty bears last year. We try not to move bears. It's not very effective when all these bears are killed in situations where they are run over trying to get back home, and they really don't stay where you put them. They just move around. . . .

"Mostly, we don't have many more bears than we had a couple of years ago. We have a lot more people than we had, particularly in the mountain region where every tract of land is being bought up, and subdivisions are being built on the sides of mountains. There is a secondary home on every inch of land, and a lot more people are using the mountains for recreational purposes. Everybody wants to go to the mountains to go on a picnic or ride around, travel, fish, or whatever. It is really putting stress on the land itself. Overuse is also going to be a problem on all of our state and federal lands. I don't know how you control it, either. As more and more people move our way, we are going to have to learn how to deal with that."

—David Carlock, Fall/Winter 1998

COUNTRY LIVING

We always felt like we was the backwoods people, and we didn't have th' chance th' city people had. So th' city people tells us now that we's th' best off. You know how th' city people used t' look at th' country people? They thought they had t' get up an' go t' work without a cup of coffee for breakfast. That's what they called mountain people—didn't even have coffee for breakfast. So when they got up here and found out what the mountain people had—their own hams and their own meat and everything—they changed their mind.

—Margaret Norton

Country living has been the source of much fantasy and many jokes. Very seldom has any media outlet given a truly accurate portrayal of country life. Rural America—specifically southern rural America—is perhaps one of the most misunderstood places on Earth.

While espousing straightforward values and a simple lifestyle, the country folk we met are anything but simple themselves. They believe in liberty of thought and deed, yet they also believe that people are obligated to do their part in this world. Hard work, honesty, integrity, charity—these characteristics are common among the people we interviewed. They believe a man's word should be his bond and that fast living and social isolation are detrimental to our modern society. Many country folk feel that their elders took better care of themselves and that modern-day life is harmful to the health of the younger generation. These people did not seek the easy life. They embraced hard work and were thankful for the good health they felt had come from it.

The people Foxfire students interviewed gave their opinions on both country living and city life as well as some insightful descriptions of the lives they lived. Roy Roberts even described for us what happened when groups of southerners, for the promise of prosperity, left the Appalachians to work in the cities up North.

Esco Pitts told us, "I was born in the country, and you can't take the country out o' me. It's not like it used to be, but still, I'd rather be here than anyplace I know." I couldn't agree with him more!

—Lacy Hunter Nix

"I don't have much company down here. I never have lived anywhere but down here and, 'course, on Hickory Knoll [North Carolina]. And this place is sorta down in a hole—never could see out. But I'd rather live in the country, instead of in a town. Country people can live 'bout like they want to."

—Belle Dryman, Winter 1976

"I've never traveled too far from home. The farthest I ever went was to Connecticut. I've got a brother-in-law that lives there. I have been to Charleston [South Carolina] and back, but that land was too level. I couldn't see nowhere down there. And it's about the same way when you get up North. It's so far up there it levels out. I never did live nowhere else, only right here. Always glad to get back home because I like it right here."

—Clarence Lusk, Summer 1985

"I like the country. I think that's the reason why I like livin' up here in the mountains so much. I was raised in the country. I think the country people are more friendly than the city people. They're more lovely, and they seem like they love each other better, and I always feel like they're more Christian-like in the country than the city people. City people have to work all the time if they have a job. In the country, on a farm, you have rest periods. In the summertime, you get through workin' your crop, and you have a little rest time. From the time you lay your crop by and from the time you have to go back to pickin' cotton, back on the farm, you have a little rest between that. So I guess that makes it a little better than livin' in the city."

—Beulah Perry, Summer 1974

"When my dad was alive—that was before 1912—he would get Mother up at four every mornin'. He was a worker! Had to work to live. She'd come in the kitchen and start her breakfast. And Dad would come up to the barn, feed his cattle, horse, and sheep, and he'd come back and wake all of us kids up to eat breakfast with them. We'd all eat together. That was pretty tough on a youngster to have to roll out in the wintertime. That came early, but we got up and had breakfast with Mom and Dad.

"We didn't have a horse here all the time. We done a lot of walkin'. Our mother walked with us to church and Sunday school over here, day or night. When I was a teenage boy, we got a horse and buggy. We also learned how to ride horseback." **—Terry Dickerson, Winter 1986**

"Well, if people would raise them somethin' to eat, they wouldn't need as much money. People have to have some kind of work to live. Country people have to work to keep the city people somethin' to eat. And, in the coun-

PLATE 163 "Had to work to live." —Terry Dickerson

try, well, people can get fresh air. People can get out and walk places. People used to walk places, and I believe they were healthier. I don't believe people gets enough exercise." —**Belle Dryman, Winter 1976**

"I don't live in the city. I wouldn't live in the city a-tall. No, I wouldn't be bound by the city. I was born in the country, and you can't take the country out o' me. It's not like it used to be, but still, I'd rather be here than anyplace I know. I was born and raised here in these mountains, and I guess I'll die here. There's too much excitement and too much selfishness in the city. Every fellow's for his own self and the devil for the hindmost! Out in the country you can have some peace. You could have good neighbors; when you meet them, they'll speak to you, and in the city they'll pass you up. No, I'm not a citified man." —**Esco Pitts, Spring 1978**

"People used to come down the road here on the way to market. There was a man from North Carolina, and he had cow dogs. He raised a lot of cattle back in the mountains, and he'd come down through here with a string of cattle. He and his helpers rode their horses, and they'd have a big gang of cattle in front of 'em. Them dogs would stay out on the outside, and if one of them cows started to get out of the road, that dog would run down around yonder and put him back in the road. He'd keep that cow in the road. They were takin' their cattle to slaughter and sellin' 'em.

"People back in the mountains would round up a lot of wild turkeys, and they'd drive them to market. I never did see that, but my daddy said he seen big gangs of turkey comin' down the road, and somebody drivin' them. When night would come, they'd fly up in the trees. They'd stay 'til daylight. The next mornin', the turkeys would come down, and they'd take off drivin' them down the road again.

"I've seen many and many of a day that they wasn't a soul in this road here but the mailman, day in and day out. Once in a while, we'd see some of those old mountain fellers comin' down the road drivin' ox and wagons. If they was from real far back in the mountains, they'd always spend the night down here with my daddy. There was an ol' feller name of Burgess that lived about a mile from here, and some of 'em would stop there sometimes. Maybe he'd have all he could keep, and my dad would have all he could keep at the same time—mountain people haulin' in the fall of the year, bringin' vegetables and what-have-you down to Anderson [South Carolina].

"Now Augusta, Georgia, was the closest place way back in my granddaddy's days when they went to market. It'd take 'em a week at a time to go down there and back, maybe more. A lot of 'em had to go in ox wagons. They'd take cabbage or whatever the people in the neighborhood (which wasn't many, just a family here and yonder) had, and they'd buy coffee, sugar, and flour to bring back. Two or three would go down there and bring back enough for everybody. They'd buy half a bushel of green coffee. Sugar would come in barrels and salt, too, I guess.

"They raised their meat, corn, milk, and butter—all like that—at home. They had old homemade looms, so they made their own cloth. Our neighbor over here, ol' lady Burgess, had a little loom, and I went over there one time and watched her stompin' that thing. She made enough cloth to make her ol' man and her boy a suit of clothes—'gray jeans', they called 'em. They was thick! Mother and Daddy both wore that kind of material.

"My mother knit. I wore homemade stockin's that come plumb up beyond my knee. Two pair would do me all winter. They was warm, too. And if I wore a hole in the heel of 'em—which a kid runnin' around will wear 'em out—she'd darn 'em. She had a big ol' bottle that she'd stick down in that sock. Then she'd take a big ol' darnin' needle and that same thread that the stockin' was made out of and darn it back, and you couldn't tell they'd ever been a hole in it. Them poor ol' people had to work for a livin'!

"And houses was open. They wasn't no such thing as an insulated house. They'd put on overcoats and underclothes and everything else in the wintertime. They was dressed for cold weather. They'd build a fire in the fireplace and open the door, maybe. Most of the houses didn't even have a glass window in them. If they did, they'd raise a window and let the wind blow through there, and sparks would get to blowin'.

"You could look down through the floor and see the chickens down under the house. Some of the people even hewed their floorboards, and you know how true cracks would be! They called them puncheon floors. If you dropped anything on the floor, it was liable to go through the floor and under the house. [**Editor's Note:** Puncheon floors were floors that mountain people made by splitting planks with a wooden glut, or wedge, and a wooden maul. They were made from trees, usually poplar. These planks were usually 2 × 6 × 3–4 inches and were finished only on one side. Because of the crude tools involved in their production, puncheon floors frequently had large cracks or holes in them as people were unable to level or straighten the planks completely.]

"It'd just be terrible to think about some of these old people comin' back here today and seein' how it was then and how it is now. On Saturday and Monday, you could hear your neighbors way over yonder just a-battlin' their clothes. They'd take their clothes outside and wash 'em and scrub 'em. A lot of people would use wooden tubs. Many didn't have metal tubs. They would buy lard that used to come in big barrels. Then they'd saw that barrel in two and make two wooden washtubs from it.

"A big iron pot would be settin' out in the yard with a big fire around it. People would put their clothes in there when they got them washed. First thing they'd do was fill the wooden tubs up with hot water and wash the clothes. Then they'd put them in the iron pot filled with water and heatin' over a fire. They'd punch the clothes down with a big stick and boil 'em for so long. Then they'd take 'em out and battle the life out of 'em. They'd rub 'em and blanch 'em out. It'd bust open some of the clothes, but that was the only way they could clean 'em up.

"They burned oak wood in the fireplace and saved the ashes in a big barrel. They made a hopper out of boards, and they'd fill that hopper full of ashes. Then they'd pour water on the ashes, and let them ashes soak up that water all night. Next mornin', they'd go out there and pour more water on 'em and let that water seep right through those ashes. Lye would run out. That lye looked dark red, just like strong coffee, and it'd burn the hound out of your tongue! Potash is what it was. They'd have to run the lye pretty clear, just like people makin' liquor. And then they'd stop it, pour them ashes out, and pour the lye in another pot. Then they'd boil it down. They'd take that old grease they had, such as hog lard, and put that lye in there and make lye soap. They'd cook the lye and lard together, then pour it into flat pans and cut it out in little cakes. 'Course, it wouldn't be hard; it'd be sorta spongy, but it sure would work. That's what they used for soap. It'd clean your clothes. If you had your hands dirty, just wash them in lye soap! I can remember my mama makin' soap, but I don't know that Alma and I ever made it." —**Clarence Lusk, Summer 1985**

"I went up to Detroit in 1927. I had a neighbor that had gone up there before, and I heard from him. I went up there and stayed with him. I went up on a train out of Marshall [North Carolina]. I borrowed twenty-five dollars from my grandma to go up there. My grandma didn't say nothin' about me goin' to Detroit. She just let me have the money. I've thought about that a lot of times. I think she thought this big store in Barnard was goin' to come up for sale, and she had a little money. She said, 'Roy, I'll let you have the money to buy that store.' But it didn't come up for sale. That was the same store I bought several years later.

"So I went up there to Detroit and went to work with a corporation which made ice cream cabinets. Later that company combined with another com-

PLATE 164 "It'd just be terrible to think about some of these old people comin' back here today and seein' how it was then and how it is now." —Clarence Lusk

pany, and they started makin' refrigerators also. I was a checker in the receivin' department checkin' the inventory of the railroad cars.

"After that, I worked for a private detective agency for six or seven years. I guarded the vice president of Chevrolet Motors for three years. I was guardin' that old boy when the Lindbergh baby was kidnapped. After that, time got pretty hard, and he discontinued our services.

"Then I started guardin' the man that financed Fisher Brothers when they went into Detroit and started makin' bodies for General Motors. I guarded his house for four years. He had a gate there, and I would close it at night. Sometimes he would come in scared to death. A lot of times, Edsel Ford's wife would be down there. I knew Edsel Ford's wife personally. I also knew a fella who was with Chrysler. I knew all of them. They visited there, you know.

"Lots of mountain people had gone to Detroit the same time I did. Generally, they tended to live in the same neighborhoods. They lived in a place called River Rouge. That was a suburb south of Detroit. It was really the same town. You would never know you was out of Detroit when you got into it. Most of the people in River Rouge were from the South. They even had a chief of police that was a southern man.

"That was probably the first time some of the mountain people had been in a town any length of time. Of course I had never been in town either. I

PLATE 165 "Indoor plumbin' was new to me." —Roy Roberts

was out of the country straight into the city. To me, it was quite a change. The numbers of people and the way they lived, of course, was different. I guess some of them hadn't been to a theater before. I don't guess I had. Indoor plumbin' was new to me. I just couldn't get used to that. I was used to sittin' on a stump! There was no indoor plumbin' in our community. Most of us didn't even have an outhouse. We had lots of woods. That's it. Young boys would sit on a stump. Be sure to get on one as high as you could get.

"And where I came from, we didn't have electricity. We didn't have a telephone. I guess at that time we didn't even have a radio. I remember the first automobile and the first radio I ever saw. I remember the first airplane that come over. I just had to guess that it was an airplane. I was hoein' corn for ten cents an hour. That airplane came over, and somebody said, 'What's that?'

"Somebody else said, 'I believe it's an airplane.' We didn't know. We just said it was an airplane." —**Roy Roberts, Spring 1985**

"Out in the country y' breathe more oxygen and more pure oxygen. Th' oxygen that we gather from th' air is more pure than it is when you're in a city or town. It's not breathed.

"They's some difference in people in the country and people in the city, but there's no *real* difference in people. People's people."

—**Annie Perry, Summer/Fall 1975**

"I believe people who live in the country get along better and seem like they're more different. You meet 'em—they'll speak howdy to y'. You take these big towns, they just go on by y' like you was a milepost. They're a lot more kinder. More kinder.

"A big town, they won't speak hardly at all. 'Course I never saw a stranger in my life. I go t' Atlanter; I talk t' somebody. But th' people in th' country is more friendlier 'n they are in town. They can't see so much meanness goin' on.

"You take like this here now . . . it's perfectly quiet. We hardly have anybody t' come up here. But you take Atlanter . . . gosh, it's rough! Too many cars bumper t' bumper. This world's full o' cars, you know it? What you goin' t' do with 'em? If they 'as all piled up, they'd be a hundred miles higher than trees!" —**Kenny Runion, Fall 1971**

"I've lived here now for eighty-four years. I sure am glad I don't live somewhere else. I don't want no part of Atlanta, no part of any big city—NO PART!—'cause I've been right here, you know, and I'm used to gettin' out here and doin' whatever I want to. If you're out in the city, you can't do that." —**J. C. Stubblefield, Fall/Winter 1998**

PLATE 166 "My uncles would always put out these big trotlines and bait them with their secret bait . . . I always caught more fish than they did." —Gary Davis

"I slept out on the screened porch in the summer. From the end of the porch to the water's edge was only about thirty yards. I had catfish hooks set all summer long. Durin' the night, if I heard any splashin' or movin' around down there, I'd go down and check my hooks, rebait them, and take the fish off. Then I got to the point where I started puttin' a bell on the end of the limbs or the poles so the bells would ring when the fish would get on them. I'd get up, go down there, and take the fish off.

"I have always been a good fisherman and hunter. As a matter of fact, my life revolved around fishin' and huntin' . . . My uncles would always put out these big trotlines and bait them with their secret bait. I would go out and put a few hooks out with my special bait, and I always caught more fish than they did . . . I think young people now are missin' out on a lot."

—Gary Davis, Fall/Winter 1999

"Mostly, I think we've come a long way since the twenties and thirties. In some ways, the livin' has improved a lot from what it was back then. And, in a way, I don't know but what people could get along just as well back then as they do now. Of course, they didn't have all the utilities and conveniences they have today. We used a spring box to keep our milk and butter in. We didn't know what a refrigerator or a freezer was, and we kept our meat in a smokehouse. But people's not as close as they used to be. Back when I was growin' up, if your cow was dry, you still got milk. If your neighbor had milk, you had milk. We'd divide the milk as long as we had it and lived close enough together. Of course, people are still neighborly. You take the people up here on Betty's Creek . . . they always come to the rescue if you need help. But I'll sure say this is unusually good up here. I don't know whether it's as good everywhere else." —**Billy Long, Winter 1987**

"I believe we'd live longer if we'd go back. We'd go slower, y' know, and study as we go along. Back then, you could meet a man with a yoke o' steers, and they'd stop and talk t' you a hour at a time—long as you wanted t' talk. We couldn't do that now. She's too fer gone. No, they's no hope.

"Me, I'm just goin' through this world th' best that I can. Don't bother nobody. Don't bother nobody. I work out what I get, just gettin' through th' best way I can. I don't claim t' be good, but I'm just doin' th' best I can. 'At's about all anybody can do, ain't it?" —**Kenny Runion, Fall 1971**

> **"But I wasn't sorry to see that way of life pass, well no, not really and truly."** —***Margaret Norton***

"Used to be they raised their own. They had their hogs and their chickens, an' they raised their garden. And whatever they bought from the store, they swapped corn for it, or they killed a hog and took th' meat in and sold it. You never heard tell of goin' to the store and buyin' things. There wasn't anything like that to sell—any meat or any chicken or anything. People raised 'em theirselves. It wasn't until after the Depression that they begun to have fatback and things like that in the store.

"Some people say the only way out now is for people to go back to th' way they's livin' fifty years ago. Wonder how th' young people'd feel about that? It'd be hard, I'll tell you, used to all the conveniences you're used to. It'd certainly be somethin'. You'd have t' go out t' th' wash place and wash your clothes an' battle 'em and boil 'em an' hang 'em out.

"But I wasn't sorry to see that way of life pass, well, no, not really and truly. 'Course, it just seemed like it didn't change all at once—gradually came on. Th' first improvement we got was electricity. Well, that was a great improvement over heatin' irons over th' fire. Then th' road come in. We knew we needed the road, and when it came in, that meant more people 'cause they could travel and they could get here.

"Y'all can't remember as far back as all that. Yeah, it's real different, I'll tell you. We always felt like we was the backwoods people, and we didn't have th' chance th' city people had. So th' city people tells us now that we's th' best off. You know how th' city people used t' look at th' country people? They thought they had t' get up an' go t' work without a cup of coffee for

PLATE 167 "Now people used to just come and see you, and now they want to be invited before they come." —Edith Darnell

breakfast. That's what they called mountain people—didn't even have coffee for breakfast. So when they got up here and found out what the mountain people had—their own hams and their own meat and everything—they changed their mind. The city people bring in new ideas and new ways of doin' which people are not used to. Some say they disturb the togetherness of the community, but they are not here to take advantage—they are here to build up." —**Margaret Norton, Spring 1975**

"I don't think it will ever go back like it used to be. Well, I don't know that it is any worse now than it was then. But there is a lot more people, and they don't visit like they used to. Now they ain't got time to stop and talk to you hardly. People used to go see one another, and they didn't have no way to go but walk or ride a horse. Now they're livin' a lot faster than we did back then. Nowadays, they ain't got no time to go see nobody. They're goin' all the time, and they don't get nowhere either."

—Claude and Edith Darnell, Spring 1975

"The school was the focus of the community. It seems like the people of the community were closer than they are now. People got together more. With the schools like they are now, you have friends from all over the county. That's very good, but unfortunately, we don't have the closeness of the community like we had then. Growing up, we lived on a farm, and we worked. But we had a lot of fun . . . It was a really tight-knit community . . .

PLATE 168 "It seems like the people of the community were closer than they are now. People got together more." —Odelle Hamby

We never thought of locking a door. We never had to put things in the house at night. We could leave things outside, and they would be there when we came back. We were just safer. We would walk home from school or at night from ballgames, and we never thought about anything bad happening. Now I don't want my grandchildren to walk anywhere alone."

—Odelle Hamby, Spring/Summer 1998

"Oh, Clayton has changed! There used to be one grocery store, I believe; one hardware store—what I call a hole in the wall, just a narrow buildin'; and real long dirt roads everywhere, and narrow at that, just wide enough

PLATE 169 J. C. Stubblefield's homeplace

for a wagon. They were just regular old wagon roads and no cars at all. It was a good long time before I'd ever seen a car. I must've been twelve or fifteen years old. That was when the mail carrier got a car. That would be all you'd see a whole week. You'd see them every day with the mail, and before he had a car, he had a horse and buggy. See, no planes at all, you know, and you didn't hear none. They've not been around too long. Now you hear one every day and three or four of them."

—J. C. Stubblefield, Fall/Winter 1998

"A lot of people would say they would have liked go back to the good old days. I guess they call them that. I don't know why. Some of it was good. There is a lot of things you would like to go back to, but there is a lot of good things that have happened that is good these days, too.

"I like the country more than I think I would like the city because it is in a slower pace and not as on the go as much. Country people have more time to stop and chat; they are friendly and show more respect than city people, I think.

"Most people these days have to work harder for the modern things that are wanted and do not really have time to spend with their children. There

PLATE 170 "I guess I was born a hundred years too late because I always like the old way of livin' when you had more time to visit and spend the afternoons, take a drive." —Dan Maxwell

is never enough time, and if you have a family, it is a lot harder than it was."

—Roberta Hicks, Spring/Summer 1994

"Times have changed over the years. I still don't have a computer. I guess I was born a hundred years too late because I always like the old way of livin' when you had more time to visit and spend the afternoons, take a drive. The people are still the same. It's just the ideas. Times have really changed, and as far as blacksmithin', people don't need their plows sharpened anymore. They don't need tools made because they can go now to the hardware store and buy the things they need. It's cheaper than gettin' them made these days. There's a lot of ornamental work to be done. That's what we blacksmiths have to go into now to make a livin' or to stay in the profession that we know and like . . . It's a dyin' art anyway, and if we don't keep younger people interested or train 'em, it's goin' by the wayside. Out of the whole North American continent, there are only three thousand of us that work full-time at it. That's not very many, so it's dwindlin'."

—Dan Maxwell, Spring/Summer 2002

"Times were different then. There wasn't any war when I was a child. I was born in 1905, and the first war that I ever heard tell of started out in 1914 and went on a year or two before the United States had to go over there. Things didn't go too high during World War I. Because we made what

PLATE 171 "You could travel miles and miles by your lone self, and you would never meet a human being." —Lillie Nix

we needed on the farm, we didn't know what it was to go buy. Things might have been scarce somewhere, but not where we lived.

"It was a happy time to live, far different from today. We didn't have any crime, no hoodlums. You could travel miles and miles by your lone self, and you would never meet a human being. There was nobody to hurt you, and you could go where you pleased. It was a peaceful time."

—Lillie Nix, *Foxfire 11*

The following letter was one shared with the Foxfire Magazine class in 1979 by Mrs. Sara Singleton, who was then an English teacher at Rabun County High School. Shortly after the turn of the twentieth century, the author, a man known only as E. E. Patton, wrote this letter expressing his longing for the good ol' days.

> **"Yes, I want to go back to the country where the air is soft and pure; where the neighbors will come in and set up with the sick. . . ."**
>
> ***—E. E. Patton***

"I have lived in the heat and dirt and smoke of this man-made town until I am ready to scram. I have heard the braying of horns and jackass politicians until I want to get back on the farm and hear the bray of a real, simon-pure jackass. The change would be sweet music to my ears. Here the land is all covered with bricks and concrete, and the hearts of people are as hard and flinty as the sidewalks.

"Yes, I want to go back to the country where the air is soft and pure; where the neighbors will come in and set up with the sick and help dig a grave and shovel the dirt on their departed friends, dropping a genuine tear of regret at their passing; where they go to meeting and pitch the tune with a tuning fork and sing through their noses with the fervor and spirit of the faithful. All church services were held at early candlelight if in the evening.

"I want to trim the lamp wicks again and fill the lamps with oil, or 'ile,' carried from the country store in a can with an Irish tater stuck in the spout. I want to eat some food cooked on the old step-stove—the old iron witch stove—sweet taters baked in an oven on the hearth over hickory and red oak coals. I want to see the small boy swing the fly brush to keep the pesky devils off the table. And right here it might be said that a family rated according to the kind of fly brush it had. The very poor used a limb out from a mulberry tree; the middle class had one cut out of newspapers; the upper-crust rich had one made of a peafowl's tail. That family rated—and rated high, brother.

"I want to go back where all the common, everyday towels were made of salt sacks and where there was only one 'store' towel, which was put out only when the preacher came. I want to see the man of the house take his table knife of chilled steel and whet it on his fork tines before he carved the sowbelly that had been cooked with the beans. Did you ever eat any lye hominy or shuck-beans? If not, you have never really lived; you have merely existed.

"I want to see the housewife reach into the salt gourd and get a pinch or two of salt to season the beans and taters. And who has not seen the 'saft' soap put in a terrapin's shell with Grandpa's initials on the side?

"Let's go into the big house and set by the fire and see the old-fashioned dog-irons and the wrought-iron shovel and tongs made in the country blacksmith's shop. And did you ever see your daddy heat the old shovel on a bitter cold day and hold it in front of the old Seth Thomas clock to thaw out the frozen oil so the old timepiece could go to ticking off the hours? And do you remember the old sun mark on the back doorsill when they had no clock? There was no such thing as daylight-saving time then. They got up at three o'clock in the morning and went to bed at seven unless it was apple-butter-making time. Then they stayed up until around eight.

"But the parlor was the sacred place: There was where all the sparkin' [courting] was done. There was the bed the preacher slept in, and what a bed—two straw ticks, one big feather bed with fat bolster and pillows. When the bed was not in use—and that was seldom—the pillows were covered with what was known as 'shams' which had mottoes worked on them. I remember this one: 'I slept and dreamed life was beauty; I woke and found that life was duty.' That was calculated to hold you for some time.

"On the center table was the old family album with plush backs. It held the pictures of the family dating back to the Civil War and, in some instances, the likeness of a great-uncle who fought with Scott in Mexico. Those in civilian clothes always had one hand on their knees and the other folded placidly over the stomach. I want to go back where all the shoe boxes were saved to make splints for the women's bonnets. Remember them?

"I want to go back and carry a few lap-links in my pocket just in case the hoss busts a trace chain; I want to tie the coon-hide hame string once more and set the colter deep by hiking the back band up just behind the hoss's withers. I want to spend Christmas in the country and get off the Christmas tree one stick of candy, one orange, and one penny pencil. The rich ones gave their children a French harp and the night was filled with music. And the cares that infested the day folded their tents like the Arabs and, as silently, stole away.

"I want to go back where they make sausage and souse meat, where the pumpkin is sliced and hung on quiltin' frames to dry. That was before germs, vitamins, and termites had been invented. I want to carry the old Barlow knife once again and whittle red cedar and soft poplar. I want to see the yaller 'thunder-mugs' drying in the sun back of the kitchen. I want to go back where only Gran'ma smoked. She used a long-stemmed clay pipe, which she fired by dipping it into the ashes on the hearth and tamping it down against the jamb of the chimney.

"I want to go back where the geese are picked every month, where the roosters are permitted to run with the hens openly and brazenly, where the corn is planted and soap is made by the signs of the moon, where walnuts and hickory nuts are gathered in the fall for winter mast, where the boys still sell peach seeds to buy their winter boots, and where said boots are greased with sheep or beef tallow, where the peggin' awl is still in use, where Arbuckle's Coffee is parched in the kitchen stove and ground in a mill hung on the wall of the kitchen, where Pap ties the brooms, where they make popguns out of elders and shoot tow wads in them, where they still order stickpins from J. Lyn & Company, where squirrel hides are tanned for family supply of shoestrings. And did you ever color Easter eggs with madder [a plant of the genus *Hubia* with roots used for dyeing]? Did you ever borrow the flutin' irons?

"Yes, I want to go back where they drink sassafack (sassafras) tea to thin their blood in the springtime, where they churn with the old up-and-down churn, where they turn the cream jar around as it sits by the fire in the big house so it will get in the right 'kelter' for churning, where they always lick their knives before they cut butter, where goose quill toothpicks are still in use, where they still battle clothes and use bluin', where they fill the straw ticks with straw right after thrashin' time and cord the bands every month, where they wear long, red flannel drawers, and where the children wear bibs.

"Yes, I want to go back to the country and get my fill of cracklin' bread. I want to see the old whatnot in the corner of the big house. I want to engage in a spelling match in Webster's old blue-back speller, the finest in the world, and read from *McGuffey's Reader*—none better. I want to see the schoolchildren, one after another, raise their hands and say, 'Teacher, may I go outdoors?'

"I want to see the people eat again and shovel it in with their knives. I want to go to the neighbors to borrow the gimlet [a small hand tool for boring holes]. I want to go back where they eat three meals a day—breakfast, dinner, and supper—and where the word 'lunch' will never be heard again.

"Yes, I want to go back and make another corn shucker out of locust. I want to strip some cane and top it and dip the skimmin's off the boiling molasses. I want to go to the neighbors for a bushel of seed corn, to pull the old trundle bed out and sleep the sleep of the just once more. I'd like to call a few doodlebugs [ant lion larvae] outen [out of] their holes, and I want to avoid the Spanish needles, the cockleburs, the seedticks, the beggar-lice [beggar's-lice, a plant bearing prickly fruit that readily clings to clothing], and the chiggers that make life unbearable—and to avoid stone bruises forever.

"Yes, I would like to see the old sidesaddle hanging on a peg on the front porch, covered by a sateen riding skirt. The women did not ride astraddle then. I would like to rime the ash-hopper [to run lye through the ash-hopper in order to make lye soap] and get a sassafack stick to stir the soap.

> *"Backward, turn backward, O Time, in thy flight*
> *Make me a child again just for tonight.*

"O Lord, let me go back once more to this land of simple things."

—E. E. Patton, Winter 1979

CONTRIBUTORS

CONTACTS

Gladys Addis
Lamar Alley
William Freeman Alley
Furman Arvey
Robert Arvey
Donna Bailey
Iris Daniel Engel Barnes
Rose Ester Shirley Barnes
Vaughn Billingsley
Gene Bingham
Arch Bishop
Addie Bleckley
Effie Mae Speed Bleckley
Mr. and Mrs. Grover Bradley
Jo Kinman Brewer
Florence Brooks
Lawton Brooks
Mr. and Mrs. Pat Brooks
Mrs. E. H. Brown
Harry Brown, Sr.
Marinda Brown
Reverend K. D. Browning
Millard Buchanan
Margaret Bulgin
Mrs. Don Burnette
Edith Burney
Mary Cabe
Ruth Cabe
Nola Campbell
Edith Cannon
Lola Cannon
Claudine Palmer Cantrell
David Carlock
Aunt Arie Carpenter
Florence Carpenter
Harley Carpenter
Mary Carpenter
Eula Carroll
Buck Carver
Joanne Carver
Leona "Dink" Carver
Annie Chastain
Ervin Chastain
Estelle Chastain
Furman Chastain
Lettie Chastain
Thomas Coy Cheek
Ruby Mae Miller Cheek
Jim W. Clark
Lara Coggins
Louise Coldren
Clay Collins
Lessie Conner
Minyard Conner
Ben Cook
Loraine Corbin
Ethel Corn
Pat Cotter
L. E. Craig
Betty Crane
Ada Crone
Minnie Dailey
Claude Darnell
Edith Darnell
Angela (Lina) dell'Arciprete Davis
Gary Davis
D. B. Dayton
Arizona Dickerson
R. M. (Mack) Dickerson
Terry Dickerson
John Peter Dillard
Malcolm Dillard
Icie Lou Ester Carpenter Dills
Bertha Dockins
Thad "Happy" Dowdle
Belle Dryman
Lois Duncan
E. H. "Hob" Duvall
Thelma Earp
Harriet Echols
Willie Elliott
Lawrence Ellis
Rutherford "Ruddy" Ellis, Jr.
Clyde English
Hilda Francis
Nora Garland
Olene Garland
O. S. Garland
Lee Garner
Lelia Gibson
Ellene Gowder

Claude "Buck" Gragg
Harley Gragg
Omie Gragg
Hillard Green
Randy Grigsby
Odelle Hamby
Kimsey Hampton
Frances Harbin
Blanche Harkins
Charley Ross Hartley
Etta Hartley
Annie Henry
Burel Henry
Carl Henry
Belle Wilburn Henslee
Roberta Hicks
Clyde Hodge
J. D. Holcomb
Ruth Holcomb
Laurence Holden
Clyde Hollifield
Frank Hollifield
Leonard Hollifield
Mary Ann Hollifield
Harold Houck
Anna Howard
Brother Huff
Andy Hunter
Eunice Hunter
Bass Hyatt
Lucy Hyatt
JoAnn Jarrio
Leonard Jones
Alex Justice
Daisy Justice
Oakley Justice
Bob Justus
Horace Justus
L. M. Keef
Mary Olive Keef
Ada Kelly
Bessie Kelly
Jimmie Kilby
Juanita Kilby
Oza Coffee Kilby
Hazel Killebrew
Mabel Kitchens
Bill Lamb
Lucy Lamb
Monroe Ledford
Virgil Ledford
Viola Lenoir
Annie Long
Billy Long
Bob Lowery
Alma Lusk
Clarence Lusk
Coleman Lyday
Wilbur Maney
Daniel Manous
Clarence Martin
Fannie Ruth Martin
J. D. Martin
Lois Martin
Pearl Martin
Dan Maxwell
Henry Harrison Mayes
Lassie McCall
Naomi Welborn McClain
Carrie McCurry
Marie Mellinger
Bessie Miller
Harvey J. Miller
Josephine Miller
R. A. Miller
Zell Miller
Johnny Mize
Rufus Morgan
Selma Mosley
Gertrude Mull
Opal Myers
G. A. Nasworthy, Jr.
Lillie Nix
Addie Norton
Lester Norton
Margaret Norton
Richard Norton
Gwen Oglesby
Sadie Owens
J. M. Parker
Burma Patterson
E. E. Patton
Harley Penland
Annie Perry
Beulah Perry
Esco Pitts
Mary Pitts
Lucille Ponder
Paul Power
Jack Prince
Ben Purcell
Gene Purcell
Clara Mae Ramey
Ode Reeves
Henrietta Reynolds
Icie Rickman
Essie Ritchie
Varina Ritchie
Ed Roane
Martha Roane
Roy Roberts
Ethel Runion
Kenny Runion
Vera Sawyer
Maude Sellars
Bettie Sellers
Sara Singleton
Floss Sitton
Fred Smith

Julia Smith
R. O. Smith
Susie Smith
Senia Southards
J. P. Speed
Mary Grace Speed
Milton Speed
Sam Stamper
Walter Stancil
Carrie Stewart
Sonja Stikeleather
Lake Stiles
Mrs. Lake Stiles
James Still
Mildred Story
Carolyn Stradley
J. C. Stubblefield
Louise Tabor
Bill Tanner
Bernice Taylor
Melvin Taylor
Bob Thomason
Anne Thurmond
Lyndall "Granny" Toothman
Amy Trammell
James Turpen, Sr.
Amanda Turpin
Jim Turpin
Anna Tutt
Charley Tyler
Bessie Underwood
Willie Underwood
Eva Vinson
Frank Vinson
Bertha Waldroop
Jake Waldroop
Ellison Wall
Julia Alice Stephens Watkins
Varney Watson
Catherine Weaver
Andy Webb
Mrs. Andy (Bashie) Webb
Dorothy Welborn
Christine Wigington
Garland Willis
Ed Wilson
Margaret Wilson
Priscilla Wilson
Celia Wood
Walker Word
Uncle Wright
Lucy York
Flora Youngblood
Magline Webb Zoellner
Will Zoellner

STUDENTS

Allison Adams
Brooks Adams
Josh Addis
Matt Alexander
Stacy Ammons
April Argoe
Glenda Arrowood
Pat Arrowood
Alicia Nicholson Aughtman
Robbie Bailey
Kim Baldwin
Rabun Baldwin
Austin Bauman
Russell Bauman
Stan Beasley
Bruce Beck
Shayne Beck
Stuart Beck
Claire Bender
Cheryl Binnie
Rhonda Black
Jessica Bleckley
Cam Bond
Clark Bowen
Alicia Brown
Ashley Brown
Cary Brown
Cody Brown
Jan Brown
Julie Brown
Harry Browne
Laurie Brunson
Nancy Bryant
Mike Burch
Tim Burgess
Libbi Burney
Andrea Burrell
Melanie Burrell
Vivian Burrell
Ruta Wilson Burt
Tony Burt
Lynn Butler
Kevin Cannon
Scott Cannon
Tom Carlton
Pam Carnes
Amanda Carpenter
Brenda Carpenter
Diana Carpenter
Jimmy Carpenter
Lee Carpenter
Maybelle Carpenter
Patricia Carpenter
Rebekah Carson
Tammy Carter
Brenda Carver
Faye "Bit" Carver
Kaye Carver

Crystal Chastain
Mary Chastain
Patti Chastain
Rosanne Chastain
Vicki Chastain
Joanna Chieves
Tessa Chieves
April Clarke
Chris Clay
Will Clay
Eddie Conner
Kyle Conway
Mike Cook
Karen Cox
Mandy Cox
John Crane
Chris Crawford
Al Crews
Ken Cronic
Ann Cross
James Crout
Debbie Crowell
Barbara Crunkleton
Wendell Culpepper
Doug Cunningham
Greg Darnell
Hedy Davalos
Emili Davis
Jenna Lauren Davis
Brandy Day
Melanie Deitz
Charles Dennis
Sidney Dennis
Julie Dickens
Amanda Dickerson
Kathy Dickerson
Leah Dickerson
Roy Dickerson
David Dillard
Anthony Dills
Becca Dills
Scott Dick
Sherie Dixon
Wesley Dockins
Dawn Dotson
Melissa Easter
Arjuna Echols
Al Edwards
Baxter Edwards
Mark Edwards
Richard Edwards
Angie English
Bridget English
Jimmy Enloe
Aubrey Eubank
Dale Ferguson
John Fincher
Holly Fisher
Ernest Flanagan
Dana Flory
Lacy Forester
Ricky Foster
Kevin Fountain
Joseph Fowler
George Freeman
Roger Freeman
Linda Garland-Page
Mary Garth
Cecelia Gentry
Taphie Galloway
Carrie Gillespie
Lorie Gillespie
Paul Gillespie
Chris Gragg
Keri Gragg
Chasity Grant
Kelli Grantham
Aimee Graves
Teresia Gravley
Jon Grewer
Wendy Guyaux
Curt Haban
Gail Hamby
Anita Hamilton
Kim Hamilton
Phil Hamilton
Randall Hardy
Richard Harmon
Josh Harrison
Suzanne Hassell
Julie Hayman
Keith Head
Kim Hendricks
Shelly Henricks
Lisa Henry
Richard Henslee
Frank Hill
Rebecca Hill
Russell Himelright
Clarissa Hodge
Frank Hoffman
Dana Holcomb
Eric Hollifield
Zack Hopper
Carla Houck
Kari Hughes
Adam Hunter
Lacy Hunter
Shanon Jackson
Debbie James
Doug James
Anita Jenkins
Stephanie Jobbitt
Andrea Johnson
Richard Jones
Julia Justice
Beverly Justus
Kristin Joy Justus
Eddie Kelly
Kara Kennedy

Karen Key
Rachel Koch
Robin Lakey
Tommy Lamb
Lewis Lane
Georgann Lanich
Linda Ledford
Tammy Ledford
Annmarie Lee
Lori Lee
Ashley Lesley
Jenny Lincoln
Sharon Littrell
Kathy Long
Hope Loudermilk
Leslie Luke
Ridg MacArthur
Heather Manter
Kelli Marcus
Matthew Marsengill
Yvette Marsh
Alan Mashburn
Jason Maxwell
Ray McBride
LouWanda McClain
Tinker McCoy
Bridget McCurry
Lori McCurry
Franz Menge
Betsy Moore
Karen Moore
Robbie Moore
Susan Mullis
Amy Nichols
John Nichols
Chris Nix
Tom Nixon
Ashley O'Shields
Juli Pankey
Kirk Patterson
Christi Patton
Ernie Payne
Paivi Peltola
Linda Phillips
Sharon Pope
Beth Pruitt
Laman Queen
Myra Queen
LeAnne Puckett
Alex Ramey
Allan Ramey
Carin Ramey
Carol Ramey
Crystal Ramey
Donna Ramey
Jennifer Ramey
Lorie Ramey
Theresa Ramey
Tommy Ramey
Peter Reddick
Annette Reems
Jeff Reeves
Jim Renfro
Mary Rhodes
Renee Richard
Alden Riesinger
Sabrina Ritchie
Nicky Robinson
Celena Rogers
Jennifer Rogers
Vaughn Rogers, Jr.
April Runion
Bruce Russell, Jr.
Brandie Rushing
Andy Ruth
Johnny Scott
Johnny Scruggs
Heather Scull
Beth Shirley
Jennie Shoemaker
Billie Shook
Kelly Shropshire
OhSoon Shropshire
John Singleton
Patsy Singleton
Seni Sise
Clay Smith
Destry Smith
Dewey Smith
Leigh Ann Smith
Steve Smith
Gabe Southards
Tracy Speed
Cindy Stewart
Cheryl Stocky
Gary Stratton
Greg Strickland
Barbara Taylor
Becky Taylor
Debbie Thomas
Mary Thomas
Ryan Thomas
Sarah Mae Thomas
Gail Thompson
Sheri Thurmond
Teresa Thurmond
John Turner
Kiki Turner
Mark Turpen
Donna Turpin
Samantha Tyler
Sue Van Petten
Marty Veal
Sheila Vinson
David Volk
April Walker
Cheryl Wall
Kim Wall
Sarah Wallace
Gary Warfield

Lacey Watkins
Dawn Watson
Greg Watts
Curtis Weaver
Rudi Webb
Chet Welch
Rose Wells
Connie Wheeler
Janice White
Frenda Wilborn
Adam Wilburn
Jennifer Wilburn
Fred Willard
Craig Williams
Lynnette Williams
Sharon Williams
David Wilson
Hobie Wood
Heather Alicia Woods
Amy York
Suzanne York
Terry York
Matt Young
Wendy Youngblood

EDITORS

PLATE 172 Foxfire editors (*left to right*): Angie Cheek, April Argoe, Diana Carpenter, Amanda Carpenter, and Lacy Hunter Nix

Angie Cheek, a Rabun County native, joined the staff at Rabun County High School in Tiger, Georgia, in 1992. She taught Advanced Placement Literature and Composition and college preparatory English and was facilitator for *The Foxfire Magazine* until she retired in May 2005. She was also coeditor of *Foxfire 12*. Lacy Hunter Nix, a former *Foxfire Magazine* senior editor and coeditor of *Foxfire 11*, graduated from Brenau University with a degree in Music. Amanda and Diana Carpenter and April Argoe served as senior editors of the Foxfire Magazine program at Rabun County High School.